6G Security Education and Multidisciplinary Implementation

Binay Kumar Pandey
Department of Information Technology, College of Technology, Govind Ballabh Pant University of Agriculture and Technology, India

Digvijay Pandey
Department of Technical Education, Government of Uttar Pradesh, India

Tanveer Ahmad
Tata Consultancy Services, UK

A volume in the Advances in Information Security, Privacy, and Ethics (AISPE) Book Series

IGI Global
PUBLISHER of TIMELY KNOWLEDGE

Published in the United States of America by
IGI Global
Information Science Reference (an imprint of IGI Global)
701 E. Chocolate Avenue
Hershey PA, USA 17033
Tel: 717-533-8845
Fax: 717-533-8661
E-mail: cust@igi-global.com
Web site: http://www.igi-global.com

Library of Congress Cataloging-in-Publication Data

CIP Data Pending
ISBN: 979-8-3693-7421-4
eISBN: 979-8-3693-7423-8

British Cataloguing in Publication Data
A Cataloguing in Publication record for this book is available from the British Library.

For electronic access to this publication, please contact: eresources@igi-global.com.

Advances in Information Security, Privacy, and Ethics (AISPE) Book Series

Manish Gupta
State University of New York, USA

ISSN:1948-9730
EISSN:1948-9749

Mission

As digital technologies become more pervasive in everyday life and the Internet is utilized in ever increasing ways by both private and public entities, concern over digital threats becomes more prevalent.

The **Advances in Information Security, Privacy, & Ethics (AISPE) Book Series** provides cutting-edge research on the protection and misuse of information and technology across various industries and settings. Comprised of scholarly research on topics such as identity management, cryptography, system security, authentication, and data protection, this book series is ideal for reference by IT professionals, academicians, and upper-level students.

Coverage

- Internet Governance
- Device Fingerprinting
- Cyberethics
- Computer ethics
- Risk Management
- Security Classifications
- IT Risk
- Cookies
- Electronic Mail Security
- Technoethics

IGI Global is currently accepting manuscripts for publication within this series. To submit a proposal for a volume in this series, please contact our Acquisition Editors at Acquisitions@igi-global.com or visit: http://www.igi-global.com/publish/.

Machine Learning and Cryptographic Solutions for Data Protection and Network Security
J. Anitha Ruth (SRM Institute of Science and Technology, Vadapalani, India) Vijayalakshmi G. V. Mahesh (BMS Institute of Technology and Management, India) P. Visalakshi (Department of Networking and Communications, College of Engineering and Technology, SRM Institute of Science and Technology, Katankulathur, India) R. Uma (Sri Sairam Engineering College, Chennai, India) and A. Meenakshi (SRM Institute of Science and Technology, Vadapalani, India)
Engineering Science Reference • copyright 2024 • 526pp • H/C (ISBN: 9798369341599) • US $355.00 (our price)

The Advances in Information Security, Privacy, and Ethics (AISPE) Book Series (ISSN 1948-9730) is published by IGI Global, 701 E. Chocolate Avenue, Hershey, PA 17033-1240, USA, www.igi-global.com. This series is composed of titles available for purchase individually; each title is edited to be contextually exclusive from any other title within the series. For pricing and ordering information please visit http://www.igi-global.com/book-series/advances-information-security-privacy-ethics/37157. Postmaster: Send all address changes to above address.

Titles in this Series

For a list of additional titles in this series, please visit: www.igi-global.com/book-series

Global Perspectives on the Applications of Computer Vision in Cybersecurity
Franklin Tchakounté (University of Ngaoundere, Cameroon) and Marcellin Atemkeng (Rhodes University, South Africa)
Engineering Science Reference • copyright 2024 • 306pp • H/C (ISBN: 9781668481271) • US $250.00 (our price)

Enhancing Security in Public Spaces Through Generative Adversarial Networks (GANs)
Sivaram Ponnusamy (Sandip University, Nashik, India) Jilali Antari (Ibn Zohr Agadir University, Morocco) Pawan R. Bhaladhare (Sandip University, Nashik, India) Amol D. Potgantwar (Sandip University, Nashik, India) and Swaminathan Kalyanaraman (Anna University, Trichy, India)
Information Science Reference • copyright 2024 • 409pp • H/C (ISBN: 9798369335970) • US $325.00 (our price)

Blockchain Applications for Smart Contract Technologies
Abdelkader Mohamed Sghaier Derbali (Taibah University, Saudi Arabia)
Engineering Science Reference • copyright 2024 • 349pp • H/C (ISBN: 9798369315118) • US $290.00 (our price)

Emerging Technologies for Securing the Cloud and IoT
Amina Ahmed Nacer (University of Lorraine, France) and Mohammed Riyadh Abdmeziem (Ecole Nationale Supérieure d'Informatique, Algeria)
Information Science Reference • copyright 2024 • 361pp • H/C (ISBN: 9798369307663) • US $275.00 (our price)

Investigating and Combating Gender-Related Victimization
Gabriela Mesquita Borges (University of Lusíada, Portugal) Ana Guerreiro (University of Maia, Portugal & School of Criminology, Faculty of Law, University of Porto, Portugal) and Miriam Pina (School of Criminology, Faculty of Law, University of Porto, Portugal & Faculté de Droit, des Sciences Criminelles et d'administration Publique, Université de Lausanne, Switzerland)
Information Science Reference • copyright 2024 • 279pp • H/C (ISBN: 9798369354360) • US $265.00 (our price)

IGI Global
PUBLISHER of TIMELY KNOWLEDGE

701 East Chocolate Avenue, Hershey, PA 17033, USA
Tel: 717-533-8845 x100 • Fax: 717-533-8661
E-Mail: cust@igi-global.com • www.igi-global.com

Table of Contents

Preface

The advent of the 6G communication network marks a significant milestone in the evolution of information and communication technologies (ICT). Spearheaded by developments in Artificial Intelligence (AI), Virtual Reality (VR), Augmented Reality (AR), Extended Reality (XR), Internet of Things (IoT), and blockchain technology, 6G represents a leap toward unprecedented connectivity and intelligence. This edited volume, *6G Security Education and Multidisciplinary Implementation*, seeks to delve into the profound impacts and multifaceted challenges presented by this next-generation network.

The intelligent connectivity envisioned in 6G encompasses deep, holographic, and ubiquitous connections, creating a landscape where security and privacy take center stage. With the increasing complexity of network architecture and the introduction of novel applications and enabling technologies, new security paradigms must be explored and established. This book addresses the anticipated security requirements and key performance indicators (KPIs) essential for the robustness of 6G networks.

The dynamic nature of 6G presents unique challenges, particularly in the context of UAV-based mobility, holographic telepresence, connected autonomous vehicles, smart grids 2.0, Industry 5.0, intelligent healthcare, digital twins, and extended reality. This book provides comprehensive insights into these challenges and proposes innovative security solutions. The exploration includes threats and countermeasures related to Distributed Ledger Technology (DLT), physical layer security, quantum communication, and distributed AI/ML systems.

For instance, DLT security threats such as majority attacks (51% attacks), double-spending attacks, re-entrance attacks, Sybil attacks, and privacy leakages are meticulously analyzed. Solutions such as appropriate access control mechanisms and the strategic selection of blockchain types tailored to specific 6G applications are discussed. Additionally, physical layer security is examined, addressing issues like line-of-sight transmission in Terahertz Technology and enhancing secrecy performance in visible light communications through multiple-input multiple-output (MIMO) technology. Quantum communication threats, including quantum cloning and collision attacks, are also explored, with proposed cryptographic solutions such as lattice-based, code-based, hash-based, and multivariate-based cryptography.

Furthermore, the book addresses security concerns in distributed AI/ML, such as poisoning attacks, evasion attacks, and API-based attacks. Techniques like adversarial training injects and defensive distillation are presented as countermeasures. The comprehensive analysis and proposed solutions aim to provide a roadmap for actualizing the security visions of 6G.

This publication is crafted to serve a diverse audience, including academics, industry managers, public and private organizations, and the general public. It is particularly beneficial for postgraduate students and researchers in social sciences and other fields, inspiring further studies and fostering a deeper understanding of the security issues and solutions in 6G communications and beyond.

We hope this book will contribute significantly to the body of knowledge on 6G security and inspire future research and development in this critical field.

ORGANIZATION OF THE BOOK

Chapter 1: Innovative Pedagogies for 6G Security: Educating the Next Generation

The introduction of 6G networks heralds unprecedented levels of innovation and connectivity in the rapidly evolving technological landscape. However, this progress necessitates robust security measures to combat emerging cyber threats. "Innovative Pedagogies for 6G Security: Educating the Next Generation" aims to transform the approach to teaching and learning security concepts related to 6G networks. This chapter delves into cutting-edge pedagogical strategies designed to foster deep understanding and practical application of security principles among future professionals. By emphasizing innovative educational methods, the chapter seeks to equip the next generation with the skills needed to navigate the complexities of 6G security.

Chapter 2: Transformative Approaches: Exploring Innovative Pedagogies for 6G Education

Pedagogical approaches in social science education are essential for fostering student engagement, deep understanding, and critical thinking. As the 6G era transforms connectivity and communication, effective pedagogies are crucial for helping students grasp complex technological concepts and develop forward-thinking problem-solving skills. This chapter highlights the constructivist approach, which emphasizes active knowledge construction through experiences, interactions, and reflections. By immersing students in real-world scenarios, this approach enhances their comprehension of 6G technologies and their ability to devise innovative solutions to emerging challenges.

Chapter 3: Securing the Digital Future: Educational Approaches in the 6G Ecosystem

With the impending introduction of 6G technology, a revolutionary era characterized by unmatched speed, connectivity, and innovation is on the horizon. As global societies increasingly rely on digital infrastructure for commerce, communication, and social advancement, the importance of securing the digital future becomes paramount. This chapter underscores the critical role of education in shaping and safeguarding this new digital landscape. It explores educational strategies that prepare individuals to address the security challenges posed by 6G networks, ensuring the resilience and integrity of the digital ecosystem.

Chapter 4: Beyond the Classroom: Integrating Cutting-Edge Pedagogies in 6G Curriculum Development

The rapid advancement of technology has significantly impacted education, transforming traditional learning environments into digital classrooms. This chapter examines the shift from conventional educational methods to innovative approaches driven by computing, communication, and information technologies. It highlights the role of digital libraries and interactive educational apps in democratizing education and enhancing accessibility worldwide. By integrating cutting-edge pedagogies into 6G curriculum development, the chapter aims to provide flexible, scalable, and personalized learning experiences that prepare students for the technological demands of the future.

Chapter 5: Educational Imperatives: Preparing Students for the Security Demands of 6G Networks

As 6G networks approach, their anticipated impact on various industries underscores the critical importance of cybersecurity. This chapter focuses on the role of educational institutions in equipping students with the knowledge and skills necessary to tackle 6G security challenges. It emphasizes the need for curriculum adaptation to address the evolving threat landscape, ensuring that students are well-prepared to manage the security demands of 6G networks. By highlighting educational imperatives, the chapter advocates for comprehensive training in cybersecurity to safeguard the digital future.

Chapter 6: Pedagogical Paradigms: Enhancing 6G Learning Experiences for Future Security Professionals

Pedagogical paradigms, encompassing the guiding principles, methods, and strategies employed by educators, play a crucial role in shaping learning experiences. This chapter explores the significance of these paradigms in the context of 6G education, focusing on how they influence students' ability to acquire and utilize knowledge effectively. By examining various pedagogical approaches, the chapter aims to enhance the learning experiences of future security professionals, equipping them with the skills necessary to navigate the opportunities and challenges of the 6G era.

Chapter 7: Commerce in the 6G Era: Adapting Business Strategies to Security Imperatives

The advent of 6G technology, characterized by increased connectivity and ultra-low latency, presents significant implications for business operations. This chapter explores the transformative potential of 6G technology and its impact on commerce. It highlights the need for stringent security measures to address the rising security challenges associated with 6G networks. By recognizing new threats, understanding the importance of data protection, and mitigating risks associated with IoT devices and edge computing, the chapter provides insights into adapting business strategies to the security imperatives of the 6G era.

Chapter 8: Commerce 5.0: Future-Proofing Businesses in the 6G Security Landscape

Commerce 5.0 represents a paradigm shift in business, driven by cutting-edge technologies that emphasize hyper-personalization, seamless connectivity, and real-time data processing. This chapter examines how Commerce 5.0 leverages AI, blockchain, IoT, AR, and other technologies to transform business interactions with customers and markets. By focusing on creating flexible and responsive ecosystems, businesses can gain valuable insights into customer behavior and preferences. The chapter discusses how companies can future-proof themselves in the 6G security landscape, ensuring robust protection and personalized customer experiences.

Chapter 9: E-Commerce Resilience: Strategies for Mitigating 6G Security Threats

As e-commerce continues to evolve, the introduction of 6G technology brings both opportunities and challenges. This chapter explores the intersection of e-commerce and 6G, highlighting the importance of robust security measures to counter new threats. It provides an overview of the e-commerce landscape in the 6G era, identifying specific risks posed by 6G technology to e-commerce platforms. The chapter then focuses on strategies to enhance the resilience of e-commerce platforms, including strengthening access controls, encrypting data, and developing effective disaster recovery plans.

Chapter 10: Blockchain Commerce: Safeguarding Transactions in the Age of 6G

The convergence of blockchain commerce and 6G networks marks the beginning of a new era in secure online transactions. This chapter delves into the fundamentals of blockchain commerce, emphasizing the significance of decentralization and cryptographic integrity. Through real-life examples, it illustrates the utility and adaptability of blockchain technology in modern business. The chapter also explores the transformative potential of 6G networks beyond connectivity, focusing on their impact on digital transactions. By examining how 6G technology reshapes transaction security, the chapter provides insights into safeguarding online commerce in this new era.

Chapter 11: Supply Chain Security in 6G Networks: Commerce's Critical Challenge

The transition to 6G networks represents a significant advancement in wireless telecommunications, offering unprecedented connectivity and technological progress. This chapter addresses the critical challenge of supply chain security in the 6G era. It examines the necessity of robust and reliable communication networks to support fast data transmission and the integration of emerging technologies. By analyzing the security implications of 6G networks on supply chains, the chapter provides strategies for ensuring the security and resilience of commerce in this advanced technological landscape.

Chapter 12: Security Roadmap for Industry 5.0: Managing Risks in the 6G Landscape

The convergence of Industry 5.0 and 6G technology represents a paradigm shift towards enhanced connectivity, efficiency, and innovation. This chapter investigates the intersection of Industry 5.0 and 6G, focusing on the critical importance of security in this evolving landscape. It analyzes the key components of 6G technology, the evolution from Industry 4.0, and the defining features of Industry 5.0. The chapter also examines the threat landscape in the 6G era, including cyber threats, system vulnerabilities, and the impact of hyper-connectivity, providing a comprehensive security roadmap for managing risks.

Chapter 13: Smart Farming in 6G: Navigating Security Challenges for Agricultural Innovations

The integration of smart farming and 6G technology signifies a major shift in agricultural innovation, enhancing productivity, sustainability, and resilience. This chapter explores the complex relationship between smart farming practices and the rise of 6G technology, emphasizing the importance of security in advancing agricultural technologies. It provides a comprehensive overview of smart farming, highlighting its role in addressing modern agricultural challenges. By examining security challenges and solutions, the chapter aims to navigate the intersection of agriculture and 6G, ensuring the protection of innovative farming methods.

Chapter 14: Digital Fields: Securing Agriculture 5.0 in the 6G Landscape

The integration of advanced technologies like 5G and 6G into agriculture heralds significant changes in the industry. This chapter discusses the importance of securing Agriculture 5.0 in the 6G landscape, focusing on the development of agricultural technology, cybersecurity challenges, and strategies for utilizing new technologies for enhanced protection. By tracing the evolution of agricultural technology from its inception to the digital age, the chapter provides insights into safeguarding agricultural innovations and ensuring the resilience of farming systems in the 6G era.

Chapter 15: IoT Solutions for Crop Protection: Safeguarding Agricultural 6G Networks

The convergence of IoT solutions and agricultural practices has revolutionized crop management and protection. This chapter examines the impact of advanced connectivity technologies like 6G networks on agricultural assets and crop protection. It highlights the transformative potential of integrating IoT solutions with 6G networks to enhance food security and optimize agricultural productivity. By exploring the opportunities presented by swift technological progress, the chapter provides strategies for safeguarding agricultural practices and ensuring the resilience of crop protection techniques in the 6G landscape.

Chapter 16: Securing Future Harvests: A Comprehensive Review of IoT Solutions for Crop Protection in Agricultural 6G Networks

Ensuring agricultural sustainability requires effective crop protection to maintain resilient and productive farming systems. This chapter provides a comprehensive review of IoT solutions in the context of agricultural 6G networks, emphasizing the enhancement of crop protection techniques. It examines the limitations of traditional methods and explores the revolutionary potential of IoT and 6G technologies in addressing diverse agricultural challenges. By analyzing the integration of these advanced technologies, the chapter offers insights into improving crop protection and ensuring the sustainability of agricultural practices.

Chapter 17: Intelligent Healthcare in 6G: Addressing Security and Privacy Concerns

The advent of 6G technology holds the promise of revolutionizing intelligent healthcare systems, enabling advanced solutions for patient care and treatment. This chapter explores the transformative potential of 6G technology in healthcare, emphasizing the importance of addressing security and privacy concerns. It provides a comprehensive analysis of the security challenges associated with intelligent healthcare systems and the measures needed to protect patient data. By examining the intersection of 6G technology and healthcare, the chapter offers strategies for ensuring the security and privacy of healthcare solutions in this new era.

Chapter 18: Telemedicine in 6G A Secure Frontier for Healthcare Transformation

The development of 6G technology is driving telemedicine, which has the potential to completely transform the way that healthcare is delivered by facilitating remote consultations, diagnosis, and treatment. This study examines how telemedicine and 6G technology interact, with an emphasis on how these developments could change patient care, increase accessibility, and strengthen security. We start by explaining what telemedicine is and giving a general review of 6G technology, emphasizing its extraordinarily dependable, latency-free communication capabilities. The thesis that telemedicine in 6G presents a secure frontier for transforming healthcare is emphasized, as is the significance of security in telemedicine.

Chapter 19: A Recent Survey on 6G Vehicular Technology, Applications and Challenges

Most cars of the future might be intelligent and self-driving. 6G will be the main technology used in automobiles. An overview of 6G enabling technologies is presented in this current study and their future application. The primary role that 6G will play in automotive technology is to accomplish this. Furthermore, a new technology called 6G wireless connection is on the rise and has the potential to completely transform automotive technology. It is anticipated that more items will be connected in the future via the new 6G technology. Therefore, it must outperform more contemporary, cutting-edge communication technologies like 5G in terms of performance. Heterogeneous object connectivity, ultra-low latency, high throughput, low power consumption, and high data reliability are the main characteristics of 6G technology. Additionally, it will use Artificial Intelligence to facilitate secure and intelligent communication.

IN CONCLUSION

As the editors of this comprehensive volume, we are both humbled and invigorated by the wealth of knowledge and innovation presented within these pages. The advent of 6G technology marks a significant milestone in our technological evolution, bringing forth transformative opportunities and unprecedented challenges across various domains. This book meticulously explores these facets, offering deep insights and practical solutions to navigate the 6G landscape.

Our journey through the intricacies of 6G security and its implications across commerce, education, healthcare, and agriculture has underscored a critical imperative: the need for a proactive and multi-disciplinary approach to safeguard our digital future. Each chapter, authored by esteemed experts in their respective fields, contributes to a holistic understanding of 6G technology's potential and the corresponding security imperatives.

From innovative pedagogies shaping the next generation of security professionals to the strategic adaptations required for businesses and industries, the chapters encapsulate a forward-thinking vision. They highlight not only the complexities and risks but also the vast potential of 6G networks to revolutionize our world.

As we conclude this volume, it is evident that the transition to 6G is not merely an upgrade but a paradigm shift that demands vigilance, adaptability, and collaborative effort. The insights provided herein are not just academic discourses but practical guides aimed at equipping stakeholders with the tools needed to thrive in this new era.

In curating this book, our goal has been to bridge the knowledge gap and foster a deeper understanding of 6G security. We hope this work serves as a valuable resource for educators, industry leaders, policymakers, and researchers, inspiring innovative solutions, and informed strategies to secure our digital future.

Thank you for embarking on this journey with us. Together, we can navigate the complexities of the 6G era and build a resilient, secure, and prosperous technological landscape.

Binay Kumar Pandey
Govind Ballabh Pant University of Agriculture and Technology, India

Digvijay Pandey
Department of Technical Education, Government of Uttar Pradesh, India

Tanveer Ahmad
Tata Consultancy Services, UK

Chapter 1
Innovative Pedagogies for 6G Security Educating the Next Generation

Anandhi Damodaraswamy
Department of Commerce With Computer Applications, PSG College of Arts and Science, India

V. Sridevi
https://orcid.org/0000-0002-1378-0507
Department of Computer Science, PSG College of Arts and Science, India

V. Revathi
https://orcid.org/0000-0002-8583-1916
Department of Applied Sciences, New Horizon College of Engineering, Bangalore, India

Lavish Kansal
Lovely Professional University, India

Melanie Lourens
Faculty of Management Sciences, Durban University of Technology, South Africa

Joshuva Arockia Dhanraj
https://orcid.org/0000-0001-5048-7775
Chandigarh University, India

ABSTRACT

The introduction of 6G networks promises previously unheard-of levels of innovation and connectivity in today's quickly changing technological environment. But this progress also means that strong security measures are desperately needed to guard against new cyberthreats. Investigating cutting-edge pedagogical strategies that promote in-depth comprehension and real-world application of security concepts is crucial as we train the next generation of professionals to handle the complexity of 6G security. The goal of the chapter is to transform the way that security is taught and learned in relation to 6G networks.

I. INTRODUCTION

The introduction of 6G networks promises previously unheard-of levels of innovation and connectivity in today's quickly changing technological environment. But this progress also means that strong security measures are desperately needed to guard against new cyberthreats. Investigating cutting-edge pedagogical strategies that promote in-depth comprehension and real-world application of security con-

DOI: 10.4018/979-8-3693-7421-4.ch001

cepts is crucial as we train the next generation of professionals to handle the complexity of 6G security. The goal of our educational (Pandey, D. et al., 2021a) project, "Innovative Pedagogies for 6G Security: Educating the Next Generation," is to transform the way that security is taught and learned in relation to 6G networks. This initiative's core value is its dedication to utilizing cutting-edge teaching strategies to provide students with the knowledge and abilities needed to protect our digital infrastructure (Swapna, H. R. et al., 2023). Our method's incorporation of simulation-based learning strategies is its main component. Through the use of realistic and simulated environments, we give students practical experience in recognizing and addressing security threats unique to 6G networks. Students can test their problem-solving skills in a risk-free environment, explore a variety of security challenges, and hone their critical thinking abilities through interactive scenarios. We engage students in an enjoyable and interactive learning experience (Saxena, A. et al., 2024) that promotes active participation and knowledge retention by introducing game-like elements into the curriculum. Students can study difficult security topics in a dynamic and captivating way with gamified activities, which promotes a deeper comprehension of 6G security principles. Program also encourages experiential learning by using real-world situations. We close the knowledge gap between theory and practice by exposing students to real-world cybersecurity challenges faced by professionals in the industry. This helps students apply their knowledge in practical settings with effectiveness. Students learn how to recognize vulnerabilities, put security measures in place, and respond to cyber threats in 6G networks through practical projects and case studies. Incorporate cutting-edge technologies into our curriculum, like blockchain (David, S. et al., 2023) and artificial intelligence (AI) (Pandey, B. K., & Pandey, D., 2023), to enhance these creative teaching methods. Students learn how to create proactive security strategies and obtain insight into the ever-evolving nature of cyber threats by utilizing AI-driven tools for threat detection and analysis. We also investigate how blockchain technology can improve privacy and security (Pandey, B. K. et al., 2022) in 6G networks, giving students a thorough understanding of state-of-the-art security solutions. Ultimately, "Innovative Pedagogies for 6G Security: Educating the Next Generation" offers a progressive method of teaching security in the context of 6G networks. By means of simulation-based learning, gamification, experiential learning, and the incorporation of cutting-edge technologies, we enable students to develop into proficient and robust cybersecurity experts who can protect our digital future (Nicolescu, L., & Tudorache, M. T., 2022).

1.1 Setting the Stage: Shift to 6G

With 5G technology (Sengupta, R. et al., 2021), mobile connectivity has reached a major milestone, opening up a huge range of social, economic, and business opportunities. Focus is already shifting to 6G, the next step in the evolution of mobile technology, as 5G continues to be widely deployed and 5G-Advanced technologies make the future clearer. Everyone in the mobile industry is paying close attention to the path of 6G development, including regulators, ministries, operators, vendors, and researchers. The importance of planning for the future of mobile connectivity is shown by the fact that spectrum policy discussions about 6G are becoming more popular. Looking ahead, 2023 will likely be the start of what will be a life-changing journey to 6G. The main mobile technology expected to appear in the 2030s is 6G, which promises to provide a better user experience than its predecessors. Central to its vision is facilitating the Sustainable Development Goals (SDGs) through global coverage, sustainability, and security. These are the building blocks that will usher in a time of meaningful connectivity for everyone. Extremely fast data rates, lower latency, significant energy efficiency, and better reliability are some of the things that 6G is expected to offer. Although 6G's exact uses haven't been decided upon yet, its main goal is to make a lot of different services and scenarios possible. As the needs of users and industries change, 6G wants to adapt to them by using a mix of different technologies to provide global connectivity, sensing connectivity, immersive communications, and critical services. Notably, the arrival of 6G brings new issues to think about when it comes to sharing spectrum. Beyond the low to very high frequency bands, more capacity and frequency ranges will be needed to support the advanced services and applications that are planned for 6G. The frequency ranges between 7 and 24 GHz, especially the 7 to 15 GHz range, have gotten a lot of attention as possible locations for 6G frequencies. Following a lot of discussion within the mobile community, the GSMA approved this frequency range as a possible solution for the upcoming 2023–2027 World Radiocommunication Conference (WRC) study cycle at the International Telecommunication Union (ITU) (Adamopoulou, E., & Moussiades, L., 2020).

1.2 Secure Education in 6G Networks

When it comes to the trustworthiness, dependability, and integrity of these cutting-edge telecommunications systems (Devasenapathy, D. et al., 2024), the importance of secure education in 6G networks is paramount. It is crucial to acknowledge that 6G networks will support numerous important applications and services, including smart cities, industrial automation, autonomous vehicles, and remote healthcare (Pandey, D. et al., 2023). Information breaches, interruptions in service, and even dangers to public safety could result from a breach in the security of these networks. From a security standpoint, there are advantages and disadvantages to 6G networks due to their unique characteristics, which include extremely fast data rates, low latency, and massive connectivity. Although these features make new use cases possible and improve user experiences, they also bring new attack vectors and vulnerabilities that need to be fixed ahead of time. Successful risk mitigation in 6G networks requires experts in cybersecurity to be well-versed in current and future threats, best practices, and principles. Because of this, security education needs to go beyond just cybersecurity courses and become more holistic and targeted. The scope of secure education in 6G networks should be broad enough to cover subjects such as regulatory compliance, secure (Pandey, B. K. et al., 2023a) coding practices, threat detection and mitigation, encryption protocols (Kumar Pandey, B. et al., 2021), and network architecture. In addition, students should gain practical experience in identifying, analyzing, and responding to security incidents in 6G environments through hands-on training exercises, real-world simulations, and case studies. Secure education in 6G networks should cover more ground than just technical skills; it should also stress the significance of privacy protection, risk management, and ethical considerations. Professionals in the field of telecommunications need to be aware of the moral weight of their decisions and make safeguarding user information and privacy a top priority, especially considering how interdependent today's systems are. A workforce prepared to tackle future cybersecurity challenges can be fostered by organizations that prioritize secure education for 6G networks. We can create a digital infrastructure (George, W. K. et al., 2023). Pedagogy for Implementation) that is more trustworthy, innovative, and economically beneficial if we equip professionals with the information, mindset, and abilities to protect 6G networks (Hwang, G. J., & Chang, C. Y., 2023).

1.3. Innovating Education

We need to innovate education to introduce new pedagogical methods for 6G networks. These advanced telecom systems will transform connectivity and require new security and technology skills. Indeed, we must rethink how we train the next generation of professionals to meet industry demands. Traditional educational methods may not prepare students for 6G networks complex challenges. Innovative pedagogical methods that encourage critical thinking, problem-solving, and knowledge application are necessary. By using new methods of education, we can help students master 6G technology and security.

Simulation-based learning immerses students in realistic scenarios to simulate real-world circumstances. Simulations teach students how to identify and mitigate 6G network security threats. Experience helps students understand and remember security principles by applying theoretical concepts in real-world situations. Gamification, which simulates games to engage and motivate students, is another innovative method. GAMification makes learning fun and competitive, encouraging active participation and achievement. Gamification can simplify complex concepts in 6G security education and encourage students to learn new skills in a dynamic and interactive environment. Experiential learning in real-world situations lets students apply their knowledge and skills. Encouraging students to experience industry professionals' real-world cybersecurity challenges can help them understand 6G security in real life. The inclusion of AI and blockchain in the curriculum can also improve learning and prepare students for 6G security. Through AI-driven threat detection and analysis, students can learn about evolving cyber threats and develop proactive security strategies. Also, exploring blockchain technology's potential to improve 6G network security and privacy can help students understand cutting-edge security solutions. Improving education through new pedagogical methods is crucial to preparing the next generation of professionals for 6G network challenges and opportunities. By using simulation-based learning, gamification, experiential learning, and emerging technologies, we can train students to be resilient, adaptable cybersecurity professionals who can protect 6G networks.

II. EVOLVING 6G THREAT LANDSCAPES

2.1 Anticipating 6G Security Hurdles

At the same time that we are looking forward to the future of mobile technology with the imminent arrival of 6G networks, it is of the utmost importance to anticipate and project the security challenges that will accompany this subsequent phase of connectivity. The fact that 6G holds a great deal of promise in terms of speed, latency, and connectivity, it also presents a number of one-of-a-kind security challenges that are shown in the figure 1, that need to be addressed in a proactive manner.

- *Scale and Complexity*: As 6G networks are widely deployed, there will be an explosion of connected devices (Sharma, M. et al., 2022), from industrial machinery and driverless cars to smartphones and Internet of Things sensors (Abdulkarim, Y. I. et al., 2024). The attack surface for possible cyber threats is increased by this enormous network of devices (Du John, H. V. et al., 2022), making it difficult to properly identify and mitigate vulnerabilities. Security measures are made more difficult by the heterogeneous nature of 6G networks, which may include a variety of technologies like massive MIMO, network slicing, and millimeter-wave spectrum.

- *Data Privacy and Confidentiality*: Although 6G networks' high-speed and low-latency capabilities allow for quick data transfer, they also give rise to worries regarding data privacy and confidentiality (Pandey, B. K. et al., 2023b). The risk of unauthorized access and interception is increased by the sheer volume of data that is transmitted over these networks as well as the possibility of real-time processing and analysis. Strict access controls, safe authentication procedures, and strong encryption protocols (Pandey, D. et al., 2021b) are needed to keep malicious actors away from sensitive data (Sharma, S. et al., 2023).
- *Landscape of Dynamic Threats*: For security professionals, the landscape is always changing due to the advancement of technology and the sophistication of cyber threats. Adversaries constantly modify their strategies and methods to take advantage of newly discovered flaws in network defenses. Organizations entrusted with safeguarding 6G networks face a formidable challenge due to the wide array of cyber threats, which includes advanced persistent threats (APTs), insider threats, and zero-day exploits.
- *International Cooperation and Regulatory Compliance*: For businesses engaged in the international telecommunications industry, it is essential to guarantee adherence to standards and regulations. But it can be difficult to navigate the complicated regulatory environment across several jurisdictions, especially as 6G networks spread globally. Furthermore, to effectively combat cyber threats on a global scale, stakeholders including governmental organizations, business associations, and law enforcement agencies must collaborate and share information with one another.

Through a thorough examination of these crucial subpoints, stakeholders can enhance their comprehension of the obstacles related to 6G network security and formulate proactive approaches to efficiently reduce risks. Identifying threats that are specific to this cutting-edge technology is an essential part of anticipating security challenges in 6G networks. When it comes to connectivity and speed, 6G promises to be unmatched, but it also brings about new vulnerabilities. New technologies, such as artificial intelligence (Anand, R. et al., 2024) driven automation, quantum encryption, and the integration of the Internet of Things (IoT) (Pandey, J. K. et al., 2022), may be associated with certain risks. On top of that, the fact that 6G relies on a complicated infrastructure and extensive data exchange could make it easier for cybercriminals to launch attacks, such as exploiting edge computing nodes or exploiting vulnerabilities in network slicing (Okonkwo, C. W., & Ade-Ibijola, A., 2021). It will be essential to gain an understanding of these distinct threats and take measures to mitigate them in order to protect the integrity, privacy, and resilience of future 6G networks.

Figure 1. 6G security: spotting special threats

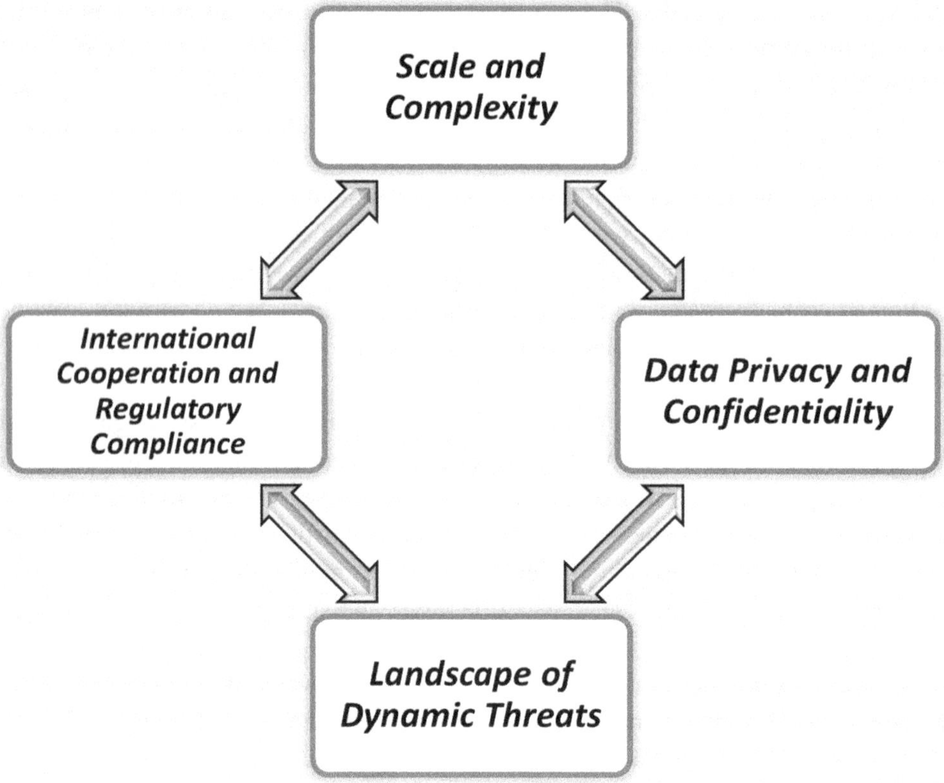

2.1 Identifying Vulnerabilities

The identification and mapping of vulnerabilities and emerging threats are crucial components in the preparation for the deployment of 6G networks. A significant area of concern pertains to the inherent vulnerabilities present within the network infrastructure. The potential vulnerabilities of 6G network architecture, which encompass base stations, core networks, and edge computing nodes, may be susceptible to exploitation by malicious entities. The implementation of software-defined networking (SDN) and network function virtualization (NFV) brings about new ways of attack that need to be addressed with caution in order to safeguard the network's security. The widespread adoption of Internet of Things (IoT) (Vinodhini, V. et al., 2022) devices in 6G networks presents a multitude of potential vulnerabilities. A significant number of IoT devices (Dhanasekar, S. et al., 2023) are deficient in strong security measures, rendering them vulnerable to exploitation by cyber assailants. The identification and mitigation of these vulnerabilities necessitate a comprehensive analysis of the firmware, communication protocols, and access control mechanisms of IoT devices (Sasidevi S et al., 2024) in order to safeguard the network's integrity and security (Menon, V. et al., 2022). The presence of software and firmware vulnerabilities in network infrastructure and IoT devices makes 6G networks highly susceptible to security risks. The growing dependence of 6G networks on software-defined technologies and virtualized infrastructure has led to an increased prevalence of vulnerabilities in operating systems, network protocols, and application software. The implementation of ongoing monitoring and analysis of software and firmware updates is imperative in order to accurately detect and effectively address these vulnerabilities. The intricate logistics network associated with the creation and implementation of 6G networks presents supplementary hazards that necessitate attention. Unscrupulous individuals can take advantage of weaknesses in the supply chain (Malhotra, P. et al., 2021) to introduce fake or compromised parts, which endangers the reliability and safety of network infrastructure. In order to safeguard 6G networks from emerging threats, it is imperative to evaluate the security practices employed by vendors and suppliers, as well as to implement appropriate measures to mitigate risks within the supply chain. The incorporation of nascent technologies (Tripathi, R. P. et al., 2023) like artificial intelligence (AI), blockchain, and quantum computing into 6G networks offers both prospects and hazards. Although these technologies present potential advantages in terms of enhanced efficiency and heightened security, they also introduce novel avenues for attacks that necessitate meticulous management. In order to protect 6G networks from emerging threats, it is crucial to comprehend the security implications of these technologies and adopt proactive measures to mitigate the associated risks (Rudolph, J., Tan, S., & Tan, S., 2023).

2.2 6G Security Breach Consequences

Assessing the effects of 6G security breaches is essential for comprehending the possible effects of cyber threats on communication systems. As 6G networks become more common, it's important to know what will happen if security is breached in order to reduce risks effectively. 6G network security breaches can affect many parts of the telecommunications infrastructure, services, and users. As a big effect, critical services and apps that depend on 6G networks could become unavailable. Communications network problems could affect emergency services, healthcare systems (Tareke, S. A. et al., 2022), and other important public services, with big effects on society and the economy. 6G network security holes can make sensitive data and information less private, less reliable, and less accessible. Theft, unauthorized access, or modification of data could cost businesses and people money, hurt their reputations, and put them in legal trouble. Additionally, breaches that expose user privacy can make people less trusting of telecom companies and digital services. Breaking into 6G networks can affect national security and the stability of world politics. Potential threats to national security and stability include cyber espionage, sabotage, and attacks on critical infrastructure that take advantage of weak spots in telecommunications infrastructure. Cybersecurity strategies and policies need to take into account the geopolitical effects of security breaches. 6G network security holes can affect other systems and networks that are connected to them. A breach in one part of the network could spread to other systems, causing problems and opening up a lot of openings. Knowing how telecommunications infrastructure is linked to each other and figuring out how security breaches might affect other systems is important for lowering risks and making cybersecurity stronger overall (Vaswani, A. et al., 2017).

III. CUSTOMIZING EDUCATION FOR 6G SECURITY

3.1 Adaptive Learning

Adaptive learning (Pandey, D., & Pandey, B. K., 2022) transforms education to meet students' needs and learning styles, especially in 6G security. Cybersecurity experts are in demand as 6G networks change the telecommunications landscape. To accommodate 6G security students' diverse backgrounds, learning paces, and proficiency levels, adaptive learning can be used. To personalize learning for each student, adaptive learning uses advanced technology and data analytics. Learning outcomes are optimized by adaptive learning systems, which continuously assess and analyze student performance to adjust course materials, pacing, and instructional strategies. This personalized approach gives students support and resources that meet their learning needs and goals. In 6G security education, where students have diverse academic backgrounds and prior knowledge, adaptive learning is invaluable. Adaptive learning platforms can tailor learning pathways to students' strengths by assessing their cybersecurity knowledge. Advanced learners may be assigned harder materials, while those who need more help can use remedial resources to improve. Adaptive learning engages students through interactive and immersive learning. Gamified activities, simulations, and virtual labs allow students to apply theoretical concepts, try different strategies, and receive immediate feedback. This hands-on approach reinforced learning and developed critical thinking, problem-solving, and decision-making skills needed for 6G security roles. By regularly assessing student performance and providing timely feedback, educators can tailor interventions and support to individual learning needs. This data-driven approach helps educators make rational decisions about instructional design, curriculum development, and resource allocation, improving 6G security education programs (Arksey, H., & O'malley, L., 2005).

3.2 Virtual Engagement

Immersive learning environments are a key strategy for connecting geographically dispersed learners in hybrid workplaces. On-premises trainers and in-class sessions are less accessible as remote work and distributed teams become more common. Thus, organisations are using immersive learning to create dynamic and engaging learning experiences that transcend physical boundaries and keep learners actively engaged. Immersive learning gives learners a sense of presence and immersion that traditional learning methods lack by simulating real-world scenarios and environments. Learners can manipulate objects, interact with virtual environments, and experience realistic simulations of their workplace using VR, AR, and MR technologies. This hands-on approach improves learning retention and develops experiential learning, problem-solving, and critical thinking skills needed in today's dynamic workplace. Immersive learning helps remote teams collaborate in hybrid workplaces with employees from different time zones. Immersive learning environments allow students to interact with peers, instructors, and learning resources in real time from anywhere. This improves remote teamwork, communication, and knowledge sharing, improving learning and effectiveness. Immersive learning also addresses hybrid workers' daily challenges and distractions. Remote workers may face many distractions and interruptions that make it hard for them to focus and learn. Immersive learning environments solve this problem by capturing students' attention and keeping them engaged in learning. To use immersive learning in hybrid workplaces, organizations must design and implement organizational-wide immersive learning experiences. CLOs, L&D teams, and technology partners must work together to create immersive learning solutions that meet the organization's learning goals. Organizations can foster continuous learning, innovation, and growth that prepares employees for the digital age by incorporating immersive learning into their learning and development strategy (Schwendimann, R. et al., 2018).

3.3 Holistic Integration

For 6G security, holistic integration, which embraces multidisciplinary perspectives, is a major educational paradigm shift. Today's rapidly changing technological landscape, where interconnected systems and networks transcend disciplinary boundaries, makes holistic education essential. Holistic integration recognizes that 6G security and other complex issues require expertise from cybersecurity, telecommunications, data science, ethics, and more. Holistic integration breaks down discipline silos and promotes interaction, creativity, and innovation across fields. By adopting multidisciplinary perspectives, learners gain a deeper understanding of complex issues and develop holistic problem-solving skills needed to address 6G security challenges. A cybersecurity expert in network security may benefit from telecommunications infrastructure and data analytics to mitigate 6G network threats. Beyond technology, 6G security should consider ethical, social, and cultural issues. The ethical implications of their work and a strong ethical framework for decision-making are enhanced by incorporating perspectives from philosophy, sociology, and anthropology. Examining complex ethical issues and ensuring ethical 6G network development and deployment requires this ethical perspective. In 6G security education, holistic integration requires interdisciplinary and project-based learning that promotes collaboration and integration across disciplines. Students may collaborate to analyze case studies, solve real-world cybersecurity problems, and present their findings to a panel of experts. This hands-on approach reinforces learning and development of critical thinking, communication, and teamwork skills needed for 6G security. Industry partnerships, research collaborations, and community engagement supplements the classroom. Through industry and community partnerships, students gain real-world experience, access to cutting-edge technologies, and meaningful ways to apply their knowledge and skills. Academic, industrial, and social collaboration promotes innovation and entrepreneurship that advances 6G security and beyond. It is possible to foster overall well-being through the utilization of a holistic approach, which incorporates aspects of physical, creative, nature, spiritual, social, emotional, and linguistic aspects are as shown in the figure 2. Through the incorporation of physical activities such as yoga or dance, one can improve their vitality and reduce their stress levels (Munn, Z. et al., 2018). Participating in creative activities has been shown to foster mental health by stimulating imagination and self-expression (Pandey, B. K. et al., 2011). It is beneficial to one's relaxation and ecological consciousness to engage in activities that take place outside and connect with nature. Meditation and other forms of spiritual practice, such as reflection, are known to foster a sense of inner peace and purpose. For the purpose of fostering a sense of belonging and support, the cultivation of social bonds through meaningful interactions is essential. Resilience and empathy are both developed through the practice of emotional awareness and regulation techniques. Last but not least, broadening one's cultural understanding and communication abilities through the study of language through literature or conversation. This holistic framework ensures that a lifestyle that is both balanced and fulfilling is fostered.

Figure 2. Holistic approach

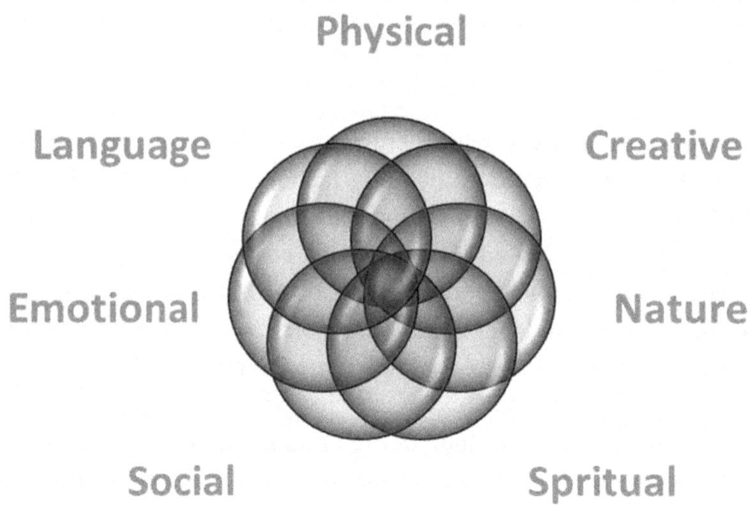

3.4 Ethical Foundations

The incorporation of ethical principles is imperative in the swiftly progressing domain of 6G security, as it guarantees that cybersecurity experts possess the requisite moral guidance to effectively navigate intricate ethical quandaries and render conscientious choices. The ethical ramifications of cybersecurity practices are becoming more significant than ever as 6G networks become more widespread and interconnected. Hence, it is imperative to incorporate moral principles into the curriculum of 6G security education in order to cultivate a climate of ethical consciousness, liability, and obligation within the upcoming cohort of cybersecurity practitioners. The fundamental basis of ethical principles in 6G security education is the acknowledgment that cybersecurity is not exclusively a technical field, but also a moral and ethical pursuit. Ethical considerations are integrated into all facets of cybersecurity, encompassing the creation and implementation of security technologies, the ethical utilization of data, and the safeguarding of individuals' rights and liberties. By incorporating morality into 6G security education, learners acquire a more profound comprehension of the ethical ramifications of their actions and cultivate the ethical reasoning abilities necessary to adeptly navigate intricate ethical dilemmas. A primary aim of incorporating morality into the curriculum of 6G security education is to foster a robust ethical framework within the cybersecurity community. Incorporating fundamental ethical principles, such as integrity, honesty, transparency, and respect for human rights, into the framework of cybersecurity education is a crucial undertaking. Teachers can empower students to uphold ethical standards and act with integrity in their professional practice by placing emphasis on the significance of ethical conduct and responsible decision-making. The process of incorporating morality into 6G security education entails an examination of the ethical aspects associated with emerging technologies and cybersecurity practices. The introduction of 6G networks brings forth novel capabilities and functionalities, including AI-driven security systems and autonomous decision-making algorithms (Bessant, Y. A. et al., 2023), thereby amplifying the complexity of ethical considerations. Learners are required to confront inquiries pertaining to privacy, equity, responsibility, and openness in the conceptualization, creation, and implementation of security technologies for 6G. The ethical underpinnings of 6G security education also involve cultivating a climate of ethical contemplation and exchange among students. Through the establishment of platforms that foster open and respectful exchanges pertaining to ethical matters, educators possess the ability to stimulate students' capacity to critically evaluate their personal ethical convictions and principles, as well as actively participate in ethical deliberation and decision-making procedures (Pollock, D. et al., 2022). Ethical reflexivity serves to not only augment students' ethical consciousness, but also furnish them with the necessary abilities and self-assurance to effectively confront ethical dilemmas within their professional endeavors. Effective incorporation of moral principles into 6G security education necessitates cooperation among academia, industry, and professional organizations to formulate ethical guidelines, codes of conduct, and optimal methodologies for cybersecurity experts. Through collaborative efforts, stakeholders have the opportunity to establish ethical standards and norms, thereby fostering a collective comprehension of ethical obligations and cultivating a climate of

IV. INNOVATIVE TEACHING TECHNIQUES

4.1 Augmented Reality

In a variety of industries, including cybersecurity, augmented reality (AR) applications have proven to be effective tools for improving the visualization of difficult concepts. Using AR technology to its full potential in the context of 6G security offers chances to give students engaging, immersive experiences that promote a deeper comprehension and interaction with important security concepts. The ability to physically and interactively visualize abstract and complex concepts is one of the main advantages of utilizing augmented reality (AR) applications in 6G security education. Learners can see and interact with virtual objects and information in real-time with augmented reality (AR), which projects digital content over the real world. Students may, for instance, scan real-world objects or surroundings with AR-capable smartphones or tablets to retrieve context-related data, graphics, and simulations about 6G security principles. By simulating real-world situations and environments, augmented reality applications can give students practical experience recognizing and reducing security threats in 6G networks. In a virtual setting, for example, students can test security protocols, discover vulnerabilities, and investigate various network configurations using augmented reality simulations. This method of experiential learning not only strengthens knowledge but also develops the critical thinking, problem-solving, and decision-making abilities necessary for working in cybersecurity. Through offering shared virtual spaces for interaction and communication, augmented reality applications can improve collaboration and knowledge sharing among students. Students can visually represent and talk about difficult security concepts, exchange ideas and viewpoints, and work together in real time to solve security challenges by utilizing AR-enabled collaborative platforms. The enhancement of overall learning experience and effectiveness of 6G security education is possible due to the collaborative learning environment that fosters teamwork, communication, and peer-to-peer learning. Personalized learning experiences catered to the requirements of each individual learner are also possible with AR applications, which can adjust to various learning preferences and styles. Depending on their preferred method of learning and learning goals, students can investigate 6G security concepts, for instance, through interactive simulations, visualizations, or gamified activities. Its adaptability enables students to interact with the material in a way that best fits their preferred method of learning, encouraging motivation, interest, and independent study (Terzopoulos, G., & Satratzemi, M., 2019).

4.2 Collaborative Problem-Solving

Real-world 6G security challenges can be dynamically addressed through group exercises that foster collaborative problem-solving. The emerging 6G networks are changing the telecom landscape, and with them, security threats are becoming more sophisticated and complex. Teachers can equip students to address these issues head-on and develop the critical thinking, cooperation, and communication skills necessary for success in the 6G security industry by involving students in cooperative problem-solving activities. Students can collaborate to analyze complex security scenarios and come up with creative solutions, which is one of the main advantages of collaborative problem-solving exercises. Collaborative problem-solving exercises enable students to evaluate various points of view, question presumptions, and think creatively about potential security threats and vulnerabilities in 6G networks by bringing together diverse perspectives, expertise, and experiences. The holistic thinking and problem-solving abilities that are fostered by this cooperative approach are critical for handling complex security issues. Group problem-solving activities give students practical experience in applying abstract ideas to actual circumstances. Students get hands-on experience in recognizing security threats, evaluating risks, and putting effective security measures in place in a controlled setting by modeling real-world security scenarios and challenges. This method of experiential learning not only helps students retain what they have learned, but it also builds their self-assurance and competence when it comes to using it to solve actual 6G security problems. Collaboration and communication skills are also fostered in students through cooperative problem-solving activities. Students gain valuable experience in group work by collaborating to solve complex problems, exchanging ideas, and communicating clearly. Learners are encouraged to use each other's skills and abilities to accomplish shared objectives by this collaborative learning environment, which also builds a sense of camaraderie and mutual support. Collaboration and cooperation are crucial in the field of 6G security to tackle complex security threats, which is where these teamwork and communication skills come in very handy. Educators can concentrate on important aspects of 6G security that match learners' interests and career goals by customizing cooperative problem-solving activities to particular learning objectives and outcomes. For instance, depending on the needs and interests of the learners, exercises may center on subjects like network security, data privacy, threat intelligence (Revathi, T. K. et al., 2022), or incident response. By being tailored to their individual needs, these programs guarantee that students are motivated and actively involved in solving problems that are pertinent to their educational path (Borenstein, J., & Howard, A., 2021).

4.3 Adaptive Assessment

By dynamically adjusting to individual learning trajectories and progress, adaptive assessment strategies bring about a revolution in the evaluation of student proficiency in 6G surveillance. Assessments that are adaptive, as opposed to traditional methods of evaluation, which adhere to a standardized approach, modify questions and tasks based on the responses of students in real time. A more accurate and comprehensive evaluation of the students' comprehension of 6G security concepts is ultimately achieved through the utilization of this personalized approach, which guarantees that every student is appropriately challenged and receives targeted support where it is required. The utilization of adaptive assessment strategies enables educators to gain valuable insights into the learning journeys of their students by harnessing the power of advanced technology and data analytics. Educators are able to identify patterns (Govindaraj, V. et al., 2023), trends, and areas for improvement by continuously monitoring the interactions that students have with assessment tasks. This provides them with the ability to make informed decisions regarding instructional interventions and intervention strategies. The ability of educators to effectively address the unique educational requirements of each student and to maximize the learning experience for each individual student is improved by this approach that is driven by data. By providing learners with immediate and pertinent feedback on their performance, adaptive assessment strategies also encourage engagement and motivation among the students. Students are able to have the ability to take ownership of their learning and make informed decisions about their study habits and approaches when they receive timely feedback on their responses. This feedback provides students with valuable insights into their strengths and weaknesses. A culture of self-directed learning and continuous improvement is fostered by this feedback loop, which ultimately results in improved learning outcomes and increased student success in 6G security education. Adaptive assessment strategies, on the other hand, provide flexibility and customization in order to cater to the varied requirements and expectations of students. Instructors have the ability to design assessments that are in line with particular learning objectives, outcomes, and instructional methods. This helps to ensure that assessments are pertinent and meaningful to the learning experiences of students. Because of this flexibility, educators are able to modify assessments to cater to the specific requirements of individual students. This helps to cultivate a learning environment that is encouraging and welcoming to all students, ensuring that every student has the opportunity to realize their full potential.

V. TRADITIONAL PEDAGOGIES IN SECURITY EDUCATION

- *Emphasis on Theoretical Knowledge*: The traditional security education pedagogies place a strong emphasis on theoretical knowledge transfer as a fundamental component. These teaching strategies cover subjects like cryptographic algorithms, access control models, and security protocols in an effort to impart a thorough understanding of basic security principles. The main form of instruction in traditional classroom settings is lectures, which are frequently complemented by readings from reputable texts and academic articles. Students gain sophisticated insights into security concepts by delving into theoretical frameworks through these readings and lectures. Students' critical thinking and conceptual understanding are developed through this interactive engagement, which also improves their capacity to successfully apply theoretical knowledge to real-world scenarios.
- *Integration of Hands-on Labs*: Hands-on labs are another essential component of traditional security education that should be incorporated. By providing students with opportunities for experiential learning, these practical exercises serve as a supplement to the theoretical instruction that they receive. Students participate in a variety of activities during lab sessions, including the configuration of network infrastructures, the conduct of vulnerability assessments, and the analysis of security incidents. Not only do these practical experiences help to reinforce theoretical concepts, but they also help to cultivate essential skills such as the ability to adapt, critical analysis, and

problem-solving. Students are able to develop their practical expertise and gain valuable insights into the complexities of security operations by using simulated environments to navigate authentic security challenges.

- *Active Engagement and Interaction*: Traditional pedagogies in security education place a strong emphasis on interaction and active engagement. Deeper engagement with security concepts is fostered by classroom environments that prioritize active participation and collaborative learning. Students are encouraged to apply theoretical knowledge to real-world scenarios and collaborate to solve complex problems through interactive activities like group projects, case studies, and role-playing exercises. Under the supervision of teachers, classroom discussions give students the chance to exchange ideas, share their perspectives, and participate in critical discourse. Students' comprehension of security concepts is deepened, and their communication and teamwork skills are improved through this interactive exchange of ideas, setting them up for success in the fast-paced field of cybersecurity.
- *Assessment Methods*: Student engagement and active learning strategies have become more important as traditional pedagogies in security education have evolved. Teaching professionals understand how critical it is to create a lively, interactive classroom where students take an active role in their own education. A range of active learning strategies, including group discussions, case studies, and hands-on activities, are now included in traditional security education in addition to lectures and readings. With these methods, students are encouraged to take charge of their education, apply abstract ideas to practical situations, and work in groups to find solutions to issues.
- *Relevance and Effectiveness*: With the evolution of traditional pedagogies in the field of security education, student engagement and active learning strategies have become increasingly important. The professionals who work in education are aware of how important it is to establish a classroom environment that is lively and interactive, and in which students play an active role in their studies. In addition to lectures and readings, traditional security education now incorporates a variety of active learning strategies. These strategies include hand-on activities, group discussions, and case studies, among others. Students are encouraged to take responsibility for their own education, to apply theoretical concepts to real-world scenarios, and to collaborate with their peers in order to find answers to problems through the use of these practices.

Standardized teaching approaches centered on fundamental ideas and procedures are included in traditional pedagogies in security education. These methods, which focus on teaching cybersecurity principles, risk management, and threat mitigation techniques, frequently include lectures, textbooks, and structured assessments. Enabling students to apply theoretical concepts in real-world scenarios, practical exercises like simulations and case studies complement theoretical learning. Additionally, learning through experience under the supervision of seasoned professionals is made possible by mentorship and apprenticeship models. These approaches which are shown in the figure 3, offers a strong foundation in security principles, but because cyber threats are constantly changing, security education curricula must also adapt to include new technologies and current issues.

Figure 3. Traditional security education pedagogies

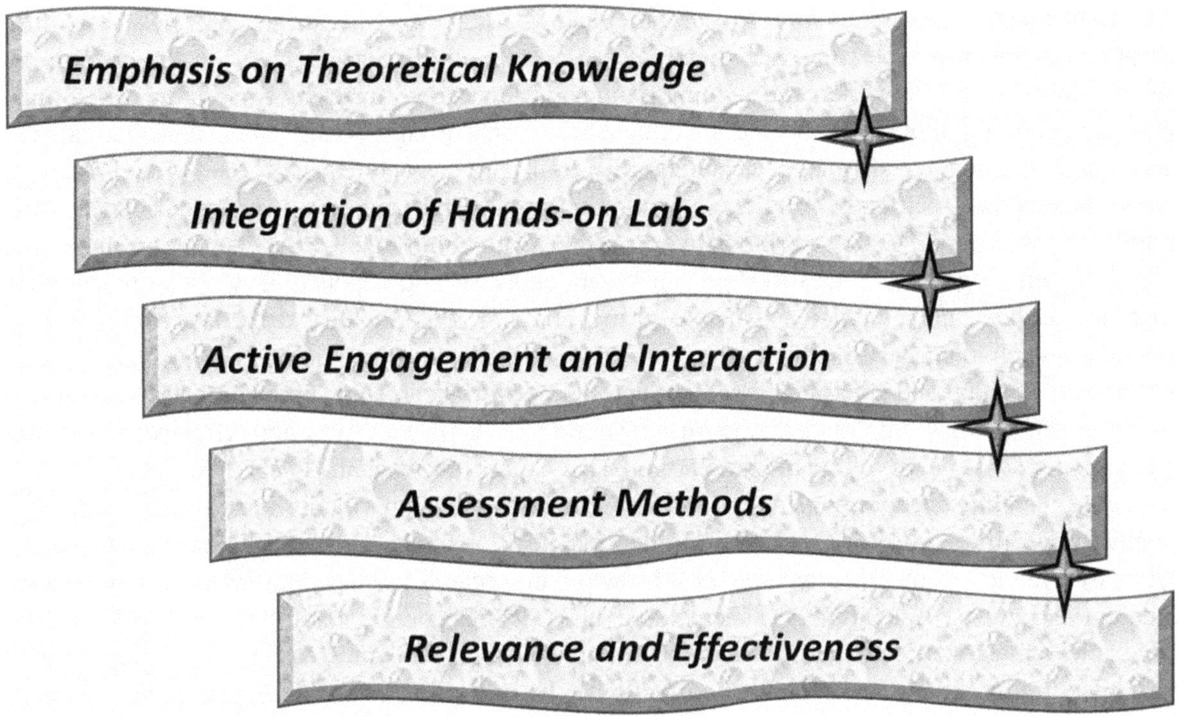

VI. CHALLENGES AND SEIZING OPPORTUNITIES

6.G networks are expected to bring ultra-fast data rates, low latency, and ubiquitous connectivity; however, in order to support these capabilities, a strong infrastructure and cutting-edge technologies are required. To fully utilize 6G networks, considerable technological obstacles must be solved in the construction of the required infrastructure, which includes high-speed transmission systems and complex network architecture. The technological landscape of 6G networks is further complicated by the integration of cutting-edge technologies like machine learning (ML) (Anand, R. et al., 2023), artificial intelligence (AI), and the Internet of Things (IoT) (Iyyanar, P. et al., 2023). The security and integrity of 6G networks must be ensured despite the fact that these technologies present previously unheard-of possibilities for efficiency and innovation. These include the introduction of new complexities and vulnerabilities, such as AI (Khan, B. et al., 2021) driven cyberattacks and IoT security breaches (Pramanik, S. et al., 2023). Resolving technical issues is essential to guaranteeing 6G networks' efficiency and dependability. This entails creating strong security protocols, putting in place efficient network management systems, and funding R&D to spur technological advancement (Deepa, R. et al., 2022). Through surmounting these obstacles, the telecom sector can unleash the complete possibilities of 6G networks and provide users across the globe with game-changing experiences. The widespread and interconnected nature of 6G networks presents important ethical issues with regard to data security, privacy, and responsible technology use. Maintaining user privacy and security is crucial since 6G networks enable the exchange of enormous volumes of sensitive and personal data. Clear ethical norms and guidelines for the telecommunications sector must be established through cooperation between industry stakeholders, regulators, and legislators. This entails creating guidelines for responsible AI and ML (Pandey, B. K. et al., 2024) use, specifying best practices for data protection, and guaranteeing accountability and openness in the creation and implementation of 6G networks. Maintaining public confidence and fostering trust in the development and implementation of 6G networks require ethical behavior. Through giving ethical considerations top priority and adhering to principles of accountability, transparency, and respect for individual rights, the telecommunications sector can show its dedication to moral behavior and cultivate confidence among stakeholders and users. The move to 6G networks offers a number of noteworthy chances for innovation, expansion, and progress. 6G networks' greater speed, capacity, and dependability open up new possibilities for services and applications, such as virtual and augmented reality, driverless cars, and smart cities. The switch to 6G networks will accelerate telecommunications technology advancements, which will promote societal and economic development. 6G networks can spur innovation across a range of industries, generate new employment opportunities, and increase productivity and efficiency by enabling faster and more dependable communication (González-Calatayud, V. et al., 2021). In order to prosper in the quickly changing telecommunications industry, businesses and individuals must embrace innovation and grasp opportunities in the 6G era. Stakeholders can position themselves for success in the 6G era and beyond by embracing emerging technologies, investing in research and development, and staying ahead of the curve. Industry stakeholders (Saxena, A. et al., 2021), academic institutions, and governmental organizations must work together to overcome obstacles and take advantage of opportunities in the 6G era. Collaboration among stakeholders can facilitate the utilisation of varied expertise and resources to tackle intricate problems and stimulate innovation within the telecommunications sector. Collaborative solutions can speed up the creation and uptake of new standards and technologies by facilitating knowledge transfer and technology adoption. Stakeholders can accomplish collective goals that would be challenging to accomplish individually by combining their resources and expertise. Stakeholders can develop a sustainable and inclusive telecommunications sector that aids society at large by cultivating a cooperative ecosystem that promotes cooperation and innovation. Stakeholders can influence the direction of telecommunications and guarantee that 6G networks fulfill their promises of connectedness, innovation, and prosperity by working together and developing a common vision.

CONCLUSION

The adoption of 6G technology brings with it previously unheard-of cybersecurity opportunities as well as challenges. Robust security measures are becoming more and more necessary to protect sensitive data and important infrastructure as 6G network advancements continue to progress. The changing threat landscape that is unique to 6G infrastructure has been studied in this paper, along with the difficulties and fallout from security breaches that are expected. The need for creative pedagogical approaches in 6G security education stems from the paradigm shift in education. In order to effectively address the complexities of 6G technology, this paper emphasizes the need to modernize security education through the promotion of adaptive learning methodologies, interactive virtual environments, multidisciplinary integration, and ethical considerations. Cutting-edge pedagogies like augmented reality and group problem-solving present viable opportunities to raise student interest and competence in 6G security principles.

To succeed in this endeavor, though, adoption barriers must be removed, effective change management techniques must be put into place, collaboration must be encouraged, and inclusivity must be guaranteed.

REFERENCES

Abdulkarim, Y. I., Awl, H. N., Muhammadsharif, F. F., Saeed, S. R., Sidiq, K. R., Khasraw, S. S., Dong, J., Pandey, B. K., & Pandey, D. (2024). Metamaterial-based sensors loaded corona-shaped resonator for COVID-19 detection by using microwave techniques. *Plasmonics*, 19(2), 595–610. 10.1007/s11468-023-02007-4

Adamopoulou, E., & Moussiades, L. (2020). Chatbots: History, technology, and applications. *Machine Learning with Applications*, 2, 100006. 10.1016/j.mlwa.2020.100006

Anand, R., Khan, B., Nassa, V. K., Pandey, D., Dhabliya, D., Pandey, B. K., & Dadheech, P. (2023). Hybrid convolutional neural network (CNN) for kennedy space center hyperspectral image. *Aerospace Systems*, 6(1), 71–78. 10.1007/s42401-022-00168-4

Anand, R., Lakshmi, S. V., Pandey, D., & Pandey, B. K. (2024). An enhanced ResNet-50 deep learning model for arrhythmia detection using electrocardiogram biomedical indicators. *Evolving Systems*, 15(1), 83–97. 10.1007/s12530-023-09559-0

Arksey, H., & O'malley, L. (2005). Scoping studies: Towards a methodological framework. *International Journal of Social Research Methodology*, 8(1), 19–32. 10.1080/1364557032000119616

Bessant, Y. A., Jency, J. G., Sagayam, K. M., Jone, A. A. A., Pandey, D., & Pandey, B. K. (2023). Improved parallel matrix multiplication using Strassen and Urdhvatiryagbhyam method. *CCF Transactions on High Performance Computing*, 5(2), 102–115. 10.1007/s42514-023-00149-9

Borenstein, J., & Howard, A. (2021). Emerging challenges in AI and the need for AI ethics education. *AI and Ethics*, 1(1), 61–65. 10.1007/s43681-020-00002-738624388

David, S., Duraipandian, K., Chandrasekaran, D., Pandey, D., Sindhwani, N., & Pandey, B. K. (2023). Impact of blockchain in healthcare system. In *Unleashing the Potentials of blockchain technology for healthcare industries* (pp. 37–57). Academic Press. 10.1016/B978-0-323-99481-1.00004-3

Deepa, R., Anand, R., Pandey, D., Pandey, B. K., & Karki, B. (2022). Comprehensive performance analysis of classifiers in diagnosis of epilepsy. *Mathematical Problems in Engineering*, 2022, 2022. 10.1155/2022/1559312

Devasenapathy, D., Madhumathy, P., Umamaheshwari, R., Pandey, B. K., & Pandey, D. (2024). Transmission-efficient grid-based synchronized model for routing in wireless sensor networks using Bayesian compressive sensing. *SN Computer Science*, 5(1), 1–11.

Dhanasekar, S., Martin Sagayam, K., Pandey, B. K., & Pandey, D. (2023). Refractive Index Sensing Using Metamaterial Absorbing Augmentation in Elliptical Graphene Arrays. *Plasmonics*, 1–11. 10.1007/s11468-023-02152-w

Du John, H. V., Jose, T., Jone, A. A. A., Sagayam, K. M., Pandey, B. K., & Pandey, D. (2022). Polarization insensitive circular ring resonator based perfect metamaterial absorber design and simulation on a silicon substrate. *Silicon*, 14(14), 9009–9020. 10.1007/s12633-021-01645-9

George, W. K., Ekong, M. O., Pandey, D., & Pandey, B. K. (2023). Pedagogy for Implementation of TVET Curriculum for the Digital World. In *Applications of Neuromarketing in the Metaverse* (pp. 117-136). IGI Global. 10.4018/978-1-6684-8150-9.ch009

González-Calatayud, V., Prendes-Espinosa, P., & Roig-Vila, R. (2021). Artificial intelligence for student assessment: A systematic review. *Applied Sciences (Basel, Switzerland)*, 11(12), 5467. 10.3390/app11125467

. Govindaraj, V., Dhanasekar, S., Martinsagayam, K., Pandey, D., Pandey, B. K., & Nassa, V. K. (2023). Low-power test pattern generator using modified LFSR. *Aerospace Systems,* 1-8.

Hwang, G. J., & Chang, C. Y. (2023). A review of opportunities and challenges of chatbots in education. *Interactive Learning Environments*, 31(7), 4099–4112. 10.1080/10494820.2021.1952615

Iyyanar, P., Anand, R., Shanthi, T., Nassa, V. K., Pandey, B. K., George, A. S., & Pandey, D. (2023). A real-time smart sewage cleaning UAV assistance system using IoT. In *Handbook of Research on Data-Driven Mathematical Modeling in Smart Cities* (pp. 24–39). IGI Global.

Khan, B., Hasan, A., Pandey, D., Ventayen, R. J. M., Pandey, B. K., & Gowwrii, G. (2021). Fusion of datamining and artificial intelligence in prediction of hazardous road accidents. In *Machine learning and iot for intelligent systems and smart applications* (pp. 201–223). CRC Press. 10.1201/9781003194415-12

Kumar Pandey, B., Pandey, D., Nassa, V. K., Ahmad, T., Singh, C., George, A. S., & Wakchaure, M. A. (2021). Encryption and steganography-based text extraction in IoT using the EWCTS optimizer. *Imaging Science Journal*, 69(1-4), 38–56. 10.1080/13682199.2022.2146885

Malhotra, P., Pandey, D., Pandey, B. K., & Patra, P. M. (2021). Managing agricultural supply chains in COVID-19 lockdown. *International Journal of Quality and Innovation*, 5(2), 109–118. 10.1504/IJQI.2021.117181

Menon, V., Pandey, D., Khosla, D., Kaur, M., Vashishtha, H. K., George, A. S., & Pandey, B. K. (2022). A Study on COVID–19, Its Origin, Phenomenon, Variants, and IoT-Based Framework to Detect the Presence of Coronavirus. In *IoT Based Smart Applications* (pp. 1–13). Springer International Publishing.

Munn, Z., Peters, M. D., Stern, C., Tufanaru, C., McArthur, A., & Aromataris, E. (2018). Systematic review or scoping review? Guidance for authors when choosing between a systematic or scoping review approach. *BMC Medical Research Methodology*, 18(1), 1–7. 10.1186/s12874-018-0611-x30453902

Nicolescu, L., & Tudorache, M. T. (2022). Human-computer interaction in customer service: The experience with AI chatbots—a systematic literature review. *Electronics (Basel)*, 11(10), 1579. 10.3390/electronics11101579

Okonkwo, C. W., & Ade-Ibijola, A. (2021). Chatbots applications in education: A systematic review. *Computers and Education: Artificial Intelligence*, 2, 100033. 10.1016/j.caeai.2021.100033

Pandey, B. K., & Pandey, D. (2023). Parametric optimization and prediction of enhanced thermoelectric performance in co-doped CaMnO3 using response surface methodology and neural network. *Journal of Materials Science Materials in Electronics*, 34(21), 1589. 10.1007/s10854-023-10954-1

Pandey, B. K., Pandey, D., & Agarwal, A. (2022). Encrypted information transmission by enhanced steganography and image transformation. *International Journal of Distributed Artificial Intelligence*, 14(1), 1–14. 10.4018/IJDAI.297110

Pandey, B. K., Pandey, D., Alkhafaji, M. A., Güneşer, M. T., & Şeker, C. (2023a). A reliable transmission and extraction of textual information using keyless encryption, steganography, and deep algorithm with cuckoo optimization. In *Micro-Electronics and Telecommunication Engineering: Proceedings of 6th ICMETE 2022* (pp. 629–636). Springer Nature Singapore. 10.1007/978-981-19-9512-5_57

Pandey, B. K., Pandey, D., Gupta, A., Nassa, V. K., Dadheech, P., & George, A. S. (2023b). Secret data transmission using advanced morphological component analysis and steganography. In *Role of data-intensive distributed computing systems in designing data solutions* (pp. 21–44). Springer International Publishing. 10.1007/978-3-031-15542-0_2

Pandey, B. K., Pandey, D., & Sahani, S. K. (2024). Autopilot control unmanned aerial vehicle system for sewage defect detection using deep learning. *Engineering Reports*, 12852. 10.1002/eng2.12852

Pandey, B. K., Pandey, S. K., & Pandey, D. (2011). A survey of bioinformatics applications on parallel architectures. *International Journal of Computer Applications*, 23(4), 21–25. 10.5120/2877-3744

Pandey, D., Hasan, A., Pandey, B. K., Lelisho, M. E., George, A. H., & Shahul, A. (2023). COVID-19 epidemic anxiety, mental stress, and sleep disorders in developing country university students. *CSI Transactions on ICT*, 11(2), 119–127. 10.1007/s40012-023-00383-0

Pandey, D., Nassa, V. K., Jhamb, A., Mahto, D., Pandey, B. K., George, A. H., & Bandyopadhyay, S. K. (2021a). An integration of keyless encryption, steganography, and artificial intelligence for the secure transmission of stego images. In *Multidisciplinary approach to modern digital steganography* (pp. 211–234). IGI Global. 10.4018/978-1-7998-7160-6.ch010

Pandey, D., Ogunmola, G. A., Enbeyle, W., Abdullahi, M., Pandey, B. K., & Pramanik, S. (2021b). COVID-19: A framework for effective delivering of online classes during lockdown. *Human Arenas*, 1-15.

Pandey, D., & Pandey, B. K. (2022). An efficient deep neural network with adaptive galactic swarm optimization for complex image text extraction. In *Process mining techniques for pattern recognition* (pp. 121–137). CRC Press. 10.1201/9781003169550-10

Pandey, J. K., Jain, R., Dilip, R., Kumbhkar, M., Jaiswal, S., Pandey, B. K., & Pandey, D. (2022). Investigating role of iot in the development of smart application for security enhancement. In *IoT Based Smart Applications* (pp. 219–243). Springer International Publishing.

Pollock, D., Tricco, A. C., Peters, M. D., Mclnerney, P. A., Khalil, H., Godfrey, C. M., Alexander, L. A., & Munn, Z. (2022). Methodological quality, guidance, and tools in scoping reviews: A scoping review protocol. *JBI Evidence Synthesis*, 20(4), 1098–1105. 10.11124/JBIES-20-0057034446668

Pramanik, S., Pandey, D., Joardar, S., Niranjanamurthy, M., Pandey, B. K., & Kaur, J. (2023, October). An overview of IoT privacy and security in smart cities. In *AIP Conference Proceedings* (Vol. 2495, No. 1). AIP Publishing 10.1063/5.0123511

Revathi, T. K., Sathiyabhama, B., Sankar, S., Pandey, D., Pandey, B. K., & Dadeech, P. (2022). An intelligent model for coronary heart disease diagnosis. In *Networking Technologies in Smart Healthcare* (pp. 309–327). CRC Press. 10.1201/9781003239888-15

Rudolph, J., Tan, S., & Tan, S. (2023). ChatGPT: Bullshit spewer or the end of traditional assessments in higher education? *Journal of Applied Learning and Teaching, 6*(1), 342-363.

Sasidevi, S., Kumarganesh, S., Saranya, S., Thiyaneswaran, B., Shree, K. V. M., & Martin Sagayam, K. (2024, May 15). Design of Surface Plasmon Resonance (SPR) Sensors for Highly Sensitive Biomolecular Detection in Cancer Diagnostics. *Plasmonics*. Advance online publication. 10.1007/s11468-024-02343-z

Saxena, A., Agarwal, A., Pandey, B. K., & Pandey, D. (2024). Examination of the Criticality of Customer Segmentation Using Unsupervised Learning Methods. *Circular Economy and Sustainability*, 1–14. 10.1007/s43615-023-00336-4

Saxena, A., Sharma, N. K., Pandey, D., & Pandey, B. K. (2021). Influence of tourists satisfaction on future behavioral intentions with special reference to desert triangle of Rajasthan. *Augmented Human Research*, 6(1), 13. 10.1007/s41133-021-00052-4

Schwendimann, R., Blatter, C., Dhaini, S., Simon, M., & Ausserhofer, D. (2018). The occurrence, types, consequences and preventability of in-hospital adverse events–a scoping review. *BMC Health Services Research*, 18(1), 1–13. 10.1186/s12913-018-3335-z29973258

Sengupta, R., Sengupta, D., Pandey, D., Pandey, B. K., Nassa, V. K., & Dadeech, P. (2021). A Systematic review of 5G opportunities, architecture and challenges. *Future Trends in 5G and 6G*, 247-269.

Sharma, M., Pandey, D., Khosla, D., Goyal, S., Pandey, B. K., & Gupta, A. K. (2022). Design of a GaN-based Flip Chip Light Emitting Diode (FC-LED) with au Bumps & Thermal Analysis with different sizes and adhesive materials for performance considerations. *Silicon*, 14(12), 7109–7120. 10.1007/s12633-021-01457-x

Sharma, S., Pandey, B. K., Pandey, D., Anand, R., Sharma, A., & Saini, S. (2023, March). Character Recognition Technique Implementation for Complicated Deteriorated Scene. In *2023 6th International Conference on Information Systems and Computer Networks (ISCON)* (pp. 1-4). IEEE. 10.1109/ISCON57294.2023.10112185

Swapna, H. R., Bigirimana, E., Madaan, G., Hasan, A., Pandey, B. K., & Pandey, D. (2023). Impact of neuromarketing on consumer psychology in digitally connected networks. In *Applications of Neuromarketing in the Metaverse* (pp. 193–205). IGI Global. 10.4018/978-1-6684-8150-9.ch015

Tareke, S. A., Lelisho, M. E., Hassen, S. S., Seid, A. A., Jemal, S. S., Teshale, B. M., & Pandey, B. K. (2022). The prevalence and predictors of depressive, anxiety, and stress symptoms among Tepi town residents during the COVID-19 pandemic lockdown in Ethiopia. *Journal of Racial and Ethnic Health Disparities*, 1–13.35028903

Terzopoulos, G., & Satratzemi, M. (2019, September). Voice assistants and artificial intelligence in education. In *Proceedings of the 9th Balkan Conference on Informatics* (pp. 1-6). 10.1145/3351556.3351588

Tripathi, R. P., Sharma, M., Gupta, A. K., Pandey, D., Pandey, B. K., Shahul, A., & George, A. H. (2023). Timely prediction of diabetes by means of machine learning practices. *Augmented Human Research*, 8(1), 1. 10.1007/s41133-023-00062-4

Vaswani, A., Shazeer, N., Parmar, N., Uszkoreit, J., Jones, L., & Gomez, A. N. (2017, December). Attention Is All You Need, Adv. Neural Inf. Process. Syst. In *Neural Inf. Process. Syst* (pp. 5999-6009). Academic Press.

Vinodhini, V., Kumar, M. S., Sankar, S., Pandey, D., Pandey, B. K., & Nassa, V. K. (2022). IoT-based early forest fire detection using MLP and AROC method. *International Journal of Global Warming*, 27(1), 55–70. 10.1504/IJGW.2022.122794

Chapter 2
Transformative Approaches:
Exploring Innovative Pedagogies for 6G Education

Freddy Ochoa-Tataje
Postgraduate Department, Universidad César Vallejo, Lima, Peru

Joel Alanya-Beltran
Universidad San Ignacio de Loyola, Peru

Jenny Ruiz-Salazar
Universidad Privada del Norte, Lima, Peru

Juan Paucar-Elera
Faculty of Economic Sciences, Universidad Nacional Federico Villarreal, Lima, Peru

Michel Mendez-Escobar
Administration Department, Universidad Autónoma del Perú, Lima, Peru

Adolfo Perez-Mendoza
Science Department, Universidad Autónoma del Perú, Lima, Peru

ABSTRACT

Pedagogical approaches guide social science education. These methods encourage student participation, deep comprehension, and critical thinking. Effective pedagogies that help students understand complex technological concepts and foster forward-thinking problem-solving skills are essential as we enter the 6G era, which will transform connectivity and communication. A cornerstone of modern pedagogy, the constructivist approach emphasizes students' active construction of knowledge through experiences, interactions, and reflections. In 6G education, this method can help students understand complex technologies. Students can learn 6G concepts and improve their problem-solving skills by participating in creation activities, experiments, and projects. Students gain a holistic view of 6G technology by immersing themselves in real-world scenarios, enabling innovative solutions to emerging challenges.

I. INTRODUCTION

Pedagogical approaches guide social science education. These methods encourage student participation, deep comprehension, and critical thinking. Effective pedagogies that help students understand complex technological concepts and foster forward-thinking problem-solving skills are essential as we enter the 6G era (Sengupta, R. et al., 2021), which will transform connectivity and communication. A

DOI: 10.4018/979-8-3693-7421-4.ch002

cornerstone of modern pedagogy, the constructivist approach emphasizes students' active construction of knowledge through experiences, interactions, and reflections. In 6G education, this method can help students understand complex technologies. Students can learn 6G concepts and improve their problem-solving skills by participating in creation activities, experiments, and projects. Students gain a holistic view of 6G technology by immersing themselves in real-world scenarios, enabling innovative solutions to emerging challenges. 6G education is interdisciplinary and based on collaboration. Students collaborate and socialize to solve complex problems and share ideas using the collaborative method. Students in 6G classrooms can form interdisciplinary teams from engineering, computer science, telecommunications, and social sciences. Students use their knowledge of 6G technology to analyze real-world case studies and propose novel solutions to emerging issues through collaborative projects and group discussions. Students learn by critically reflecting on their experiences and identifying areas for growth. In 6G education, the reflective method encourages students to consider the social and ethical implications of advanced technologies. Journaling, group discussions, and peer feedback help students understand 6G technology ethics. Self-reflection helps students identify their strengths and weaknesses, improve their problem-solving skills, and develop responsibility as future technologists and policymakers. Integrating multiple fields of study and perspectives helps explain complex phenomena. 6G from multiple perspectives, students learn about its technological, economic, social, and ethical aspects and can better address real-world issues. The inquiry-based method encourages students to ask questions, investigate, and experiment to learn. In 6G education, where innovation and problem-solving are key, inquiry-based learning fosters students' curiosity and initiative. Students improve their critical thinking, research, and 6G technology knowledge through inquiry-driven projects. Students learn the skills and competencies needed to succeed in 6G technology through hands-on activities and cutting-edge research (Kaur, M. J. et al., 2020).

1.1 Innovative Pedagogies in 6G Education

The sixth-generation wireless technology is the next step forward in the evolution of wireless communication systems (Devasenapathy, D. et al., 2024). Its primary objective is to revolutionize connectivity, data (Sharma, S. et al., 2023) transmission, and network capabilities beyond those of its predecessors. Experts and researchers are already envisioning the potential of 6G to enable even faster data speeds, ultra-low latency, massive device (Du John, H. V. et al., 2022) connectivity, and seamless integration with emerging technologies such as artificial intelligence (Anand, R. et al., 2023), Internet of Things (IoT) (Menon, V. et al., 2022), and quantum computing. This is despite the fact that 5G technology is still in the process of being deployed on a global scale. An era of unprecedented connectivity and innovation is anticipated to be ushered in by the advent of 6G, which is anticipated to unlock new possibilities in a variety of industries, including healthcare (Revathi, T. K. et. al., 2022), transportation (Sahani, K. et al., 2023), entertainment, and manufacturing. For the purpose of preparing the next generation of professionals to comprehend, develop, and make use of the potential of 6G technology, innovative pedagogies play a crucial role (Singh, S. et al., 2023). When it comes to addressing the multifaceted nature of 6G, which necessitates a profound comprehension of advanced telecommunications concepts, the ability to collaborate across disciplines, and critical thinking skills, traditional teaching methods frequently fall short. Teachers are able to create engaging learning experiences for their students by incorporating innovative pedagogies such as project-based learning, collaborative activities, and hands-on experimentation. These pedagogies enable students to investigate 6G technology in depth, apply theoretical knowledge to practical scenarios, and develop creative solutions to complex problems. Innovative pedagogies cultivate skills such as adaptability, resilience, and lifelong learning, all of which are essential for thriving in a technological landscape that is constantly evolving (KVM, S. et al., 2024). It is essential to investigate transformative approaches in the field of 6G education in order to address the one-of-a-kind challenges and opportunities that are presented by this emerging technology. Students are encouraged to engage in deep learning (Pandey, B. K., & Pandey, D., 2023). Parametric), critical thinking, and innovative thinking through the use of transformative approaches, which go beyond traditional teaching methods. It is possible for educators to cultivate an environment in which students are encouraged to question assumptions, think creatively, and collaborate across disciplines in order to address real-world problems if they embrace transformative approaches. Transformative approaches give students the ability to become active participants in their own learning journey, which helps to cultivate a sense of ownership and responsibility for their education as well as their future careers in the field of 6G technology. When all is said and done, the objective of investigating transformative approaches is to provide students with the information (Pandey, B. K. et al., 2022), abilities, and mentality that will enable them to navigate the complexities of 6G technology and make a meaningful contribution to its development and implementation (Wang, K. J. et al., 2021).

1.2 6G Education Scope and Skills

A comprehensive understanding of the next evolution in wireless communication technology (Gupta, A. K. et al., 2023) is what is encompassed by a 6G education. This understanding goes beyond simple technical proficiency and encompasses a wide range of knowledge and skills that apply to a variety of fields. The study of advanced telecommunications concepts is at the heart of 6G education. These concepts include, but are not limited to, information about terahertz frequency bands, integrated satellite-terrestrial networks, and communication systems that are driven by artificial intelligence (Tripathi, R. P. et al., 2023). Its scope, on the other hand, extends far beyond these technical aspects, branching out into a variety of fields such as computer science, engineering, mathematics, physics, social sciences, and policy interpretation. Examining the societal implications, ethical considerations, and economic impacts of the deployment of 6G technology is an essential component of the education that is provided for 6G. Concerns about privacy, data security (David, S. et al., 2023), the digital divide, and the potential socioeconomic disparities that could result from unequal access to advanced communication technologies are some of the issues that will be investigated as part of this exercise (Pandey, B. K. et al., 2023a). To ensure that technological advancements are in accordance with ethical principles and the well-being of society, students are also tasked with analyzing the ethical dilemmas that are inherent in 6G technology and developing strategies to address them in a responsible manner. The development of skills such as critical thinking, problem-solving, and innovation is emphasized in 6G education. These skills are essential for successfully navigating the complexities of future technological landscapes. Students are strongly encouraged to participate in collaborative projects that span multiple disciplines, to think creatively, and to adapt to technology and industry trends that are constantly evolving. This requires not only the acquisition of theoretical knowledge but also the acquisition of practical experience through the pursuit of research projects, hands-on experimentation, and applications in the real world. By incorporating industry partnerships, research collaborations, and opportunities for experiential learning, 6G education goes beyond the framework of traditional classroom settings. For the purpose of gaining hands-on experience and gaining an understanding of the most recent advancements in 6G technology, students have the opportunity to interact with professionals from the industry, take part in internships or co-op programs, and execute research projects. Students will be well-equipped to address the challenges and opportunities presented by the next generation of wireless communication technology if they receive a 6G education because it bridges the gap between the academic world and the business world (Malhotra, P. et al., 2021). Sixth Generation (6G) education places an emphasis on learning that continues throughout one's life and adaptability, acknowledging the dynamic nature of the field of telecommunications (Raja, D. et al., 2024). Continual learning and professional development initiatives are some of the ways in which students are encouraged to keep themselves abreast of the most recent technological advancements, research findings, and industry trends. That graduates will continue to be competitive and well-prepared to navigate the ever-changing landscape of 6G technology throughout their careers is a result of this commitment to lifelong learning, which also contributes to the ongoing innovation and advancement in the field (Laubenbacher, R. et al., 2021).

1.3 Challenges and Opportunities

Challenge

One of the main challenges in teaching 6G concepts is their complexity. Teachers must be able to explain extremely complex technological concepts to students with different levels of technical proficiency. For students who don't have a strong background in telecommunications or related fields, concepts like intelligent networking, quantum (Du John, H. V. et al., 2023) computing, and terahertz communication can be intimidating. Educators may face a great difficulty in simplifying these difficult concepts and offering pertinent examples and analogies. Furthermore, careful planning and instructional design are needed to guarantee that students understand not only the theoretical foundations but also the real-world applications of these concepts. Teachers need to find creative ways to make difficult concepts interesting and approachable for all students, while also making sure that students have a sufficient depth of understanding without overloading them with technical jargon. It can be difficult for teachers to maintain current course materials given the quick speed at which technology is developing in the telecommunications industry. Teachers need to constantly review and modify their curricula to reflect the most recent advancements because new discoveries and research findings are made on a regular basis. To make sure that course material stays current and reflective of industry practices, this calls for attending conferences and workshops, keeping up with current research and trends in the field, and interacting with professionals in the field. Nevertheless, juggling this steady stream of new textual information (Pandey, D., & Pandey, B. K., 2022) with the curriculum's coherence and continuity can be a difficult task, necessitating educators to be adaptable, creative, and proactive in their approach to curriculum development and delivery (Santos, J. A. et al., 2020).

Opportunities

Teaching 6G concepts gives teachers a chance to experiment with cutting-edge teaching strategies that encourage engagement, critical thinking, and active learning. For instance, project-based learning encourages creativity and teamwork by allowing students to explore real-world issues and devise solutions utilizing 6G technologies. Simulators, virtual labs, and practical experiments are examples of experiential learning opportunities that give students practical skills and insights into the operation of

6G networks. Teachers can enhance student motivation and learning outcomes by implementing these cutting-edge pedagogies into their lessons to create dynamic, interactive learning environments that accommodate a variety of learning preferences and styles. The interdisciplinary nature of 6G technology also gives teachers a chance to encourage cooperation amongst students with various academic backgrounds. Teachers can assist students in understanding the complexity of 6G technology and help them develop their communication, problem-solving, and collaborative skills by promoting interdisciplinary teamwork and projects. Industry collaborations also provide students with excellent chances to obtain practical experience and understanding of the useful applications of 6G technology. Students are exposed to current industry practices, trends, and challenges through research projects, internships, and guest lectures. This improves their employability and gives them invaluable networking opportunities. Teachers can equip students to become proficient, flexible, and creative professionals in the field of 6G technology by taking advantage of these opportunities.

II. TRADITIONAL VS. NEW METHODS

2.1 Legacy vs. Innovation

In the rapidly changing educational landscape of today, traditional teaching methods frequently take a back seat to those that are more contemporary and innovative. The conventional approach to instruction, on the other hand, continues to be applicable in a variety of educational settings, particularly in the field of STEM (science, technology, engineering, and mathematics) education. In order to provide a comprehensive overview of traditional teaching methods in STEM education, the purpose of this article is to investigate the benefits and drawbacks of these methods in comparison to contemporary approaches. The more we investigate the complexities of traditional teaching, the more we will be able to comprehend the role that it plays and the significance it holds in the educational practices of today.

Traditional teaching methods are still widely used in many classrooms around the world, despite the widespread belief that they are no longer prevalent. For the most part, these approaches involve teacher-centered instruction, in which the instructor acts as the primary source of knowledge and imparts information to students through the use of lectures, textbooks, and structured assignments within the classroom. The traditional method of instruction in the STEM fields frequently places an emphasis on rote memorization, problem-solving through algorithms (Pandey, B. K. et al., 2011), and the mastery of fundamental concepts before moving on to more complex subjects. The continued popularity of traditional teaching methods in STEM education can be attributed to the fact that they offer a number of benefits. First and foremost, the structured nature of traditional instruction gives students a distinct framework for learning, which assists in the establishment of a solid foundation of fundamental concepts and principles. Additionally, the direct guidance and expertise of the instructor can provide students with an invaluable support system, particularly in subjects that require students to solve complex problems and develop abstract reasoning skills. As a result of the fact that students are expected to adhere to the rules and procedures that have been established within the classroom environment, traditional methods further encourage students to develop discipline and accountability.

Students are able to delve deeply into fundamental concepts and develop a comprehensive understanding of fundamental principles when they apply traditional teaching methods, which frequently prioritize depth of understanding over breadth of coverage. Having such a profound comprehension is especially important in the STEM fields, as it is the mastery of fundamental concepts that serves as the foundation for more advanced research and study. Furthermore, traditional teaching methods have the potential to instill a sense of discipline, perseverance, and work ethic in students. This is because students are required to engage in rigorous study and practice in order to gain academic success. While traditional teaching methods do have some benefits, they also have a number of significant drawbacks, which have resulted in criticism of these methods and a gradual decline in their popularity. Students, who are frequently relegated to the role of passive recipients of knowledge rather than active participants in the learning process, are often assigned a passive role, which is one of the substantial disadvantages of the system. Students may become disinterested or disengaged from the material that is being presented, which can be detrimental to student engagement, creativity, and critical thinking skills. This approach to learning can be considered passive. It is common for traditional teaching methods to place a greater emphasis on rote memorization and the repetition of facts than they do on in-depth comprehension and the relevance of knowledge. As a result of this approach to learning, students may focus on memorizing information without fully comprehending its significance or relevance, which can lead to a surface-level understanding and a lack of critical thinking skills within the student body. Furthermore, it is possible that traditional methods of instruction do not adequately prepare students for the requirements of the modern workforce, which places a greater emphasis on transferable skills such as adaptability, creativity, and collaboration (Holland, J. et al., 2021).

2.2 Limitations of Old Ways

Figure 1. Key components and skills required

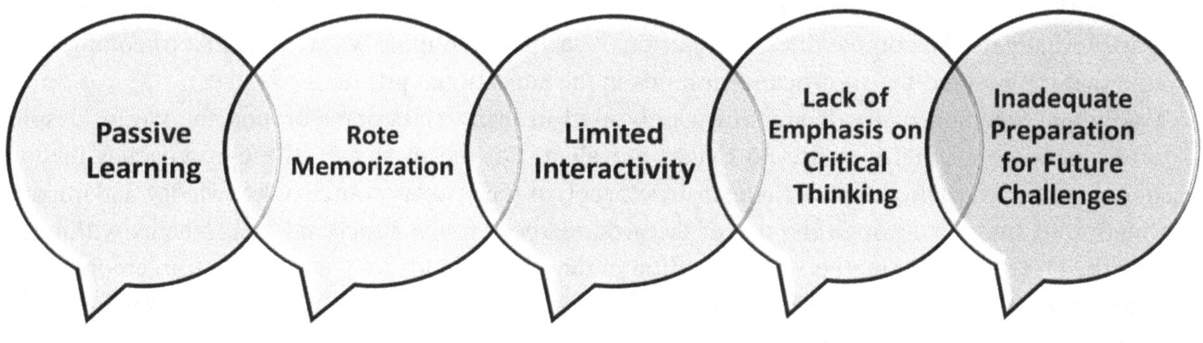

Key parts and skills needed for 6G education are shown in the figure 1, which include a wide range of technical knowledge, the ability to think critically, and information from different fields (Pandey, B. K. et al., 2023b). It's important to be good at things like wireless communication, artificial intelligence (Deepa, R. et al., 2022), hacking, and data analytics (Pandey, B. K. et al., 2024). You should also be able to solve problems, work with others, be flexible, and make moral decisions.

- *Passive Learning*: Traditional methods of instruction frequently encourage passive learning, in which students are primarily passive recipients of information rather than active participants in the process of learning. When it comes to the teaching of concepts related to 6G, passive learning can be especially detrimental because it hinders the ability of students to engage deeply with the material and develop a comprehensive understanding of complex concepts. Students may passively absorb information without fully comprehending its significance or relevance. This indicates that they are not actively questioning, analyzing, or synthesizing the information they are being presented with. Taking a passive approach to learning can result in students having a surface-level understanding and a lack of critical thinking skills, which hinders their ability to apply their knowledge to real-world scenarios or adapt to new challenges in the field of 6G technology, which is rapidly evolving.

- *Rote Memorization*: The conventional methods of teaching 6G concepts frequently involve the memorization of technical details and terminology through rote learning, rather than fostering an in-depth comprehension of the fundamental principles that underlie the technology. It's possible that students will be expected to memorize formulas, definitions, and protocols without fully comprehending the significance of these things or how they can be applied in the real world. As a result of this emphasis on memorization, students may have difficulty making connections between various concepts or applying their knowledge in novel ways, which can lead to a superficial understanding of the concepts pertaining to 6G. It is possible that students' ability to think critically, solve problems creatively, and adapt to new challenges in the rapidly changing landscape of 6G technology may be hindered if they rely solely on rote memorization.
- *Limited Interactivity*: When it comes to STEM education, traditional teaching methods, which include concepts related to 6G, frequently place a greater emphasis on lectures and textbooks than they do on interactive and experiential learning experiences. The limited amount of interaction that students have with the material can make it more difficult for them to actively engage with the content, explore hands-on experiments, and work together with their classmates to find solutions to problems. In the context of teaching 6G concepts, which involve intricate technical concepts and emerging technologies, interactive learning experiences are essential for fostering creativity and innovation among students, as well as for deepening their understanding of the material. Students may have difficulty developing the practical skills and critical thinking abilities necessary to be successful in the field of 6G technology if they are not provided with opportunities for hands-on experimentation, collaborative problem-solving, and real-world applications.
- *Lack of Emphasis on Critical Thinking*: Critical thinking abilities like analysis, synthesis, and evaluation may not be sufficiently emphasized in traditional teaching methods. These abilities are crucial for comprehending difficult ideas and resolving practical issues. Critical thinking abilities are crucial when teaching 6G concepts because students will need to predict future advancements and maneuver through complex technological systems. Traditional methods, however, frequently place more emphasis on memorization and recall than on more in-depth comprehension and analysis. Students may as a result passively accept information without challenging presumptions or critically assessing the data (Khan, B. et al., 2021). Without a strong focus on critical thinking, students might find it difficult to acquire the analytical and problem-solving skills required to handle the intricate challenges presented by 6G technology.
- *Inadequate Preparation for Future Challenges*: The dynamic and multidisciplinary nature of the 6G technology landscape may not be sufficiently addressed by traditional teaching methods. Students must acquire a wide range of abilities beyond technical knowledge, such as flexibility, teamwork, and creativity, as the field of 6G continues to develop quickly. Traditional methods of teaching 6G concepts, however, might prioritize content delivery over chances for students to

acquire these crucial abilities. Furthermore, the interdisciplinary nature of 6G technology—which includes social, economic, and ethical issues in addition to technical concepts—might not be sufficiently covered by conventional methods for students. Students might not be well-equipped to handle the many opportunities and challenges that come with 6G technology in their future careers if they are not exposed to these wider viewpoints. Therefore, in order to effectively prepare students for success in the field of 6G technology, educators must take into account the shortcomings of traditional teaching methods and investigate alternative approaches that prioritize critical thinking, interdisciplinary collaboration, active learning, and real-world applications over traditional methods.

2.3 New Pedagogical Strategies

Exploring transformative pedagogical strategies is a result of the current educational discourse's pursuit of more impactful and effective teaching methods. Transformative pedagogy aims to go beyond these constraints by encouraging students' deeper engagement, critical thinking, and holistic development. Traditional approaches to education frequently place a higher priority on content delivery and standardized assessment. This introduction gives a general overview of transformative pedagogy, emphasizing its fundamental ideas, guiding principles, and possible effects on methods of instruction and learning. Education has historically been defined by a one-size-fits-all methodology in which teachers serve as the main knowledge distributors and students are expected to absorb knowledge passively. But because it ignores the wide range of needs, interests, and skill levels among students, this educational approach has drawn criticism. An alternate framework made possible by transformative pedagogy places a higher value on student agency, autonomy, and empowerment. Transformative pedagogy, which questions established power dynamics in the classroom and aims to create more inclusive, equitable, and transformative learning environments, has its roots in critical theory, social justice, and constructivism. The idea that education should stimulate social and personal change in addition to imparting knowledge forms the basis of transformative pedagogy. Transformative pedagogy helps students become engaged citizens who can positively impact their communities and society as a whole by urging them to critically analyze their experiences, question prevailing narratives, and take action to address social injustices. The theoretical underpinnings, real-world applications, and potential drawbacks of transformative pedagogical strategies are examined in the following chapters, with this introduction providing context (Lopes, D. et al., 2023).

IV. INNOVATIVE PEDAGOGIES FOR 6G

Creative teaching strategies that equip students with the 6G technology comprise innovative pedagogies for 6G education are shown in the Figure 2. In order to develop the critical thinking, problem-solving, and adaptability abilities necessary for navigating the changing terrain of next-generation wireless communication, these approaches make use of active learning, technological integration, and collaborative environments.

Figure 2. Innovative pedagogies for 6G education

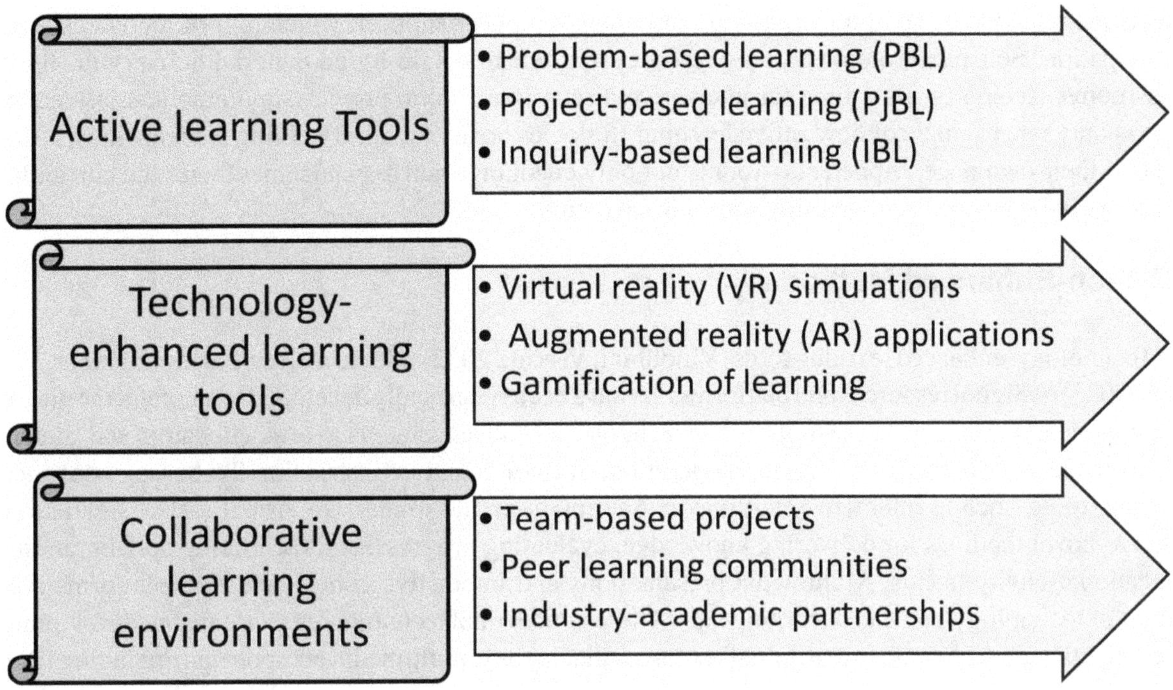

4.1 Active Learning Tools

Students are expected to actively participate with the course material through a range of interactive and participatory activities, which is a break from typical lecture-based teaching styles. This is known as an active learning strategy. These approaches include many different strategies intended to help students gain a deeper comprehension, develop their critical thinking skills, and retain information. Active learning approaches try to create a more dynamic and engaging learning environment that better equips students for success in the modern world by encouraging students to take a more active part in their education. Problem-based learning (PBL) is a popular approach to active learning in which students are given real-world scenarios or problems and are required to problem-solve and engage in collaborative inquiry to create solutions. Critical thinking, communication, and teamwork are just a few of the vital qualities that PBL fosters in addition to encouraging the application of information in real-world situations. PBL allows for a deeper comprehension of fundamental ideas and concepts by involving students in real-world problem-solving scenarios. Inquiry-based learning, which allows students to conduct independent research and discovery on interesting subjects, is another popular active learning approach. An increasingly individualized and student-driven learning process is made possible by inquiry-based learning, which encourages students to pose questions, carry out research, and come to their own conclusions. Through granting students the freedom to follow their own passions and curiosities, inquiry-based learning fosters a sense of ownership over the learning process and intrinsic motivation. Collaboration among students is emphasized through collaborative learning, an additional efficacious active learning approach. Small groups of students collaborate in collaborative learning settings to solve issues, talk about the course material, and exchange ideas. Collaborative learning promotes social contact and the development of interpersonal skills by creating a sense of community and peer support, which in turn motivates active participation. Self-paced online training replaces traditional lecture-based material delivery in flipped classrooms, freeing up class time for interactive discussions, group projects, and practical instruction. This is only one example of how active learning strategies are included. By giving students the freedom to go at their own pace, flipped classrooms not only encourage active engagement with the curriculum but also give them more ownership over their education.

4.2 Tech-Enhanced Methods

Technology-enhanced learning tools (Vinodhini, V. et al., 2022) refer to a diverse array (Bessant, Y. A. et al., 2023) of digital resources and platforms that have been specifically developed to augment the process of teaching and learning. These tools utilize technological advancements to offer educators and students novel prospects for active participation, cooperation, and individualized instruction. Technology-enhanced learning tools, such as interactive multimedia presentations and immersive virtual reality simulations, provide novel methods for delivering knowledge, evaluating progress, and facilitating collaboration in educational environments. Multimedia presentations and interactive content creation platforms are a subset of technology-enhanced learning aids. These educational technologies facilitate the development of captivating and dynamic instructional resources that include multimedia components, including films, animations, audio recordings, and interactive features like quizzes and simulations. By employing a visually engaging and interactive medium, these educational tools have the ability to captivate students' interest and enhance their comprehension of intricate ideas. Collaborative online platforms and communication tools represent an additional classification of technology-enhanced learning resources. These digital platforms (Swapna, H. R. et al., 2023) facilitate student collaboration on collective assignments, resource sharing, and real-time communication with both classmates and teachers. These tools facilitate cooperation, teamwork, and communication skills that are crucial for achieving success in the digital era, whether through the utilization of discussion forums, video conferencing, or shared document editing. Evaluation and feedback instruments are essential components of technology-enhanced learning. These educational tools facilitate the evaluation of student advancement, monitoring of learning achievements, and provision of prompt feedback on assignments and exams. Adaptive learning platforms (Saxena, A. et al., 2024) employ algorithms to customize learning experiences according to the unique performance of individual students, thereby offering focused interventions and assistance in areas that require attention. Both virtual reality (VR) and augmented reality (AR) technologies provide students with immersive learning experiences, enabling them to engage with digital content (George, W. K. et al., 2023) and explore virtual settings in a realistic manner. Virtual reality (VR) simulations have the capability to mimic historical events, scientific phenomena, and intricate processes, so affording students with experiential learning opportunities that would be challenging or unattainable to replicate within the confines of a conventional classroom environment. AR apps have the capability to superimpose digital information (Ekong, M. O. et al., 2023) onto the physical world, enabling students to engage with digital content within their immediate surroundings. Mobile learning applications and online learning management systems (LMS) are widely utilized technological solutions that contribute to the enhancement of learning experiences. These platforms offer students convenient access to educational resources at any time and from any location. These platforms provide students with the ability to interact with course materials, take part in conversations, and finish assignments using their cellphones, tablets, or PCs, offering both flexibility and convenience (Salameh, A. I., & El Tarhuni, M., 2022).

4.3 Collaborative Environments

When students collaborate in small groups or teams to accomplish shared learning objectives, they are learning in collaborative learning environments. These learning settings encourage active participation and shared accountability for learning objectives by fostering cooperation, communication, and teamwork among students. Virtual learning environments, in-person instruction, and hybrid models fusing digital and in-person interactions are just a few examples of the diverse types of collaborative learning environments that exist. In a typical classroom, students work together to solve issues, share ideas, and learn from one another in groups through projects, conversations, and activities. Through active participation in the learning process, students are able to develop their critical thinking abilities and gain a deeper comprehension of the course material. Additionally, students can develop critical interpersonal and social skills including leadership, communication, and conflict resolution in collaborative learning situations. Student freedom and accessibility are increased in online collaborative learning settings, which are enabled by digital platforms and communication technologies. From any location with an internet connection (Kumar Pandey, B. et al., 2021), students may work together on group projects, share materials, and interact with peers and teachers using these platforms. Due to scheduling difficulties or geographic restrictions, students who are unable to attend traditional in-person classes may find special benefit from online collaborative learning environments. With the best of both worlds, students can benefit from hybrid methods of collaborative learning that incorporate parts of online and traditional classroom training. Students may participate in online collaboration and discussion outside of class hours in addition to in-person discussions and activities during meetings in a hybrid collaborative learning environment. With the use of a blended learning method, the learning process can be more easily tailored to the individual preferences and styles of learning. Establishing a welcoming and inclusive climate, outlining expectations and goals for group work, and encouraging active participation from all students are all essential components of successful collaborative learning environments. When they offer direction, criticism, and encouragement to students as they collaborate to accomplish learning objectives, educators are essential in creating collaborative learning environments (Dao, N. N., 2023).

4.4 Hurdles and Solutions for Collaborative Learning

When implementing collaborative learning environments, educators may run into a number of obstacles that they must successfully overcome. Resistance to change is a major obstacle, especially among educators who are used to using conventional teaching techniques. Some may be reluctant to implement collaborative learning because they don't know how to incorporate it into their current curriculum or have doubts about its efficacy. Giving teachers and students thorough training and assistance is crucial to removing this obstacle. Workshops, seminars, and chances for professional development can assist educators in comprehending the advantages of collaborative learning and providing them with the tools and techniques they need to successfully execute it. Furthermore, encouraging an honest conversation and communicating openly to resolve concerns can lessen opposition and increase buy-in from stakeholders. Student involvement disparities are another typical obstacle to the implementation of collaborative learning environments. Certain students may take the lead in group conversations or activities, leaving others feeling excluded or uninterested. This disparity may reduce collaborative learning's potential advantages and reduce its efficacy. Teachers can reduce this obstacle by setting up procedures that encourage equal involvement from all group members and by clearly outlining expectations for participation. Ensuring that every student has the chance to participate meaningfully in collaborative activities can be achieved through setting up norms for inclusive communication, rotating leadership positions, and assigning specific tasks or duties within groups. Teachers can also foster an environment in the classroom that is inclusive, supportive, and appreciates a variety of viewpoints and motivates all students to participate actively. The implementation of collaborative learning environments may face logistical hurdles such as resource limitations, time limits, and technological difficulties. Inadequate assistance or lack of access to suitable technology can impede instructors' capacity to design successful cooperative learning environments. In order to get above these obstacles, educators should make innovative use of the infrastructure and resources already in place. They should look for free or inexpensive digital tools and platforms that promote teamwork. Time management and careful scheduling can also help maximize class time and guarantee that group projects complement learning goals. Working together with IT support personnel or instructional technology specialists can also be very helpful in resolving technical issues and maximizing the success of collaborative learning projects. Through proactive resolution of these obstacles and implementation of focused tactics for alleviation, educators can establish cooperative learning settings that promote student involvement, critical thinking, and significant learning results.

CONCLUSION

The landscape of education is fast altering with breakthroughs in technology, with 6G technology ready to revolutionize the way in which we communicate, cooperate, and invent at the same time. During the process of preparing for this future, it is becoming increasingly apparent that existing pedagogies are not adequate for properly teaching concepts related to 6G infrastructure. The implementation of ways that are both innovative and transformative is essential in order to provide students with the knowledge, skills, and mindset that are necessary for them to prosper in this dynamic world. As a result of this investigation into 6G education, we have acquired a more profound comprehension of the significance of new pedagogies in the process of preparing students for the difficulties and opportunities that are given by 6G technology. By embracing active learning approaches, employing technology-enhanced learning tools, and cultivating collaborative learning settings, educators are able to create learning experiences that are not only successful but also interesting, so empowering students to become critical thinkers, problem solvers, and learners who continue to learn throughout their lives. The fact that transformative approaches present a substantial number of advantages for 6G education, they also come with their own unique set of difficulties. Educators are able to overcome these hurdles and unlock the full potential of transformative pedagogies in 6G education if they take a proactive approach to addressing potential barriers and implement measures for mitigating their effects.

REFERENCES

Anand, R., Khan, B., Nassa, V. K., Pandey, D., Dhabliya, D., Pandey, B. K., & Dadheech, P. (2023). Hybrid convolutional neural network (CNN) for kennedy space center hyperspectral image. *Aerospace Systems*, 6(1), 71–78. 10.1007/s42401-022-00168-4

Bessant, Y. A., Jency, J. G., Sagayam, K. M., Jone, A. A. A., Pandey, D., & Pandey, B. K. (2023). Improved parallel matrix multiplication using Strassen and Urdhvatiryagbhyam method. *CCF Transactions on High Performance Computing*, 5(2), 102–115. 10.1007/s42514-023-00149-9

Dao, N. N. (2023). Internet of wearable things: Advancements and benefits from 6G technologies. *Future Generation Computer Systems*, 138, 172–184. 10.1016/j.future.2022.07.006

David, S., Duraipandian, K., Chandrasekaran, D., Pandey, D., Sindhwani, N., & Pandey, B. K. (2023). Impact of blockchain in healthcare system. In *Unleashing the Potentials of blockchain technology for healthcare industries* (pp. 37–57). Academic Press. 10.1016/B978-0-323-99481-1.00004-3

Deepa, R., Anand, R., Pandey, D., Pandey, B. K., & Karki, B. (2022). Comprehensive performance analysis of classifiers in diagnosis of epilepsy. *Mathematical Problems in Engineering*, 2022, 2022. 10.1155/2022/1559312

Devasenapathy, D., Madhumathy, P., Umamaheshwari, R., Pandey, B. K., & Pandey, D. (2024). Transmission-efficient grid-based synchronized model for routing in wireless sensor networks using Bayesian compressive sensing. *SN Computer Science*, 5(1), 1–11.

Du John, H. V., Jose, T., Jone, A. A. A., Sagayam, K. M., Pandey, B. K., & Pandey, D. (2022). Polarization insensitive circular ring resonator based perfect metamaterial absorber design and simulation on a silicon substrate. *Silicon*, 14(14), 9009–9020. 10.1007/s12633-021-01645-9

Du John, H. V., Sagayam, K. M., Jose, T., Pandey, D., Pandey, B. K., Kotti, J., & Kaur, P. (2023). Design simulation and parametric investigation of a metamaterial light absorber with tungsten resonator for solar cell applications using silicon as dielectric layer. *Silicon*, 15(9), 4065–4079. 10.1007/s12633-023-02321-w

Ekong, M. O., George, W. K., Pandey, B. K., & Pandey, D. (2023). Enhancing the Fundamentals of Industrial Safety Management in TVET for Metaverse Realities. In *Applications of Neuromarketing in the Metaverse* (pp. 19-41). IGI Global. 10.4018/978-1-6684-8150-9.ch002

George, W. K., Ekong, M. O., Pandey, D., & Pandey, B. K. (2023). Pedagogy for Implementation of TVET Curriculum for the Digital World. In *Applications of Neuromarketing in the Metaverse* (pp. 117-136). IGI Global. 10.4018/978-1-6684-8150-9.ch009

Gupta, A. K., Sharma, R., Pandey, D., Nassa, V. K., Pandey, B. K., George, A. S., & Dadheech, P. (2023). Performance analysis of eight-channel WDM optical network with different optical amplifiers for industry 4.0. In *Innovation and Competitiveness in Industry 4.0 Based on Intelligent Systems* (pp. 197–212). Springer International Publishing. 10.1007/978-3-031-29775-5_9

Holland, J., Kingston, L., McCarthy, C., Armstrong, E., O'Dwyer, P., Merz, F., & McConnell, M. (2021). Service robots in the healthcare sector. *Robotics (Basel, Switzerland)*, 10(1), 47. 10.3390/robotics10010047

. Kaur, M. J., Mishra, V. P., & Maheshwari, P. (2020). The convergence of digital twin, IoT, and machine learning: transforming data into action. *Digital twin technologies and smart cities*, 3-17.

Khan, B., Hasan, A., Pandey, D., Ventayen, R. J. M., Pandey, B. K., & Gowwrii, G. (2021). Fusion of datamining and artificial intelligence in prediction of hazardous road accidents. In *Machine learning and iot for intelligent systems and smart applications* (pp. 201–223). CRC Press. 10.1201/9781003194415-12

Kumar Pandey, B., Pandey, D., Nassa, V. K., Ahmad, T., Singh, C., George, A. S., & Wakchaure, M. A. (2021). Encryption and steganography-based text extraction in IoT using the EWCTS optimizer. *Imaging Science Journal*, 69(1-4), 38–56. 10.1080/13682199.2022.2146885

KVM, S., Pandey, B. K., & Pandey, D. (2024). Design of Surface Plasmon Resonance (SPR) Sensors for Highly Sensitive Biomolecular Detection in Cancer Diagnostics. *Plasmonics*, 1–13.

Laubenbacher, R., Sluka, J. P., & Glazier, J. A. (2021). Using digital twins in viral infection. *Science*, 371(6534), 1105–1106. 10.1126/science.abf337033707255

Lopes, D., Coelho, L., & Silva, M. F. (2023). Development of a collaborative robotic platform for autonomous auscultation. *Applied Sciences (Basel, Switzerland)*, 13(3), 1604. 10.3390/app13031604

Malhotra, P., Pandey, D., Pandey, B. K., & Patra, P. M. (2021). Managing agricultural supply chains in COVID-19 lockdown. *International Journal of Quality and Innovation*, 5(2), 109–118. 10.1504/IJQI.2021.117181

Menon, V., Pandey, D., Khosla, D., Kaur, M., Vashishtha, H. K., George, A. S., & Pandey, B. K. (2022). A Study on COVID–19, Its Origin, Phenomenon, Variants, and IoT-Based Framework to Detect the Presence of Coronavirus. In *IoT Based Smart Applications* (pp. 1–13). Springer International Publishing.

Pandey, B. K., & Pandey, D. (2023). Parametric optimization and prediction of enhanced thermoelectric performance in co-doped CaMnO3 using response surface methodology and neural network. *Journal of Materials Science Materials in Electronics*, 34(21), 1589. 10.1007/s10854-023-10954-1

Pandey, B. K., Pandey, D., & Agarwal, A. (2022). Encrypted information transmission by enhanced steganography and image transformation. *International Journal of Distributed Artificial Intelligence*, 14(1), 1–14. 10.4018/IJDAI.297110

Pandey, B. K., Pandey, D., Alkhafaji, M. A., Güneşer, M. T., & Şeker, C. (2023a). A reliable transmission and extraction of textual information using keyless encryption, steganography, and deep algorithm with cuckoo optimization. In *Micro-Electronics and Telecommunication Engineering: Proceedings of 6th ICMETE 2022* (pp. 629–636). Springer Nature Singapore. 10.1007/978-981-19-9512-5_57

Pandey, B. K., Pandey, D., Gupta, A., Nassa, V. K., Dadheech, P., & George, A. S. (2023b). Secret data transmission using advanced morphological component analysis and steganography. In *Role of data-intensive distributed computing systems in designing data solutions* (pp. 21–44). Springer International Publishing. 10.1007/978-3-031-15542-0_2

Pandey, B. K., Pandey, D., & Sahani, S. K. (2024). Autopilot control unmanned aerial vehicle system for sewage defect detection using deep learning. *Engineering Reports*, 12852. 10.1002/eng2.12852

Pandey, B. K., Pandey, S. K., & Pandey, D. (2011). A survey of bioinformatics applications on parallel architectures. *International Journal of Computer Applications*, 23(4), 21–25. 10.5120/2877-3744

Pandey, D., & Pandey, B. K. (2022). An efficient deep neural network with adaptive galactic swarm optimization for complex image text extraction. In *Process mining techniques for pattern recognition* (pp. 121–137). CRC Press. 10.1201/9781003169550-10

Raja, D., Kumar, D. R., Santhiyakumari, N., Kumarganesh, S., Sagayam, K. M., Thiyaneswaran, B., Pandey, B. K., & Pandey, D. (2024). A compact dual-feed wide-band slotted antenna for future wireless applications. *Analog Integrated Circuits and Signal Processing*, 1–15. 10.1007/s10470-023-02233-0

Revathi, T. K., Sathiyabhama, B., Sankar, S., Pandey, D., Pandey, B. K., & Dadeech, P. (2022). An intelligent model for coronary heart disease diagnosis. In *Networking Technologies in Smart Healthcare* (pp. 309–327). CRC Press. 10.1201/9781003239888-15

Sahani, K., Khadka, S. S., Sahani, S. K., Pandey, B. K., & Pandey, D. (2023). A possible underground roadway for transportation facilities in Kathmandu Valley: A racking deformation of underground rectangular structures. *Engineering Reports*, 12821. 10.1002/eng2.12821

Salameh, A. I., & El Tarhuni, M. (2022). From 5G to 6G—Challenges, technologies, and applications. *Future Internet*, 14(4), 117. 10.3390/fi14040117

Santos, J. A., Lopes, M. R., Viegas, J. L., Vieira, S. M., & Sousa, J. M. (2020). Internal supply chain digital twin of a pharmaceutical company. *IFAC-PapersOnLine*, 53(2), 10797–10802. 10.1016/j.ifacol.2020.12.2864

Saxena, A., Agarwal, A., Pandey, B. K., & Pandey, D. (2024). Examination of the Criticality of Customer Segmentation Using Unsupervised Learning Methods. *Circular Economy and Sustainability*, 1–14. 10.1007/s43615-023-00336-4

. Sengupta, R., Sengupta, D., Pandey, D., Pandey, B. K., Nassa, V. K., & Dadeech, P. (2021). A Systematic review of 5G opportunities, architecture and challenges. *Future Trends in 5G and 6G,* 247-269.

Sharma, S., Pandey, B. K., Pandey, D., Anand, R., Sharma, A., & Saini, S. (2023, March). Character Recognition Technique Implementation for Complicated Deteriorated Scene. In *2023 6th International Conference on Information Systems and Computer Networks (ISCON)* (pp. 1-4). IEEE. 10.1109/ISCON57294.2023.10112185

Singh, S., Madaan, G., Kaur, J., Swapna, H. R., Pandey, D., Singh, A., & Pandey, B. K. (2023). *Bibliometric Review on Healthcare Sustainability. Handbook of Research on Safe Disposal Methods of Municipal Solid Wastes for a Sustainable Environment*, 142-161. 10.4018/978-1-6684-8117-2.ch011

Swapna, H. R., Bigirimana, E., Madaan, G., Hasan, A., Pandey, B. K., & Pandey, D. (2023). Impact of neuromarketing on consumer psychology in digitally connected networks. In *Applications of Neuromarketing in the Metaverse* (pp. 193–205). IGI Global. 10.4018/978-1-6684-8150-9.ch015

Tripathi, R. P., Sharma, M., Gupta, A. K., Pandey, D., Pandey, B. K., Shahul, A., & George, A. H. (2023). Timely prediction of diabetes by means of machine learning practices. *Augmented Human Research*, 8(1), 1. 10.1007/s41133-023-00062-4

Vinodhini, V., Kumar, M. S., Sankar, S., Pandey, D., Pandey, B. K., & Nassa, V. K. (2022). IoT-based early forest fire detection using MLP and AROC method. *International Journal of Global Warming*, 27(1), 55–70. 10.1504/IJGW.2022.122794

Wang, K. J., Lee, Y. H., & Angelica, S. (2021). Digital twin design for real-time monitoring–a case study of die cutting machine. *International Journal of Production Research*, 59(21), 6471–6485. 10.1080/00207543.2020.1817999

Chapter 3
Securing the Digital Future:
Educational Approaches in the 6G Ecosystem

T. Faisal
Karpagam Academy of Higher Education, Coimbatore, India

A. Dharmaraj
Department of Management, Karpagam Academy of Higher Education, Coimbatore, India

ABSTRACT

A revolutionary era marked by unmatched speed, connectivity, and game-changing innovation is about to dawn in the rapidly evolving field of telecommunications with the impending introduction of 6G technology. Security of the digital future is becoming more and more important as societies around the world depend more and more on digital infrastructure for commerce, communication, and social advancement. Notwithstanding the excitement and expectation that accompany technological developments, it is crucial to acknowledge the fundamental function that education performs in molding and preserving this new digital landscape.

I. INTRODUCTION

A revolutionary era marked by unmatched speed, connectivity, and game-changing innovation is about to dawn in the rapidly evolving field of telecommunications with the impending introduction of 6G technology. Security of the digital future is becoming more and more important as societies around the world depend more and more on digital infrastructure for commerce (Swapna, H. R. et al., 2023), communication, and social advancement. Notwithstanding the excitement and expectation that accompany technological developments, it is crucial to acknowledge the fundamental function that education performs in molding and preserving this new digital landscape. Fundamentally, the adoption of 6G technology represents a significant change in thinking that goes beyond technical expertise. Comprehending the ramifications, potential uses, and moral dilemmas associated with this emerging digital environment is imperative (George, W. K. et al., 2023). A concentrated effort to inform and empower people across numerous domains is necessary to attain this understanding; it cannot be done in isolation. Beyond conventional learning paradigms (Saxena, A. et al., 2024), education in the context of 6G encompasses

DOI: 10.4018/979-8-3693-7421-4.ch003

a multifaceted approach. It includes giving people the mindset, abilities, and information needed to successfully negotiate the complexity of the 6G ecosystem. The implementation and application of 6G technology requires not only technical know-how but also critical thinking, problem-solving skills, and ethical considerations. Against these backdrops, the purpose of this paper is to investigate the role that educational strategies play in safeguarding the digital future in the context of 6G technology. In order to clarify the way forward, we will explore the intricacies of 6G technology, comprehend its possible uses, and outline efficacious instructional approaches. This conversation revolves around the understanding that, in the digital age, education is the foundation for advancement and growth. By allocating resources towards educational programs that facilitate a more profound comprehension of 6G technology, we can develop a labor force that is not only capable of fully utilizing its potential but also proficiently managing its hazards and obstacles. In order to guarantee that everyone in society can take advantage of the advantages of 6G technology, education is vital. We can mitigate the risk of exacerbating existing disparities and guarantee that everyone benefits from the digital future by promoting digital literacy, inclusivity, and equitable access to educational opportunities.

1.1 Education in 6G's Future

Educational strategies play a crucial role in determining the future of 6G technology, as they serve as the foundation for the technology's development, deployment, and widespread application. The significance of education in this context is of the utmost importance, as the entire world is eagerly anticipating the arrival of 6G. In order for individuals to have the necessary foundation to comprehend the complexities of 6G technology, educational approaches are implemented. 6G is a paradigm shift in comparison to its predecessors, as it incorporates novel concepts and capabilities such as terahertz frequencies, the integration of artificial intelligence (AI) (Pandey, B. K., & Pandey, D., 2023), and holographic communication. Education provides individuals with the knowledge and skills necessary to comprehend these more advanced concepts, which in turn fosters a deeper understanding of the potential and possibilities that 6G has to offer. Education plays a significant part in the process of cultivating the talent pool that is necessary for the innovation of 6G. The development of a skilled labor force that is capable of driving advancements in 6G technology is accomplished by educational institutions through the provision of specialized courses, opportunities for research, and practical training programs. When it comes to the holistic development and responsible deployment of 6G solutions, this talent pool includes not only engineers and scientists but also policymakers, ethicists, and entrepreneurs who contribute to the process. Educational strategies make it easier for people from different fields to work together, which is absolutely necessary in order to address the myriad of challenges and opportunities that are associated with 6G (Ismail, L., & Materwala, H., 2019). Due to the fact that it has a wide range of applications across industries such as healthcare (Tareke, S. A. et al., 2022), transportation, and entertainment, 6G necessitates (Sengupta, R. et al., 2021) a collaborative approach that goes beyond the boundaries of individual disciplines. Educational initiatives that encourage learning across disciplines and collaboration foster innovation at the intersection of technology, policy, and society, which ultimately results in solutions that are more comprehensive and have a greater impact on the world. Through education and technical expertise, ethical considerations and societal implications are incorporated into the process of developing and deploying 6G technology. As the capabilities of 6G continue to expand to include ubiquitous connectivity, immersive experiences, and automation driven by artificial intelligence (Anand, R. et al., 2023), ethical dilemmas concerning privacy (Pramanik, S. et al., 2023), security, and algorithmic (Bessant, Y. A. et al., 2023) bias are becoming more prevalent. The incorporation of ethics, social sciences, and humanities into 6G curricula provides individuals with the ability to navigate these complex ethical landscapes in a responsible manner. This helps to ensure that 6G technology is in line with the values and aspirations of society. By acting as a catalyst for inclusive innovation, education helps to ensure that the benefits of 6G technology are accessible to all sectors of society. Educational approaches that encourage diversity, equity, and accessibility in STEM education create opportunities for underrepresented groups to participate in and contribute to the innovation of 6G networks. This approach, which is inclusive, not only promotes social equity but also enriches the ecosystem of innovation by utilizing a wide range of perspectives and experiences. When it comes to fostering lifelong learning and adaptability in the face of rapid technological change, educational approaches are absolutely necessary. In order to maintain their relevance in the digital economy, individuals are required to continually update their skills and knowledge as 6G continues to develop and mature. Educational initiatives that place an emphasis on continuous learning, reskilling, and upskilling equip individuals with the ability to navigate dynamic career landscapes and seize emerging opportunities in the era of 6G (Cao, K. et al., 2021).

1.2 Securing the Digital Future

Digital technologies are used in every part of society and our world is becoming more interconnected, safeguarding the digital future is crucial." The digital sphere is essential to modern living, influencing everything from commerce to healthcare (Pandey, D. et al., 2023) to entertainment. Cyberthreats and vulnerabilities are constantly growing and changing, this reliance also brings with it vulnerability. In order to strengthen our digital future, education is essential. Education works as a first line of defense against cyber threats by providing people with the information, abilities, and awareness needed to navigate cyberspace safely. Digital literacy, critical thinking, and cybersecurity awareness are all included in addition to technical proficiency. The fundamental goal of education is to enable people to use safe online behavior and make educated decisions (Pandey, D. et al., 2021a). Education instils best practices that promote resilience and cyber hygiene, from identifying phishing attempts to protecting personal information. A culture of cybersecurity consciousness is also fostered by education, where people value security in their digital interactions and promote group awareness. Education encourages teamwork and creativity in tackling cybersecurity challenges, going beyond personal empowerment. The creation of successful cybersecurity strategies, laws, and technologies is aided by education, which promotes interdisciplinary collaboration between researchers, educators, legislators, and industry stakeholders (Saxena, A. et al., 2021). To stay ahead of changing threats and adjust to new technologies and attack vectors, a collaborative approach is absolutely necessary. By guaranteeing a pipeline of qualified professionals ready to fend off cyberattacks, education is essential to closing the cybersecurity skills gap. Educational establishments and business associates train the next generation of cybersecurity specialists with the know-how to address challenging cybersecurity issues through cybersecurity education and training programs. Technological know-how, ethics, and responsible digital citizenship are emphasized in the curriculum. Education creates an environment of digital trust and accountability by advancing human rights, privacy (Pandey, B. K. et al., 2022), and ethical principles in cyberspace. The protection of individual rights, the integrity of digital ecosystems, and the reduction of the likelihood of cyber conflicts are all made possible by this ethical framework (Burns, R. et al., 2021).

1.3 6G Landscape: Applications and Impact

Imagining the landscape of 6G requires investigating the possible applications of the technology and gaining an understanding of the impact it will have on society. 6G, which is the next generation of wireless technology (Devasenapathy, D. et al., 2024), promises revolutionary advancements that will reimagine the ways in which we interact with electronic devices (Sharma, M. et al., 2022a) and with one another. The capability of 6G to support augmented reality (AR) and virtual reality (VR) experiences at levels of immersion and realism that have never been seen before is quickly becoming one of the most anticipated applications of this technology (Ekong, M. O. et al., 2023). Imagine having the ability to combine digital information with the real world in a seamless manner, whether for the purpose of providing entertainment, educating students, or implementing professional applications. It is possible that augmented reality and virtual reality powered by 6G will revolutionize the way in which we experience and interact with digital content. This could include everything from immersive learning environments and virtual meetings to interactive gaming. It is anticipated that 6G will make it possible for the Internet of Things (IoT) (Pandey, J. K.et al., 2022) to spread on a scale that has never been seen before, when billions of connected semiconductor devices (Sharma, M. et al., 2022b). will be able to communicate and coordinate with one another in real time smoothly. This has the potential to result in revolutionary developments in smart cities, which are characterized by the utilization of resources, the enhancement of public services, and the improvement of residents' quality of life through the utilization of interconnected sensors and electronics. The Internet of Things (IoT) (Vinodhini, V. et al., 2022) that is enabled by 6G has the potential to address some of the most pressing challenges that modern societies are currently facing (Iyyanar, P. et al., 2023). These challenges include smart infrastructure and transportation systems (Sahani, K. et al., 2023), healthcare monitoring (KVM, S., 2024), and environmental sustainability campaigns (Materwala, H. et al., 2022). Utilizing telemedicine, remote patient monitoring, and personalized healthcare solutions (Pandey, B. K. et al., 2011), 6G is poised to bring about a revolution in the delivery of healthcare. Patients can be remotely monitored in real time by medical professionals, virtual consultations can be facilitated, and timely interventions can be administered when necessary thanks to connectivity that is both extremely reliable and low in latency. The provision of proactive and individualized care is made possible as a result of this, which not only improves access to healthcare services (Singh, S. et al., 2023), particularly in areas that are underserved, but also improves patient outcomes. Autonomous systems, such as self-driving vehicles, drones, and robotic systems, are anticipated to experience significant advancements as a result of sixth-generation wireless technology. With their extremely low latency and high reliability, 6G networks are able to support real-time communication and coordination among autonomous entities. This makes it possible for these networks to operate in a manner that is both safer and more efficient across a variety of categories. Autonomous systems that are powered by 6G have the potential to revolutionize a wide range of industries (Malhotra, P. et al., 2021), including industrial automation and disaster response, as well as transportation and delivery systems that are in charge of themselves (Zeng, X. et al., 2020).

II. THE EDUCATION IMPERATIVE

2.1 Closing the Skills Gap

It is essential to educate the workforce in order to bridge the gap in skills and knowledge that is necessary for the successful adoption and implementation of 6G technology. As the next generation of wireless communication (Gupta, A. K. et al., 2023), 6G will introduce advanced concepts and technologies that will necessitate a workforce that possesses specialized expertise and capabilities. One of the most important areas in which education plays a significant role is in the process of preparing individuals with the technical skills necessary to design, develop, and maintain 6G networks and systems. In this context, it is important to have an understanding of concepts such as terahertz frequencies, massive MIMO (Multiple-Input Multiple-Output), and AI (Anand, R. et al., 2024) driven network optimization, all of which are essential to the operation of 6G technology. Educational programs and training initiatives that are specifically designed to meet these technical requirements can assist in the process of upskilling existing professionals and preparing new entrants to meet the requirements of the 6G workforce. Education is also an important factor in fostering a deeper understanding of the broader implications and applications of 6G technology. Technical skills are also an important factor. This includes investigating the ways in which 6G can propel innovation and transformation across a wide range of industries, including healthcare, transportation, entertainment, and manufacturing, among others (Pandey, D., & Pandey, B. K., 2022). Education gives individuals the ability to make meaningful contributions to the development and deployment of 6G technology in their respective fields by providing them with a comprehensive understanding of the potential benefits and challenges of 6G. Education is absolutely necessary in order to cultivate critical thinking, problem-solving skills, and adaptability among the workforce. Individuals need to be equipped with the skills necessary to navigate complex situations and find innovative solutions in order to keep up with the ongoing evolution of 6G technology and the emergence of new challenges. It is possible to cultivate these essential skills through educational methods that place an emphasis on hands-on learning, real-world applications, and interdisciplinary collaboration. This will help to ensure that the workforce continues to be adaptable and resilient in the face of technological change. When it comes to addressing inequalities in access to opportunities related to 6G and ensuring equitable participation in the digital economy, education is an extremely important factor to consider. Education contributes to the closing of the digital divide and the promotion of social and economic inclusion by providing educational programs and initiatives that are inclusive and that cater to individuals who come from a variety of communities and backgrounds. This is of utmost significance in order to guarantee that underserved communities are able to reap the benefits of the technological advancements and opportunities that are brought about by the implementation of 6G technology.

2.2 Fostering 6G Innovation

The development of innovative ideas is essential to the progression of 6G technology, and education is an essential component in the process of cultivating future leaders in this area. Considering that 6G is the next generation of wireless communication (Raja, D. et al., 2024), it will require pioneers, problem solvers, and visionaries who are able to push the boundaries of what is possible and make significant progress. Education acts as a catalyst for innovation because it equips individuals with the knowledge, skills, and mindset that are necessary to think outside the box and investigate new possibilities. Educational institutions cultivate an atmosphere that encourages curiosity, experimentation, and bold thinking by providing students with opportunities to participate in hands-on learning experiences, collaborative projects, and exposure to cutting-edge research. In the interest of advancing 6G technology, this helps to cultivate a new generation of innovators who are not afraid to challenge the status quo and pursue ideas that are ground-breaking. Education helps to cultivate an entrepreneurial spirit among future leaders of 6G networks, which enables them to transform innovative ideas into tangible solutions and products that address challenges that are encountered in the real world. In order to equip students with the knowledge, abilities, and resources necessary to launch successful businesses and drive economic growth within the 6G ecosystem, educational programs provide training in entrepreneurship, business management, and technology commercialization. The field of 6G technology is a complex and multifaceted field, and education plays a crucial role in fostering interdisciplinary collaboration, which is essential for driving innovation in this field. Educational programmes create opportunities for the cross-pollination of ideas and the synthesis of knowledge from a variety of fields by bringing together individuals who come from a variety of backgrounds, have a variety of expertise, and have different points of view. This multidisciplinary approach inspires creativity, generates fresh insights, and ultimately results in ground-breaking innovations that have the potential to revolutionize the way we think about and make use of 6G technology (Ismail, L., & Materwala, H., 2021). Education instills values such as resiliency, perseverance, and ethical responsibility, which are essential qualities for effective innovation leadership in the era of 6G that we are currently living in. Educational programmes prepare future leaders to navigate the ethical and moral complexities that are inherent in the process of developing and deploying advanced technologies such as 6G by placing an emphasis on the importance of integrity, social responsibility, and ethical decision-making.

2.3 Ensuring Digital Inclusivity

The digital literacy and accessibility and enable widespread participation and equitable opportunities in the digital age, it is imperative that 6G education be inclusive. As 6G technology develops further, it is critical to guarantee that everyone, regardless of background or situation, has the resources, knowledge, and abilities necessary to fully utilize and benefit from 6G technology. The cornerstone of ensuring inclusivity in 6G education is digital literacy. It includes having the capacity to successfully access, comprehend, assess, and use digital information and technologies. Prioritizing digital literacy training is imperative for educational initiatives to equip individuals with the necessary skills to navigate the complex digital landscape. These skills include understanding 6G technology, accessing online resources, and protecting personal information. In order to ensure that people with disabilities can fully participate in 6G education and benefit from its advancements, it is imperative that accessibility challenges are addressed. This involves making certain that learning environments, platforms, and instructional materials are accessible to people with a range of needs, including those who need accommodations or assistive technology. In order to establish inclusive learning environments that are friendly and open to all students, educators also need to be trained in inclusive teaching practices. Encouraging diversity and representation in 6G education is crucial to making sure that every person's experiences and viewpoints are respected and included in the educational process (Liu, Y. et al., 2020). This entails actively seeking out and keeping teachers and students from underrepresented groups in STEM fields, as well as incorporating a variety of viewpoints into the creation of curricula and teaching resources. To more effectively address the issues of digital literacy and accessibility, cooperative partnerships between educational institutions, government agencies, non-profit organizations, and industry stakeholders can be formed. Through the combined use of resources, knowledge, and best practices, these collaborations are able to create and carry out all-encompassing plans that support equity and digital inclusion in 6G education (Belkhir, L., & Elmeligi, A., 2018).

III. THE EDUCATION IMPERATIVE

3.1 Fostering 6G Innovation

Fundamental components of innovation, economic growth, and workforce development are education and skill development. Through the provision of appropriate knowledge, skills, and mindsets, educational systems across the globe facilitate the development of an innovative culture. The critical roles that education and skill development play in promoting innovation are as shown in the figure 1.:

- *STEM Education*: The foundation of innovation-driven industries is Science, Technology, Engineering, and Mathematics (STEM) education. By placing a strong emphasis on these subjects at every educational level, from elementary schools to universities, nations can develop a talent pool with the know-how and technical proficiency required to propel innovation forward. In addition to giving people a solid foundation in critical thinking and problem-solving, STEM education equips students to take on real-world challenges and advance technological advancements in a variety of fields.
- *Entrepreneurship Education*: Individuals are encouraged to think creatively, take calculated risks, and pursue novel ideas in an environment that is fostered by entrepreneurship education. Education systems foster an entrepreneurial mindset that is critical for promoting innovation by teaching would-be business owners how to recognize opportunities, validate concepts, and negotiate the complexities of the business environment. By enabling people to realize their ideas, entrepreneurship education promotes an innovative and risk-taking culture that is advantageous to prosperity and economic growth.
- *Programs for Lifelong Learning*: Innovation is a constant process in the quickly changing world of today, requiring people to learn, adapt, and pick up new skills all throughout their careers. Initiatives promoting lifelong learning are crucial for enabling people to keep up with changes in the market, industry trends, and technology. Governments and educational establishments ought to support lifelong learning initiatives that give people the chance to reskill, upskill, and maintain their competitiveness in the labor market. Countries can guarantee that their workforce is flexible, adaptive, and ready to tackle the challenges of a constantly evolving economy by allocating resources towards lifelong learning.
- *Collaboration with Industry*: In order to create educational programs that meet the demands of the labor market, educational institutions and industry partners must work together. Educational institutions can learn about new technologies, changing skill requirements, and industry trends by interacting with businesses. Through this partnership, academic institutions can customize their training programs and curricula to give students the knowledge and skills that employers are looking for. Education systems can guarantee that graduates are well-prepared to succeed in the

workforce and foster innovation in their respective fields by collaborating closely with industry partners.

Innovation and economic growth are largely fueled by education and skill development. Global education systems can develop a workforce capable of meeting future challenges and propelling innovation forward by supporting STEM education, encouraging entrepreneurship, funding lifelong learning programs, and working with industry partners.

Figure 1. The role of education and skills development in fostering innovation

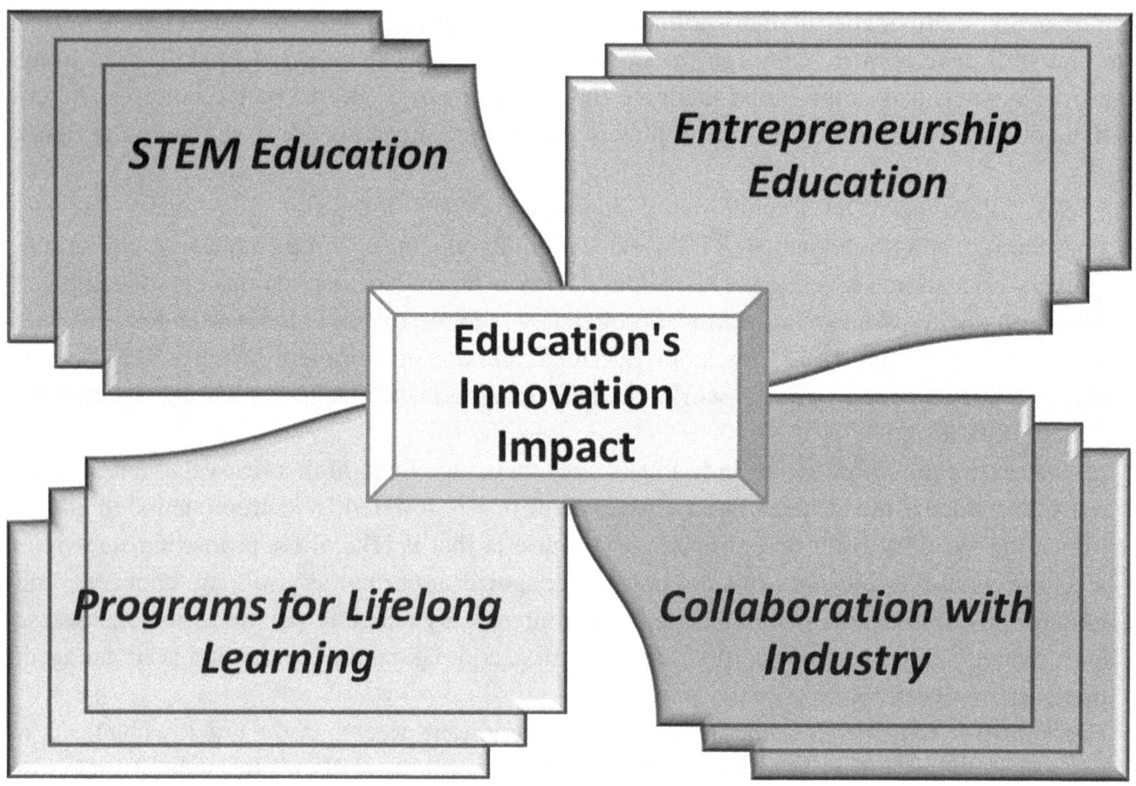

3.2 Ensuring Digital Inclusivity

Improving digital literacy and accessibility issues through 6G education must include everyone. This will encourage widespread participation and fair opportunities in the digital age. To make sure that everyone, no matter their background or situation, has the knowledge, skills, and resources they need to fully engage with and benefit from 6G technology as it continues to develop. To give people the skills they need to use and understand 6G technology, digital literacy programs are essential. Federal and state governments should put a high priority on digital literacy programs that teach people how to find, evaluate, and use digital resources and information. So that everyone can have a meaningful experience in the digital world, these programs should cover things like internet safety, how to communicate online, how to use information effectively, and basic computer skills. Individuals with disabilities must be able to fully participate in 6G education and benefit from its advances. All educational materials, platforms, and learning spaces must be created with accessibility in mind, making sure that everyone can access and participate in 6G education equally, even if they need help or special accommodations. Teachers should get training on how to make learning environments that are welcoming and easy for all students, no matter what abilities they have. Making sure that everyone's ideas and experiences are valued and used in 6G education means promoting diversity and representation. Educational programs should actively recruit and keep teachers and students from underrepresented groups in STEM fields. They should also make sure that learning materials and curriculum are developed with a variety of perspectives in mind. Academic institutions can make sure that everyone can contribute to and benefit from 6G education by creating a learning space that is diverse and welcoming. Educational institutions, government agencies, non-profits, and industry stakeholders must work together to solve problems with digital literacy and accessibility. Together, these partnerships can create all-encompassing plans to enhance digital equality and inclusion in 6G education by sharing resources, knowledge, and the very best ways to do things. Working together with partners in the industry can help make sure that educational programs match the needs of the industry and prepare students for successful careers in the 6G ecosystem (Akhtar, M. W. et al., 2020).

IV. EDUCATIONAL APPROACHES

4.1 Integrating 6G in Curriculum

The incorporation of 6G concepts into educational programs is an essential component of curriculum enhancement. This helps to ensure that students are prepared for the era of 6G. The sixth-generation wireless technology, also known as 6G, holds the promise of revolutionary advancements that will reshape both industries and society. It is possible for educational institutions to accomplish this by modernizing programs that are already in place, introducing new ones, and placing an emphasis on research and hands-on projects. It is essential to bring existing courses in fields such as engineering, computer science, and telecommunications up to date to meet current standards. Students should be provided with a comprehensive understanding of the basic principles, technologies, and applications of 6G technology through the implementation of these updates, which should include dedicated modules or units on the subject. By incorporating concepts related to 6G into the curriculum that is already in place, educational institutions can guarantee that students receive knowledge that is current, pertinent, and in line with the trends that are occurring in the industry. Additionally, the introduction of new courses that are specifically focused on 6G technology can further improve students' understanding and abilities. Students will be better prepared for specialized roles within the 6G ecosystem if they take these specialized courses, which can more deeply delve into advanced concepts and applications that are specific to 6G. Educational institutions are able to demonstrate their dedication to remaining at the forefront of technological innovation and providing students with an education that is modern by offering courses that are specifically focused on sixth-generation wireless networks (also known as 6G).

For the purpose of enhancing theoretical knowledge and developing practical skills, it is essential to place an emphasis on research opportunities and projects that require hands-on participation. Students are able to acquire valuable experience by participating in real-world projects that are related to 6G technology. These projects allow students to apply their knowledge to solve complex problems and develop innovative solutions. In addition, it is possible for students to make contributions to the development of 6G technology through participation in research initiatives, which helps to cultivate an environment within educational institutions that encourages innovation and exploration (Tataria, H. et al., 2021).

4.2 Industry-Academia Partnerships

In order to promote knowledge exchange and practical learning opportunities between academic institutions and industry, industry-academia partnerships are crucial. The theoretical knowledge gained in academic settings and the practical skills needed in real-world work environments are greatly aided by these collaborations. The provision of co-ops and internships is a noteworthy feature of these collaborations. Through these programs, students can interact with business professionals face-to-face and acquire practical experience as well as insights into the various sectors' daily operations. Students can hone their skills and deepen their understanding of industry practices by applying the theoretical concepts they have learned in the classroom to real-world projects and tasks. Collaborative research projects and initiatives are facilitated by partnerships between industry and academia. Collaborating on research projects, experts from the academic and industry sectors can combine their strengths and resources to tackle intricate problems and produce novel solutions. This cooperative approach develops a culture of innovation and encourages cross-disciplinary learning in addition to increasing knowledge in particular fields. Industry professionals frequently lead seminars, workshops, and guest lectures as part of partnerships. By giving students access to industry trends, best practices, and emerging technologies, these events enhance their academic curriculum with practical insights. These events provide networking opportunities for students to interact with professionals in their field of interest, which may result in opportunities for internships, jobs, or mentorship. Partnerships between industry and academia benefit participating industries as well as students. Companies can identify future employees or collaborators by interacting with educational institutions, which gives them access to a talented and motivated pool of people. Additionally, by participating in these partnerships, businesses can help shape the careers of upcoming professionals, guaranteeing a workforce with the skills necessary to meet industry demands and spur innovation (Yang, H. et al., 2020).

4.3 Lifelong Learning Initiatives

Continuous education and upskilling in 6G technology are crucial for individuals to stay skilled and competitive in a rapidly changing digital environment, making lifelong learning initiatives essential. These initiatives acknowledge the continuous nature of learning, which is crucial for individuals to thrive in the face of technological progress and maintain their professional relevance. The contribution of lifelong learning initiatives to the promotion of continuous education and upskilling in 6G technology can be elucidated as follows. Long-term learning initiatives offer individuals the chance to acquire additional knowledge and skills pertaining to 6G technology over the course of their professional lives. These initiatives provide a range of flexible learning opportunities, such as online courses, workshops, seminars, and certification programs, enabling individuals to conveniently and on-demand access educational resources. By facilitating the accessibility and flexibility of learning to accommodate individual schedules and preferences, lifelong learning initiatives enable individuals to enhance their skills and remain informed about the most recent advancements in 6G technology. Through the promotion of lifelong learning initiatives, employers have the opportunity to foster a proficient workforce that possesses the ability to effectively utilize 6G technology in order to stimulate innovation and enhance competitiveness. Investing in the upskilling of employees not only has a positive impact on individual performance, but also serves to bolster organizational capabilities and resilience in response to technological advancements. Lifelong learning initiatives foster collaboration and facilitate the exchange of knowledge among professionals engaged in the domain of 6G technology. Through engagement in networking events, conferences, and community forums, individuals have the opportunity to share ideas, insights, and best practices with colleagues and industry experts. The collective endeavors mentioned above serve to enhance the exchange of knowledge between different fields, foster creativity, and expedite the integration and execution of 6G technology in diverse industries. Long-term educational endeavors are of utmost importance in tackling the digital divide and fostering inclusivity within the realm of 6G technology. These initiatives guarantee universal access to the knowledge and skills necessary for participation in the digital economy by providing educational resources and training opportunities to individuals from various backgrounds and communities. Addressing the digital divide not only facilitates social and economic fairness, but also cultivates a workforce that is more diverse and inclusive, thereby stimulating innovation and advancement within the 6G framework (Letaief, K. B. et al., 2019).

V. NAVIGATING CHALLENGES AND OPTIMIZING OPPORTUNITIES

5.1 Barrier Breakdown

6G Education Barriers discusses the challenges that are shown in the Figure 2, which remain in the way of 6G education initiatives becoming widely adopted. Some of the issues covered in the conversation include infrastructure limitations, specialized training programs, and restricted access to resources. The goal is to enable more people to participate and engage in 6G education by recognizing and removing these barriers.

- *Electrical Power*: In many developing nations, obtaining dependable electricity is still a major obstacle, which prevents educational technology from being widely used. Distant communities are increasingly being served by decentralized electricity access initiatives like microgrids and off-grid solar power systems. Collaborating with governmental bodies, global associations, and commercial enterprises can expedite the implementation of sustainable energy remedies, such as photovoltaic cells and energy-storage infrastructure, to supply energy to academic establishments. In underprivileged areas, community-based initiatives that improve access to electricity for educational purposes like the installation of solar-powered charging stations or shared energy resources can improve school access.
- *Internet Connectivity*: Although the installation of submarine cables has increased internet connectivity worldwide, nations that are landlocked or have poor infrastructure still have difficulty getting high-speed internet. It is now possible to use mobile networks to deliver educational resources and content because mobile internet penetration has grown dramatically in many developing nations. Access to the internet can be enhanced in underserved areas, such as rural communities and m marginalized populations, through public-private partnerships that facilitate the deployment of broadband infrastructure. New technologies that have the potential to extend in-

ternet coverage to remote areas where traditional infrastructure deployment is not feasible include wireless mesh networks and low-earth orbit (LEO) satellites.

- *Training and Professional Development*: Educational programs that prepare teachers for the classroom should emphasize pedagogical approaches for incorporating technology into instruction as well as technical skills. Peer networks and mentoring initiatives can offer educators continuous assistance and chances for cooperation to share creative teaching strategies and best practices. Collaborations among academic institutions, governmental organizations, and tech firms can simplify the creation and provision of excellent workshops and resources for teacher professional development. Digital literacy skills for teachers and students should be covered in training programs as well, to guarantee that they can use digital tools and resources efficiently.
- *Value Teachers*: As a result of the realization of the vital role that teachers play in education, governments and other stakeholders in the field of education need to place a high priority on funding teacher recruitment, retention, and professional development. For the teaching profession to draw and keep talented individuals, competitive salaries and opportunities for professional development are crucial. Programs, prizes, and incentives designed to show appreciation for teachers can foster an environment where educators are valued and respected, which will inspire them to perform to the best of their abilities. Promoting a greater understanding of teaching among the public and policymakers requires advocacy campaigns to highlight the value of education to society and the beneficial effects that teachers have on students' lives.
- *Sustainability*: To guarantee ongoing success after initial implementation, sustainable educational technology projects should take into account long-term funding sources, maintenance schedules, and capacity-building activities. It is possible to co-create and take ownership of educational technology solutions that are customized to the unique requirements and environments of the target populations by working in partnership with regional communities, educational stakeholders, and pertinent institutions. Adaptive management strategies for sustainable implementation should be informed by monitoring and evaluation frameworks, which should be incorporated into project design to assess impact and identify challenges. The incorporation of open-source technologies and open educational resources (OER) can facilitate community-driven innovation, cost-effectiveness, and scalability in educational technology initiatives, thereby enhancing their future viability.
- *Global Cooperation*: In order to address complex issues and achieve global sustainable development goals, cooperation on a global scale for knowledge exchange and capacity building is essential. Partnerships between countries, organizations, and stakeholders are essential in today's interconnected world because they allow for the efficient sharing of resources, knowledge, and best practices in order to address common problems. Countries and institutions can share important knowledge, expertise, and innovations across international boundaries by promoting collaboration. International conferences, research networks, and online forums provide a platform for experts and practitioners with varying backgrounds to work together, exchange findings, and jointly generate new knowledge. The exchange of ideas facilitates the discovery of novel approaches to urgent global issues, including those related to healthcare, education, environmental preservation, and technological advancement.

Figure 2. 6G education barriers

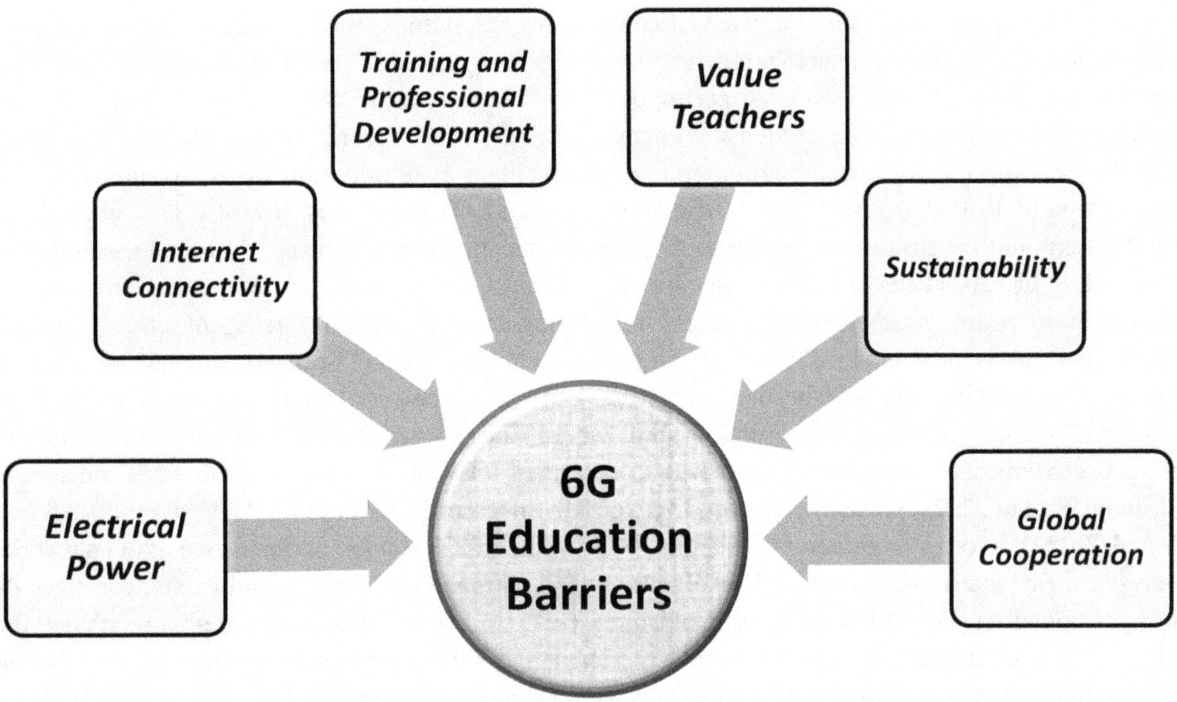

International cooperation helps capacity building by supporting programs for education and training, especially in areas with limited resources or that are experiencing developmental obstacles. Partnerships between developed and developing nations allow capacity-building initiatives to be customized to meet particular priorities and needs. Through the provision of technical expertise, funding, and educational resources, these initiatives enable individuals and communities to foster skill development, improve resilience, and stimulate local efforts towards sustainable development. By utilizing a variety of viewpoints and resources, global cooperation improves the efficacy of capacity-building programs. Countries and organizations can reach a wider audience and maximize impact by pooling their resources. By fostering a culture of mutual support and shared learning, this approach enables stakeholders to take advantage of each other's experiences and strengths. Experimentation and the adoption of best practices from various contexts are encouraged by global cooperation, which promotes innovation and results in more sustainable and effective solutions to global problems.

5.2 Leveraging Tech for Education

The utilization of emerging technologies to augment educational methodologies for 6G presents considerable promise in equipping individuals with the necessary skills to effectively navigate and thrive in the swiftly changing digital environment (Deepa, R. et al., 2022). The forthcoming wireless technology, known as 6G, holds the potential to bring about significant advancements that will have a profound impact on various industries and society at large. VR and AR technologies provide students with immersive learning experiences, enabling them to visualize intricate concepts pertaining to 6G technology within three-dimensional environments. By utilizing virtual reality (VR) simulations, students have the opportunity to investigate virtual 6G networks, witness the interactions between various components, and address potential problems, thereby gaining valuable practical experience. Likewise, augmented reality (AR) applications superimpose digital data (Kumar Pandey, B. et al., 2021) onto the physical environment, allowing students to engage with 6G infrastructure and devices (KVM, S. et al., 2024) in real-time, thereby improving comprehension and memory of important ideas. Machine Learning (ML) (Tripathi, R. P. et al., 2023) and Artificial Intelligence (AI) algorithms (Revathi, T. K. et al., 2022) are of paramount importance in the customization of educational experiences. AI based methodology (Khan, B. et al., 2021) can customize educational content based on students' performance data, tailoring it to their specific needs and preferences. AI (Pandey, D. et al., 2021b) intelligent tutoring systems offer focused assistance and feedback to students as they interact with 6G-related coursework, fostering enhanced comprehension and expertise in intricate subjects. AI-powered analytics tools (Pandey, B. K. et al., 2024) assist educators in identifying areas where students may be encountering difficulties and take proactive measures to offer support. The utilization of Internet of Things (IoT) devices and sensors (Sasidevi, S. et al., 2024) presents prospects for experiential learning and empirical investigation (Menon, V. et al., 2022). In order to gather data (Pandey, B. K. et al., 2023a) on the performance of 6G networks, analyze traffic patterns (Govindaraj, V. et al., 2023), and optimize resource allocation, students have the ability to construct and implement Internet of Things (IoT) solutions. Through engagement with tangible IoT applications, students acquire hands-on experience and cultivate problem-solving abilities that are relevant to the implementation of 6G technology. Blockchain technology (David, S. et al., 2023) plays a crucial role in safeguarding the confidentiality and authenticity (Pandey, B. K. et al., 2023b) of educational records and credentials. Educational institutions can utilize blockchain-based systems to securely store and authenticate (Sharma, S. et al., 2023) students' academic accomplishments, certifications, and qualifications pertaining to 6G technology. This promotes transparency and confidence in educational qualifications, making it easier for students to transition into the workforce or pursue higher education in fields related to 6G.

CONCLUSION

6G technology and education highlight the importance of educational approaches in shaping its future. After studying the evolution from 1G to 6G, 6G's potential applications and societal impact stand out, presenting both challenges and opportunities. Education is a key pillar of 6G development, focusing on skills, innovation, and digital literacy and accessibility. Curriculum enhancement, research collaboration, and industry-academia partnerships can prepare students for the 6G ecosystem. Lifelong learning programmes promote 6G technology education and upskilling, keeping people adaptable and competitive in a rapidly changing digital landscape. Future goals include overcoming 6G education adoption barriers and leveraging global cooperation for knowledge sharing and capacity building. Additionally, virtual reality, artificial intelligence, and blockchain can improve 6G education by providing immersive learning experiences and securing educational credentials.

REFERENCES

Akhtar, M. W., Hassan, S. A., Ghaffar, R., Jung, H., Garg, S., & Hossain, M. S. (2020). The shift to 6G communications: Vision and requirements. *Human-centric Computing and Information Sciences*, 10(1), 1–27. 10.1186/s13673-020-00258-2

Anand, R., Khan, B., Nassa, V. K., Pandey, D., Dhabliya, D., Pandey, B. K., & Dadheech, P. (2023). Hybrid convolutional neural network (CNN) for kennedy space center hyperspectral image. *Aerospace Systems*, 6(1), 71–78. 10.1007/s42401-022-00168-4

Anand, R., Lakshmi, S. V., Pandey, D., & Pandey, B. K. (2024). An enhanced ResNet-50 deep learning model for arrhythmia detection using electrocardiogram biomedical indicators. *Evolving Systems*, 15(1), 83–97. 10.1007/s12530-023-09559-0

Belkhir, L., & Elmeligi, A. (2018). Assessing ICT global emissions footprint: Trends to 2040 & recommendations. *Journal of Cleaner Production*, 177, 448–463. 10.1016/j.jclepro.2017.12.239

Bessant, Y. A., Jency, J. G., Sagayam, K. M., Jone, A. A. A., Pandey, D., & Pandey, B. K. (2023). Improved parallel matrix multiplication using Strassen and Urdhvatiryagbhyam method. *CCF Transactions on High Performance Computing*, 5(2), 102–115. 10.1007/s42514-023-00149-9

Burns, R., Fast, V., Levenda, A., & Miller, B. (2021). Smart cities: Between worlding and provincialising. *Urban Studies (Edinburgh, Scotland)*, 58(3), 461–470. 10.1177/0042098020975982

Cao, K., Hu, S., Shi, Y., Colombo, A. W., Karnouskos, S., & Li, X. (2021). A survey on edge and edge-cloud computing assisted cyber-physical systems. *IEEE Transactions on Industrial Informatics*, 17(11), 7806–7819. 10.1109/TII.2021.3073066

David, S., Duraipandian, K., Chandrasekaran, D., Pandey, D., Sindhwani, N., & Pandey, B. K. (2023). Impact of blockchain in healthcare system. In *Unleashing the Potentials of blockchain technology for healthcare industries* (pp. 37–57). Academic Press. 10.1016/B978-0-323-99481-1.00004-3

Deepa, R., Anand, R., Pandey, D., Pandey, B. K., & Karki, B. (2022). Comprehensive performance analysis of classifiers in diagnosis of epilepsy. *Mathematical Problems in Engineering*, 2022, 2022. 10.1155/2022/1559312

Devasenapathy, D., Madhumathy, P., Umamaheshwari, R., Pandey, B. K., & Pandey, D. (2024). Transmission-efficient grid-based synchronized model for routing in wireless sensor networks using Bayesian compressive sensing. *SN Computer Science*, 5(1), 1–11.

Ekong, M. O., George, W. K., Pandey, B. K., & Pandey, D. (2023). Enhancing the Fundamentals of Industrial Safety Management in TVET for Metaverse Realities. In *Applications of Neuromarketing in the Metaverse* (pp. 19-41). IGI Global. 10.4018/978-1-6684-8150-9.ch002

George, W. K., Ekong, M. O., Pandey, D., & Pandey, B. K. (2023). Pedagogy for Implementation of TVET Curriculum for the Digital World. In *Applications of Neuromarketing in the Metaverse* (pp. 117-136). IGI Global. 10.4018/978-1-6684-8150-9.ch009

. Govindaraj, V., Dhanasekar, S., Martinsagayam, K., Pandey, D., Pandey, B. K., & Nassa, V. K. (2023). Low-power test pattern generator using modified LFSR. *Aerospace Systems*, 1-8.

Gupta, A. K., Sharma, R., Pandey, D., Nassa, V. K., Pandey, B. K., George, A. S., & Dadheech, P. (2023). Performance analysis of eight-channel WDM optical network with different optical amplifiers for industry 4.0. In *Innovation and Competitiveness in Industry 4.0 Based on Intelligent Systems* (pp. 197–212). Springer International Publishing. 10.1007/978-3-031-29775-5_9

Ismail, L., & Materwala, H. (2019). A review of blockchain architecture and consensus protocols: Use cases, challenges, and solutions. *Symmetry*, 11(10), 1198. 10.3390/sym11101198

Ismail, L., & Materwala, H. (2021). IoT-edge-cloud computing framework for QoS-aware computation offloading in autonomous mobile agents: modeling and simulation. In *Mobile, Secure, and Programmable Networking: 6th International Conference, MSPN 2020, Paris, France, October 28–29, 2020, Revised Selected Papers 6* (pp. 161-176). Springer International Publishing. 10.1007/978-3-030-67550-9_11

Iyyanar, P., Anand, R., Shanthi, T., Nassa, V. K., Pandey, B. K., George, A. S., & Pandey, D. (2023). A real-time smart sewage cleaning UAV assistance system using IoT. In *Handbook of Research on Data-Driven Mathematical Modeling in Smart Cities* (pp. 24–39). IGI Global.

Khan, B., Hasan, A., Pandey, D., Ventayen, R. J. M., Pandey, B. K., & Gowwrii, G. (2021). Fusion of datamining and artificial intelligence in prediction of hazardous road accidents. In *Machine learning and iot for intelligent systems and smart applications* (pp. 201–223). CRC Press. 10.1201/9781003194415-12

Kumar Pandey, B., Pandey, D., Nassa, V. K., Ahmad, T., Singh, C., George, A. S., & Wakchaure, M. A. (2021). Encryption and steganography-based text extraction in IoT using the EWCTS optimizer. *Imaging Science Journal*, 69(1-4), 38–56. 10.1080/13682199.2022.2146885

KVM, S., Pandey, B. K., & Pandey, D. (2024). Design of Surface Plasmon Resonance (SPR) Sensors for Highly Sensitive Biomolecular Detection in Cancer Diagnostics. *Plasmonics*, 1–13.

Letaief, K. B., Chen, W., Shi, Y., Zhang, J., & Zhang, Y. J. A. (2019). The roadmap to 6G: AI empowered wireless networks. *IEEE Communications Magazine*, 57(8), 84–90. 10.1109/MCOM.2019.1900271

Liu, Y., Wei, X., Xiao, J., Liu, Z., Xu, Y., & Tian, Y. (2020). Energy consumption and emission mitigation prediction based on data center traffic and PUE for global data centers. *Global Energy Interconnection*, 3(3), 272–282. 10.1016/j.gloei.2020.07.008

Malhotra, P., Pandey, D., Pandey, B. K., & Patra, P. M. (2021). Managing agricultural supply chains in COVID-19 lockdown. *International Journal of Quality and Innovation*, 5(2), 109–118. 10.1504/IJQI.2021.117181

Materwala, H., Ismail, L., Shubair, R. M., & Buyya, R. (2022). Energy-SLA-aware genetic algorithm for edge–cloud integrated computation offloading in vehicular networks. *Future Generation Computer Systems*, 135, 205–222. 10.1016/j.future.2022.04.009

Menon, V., Pandey, D., Khosla, D., Kaur, M., Vashishtha, H. K., George, A. S., & Pandey, B. K. (2022). A Study on COVID–19, Its Origin, Phenomenon, Variants, and IoT-Based Framework to Detect the Presence of Coronavirus. In *IoT Based Smart Applications* (pp. 1–13). Springer International Publishing.

Pandey, B. K., & Pandey, D. (2023). Parametric optimization and prediction of enhanced thermoelectric performance in co-doped CaMnO3 using response surface methodology and neural network. *Journal of Materials Science Materials in Electronics*, 34(21), 1589. 10.1007/s10854-023-10954-1

Pandey, B. K., Pandey, D., & Agarwal, A. (2022). Encrypted information transmission by enhanced steganography and image transformation. *International Journal of Distributed Artificial Intelligence*, 14(1), 1–14. 10.4018/IJDAI.297110

Pandey, B. K., Pandey, D., Alkhafaji, M. A., Güneşer, M. T., & Şeker, C. (2023a). A reliable transmission and extraction of textual information using keyless encryption, steganography, and deep algorithm with cuckoo optimization. In *Micro-Electronics and Telecommunication Engineering: Proceedings of 6th ICMETE 2022* (pp. 629–636). Springer Nature Singapore. 10.1007/978-981-19-9512-5_57

Pandey, B. K., Pandey, D., Gupta, A., Nassa, V. K., Dadheech, P., & George, A. S. (2023b). Secret data transmission using advanced morphological component analysis and steganography. In *Role of data-intensive distributed computing systems in designing data solutions* (pp. 21–44). Springer International Publishing. 10.1007/978-3-031-15542-0_2

Pandey, B. K., Pandey, D., & Sahani, S. K. (2024). Autopilot control unmanned aerial vehicle system for sewage defect detection using deep learning. *Engineering Reports*, 12852. 10.1002/eng2.12852

Pandey, B. K., Pandey, S. K., & Pandey, D. (2011). A survey of bioinformatics applications on parallel architectures. *International Journal of Computer Applications*, 23(4), 21–25. 10.5120/2877-3744

Pandey, D., Hasan, A., Pandey, B. K., Lelisho, M. E., George, A. H., & Shahul, A. (2023). COVID-19 epidemic anxiety, mental stress, and sleep disorders in developing country university students. *CSI Transactions on ICT*, 11(2), 119–127. 10.1007/s40012-023-00383-0

Pandey, D., Nassa, V. K., Jhamb, A., Mahto, D., Pandey, B. K., George, A. H., & Bandyopadhyay, S. K. (2021a). An integration of keyless encryption, steganography, and artificial intelligence for the secure transmission of stego images. In *Multidisciplinary approach to modern digital steganography* (pp. 211–234). IGI Global. 10.4018/978-1-7998-7160-6.ch010

Pandey, D., Ogunmola, G. A., Enbeyle, W., Abdullahi, M., Pandey, B. K., & Pramanik, S. (2021b). COVID-19: A framework for effective delivering of online classes during lockdown. *Human Arenas*, 1-15.

Pandey, D., & Pandey, B. K. (2022). An efficient deep neural network with adaptive galactic swarm optimization for complex image text extraction. In *Process mining techniques for pattern recognition* (pp. 121–137). CRC Press. 10.1201/9781003169550-10

Pandey, J. K., Jain, R., Dilip, R., Kumbhkar, M., Jaiswal, S., Pandey, B. K., & Pandey, D. (2022). Investigating role of iot in the development of smart application for security enhancement. In *IoT Based Smart Applications* (pp. 219–243). Springer International Publishing.

Pramanik, S., Pandey, D., Joardar, S., Niranjanamurthy, M., Pandey, B. K., & Kaur, J. (2023, October). An overview of IoT privacy and security in smart cities. In *AIP Conference Proceedings* (Vol. 2495, No. 1). AIP Publishing 10.1063/5.0123511

Raja, D., Kumar, D. R., Santhiyakumari, N., Kumarganesh, S., Sagayam, K. M., Thiyaneswaran, B., Pandey, B. K., & Pandey, D. (2024). A compact dual-feed wide-band slotted antenna for future wireless applications. *Analog Integrated Circuits and Signal Processing*, 118(2), 1–15. 10.1007/s10470-023-02233-0

Revathi, T. K., Sathiyabhama, B., Sankar, S., Pandey, D., Pandey, B. K., & Dadeech, P. (2022). An intelligent model for coronary heart disease diagnosis. In *Networking Technologies in Smart Healthcare* (pp. 309–327). CRC Press. 10.1201/9781003239888-15

Sahani, K., Khadka, S. S., Sahani, S. K., Pandey, B. K., & Pandey, D. (2023). A possible underground roadway for transportation facilities in Kathmandu Valley: A racking deformation of underground rectangular struct es. *Engineering Reports*, 12821. 10.1002/eng2.12821

Saxena, A., Agarwal, A., Pandey, B. K., & Pandey, D. (2024). Examination of the Criticality of Customer Segmentation Using Unsupervised Learning Methods. *Circular Economy and Sustainability*, 1–14. 10.1007/s43615-023-00336-4

Saxena, A., Sharma, N. K., Pandey, D., & Pandey, B. K. (2021). Influence of tourists satisfaction on future behavioral intentions with special reference to desert triangle of Rajasthan. *Augmented Human Research*, 6(1), 13. 10.1007/s41133-021-00052-4

Sengupta, R., Sengupta, D., Pandey, D., Pandey, B. K., Nassa, V. K., & Dadeech, P. (2021). A Systematic review of 5G opportunities, architecture and challenges. *Future Trends in 5G and 6G*, 247-269.

Sharma, M., Pandey, D., Khosla, D., Goyal, S., Pandey, B. K., & Gupta, A. K. (2022a). Design of a GaN-based Flip Chip Light Emitting Diode (FC-LED) with au Bumps & Thermal Analysis with different sizes and adhesive materials for performance considerations. *Silicon*, 14(12), 7109–7120. 10.1007/s12633-021-01457-x

Sharma, M., Pandey, D., Palta, P., & Pandey, B. K. (2022b). Design and power dissipation consideration of PFAL CMOS V/S conventional CMOS based 2: 1 multiplexer and full adder. *Silicon*, 14(8), 4401–4410. 10.1007/s12633-021-01221-1

Sharma, S., Pandey, B. K., Pandey, D., Anand, R., Sharma, A., & Saini, S. (2023, March). Character Recognition Technique Implementation for Complicated Deteriorated Scene. In *2023 6th International Conference on Information Systems and Computer Networks (ISCON)* (pp. 1-4). IEEE. 10.1109/ISCON57294.2023.10112185

Singh, S., Madaan, G., Kaur, J., Swapna, H. R., Pandey, D., Singh, A., & Pandey, B. K. (2023). *Bibliometric Review on Healthcare Sustainability. Handbook of Research on Safe Disposal Methods of Municipal Solid Wastes for a Sustainable Environment*, 142-161. 10.4018/978-1-6684-8117-2.ch011

Swapna, H. R., Bigirimana, E., Madaan, G., Hasan, A., Pandey, B. K., & Pandey, D. (2023). Impact of neuromarketing on consumer psychology in digitally connected networks. In *Applications of Neuromarketing in the Metaverse* (pp. 193–205). IGI Global. 10.4018/978-1-6684-8150-9.ch015

Tareke, S. A., Lelisho, M. E., Hassen, S. S., Seid, A. A., Jemal, S. S., Teshale, B. M., & Pandey, B. K. (2022). The prevalence and predictors of depressive, anxiety, and stress symptoms among Tepi town residents during the COVID-19 pandemic lockdown in Ethiopia. *Journal of Racial and Ethnic Health Disparities*, 1–13.35028903

Tataria, H., Shafi, M., Molisch, A. F., Dohler, M., Sjöland, H., & Tufvesson, F. (2021). 6G wireless systems: Vision, requirements, challenges, insights, and opportunities. *Proceedings of the IEEE*, 109(7), 1166–1199. 10.1109/JPROC.2021.3061701

Tripathi, R. P., Sharma, M., Gupta, A. K., Pandey, D., Pandey, B. K., Shahul, A., & George, A. H. (2023). Timely prediction of diabetes by means of machine learning practices. *Augmented Human Research*, 8(1), 1. 10.1007/s41133-023-00062-4

Vinodhini, V., Kumar, M. S., Sankar, S., Pandey, D., Pandey, B. K., & Nassa, V. K. (2022). IoT-based early forest fire detection using MLP and AROC method. *International Journal of Global Warming*, 27(1), 55–70. 10.1504/IJGW.2022.122794

Yang, H., Alphones, A., Xiong, Z., Niyato, D., Zhao, J., & Wu, K. (2020). Artificial-intelligence-enabled intelligent 6G networks. *IEEE Network*, 34(6), 272–280. 10.1109/MNET.011.2000195

Zeng, X., Garg, S., Barika, M., Zomaya, A. Y., Wang, L., Villari, M., Chen, D., & Ranjan, R. (2020). SLA management for big data analytical applications in clouds: A taxonomy study. *ACM Computing Surveys*, 53(3), 1–40. 10.1145/3383464

Chapter 4
Beyond the Classroom:
Integrating Cutting-Edge Pedagogies in 6G Curriculum Development

Freddy Ochoa-Tataje
Postgraduate Department, Universidad César Vallejo, Lima, Peru

Luis Velarde-Vela
Science Department, Universidad Peruana de Ciencias Aplicadas, Lima, Peru

Joel Alanya-Beltran
Universidad San Ignacio de Loyola, Peru

Eladia Perez-Peralta
IE Los Precursores, Lima, Peru

Jenny Ruiz-Salazar
Universidad Privada del Norte, Lima

Monica La-Chira-Loli
Engineering Department, Universidad Autónoma del Perú, Lima, Peru

ABSTRACT

Technology has advanced so quickly that it has had a significant impact on all facets of our lives, including education. Technology has changed how we learn, teach, and engage with educational materials over the years. Innovations in computing, communication, and information technologies have caused a dramatic shift in the educational landscape, moving away from traditional chalkboards and toward digital classrooms. The democratization of education in the last few decades has been brought about by the widespread use of mobile devices, the internet, and digital platforms. This has eliminated regional barriers and increased access to education for people all over the world. With their flexibility, scalability, and ability to provide individualized learning experiences, digital libraries and interactive educational apps have established themselves as essential elements of contemporary education.

I. INTRODUCTION

Technology has advanced so quickly that it has had a significant impact on all facets of our lives, including education. Technology has changed how we learn, teach, and engage with educational materials over the years. Innovations in computing, communication, and information technologies have caused a dramatic shift in the educational landscape, moving away from traditional chalkboards and toward digital classrooms. The democratization of education in the last few decades has been brought about by

DOI: 10.4018/979-8-3693-7421-4.ch004

the widespread use of mobile semi-conductor devices (Sharma, M. et al., 2022), the internet, and digital platforms. This has eliminated regional barriers and increased access to education for people all over the world. With their flexibility, scalability, and ability to provide individualized learning experiences, digital libraries (Swapna, H. R. et al., 2023), and interactive educational apps have established themselves as essential elements of contemporary education. Emerging technologies like virtual reality, augmented reality, and artificial intelligence (Pandey, D. et al., 2021) are changing the face of education and creating new opportunities for immersive and engaging learning. AI-powered adaptive learning platforms can provide customized feedback and suggestions to improve learning (Pandey, B. K. et al., 2024) outcomes while adapting instructional materials to each student's unique needs. Through the use of immersive simulations and virtual environments, augmented reality (AR) and virtual reality (VR) technologies allow students to investigate difficult ideas, carry out experiments, and participate in interactive learning (Anand, R. et al., 2023) activities in virtual environments. The incorporation of technology into education has additionally enabled cooperative learning opportunities, enabling learners to establish connections, exchange information, and cooperate with classmates and teachers from different places and backgrounds. Students are prepared for success in a globally interconnected world through the use of online discussion forums, collaborative projects, and virtual group activities that promote teamwork, communication skills, and cross-cultural understanding. Thanks to technology, teachers are now able to implement cutting-edge pedagogical strategies that encourage problem-solving, critical thinking, and active learning (Chard, R. et al., 2017). Healthcare is one of 6G's biggest application areas. SixG networks can support real-time remote medical consultations, telemedicine, and remote patient monitoring due to their fast data transfer speeds and low latency. This allows providers to provide high-quality care to remote or underserved patients, improving access and reducing differences in outcomes. Healthcare (Abdulkarim, Y. I. et al., 2024) applications like personalised medicine and predictive analytics can benefit from 6G technology (Kirubasri, G. et al., 2021). Doctors can use big data analytics and AI to identify trends, predict disease outbreaks, and create targeted treatments (Tripathi, R. P. et al., 2023). This proactive approach to healthcare improves patient outcomes, costs, and population health (Pandey, B. K. et al., 2011). Through immersive and interactive learning, 6G technology (Sengupta, R. et al., 2021) could transform education as well as healthcare (Singh, S. et al., 2023). Virtual reality, augmented reality, and holographic technologies allow 6G networks to create virtual classrooms, simulations, and collaborative learning environments that surpass traditional classrooms. This empowers students for digital success by encouraging creativity, critical thinking, and engagement (George, W. K. et al., 2023). The development of new products, services, and business models enabled by 6G technology can boost economic growth. 6G networks enable groundbreaking applications and services like autonomous vehicles, smart cities, advanced manufacturing, and precision agriculture. Entrepreneurs, startups, and businesses can benefit from emerging technologies and disrupt traditional industries. 6G can improve resource management and energy consumption, promoting environmental sustainability. A more sustainable and resilient energy infrastructure can be achieved with 6G-powered smart grids that optimise energy distribution, reduce waste, and promote renewable energy. Traffic congestion, emissions, and air quality can be improved by 6G-enabled smart transportation systems (Sahani, K. et al., 2023)), making the environment cleaner. Utilizing technology to involve students in real-world problems and useful problem-solving exercises, project-based learning, flipped classrooms, and gamification techniques increase the relevance, significance, and enjoyment of learning. Future developments in education could be even more significant with the introduction of 6G technology, which would open up new avenues for individualized, immersive, and interactive learning experiences. Virtual reality, augmented reality, and holographic technologies will be able to be seamlessly integrated into educational environments thanks to 6G technology's ultra-fast connectivity, ultra-low latency, and massive network capacity (Kirubasri, G. et al., 2022). This will allow for immersive and interactive learning experiences that go beyond the confines of traditional classrooms (Alshammari, S. 2021).

1.1 Adaptable Pedagogies in 6G

As the 6G curriculum is being made, combining dynamic and flexible teaching methods is a one-of-a-kind chance to use artificial intelligence (AI) (Pandey, B. K., & Pandey, D., 2023) to make learning more personalized. With the progress of AI technologies, school systems can use machine learning algorithms (Anand, R. et al., 2024) to look at huge amounts of data about each student and make lessons fit their specific learning styles, preferences, and levels of performance. By using AI (Pandey, D., & Pandey, B. K., 2022) powered adaptive learning platforms in the classroom, teachers can make personalized learning paths for each student. This way, each student can learn at their own pace and focus on areas where they need more help or challenge. Adaptive learning systems can change the level of difficulty of learning activities on the fly, give real-time feedback, and make personalized suggestions for more work to be done. This way, each student gets the one-on-one help they need to succeed. AI (Deepa, R. et al., 2022) powered educational chatbots can help and tutor students whenever they need it, even when school isn't in session. They can answer questions, explain things, and lead students through real-time problem-solving activities. These virtual assistants can help to supplement what is taught in the classroom, extend learning beyond the school day, and give extra help to students who may need it. Through the use of virtual reality (VR) and augmented reality (AR) simulations, AI technologies can make learning more immersive and interactive. By using AI-powered intelligent agents (Revathi, T. K. et al., 2022) in virtual worlds, teachers can make realistic situations and challenges that change based on what students do and choose, giving them hands-on learning opportunities that are like those in the real world. AI programs can look at student performance data to find patterns (Govindaraj, V. et al., 2023), trends, and areas where students can improve. This helps teachers make decisions about what to teach, how to teach, and how to help students who are having trouble. AI-powered assessment tools can also grade assignments automatically, give students feedback right away, and gather information about how well students are learning, which helps teachers see how they're doing, find learning gaps, and adjust their lessons as needed (Sithipolvanichgul, J. et al., 2021).

1.2 Interdisciplinary and Curriculum Design

The ultimate in wireless communication networks (Gupta, A. K. et al., 2023), 6G technology has the potential to completely change our lives in terms of connectivity (Raja, D. et al., 2024). Building upon the foundations set by its predecessors, especially 5G, it promises to surpass current capabilities with revolutionary advancements. Fundamentally, the goals of 6G technology are to provide extremely rapid data transfer rates (Devasenapathy, D. et al., 2024). extremely low latency, and widespread global connectivity. Known as the "era of terabits per second," 6G technology promises to provide lag-free real-time communication, immersive virtual reality experiences, and flawless streaming of high-definition video. But the importance of 6G technology goes beyond improved connectivity and speed. Its interdisciplinary nature is highlighted by the convergence of multiple technological innovations and disciplines. When creating curricula centered around 6G technology, educators must consider this multidisciplinary component. It requires the synthesis of techniques and knowledge from a variety of disciplines, including mathematics (Bessant, Y. A. et al., 2023), physics, computer science, engineering, and telecommunications. The interdisciplinary nature of 6G technology offers opportunities and challenges for curriculum designers. On the one hand, it enables instructors to design all-encompassing lesson plans that provide learners a thorough grasp of the fundamental ideas, innovations, and uses of 6G networks. Through the integration of insights from various disciplines, educators can provide students with a comprehensive understanding of the intricacies and consequences associated with 6G technology. Working together across disciplines, educators can create an effective interdisciplinary curriculum for 6G education. In order to ensure relevance and alignment with current trends and needs in the real world, it also necessitates engagement with industry experts and stakeholders. In order to navigate the various disciplinary perspectives, methodologies, and terminologies, collaboration is crucial. The necessity of developing interdisciplinary skills and competencies in students is highlighted by the interdisciplinary nature of 6G technology. Teachers need to create learning opportunities that push students to synthesize information from different fields, evaluate difficult issues from several angles, and effectively present their conclusions to a range of audiences. With a focus on interdisciplinary skills, students are better prepared for the dynamic and interconnected 6G era, where creativity and teamwork are crucial for solving difficult problems and bringing about positive change (Pesek, I. et al., 2022).

II. EVOLUTION OF PEDAGOGIES IN EDUCATION

2.1 Historical Pedagogical Shifts

The field of education has seen a number of pedagogical paradigms shifts over time, each of which was influenced by the dominant technological, societal, and cultural contexts. As opinions about the nature of learning (Saxena, A. et al., 2024), the function of teachers, and the goal of education itself have changed, so too have these paradigms. The move from traditional teacher-centric approaches to more personalized and participatory instructional methods known as student-centered learning has been one of the major trends to emerge in recent decades. Throughout antiquated societies like Greece and Rome, education was mainly restricted to the upper classes and concentrated on the transfer of knowledge from instructor to pupil via lectures, memorization, and recitation. Throughout much of history, this teacher-centered approach was prevalent. During the Middle Ages, for example, religious institutions and monasteries served as centers of learning, with the emphasis of instruction being on memorization of sacred texts and religious doctrine. Aiming to prepare citizens for the workforce, compulsory education systems were established as a result of the profound social changes brought about by the Industrial Revolution of the 18th and 19th centuries. During this time, standardized testing, large class sizes, and a uniform curriculum gave rise to the factory model of education. Students were supposed to passively absorb knowledge in a one-size-fits-all manner, with teachers acting as information distributors. Education underwent a paradigm shift in the late 20th and early 21st centuries as the value of student agency, engagement, and autonomy in the learning process was increasingly acknowledged. Student-centered approaches prioritise the needs, interests, and experiences of individual learners, promoting active participation, critical thinking, and collaboration. They are influenced by educational theorists such as Lev Vygotsky, Maria Montessori, and John Dewey. As well-known pedagogical frameworks, constructivism and inquiry-based learning emphasize the value of practical exploration, problem-solving, and discovery in the learning process. Rather than having students passively absorb knowledge from teachers, these methods encourage students to actively construct their understanding of concepts through experience and reflection. Technological developments have accelerated the transition to student-centered learning in recent years by giving teachers the means to differentiate instruction, personalize lessons, and involve students as co-authors of knowledge. Because they provide flexibility and customization to accommodate students' varied needs and learning styles, blended learning models, flipped classrooms, and project-based approaches have become more and more popular.

2.2. Limits of Traditional Methods for 6G

It is extremely difficult for traditional pedagogies which are defined by teacher-centered instruction, standardized curricula, and passive learning experiences to sufficiently prepare students for the difficulties that the introduction of 6G technology will present. Even though these pedagogical strategies might have been adequate in earlier times, the quick speed of technological development and the intricate, multidisciplinary nature of 6G call for a review of teaching methods in order to better meet the needs of the future. Traditional methods 6G limitations are shown in the figure 1.

Figure 1. Traditional methods' 6G limitations

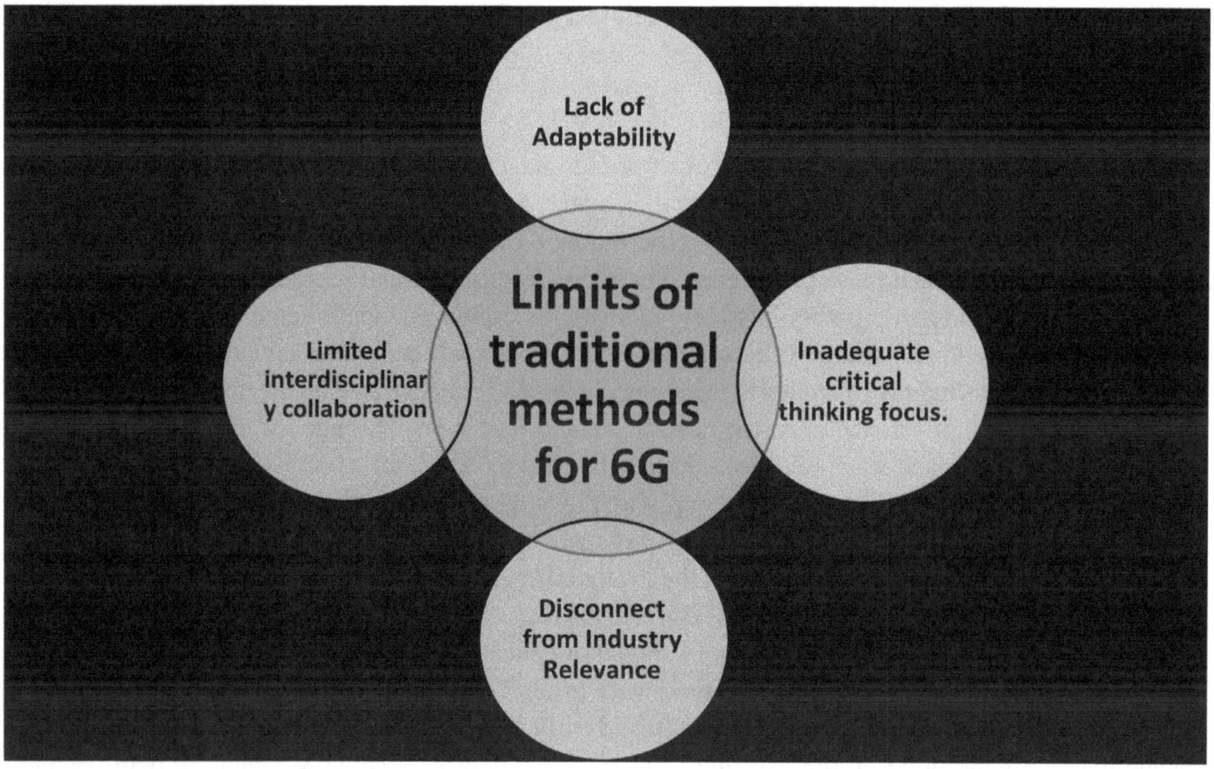

1. *Lack of Adaptability*: Conventional pedagogies frequently adhere to strict frameworks and uniform curriculums that may make it difficult to adapt to new technologies and changing skill requirements. In the ever-evolving field of 6G technology, where new ideas, instruments, and uses appear all the time, teachers must be flexible and adaptive in order to modify their lesson plans and curriculum in order to stay up to date with the latest developments. It may be difficult for traditional pedagogies to offer the flexibility required to quickly and adaptably incorporate 6G-related topics into the curriculum.
2. *Inadequate critical thinking focus:* Passive learning and rote memorization are usually given precedence over critical thinking, problem-solving, and practical experimentation in traditional pedagogies. However, students must acquire analytical skills, creative problem-solving abilities, and the ability to apply theoretical knowledge to real-world situations due to the complex challenges associated with 6G technology. Conventional methods that place a strong emphasis on lectures and standardized tests might not be able to sufficiently foster these fundamental skills, leaving students unprepared to deal with the complex issues raised by 6G.
3. *Disconnect from Industry Relevance*: Conventional pedagogies frequently function independently of current business trends and practical applications, which causes a gulf between professional practice and classroom instruction. In the era of 6G technology, where creativity and real-world application are critical, students require chances to interact with professionals in the field, complete real-world projects, and obtain practical experience with state-of-the-art equipment. The ability of students to successfully transition into 6G-related careers may be hampered by traditional pedagogies that place a high priority on the delivery of theoretical content without making meaningful connections to industry practices.
4. *Limited interdisciplinary collaboration;* Conventional pedagogies frequently reinforce disciplinary boundaries and knowledge that is compartmentalized, which reduces the possibility of interdisciplinary collaboration and holistic understanding. However, knowledge from a variety of fields, including mathematics, computer science, engineering, and telecommunications, is needed for the development and implementation of 6G technology. To tackle complex 6G challenges, students need to develop their ability to collaborate across disciplinary boundaries, integrate diverse perspectives, and apply knowledge from various fields. The emphasis on isolated learning experiences in traditional pedagogies may prevent students from acquiring the interdisciplinary abilities and mindset required for success in the 6G era.

To effectively prepare students for success in the dynamic and interconnected world of 6G, educators must acknowledge these limitations and adopt pedagogical approaches that prioritize adaptability, critical thinking, industry relevance, and interdisciplinary collaboration.

2.3 Cutting-Edge Pedagogies

The traditional educational approaches are failing to adequately prepare students for the many opportunities and challenges that await them as we stand on the cusp of the 6G era, which will be marked by unprecedented levels of connectivity, data exchange (Khan, B. et al., 2021), and technological innovation. To better prepare students for the demands of the future and reshape curriculum development, educators and policymakers are looking to cutting-edge pedagogies as creative solutions. Modern pedagogies are a shift from traditional teacher-centered teaching strategies to ones that emphasize more individualized, dynamic, and interactive learning. These teaching strategies make use of the most recent developments in educational theory, technology, and research to encourage students' critical thinking, creativity, teamwork, and adaptability. Innovative teaching methods provide a revolutionary framework for incorporating difficult ideas, multidisciplinary competencies, and practical applications into 6G curricula. Experiential learning is one such innovative pedagogy that lets students actively interact with 6G technology in real-world settings by emphasizing immersive, hands-on experiences. Students acquire real-world experience, problem-solving skills, and a deeper comprehension of 6G concepts and applications through experiential learning activities like case studies, simulations, and project-based assignments. By encouraging students to explore, experiment, and learn from mistakes, experiential learning not only improves retention and comprehension but also stimulates creativity and innovation. Project-based learning is another innovative approach to education that gives students the tools they need to work together to solve real-world problems (Lee, B. H., & Park, S. H., 2021). Within the framework of creating a 6G curriculum, project-based learning gives students the chance to use their understanding of computer science, engineering, telecommunications, and other subjects to create and carry out 6G-related projects. Students acquire practical experience and an understanding of the intricacies of 6G technology by engaging in real-world, multidisciplinary projects that foster critical thinking, communication, and teamwork abilities. A crucial element of state-of-the-art pedagogies for 6G curriculum development is collaborative learning. Collaborative learning encourages information sharing, group problem-solving, and the co-creation of new concepts and solutions by promoting cooperation among students, instructors, business partners, and other stakeholders. Within the framework of 6G education, collaborative learning allows students to take advantage of a variety of viewpoints, knowledge bases, and tools to tackle difficult problems and spur innovation in the telecom industry and other fields. Developing cutting-edge pedagogies for 6G curriculum development heavily relies on technology-enhanced learning. Teachers can design immersive, interactive, and customized learning experiences that meet the needs and preferences of each individual student by utilizing digital tools (Ekong, M. O. et al., 2023), virtual reality, augmented reality, and other technologies. In addition to facilitating remote collaboration, technology-enhanced learning gives educators access to cutting-edge resources and knowledge while removing geographical barriers (Yang, Y., & Yu, D., 2022).

III. CUTTING-EDGE PEDAGOGIES IN 6G CURRICULUM DEVELOPMENT

3.1 Experiential Learning

a) Immersive Learning Experiences

One new educational strategy that aims to give students fully immersive and experience situations is called immersive learning. Through the use of cutting-edge technology, students can experience real-life problems and circumstances in a secure (Pandey, B. K. et al., 2023a), regulated setting by immersing them in virtual spaces or scenarios. Because it has been shown to improve learning outcomes, engagement, and retention of information, immersive learning has become more and more popular in recent years. The growing accessibility of virtual reality (VR) technology is a major driver propelling the use of immersive learning. Immersion experiences are becoming more and more common in a variety of industries, including training and education, as virtual reality technology gets more generally available and more reasonably priced. As a result, immersive learning will likely become a standard practice and vital resource for trainers and educators alike. The capacity to replicate real-world situations in which students can use their knowledge, skills, and abilities in useful contexts is what makes immersive learning so effective. This method leads to better knowledge retention, quicker skill acquisition, and increased problem-solving skills by immersing learners in immersive settings where they may interact with the material at a deeper level. A secure (Sharma, S. et al., 2023) environment to hone abilities without the dangers of real-world scenarios is another benefit of immersive learning for students. For training in complicated or high-risk contexts like emergency response, aviation, or healthcare (Tareke, S. A. et al., 2022), this portion of experiential learning is very beneficial. Immersion learning increases students' competency and self-assurance in addressing problems in the real world by letting them experience and learn from simulated circumstances. Immersion learning also offers individualized and flexible learning experiences since it can be customized to match the unique requirements and preferences of students. Instructors and trainers can design immersive scenarios that accommodate varying learning preferences, proficiency levels, and learning goals. This guarantees that students receive education that is both pertinent and focused. The ability to provide accessible and affordable education and training options is another important benefit of immersive learning. Anyone can produce inexpensive, immersive learning resources with little technical knowledge thanks to the accessibility of user-friendly authoring tools and platforms. In order to provide personalized and captivating learning experiences for their audiences, educators, trainers, and subject matter experts are now able to create content more easily and more rapidly (Rani, S. et al., 2023).

b) Real-World Applications and Simulations

Immersion learning is based on the integration of real-world applications and simulations, which enhances the learning process and helps students comprehend intricate ideas more thoroughly. Teachers can close the gap between theory and practice by immersing students in real-world situations and places. This will increase students' comprehension and engagement levels. Learning becomes more relevant and meaningful when students are able to contextualize abstract concepts in familiar contexts through real-world applications. Students may participate in a simulation, for instance, where they must make strategic decisions for a virtual corporation and personally feel the effects of their actions, in a business management course. Similar to this, simulations can mimic real-world clinical settings in a medical education program, giving students a safe setting to hone their diagnostic and treatment techniques. By giving students the chance to apply theoretical information in real-world situations, these simulations foster critical thinking, problem-solving, and decision-making abilities. Through navigating obstacles and reaching judgments in virtual worlds, students get practical experience that they can use to real-world situations and a greater comprehension of difficult subjects. By using simulations, educators may design immersive learning environments that are flexible, scalable, and configurable to accommodate a wide range of student needs. Learners can practice skills in varied degrees of complexity and difficulty by using virtual environments that can be constructed to imitate a wide range of events, from mundane jobs to high-stakes emergencies. This adaptability guarantees that learning experiences stay interesting and difficult regardless of the backgrounds or skill levels of learners. It has been demonstrated that integrating real-world applications and simulations improves learning outcomes by encouraging experiential learning and active learning. Learners actively interact with the material, making choices, resolving issues, and thinking back on their experiences rather than merely absorbing it. As students make connections between theoretical concepts and real-world circumstances and experiences, their active engagement fosters deeper understanding and long-term retention of knowledge. This portion of experience learning is especially helpful in complex or high-risk industries like engineering, aviation, and healthcare where errors can have catastrophic consequences. Simulations enhance confidence and competence by providing a risk-free environment for learners to hone their abilities, so equipping them for success in their future employment.

3.2 Project-Based Learning

a) Critical Thinking and Problem-Solving Skills

Project-based learning strategies are effective in developing students' critical thinking and problem-solving abilities because they provide them the chance to participate in practical, real-world situations that mimic the intricacies of work settings. Teachers can help students develop a variety of critical skills that are useful in both academic and professional settings by including them in real-world, project-based assignments. The potential of project-based learning to foster critical thinking in students is one of its main advantages. It does this by pushing students to examine, assess, and synthesize data in order to tackle challenging challenges. Students actively interact with the material, solving problems in the real world and putting theoretical knowledge to use in useful situations, as opposed to passively taking in information. Higher-order thinking abilities like analysis, assessment, and synthesis are sparked by this process as students work through open-ended challenges and make deft decisions to complete projects. Working together with peers who have different backgrounds and viewpoints helps students develop their communication, teamwork, and empathy skills. Students that collaborate well are better able to work in interdisciplinary and cross-functional teams because they learn how to utilize collective expertise, share ideas, and negotiate solutions—a crucial skill in todays linked and globalized world. Project-based learning methods not only encourage critical thinking and teamwork, but they also help students develop their problem-solving abilities by putting them in real-world situations where they have to recognize, evaluate, and solve complicated issues. Students learn how to think creatively, adaptably, and innovatively to overcome obstacles and accomplish goals by working on projects that demand them to apply theoretical knowledge to real-world scenarios. Students get invested in their education and motivated to succeed when they actively participate in the planning, designing, and carrying out of projects. As a result of taking accountability for goal-setting, time management, and progress evaluation, children develop intrinsic motivation and self-directed learning (Zou, J., & Chen, Y.).

b) Industry-Relevant Projects

Integrating industry-relevant projects into educational courses boosts student engagement and relevance. Teachers engage students and apply academic principles by incorporating real-world industry initiatives into curricula. Contextual learning immerses students in professional contexts, helping them understand how their studies relate to their careers. Through industry examples and applications, students learn course material better as they work on these projects. Students gain hands-on experience in problem-solving and skill development through industry-relevant projects. Writing software, devising marketing campaigns, and performing scientific research let students apply theory to practice. Student success in their industries depends on critical thinking, communication, and cooperation abilities developed through experiential learning. These immersive projects encourage research and experimentation, enabling students to take responsibility of their learning and invest in their academic advancement. Industry partnerships on project-based learning give students access to real-world professionals' thoughts and advice. Mentors, comments, and industry viewpoints help students grasp industry practices and expectations. In addition, industry partnerships allow students to build professional networks, explore career paths, and experience industry trends and problems. These collaborations give students industry-relevant skills and expertise. Relevant industrial projects to students' professional aspirations boost motivation and purpose in school. Students learn the practical applications of their studies by working on projects they enjoy. This alignment gives students direction and incentives to work hard toward their academic and career goals. Industrial initiatives also give students a sense of success and fulfillment, strengthening their academic commitment (Doughan, Z. et al., 2022).

3.3 Collaborative Learning

a) Virtual Collaboration Tools

Virtual collaboration amongst students relies on digital platforms and tools to enable smooth communication, cooperation, and knowledge sharing. Digital collaboration systems let students collaborate efficiently in virtual environments in today's interconnected world of remote learning. Digital collaboration solutions concentrate student communication, file sharing, and project management. Instant chat, video conferencing, and discussion boards allow students to collaborate in real time. These platforms let students exchange ideas, collaborate on assignments, and interact with peers from anywhere with an internet connection, breaking down time and space barriers. Digital collaboration technologies allow students to work together asynchronously at their own pace. Shared documents, collaborative editing, and version control allow students to work on assignments and projects asynchronously, fitting different schedules and learning styles. Asynchronous collaboration allows students to participate in group work and conversations on their own schedule, encouraging flexibility and inclusivity in virtual learning. Digital collaboration systems also help manage collaborative projects by assigning tasks, managing deadlines, and tracking progress. Task lists, calendars, and kanban boards help students collaborate, measure milestones, and hold each other accountable. These tools improve virtual collaborative workflow, productivity, and project management. Interactive elements and multimedia material encourage active learning and participation on digital collaboration platforms. Digital tools enable students to create immersive learning experiences by collaborating on multimedia presentations, interactive quizzes, and multimedia projects. Polling, surveys, and quizzes stimulate student participation and feedback, creating a dynamic learning environment. Digital collaboration platforms also allow students to give and receive critical criticism from peers. Peer review assignments and discussion forums allow students to assess each other's work, make comments, and reflect. Peer feedback improves student work and fosters ongoing growth by developing critical thinking, communication, and metacognition (Luo, X., & Xie, L., 2018).

b) Fostering Innovation and Diversity

Collaboration promotes innovation, problem-solving, and knowledge development in the 6G workforce by using a diverse group's information, experiences, and perspectives. In the rapidly changing world of 6G technology, where interdisciplinary collaboration is essential for addressing complex challenges and improving technology, collaborative learning sparks innovation and diversity. Collaborative learning fosters 6G workforce innovation by promoting interdisciplinary collaboration and information sharing. In a collaborative learning setting, people from diverse fields work on projects and goals. Interdisciplinary teams can generate new ideas, strategies, and solutions by combining their knowledge and views. Cross-pollination generates creative ideas and perspectives that drive 6G ecosystem product and service development. A creative workforce requires open communication, teamwork, and information exchange, which collaborative learning promotes. In collaborative learning contexts, people feel more comfortable sharing their views, opinions, and contributions. Candor and cooperation foster experimentation, invention, and open communication. Collaborative learning encourages 6G workers to think creatively, question conventional thinking, and try new things in a respectful and inclusive environment. Collective learning allows people from different backgrounds to work together and exchange knowledge, promoting diversity and inclusivity in the 6G business. Participants from diverse cultural, ethnic, gender, and socioeconomic backgrounds collaborate on projects, share ideas, and learn from one other. Different perspectives offer a vibrant learning environment where people can learn new ways to solve problems, think, and face challenges. Diversity and inclusion in collaborative learning promote empathy, respect, and understanding. Creating inclusive and innovative 6G teams requires these traits. Collaboration skills including leadership, teamwork, communication, and dispute resolution are valued in the 6G business. Collaboration skills help people create innovation and foster a collaborative culture in the 6G ecosystem by efficiently collaborating with colleagues, partners, and stakeholders across disciplines, organizations, and geographies.

3.4 Technology-Enhanced Learning

a) Emerging Technologies in Education

Discovering new technologies like AI, IoT (Kumar Pandey, B. et al., 2021), and blockchain is transforming education by improving learning results, personalizing instruction, and streamlining administrative operations. These technologies can revolutionize education by creating immersive, adaptive, and accessible learning environments suited to individual learners. AI is transforming education with tailored learning pathways, adaptive assessments, and intelligent tutoring. AI systems assess student data, including learning preferences, strengths, and limitations, to adapt learning experiences for each learner's style and pace. Adaptive learning platforms use AI to alter material and activities based on student performance and comprehension for best learning. Additionally, AI-driven teaching tools help pupils understand complicated ideas and learn independently by providing individualized feedback. Through interconnected ecosystems that improve cooperation, participation, and efficiency, the Internet of Things (IoT) (Pandey, J. K. et al., 2022) is changing education. Connected smartboards, wearables, and interactive learning tools offer immersive learning experiences that encourage student participation. We also track student interactions, learning progress, and preferences using IoT devices (Iyyanar, P. et al., 2023) and data analytics. Real-time data helps instructors make data-driven decisions, improve, and adapt instruction to students' changing needs. Blockchain (David, S. et al., 2023) improves security, transparency, and certification in education. Blockchain-based solutions securely (Pandey, B. K. et al., 2022) store and verify diplomas, certifications, and transcripts, preventing fraud and misrepresentation. Blockchain-powered digital credentials allow students to demonstrate their abilities and certifications to prospective companies and academic institutions thanks to portable, tamper-proof records. Blockchain allows transparent, decentralized learning environments with peer-to-peer collaboration, certification, and micropayments for educational content and services. These developing technologies improve personalization, engagement, and accessibility in education. We must address data privacy (Pandey, B. K. et al., 2023b), security, and digital equity issues to enable fair access and ethical use of technology in education. AI, IoT (Vinodhini, V. et al., 2022), and blockchain can help educators and institutions create dynamic and inclusive learning environments that prepare students for the digital age. These technologies (Menon, V. et al., 2022) can transform education and open up new teaching and learning opportunities as they progress (Li & Wu, 2023).

b) Adaptive Learning Platforms

The 6G curriculum's individualized learning paths and adaptive learning platforms are ground breaking, tailoring learning to each student's needs, interests, and talents. Through personalized learning pathways and adaptive learning technologies, educators can create dynamic and responsive learning environments that optimize learning outcomes, foster student engagement, and help students reach their full potential in the rapidly changing 6G technology landscape. Adaptive learning systems leverage AI algorithms and data analytics to adjust speed, topic content, and manner of education to student preferences, performance, and advancement. These platforms assess students' strengths, weaknesses, and learning styles with diagnostic exams, adaptive quizzes, and real-time feedback. This information lets teachers customize classes and interventions for each kid. Personalized advice and remediation help students overcome learning difficulties, fill knowledge gaps, and progress at their own pace using adaptive learning platforms. This boosts learning and retention. With personalized learning pathways, students can explore topics of interest, work toward individualized learning goals, and engage in self-directed learning activities tailored to their interests, aspirations, and learning preferences. To accommodate different learning styles and skills, instructors can construct tailored learning paths that integrate learning resources, activities, and evaluations. Giving learners the power to choose their own routes, set goals, and track their progress fosters agency and ownership. Adaptive learning systems help teachers track student progress, differentiate instruction, and give personalized feedback. This lets teachers focus on student needs. Through personalized learning pathways, students can take command of their education, improve self-control, and explore 6G technology areas of interest or competence (Soodtoetong, N., & Rattanasiriwongwut, M., 2022). Individualized learning routes and adaptable learning platforms promote justice and diversity by considering a variety of learning needs, preferences, and talents. Students of all learning styles, backgrounds, and skills can access individualized learning experiences that meet their needs, giving them equal chances to succeed. Adaptive learning technology can also help underprivileged and underrepresented kids succeed academically by providing targeted interventions and support.

CONCLUSION

Integrating multiple cutting-edge pedagogies into 6G curriculum creation transforms education and prepares students for future problems and possibilities. As technology advances, especially with 6G technology, educators must adjust their educational methods to give students the skills, knowledge, and competencies they need to succeed. Using immersive, project-based, collaborative, and technology-enhanced learning, educators may create dynamic and engaging learning environments that promote critical thinking, problem-solving, innovation, and teamwork. Innovative teaching methods improve student engagement, relevance, inclusivity, diversity, and equity. AI, IoT, and blockchain can transform education and help students reach their full potential. Ethical and privacy problems must be considered to use technology in education responsibly. Educators may educate students for the 6G future by using varied cutting-edge pedagogies and technology. Educators, governments, and stakeholders must work together to promote innovation, equity, and excellence in education to ensure that all students have high-quality learning experiences that equip them for success in the 6G age and beyond.

REFERENCES

Abdulkarim, Y. I., Awl, H. N., Muhammadsharif, F. F., Saeed, S. R., Sidiq, K. R., Khasraw, S. S., Dong, J., Pandey, B. K., & Pandey, D. (2024). Metamaterial-based sensors loaded corona-shaped resonator for COVID-19 detection by using microwave techniques. *Plasmonics*, 19(2), 595–610. 10.1007/s11468-023-02007-4

Alshammari, S. (2021). Determining the factors that affect the use of virtual classrooms: A modification of the UTAUT model. *Journal of Information Technology Education*, 20, 117–135. 10.28945/4709

Anand, R., Khan, B., Nassa, V. K., Pandey, D., Dhabliya, D., Pandey, B. K., & Dadheech, P. (2023). Hybrid convolutional neural network (CNN) for kennedy space center hyperspectral image. *Aerospace Systems*, 6(1), 71–78. 10.1007/s42401-022-00168-4

Anand, R., Lakshmi, S. V., Pandey, D., & Pandey, B. K. (2024). An enhanced ResNet-50 deep learning model for arrhythmia detection using electrocardiogram biomedical indicators. *Evolving Systems*, 15(1), 83–97. 10.1007/s12530-023-09559-0

Bessant, Y. A., Jency, J. G., Sagayam, K. M., Jone, A. A. A., Pandey, D., & Pandey, B. K. (2023). Improved parallel matrix multiplication using Strassen and Urdhvatiryagbhyam method. *CCF Transactions on High Performance Computing*, 5(2), 102–115. 10.1007/s42514-023-00149-9

Chard, R., Chard, K., Wolski, R., Madduri, R., Ng, B., Bubendorfer, K., & Foster, I. (2017). Cost-aware cloud profiling, prediction, and provisioning as a service. *IEEE Cloud Computing*, 4(4), 48–59. 10.1109/MCC.2017.3791025

David, S., Duraipandian, K., Chandrasekaran, D., Pandey, D., Sindhwani, N., & Pandey, B. K. (2023). Impact of blockchain in healthcare system. In *Unleashing the Potentials of blockchain technology for healthcare industries* (pp. 37–57). Academic Press. 10.1016/B978-0-323-99481-1.00004-3

Deepa, R., Anand, R., Pandey, D., Pandey, B. K., & Karki, B. (2022). Comprehensive performance analysis of classifiers in diagnosis of epilepsy. *Mathematical Problems in Engineering*, 2022, 2022. 10.1155/2022/1559312

Devasenapathy, D., Madhumathy, P., Umamaheshwari, R., Pandey, B. K., & Pandey, D. (2024). Transmission-efficient grid-based synchronized model for routing in wireless sensor networks using Bayesian compressive sensing. *SN Computer Science*, 5(1), 1–11.

Doughan, Z., Al Mubasher, H., El Bizri, M., & Haidar, A. (2022). The metaverse: A virtual world in the palm of your hand. *BAU Journal-Science and Technology*, 4(1), 10. 10.54729/KXRC1143

Ekong, M. O., George, W. K., Pandey, B. K., & Pandey, D. (2023). Enhancing the Fundamentals of Industrial Safety Management in TVET for Metaverse Realities. In *Applications of Neuromarketing in the Metaverse* (pp. 19-41). IGI Global. 10.4018/978-1-6684-8150-9.ch002

George, W. K., Ekong, M. O., Pandey, D., & Pandey, B. K. (2023). Pedagogy for Implementation of TVET Curriculum for the Digital World. In *Applications of Neuromarketing in the Metaverse* (pp. 117-136). IGI Global. 10.4018/978-1-6684-8150-9.ch009

. Govindaraj, V., Dhanasekar, S., Martinsagayam, K., Pandey, D., Pandey, B. K., & Nassa, V. K. (2023). Low-power test pattern generator using modified LFSR. *Aerospace Systems*, 1-8.

Gupta, A. K., Sharma, R., Pandey, D., Nassa, V. K., Pandey, B. K., George, A. S., & Dadheech, P. (2023). Performance analysis of eight-channel WDM optical network with different optical amplifiers for industry 4.0. In *Innovation and Competitiveness in Industry 4.0 Based on Intelligent Systems* (pp. 197–212). Springer International Publishing. 10.1007/978-3-031-29775-5_9

Iyyanar, P., Anand, R., Shanthi, T., Nassa, V. K., Pandey, B. K., George, A. S., & Pandey, D. (2023). A real-time smart sewage cleaning UAV assistance system using IoT. In *Handbook of Research on Data-Driven Mathematical Modeling in Smart Cities* (pp. 24–39). IGI Global.

Khan, B., Hasan, A., Pandey, D., Ventayen, R. J. M., Pandey, B. K., & Gowwrii, G. (2021). Fusion of datamining and artificial intelligence in prediction of hazardous road accidents. In *Machine learning and iot for intelligent systems and smart applications* (pp. 201–223). CRC Press. 10.1201/9781003194415-12

Kirubasri, G., Sankar, S., Pandey, D., Pandey, B. K., Nassa, V. K., & Dadheech, P. (2022). Software-defined networking-based Ad hoc networks routing protocols. In *Software defined networking for Ad Hoc networks* (pp. 95–123). Springer International Publishing. 10.1007/978-3-030-91149-2_5

Kirubasri, G., Sankar, S., Pandey, D., Pandey, B. K., Singh, H., & Anand, R. (2021, September). A recent survey on 6G vehicular technology, applications and challenges. In *2021 9th International Conference on Reliability, Infocom Technologies and Optimization (Trends and Future Directions)(ICRITO)* (pp. 1-5). IEEE.

Kumar Pandey, B., Pandey, D., Nassa, V. K., Ahmad, T., Singh, C., George, A. S., & Wakchaure, M. A. (2021). Encryption and steganography-based text extraction in IoT using the EWCTS optimizer. *Imaging Science Journal*, 69(1-4), 38–56. 10.1080/13682199.2022.2146885

Lee, B. H., & Park, S. H. (2021). *A study on the NCS based curriculum for educating Technical Director for VFX industry with Artificial Intelligence*. Cartoon and Animation Studies.

Liu, H., Tai, Y., Lin, H., & Du, X. (2022, January). Analysis of technology hotspots in artificial intelligence field based on Patent Map. In *2022 International Seminar on Computer Science and Engineering Technology (SCSET)* (pp. 141-144). IEEE. 10.1109/SCSET55041.2022.00041

Luo, X., & Xie, L. (2018, January). Research on artificial intelligence-based sharing education in the era of Internet+. In *2018 International conference on intelligent transportation, big data & smart city (ICITBS)* (pp. 335-338). IEEE.

Malhotra, P., Pandey, D., Pandey, B. K., & Patra, P. M. (2021). Managing agricultural supply chains in COVID-19 lockdown. *International Journal of Quality and Innovation*, 5(2), 109–118. 10.1504/IJQI.2021.117181

Menon, V., Pandey, D., Khosla, D., Kaur, M., Vashishtha, H. K., George, A. S., & Pandey, B. K. (2022). A Study on COVID–19, Its Origin, Phenomenon, Variants, and IoT-Based Framework to Detect the Presence of Coronavirus. In *IoT Based Smart Applications* (pp. 1–13). Springer International Publishing.

Pandey, B. K., & Pandey, D. (2023). Parametric optimization and prediction of enhanced thermoelectric performance in co-doped CaMnO3 using response surface methodology and neural network. *Journal of Materials Science Materials in Electronics*, 34(21), 1589. 10.1007/s10854-023-10954-1

Pandey, B. K., Pandey, D., & Agarwal, A. (2022). Encrypted information transmission by enhanced steganography and image transformation. *International Journal of Distributed Artificial Intelligence*, 14(1), 1–14. 10.4018/IJDAI.297110

Pandey, B. K., Pandey, D., Alkhafaji, M. A., Güneşer, M. T., & Şeker, C. (2023b). A reliable transmission and extraction of textual information using keyless encryption, steganography, and deep algorithm with cuckoo optimization. In *Micro-Electronics and Telecommunication Engineering: Proceedings of 6th ICMETE 2022* (pp. 629–636). Springer Nature Singapore. 10.1007/978-981-19-9512-5_57

Pandey, B. K., Pandey, D., Gupta, A., Nassa, V. K., Dadheech, P., & George, A. S. (2023a). Secret data transmission using advanced morphological component analysis and steganography. In *Role of data-intensive distributed computing systems in designing data solutions* (pp. 21–44). Springer International Publishing. 10.1007/978-3-031-15542-0_2

Pandey, B. K., Pandey, D., & Sahani, S. K. (2024). Autopilot control unmanned aerial vehicle system for sewage defect detection using deep learning. *Engineering Reports*, 12852. 10.1002/eng2.12852

Pandey, B. K., Pandey, S. K., & Pandey, D. (2011). A survey of bioinformatics applications on parallel architectures. *International Journal of Computer Applications*, 23(4), 21–25. 10.5120/2877-3744

Pandey, D., & Pandey, B. K. (2022). An efficient deep neural network with adaptive galactic swarm optimization for complex image text extraction. In *Process mining techniques for pattern recognition* (pp. 121–137). CRC Press. 10.1201/9781003169550-10

Pandey, D., Pandey, B. K., & Wairya, S. (2021). Hybrid deep neural network with adaptive galactic swarm optimization for text extraction from scene images. *Soft Computing*, 25(2), 1563–1580. 10.1007/s00500-020-05245-4

Pandey, J. K., Jain, R., Dilip, R., Kumbhkar, M., Jaiswal, S., Pandey, B. K., & Pandey, D. (2022). Investigating role of iot in the development of smart application for security enhancement. In *IoT Based Smart Applications* (pp. 219–243). Springer International Publishing.

Pesek, I., Nosović, N., & Krašna, M. (2022, June). The Role of AI in the Education and for the Education. In *2022 11th Mediterranean Conference on Embedded Computing (MECO)* (pp. 1-4). IEEE. 10.1109/MECO55406.2022.9797189

Raja, D., Kumar, D. R., Santhiyakumari, N., Kumarganesh, S., Sagayam, K. M., Thiyaneswaran, B., Pandey, B. K., & Pandey, D. (2024). A compact dual-feed wide-band slotted antenna for future wireless applications. *Analog Integrated Circuits and Signal Processing*, 118(2), 1–15. 10.1007/s10470-023-02233-0

Rani, S., Bhambri, P., & Kataria, A. (2023). Integration of IoT, Big Data, and Cloud Computing Technologies: Trend of the Era. In *Big Data, Cloud Computing and IoT* (pp. 1-21). Chapman and Hall/CRC.

Revathi, T. K., Sathiyabhama, B., Sankar, S., Pandey, D., Pandey, B. K., & Dadeech, P. (2022). An intelligent model for coronary heart disease diagnosis. In *Networking Technologies in Smart Healthcare* (pp. 309–327). CRC Press. 10.1201/9781003239888-15

Sahani, K., Khadka, S. S., Sahani, S. K., Pandey, B. K., & Pandey, D. (2023). A possible underground roadway for transportation facilities in Kathmandu Valley: A racking deformation of underground rectangular structures. *Engineering Reports*, 12821. 10.1002/eng2.12821

Saxena, A., Agarwal, A., Pandey, B. K., & Pandey, D. (2024). Examination of the Criticality of Customer Segmentation Using Unsupervised Learning Methods. *Circular Economy and Sustainability*, 1–14. 10.1007/s43615-023-00336-4

. Sengupta, R., Sengupta, D., Pandey, D., Pandey, B. K., Nassa, V. K., & Dadeech, P. (2021). A Systematic review of 5G opportunities, architecture and challenges. *Future Trends in 5G and 6G,* 247-269.

Sharma, M., Pandey, D., Khosla, D., Goyal, S., Pandey, B. K., & Gupta, A. K. (2022). Design of a GaN-based Flip Chip Light Emitting Diode (FC-LED) with au Bumps & Thermal Analysis with different sizes and adhesive materials for performance considerations. *Silicon*, 14(12), 7109–7120. 10.1007/s12633-021-01457-x

Sharma, S., Pandey, B. K., Pandey, D., Anand, R., Sharma, A., & Saini, S. (2023, March). Character Recognition Technique Implementation for Complicated Deteriorated Scene. In *2023 6th International Conference on Information Systems and Computer Networks (ISCON)* (pp. 1-4). IEEE. 10.1109/ISCON57294.2023.10112185

Singh, S., Madaan, G., Kaur, J., Swapna, H. R., Pandey, D., Singh, A., & Pandey, B. K. (2023). *Bibliometric Review on Healthcare Sustainability. Handbook of Research on Safe Disposal Methods of Municipal Solid Wastes for a Sustainable Environment*, 142-161. 10.4018/978-1-6684-8117-2.ch011

Sithipolvanichgul, J., Chen, C., Land, J., & Ractham, P. (2021). Factors affecting cloud computing adoption and continuance intention of students in Thailand. *International Journal on Management of Innovation & Technology*, 18(07), 2150037. 10.1142/S0219877021500371

Soodtoetong, N., & Rattanasiriwongwut, M. (2022). Educational Transformation with Virtual Classroom: Integrated between TTF and Social Motivation. *TEM Journal*, 11(1), 439–445. 10.18421/TEM111-56

Swapna, H. R., Bigirimana, E., Madaan, G., Hasan, A., Pandey, B. K., & Pandey, D. (2023). Impact of neuromarketing on consumer psychology in digitally connected networks. In *Applications of Neuromarketing in the Metaverse* (pp. 193–205). IGI Global. 10.4018/978-1-6684-8150-9.ch015

Tareke, S. A., Lelisho, M. E., Hassen, S. S., Seid, A. A., Jemal, S. S., Teshale, B. M., & Pandey, B. K. (2022). The prevalence and predictors of depressive, anxiety, and stress symptoms among Tepi town residents during the COVID-19 pandemic lockdown in Ethiopia. *Journal of Racial and Ethnic Health Disparities*, 1–13.35028903

Tripathi, R. P., Sharma, M., Gupta, A. K., Pandey, D., Pandey, B. K., Shahul, A., & George, A. H. (2023). Timely prediction of diabetes by means of machine learning practices. *Augmented Human Research*, 8(1), 1. 10.1007/s41133-023-00062-4

Vinodhini, V., Kumar, M. S., Sankar, S., Pandey, D., Pandey, B. K., & Nassa, V. K. (2022). IoT-based early forest fire detection using MLP and AROC method. *International Journal of Global Warming*, 27(1), 55–70. 10.1504/IJGW.2022.122794

Yang, Y., & Yu, D. (2022, January). Research and Exploration on the Training of New Engineering Personnel from the Perspective of Artificial Intelligence. In *2022 2nd Asia Conference on Information Engineering (ACIE)* (pp. 102-106). IEEE 10.1109/ACIE55485.2022.00029

Zou, J., & Chen, Y. (2022, December). Online Aesthetic Education Information Teaching System Based On Big Data Cloud Platform. In *2022 International Conference on Knowledge Engineering and Communication Systems (ICKES)* (pp. 1-6). IEEE. 10.1109/ICKECS56523.2022.10059986

Chapter 5
Educational Imperatives:
Preparing Students for the Security Demands of 6G Networks

V. Rekha
Department of Bachelor of Computer Applications, Agurchand Manmull Jain College, Chennai, India

N. Indumathi
Department of Commerce, B.S. Abdur Rahman Crescent Institute of Science and Technology, Chennai, India

Krupa B. Nair
Department of Commerce, B.S. Abdur Rahman Crescent Institute of Science and Technology, Chennai, India

R. Rajmohan
Department of English, K.S. Rangasamy College of Technology, India

Amara S. A. L. G. Gopala Gupta
https://orcid.org/0000-0002-5033-002X
Department of Computer Science and Engineering, Koneru Lakshmaiah Education Foundation, Vaddeswaram, India

Sandeep Gupta
https://orcid.org/0000-0002-3734-3723
Graphic Era University (Deemed), India

ABSTRACT

The impending arrival of 6G networks and the anticipated impact they will have on a variety of industries are the topics that are investigated in this chapter. The chapter also highlights the critical importance of cybersecurity in this newly evolving landscape. With a particular emphasis on the role that educational institutions play, the study emphasizes how important it is to provide students with the knowledge and abilities they need to effectively address the challenges that are associated with 6G security. This chapter highlights the necessity of curriculum adaptation in order to accommodate the ever-changing threat landscape.

I. INTRODUCTION

The next big thing in wireless communication (Devasenapathy, D. et al., 2024) technology, 6G networks, is expected to change a lot of industries with its predicted capabilities and breakthroughs. Expanding on the groundwork established by 5G networks, 6G is anticipated to provide unmatched data rates, extremely low latency, and extensive connectivity, opening the door for revolutionary applications

DOI: 10.4018/979-8-3693-7421-4.ch005

in a variety of sectors. Operating at terahertz frequencies (Govindaraj, V. et al., 2023), which enables previously unheard-of data transmission rates (JayaLakshmi, G. et al., 2024), is one of the distinguishing characteristics of 6G networks. High-speed, low-latency connections could be extremely helpful for telemedicine and real-time monitoring in the healthcare industry (Singh, S. et al., 2023), which is one area where this development has enormous potential (KVM, S., 2024). Additionally, improved communication (Raja, D. et al., 2024) networks will benefit sectors such as transportation (Sahani, K. et al., 2023) since they will allow autonomous vehicles to exchange large amounts of data quickly, increasing road safety and efficiency. It is anticipated that 6G networks will make use of massive MIMO (Multiple Input Multiple Output) technology, which will allow for the simultaneous transmission and reception of several data streams. With the ability to support multiple devices (Du John, H. V. et al., 2024) with ease, this capability promises to meet the increasing demand for connectivity in high-traffic areas and densely populated areas. Consequently, there is potential for substantial advancement in smart city projects, since networked infrastructure will enable effective resource management, traffic regulation, and provision of public services. 6G networks are expected to incorporate artificial intelligence (AI) (Anand, R. et al., 2024) at a fundamental level in addition to these technological advancements. Network efficiency, flexibility, and dependability should all be improved by AI-driven resource allocation and optimization algorithms. This combination of wireless communication (Gupta, A. K. et al., 2023) and artificial intelligence (AI) (Pandey, B. K., & Pandey, D., 2023) has potential applications in everything from intelligent automation in industrial settings to personalized user experiences in gaming and entertainment. The likelihood of security lapses and cyberattacks increases as these networks become more interconnected and essential services depend on them. The interconnectivity of 6G systems with newer technologies such as the Internet of Things (IoT) (Pramanik, S. et al., 2023) increases attack surface area and creates new vulnerabilities. For the protection of sensitive data, vital infrastructure, and public safety, 6G network security and integrity must be guaranteed. Strong encryption (Pandey, B. K. et al., 2023a), authentication procedures, and intrusion detection systems are going to be crucial parts of 6G security plans. To further anticipate and mitigate emerging threats, industry stakeholders (George, W. K. et al., 2024), researchers, and policymakers must work together and provide proactive threat intelligence.

1.1 Educational Role in 6G Security

The role of educational institutions is crucial in equipping the workforce of the future to meet the security requirements of 6G networks. With the speed at which wireless communication is changing, educational institutions must make sure that students have the skills and knowledge needed to handle the complexities of 6G security. The following are a few ways that are educational establishments can carry out this function are as shown in the Figure 1.

Figure 1. Education's role in 6G security skills

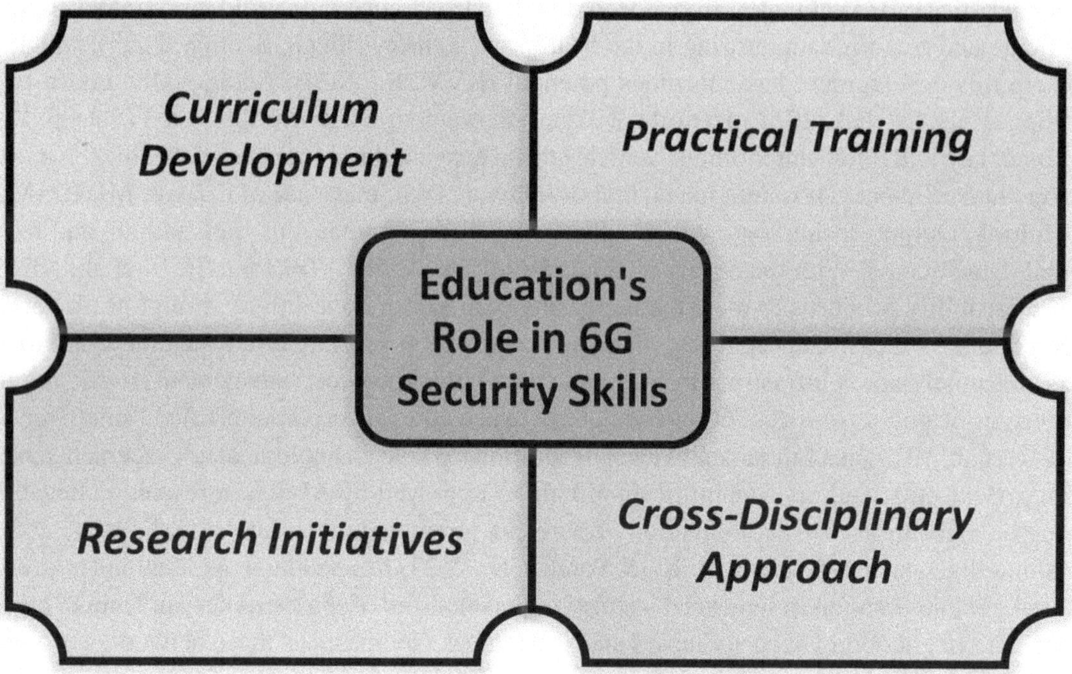

1. *Curriculum Development*: incorporating 6G security concepts into the current cybersecurity and telecom curricula. creation of specialized training programs or modules with a focus on 6G security, including subjects like risk mitigation techniques, network architecture, encryption protocols (Sharma, S. et al., 2023), and threat analysis. Working in tandem with industry partners to guarantee that curriculum content stays current and in line with industry demands for 6G security and the newest developments (Sharma, M. et al., 2024).
2. *Practical Training*: By implementing practical labs and simulation exercises that mimic 6G network environments, students will be able to gain practical experience in setting up, protecting, and debugging 6G networks. promotion of cooperative education and internships with businesses developing 6G technology, giving students practical experience with 6G security issues and recommended procedures. organization of cybersecurity challenges and capture-the-flag events with an emphasis on 6G security scenarios, which encourages student participation, critical thinking, and problem-solving abilities.
3. *Research Initiatives*: Encouragement of student-led research projects that tackle important 6G security issues, with a focus on innovation and the investigation of new approaches and technologies. Creation of research facilities or projects devoted to 6G security studies, giving students the chance to work with academics and professionals in the field while conducting cutting-edge research. Cooperation on 6G security research projects with industry and government organizations, knowledge sharing, and building a cooperative ecosystem to tackle 6G security issues.

4. *Cross-Disciplinary Approach*: The need for multidisciplinary collaboration between cybersecurity, computer science, telecommunications, and other relevant departments is emphasized. This is because 6G security is complex and requires a range of perspectives and expertise. In order to ensure that students are prepared to handle legal and ethical complexities in their future careers, regulatory and ethical considerations in 6G security will be addressed in collaboration with legal and policy experts. Involvement in networks and consortiums that promote cooperation in the field of 6G security between the government, business, and academia; these initiatives also facilitate knowledge exchange and cultivate an innovative and cooperative culture (George, W. K. et al., 2023).

Through the implementation of these strategies, educational establishments can adequately equip students to tackle the security requirements of 6G networks, guaranteeing that they possess the abilities, know-how, and hands-on experience required to thrive in a digital (Swapna, H. R. et al., 2023) landscape that is rapidly changing and becoming more interconnected.

II. MAPPING THE LANDSCAPE OF 6G SECURITY EDUCATION

2.1 Cybersecurity Education Programs

A comprehensive analysis of the various factors that shape the readiness of educational institutions to prepare students for the security demands of next-generation networks is required in order to evaluate the current cybersecurity education programs in relation to the security of 6G networks. It is essential to take into consideration the changing nature of the threat landscape. This involves determining whether or not the cybersecurity education programs that are currently in place are in line with the ever-evolving dangers that are posed by 6G networks. Evaluators are tasked with determining whether or not programs adequately cover emerging threats that are specific to 6G. These threats include attacks driven by artificial intelligence (Anand, R. et al., 2023), vulnerabilities in supply chains, and the exploitation of edge computing resources. The ability of students to anticipate, detect, and effectively respond to these threats can be improved through the incorporation of scenario-based learning (Saxena, A. et al., 2024) and threat intelligence into the educational curriculum. Regulatory and compliance requirements are yet another important factor to take into consideration. It is necessary for evaluators to investigate whether or not the existing cybersecurity education programs discuss the regulations and compliance standards that are pertinent to 6G networks. This encompasses regulations pertaining to privacy, laws pertaining to data protection, and industry standards. Legal and ethical considerations ought to be incorporated into the curriculum of programs, with topics such as data privacy, consent management, and compliance with international standards being included. Providing students with the tools they need to navigate the regulatory complexities of 6G security can be accomplished through collaboration with legal and policy experts (Hassan, R. et al., 2020). Collaborating across disciplines is absolutely necessary in order to adequately prepare students for the complex challenges that are associated with 6G security. It is important for educational institutions to evaluate the level of collaboration that exists within cybersecurity programs, particularly in fields that intersect with 6G security, such as engineering, computer science, and telecommunications. In order to encourage collaboration and the sharing of knowledge among students and faculty members from a variety of fields, it is important to investigate the possibility of interdisciplinary research projects, joint classes, and shared resources. It is possible to provide students with a comprehensive understanding of the technical, social, and ethical aspects of 6G security by incorporating interdisciplinary perspectives into the curriculum. It is important for educational institutions to evaluate their role in promoting innovation and entrepreneurship in this sector. This involvement should include providing assistance to student-led startups, technology transfer initiatives, and research projects sponsored by industry. When it comes to shaping the curriculum, providing guest lectures, and offering internship opportunities, collaboration with industry partners is absolutely necessary. The maintenance of programs that are in line with industry trends, best practices, and emerging technologies in 6G security can be accomplished through the formation of partnerships with industry consortia, standards bodies, and professional associations. As a final point of discussion, it is becoming increasingly important for cybersecurity education to incorporate a global perspective and cultural awareness, particularly in the context of 6G networks. In order to determine whether or not their programs incorporate a global perspective and cultural awareness into the curriculum, institutions should conduct an assessment. In order to accomplish this, it is necessary to incorporate case studies, examples, and guest lectures who come from a variety of geographical regions and cultural backgrounds. Students can be exposed to global cybersecurity issues and cross-cultural understanding in the context of 6G security through the opportunities for international collaboration, exchange programs, and research partnerships that are available to them (Snehi, J. et al., 2022).

2.2. Identify Gaps in Education

Enhancing the efficacy and relevance of cybersecurity education programs requires identifying the gaps and difficulties in current approaches to cybersecurity education, especially with regard to preparing students for the security requirements of 6G networks. First and foremost, it is imperative to critically evaluate how well current cybersecurity curricula match the particular knowledge and abilities needed to secure 6G networks. This comprises assessing how well emerging technologies, network architectures, cryptography methods, and threat intelligence are covered in relation to 6G security. It also entails evaluating how multidisciplinary subjects from disciplines like computer science, engineering, and telecommunications are incorporated to give students a comprehensive grasp of the difficulties associated with 6G security. There might be gaps in the cybersecurity education curriculum when it comes to offering opportunities for practical training and hands-on experience related to 6G security. In order to guarantee that students receive hands-on experience in configuring, securing, and monitoring 6G networks, it is essential to evaluate the accessibility and efficacy of practical labs, simulation exercises, and real-world projects. Furthermore, recognizing any deficiencies in opportunities for hands-on training in the real world, such as restricted availability of specialized equipment and simulation software, encourages the investigation of novel ways to offer practical experience, such as online laboratories, remote access to network environments, and industry collaborations. Collaboration and industry relevance are key factors that influence cybersecurity education initiatives. Gaps in industry relevance and alignment with current industry practices and standards in 6G security can be found by evaluating the degree of industry engagement and collaboration. Addressing these gaps and making sure that educational programs stay current and responsive to industry needs require strengthening industry partnerships, creating advisory boards, and incorporating industry feedback into curriculum development efforts. Innovation and research are essential to cybersecurity education, and it is important to find and close any gaps that exist in order to support student-led research projects and technology transfer initiatives that are pertinent to 6G security. These gaps can be filled and an innovative culture can be fostered within educational institutions by leveraging external funding sources, fostering interdisciplinary collaboration, and improving research capacity. For the purpose of providing top-notch cybersecurity education, faculty experience and professional development are essential. In order to improve faculty knowledge and skills in this field, it is critical to offer professional development opportunities and industry partnerships. This is highlighted by the identification of gaps in faculty expertise and training with regard to emerging technologies, research methodologies, and industry trends in 6G security. Finding gaps and chances for improvement in this area is made easier by evaluating the availability of professional development materials, career counselling, and student support services catered to students interested in pursuing careers in 6G security. Students can succeed in 6G security-related fields by increasing their engagement, retention, and success through networking events, mentorship programs, and help finding jobs (Katz, M. et al., 2018).

2.3 Evolving Threats Landscape

To develop effective cybersecurity education programs, it is essential to have a solid understanding of the ever-changing threat landscape. This is especially true when it comes to preparing students for the security challenges that 6G networks present. Threats and vulnerabilities are constantly evolving alongside the development of new communication paradigms and technological advancements. By gaining an understanding of the various types of cybersecurity threats that 6G networks might be exposed to, educators are able to tailor their curriculum and training to effectively address these challenges. This is made possible by the examination of the evolving threat landscape. There is a growing level of sophistication in cyberattacks, which is one facet of the new threat landscape that is emerging. As the data speeds of 6G networks increase, the latency decreases, and the capacity increases, these networks also become more appealing targets for malicious actors who are looking to exploit vulnerabilities for the purpose of financial gain, espionage, or sabotage. For students to be able to effectively detect, prevent, and respond to advanced attack techniques, such as zero-day exploits, advanced persistent threats (APTs), and supply chain attacks, educators need to educate them on these advanced attack techniques and equip them with the knowledge and skills necessary to do so. The expanding number of connected devices and the Internet of Things (IoT) (Iyyanar, P. et al., 2023) is another facet of the ever-changing nature of the threat landscape. It is anticipated that 6G networks will be able to support a vast array of Internet of Things devices, which will include something as diverse as autonomous vehicles and industrial machinery to smart sensors (Abdulkarim, Y. I. et al., 2023) and wearable devices. In order to gain unauthorized access to network infrastructure or to launch distributed denial-of-service (DDoS) attacks, cybercriminals exploit vulnerabilities in poorly secured Internet of Things devices. This interconnectedness has the effect of introducing new attack vectors and potential points of failure. The importance of securing Internet of Things devices, implementing robust access controls, and monitoring network traffic for suspicious activity is something that educators need to emphasize in order to effectively mitigate these risks. As an additional point of interest, the incorporation of artificial intelligence (AI) and machine learning (ML) (Muniandi, B. et al., 2024) technologies into 6G networks presents both opportunities and challenges for the field of cybersecurity (Pandey, B. K. et al., 2024). The use of artificial intelligence and machine learning (Pandey, B. K. et al., 2023b) can improve network efficiency, automate threat detection, and enhance incident response; however, these technologies also introduce new security risks, such as adversarial attacks, data poisoning, and algorithmic bias. By teaching students about the security implications of artificial intelligence and machine learning (Tripathi, R. P. et al., 2023) in 6G networks, educators should equip students with the skills necessary to effectively develop and deploy AI-driven security solutions. Because it is anticipated that 6G networks will be deployed all over the world, it is essential for students to have an understanding of the various regulatory environments, cultural norms, and geopolitical tensions that can have an effect on cybersecurity practices and policies. Educators should provide students with a global perspective on cybersecurity issues, highlighting the significance of complying with international standards, data privacy regulations, and ethical considerations in their professional practice during the course of their studies (Brito, J. M. C. et al., 2020).

III. BUILDING CURRICULUM AND TRAINING PROGRAMS

3.1 Integrate 6G Security Into Existing Programs

Incorporating 6G security concepts into current cybersecurity curricula which are shown in the figure 2, is imperative in order to equip students with the necessary skills to tackle the distinct obstacles presented by next-generation networks. The following techniques can be used to successfully integrate 6G security topics into currently running cybersecurity programs:

- *Curriculum Mapping*: Identify opportunities for integrating 6G security topics by conducting a thorough analysis of the current cybersecurity curriculum. Seek out coverage gaps or overlaps that correspond with the specialized knowledge and abilities needed to secure 6G networks. Determine how to integrate 6G security concepts into pertinent courses by mapping out the current course structure. Make sure the addition of 6G security topics strengthens and completes the cybersecurity curriculum's overall learning objectives. Create a coherent plan that takes learning objectives, prerequisites, and sequencing into consideration when incorporating 6G security topics into the current curriculum.
- *Integration of Fundamental Concepts*: Incorporate network architecture and encryption protocols (Kumar Pandey, B. et al., 2021) two key components of 6G security into the cybersecurity curriculum's core courses. Include talks about the particular security issues raised by massive MIMO technology, terahertz frequencies (Bruntha, P. M. et al., 2023), and AI-driven networks. Make sure that students get a clear understanding of how these fundamental ideas relate to 6G network security in particular. In order to help students apply their knowledge in real-world situations and to reinforce important concepts, give them practical examples and hands-on exercises (Jayapoorani, S. et al., 2023).
- *Particularized Modules or Courses*: Create specialized 6G security courses or modules to give students in-depth knowledge of cutting-edge subjects and new dangers. Create courses that concentrate on particular facets of 6G security, like secure software development for 6G networks, edge computing security, and AI-driven security. Use case studies, role-playing, and hands-on activities to give students real-world experience and to help them develop the necessary skills. Ask business leaders to give guest lectures to students so they can impart their knowledge and experiences about 6G security. Give students the option to customize their education to fit their unique interests and professional aspirations by offering elective courses or concentrations in 6G security.
- *Case Studies and Real-World Uses*: Incorporate practical applications of 6G security principles and real-world case studies into the curriculum to give students practical experience and context.

Examine current cyberattacks on 5G networks and talk about how 6G environments might be vulnerable to similar attacks. Examine real-world situations and use cases where students can solve issues and reach well-informed conclusions by utilizing their understanding of 6G security concepts. To improve their abilities and obtain real-world experience, encourage students to take part in 6G security-focused capture-the-flag events and cybersecurity competitions. Give students the chance to participate in research projects or internships with business partners so they can get practical experience solving 6G security issues.

- *Industry Experts and Guest Lecturers*: Get students' insights, experiences, and best practices from industry experts and guest lecturers in the field of 6G security. Through industry seminars and guest lectures, expose students to a range of viewpoints and practical applications of 6G security concepts. Promote communication and interaction between professionals in the industry and students to enable networking and the transfer of knowledge. Arrange symposiums, panel discussions, or workshops with professionals from government, business, and academia to talk about the issues and trends facing 6G security today.
- *Research Projects and Capstone Experiences*: To expand their knowledge and hone their practical skills, we strongly advise students to undertake research projects and capstone experiences centered around 6G security issues. As students work on research projects, mentor and advise them, assisting with the formulation of research questions, the creation of experiments, and the analysis of data. Through industry partnerships and research collaborations, support student-led initiatives to investigate cutting-edge technologies and emerging trends in 6G security. Highlight student research accomplishments at conferences, in publications, and in presentations to increase awareness and add to the corpus of information about 6G security. Encourage students from various backgrounds to collaborate across disciplines and work as a team to solve challenging research problems and practical 6G security issues.
- *Continuous Curriculum Review and Update*: To guarantee that lessons on 6G security are up to date and pertinent, develop a methodical procedure for curriculum review and update on a regular basis. Keep an eye out for changes in the industry, new risks, and technological breakthroughs to spot opportunities for continuous curriculum improvement and revision. Get input from industry partners, educators, students, and other relevant parties to evaluate the success of 6G security education programs and pinpoint areas that need improvement. Make sure all of your reading materials—including textbooks, course materials, and learning resources reflect the most recent advancements in 6G security trends, technologies, and best practices. Participate in professional development events, such as conferences, seminars, and workshops, to keep up with the latest advancements and growing themes in 6G security education.

Figure 2. 6G security in cyber curriculum

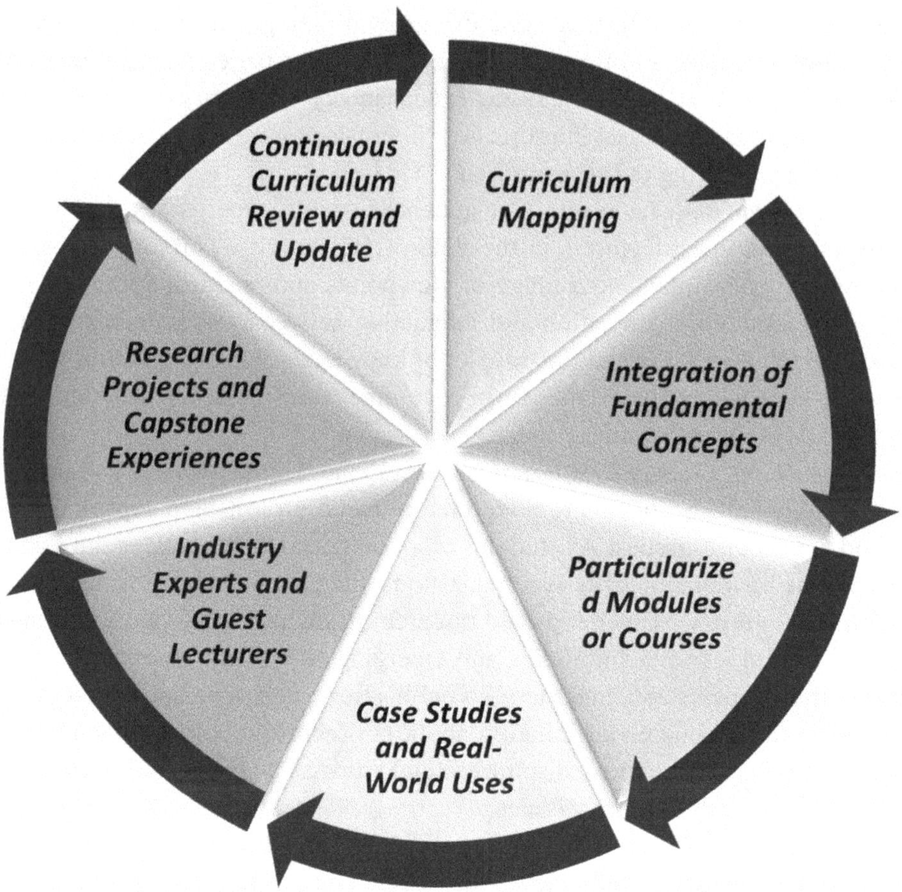

3.2. Develop Specialized Courses

The development of specialized courses or modules that are specifically focused on 6G security is an example of a strategic response to the changing landscape of cybersecurity. In order to provide students with the knowledge and abilities they need to address the specific challenges that are posed by next-generation networks, these classes have been intentionally designed. Conducting a comprehensive needs assessment is an essential first step in this process. The purpose of this assessment is to determine the specific requirements and priorities that pertain to the implementation of 6G security. Contributions from industry professionals, cybersecurity experts, and other stakeholders are helpful in identifying the most important areas of concentration and shaping the course objectives in accordance with those areas.

Following the establishment of the objectives, the curriculum is meticulously designed to cover a wide range of subjects that are pertinent to the security of 6G networks. Fundamental ideas such as network architecture, encryption protocols, threat intelligence, and risk management are included in this category. Hands-on exercises, case studies, and simulation exercises are all incorporated into the curriculum in order to effectively reinforce learning outcomes. The curriculum is designed to strike a balance between theoretical understanding and practical application. Methods of instruction are chosen with great care in order to keep students interested and to make active learning possible throughout the entirety of the course. Students are given the opportunity to participate in hands-on labs, group projects, and cybersecurity competitions in addition to the traditional lectures and discussions that are offered to them. In order to enrich the learning experience and bridge the gap between academia and industry, guest lectures from industry experts provide valuable insights and real-world perspectives on the challenges and solutions related to 6G security. It is the purpose of assessment and evaluation strategies to determine whether or not students have a comprehension of key concepts, critical thinking skills, problem-solving abilities, and practical proficiency in 6G security. A wide range of assessment strategies, such as quizzes, examinations, research projects, presentations, and hands-on demonstrations, are utilized in order to accurately gauge the learning and progress of students. The instructors are able to identify areas for improvement and make adjustments to the curriculum as necessary to ensure that it continues to be relevant and effective. This is made possible through the regularly scheduled review and evaluation of the course outcomes and the performance of the students. Validating course objectives, providing input for curriculum development, and ensuring alignment with industry needs and best practices are all accomplished with the assistance of industry input. Students receive valuable exposure to real-world scenarios and challenges in 6G security through the contributions of guest speakers from the industry who share their firsthand insights, experiences, and case studies. The creation of specialized courses or modules that concentrate on 6G security is an example of a proactive approach to preparing students for the complexities and requirements of securing networks of the next generation (Dang, S. et al., 2020).

3.3 Collaborate With Industry for Relevance

Particularly in the context of preparing students for the security requirements of 6G networks, collaboration with industry partners is an essential component in ensuring that cybersecurity curricula are relevant and aligned with the needs of the industry. These kinds of partnerships provide valuable insights into the practices that are currently being used in the industry, emerging technologies, and evolving threats. These insights can enhance the educational experience for students and help inform the development of curriculum. Participation of industry professionals in the process of curriculum design and review is an essential component of working together with members of the industry. Educational institutions are able to acquire first-hand knowledge of the skills and competencies that are most valued in the workforce if they bring in cybersecurity experts, network engineers, and technology leaders from industry to participate in discussions and workshops. That the curriculum is aligned with industry standards, best practices, and emerging trends in 6G security is made possible with the help of this input. Real-world case studies, practical exercises, and hands-on projects can also be incorporated into the curriculum with the help of industry partnerships, which enable this integration. Education institutions are able to gain access to a vast array of industry-specific scenarios and challenges through collaboration with industry partners. These can be utilized to enhance classroom instruction and provide students with valuable opportunities for experiential learning. Students acquire knowledge and practical skills that are directly applicable to their future careers in 6G security from the incorporation of industry-relevant content into their academic coursework. Students are able to gain valuable hands-on experience in real-world settings through internships and cooperative education opportunities, which are frequently developed as a result of industry partnerships. Students are able to apply what they have learned in the classroom to real-world situations when educational institutions form partnerships with businesses. These partnerships allow for the establishment of internship programs, cooperative education initiatives, and work-study arrangements (Qamar, F. et al., 2019). Not only do these hands-on experiences help students develop essential professional skills and networks that can make it easier for them to transition into the workforce, but they also improve students' understanding of the concepts underlying 6G security. Partnerships with businesses can provide support for research and innovation in the field of cybersecurity, in addition to the development of curricula and opportunities for experiential learning. It is possible for educational institutions to address challenges that are specific to the industry, investigate cutting-edge technologies, and contribute to the advancement of knowledge in 6G security by working together with industry partners on research projects, technology transfer initiatives, and joint ventures. In order to ensure that cybersecurity education continues to be relevant, responsive, and forward-thinking in the face of evolving industry needs and technological advancements, industry partnerships help to ensure that a culture of collaboration and innovation is fostered.

IV. EXPERIENTIAL LEARNING AND PRACTICAL TRAINING

4.1 Hands-On Labs and Simulations

In cybersecurity education, the use of interactive labs and simulation exercises that mimic 6G network environments is essential because it provides students with invaluable real-world experience and exposure to various scenarios. As crucial elements of an all-encompassing educational strategy, these interactive learning exercises allow students to put their theoretical knowledge into practice, hone their technical abilities, and try out various security solutions in a safe and authentic environment. It is essential to set up a specific lab space with the required networking, software, and hardware. Virtualization platforms like VMware and VirtualBox, which generate virtualized instances of 6G network components like base stations, mobile devices, and edge computing nodes, are part of this infrastructure. In order to simulate different network configurations and scenarios and to mimic the behavior of 6G networks, additional simulation tools and emulators are installed, such as ns-3 or OPNET. The carefully crafted lab exercises cover every facet of 6G security, from threat detection and incident response to network configuration. These exercises include scenarios like DDoS attacks, malware infections, data breaches, and insider threats in order to replicate real-world 6G security challenges. Students' learning experience is enhanced by the incorporation of case studies and real-world examples from recent cyber incidents in 6G networks, which give context and relevance to the lab exercises. Students are encouraged to experiment in the lab setting with various security tools, approaches, and procedures in order to reduce risks and safeguard 6G network environments. As they investigate different security configurations, carry out vulnerability analyses, and put countermeasures in place, they get direction and assistance. In addition, an environment of inquiry and curiosity is promoted, pushing students to exercise critical thinking, evaluate information, and make inferences from their observations and research. An essential part of learning is reflection and feedback. As students complete the lab exercises, they receive timely feedback that includes constructive criticism and recommendations for improvement. It is encouraged of students to think back on their experiences, note the lessons they've learned, and share their observations and insights. Peer reviews and group discussions encourage students to share their knowledge, work together, and solve problems as a group, which improves their overall learning experience. It is crucial to incorporate practical labs and simulation exercises into already-existing cybersecurity courses or modules. These exercises should support the theoretical ideas presented in lectures and readings by being in line with the learning objectives and course objectives. All students, regardless of their technical background or experience level, can be made to feel included by offering assistance, resources, and clear instructions.

To give students practical experience and exposure to cybersecurity principles in the context of next-generation networks, it makes sense to support internships and cooperative education programs with industry partners working on 6G technology. Collaborations between academic institutions and business executives provide students with chances to put their theoretical knowledge to use in real-world situations, hone their professional skills, and create industry connections that may open doors to future employment. Students can work directly with industry partners on projects related to network infrastructure, cybersecurity, and 6G technology through internships. Through first-hand exposure to industry practices, methodologies, and technologies, these experiences give students insights and practical skills that they cannot acquire through classroom instruction alone. Furthermore, internships give students the chance to collaborate with researchers, mentors, and seasoned professionals, developing professional networks and mentoring relationships. Cooperative education programs, also known as "coops," give students the opportunity to pursue their academic goals while simultaneously gaining extensive work experience in an industry partner organization. Co-op programs allow students to combine classroom learning with real-world work experience by alternating between periods of full-time work and study. With the help of this immersive approach, students can obtain academic credit and valuable professional experience in addition to developing a deeper understanding of the opportunities, challenges, and processes of the industry (Nayak, S., & Patgiri, R, 2020). Cooperative education and internship partnerships with business partners benefit both educational institutions and business partners. By gaining access to resources, industry expertise, and real-world projects, educational institutions can improve the caliber and applicability of their cybersecurity education programs. Conversely, industry partners have access to a pool of bright and driven students who can bring new insights, concepts, and abilities to their companies. Additionally, co-ops and internships are useful hiring channels for locating and developing future talent in the 6G security space. Educational institutions can be proactive in promoting internships and cooperative education programs with industry partners developing 6G technology by doing the following:

Formal agreements and partnerships should be established with industry organizations: Academic institutions should aggressively pursue collaborations with businesses engaged in the development, testing, and deployment of 6G technology. In order to investigate potential collaborations, this entails contacting businesses, academic institutions, governmental organizations, and other pertinent entities. To guarantee transparency and accountability, formal agreements specifying the parameters of the partnership—including duties, obligations, and rewards for each party should be set up. These collaborations can take many different forms, depending on the objectives and preferences of the parties involved, including joint projects, sponsorship agreements, advisory boards, and research collaborations.

Promoting internship and cooperative education opportunities: Through a variety of channels, educational institutions should aggressively promote internship and cooperative education opportunities with industry partners. In order to connect students with potential employers and increase awareness of available opportunities, career services offices, academic advisors, and industry networking events can be utilized. In order to help students apply for internships and coops and to spread information about these opportunities, job boards, social media, and online platforms can all be used. Enhancing student engagement and participation in internship and co-op programs can also be achieved by working with industry partners to organize information sessions, workshops, or recruitment events on campus.

Providing direction and assistance to students: Academic establishments ought to provide students with all-encompassing assistance during the application process for internships and cooperative education. To help students effectively present themselves to potential employers, this includes offering advice on how to write a resume, prepare a cover letter, and practice interview techniques. Academic advisors, career counselors, and faculty mentors can provide students with customized guidance and support, assisting them in locating appropriate opportunities and navigating the application process. Furthermore, career-ready workshops, seminars, and networking events that concentrate on internship and co-op preparation can offer students insightful information and tools to improve their professional growth.

Encouraging communication and cooperation: In order to ensure that students, instructors, and business partners engaged in co-ops and internships can effectively communicate with one another, educational institutions are essential. To guarantee that internship and co-op experiences are in line with academic goals and learning outcomes, this entails creating clear lines of communication and coordination. In order to track students' development, offer feedback, and handle any problems or worries that might come up during the internship or co-op term, faculty mentors and industry supervisors should stay in regular communication. In order to promote communication and information sharing among stakeholders and create a collaborative and supportive environment for professional and student learning, collaboration platforms, project management tools, and online forums can be employed.

Financial aid, stipends, or other incentives: Academic institutions may provide financial aid, stipends, or other incentives to students in order to encourage their involvement in internship and cooperative education programs. Students who successfully complete an internship or co-op program can receive academic credit, which enables them to obtain course credits while gaining real-world work experience. In order to assist with living expenses and transportation costs (Sahani, K. et al., 2023) related to taking part in unpaid or low-paid internships, stipends or other forms of financial support may be offered. In addition, exceptional co-ops or interns may receive awards or recognition for their accomplishments and contributions during their placements. Educational institutions can optimize the advantages of experiential learning opportunities by providing incentives to encourage a greater number of students to participate in internship and co-op programs.

V. RESEARCH AND INNOVATION

5.1 Promote Student-Led Research

One of the most important ways to encourage innovation and advance knowledge in the field of 6G security is to support student-led research projects that tackle important problems. In order to inspire students to investigate cutting-edge subjects, create original solutions, and give back to the larger cybersecurity community, educational institutions are essential. Institutions foster a culture of inquiry and discovery as well as critical thinking and problem-solving abilities by allowing students to take charge of their research projects. Creating initiatives, centers, or research programs specifically focused on 6G (Kirubasri, G. et al., 2021) security is one way to support student-led research projects. These platforms give students the tools, opportunities for collaboration, and guidance they need to follow their research interests in a safe setting. Cybersecurity-focused faculty members can act as mentors and advisors, helping students with their research, offering technical support, and giving feedback on project proposals and results. Academic institutions have the ability to foster interdisciplinary cooperation between students with different backgrounds in computer science, engineering, mathematics (Sahani, S. K. et al., 2024), and social sciences. A comprehensive approach to addressing complex challenges in 6G security is made possible by collaborative research projects that bring together students with complementary skills and perspectives (Bessant, Y. A. et al.,2023). Institutions can harness the collective expertise of students to address complex issues and produce creative solutions by encouraging cross-disciplinary collaboration. Educational institutions can also offer funding opportunities, grants, or scholarships to support student research endeavors in order to encourage student-led research projects. Financial support enables students to fully engage in their research activities without financial constraints by helping to cover costs associated with data collection, equipment, software, conference attendance, and publication fees. Institutions may also provide assistantships, fellowships, or research internships that give students financial aid or academic credit in return for their participation in continuing research projects. Institutions can also honor and display the accomplishments of student research through a variety of venues, including publications, research forums, conferences, and symposiums. Giving students the chance to present their research, exchange ideas, and get feedback from teachers and peers not only validates their contributions but also aids in the dissemination of fresh ideas and knowledge both inside and outside of the academic community (Wang, J. et al., 2022).

5.2 Collaborate With Industry and Government

Working together with government and industry organizations on 6G security research projects is essential to knowledge advancement, tackling new problems, and guaranteeing the creation of strong defenses for the networks of the future. These partnerships take advantage of the knowledge, assets, and practical experience of government and business partners to promote innovation, guide policy choices, and improve cybersecurity procedures in the context of the sixth-generation network. In order to address complex issues in 6G security, academic institutions are essential in fostering collaboration between researchers, industry stakeholders, and government agencies. Institutions can generate synergies that expedite research progress and facilitate the translation of research findings into practical applications by forming partnerships and promoting interdisciplinary cooperation. Access to industry-specific data, infrastructure, and expertise that can guide research initiatives and validate research findings is a major advantage of working with industry partners. Researchers can create more accurate risk assessments, threat models, and mitigation strategies by working with industry partners who frequently have valuable insights into emerging threats, vulnerabilities, and best practices in 6G security. Students can enhance their education and professional development by participating in collaborative research projects with industry partners, which expose them to real-world challenges and firsthand experience. Governmental organizations frequently offer funding for research projects, access to resources and data that are owned by the government, and their expertise in developing and enforcing policies. In order to guarantee that research results are in line with national security priorities, legal frameworks, and regulatory requirements, collaborative research projects with government agencies can aid in bridging the gap between academic research and real-world applications. For industry and government agencies to collaborate effectively, all parties involved must be proactive, communicate openly, and have mutual trust. A variety of strategies, including cooperative research projects, sponsored research agreements, cooperative workshops, and advisory boards, can be used by educational institutions to promote collaboration. Institutions can guarantee that collaboration efforts are targeted, fruitful, and advantageous to all involved by setting clear objectives, standards, and governance frameworks.

VI. CROSS-DISCIPLINARY APPROACH

Collaboration and a cross-disciplinary approach are crucial tactics for successfully tackling the complex issues surrounding 6G security. Through the integration of specialists from various domains, including cybersecurity, telecommunications, computer science, law, policy, and social sciences, educational establishments can stimulate creativity, encourage comprehensive problem-solving, and formulate all-encompassing solutions that take into account ethical, legal, technical, and societal factors. Leveraging diverse perspectives and expertise to gain a more comprehensive understanding of complex issues in 6G security is one of the main advantages of a cross-disciplinary approach. While telecommunications specialists offer knowledge of network architecture, protocol design, and wireless communications, cybersecurity experts can offer technical insights into threat detection, encryption, and network defense mechanisms. To guarantee that security solutions (Pandey, B. K. et al., 2021a) are in line with legal frameworks and societal values, legal and policy experts offer advice on matters pertaining to regulatory compliance, privacy laws, liability concerns, and ethical issues. Working together across disciplines facilitates the sharing of ideas, approaches, and best practices (Pandey, D. et al., 2021), which further fosters innovation. Multidisciplinary research groups can investigate cutting-edge strategies for 6G security, like creating cryptographic algorithms that are resistant to quantum fluctuations, utilizing blockchain technology (David, S. et al., 2023) for secure transactions, and utilizing artificial intelligence and machine learning for threat detection (Pandey, B. K. et al., 2021b). Through the integration of specialized knowledge from various domains, scientists can expand their understanding and create innovative solutions to tackle new risks and difficulties in 5G networks. Researchers might look into the ethical ramifications of data privacy and surveillance, the social and economic effects of 6G technologies, or the geopolitical aspects of cybersecurity in a hyperconnected world. Educational institutions can produce more well-rounded cybersecurity professionals who are capable of navigating the intricate and interconnected nature of 6G security challenges by incorporating social sciences, humanities, and policy perspectives into cybersecurity education and research. Educational institutions can establish interdisciplinary research centers, institutes, or collaborative networks devoted to 6G security in order to promote cross-disciplinary collaboration. These platforms give researchers from various fields a place to meet, exchange ideas, and work together on collaborative projects. Institutions of higher learning can also provide interdisciplinary seminars, workshops, and courses that unite teachers and students from various backgrounds to investigate interdisciplinary approaches to 6G security issues.

CONCLUSION

The impending arrival of 6G networks and the transformative impact that these networks are expected to have across a variety of industries are called attention to. Nevertheless, this technological advancement also highlights the critical importance of cybersecurity, demanding that proactive measures be taken in order to address emerging vulnerabilities and threats. As a result of this landscape, educational institutions have emerged as key players, and they have been tasked with the responsibility of providing students with the knowledge and skills necessary to navigate the complexities caused by 6G security. Examining the existing cybersecurity education programs reveals areas that could be improved, highlighting the necessity of modifying the curriculum in order to accommodate the ever-changing threat landscape. Among the essential strategies that emerge from this endeavor are the incorporation of topics related to 6G security, the development of specialized courses, and the collaboration with industry partners. Additionally, students are provided with opportunities for practical training through experiential learning initiatives such as hands-on labs and internships. Also, research and innovation efforts are driving forward progress in addressing key challenges. Adopting a multidisciplinary approach not only promotes holistic comprehension but also encourages the development of innovative solutions that go beyond the boundaries of traditional disciplines. As a result, educational institutions play a pivotal role in preparing students for the security demands of 6G networks and shaping a skilled workforce that is capable of navigating the complexities of the digital era. This is accomplished by embracing specific strategies and encouraging collaboration.

REFERENCES

Abdulkarim, Y. I., Awl, H. N., Muhammadsharif, F. F., Saeed, S. R., Sidiq, K. R., Khasraw, S. S., & Pandey, D. (2023). Metamaterial-based sensors loaded corona-shaped resonator for COVID-19 detection by using microwave techniques. *Plasmonics*, 1–16.

Anand, R., Khan, B., Nassa, V. K., Pandey, D., Dhabliya, D., Pandey, B. K., & Dadheech, P. (2023). Hybrid convolutional neural network (CNN) for kennedy space center hyperspectral image. *Aerospace Systems*, 6(1), 71–78. 10.1007/s42401-022-00168-4

Anand, R., Lakshmi, S. V., Pandey, D., & Pandey, B. K. (2024). An enhanced ResNet-50 deep learning model for arrhythmia detection using electrocardiogram biomedical indicators. *Evolving Systems*, 15(1), 83–97. 10.1007/s12530-023-09559-0

Bessant, Y. A., Jency, J. G., Sagayam, K. M., Jone, A. A. A., Pandey, D., & Pandey, B. K. (2023). Improved parallel matrix multiplication using Strassen and Urdhvatiryagbhyam method. *CCF Transactions on High Performance Computing*, 5(2), 102–115. 10.1007/s42514-023-00149-9

Brito, J. M. C., Mendes, L. L., & Gontijo, J. G. S. (2020, March). Brazil 6G project-an approach to build a national-wise framework for 6G networks. In *2020 2nd 6G Wireless Summit (6G SUMMIT)* (pp. 1-5). IEEE.

. Bruntha, P. M., Dhanasekar, S., Hepsiba, D., Sagayam, K. M., Neebha, T. M., Pandey, D., & Pandey, B. K. (2023). Application of switching median filter with L 2 norm-based auto-tuning function for removing random valued impulse noise. *Aerospace Systems, 6*(1), 53-59.

Dang, S., Amin, O., Shihada, B., & Alouini, M. S. (2020). What should 6G be? *Nature Electronics*, 3(1), 20–29. 10.1038/s41928-019-0355-6

David, S., Duraipandian, K., Chandrasekaran, D., Pandey, D., Sindhwani, N., & Pandey, B. K. (2023). Impact of blockchain in healthcare system. In *Unleashing the Potentials of blockchain technology for healthcare industries* (pp. 37–57). Academic Press. 10.1016/B978-0-323-99481-1.00004-3

Devasenapathy, D., Madhumathy, P., Umamaheshwari, R., Pandey, B. K., & Pandey, D. (2024). Transmission-efficient grid-based synchronized model for routing in wireless sensor networks using Bayesian compressive sensing. *SN Computer Science*, 5(1), 1–11.

Du John, H. V., Jose, T., Sagayam, K. M., Pandey, B. K., & Pandey, D. (2024). Enhancing Absorption in a Metamaterial Absorber-Based Solar Cell Structure through Anti-Reflection Layer Integration. *Silicon*, 1-11.

George, W. K., Ekong, M. O., Pandey, D., & Pandey, B. K. (2023). Pedagogy for Implementation of TVET Curriculum for the Digital World. In *Applications of Neuromarketing in the Metaverse* (pp. 117-136). IGI Global. 10.4018/978-1-6684-8150-9.ch009

George, W. K., Silas, E. I., Pandey, D., & Pandey, B. K. (2024). Utilization of Industry 4.0 Technologies in Nigerian Technical and Vocational Education: A Conundrum for Educators. In *Examining the Rapid Advance of Digital Technology in Africa* (pp. 270–293). IGI Global. 10.4018/978-1-6684-9962-7.ch014

Govindaraj, V., Dhanasekar, S., Martinsagayam, K., Pandey, D., Pandey, B. K., & Nassa, V. K. (2023). Low-power test pattern generator using modified LFSR. *Aerospace Systems*, 1-8.

Gupta, A. K., Sharma, R., Pandey, D., Nassa, V. K., Pandey, B. K., George, A. S., & Dadheech, P. (2023). Performance analysis of eight-channel WDM optical network with different optical amplifiers for industry 4.0. In *Innovation and Competitiveness in Industry 4.0 Based on Intelligent Systems* (pp. 197–212). Springer International Publishing. 10.1007/978-3-031-29775-5_9

Iyyanar, P., Anand, R., Shanthi, T., Nassa, V. K., Pandey, B. K., George, A. S., & Pandey, D. (2023). A real-time smart sewage cleaning UAV assistance system using IoT. In *Handbook of Research on Data-Driven Mathematical Modeling in Smart Cities* (pp. 24–39). IGI Global.

JayaLakshmi, G., Pandey, D., Pandey, B. K., Kaur, P., Mahajan, D. A., & Dari, S. S. (2024). Smart Big Data Collection for Intelligent Supply Chain Improvement. In *AI and Machine Learning Impacts in Intelligent Supply Chain* (pp. 180-195). IGI Global.

Jayapoorani, S., Pandey, D., Sasirekha, N. S., Anand, R., & Pandey, B. K. (2023). Systolic optimized adaptive filter architecture designs for ECG noise cancellation by Vertex-5. *Aerospace Systems*, 6(1), 163–173. 10.1007/s42401-022-00177-3

Katz, M., Matinmikko-Blue, M., & Latva-Aho, M. (2018, November). 6Genesis flagship program: Building the bridges towards 6G-enabled wireless smart society and ecosystem. In *2018 IEEE 10th Latin-American Conference on Communications (LATINCOM)* (pp. 1-9). IEEE.

Kirubasri, G., Sankar, S., Pandey, D., Pandey, B. K., Singh, H., & Anand, R. (2021, September). A recent survey on 6G vehicular technology, applications and challenges. In *2021 9th International Conference on Reliability, Infocom Technologies and Optimization (Trends and Future Directions)(ICRITO)* (pp. 1-5). IEEE.

Kumar Pandey, B., Pandey, D., Nassa, V. K., Ahmad, T., Singh, C., George, A. S., & Wakchaure, M. A. (2021). Encryption and steganography-based text extraction in IoT using the EWCTS optimizer. *Imaging Science Journal*, 69(1-4), 38–56. 10.1080/13682199.2022.2146885

KVM, S., Pandey, B. K., & Pandey, D. (2024). Design of Surface Plasmon Resonance (SPR) Sensors for Highly Sensitive Biomolecular Detection in Cancer Diagnostics. *Plasmonics*, 1-13.

Muniandi, B., Nassa, V. K., Pandey, D., Pandey, B. K., Dadheech, P., & George, A. S. (2024). Pattern Analysis for Feature Extraction in Complex Images. In *Using Machine Learning to Detect Emotions and Predict Human Psychology* (pp. 145-167). IGI Global. 10.4018/979-8-3693-1910-9.ch007

Nayak, S., & Patgiri, R. (2020). 6G communication: Envisioning the key issues and challenges. arXiv preprint arXiv:2004.04024.

Pandey, B. K., & Pandey, D. (2023). Parametric optimization and prediction of enhanced thermoelectric performance in co-doped CaMnO3 using response surface methodology and neural network. *Journal of Materials Science Materials in Electronics*, 34(21), 1589. 10.1007/s10854-023-10954-1

Pandey, B. K., Pandey, D., Alkhafaji, M. A., Güneşer, M. T., & Şeker, C. (2023a). A reliable transmission and extraction of textual information using keyless encryption, steganography, and deep algorithm with cuckoo optimization. In *Micro-Electronics and Telecommunication Engineering: Proceedings of 6th ICMETE 2022* (pp. 629–636). Springer Nature Singapore. 10.1007/978-981-19-9512-5_57

Pandey, B. K., Pandey, D., Dadheech, P., Mahajan, D. A., George, A. S., & Hameed, A. S. (2023b). Review on Smart Sewage Cleaning UAV Assistance for Sustainable Development. In *Handbook of Research on Safe Disposal Methods of Municipal Solid Wastes for a Sustainable Environment* (pp. 69–79). IGI Global. 10.4018/978-1-6684-8117-2.ch005

Pandey, B. K., Pandey, D., & Sahani, S. K. (2024). Autopilot control unmanned aerial vehicle system for sewage defect detection using deep learning. *Engineering Reports*, 12852. 10.1002/eng2.12852

Pandey, B. K., Pandey, D., Wairya, S., & Agarwal, G. (2021a). An advanced morphological component analysis, steganography, and deep learning-based system to transmit secure textual data. *International Journal of Distributed Artificial Intelligence*, 13(2), 40–62. 10.4018/IJDAI.2021070104

Pandey, B. K., Pandey, D., Wariya, S., & Agarwal, G. (2021b). A deep neural network-based approach for extracting textual images from deteriorate images. *EAI Endorsed Transactions on Industrial Networks and Intelligent Systems*, 8(28), e3–e3. 10.4108/eai.17-9-2021.170961

Pandey, D., Pandey, B. K., & Wairya, S. (2021). Hybrid deep neural network with adaptive galactic swarm optimization for text extraction from scene images. *Soft Computing*, 25(2), 1563–1580. 10.1007/s00500-020-05245-4

Pramanik, S., Pandey, D., Joardar, S., Niranjanamurthy, M., Pandey, B. K., & Kaur, J. (2023, October). An overview of IoT privacy and security in smart cities. In *AIP Conference Proceedings* (Vol. 2495, No. 1). AIP Publishing. 10.1063/5.0123511

Qamar, F., Hindia, M. N., Abbas, T., Dimyati, K. B., & Amiri, I. S. (2019). Investigation of QoS performance evaluation over 5G network for indoor environment at millimeter wave bands. *International Journal of Electronics and Telecommunications*, 65(1), 95–101. 10.24425/ijet.2019.126288

Raja, D., Kumar, D. R., Santhiyakumari, N., Kumarganesh, S., Sagayam, K. M., Thiyaneswaran, B., Pandey, B. K., & Pandey, D. (2024). A compact dual-feed wide-band slotted antenna for future wireless applications. *Analog Integrated Circuits and Signal Processing*, 1–15. 10.1007/s10470-023-02233-0

Sahani, K., Khadka, S., Sahani, S. K., Pandey, B. K., & Pandey, D. (2023). *A Possible Underground Roadway for Transportation Facilities in Kathmandu Valley Ring Road: A Racking Deformation of Underground Rectangular Structures*. Academic Press.

Sahani, K., Khadka, S. S., Sahani, S. K., Pandey, B. K., & Pandey, D. (2023). A possible underground roadway for transportation facilities in Kathmandu Valley: A racking deformation of underground rectangular structures. *Engineering Reports*, 12821. 10.1002/eng2.12821

Sahani, S. K., Pandey, B. K., & Pandey, D. (2024). *Single-valued Signals, Multi-valued Signals and Fixed-Point of Contractive Signals*. Mathematics Open. 10.1142/S2811007224500020

Saxena, A., Agarwal, A., Pandey, B. K., & Pandey, D. (2024). Examination of the Criticality of Customer Segmentation Using Unsupervised Learning Methods. *Circular Economy and Sustainability*, 1–14. 10.1007/s43615-023-00336-4

Sharma, M., Talwar, R., Pandey, D., Nassa, V. K., Pandey, B. K., & Dadheech, P. (2024). A Review of Dielectric Resonator Antennas (DRA)-Based RFID Technology for Industry 4.0. *Robotics and Automation in Industry*, 4(0), 303–324.

Sharma, S., Pandey, B. K., Pandey, D., Anand, R., Sharma, A., & Saini, S. (2023, March). Character Recognition Technique Implementation for Complicated Deteriorated Scene. In *2023 6th International Conference on Information Systems and Computer Networks (ISCON)* (pp. 1-4). IEEE. 10.1109/ISCON57294.2023.10112185

Singh, S., Madaan, G., Kaur, J., Swapna, H. R., Pandey, D., Singh, A., & Pandey, B. K. (2023). *Bibliometric Review on Healthcare Sustainability. Handbook of Research on Safe Disposal Methods of Municipal Solid Wastes for a Sustainable Environment*, 142-161. 10.4018/978-1-6684-8117-2.ch011

Snehi, J., Snehi, M., Prasad, D., Simaiya, S., Kansal, I., & Baggan, V. (2022). SDN-Based Cloud Combining Edge Computing for IoT Infrastructure. *Software Defined Networks: Architecture and Applications*, 497-540.

Swapna, H. R., Bigirimana, E., Madaan, G., Hasan, A., Pandey, B. K., & Pandey, D. (2023). Impact of neuromarketing on consumer psychology in digitally connected networks. In *Applications of Neuromarketing in the Metaverse* (pp. 193–205). IGI Global. 10.4018/978-1-6684-8150-9.ch015

Tripathi, R. P., Sharma, M., Gupta, A. K., Pandey, D., Pandey, B. K., Shahul, A., & George, A. H. (2023). Timely prediction of diabetes by means of machine learning practices. *Augmented Human Research*, 8(1), 1. 10.1007/s41133-023-00062-4

Wang, J., Wang, C. X., Huang, J., & Chen, Y. (2022). 6G THz propagation channel characteristics and modeling: Recent developments and future challenges. *IEEE Communications Magazine*.

Chapter 6
Pedagogical Paradigms:
Enhancing 6G Learning Experiences for Future Security Professionals

Freddy Ochoa-Tataje
Postgraduate Department, Universidad César Vallejo, Lima, Peru

Luis Velarde-Vela
Science Department, Universidad Peruana de Ciencias Aplicadas, Lima, Peru

Joel Alanya-Beltran
Universidad San Ignacio de Loyola, Peru

Eladia Perez-Peralta
IE Los Precursores, Lima, Peru

Jenny Ruiz-Salazar
Universidad Privada del Norte, Lima, Peru

Monica La-Chira-Loli
Engineering Department, Universidad Autónoma del Perú, Lima, Peru

ABSTRACT

The guiding concepts, procedures, and strategies that teachers employ to promote learning are known as pedagogical paradigms. They support the entire educational process and have an impact on how knowledge is organized, disseminated, and assimilated by students. Comprehending the importance of pedagogical paradigms is crucial, as they influence students' learning experiences and their capacity to acquire and utilize knowledge efficiently. The primary goal of education is to equip people with the skills and knowledge necessary to meet the opportunities and challenges of both their personal and professional lives.

I. INTRODUCTION

Implementing customized learning experiences are then looked at, with an emphasis on developing a variety of skill sets, encouraging learner engagement and motivation, and tailoring instructional content. These tactics stress the significance of encouraging communication, teamwork, and adaptability skills, allowing students to take charge of their education, and striking a balance between theoretical knowledge and real-world application. Teachers may equip students to successfully traverse the challenges of the digital age and make meaningful contributions to a safer and more secure environment (Pandey, B. K. et al., 2023a) by embracing pedagogical innovation and utilizing a variety of instructional meth-

DOI: 10.4018/979-8-3693-7421-4.ch006

odologies. The guiding concepts, procedures, and strategies that teachers employ to promote learning are known as pedagogical paradigms. They support the entire educational process and have an impact on how knowledge is organized, disseminated, and assimilated by students. Comprehending the importance of pedagogical paradigms is crucial, as they influence students' learning experiences and their capacity to acquire and utilize knowledge efficiently. The primary goal of education is to equip people with the skills and knowledge necessary to meet the opportunities and challenges of both their personal and professional lives. The cornerstone of educational systems around the world for a long time has been traditional pedagogical approaches like rote memorization and lecture-based instruction. While there are benefits to these approaches, they frequently fall short of meeting students' various needs and learning preferences. This restriction has sparked a move toward more creative pedagogical paradigms that place an emphasis on group projects, critical thinking, and active participation. This means that in order to empower students to become self-directed, lifelong learners, pedagogical paradigms that replace antiquated teaching methodologies must be adopted. Teachers can foster critical abilities like creativity, adaptability, and resilience by adopting cutting-edge teaching strategies like inquiry-based learning, project-based learning, and problem-based learning. In order to promote equity and inclusivity in education, pedagogical paradigms are essential. Teachers can establish supportive learning environments that promote academic success by implementing learner-centered approaches that acknowledge and value the diverse backgrounds, experiences, and perspectives of their students. To further ensure that every learner has the chance to succeed, using technology to personalize learning experiences can help close the achievement gap for students with a variety of learning needs. The need for cutting-edge connectivity solutions is higher than ever as society continues to embrace digital transformation (George, W. K. et al., 2023). With its unprecedented speeds, extremely low latency, and widespread connectivity, 6G technology is the next big thing in wireless communication (Devasenapathy, D. et al., 2024). 6G technology is set to transform a number of industries, including manufacturing, transportation, healthcare (Revathi, T. K. et al., 2022), and more, building on the groundwork established by its predecessors. The arrival of 6G technology presents opportunities as well as challenges for aspiring security professionals. 6G technology has the potential to facilitate creative security solutions that make use of cutting-edge features like augmented reality, artificial intelligence (Tripathi, R. P. et al., 2023), and real-time data analytic (Chettri & Bera, 2019). 6G technology has the power to completely change the way security operations (Pandey, B. K. et al., 2023b) are carried out, improving situational awareness and response times through improved surveillance systems and secure communication networks (Sharma, S. et al., 2023). But the widespread adoption of 6G technology (Sengupta, R. et al., 2021) also presents a fresh set of risks and difficulties related to cybersecurity. The proliferation of connected semiconductor devices (Sharma, M. et al., 2022) and the growth of the Internet of Things (IoT) (Menon, V. et al., 2022) create an unprecedented attack surface for malevolent actors, posing threats to sensitive data (Singh, S. et al., 2023), critical infrastructure, and individual privacy (Pandey, B. K. et al., 2022). In addition, new vulnerabilities posed by the ultra-low latency and high data transfer rates of 6G networks need to be addressed in order to guarantee the integrity and security of communication systems (Gupta, A. K. et al., 2023). Future security professionals must have a thorough understanding of 6G technology and its implications for cybersecurity (David, S. et al., 2023) in light of these developments. Proficiency in safeguarding IoT devices (Du John, H. V. et al., 2022) and networks, awareness of new threats and attack methods, and know-how in utilizing cutting-edge technologies to reduce risks and safeguard digital assets (Swapna, H. R. et al., 2023) are all examples of this. Network engineers, cybersecurity (Pandey, J. K.

et al., 2022). specialists, and policymakers will need to work together interdisciplinary to create strong security plans that protect the integrity and robustness of 6G networks (Saad et al., 2019).

II. PEDAGOGICAL PARADIGMS

2.1 Historical Overview

The development of educational philosophy and practice over millennia is reflected in the rich tapestry of pedagogical approaches' history. Many pedagogical philosophies have evolved from ancient civilizations to contemporary educational systems, each shaped by the philosophical, social, and cultural contexts of its day. Gaining an understanding of the historical development of pedagogical approaches can help one better understand the principles of education and how modern educational practices have evolved. Ancient societies like Mesopotamia, Egypt, Greece, and China are the origins of pedagogical practices. With an emphasis on teaching vital skills and knowledge for governance, religious rituals, and societal roles, education in these early societies was frequently restricted to the elite. Oral instruction, memorization, and apprenticeship-based learning were hallmarks of this era's pedagogical approaches, in which teachers acted as mentors and advisors for their students. Important educational philosophers like Socrates, Plato, and Aristotle rose to prominence during the classical era in ancient Greece and Rome. Socrates promoted dialogue-based teaching strategies that use the Socratic method to get students to think critically and ask questions. Aristotle stressed observation, categorization, and logical analysis as the foundation of learning, whereas Plato highlighted the value of methodical investigation and the pursuit of knowledge through dialectic reasoning. As Christianity spread throughout the Middle Ages, monastic and cathedral schools were established, placing a strong emphasis on religious instruction. Education discourse was dominated by Scholasticism, a philosophical and theological system that attempted to reconcile faith and reason. Thomas Aquinas, among other Scholastic scholars, combined Christian theology and classical philosophy, emphasizing the pursuit of truth via dialectical reasoning and reasoned inquiry. Education made tremendous strides during the Renaissance as humanistic ideals and classical education were revived. To create well-rounded people with a wide range of moral and intellectual qualities, humanist educators like Erasmus and Vittorino da Feltre pushed for a curriculum that prioritized the study of classical literature, history, and the arts. Individualism, critical thinking, and the realization of human potential were all highly valued aspects of humanism. The 17th and 18th century Enlightenment brought in a new age of rationalism and empiricism that challenged established wisdom and doctrine. Philosophers of education like Jean-Jacques Rousseau and John Locke highlighted the value of experience-based learning and the inherent goodness of people (Zhang et al., 2019). While Rousseau promoted child-centered education that honored children's natural development, Locke proposed the idea of tabula rasa, which holds that knowledge is imprinted on the mind through sensory experiences. The 19th-century Industrial Revolution brought about profound social and economic shifts, which made a more methodical approach to education necessary to keep up with the demands of an industrial society. Innovative pedagogical approaches that prioritized experiential learning, student-centered instruction, and hands-on activities were pioneered by progressive educators like Maria Montessori and John Dewey. Montessori's method concentrated on encouraging independence, self-discipline, and individualized learning, while Dewey's pragmatism promoted learning via inquiry and problem-solving. Educational theories and practices have continued to change in the 20th and 21st centuries in response to shifting societal demands and technological breakthroughs. Constructivist theories which draw inspiration from thinkers like Jean Piaget and Lev Vygotsky place a strong emphasis on how social interaction and cognitive development enable people to actively construct knowledge. In order to personalize learning experiences and foster lifelong learning skills, there has been an increasing focus in recent years on learner-centered pedagogies, digital learning environments (Ekong, M. O. et al., 2023), and the integration of technology. Educational practices and philosophies are guided by pedagogical paradigms, which are fundamental frameworks and theories that make up the educational system. Educators use a wide variety of approaches, theories, and methodologies to facilitate learning and promote student development. These paradigms encompass a wide range of these approaches, theories, because they influence the manner in which knowledge is organized, transmitted (Raja, D. et al., 2024), and internalized by students, it is essential for educators to have a solid understanding of pedagogical paradigms (You et al., 2021).

2.2. Importance in Innovation

Innovative pedagogy is essential to tackling the problems and seizing the chances that come with new technologies like 6G. The intricate ideas and cutting-edge applications presented by these technologies may be too complex for traditional teaching methods to fully explain. Teachers can create engaging learning experiences that aid students in more effectively understanding abstract concepts by embracing pedagogical innovation. By means of interactive simulations, practical experiments, and multimedia resources, educators can furnish students with concrete experiences that foster a more profound comprehension of 6G technology and its fundamental concepts. The development of critical thinking and problem-solving abilities both necessary for navigating the complexities of 6G technology is facilitated by innovative pedagogy. Students must have a creative and flexible mindset because these technologies frequently call for original solutions to new problems. Teachers can develop the critical thinking and teamwork skills necessary to tackle challenging problems by integrating real-world, authentic tasks pertaining to 6G technology into the curriculum. Students can gain the competence and confidence to navigate the ever-changing world of emerging technologies through projects, case studies, and group problem-solving exercises. In light of new technologies like 6G, ethical issues and responsible use are essential components of education. Teachers can incorporate ethical dilemmas, privacy concerns, and societal implications into their curricula through the use of pedagogical innovation. Teachers can help students understand the ethical implications of technology and develop a sense of responsibility by involving them in thoughtful discussions and ethical debates. Students develop the ethical framework required for responsible innovation and decision-making through these discussions, which also help them understand the ethical implications of their actions on a deeper level.

Innovative teaching methods help students become more adaptive and lifelong learners, preparing them for the 6G technology industry's ongoing development. Educators can foster a lifelong love of learning and equip students with the skills they need to adjust to new challenges and technologies by implementing learner-centered approaches that encourage curiosity, exploration, and self-directed learning. By incorporating cutting-edge technologies like 6G into the educational process, instructors can better prepare their students for the ever-changing demands of the digital age by developing their autonomous learning, creative thinking, and adaptability skills in addition to improving their technical proficiency (Chowdhury et al., 2020).

III. ENHANCED LEARNING EXPERIENCES

3.1 Challenges in Traditional Approaches

When it comes to efficiently teaching issues connected to 6G, traditional educational methodologies confront challenges due to the fact that they are static and lack the flexibility to adapt. These techniques which are shown in the Figure 1, may have difficulty keeping up with the rapid changes in technology, may impede student participation, and may fail to deliver the practical, real-world applications that are important for preparing future security professionals.

Figure 1. Traditional approaches in teaching 6G topics

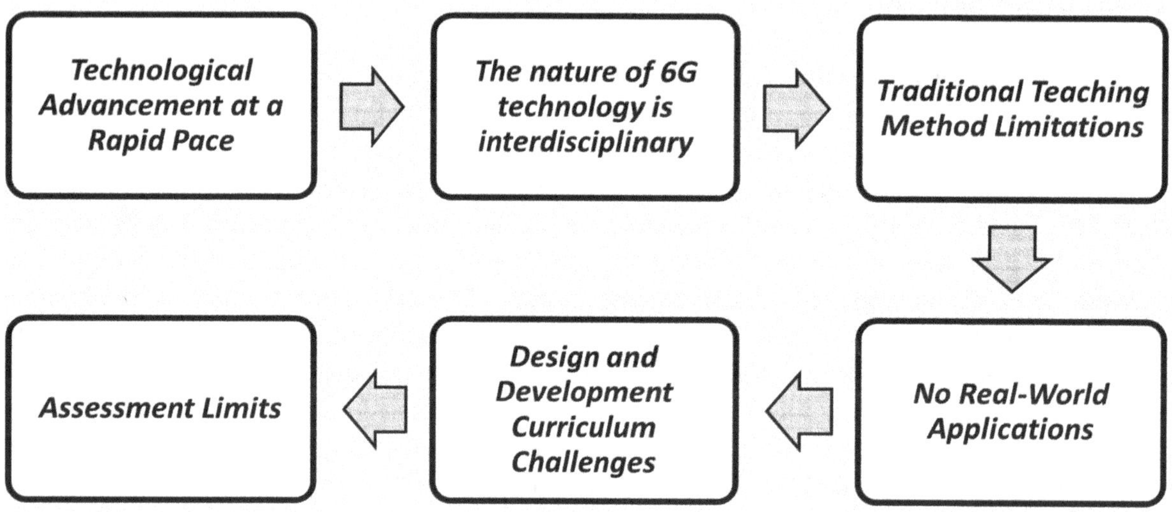

1. *Technological Advancement at a Rapid Pace:* Regarding the teaching of 6G-related topics, the quick speed of technological development presents a major obstacle for conventional teaching methods. Educational materials and curricula may find it difficult to stay current with the most recent advancements in 6G technology due to the constantly emerging discoveries and innovations. Due to this, students may be taught material that is out-of-date or lacking, which will make it more difficult for them to understand the most recent ideas and theories in the industry. It is also more difficult to remain current in educational settings because of the dynamic nature of 6G technology, which implies that what is deemed cutting-edge today could become outdated tomorrow. Also, when it comes to adding new content and updating curricula, traditional educational institutions frequently encounter sluggish and bureaucratic procedures. The updated materials may become outdated again when changes are put into practice because technology may have advanced by then. There may be a gap between what is taught in the classroom and the realities of the industry as a result of educators finding it difficult to keep up with the quick development of 6G technology (Zhao et al., 2021).

2. *The nature of 6G technology is interdisciplinary.* Multidisciplinary nature of 6G technology presents another obstacle for conventional educational approaches. Sixth generation (6G) technology combines ideas from multiple fields like cybersecurity, computer science, engineering, and telecommunications, unlike traditional subjects that can be easily divided into discrete disciplines. A comprehensive understanding that may be difficult to come by in traditional educational structures is required by this multidisciplinary nature. A lack of awareness of the connections between various concepts and disciplines in the context of 6G technology could lead to gaps in students' knowledge as a result of siloed approaches to education. To further address the intricate problems raised by 6G technology, interdisciplinary cooperation is crucial. Collaboration between departments and faculties may be difficult to establish in traditional educational institutions, which could make it more difficult for students to acquire a thorough understanding of 6G-related subjects. Traditional methods of teaching knowledge compartmentalize it into distinct disciplines, which may prevent students from being exposed to a variety of viewpoints and methods and thus hinder their capacity for critical and innovative thought. Because 6G technology is interdisciplinary, creative pedagogical strategies that dismantle established divisions and promote cooperation amongst disciplines are needed to address this aspect of the technology.
3. *Traditional Teaching Method Limitations*: Lecture-based instruction and rote memorization may not engage students or accommodate diverse learning styles when teaching 6G topics. 6G technology is complex and abstract, so students need more interactive and hands-on learning to understand and retain it. Traditional methods emphasize passive learning, where students receive information rather than actively participate. Student disengagement and limited comprehension of 6G concepts may result from struggling to connect theoretical knowledge with real-world applications. Traditional teaching methods may also neglect 6G technology's practical skills. Practical experience and problem-solving skills are as important as theoretical knowledge for industry success. Traditional theoretical instruction may leave students unprepared to solve real-world problems and apply their knowledge. To better prepare students for industry demands, pedagogical innovation must emphasize active learning, critical thinking, and practical application of 6G concepts.
4. *No Real-World Applications*: Traditional education may struggle to give students real-world 6G experiences. While theoretical instruction builds foundational knowledge, practical application deepens understanding and develops skills. Traditional methods emphasize theoretical content over practical experiences, limiting students' real-world application. This can disconnect classroom learning from real-world applications, hindering students' ability to apply their skills to the workplace. Due to the rapid evolution of 6G technology, educational materials and curricula may not reflect the latest advances and industry practices. So, students may graduate with outdated or irrelevant skills that don't match 6G employers' needs. To prepare students for the 6G workforce, educators must include real-world applications, case studies, and hands-on projects in the curriculum. Educators can prepare students for the fast-paced world of 6G technology by connecting theory and practice (Mutichiro et al., 2021).
5. *Design and Development Curriculum Challenges:* Traditional schools often struggle to incorporate 6G topics into their curricula. The interdisciplinary nature and rapid evolution of 6G technology complicate curriculum development. Teachers must explain complex technical concepts while following industry standards. Traditional bureaucracy and slow decision-making may delay curriculum changes. This can result in outdated or inadequate educational materials that fail to prepare students for 6G careers. Curriculum design is further complicated by 6G technology's diverse skills and

competencies. Teachers must balance theory, practice, interdisciplinary understanding, and ethics. For relevance and efficacy, educators, industry experts, and stakeholders must collaborate on a 6G technology curriculum. However, traditional educational institutions may struggle to foster such collaboration, resulting in curricula that don't meet student or industry needs.

6. *Assessment Limits*: Traditional assessment methods may not accurately assess students' 6G knowledge and real-world application. Standardised tests, written exams, and quizzes may not capture 6G technology's complexity or students' practical skills. The dynamic nature of 6G technology means that traditional assessment methods may quickly become outdated and fail to reflect industry practices. Traditional assessments may also not match 6G employers' skills and competencies. Employers value practical skills, critical thinking, and technology adaptability as well as theoretical knowledge. Traditional assessments may miss these crucial traits, causing educational outcomes to fall short of industry expectations. Educators must use project-based assessments, simulations, and real-world challenges to better assess students' workforce readiness and reflect 6G technology's complexity and dynamic nature.

3.1 Tailored Learning

In order to effectively navigate the ever-changing landscape of security threats and challenges, future security professionals must have access to tailored learning experiences. Tailoring educational content and approaches to each learner's unique needs, interests, and learning style is a crucial component of tailored learning. Within the security domain, given the constantly evolving and heterogeneous nature of both threats and technologies, a uniform approach to education might prove inadequate. In order to guarantee that aspiring security professionals gain the knowledge and abilities needed to succeed in their chosen career paths, tailored learning experiences enable them to go deeper into areas of interest or specialization. Future security professionals can keep up with the latest innovations in the field by taking advantage of customized learning opportunities. Technological developments, alterations in the geopolitical environment, and changes in societal norms are the driving forces behind the continuous evolution of security threats. Teachers can make sure that students have the most current and pertinent knowledge and skills by customizing learning experiences to address specific areas of focus, such as risk management, physical security, cybersecurity, or data privacy (Khan, B. et al., 2021). By adopting a proactive approach to learning, aspiring security professionals can effectively anticipate and adjust to new threats, ultimately strengthening the overall resilience and efficacy of security protocols. More motivation and deeper engagement are fostered in aspiring security professionals through customized learning experiences. Teachers can encourage a sense of ownership and investment in students' learning journeys by letting them explore topics that are relevant to their interests and career goals. Students are therefore more likely to actively seek out opportunities for learning and professional development, which in turn results in increased motivation, curiosity, and initiative. In addition to facilitating individualized feedback and support, tailored learning experiences allow teachers to mentor and guide specific students according to their individual needs and objectives. It assists aspiring security specialists in acquiring a broad skill set that can be tailored to a variety of situations and difficulties. Security professionals need to be highly skilled in critical thinking, problem-solving, communication, and decision-making in addition to having strong technical knowledge in today's interconnected world. With projects, case studies, simulations, and real-world scenarios that are customized to their interests and professional objectives, students can gain these fundamental skills through tailored learning experiences. By taking a comprehensive approach to education, security professionals of the future will be well-rounded and adaptable, able to handle the complex threats and difficulties associated with modern security (Saxena et al., 2021).

3.2 Role of Pedagogical Paradigms

Pedagogical paradigms are very important for figuring out how to give future security professionals the best learning experiences possible. Teachers can use these paradigms as guides to come up with, use, and evaluate teaching methods that meet the unique interests and needs of each student. Teachers can make dynamic and flexible learning spaces that prepare future security professionals to do well in a world that is changing quickly by understanding and using different ways of teaching. One way that pedagogical paradigms deal with these problems is by supporting teaching methods that focus on the learner. Some learning theories, like constructivism and experiential learning, stress how important it is for students to actively build their own knowledge and understanding. By giving students hands-on tasks, problem-solving assignments, and group projects, teachers can make sure that each student's learning fits with their interests, background, and preferred way of learning. This method helps students feel like they own their learning and gives them the freedom to choose their own path and explore areas of interest in the field of security. Adding technology and digital tools to the learning process, which makes personalized learning more effective. Concepts like connectivism and blended learning acknowledge that technology has the power to change education and support the use of digital resources to help students learn in their own way. Teachers can give students who want to become security professionals access to a lot of resources and chances to learn on their own by using online platforms, simulations, virtual reality, and other digital tools. This lets students explore topics that interest them, take part in hands-on activities for learning, and work together with classmates and experts from all over the world, even if they live in different places. It talks about the different kinds of skills that are needed to be successful in the field of security and how important it is to teach in a way that includes all of these areas. Problem-based learning and inquiry-based learning are two learning models that push students to use their knowledge and skills from different subjects to solve difficult problems in the real world. Teachers can help future security professionals learn how to think critically, solve problems, and make decisions by using cross-disciplinary projects, case studies, and simulations in the classroom. This will help them deal with the complex nature of security threats and challenges. This method also improves students' ability to work together and talk to others, which helps them do well in teams with people from different fields and in different professional settings. Implementation of formative assessment methods that give students ongoing feedback and help as they go through school. Assessment for learning and authentic assessment are two paradigms that stress how important it is to check on students' progress and understanding all the time, instead of just using summative tests. Formative assessment methods, like peer feedback, self-assessment, and performance-based assessments, help teachers figure out what each student needs to learn, keep track of their progress, and adjust their lessons to focus on their strengths and weaknesses. This customized way of testing makes sure that students who want to become security professionals get the help and direction they need to reach their learning goals and do well in their chosen careers (De Mattos & Gondim, 2016).

IV. APPROACHES FOR TAILORING LEARNING EXPERIENCES

The process of adjusting instructional materials and activities to each learners' unique requirements, interests, and skill level is known as "tailoring." Personalized learning paths that maximize engagement and learning results are the goal of this strategy, which recognizes that learners have a variety of learning styles, interests, and prior knowledge. Customized learning experiences can include modifying course content, adding examples and applications from the real world, giving students opportunities for freedom and autonomy, and providing them with individualized feedback and assistance. Tailoring learning experiences to each individual student's needs results in increased motivation, retention, and understanding, which in turn creates a more productive and welcoming learning environment. Customized Learning Approaches are shown in the figure 2.

Figure 2. Customized learning approaches

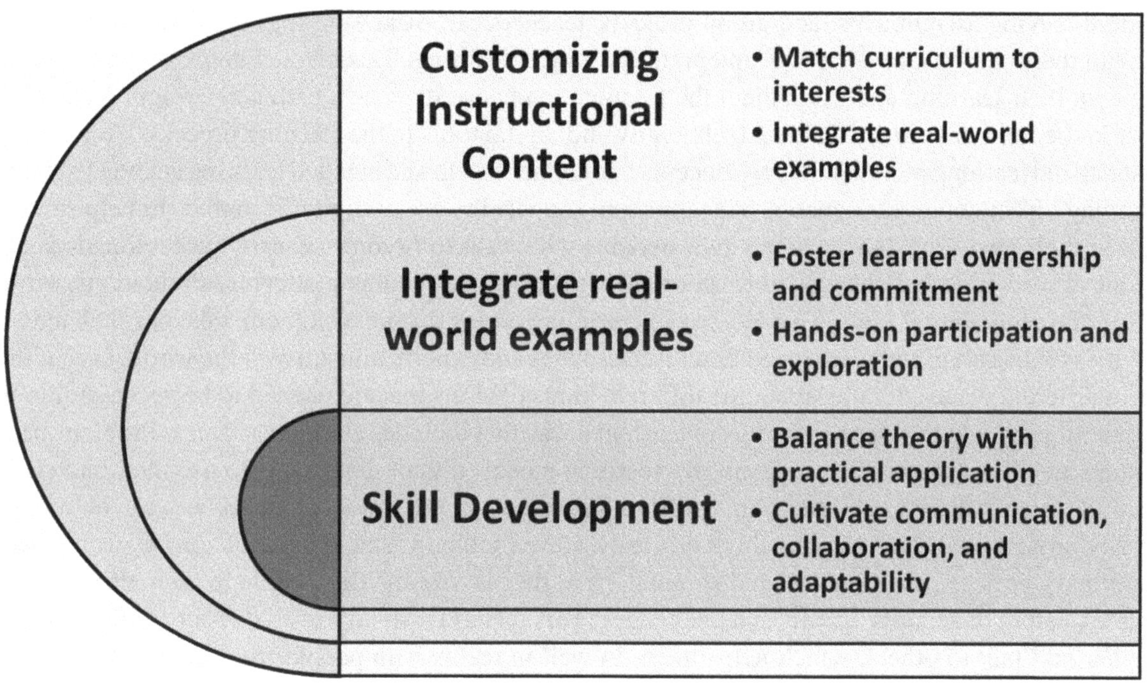

4.1 Customizing Instructional Content

a) Match Curriculum to Interests

In education, one of the most important aspects of customizing learning experiences is curriculum adaptation to students' interests and career aspirations. It is impossible to overestimate the significance of curriculum customization in the quickly changing educational environment, where a diverse student body brings a range of backgrounds, goals, and learning preferences to the classroom. This methodology acknowledges that students are not uniform entities but rather distinct individuals with distinct requirements and incentives. Teachers can improve student engagement, motivation, and ultimately the efficacy of learning outcomes by matching the curriculum to the interests and career goals of their students. Recognizing students' varied interests and aspirations for their careers is the first step in curriculum adaptation. Teachers need to make the effort to interact with students and find more about their interests, histories, and goals for the future. This can be done through surveys, interviews, or casual conversations, giving teachers insight into the wide range of interests and objectives that students have. Teachers can customize the curriculum to target certain interests and career routes by recognizing the different needs and motivations of their pupils. This ensures that the learning process is relevant and meaningful. Customizing the curriculum is the next step for instructors after learning about the interests and professional aspirations of their students. This entails finding ways to incorporate activities, examples, and pertinent content that speak to the interests and goals of the pupils. In a science classroom, for instance, teachers can include practical applications of scientific ideas that correspond with the professional goals of their students, such medical research or environmental preservation. Similar to this, teachers can encourage more student involvement and relevance in the language arts classroom by assigning readings and writing projects that are related to the cultural backgrounds or personal interests of the students. Options for inquiry and specialization are necessary in order to modify the curriculum to fit students' interests and career aspirations. Teachers can provide extracurricular activities, independent study projects, and optional courses to help students explore their interests more deeply or follow particular career paths (Henrique & Prasad, 2020). For example, to accommodate pupils interested in technology-related vocations, a high school may offer elective classes in robotics, graphic design, or computer programming. Teachers can enable students to follow their hobbies and gain competence in fields that are in line with their future goals by giving them these opportunities for exploration and specialization.

b) Integrate Real-World Examples

The incorporation of real-world examples and case studies into the curriculum is an effective approach to augmenting learning experiences and equipping students with the necessary skills to navigate the intricacies of the real world outside of the educational setting. Real-world illustrations offer tangible contexts that facilitate the integration of academic concepts with practical applications, hence enhancing the significance and applicability of the learning process. Case studies provide comprehensive examinations of actual circumstances or issues, enabling students to scrutinize, resolve, and employ their understanding in genuine contexts. Educators have the ability to enhance the understanding of abstract concepts and theories by integrating concrete, relatable scenarios into the curriculum. In a scientific class, educators can employ real-world illustrations, such as the design of amusement park rides or the construction of bridges, to illustrate the practical application of physics principles, rather than solely focusing on theoretical concepts. In a historical classroom setting, instructors have the ability to employ primary materials, artifacts, and human narratives as pedagogical tools to imbue historical occurrences with vitality and facilitate students' comprehension of their contextual significance. Case studies extend this methodology by exposing students to intricate, authentic situations that necessitate the application of critical thinking, analysis, and problem-solving abilities. In the context of a business course, students may encounter a case study pertaining to a corporation encountering financial difficulties, wherein they are assigned the responsibility of formulating a strategy plan to effectively tackle the identified concerns. Through active participation in case studies, students have the opportunity to apply theoretical principles to real-world scenarios, cultivate their analytical abilities, and get a more profound comprehension of the intricacies inherent in the realm of business (Malhotra, P. et al., 2021). The use of real-world illustrations and case studies within the educational framework promotes interdisciplinary learning and stimulates students to establish links among diverse subject domains. For instance, a case study on climate change may encompass scientific, economic, political, and ethical aspects, encouraging students to examine the topic from diverse viewpoints and utilize insights from other fields of study. This interdisciplinary approach reflects the interrelatedness of real-world issues and equips students to address intricate challenges that necessitate cooperation and specialized knowledge from other professions. The utilization of real-world examples and case studies affords students the chance to cultivate fundamental competencies, including critical thinking, problem-solving, communication, and cooperation. Through engaging with authentic scenarios and ethical quandaries, students acquire the skills to scrutinize data (Pandey, B. K. et al., 2024), assess substantiation, consider conflicting viewpoints, and articulate their thoughts proficiently. Case studies, specifically, present students with the opportunity to engage in creative and imaginative thinking as they develop resolutions to intricate issues, equipping them with the necessary skills to navigate the uncertainties and difficulties that lie ahead (Sodhro et al., 2020).

4.2 Engagement and Motivation

a) Foster Learner Ownership and Commitment

Tailoring learning to students needs and interests requires encouraging learner ownership and commitment. Student ownership of their learning increases engagement, motivation, and investment in the educational process, leading to better learning outcomes and academic success. Giving pupils choices and accountability for their learning can promote learner ownership. Teachers can let students choose topics, projects, and tasks to explore their passions. Educators inspire students to own their education and become active learners by providing them agency. By giving students resources, support, and advice to explore their interests outside of class, instructors may foster self-directed learning. This may include providing books, articles, websites, or other instructional materials linked to students' interests or professional objectives. Teachers can also help students conduct independent study, inquiry, or creative projects on personal interests. By encouraging curiosity and inquiry, educators empower students to take charge of their learning and explore their passions outside of class. By including students in goal-setting and assessment, instructors may foster learner ownership. Teachers and students can set clear objectives and performance standards by defining learning goals together. Students can then track their progress, remark on their learning, and own their academic improvement. Educators can also help students self-assess, improve, and create learning goals. Students take ownership of their learning outcomes and become active participants in their academic journey when educators involve them in evaluation. By providing a supportive and inclusive learning environment where students feel valued, respected, and empowered to express themselves, educators may foster learner ownership. By creating a feeling of community in the classroom, instructors may inspire students to take risks, share ideas, and own their learning. Implement collaborative learning activities, encourage peer feedback, and celebrate students' successes. Creating a healthy and inclusive classroom culture empowers students to take control of their learning and become active learners.

b) Hands-On Participation and Exploration

To personalize learning to kids' needs and interests, encourage hands-on participation and discovery. Active learning, applying theoretical concepts in practical settings, and developing important abilities through experiential learning are possible with hands-on activities. The curriculum can include interactive learning (Saxena, A. et al., 2024) activities to encourage hands-on participation. Experimental, simulation, demonstration, and problem-solving activities require students to actively manipulate materials, collect data (Vinodhini, V. et al., 2022), and solve problems in real time. Students can practice critical thinking, explore concepts, and learn course material through hands-on experiences. Science classes may require students to develop and conduct experiments to investigate scientific concepts. Through investigation and curiosity, educators allow children to own their learning and create agency. Authentic learning activities that relate classroom learning to real-world applications can also encourage hands-on participation. It may incorporate field trips, guest speakers, or industry partnerships to give students real-world experience. Environmental science and engineering students may visit a local ecosystem to collect data (Deepa, R. et al., 2022) or work with professionals to design and build prototypes of their creations. By applying classroom learning to real-world situations, educators inspire students to explore and learn more. Teachers can encourage hands-on engagement by fostering a supportive and inclusive learning atmosphere where students feel comfortable taking chances and trying new things. Collaboration, peer contact, and teamwork may help students share ideas, learn from one other, and work together on projects and tasks. By encouraging cooperation and inquiry, educators help students take charge of their learning and gain the confidence and skills they need to succeed in school and work (Fiedler & Hossfeld, 2010).

4.3 Skill Development

a) Balance Theory With Practical Application

Providing students with well-rounded learning experiences that equip them for success in the real world requires a balance between theory and practical application. Practical application enables students to observe the theories' applications in real-life situations, which promotes deeper understanding, critical thinking, and skill development, while theoretical knowledge offers the groundwork for comprehending concepts and principles. A curriculum that incorporates hands-on exercises, experiments, or projects that enable students to apply theoretical concepts in real-world circumstances is one approach to balancing theory with practical application. In a science class, for instance, students have the opportunity to learn by doing, analyzing data (Pandey, D., & Pandey, B. K., 2022), and drawing conclusions from experiments designed to test scientific ideas and hypotheses. Practical skills like problem-solving, data analysis (Iyyanar, P. et al., 2023), and experimental design are developed by students through participation in hands-on exercises, which also help them retain theoretical concepts. To further immerse students in real-world challenges and settings, educators can include case studies, simulations, or role-playing exercises into their lessons. Students can enhance their critical thinking abilities, see the intricacies of the working world, and apply theoretical concepts to real-world scenarios through active engagement with these types of content. Students can acquire practical experience in their chosen fields through internships, field experiences, or hands-on projects, all of which can be arranged by educators. Engineering students, for instance, might get practical experience and put their classroom learning into practice by interning with local businesses. Internships and field experiences assist students make the transition from classroom learning to real-world application, allowing them to get a better understanding of the business world and hone the abilities employers want. Virtual simulations, online labs, or interactive software can further help teachers improve students' practical learning experiences by letting them investigate ideas and principles in a more hands-on way. As an example, students of physiology and anatomy can learn about the human body's components and functions through virtual dissection software. To help students make the transition from theory to practice, teachers can use technology to create interactive and immersive learning environments (Chen et al., 2014).

b) Cultivate Communication, Collaboration, and Adaptability

Students need to be prepared to succeed in a variety of academic, professional, and personal contexts by developing their communication, teamwork, and adaptability abilities. These abilities allow people to collaborate with others toward shared objectives, engage with others in an effective manner, and adjust to shifting conditions and surroundings. Providing children with opportunities to participate in writing and oral communication activities is one strategy to foster communication skills. Teachers might include activities in the curriculum that force students to clearly explain themselves, articulate their thoughts, and interact with others, such as debates, presentations, and writing assignments. Students gain the competence and confidence necessary to convey concepts, details, and viewpoints with accuracy and clarity by engaging in communication practice across a range of formats and situations. Incorporating cooperative learning activities, team-based assignments, and group projects into the curriculum is another way that educators can promote collaborative abilities. Students might collaborate in small groups to finish tasks, find solutions to issues, or carry out research, for instance. Students gain experience in active listening, idea sharing, conflict resolution, and working toward common objectives through peer collaboration. Along with these benefits, collaboration gives kids the chance to practice interpersonal skills like empathy, respect, and dispute resolution all of which are critical for fostering healthy relationships and cooperating with others. By exposing kids to a variety of viewpoints, experiences, and obstacles, instructors can help them develop their capacity for adaptation. To encourage critical thinking, problem-solving, and situational adaptation in their pupils, educators can integrate multicultural perspectives, multidisciplinary approaches, and real-world challenges into the curriculum (Baraković & Skorin-Kapov, 2013). In order to help students navigate ambiguity and complexity in a world that is constantly changing, educators should expose them to new or challenging situations. This helps kids build resilience, flexibility, and resourcefulness. Teachers can also use technology to improve their student's communication, teamwork, and adaptation skills by giving them access to digital tools and platforms that promote learning, communication, and teamwork. Teachers might encourage virtual contact and collaboration among students by using online discussion boards, video conferencing, and collaborative document editing tools. Utilizing technology, teachers can provide students the chance to interact with others, work together on projects, and become accustomed to new methods of learning and working in digital settings.

CONCLUSION

The need of pedagogical paradigms in forming learning experiences for future security professionals is greater than ever in a time of fast technology breakthroughs and changing security threats. The importance of educational paradigms in light of new technologies like 6G has been examined in this work. We have shown the necessity of improved learning experiences catered to the particular requirements of future security professionals by looking at the historical development of pedagogical techniques and the difficulties presented by incorporating 6G-related subjects into conventional educational frameworks. For security experts, 6G technology presents both previously unheard-of possibilities and difficulties. It is critical that instructional strategies change as students negotiate this complicated terrain in order to provide them the information, abilities, and flexibility needed to properly counter new threats. In this sense, customized learning experiences are essential since they enable teachers to develop a variety of skill sets that meet the needs of the contemporary security environment, encourage motivation and involvement, and personalize the content of education. Future security professionals can flourish in the age of 6G technology if educators embrace pedagogical innovation and use a variety of teaching techniques to build dynamic learning environments. Pedagogical paradigms provide a route to improving learning experiences and preparing students for success in the quickly developing field of security, whether through the integration of real-world examples and case studies, fostering learner ownership and commitment, or developing communication, collaboration, and adaptability skills.

REFERENCES

Baraković, S., & Skorin-Kapov, L. (2013). Survey and challenges of QoE management issues in wireless networks. *Journal of Computer Networks and Communications*, 2013, 165146. 10.1155/2013/165146

Chen, Y., Wu, K., & Zhang, Q. (2014). From QoS to QoE: A tutorial on video quality assessment. *IEEE Communications Surveys and Tutorials*, 17(2), 1126–1165. 10.1109/COMST.2014.2363139

Chettri, L., & Bera, R. (2019). A comprehensive survey on Internet of Things (IoT) toward 5G wireless systems. *IEEE Internet of Things Journal*, 7(1), 16–32. 10.1109/JIOT.2019.2948888

Chowdhury, M. Z., Shahjalal, M., Ahmed, S., & Jang, Y. M. (2020). 6G wireless communication systems: Applications, requirements, technologies, challenges, and research directions. *IEEE Open Journal of the Communications Society*, 1, 957–975. 10.1109/OJCOMS.2020.3010270

David, S., Duraipandian, K., Chandrasekaran, D., Pandey, D., Sindhwani, N., & Pandey, B. K. (2023). Impact of blockchain in healthcare system. In *Unleashing the Potentials of blockchain technology for healthcare industries* (pp. 37–57). Academic Press. 10.1016/B978-0-323-99481-1.00004-3

De Mattos, W. D., & Gondim, P. R. (2016). m-health solutions using 5G networks and M2M communications. *IT Professional*, 18(3), 24–29. 10.1109/MITP.2016.52

Deepa, R., Anand, R., Pandey, D., Pandey, B. K., & Karki, B. (2022). Comprehensive performance analysis of classifiers in diagnosis of epilepsy. *Mathematical Problems in Engineering*, 2022, 2022. 10.1155/2022/1559312

Devasenapathy, D., Madhumathy, P., Umamaheshwari, R., Pandey, B. K., & Pandey, D. (2024). Transmission-efficient grid-based synchronized model for routing in wireless sensor networks using Bayesian compressive sensing. *SN Computer Science*, 5(1), 1–11.

Ekong, M. O., George, W. K., Pandey, B. K., & Pandey, D. (2023). Enhancing the Fundamentals of Industrial Safety Management in TVET for Metaverse Realities. In *Applications of Neuromarketing in the Metaverse* (pp. 19-41). IGI Global. 10.4018/978-1-6684-8150-9.ch002

Fiedler, M., Hossfeld, T., & Tran-Gia, P. (2010). A generic quantitative relationship between quality of experience and quality of service. *IEEE Network*, 24(2), 36–41. 10.1109/MNET.2010.5430142

George, W. K., Ekong, M. O., Pandey, D., & Pandey, B. K. (2023). Pedagogy for Implementation of TVET Curriculum for the Digital World. In *Applications of Neuromarketing in the Metaverse* (pp. 117-136). IGI Global. 10.4018/978-1-6684-8150-9.ch009

Gupta, A. K., Sharma, R., Pandey, D., Nassa, V. K., Pandey, B. K., George, A. S., & Dadheech, P. (2023). Performance analysis of eight-channel WDM optical network with different optical amplifiers for industry 4.0. In *Innovation and Competitiveness in Industry 4.0 Based on Intelligent Systems* (pp. 197–212). Springer International Publishing. 10.1007/978-3-031-29775-5_9

Henrique, P. S. R., & Prasad, R. (2020). The Road for 6G Multimedia Applications. *Proceedings of the 2020 23rd International Symposium on Wireless Personal Multimedia Communications (WPMC),* 1–6.

Iyyanar, P., Anand, R., Shanthi, T., Nassa, V. K., Pandey, B. K., George, A. S., & Pandey, D. (2023). A real-time smart sewage cleaning UAV assistance system using IoT. In *Handbook of Research on Data-Driven Mathematical Modeling in Smart Cities* (pp. 24–39). IGI Global.

Khan, B., Hasan, A., Pandey, D., Ventayen, R. J. M., Pandey, B. K., & Gowwrii, G. (2021). Fusion of datamining and artificial intelligence in prediction of hazardous road accidents. In *Machine learning and iot for intelligent systems and smart applications* (pp. 201–223). CRC Press. 10.1201/9781003194415-12

Malhotra, P., Pandey, D., Pandey, B. K., & Patra, P. M. (2021). Managing agricultural supply chains in COVID-19 lockdown. *International Journal of Quality and Innovation*, 5(2), 109–118. 10.1504/IJQI.2021.117181

Menon, V., Pandey, D., Khosla, D., Kaur, M., Vashishtha, H. K., George, A. S., & Pandey, B. K. (2022). A Study on COVID–19, Its Origin, Phenomenon, Variants, and IoT-Based Framework to Detect the Presence of Coronavirus. In *IoT Based Smart Applications* (pp. 1–13). Springer International Publishing.

Mutichiro, B., Tran, M. N., & Kim, Y. H. (2021). QoS-based service-time scheduling in the IoT-edge cloud. *Sensors (Basel)*, 21(17), 5797. 10.3390/s2117579734502688

Pandey, B. K., Pandey, D., & Agarwal, A. (2022). Encrypted information transmission by enhanced steganography and image transformation. *International Journal of Distributed Artificial Intelligence*, 14(1), 1–14. 10.4018/IJDAI.297110

Pandey, B. K., Pandey, D., Alkhafaji, M. A., Güneşer, M. T., & Şeker, C. (2023a). A reliable transmission and extraction of textual information using keyless encryption, steganography, and deep algorithm with cuckoo optimization. In *Micro-Electronics and Telecommunication Engineering: Proceedings of 6th ICMETE 2022* (pp. 629–636). Springer Nature Singapore. 10.1007/978-981-19-9512-5_57

Pandey, B. K., Pandey, D., Gupta, A., Nassa, V. K., Dadheech, P., & George, A. S. (2023b). Secret data transmission using advanced morphological component analysis and steganography. In *Role of data-intensive distributed computing systems in designing data solutions* (pp. 21–44). Springer International Publishing. 10.1007/978-3-031-15542-0_2

Pandey, B. K., Pandey, D., & Sahani, S. K. (2024). Autopilot control unmanned aerial vehicle system for sewage defect detection using deep learning. *Engineering Reports*, 12852. 10.1002/eng2.12852

Pandey, D., & Pandey, B. K. (2022). An efficient deep neural network with adaptive galactic swarm optimization for complex image text extraction. In *Process mining techniques for pattern recognition* (pp. 121–137). CRC Press. 10.1201/9781003169550-10

Pandey, J. K., Jain, R., Dilip, R., Kumbhkar, M., Jaiswal, S., Pandey, B. K., & Pandey, D. (2022). Investigating role of iot in the development of smart application for security enhancement. In *IoT Based Smart Applications* (pp. 219–243). Springer International Publishing.

Raja, D., Kumar, D. R., Santhiyakumari, N., Kumarganesh, S., Sagayam, K. M., Thiyaneswaran, B., Pandey, B. K., & Pandey, D. (2024). A compact dual-feed wide-band slotted antenna for future wireless applications. *Analog Integrated Circuits and Signal Processing*, 118(2), 1–15. 10.1007/s10470-023-02233-0

Revathi, T. K., Sathiyabhama, B., Sankar, S., Pandey, D., Pandey, B. K., & Dadeech, P. (2022). An intelligent model for coronary heart disease diagnosis. In *Networking Technologies in Smart Healthcare* (pp. 309–327). CRC Press. 10.1201/9781003239888-15

Saad, W., Bennis, M., & Chen, M. (2019). A vision of 6G wireless systems: Applications, trends, technologies, and open research problems. *IEEE Network*, 34(3), 134–142. 10.1109/MNET.001.1900287

Saxena, A., Agarwal, A., Pandey, B. K., & Pandey, D. (2024). Examination of the Criticality of Customer Segmentation Using Unsupervised Learning Methods. *Circular Economy and Sustainability*, 1–14. 10.1007/s43615-023-00336-4

Saxena, N., Rastogi, E., & Rastogi, A. (2021). *6G Use Cases, Requirements, and Metrics. In 6G Mobile Wireless Networks*. Springer.

Sengupta, R., Sengupta, D., Pandey, D., Pandey, B. K., Nassa, V. K., & Dadeech, P. (2021). A Systematic review of 5G opportunities, architecture and challenges. *Future Trends in 5G and 6G,* 247-269.

Sharma, M., Pandey, D., Khosla, D., Goyal, S., Pandey, B. K., & Gupta, A. K. (2022). Design of a GaN-based Flip Chip Light Emitting Diode (FC-LED) with au Bumps & Thermal Analysis with different sizes and adhesive materials for performance considerations. *Silicon*, 14(12), 7109–7120. 10.1007/s12633-021-01457-x

Sharma, S., Pandey, B. K., Pandey, D., Anand, R., Sharma, A., & Saini, S. (2023, March). Character Recognition Technique Implementation for Complicated Deteriorated Scene. In *2023 6th International Conference on Information Systems and Computer Networks (ISCON)* (pp. 1-4). IEEE. 10.1109/ISCON57294.2023.10112185

Singh, S., Madaan, G., Kaur, J., Swapna, H. R., Pandey, D., Singh, A., & Pandey, B. K. (2023). *Bibliometric Review on Healthcare Sustainability. Handbook of Research on Safe Disposal Methods of Municipal Solid Wastes for a Sustainable Environment*, 142-161. 10.4018/978-1-6684-8117-2.ch011

Sodhro, A. H., Zahid, N., Pirbhulal, S., Garcia, N. M., & Wang, L. (2020). Towards QoE Optimization in Medical Multimedia Services for Decentralized IoT-based Applications. *Proceedings of the 2020 IEEE 91st Vehicular Technology Conference (VTC2020-Spring),* 1–5. 10.1109/VTC2020-Spring48590.2020.9129227

Swapna, H. R., Bigirimana, E., Madaan, G., Hasan, A., Pandey, B. K., & Pandey, D. (2023). Impact of neuromarketing on consumer psychology in digitally connected networks. In *Applications of Neuromarketing in the Metaverse* (pp. 193–205). IGI Global. 10.4018/978-1-6684-8150-9.ch015

Tripathi, R. P., Sharma, M., Gupta, A. K., Pandey, D., Pandey, B. K., Shahul, A., & George, A. H. (2023). Timely prediction of diabetes by means of machine learning practices. *Augmented Human Research*, 8(1), 1. 10.1007/s41133-023-00062-4

Vinodhini, V., Kumar, M. S., Sankar, S., Pandey, D., Pandey, B. K., & Nassa, V. K. (2022). IoT-based early forest fire detection using MLP and AROC method. *International Journal of Global Warming*, 27(1), 55–70. 10.1504/IJGW.2022.122794

You, X., Wang, C. X., Huang, J., Gao, X., Zhang, Z., Wang, M., Huang, Y., Zhang, C., Jiang, Y., Wang, J., Zhu, M., Sheng, B., Wang, D., Pan, Z., Zhu, P., Yang, Y., Liu, Z., Zhang, P., Tao, X., & Liang, Y.-C. (2021). Towards 6G wireless communication networks: Vision, enabling technologies, and new paradigm shifts. *Science China. Information Sciences*, 64(1), 1–74. 10.1007/s11432-020-2955-6

Zhang, Z., Xiao, Y., Ma, Z., Xiao, M., Ding, Z., Lei, X., Karagiannidis, G. K., & Fan, P. (2019). 6G wireless networks: Vision, requirements, architecture, and key technologies. *IEEE Vehicular Technology Magazine*, 14(3), 28–41. 10.1109/MVT.2019.2921208

Zhao, Y., Zhao, J., Zhai, W., Sun, S., Niyato, D., & Lam, K. Y. (2021). A survey of 6G wireless communications: Emerging technologies. *Proceedings of the Future of Information and Communication Conference,* 150–170. 10.1007/978-3-030-73100-7_12

Chapter 7
Commerce in the 6G Era:
Adapting Business Strategies to Security Imperatives

Ashutosh Singh
Institute of Business Management, GLA University, India

K. Sankara Moorthy
https://orcid.org/0000-0002-6853-6878
Faculty of Management, SRM Institute of Science and Technology, India

Kavitha Rani Thipparaju
Department of Commerce, TSWR Degree College (W), India

S. Bathrinath
https://orcid.org/0000-0002-5502-6203
Department of Mechanical Engineering, Kalasalingam Academy of Research and Education, Krishnankoil, India

Sanjeev Kumar Singh
P.R. Pote Patil College of Engineering and Management, Amravati, India

Gourav Kalra
Department of Mechanical Engineering, Maharishi Markandeshwar University (Deemed), India

Pankaj Dadheech Dadheech
https://orcid.org/0000-0001-5783-1989
Swami Keshvanand Institute of Technology, Management, and Gramothan, India

ABSTRACT

Significant implications for business are brought about by the advent of the 6G era, which is characterized by increased connectivity and extremely low latency. This chapter investigates the transformative potential of 6G technology and highlights the impact that it has on the operations of businesses. Nevertheless, the promises of 6G are accompanied by an increase in the number of security challenges, which calls for the incorporation of stringent security measures into business strategies. In the era of 6G, it is absolutely necessary to recognize new dangers that are specific to 6G networks to comprehend the significance of data protection and to reduce the risks that are associated with internet of things devices and edge computing.

DOI: 10.4018/979-8-3693-7421-4.ch007

I. INTRODUCTION

The emergence of 6G (Kirubasri, G. et al., 2021) heralds a new era in wireless communication (Devasenapathy, D. et al., 2024), offering previously unheard-of improvements in latency, speed, and capacity over 5G. 6G networks, which represent the sixth generation of cellular technology, are expected to function at higher frequencies (Du John, H. V. et al., 2023), opening the door to greatly improved capabilities that will completely transform a number of business and industrial sectors. The importance of the 6G era for commerce is found in its ability to completely change how companies function and communicate in the digital sphere (Raja, D. et al., 2024). 6G networks offer a significant advancement in terms of responsiveness and real-time data processing (JayaLakshmi, G. et al., 2024), as they can support communications with a latency of just one microsecond. This amazing speed creates a lot of opportunities for businesses to improve customer experiences, streamline operations, and spur innovation across industries—it is 1,000 times faster than current millisecond throughput rates. The potential of 6G technology to enable advanced imaging, location awareness, and presence technology is one of its most significant effects on commerce. Businesses will be able to process, store, and share data (Iyyanar, P. et al., 2023) with previously unheard-of levels of accuracy and efficiency thanks to 6G's computational infrastructure. This implies that activities like location-based services, real-time image analysis, and immersive virtual presence will become possible and easily incorporated into regular business operations. Businesses will be able to make more informed decisions and optimize their processes like never before thanks to the combination of artificial intelligence (AI) (Anand, R. et al., 2024) and the optimization of computing resources made possible by 6G networks. Cost-effective solutions and more efficient resource allocation will arise from the ability to identify the best location for computing tasks (Bessant, Y. A. et al., 2023), taking into account variables like data sensitivity, processing requirements, and network congestion. 6G networks are more susceptible to cyberthreats and attacks as a result of using higher frequencies and transmitting exponentially more data (Bruntha, P. M. et al., 2023). 6G networks' increased capacity and decreased latency could unintentionally magnify the effects of security breaches, putting companies at previously unheard-of risk. It will take several years before industry standards (George, W. K. et al., 2024) are established and 6G-enabled network products become commercially available, even with vendor investments and continuous research and development efforts. Businesses must therefore approach the move to 6G with cautious optimism, giving careful risk assessments and strategic planning top priority in order to reduce potential security vulnerabilities and guarantee a seamless transfer to the upcoming wireless communication technology (Gupta, A. K. et al., 2023).

1.1 Security Challenges With 6G Transition

Considering the current state of the digital age (Swapna, H. R. et al., 2023), it is impossible to overstate the significance of cybersecurity for businesses. These cyber threats are becoming more sophisticated and more frequent as a result of the growing reliance on technology and the internet. They pose a significant risk to businesses of all sizes. The importance of incorporating strong security measures into business strategies is outlined in the following figure 1.

1. *Protection of Sensitive Data*: Sensitive data is a broad category that includes financial information (Sharma, S. et al., 2023), trade secrets, intellectual property, and personally identifiable information (PII). Sensitive data breaches can have serious repercussions, such as monetary loss, legal obligations,

reputational harm, and loss of competitive advantage. Implementing encryption (Kumar Pandey, B. et al., 2021), access controls, data loss prevention (DLP) programs, and routine security audits are all part of integrating strong security measures to protect sensitive data from theft, unauthorized access, and manipulation. Maintaining customer privacy and avoiding expensive fines require adherence to data protection laws like the California Consumer Privacy Act (CCPA) and the General Data Protection Regulation (GDPR).

2. *Safeguarding Reputation and Trust*: Businesses need both a solid reputation and the trust of their customers in order to establish and preserve fruitful partnerships with customers, partners, and stakeholders. Cyberattacks, data breaches, and privacy violations are examples of security incidents that can seriously harm an organization's brand and undermine consumer trust. Including strong security measures shows a dedication to safeguarding client information and upholding information availability, confidentiality, and integrity, which builds stakeholder and customer loyalty (Pandey, B. K. et al., 2023a).
3. *Compliance with Regulatory Requirements*: Strict regulatory requirements covering data security, privacy, and compliance apply to many industries. Serious fines, legal ramifications, and reputational harm may arise from breaking laws like the Health Insurance Portability and Accountability Act (HIPAA), the Payment Card Industry Data Security Standard (PCI DSS), and the Sarbanes-Oxley Act (SOX). In order to protect sensitive data, assure regulatory compliance, and reduce the risk of non-compliance, integrating strong security measures necessitates putting controls, policies, and procedures in place.
4. *Prevention of Financial Loss*: Businesses may suffer large financial losses as a result of cyberattacks and security breaches. These losses can be attributed to both direct and indirect factors, such as lost revenue, customer attrition, and harm to a company's reputation, as well as direct costs like remediation costs, legal fees, and regulatory fines. The average cost of a data breach keeps going up, with annual increases in costs for detection, containment, notification, and recovery. By protecting vital assets and resources, reducing the possibility and impact of security incidents, and facilitating quick detection and response to cyber threats, integrating strong security measures helps reduce the risk of financial loss.
5. *Protection Against Emerging Threats*: The field of cybersecurity is always changing as a result of cybercriminals using more advanced tactics, techniques, and procedures (TTPs) to get around established security measures and exploit vulnerabilities. Businesses of all sizes and industries are at serious risk from emerging threats like supply chain attacks, phishing, ransomware, and zero-day exploits. By implementing advanced threat detection, prevention, and response capabilities, utilizing threat intelligence, and working with industry peers (Saxena, A. et al., 2024) and security experts to share best practices and mitigate risks, organizations can stay ahead of emerging threats by integrating robust security measures.
6. *Support for Business Growth and Innovation*: Businesses can confidently pursue growth opportunities and innovation with a strong security posture, knowing that their assets, data, and systems are sufficiently safeguarded. Digital transformation is made possible by security, which enables businesses to take advantage of cutting-edge innovations like blockchain (David, S. et al., 2023), cloud computing, Internet of Things (IoT) (Pramanik, S. et al., 2023), and artificial intelligence (AI) to boost productivity, innovate, and become more competitive (Pandey, B. K., & Pandey, D., 2023).

To enable secure innovation and sustainable growth, integrating security into business strategies entails coordinating security objectives with business goals, creating a culture of security awareness and accountability, and incorporating security into the product, service, and solution development lifecycle.

Security lapses can cause downtime, interfere with essential services, and affect business operations, which can cost an organization money and negatively impact customer satisfaction, productivity, and revenue (Muñoz-Saavedra, L., 2020). Disruptions to operations can have far-reaching effects on supply chain partners, customer relations, employee morale, and regulatory compliance. Resilience, redundancy, and contingency planning are implemented as part of integrating strong security measures to reduce the impact of security incidents, preserve business continuity, and guarantee the dependability and availability of crucial services and systems

Figure 1. Security business strategies

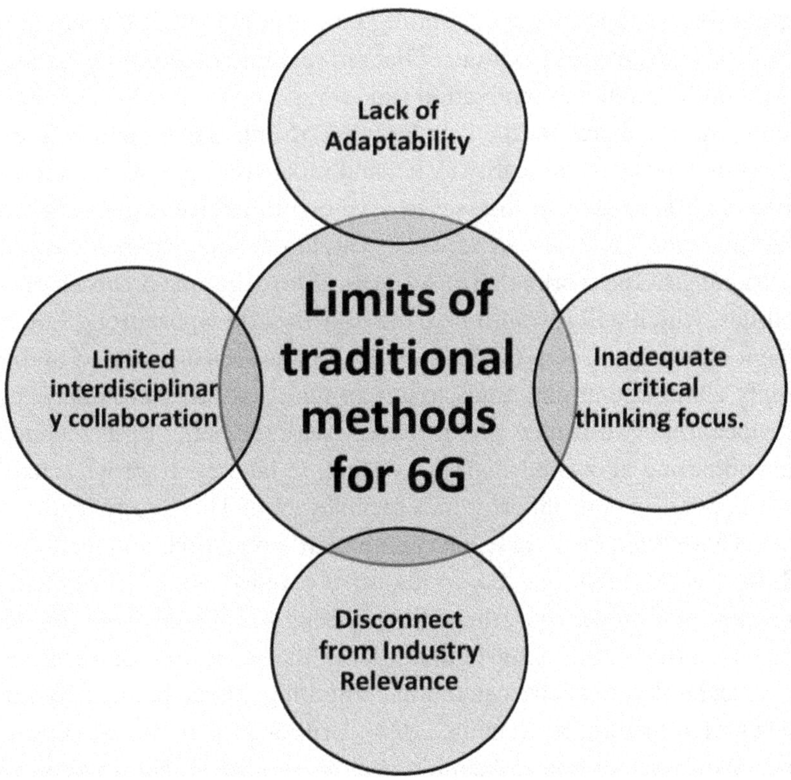

II. 6G TECHNOLOGY LANDSCAPE

2.1 Transformative Potential in Commerce

Exploring the transformative potential of 6G technology in the commercial sector reveals a landscape of opportunities and advancements that have never been seen before. These advancements and opportunities have the potential to revolutionize the way in which businesses act, interact, and innovate.

Businesses will be able to transmit and process data at lightning-fast speeds thanks to the 6G technology, which is poised to deliver connection and speed levels that have never been seen before. In comparison to its predecessors, 6G networks will have a significantly higher capacity and lower latency, which will make it possible for businesses to communicate and collaborate in a seamless manner across a wide range of territories and business operations. Real-time data processing and analysis are made possible by the ultra-low latency of 6G networks. This gives businesses the ability to make well-informed decisions and react quickly to shifting market dynamics. Through the utilization of 6G technology, businesses are able to gain access to and analyze vast amounts of data in real time, thereby revealing valuable insights and opportunities for optimization and innovation (Pandey, D. et al., 2021). The technology of 6G has the potential to open up new avenues for the development of immersive technologies and experiences, such as augmented reality (AR), virtual reality (VR), and mixed reality with mixed reality (MR). Sixth-generation networks can be utilized by businesses to develop immersive experiences for their customers, employees, and other stakeholders. These experiences can improve engagement, training, visualization, and product demonstrations. 6G networks also make it possible to provide precise location-based services and tracking capabilities, which will revolutionize the logistics, transportation (Sahani, K. et al., 2023), and asset management industries. Using 6G technology, businesses are able to optimize (Jayapoorani, S. et al., 2023) supply chain operations, track assets in real time, and provide personalized services based on the precise location of customers and resources with the help of this technology. Utilizing the capabilities of edge computing allows businesses to decrease latency, improve reliability, and enhance security, which in turn opens up new opportunities for Internet of Things applications, automation, and autonomous systems. These features include encryption, authentication, and technologies that enhance privacy (Pandey, B. K. et al., 2021a). The incorporation of sophisticated security and privacy measures safeguards sensitive data and transactions, thereby protecting businesses from the dangers and vulnerabilities that originate from the internet. Last but not least, the 6G technology features a seamless integration with emerging technologies such as quantum computing, blockchain, artificial intelligence (AI), and machine learning (ML) (Pandey, B. K. et al., 2024). Utilizing the power of 6G networks, businesses have the ability to speed up the adoption and deployment of emerging technologies, which in turn drives innovation, efficiency, and competitiveness (Elliott, D. et al., 2019).

2.2 Impacts on Business Operations

There will be a significant impact on business operations across a variety of industries as a result of the introduction of 5G technology, which ushers in a new era of hyperconnectivity and promises extraordinarily high speeds, decreased latency, and increased capacity. Understanding how 5G will affect operations is becoming increasingly important as businesses work to capitalize on the transformative potential of the technology. We delve into the implications of hyperconnectivity and ultra-low latency on business operations in this article. We also investigate how 5G technology is going to revolutionize industries and reshape the way in which we connect with one another and communicate with one another. The ability of 5G technology to deliver lightning-fast speeds and significantly increased bandwidth is the fundamental feature that sets it apart from other technologies. Real-time data transmission, seamless streaming, and high-quality video conferencing are all made possible by 5G's utilization of higher-frequency spectrum (Govindaraj, V. et al., 2023) and advanced modulation techniques, which allow for data transfer speeds of up to 10 gigabits per second. Productivity, collaboration, and efficiency in business operations are all improved as a result of this unparalleled speed, which enables organizations to provide customers with services that are both more responsive and less time consuming. Because of the dramatic reduction in latency that 5G technology offers, it is ideal for applications that require instant responsiveness. This is one of the most significant implications of 5G technology. 5G enables nearly instantaneous communication between devices, the latency of which can be as low as one millisecond. This opens up new possibilities for immersive experiences and applications that are essential to the operation of the business. Because of its low latency, 5G has the potential to significantly benefit industries such as autonomous vehicles, remote surgery, and virtual reality. This technology will make it possible to engage in interactions in real time, thereby improving safety, efficiency, and the overall user experience (Khan, W. Z. et al., 2020). The expansion of Internet of Things based semiconductor devices (Du John, H. V. et al., 2024) at an exponential rate calls for a network infrastructure that is dependable and robust, which is something that 5G offers. By virtue of its high capacity and low latency, 5G makes it possible to integrate billions of Internet of Things devices in a seamless manner, thereby fostering the development of smart homes, smart cities, and factories. 5G enables Internet of Things-driven innovations, such as smart sensors and autonomous systems, which result in improved decision-making, optimized resource utilization, and increased operational efficiency across all industries. Edge computing and fifth-generation wireless networks have come together to form a formidable combination for the transformation of industries. Real-time data processing, edge artificial intelligence, and augmented reality applications are all made possible by edge computing, which is located at the network's edge. Additionally, 5G's high bandwidth and low latency make this possible. Productivity is increased, predictive maintenance is made possible, and industries like manufacturing, healthcare (Singh, S. et al., 2023), and logistics are given the ability to optimize processes, improve decision-making, and provide customers with personalized experiences as a result of this convergence. The adoption of emerging technologies and driving advancements in fields such as artificial intelligence, augmented reality, and the Internet of Medical Things (IoMT). For example, 5G speeds up the adoption of emerging technologies. Innovations in areas such as autonomous vehicles, smart grids, remote robotics, and healthcare delivery are made possible by the high-speed connectivity and ultra-low latency of 5G, which opens up new frontiers for research and development (Strinati, E. C. et al., 2019).

III. SECURITY IMPERATIVES

3.1 Emerging Threats in 6G Networks

Ensuring the security and resilience of these next-generation communication systems requires identifying emerging threats and vulnerabilities specific to 6G networks. As 6G technology develops and spreads, it presents a number of new risks and difficulties that need to be anticipated and handled early on. New issues with signal propagation, coverage, and security arise with the use of higher frequency (Du John,

H. V. et al., 2023) spectrum bands, such as terahertz and millimeter-wave frequencies. The increased vulnerability of these higher frequency bands to jamming, eavesdropping, and signal interference raises questions about how to protect communication channels from illegal access. Vulnerabilities are introduced by the intricacy of managing heterogeneous networks in the 6G ecosystem. In order to mitigate potential threats like protocol vulnerabilities and interoperability issues, it is imperative to ensure interoperability and coordination between various network elements. This is made possible by the combination of traditional cellular networks, satellite communications, and emerging technologies such as mesh networks and unmanned aerial vehicles (UAVs). There are more opportunities for malicious actors to exploit vulnerabilities and launch large-scale attacks due to the widespread deployment of Internet of Things (IoT) devices in 6G networks, which increases the attack surface. IoT infrastructure is more vulnerable to cyberattacks such as distributed denial-of-service (DDoS) attacks, botnets, and other cyberthreats due to the wide variety of IoT devices, ranging from sensors (Abdulkarim, Y. I. et al., 2023) to driverless cars. Even though edge computing has advantages like increased scalability and performance, it also raises issues like endpoint security, data privacy, and unauthorized access to edge devices and resources. As a result, strong security measures are needed to reduce any potential risks. The possible integration of quantum communication technologies in 6G networks. While quantum key distribution (QKD) in quantum communication provides theoretically unbreakable encryption (Pandey, B. K. et al., 2021b), practical implementation, key management, and interoperability issues need to be resolved to guarantee the security and dependability of quantum communication in 6G networks. As 6G networks proliferate, privacy and data protection issues become more pressing. Strong privacy-preserving techniques, like encryption, anonymization, and access controls, are required as 6G enables ubiquitous connectivity and real-time monitoring in order to safeguard user privacy and stop illegal data access. Supply chain risks and trustworthiness issues present serious obstacles to 6G network security. The integrity, authenticity, and reliability of hardware, software, and firmware components are at risk in the global supply chain for 6G infrastructure components. As a result, precautions against supply chain attacks, fake parts, and malicious firmware modifications are required (Elmeadawy, S., & Shubair, R. M., 2019).

3.2 Data Protection in Interconnected Systems

Today's digital landscape, where large amounts of sensitive data are exchanged and processed across networks and platforms, makes it imperative to understand the criticality of data protection and privacy in an interconnected ecosystem. The confidentiality, integrity, and availability of data are critical for upholding trust, reducing risks, and meeting regulatory requirements in an interconnected ecosystem where data flows effortlessly between devices, systems, and users. Protecting sensitive information from unauthorized access, disclosure, or manipulation is the primary reason why data protection is so important. There is an increased risk of data breaches and cyberattacks in an interconnected ecosystem where data moves across networks and is stored on different devices and servers. Data protection is crucial to preventing unwanted access and lessening the effects of possible security incidents. It can be achieved through encryption, access controls, and other security measures. The autonomy of individuals to manage their personal data and guaranteeing adherence to privacy laws and guidelines depend on privacy protection. It takes openness, permission, and responsibility to manage data responsibly in an interconnected ecosystem where information is gathered, processed, and shared amongst several entities in order to preserve privacy. To uphold individuals' right to privacy and reduce the likelihood of privacy violations, organizations need to incorporate privacy-preserving technologies and practices, such as data anonymization, pseudonymization, and privacy-enhancing protocols. Preserving confidence and trust among stakeholders including clients, business associates, and government authorities—requires privacy and data protection. Data security and privacy must be given top priority by organizations as essential components of their business strategy in an interconnected ecosystem where violations of these rights can have far-reaching effects, including financial loss, reputational harm, and legal liabilities. Organisations can establish credibility with stakeholders and set themselves apart in the market by showcasing their dedication to safeguarding data and upholding privacy rights. Businesses must maintain compliance to avoid fines, penalties, and other legal repercussions in an interconnected ecosystem where data is subject to numerous laws and regulations, including the California Consumer Privacy Act (CCPA), the General Data Protection Regulation (GDPR), and sector-specific regulations. To prove compliance and reduce regulatory risks, it is imperative to put strong data protection and privacy controls in place, carry out frequent audits and assessments, and keep up with documentation and records (Yang, P. et al., 2019).

3.3 Risks From IoT and Edge Computing

IoT devices and edge computing in commerce have ushered in a new era of connectivity, efficiency, and innovation. Technology presents many opportunities, but it also poses many challenges and risks that businesses must overcome to reach their full potential. We examine the interconnected ecosystems, security concerns, scalability issues, data management issues, and regulatory compliance requirements of IoT devices and edge computing in commerce in this comprehensive exploration. IoT sensors, actuators, smart appliances, and industrial machinery are changing how businesses operate and interact with their environments (Pandey, B. K. et al., 2023b). Sensors and connectivity allow these devices to collect massive amounts of physical data for real-time monitoring, analysis, and automation. IoT devices can improve supply chain operations, customer experiences, predictive maintenance, and energy efficiency across industries. Edge computing provides computational resources and processing power at the network edge, closer to data generation and consumption, enabling IoT-driven innovation. Edge computing enables real-time processing, decision-making, and responsiveness by decentralizing computing tasks and distributing workloads across edge devices, reducing latency, bandwidth usage, and data center dependence. Autonomous vehicles, industrial automation, and augmented reality benefit from this distributed computing paradigm's low latency, high throughput, and network resilience. IoT devices and edge computing pose significant challenges and risks that businesses must address to ensure system security, reliability, and scalability. IoT devices' limited processing power and memory make them vulnerable to malware attacks, unauthorized access, and data breaches. Malicious actors can exploit devices and data due to weak authentication, insecure firmware, and lack of encryption. IoT deployments are growing rapidly, raising concerns about infrastructure scalability and resilience. Traditional network architectures may struggle to handle the increased traffic and processing demands of more connected devices, causing network congestion, latency, and performance degradation. Edge computing's dynamic nature, where computing resources are distributed across a network of edge devices, presents scalability challenges as businesses must ensure adequate resources to meet IoT and edge computing deployment needs. Integration of IoT devices and edge computing complicates data management and governance. Businesses must address data sovereignty, ownership, and lifecycle management as data is generated and processed at the network edge. As data flows across devices and environments, complying with data protection laws like the GDPR and CCPA becomes harder. Encryption, access controls, and data lifecycle management policies are necessary to reduce data breaches, unauthorized access, and regulatory non-compliance.

Businesses must also deal with IoT device and edge computing interoperability issues in addition to security and scalability issues. Integrating and interoperating devices from different manufacturers, protocols, and standards is difficult. Interoperability issues can slow data exchange, device communication, and system compatibility, causing integration bottlenecks, higher implementation costs, and operational inefficiencies. IoT devices also pose physical security risks. These devices are vulnerable to physical tampering, theft, and vandalism in retail stores, warehouses, and manufacturing facilities. Poor physical security, such as weak access controls and unprotected communication channels, can compromise IoT device integrity and reliability, threatening business operations and data security. Businesses must comply with IoT and edge computing data collection, processing, and storage regulations. Data protection, privacy, and consumer rights regulations apply to organizations using IoT devices and edge computing technologies. Businesses must implement comprehensive data protection measures, conduct regular audits, and maintain meticulous documentation to comply with these regulations (Giordani, M. et al., 2020).

IV. ADAPTING BUSINESS STRATEGIES

4.1 Security by Design Approach

By incorporating security practices and principles into each phase of the product development lifecycle, security can be incorporated by design into business processes, thereby solidifying its position as a fundamental component of organizational operations. By taking a proactive stance, security concerns are taken into account early on rather than being added later as an afterthought. Organizations can effectively reduce risks, improve resilience, and cultivate stakeholder trust by incorporating security by design Performing thorough risk assessments and threat modeling exercises early in the development process is a crucial part of integrating security by design. Organizations can identify potential security threats and vulnerabilities ahead of time and implement proactive risk mitigation strategies by evaluating potential attack vectors, evaluating the impact of security breaches, and prioritizing security controls based on risk level. Using secure development practices at every stage of the software development lifecycle is another essential element. To reduce the introduction of security flaws and vulnerabilities during the development phase, this involves following secure coding standards, doing code reviews, and using vulnerability scanning tools. Organizations can guarantee that security is embedded into the development process from the beginning by providing developers with secure coding techniques and best practices training. When designing systems and applications, organizations need to take security architecture and design into account in addition to secure development practices. By incorporating security features like encryption, secure communication protocols, authentication, and authorization into the system architecture, enterprises can employ defense-in-depth tactics to progressively assemble security controls across the architecture, offering a multitude of defenses against possible attacks. Organizations can routinely evaluate the security posture of their systems and fix any vulnerabilities or weaknesses found during testing by implementing continuous security testing throughout the development lifecycle, which includes static code analysis, dynamic application testing, and penetration testing. Integrating security by design also requires secure operations and deployment. Organizations can guarantee that systems are securely deployed, configured, and maintained throughout their lifecycle by putting in place secure deployment pipelines, promptly applying security patches and updates, and keeping an eye out for security incidents and anomalies. Organizations can increase awareness about common security threats, best practices for secure development and deployment, and the significance of security in protecting sensitive data and assets by offering ongoing security awareness training and education to all stakeholders involved in the development and operation of systems. Last but not least, safe supply chain management is necessary to guarantee security at every stage of the supply chain, from internal development teams to external suppliers and vendors. Organizations can reduce the risk of security breaches and vulnerabilities introduced through the supply chain by evaluating third-party vendors' security practices and controls, putting contractual obligations for security compliance in place, and conducting due diligence on them (Han, C. et al., 2019).

4.2 Proactive Risk Assessments

In the hyperconnected world of today, where cyber threats are real and organizations must deal with a constantly changing set of risks, investing in thorough risk assessments and threat intelligence is critical. Businesses need to take a proactive approach to security in order to protect their most important assets and guarantee cyber resilience, as cyberattacks are becoming more complex and widespread. In order to detect possible threats, weaknesses, and security holes before malevolent actors take advantage of them, this proactive strategy collects, examines, and makes use of cyber threat intelligence. Information about potential adversaries, their tactics, techniques, and procedures (TTPs), and the risks they might pose to organizations is gathered, analyzed, and disseminated through the process of cyber threat intelligence. Businesses may acquire important insights into the changing threat landscape by utilizing cyber threat intelligence, which enables them to decide on their cybersecurity posture and tactics with knowledge. Investing in thorough risk assessments and threat intelligence can assist organizations in anticipating vulnerabilities and reducing associated risks. By using thorough risk assessments and threat intelligence, organizations can find potential points of attack, weak points in their systems, and security holes in their networks. Businesses can gain visibility into emerging threats and anticipate potential cyberattacks by conducting risk assessments and analyzing threat intelligence feeds. This enables them to take preventive measures before an incident occurs. In the event of a security incident, security teams can react more swiftly and efficiently by using cyber threat intelligence to give them important context and insights. Organizations can customize their incident response strategies to minimize the impact of attacks and avert future breaches by comprehending the tactics, techniques, and procedures (TTPs) utilized by threat actors. Organizations can raise their level of awareness about potential risks and their threat landscape by utilizing cyber threat intelligence (Rappaport, T. S. et al, 2019). This helps them to improve their overall cyber resilience and fortify their defenses by implementing proactive security measures like patch management, vulnerability scanning, and security awareness training. An important factor in strengthening the collective defense of businesses against cyber threats is the sharing of intelligence among them. Organizations can obtain important insights into new threats and adversary strategies by working with industry peers, exchanging threat intelligence, and taking part in information-sharing programs (Sharma, M. et al., 2024). This improves their capacity to identify, stop, and mitigate cyberattacks. By funding thorough risk analyses and threat intelligence, companies can decide more wisely where to allocate their resources for security. Businesses may maximize their cybersecurity budgets and resources by prioritizing security initiatives based on the most pertinent and practical solutions. This way, they can make sure that resources are allocated where they are most needed to successfully reduce risks and safeguard their vital assets. To sum up, in today's intricate and ever-changing threat landscape, organizations that want to proactively identify vulnerabilities, mitigate risks, and improve their cyber resilience must invest in thorough risk assessments and threat intelligence. Organizations can enhance their incident response capabilities, fortify their defenses, and work with industry peers to jointly thwart cyberattacks by utilizing cyber threat intelligence to obtain insights into new and emerging threats. Investing in thorough risk assessments and threat intelligence ultimately helps organizations to safeguard their vital assets from potential security breaches and cyberattacks while also keeping ahead of the constantly changing landscape of cyber threats.

4.3 Resilient Cybersecurity Frameworks

Organizations are realizing that, in order to effectively mitigate risks and defend against possible attacks, they must put in place robust cybersecurity frameworks in response to the constantly changing cyber threat landscape. Historically, the main focus of cybersecurity efforts has been on developing and implementing cyber controls to limit the scope and lessen the impact of cyberattacks. But as cyberattacks become more frequent and sophisticated, businesses need to take a proactive stance when it comes to cybersecurity resilience. Sturdy frameworks for thwarting cyberattack, like the NIST Cybersecurity Framework, have surfaced to offer organizations best practices and guidelines for improving their cybersecurity posture. Nevertheless, these frameworks frequently lag behind in adopting fresh approaches and industry insights, which reduces their usefulness in effectively combating cybercrime. In addition, a lot of top-tier companies have trouble achieving their own cybersecurity goals in all impacted areas of the business, which emphasizes the necessity of both tactical and strategic resilience models to completely handle system risks. Models of strategic and tactical resilience consider a number of variables, such as the degree of vulnerability and dependability of hardware and software resources, as well as networking and physical proximity-related features. Organizations can assess their cybersecurity resilience in-depth and pinpoint areas for development by developing a strong matrix framework based on a four-stage lifecycle model: planning/preparation, absorption, recovery, and adaptation. These frameworks place a strong emphasis on the necessity of comprehending the surrounding context, picking up new skills, and developing specialized knowledge in order to effectively manage known and unknown risks. Improving cybersecurity resilience also requires cooperation between institutions, governmental bodies, and business stakeholders. Through the exchange of threat intelligence, best practices, and insights gained, the community can effectively fend off sophisticated cyberattacks that could target numerous targets. Public relations campaigns, consumer education programs, and financial incentives like "cyber premiums" in insurance policies can motivate companies to follow voluntary standards and strengthen their cybersecurity defenses.n The creation of thorough frameworks for managing cybersecurity resilience, like the Cyber-Physical Security System (CPSS) architecture, also gives organizations direction on how to invest and take the right actions to improve their cybersecurity resilience. These frameworks provide a comprehensive approach to cybersecurity resilience management, taking into account elements like information security, control, physical security, and recovery plans (Hong, W. et al., 2021).

V. COLLABORATIVE SECURITY APPROACHES

5.2 Information Sharing With Stakeholders

Maintaining an open, equitable, and compliant business environment requires encouraging information sharing and cooperation between corporations, governmental organizations, and regulatory bodies. These organizations are essential for monitoring many facets of company operations, upholding laws, defending the rights of consumers, and encouraging healthy competition. Businesses can guarantee legal and regulatory compliance, reduce risks, and help create a level playing field for all market players by promoting cooperation and exchanging pertinent information. Enforcing laws and regulations that regulate particular industries or business activities is the responsibility of government agencies and regulatory bodies. These organizations guarantee that the law is followed and encourage conformity to norms that protect the interests of consumers and the integrity of the market. In the United States, for instance, the Food and Drug Administration (FDA) regulates pharmaceuticals and medical devices, while organizations like the Securities and Exchange Commission (SEC) supervise the financial markets. To maintain legal compliance in their contracts and business operations, businesses must abide by these regulations. Federal Trade Commissions (FTCs) and other similar organizations keep an eye out for and combat unfair or deceptive business practices, like fraud and false advertising. To avoid engaging in activities that could endanger customers or violate their rights, businesses must include consumer protection laws into their contracts. This will help them retain their credibility and trust in the marketplace. By prohibiting monopolistic practices and guaranteeing an even playing field for all market participants, regulatory bodies also work to encourage fair competition among businesses. To maintain competition, agencies such as the Competition and Markets Authority (CMA) look into anti-competitive activity and implement corrective actions. To promote fair market competition, businesses should be aware of anti-competitive regulations and refrain from engaging in actions that could result in legal ramifications or harm their reputation. By establishing norms and guidelines for moral behavior and accountability, governmental organizations and regulatory bodies help to preserve the general integrity of the business environment. Organizations that oversee financial markets and establish guidelines for behavior to safeguard consumers and preserve market integrity include the Financial Conduct Authority (FCA). Businesses show their dedication to moral behavior and foster a reliable business environment by implementing these standards into their contracts and daily operations. Several crucial tactics can be used in order to successfully encourage information sharing and cooperation between corporations, governmental organizations, and regulatory bodies:

1. *Establish Communication Channels*: Opening lines of communication with pertinent regulatory and governmental organizations promotes cooperation and gives companies the ability to proactively handle compliance-related concerns. Frequent communication and interaction promote the development of trust and make it easier for ideas and information to be shared.
2. *Seek Legal Advice*: It is advisable to obtain legal counsel when drafting intricate contracts or managing regulatory requirements. Legal experts can help businesses effectively navigate the legal landscape, interpret complex regulations, and offer insights into industry-specific requirements.

3. *Participate in Industry Initiatives*: Companies can take part in industry forums, working groups, and initiatives that help them collaborate and share information with government and regulatory agencies. These forums offer chances to talk about regulatory difficulties, exchange best practices, and influence the creation of policies.
4. *Stay Updated*: It is imperative for businesses to remain up to date with the rules and policies established by pertinent governmental entities and regulatory authorities. Monitoring legislation and regulation changes on a regular basis promotes compliance and reduces the risk of legal trouble or damage to one's reputation from non-compliance.

Organizations can improve compliance, reduce risks, and support an open, equitable, and moral business environment by encouraging information sharing and cooperation amongst corporations, governmental bodies, and regulatory bodies. Cooperation amongst interested parties promotes trust, fortifies regulatory supervision, and eventually helps consumers and the overall economy.

VI. INNOVATION IN SECURITY TECHNOLOGIES

6.1 AI and ML for Threat Detection

One of the most significant paradigms shifts in cybersecurity is the utilization of artificial intelligence (AI) and machine learning (ML) (Anand, R. et al., 2023) for the purpose of detecting threats in advance and developing defense mechanisms that can adapt to changing circumstances. The implementation of these cutting-edge technologies gives organizations the ability to proactively identify and respond to cyber threats in real time, thereby improving their overall security posture and strengthening their resilience. Businesses are able to analyze vast amounts of data, recognize patterns, and automate decision-making processes by utilizing artificial intelligence and machine learning algorithms (Muniandi, B. et al., 2024). This allows them to stay ahead of evolving cyber threats. AI and ML have the ability to enable predictive threat detection, which is one of the most important benefits they bring to the field of cybersecurity. Reactive approaches are frequently utilized in traditional cybersecurity measures. These approaches involve the activation of security controls in response to threats that have been identified. Artificial intelligence and machine learning algorithms (Tripathi, R. P. et al., 2023), on the other hand, are able to examine historical data, recognize trends, and anticipate potential future threats before they occur. Organizations have the ability to take preventative measures to mitigate risks and prevent security breaches if they possess the ability to recognize patterns that are indicative of malicious activity. On the other hand, adaptive defense mechanisms are able to continuously learn and adapt based on real-time threat intelligence, in contrast to static security measures, which may become obsolete as cyber threats evolve. With the help of this proactive approach, organizations are able to swiftly react to shifting threat landscapes and implement targeted countermeasures in order to effectively mitigate risks. It improve the efficiency and effectiveness of security operations by automating tasks that are repetitive and by augmenting the decision-making processes of humans. As an illustration, threat detection systems that are powered by artificial intelligence are able to analyze patterns of network traffic, recognize anomalies, and flag potential security incidents for further investigation. Not only does this lessen the workload of cybersecurity teams, but it also makes it possible for them to reduce response times and conduct threat assessments with greater precision. Artificial intelligence and machine learning algorithms are able to identify potential security vulnerabilities by analyzing data from a variety of sources, such as network logs, system logs, and user behavior. These algorithms can then prioritize remediation efforts based on the severity of the risk. To effectively prioritize resources and address critical security gaps before they can be exploited by attackers, this proactive approach provides organizations with the ability to prioritize resources. The effectiveness of fraud detection and identity verification procedures can also be improved by security solutions that are based on artificial intelligence and machine learning. These technologies have the ability to detect suspicious behavior through the analysis of user behavior patterns and the identification of deviations from normal activity. This behavior may be indicative of fraudulent activity or attempts to gain unauthorized access. This provides organizations with the ability to detect and prevent fraud in real time, thereby protecting sensitive data and financial assets from being accessed or misused by unauthorized parties. Cybersecurity is represented by the utilization of artificial intelligence and machine learning for the purpose of detecting threats in advance and implementing defense mechanisms that are adaptable to changing circumstances. Organisations are able to proactively identify and respond to cyber threats, improve the efficiency of security operations, and effectively mitigate risks when they make use of advanced algorithms and analytics capabilities. It is expected that artificial intelligence and machine learning technologies will play an increasingly important role in the protection of digital assets and the maintenance of cyber resilience as the complexity and sophistication of cyber threats continues to increase (Chaudhary, S. et al., 2014).

6.2 Decentralized Architectures for Resilience

Improving resistance to cyberattacks by combining distributed and decentralized architectures is a major advancement. Single points of failure and targeted attacks have long been threats to traditional centralized architectures. Organizations can reduce these risks by switching to decentralized and distributed architectures, which spread data and computational resources among several nodes or locations, making it more difficult for attackers to compromise the system as a whole. Decentralized architectures do away with the need for a single central authority by dividing control and decision-making functions among several nodes. With this distributed approach, even if some nodes are compromised, the system as a whole can still function, minimizing the impact of potential breaches or disruptions to individual nodes. Through the distribution of data and processing power among a network of linked nodes, enterprises can strengthen their defenses against cyberattacks while maintaining data integrity and business continuity. In a similar vein, distributed architectures disperse information and computational power (Sahani, S. K. et al., 2024) among several sites or servers, lowering the possibility of data loss or system outages brought on by isolated malfunctions or intrusions. Even in the event of an infrastructure breakdown or cyberattack, enterprises can guarantee high availability and fault tolerance by distributing data across several nodes and putting redundancy measures in place. By distributing risk and reducing the effect of possible disruptions on overall system performance, this distributed approach improves resilience. By decreasing the attack surface and limiting the possible impact of successful cyberattacks, integrating distributed and decentralized architectures can improve security. A single breach or compromise in a centralized architecture may have far-reaching effects, exposing confidential information or jeopardizing vital systems. Decentralized and distributed architectures, on the other hand, divide up data and functionality so that the effects of security breaches are limited to particular nodes or components. Because of this isolation, the possibility of cascading failures is decreased, and the potential damage from cyberattacks is constrained (Zhao, J., 2019). Organizations can absorb and lessen the effects of volumetric attacks by distributing incoming traffic and dynamically adjusting resource allocation to reduce congestion and guarantee continuous service availability. This is achieved by distributing data and processing capabilities across multiple nodes. Better scalability, flexibility, and performance are just a few advantages of decentralized and distributed architectures, which also increase resilience against cyberattacks. Organizations can maximize resource utilization, provide better performance and responsiveness to end users, and dynamically scale resources in response to fluctuating demand by utilizing a network of interconnected nodes. Organizations can adjust to changing business needs and technology trends thanks to this scalability and flexibility, which ensures their long-term viability and competitiveness in the digital age.

CONCLUSION

The future of commerce is clearly going to undergo tremendous change, as we approach the arrival of the 6G era. The emergence of 6G technology presents enormous potential for businesses to innovate and prosper in the digital environment by delivering hyper-connectivity and ultra-low latency. It is impossible to overlook the serious security risks that these developments bring with them. For business strategies to effectively mitigate emerging threats, the move to 6G requires the integration of strong security measures. Businesses need to put security first in order to protect their operations and keep customers' trust. This includes knowing what vulnerabilities are specific to 6G networks and how important data protection and privacy are in an interconnected ecosystem. Information sharing and cooperation between corporations, governmental organizations, and regulatory bodies are crucial components of collaborative approaches to security. Together, the stakeholders can fortify the resilience of the larger ecosystem and remain ahead of ever-changing threats. A number of innovative security technologies, including decentralized architectures, quantum-resistant cryptography, and artificial intelligence, present promising ways to strengthen cyberattack resistance in the 6G era. Assuring the integrity and security of their digital assets, these developments enable organizations to proactively detect and respond to threats. Businesses must continue to be alert, flexible, and proactive in facing security issues as they navigate the complexities of the 6G landscape. Organisations can achieve a competitive edge in the highly interconnected and dynamic realm of 6G commerce by adopting a comprehensive security strategy and utilising cutting-edge technologies.

REFERENCES

Abdulkarim, Y. I., Awl, H. N., Muhammadsharif, F. F., Saeed, S. R., Sidiq, K. R., Khasraw, S. S., & Pandey, D. (2023). Metamaterial-based sensors loaded corona-shaped resonator for COVID-19 detection by using microwave techniques. *Plasmonics*, 1–16.

Anand, R., Khan, B., Nassa, V. K., Pandey, D., Dhabliya, D., Pandey, B. K., & Dadheech, P. (2023). Hybrid convolutional neural network (CNN) for kennedy space center hyperspectral image. *Aerospace Systems*, 6(1), 71–78. 10.1007/s42401-022-00168-4

Anand, R., Lakshmi, S. V., Pandey, D., & Pandey, B. K. (2024). An enhanced ResNet-50 deep learning model for arrhythmia detection using electrocardiogram biomedical indicators. *Evolving Systems*, 15(1), 83–97. 10.1007/s12530-023-09559-0

Bessant, Y. A., Jency, J. G., Sagayam, K. M., Jone, A. A. A., Pandey, D., & Pandey, B. K. (2023). Improved parallel matrix multiplication using Strassen and Urdhvatiryagbhyam method. *CCF Transactions on High Performance Computing*, 5(2), 102–115. 10.1007/s42514-023-00149-9

Bruntha, P. M., Dhanasekar, S., Hepsiba, D., Sagayam, K. M., Neebha, T. M., Pandey, D., & Pandey, B. K. (2023). Application of switching median filter with L 2 norm-based auto-tuning function for removing random valued impulse noise. *Aerospace Systems, 6*(1), 53-59.

Chaudhary, S., & Amphawan, A. (2014). The role and challenges of free-space optical systems. *Journal of Optical Communications*, 35(4), 327–334. 10.1515/joc-2014-0004

David, S., Duraipandian, K., Chandrasekaran, D., Pandey, D., Sindhwani, N., & Pandey, B. K. (2023). Impact of blockchain in healthcare system. In *Unleashing the Potentials of blockchain technology for healthcare industries* (pp. 37–57). Academic Press. 10.1016/B978-0-323-99481-1.00004-3

Devasenapathy, D., Madhumathy, P., Umamaheshwari, R., Pandey, B. K., & Pandey, D. (2024). Transmission-efficient grid-based synchronized model for routing in wireless sensor networks using Bayesian compressive sensing. *SN Computer Science*, 5(1), 1–11.

Du John, H. V., Ajay, T., Reddy, G. M. K., Ganesh, M. N. S., Hembram, A., Pandey, B. K., & Pandey, D. (2023). Design and simulation of SRR-based tungsten metamaterial absorber for biomedical sensing applications. *Plasmonics*, 18(5), 1903–1912. 10.1007/s11468-023-01910-0

Du John, H. V., Jose, T., Sagayam, K. M., Pandey, B. K., & Pandey, D. (2024). Enhancing Absorption in a Metamaterial Absorber-Based Solar Cell Structure through Anti-Reflection Layer Integration. *Silicon*, 1-11.

Du John, H. V., Sagayam, K. M., Jose, T., Pandey, D., Pandey, B. K., Kotti, J., & Kaur, P. (2023). Design simulation and parametric investigation of a metamaterial light absorber with tungsten resonator for solar cell applications using silicon as dielectric layer. *Silicon*, 15(9), 4065–4079. 10.1007/s12633-023-02321-w

Elliott, D., Keen, W., & Miao, L. (2019). Recent advances in connected and automated vehicles. *Journal of Traffic and Transportation Engineering (English Edition), 6*(2), 109-131.

Elmeadawy, S., & Shubair, R. M. (2019, November). 6G wireless communications: Future technologies and research challenges. In *2019 international conference on electrical and computing technologies and applications (ICECTA)* (pp. 1-5). IEEE.

George, W. K., Ekong, M. O., Pandey, D., & Pandey, B. K. (2023). Pedagogy for Implementation of TVET Curriculum for the Digital World. In *Applications of Neuromarketing in the Metaverse* (pp. 117-136). IGI Global. 10.4018/978-1-6684-8150-9.ch009

George, W. K., Silas, E. I., Pandey, D., & Pandey, B. K. (2024). Utilization of Industry 4.0 Technologies in Nigerian Technical and Vocational Education: A Conundrum for Educators. In *Examining the Rapid Advance of Digital Technology in Africa* (pp. 270–293). IGI Global. 10.4018/978-1-6684-9962-7.ch014

Giordani, M., Polese, M., Mezzavilla, M., Rangan, S., & Zorzi, M. (2020). Toward 6G networks: Use cases and technologies. *IEEE Communications Magazine*, 58(3), 55–61. 10.1109/MCOM.001.1900411

. Govindaraj, V., Dhanasekar, S., Martinsagayam, K., Pandey, D., Pandey, B. K., & Nassa, V. K. (2023). Low-power test pattern generator using modified LFSR. *Aerospace Systems*, 1-8.

Gupta, A. K., Sharma, R., Pandey, D., Nassa, V. K., Pandey, B. K., George, A. S., & Dadheech, P. (2023). Performance analysis of eight-channel WDM optical network with different optical amplifiers for industry 4.0. In *Innovation and Competitiveness in Industry 4.0 Based on Intelligent Systems* (pp. 197–212). Springer International Publishing. 10.1007/978-3-031-29775-5_9

Han, C., Wu, Y., Chen, Z., & Wang, X. (2019). Terahertz communications (TeraCom): Challenges and impact on 6G wireless systems. arXiv preprint arXiv:1912.06040.

Hong, W., Jiang, Z. H., Yu, C., Hou, D., Wang, H., Guo, C., Hu, Y., Kuai, L., Yu, Y., Jiang, Z., Chen, Z., Chen, J., Yu, Z., Zhai, J., Zhang, N., Tian, L., Wu, F., Yang, G., Hao, Z.-C., & Zhou, J. Y. (2021). The role of millimeter-wave technologies in 5G/6G wireless communications. *IEEE Journal of Microwaves*, 1(1), 101–122. 10.1109/JMW.2020.3035541

Iyyanar, P., Anand, R., Shanthi, T., Nassa, V. K., Pandey, B. K., George, A. S., & Pandey, D. (2023). A real-time smart sewage cleaning UAV assistance system using IoT. In *Handbook of Research on Data-Driven Mathematical Modeling in Smart Cities* (pp. 24–39). IGI Global.

JayaLakshmi, G., Pandey, D., Pandey, B. K., Kaur, P., Mahajan, D. A., & Dari, S. S. (2024). Smart Big Data Collection for Intelligent Supply Chain Improvement. In *AI and Machine Learning Impacts in Intelligent Supply Chain* (pp. 180-195). IGI Global.

Jayapoorani, S., Pandey, D., Sasirekha, N. S., Anand, R., & Pandey, B. K. (2023). Systolic optimized adaptive filter architecture designs for ECG noise cancellation by Vertex-5. *Aerospace Systems*, 6(1), 163–173. 10.1007/s42401-022-00177-3

Khan, W. Z., Rehman, M. H., Zangoti, H. M., Afzal, M. K., Armi, N., & Salah, K. (2020). Industrial internet of things: Recent advances, enabling technologies and open challenges. *Computers & Electrical Engineering*, 81, 106522. 10.1016/j.compeleceng.2019.106522

Kirubasri, G., Sankar, S., Pandey, D., Pandey, B. K., Singh, H., & Anand, R. (2021, September). A recent survey on 6G vehicular technology, applications and challenges. In *2021 9th International Conference on Reliability, Infocom Technologies and Optimization (Trends and Future Directions)(ICRITO)* (pp. 1-5). IEEE.

Kumar Pandey, B., Pandey, D., Nassa, V. K., Ahmad, T., Singh, C., George, A. S., & Wakchaure, M. A. (2021). Encryption and steganography-based text extraction in IoT using the EWCTS optimizer. *Imaging Science Journal*, 69(1-4), 38–56. 10.1080/13682199.2022.2146885

Muniandi, B., Nassa, V. K., Pandey, D., Pandey, B. K., Dadheech, P., & George, A. S. (2024). Pattern Analysis for Feature Extraction in Complex Images. In *Using Machine Learning to Detect Emotions and Predict Human Psychology* (pp. 145-167). IGI Global. 10.4018/979-8-3693-1910-9.ch007

Muñoz-Saavedra, L., Miró-Amarante, L., & Domínguez-Morales, M. (2020). Augmented and virtual reality evolution and future tendency. *Applied Sciences (Basel, Switzerland)*, 10(1), 322. 10.3390/app10010322

Pandey, B. K., & Pandey, D. (2023). Parametric optimization and prediction of enhanced thermoelectric performance in co-doped CaMnO3 using response surface methodology and neural network. *Journal of Materials Science Materials in Electronics*, 34(21), 1589. 10.1007/s10854-023-10954-1

Pandey, B. K., Pandey, D., Alkhafaji, M. A., Güneşer, M. T., & Şeker, C. (2023a). A reliable transmission and extraction of textual information using keyless encryption, steganography, and deep algorithm with cuckoo optimization. In *Micro-Electronics and Telecommunication Engineering: Proceedings of 6th ICMETE 2022* (pp. 629–636). Springer Nature Singapore. 10.1007/978-981-19-9512-5_57

Pandey, B. K., Pandey, D., Dadheech, P., Mahajan, D. A., George, A. S., & Hameed, A. S. (2023b). Review on Smart Sewage Cleaning UAV Assistance for Sustainable Development. In *Handbook of Research on Safe Disposal Methods of Municipal Solid Wastes for a Sustainable Environment* (pp. 69–79). IGI Global. 10.4018/978-1-6684-8117-2.ch005

Pandey, B. K., Pandey, D., & Sahani, S. K. (2024). Autopilot control unmanned aerial vehicle system for sewage defect detection using deep learning. *Engineering Reports*, 12852. 10.1002/eng2.12852

Pandey, B. K., Pandey, D., Wairya, S., & Agarwal, G. (2021a). An advanced morphological component analysis, steganography, and deep learning-based system to transmit secure textual data. *International Journal of Distributed Artificial Intelligence*, 13(2), 40–62. 10.4018/IJDAI.2021070104

Pandey, B. K., Pandey, D., Wariya, S., & Agarwal, G. (2021b). A deep neural network-based approach for extracting textual images from deteriorate images. *EAI Endorsed Transactions on Industrial Networks and Intelligent Systems*, 8(28), e3–e3. 10.4108/eai.17-9-2021.170961

Pandey, D., Pandey, B. K., & Wairya, S. (2021). Hybrid deep neural network with adaptive galactic swarm optimization for text extraction from scene images. *Soft Computing*, 25(2), 1563–1580. 10.1007/s00500-020-05245-4

Pramanik, S., Pandey, D., Joardar, S., Niranjanamurthy, M., Pandey, B. K., & Kaur, J. (2023, October). An overview of IoT privacy and security in smart cities. In *AIP Conference Proceedings* (Vol. 2495, No. 1). AIP Publishing. 10.1063/5.0123511

Raja, D., Kumar, D. R., Santhiyakumari, N., Kumarganesh, S., Sagayam, K. M., Thiyaneswaran, B., Pandey, B. K., & Pandey, D. (2024). A compact dual-feed wide-band slotted antenna for future wireless applications. *Analog Integrated Circuits and Signal Processing*, 1–15. 10.1007/s10470-023-02233-0

Rappaport, T. S., Xing, Y., Kanhere, O., Ju, S., Madanayake, A., Mandal, S., Alkhateeb, A., & Trichopoulos, G. C. (2019). Wireless communications and applications above 100 GHz: Opportunities and challenges for 6G and beyond. *IEEE Access : Practical Innovations, Open Solutions*, 7, 78729–78757. 10.1109/ACCESS.2019.2921522

Sahani, K., Khadka, S. S., Sahani, S. K., Pandey, B. K., & Pandey, D. (2023). A possible underground roadway for transportation facilities in Kathmandu Valley: A racking deformation of underground rectangular structures. *Engineering Reports*, 12821. 10.1002/eng2.12821

Sahani, S. K., Pandey, B. K., & Pandey, D. (2024). *Single-valued Signals, Multi-valued Signals and Fixed-Point of Contractive Signals*. Mathematics Open. 10.1142/S2811007224500020

Saxena, A., Agarwal, A., Pandey, B. K., & Pandey, D. (2024). Examination of the Criticality of Customer Segmentation Using Unsupervised Learning Methods. *Circular Economy and Sustainability*, 1–14. 10.1007/s43615-023-00336-4

Sharma, M., Talwar, R., Pandey, D., Nassa, V. K., Pandey, B. K., & Dadheech, P. (2024). A Review of Dielectric Resonator Antennas (DRA)-Based RFID Technology for Industry 4.0. *Robotics and Automation in Industry*, 4(0), 303–324.

Sharma, S., Pandey, B. K., Pandey, D., Anand, R., Sharma, A., & Saini, S. (2023, March). Character Recognition Technique Implementation for Complicated Deteriorated Scene. In *2023 6th International Conference on Information Systems and Computer Networks (ISCON)* (pp. 1-4). IEEE. 10.1109/ISCON57294.2023.10112185

Singh, S., Madaan, G., Kaur, J., Swapna, H. R., Pandey, D., Singh, A., & Pandey, B. K. (2023). *Bibliometric Review on Healthcare Sustainability. Handbook of Research on Safe Disposal Methods of Municipal Solid Wastes for a Sustainable Environment*, 142-161. 10.4018/978-1-6684-8117-2.ch011

Strinati, E. C., Barbarossa, S., Gonzalez-Jimenez, J. L., Ktenas, D., Cassiau, N., Maret, L., & Dehos, C. (2019). 6G: The next frontier: From holographic messaging to artificial intelligence using subterahertz and visible light communication. *IEEE Vehicular Technology Magazine*, 14(3), 42–50. 10.1109/MVT.2019.2921162

Swapna, H. R., Bigirimana, E., Madaan, G., Hasan, A., Pandey, B. K., & Pandey, D. (2023). Impact of neuromarketing on consumer psychology in digitally connected networks. In *Applications of Neuromarketing in the Metaverse* (pp. 193–205). IGI Global. 10.4018/978-1-6684-8150-9.ch015

Tripathi, R. P., Sharma, M., Gupta, A. K., Pandey, D., Pandey, B. K., Shahul, A., & George, A. H. (2023). Timely prediction of diabetes by means of machine learning practices. *Augmented Human Research*, 8(1), 1. 10.1007/s41133-023-00062-4

Yang, P., Xiao, Y., Xiao, M., & Li, S. (2019). 6G wireless communications: Vision and potential techniques. *IEEE Network*, 33(4), 70–75. 10.1109/MNET.2019.1800418

Zhao, J. (2019). A survey of intelligent reflecting surfaces (IRSs): Towards 6G wireless communication networks. arXiv preprint arXiv:1907.04789.

Chapter 8
Commerce 5.0:
Future-Proofing Businesses in the 6G Security Landscape

Uchit Kapoor
Arthkalp, India

S. Thilaga
Coimbatore Institute of Technology, India

Manish Gupta
Lovely Professional University, India

Nikhil Polke
https://orcid.org/0000-0001-8986-3715
Symbiosis Law School, Symbiosis International University (Deemed), Pune, India

Joshuva Arockia Dhanraj
https://orcid.org/0000-0001-5048-7775
Chandigarh University, India

ABSTRACT

Commerce 5.0 is the newest step forward in business. It's a paradigm shift made possible by the use of cutting-edge technologies. It's a move away from traditional transactional models and toward dynamic, digitally driven ecosystems that put an emphasis on hyper-personalization, seamless connectivity, and processing data in real time. Commerce 5.0 uses new technologies like AI, blockchain, IoT, AR, and others to change how businesses work with customers and the market. One thing that makes Commerce 5.0 unique is that it focuses on making ecosystems that are very flexible and quick to respond. Businesses can learn a lot about customer behavior, preferences, and trends by using AI-driven analytics and predictive modeling. In this way, they can give each customer a more customized experience and make offerings that really speak to them. Companies can get real-time data from all along the supply chain by using IoT devices and sensors.

DOI: 10.4018/979-8-3693-7421-4.ch008

I. INTRODUCTION

Commerce 5.0 is the newest step forward in business. It's a paradigm shift made possible by the use of cutting-edge technologies. It's a move away from traditional transactional models and toward dynamic, digitally-driven ecosystems that put an emphasis on hyper-personalization, seamless connectivity, and processing data in real time. Commerce 5.0 uses new technologies like AI, blockchain, IoT (Pandey, J. K. et al., 2022), AR, and others to change how businesses work with customers and the market. One thing that makes Commerce 5.0 unique is that it focuses on making ecosystems that are very flexible and quick to respond. Businesses (Saxena, A. et al., 2021) can learn a lot about customer behavior, preferences, and trends by using AI-driven analytics and predictive modelling (Anand, R. et al., 2024). In this way, they can give each customer a more customized experience and make offerings that really speak to them. Companies can get real-time data (Sharma, S. et al., 2023) from all along the supply chain by using IoT (Iyyanar, P. et al., 2023) devices and sensors. This helps them improve processes, cut down on waste, and work more efficiently overall. For Commerce 5.0 to work, blockchain technology (David, S. et al., 2023) is essential because it makes transactions clear and safe. Because it is decentralized, there are no middlemen needed. This lowers the cost of transactions and builds trust between parties. Blockchain also makes it possible to keep records that can't be changed. This makes sure that transactions, contracts, and product provenance are honest and correct. This not only makes things more open and accountable, but it also lowers the risk of fraud and fake goods, which makes customers trust and stay loyal. Augmented reality (AR) is another game-changing technology that is pushing Commerce 5.0 forward and changing how people interact with brands and products. AR lets people have more immersive shopping experiences by adding digital content on top of the real world. This lets people see how products will look in real life before they buy them. This not only makes people more interested, but it also lowers the chance of them going back and raises the conversion rate. AR-powered marketing campaigns and virtual try on experiences can also help people learn more about a brand and connect with it on a deeper level. As Commerce 5.0 continues to take shape, companies must find their way through the complicated sixth generation (6G) security environment. With 6G (Kirubasri, G. et al., 2021) networks set to offer speeds, latency, and device connectivity that have never been seen before, security issues become more important than ever. 6G ecosystems are more vulnerable than ever because they are connected to each other. There are new risks to data privacy, network integrity, and system resilience. To deal with these problems, companies need to take proactive security steps that are designed to work with 6G technology. To keep private information safe while it's being sent over fast 6G networks, you need advanced encryption (Kumar Pandey, B. et al., 2021) protocols and strong authentication systems. Leveraging artificial intelligence (AI) (Pandey, B. K., & Pandey, D., 2023) and machine learning (ML) (Saxena, A. et al., 2024) for threat detection and response can also help businesses find and fix security holes in real time, which lowers the damage from cyberattacks. As security threats change, it's important to make sure that the supply chain is resilient. Adding blockchain technology to the management of the supply chain can make the whole process more open, tracable, and trustworthy. Blockchain records every transaction and movement of goods in a way that can't be changed. This creates an auditable trail that helps businesses find and fix security problems like fake goods or unauthorized access.

1.1 Future-Proofing Businesses Importance

Future-proofing your company means getting ready for the opportunities and challenges that lie ahead, not just adjusting to the circumstances of the here and now. It entails acting proactively to make sure your company adapts to the quickly changing markets, technologies, and consumer preferences while staying resilient, competitive, and relevant. The ability to adapt to change is a strong argument for future-proofing your company. Change is a constant in the fast-paced business world of today. Your company's operations may be impacted by changes in the economy, in technology, and in customer behavior. Your company can reduce disruptions and maximize opportunities by future-proofing it so you can anticipate and respond to these changes more skillfully. Future-proofing guarantees the durability and viability of your company. Developing a long-lasting and sustainable business model is more important than simply surviving in the near term. You can position your company for long-term success and guarantee its viability and relevance for years to come by making investments in innovation, diversification, and strategic planning. Acquiring a competitive edge is another important benefit of future-proofing. Companies are better positioned to obtain a competitive edge in the market if they embrace innovation and foresee emerging trends. By introducing new goods or services, increasing operational effectiveness, and better satisfying changing customer needs, future-proofing helps you stay one step ahead of the competition. Proactive risk management is necessary to future-proof your company. There are many risks in the business world, from cybersecurity threats to economic downturns. The process of future-proofing entails determining possible risks and putting mitigation measures in place. Proactive risk management is crucial to shielding your company from unanticipated difficulties, whether that means increasing cash reserves, making investments in cybersecurity defenses, or diversifying your sources of income. Talented workers are drawn to organizations that exhibit a commitment to innovation and growth in an increasingly dynamic and competitive job market. You can attract top talent and cultivate employee engagement and loyalty by future-proofing your business. Putting money into training and development initiatives can also assist your staff in staying innovative and adjusting to shifting job requirements and technological advancements. Global trends, cultural shifts, and technology improvements all contribute to the continuous evolution of consumer preferences and expectations (Kychkin, A., et al., 2019). By future-proofing your business, you can prepare for these changes in the future and adjust your offerings to better serve your clients and enhance their experiences. You can sustain client loyalty and promote business expansion by remaining aware of the requirements and preferences of your customers. Businesses that had already embraced digital transformation and broadened their sources of income were better positioned to

1.2 Commerce Evolution

Throughout the course of human history, commerce has been a driving force behind the progression of human civilization. It has been responsible for both remarkable advancements and turbulent upheavals. The exchange of cultures, ideas, and ways of life is what commerce is all about; it is more than just the exchange of goods and services; it is what shapes the path that nations and civilizations take. Commerce has been an essential factor in the development of global events and interactions ever since the beginning of human history. It was the exchange of goods along ancient trade routes like the Silk Road that made it possible for cultures to spread and for economies to flourish across geographical regions. It was not enough for commerce to simply involve the acquisition of goods; it evolved into a medium through which information, technologies, and philosophies could be traded, thereby laying the groundwork for intercultural understanding and innovation. During the Age of Exploration, which was associated with the discovery of new lands and the establishment of trade networks that extended across the entire world, one of the most significant epochs in the development of commerce occurred. The search for new trade routes and sources of wealth was the impetus behind the expeditions of explorers such as Christopher Columbus and Vasco da Gama. This led to the colonization of faraway lands and the exchange of goods between geographically distinct continents. Mechanization of production processes and the rise of mass manufacturing were two of the hallmarks of the Industrial Revolution, which was a period of time that marked a significant turning point in the history of commerce. Innovations such as the steam engine and the assembly line were instrumental in revolutionizing various industries and making it possible to produce goods in mass quantities on a scale that had never been seen before. Businesses were no longer restricted to the confines of local markets; rather, they became increasingly globalized as a result of the fact that goods were produced in one region of the world and consumed in another region. Providing a standardized medium of exchange that facilitated trade and economic growth, the invention of money further revolutionized commerce by providing a tool for it. The shift from barter economies to monetary economies made it possible to increase the degree of specialization and division of labor, which ultimately resulted in an increase in the level of productivity and efficiency in commercial transactions. The landscape of commerce has been reshaped in the modern era as a result of technological advancements, which have enabled new interactions and modes of exchange. The proliferation of e-commerce and digital payment systems has brought about a significant change in the manner in which goods and services are purchased and sold, thereby presenting companies and customers with new opportunities. Access to commerce has been democratized as a result of the proliferation of mobile applications and online (Pandey, D. et al., 2021a) marketplaces, which have made it possible for individuals to undertake transactions from virtually any location on the planet. As a result of these advancements, various new challenges and complexities have emerged. Concerns about issues such as cybersecurity, data privacy, and ethical consumption have been heightened as a result of the growing interconnectedness of the World Economy. It is imperative that these challenges be addressed and that efforts be made toward a future that is more sustainable and equitable as commerce continues to undergo an extraordinary amount of change (Shah, K., et al., 2022).

II. KEY CHARACTERISTICS OF COMMERCE 5.0

The digitalization, connection, and innovation that define Commerce 5.0 are its defining characteristics are as shown in the figure 1. Some of the most important qualities include the seamless integration of technology into business models, the ability to provide tailored consumer experiences, decision-making that is driven by real-time data, and global reach. Businesses are able to thrive in this era of increased connectivity and evolving technologies because it places an emphasis on agility, adaptability, and sustainability.

1. *Hyper-personalization*: Commerce 5.0 ushers in a new era of customer-centricity, one in which personalization is of the utmost importance. It is possible for businesses to gain a comprehensive understanding of the preferences, behaviors, and purchase histories of individual customers by utilizing sophisticated data analytics and machine learning algorithms. The delivery of highly tailored

products, services, and marketing messages that resonate with customers on a personal level is made possible as a result of this. The use of hyper-personalization, which includes the recommendation of products based on previous purchases, the customization of marketing emails to match specific interests, and the provision of personalized discounts, all contribute to an increase in customer engagement, which in turn fosters loyalty and ultimately drives sales. Businesses use technology in Commerce 5.0 not only to understand their customers but also to anticipate their needs and exceed their expectations. This allows them to create interactions that are memorable and meaningful, which differentiates them from their competitors.

2. *Seamless Connectivity*: Commerce 5.0 is predicated (Tripathi, R. P. et al., 2023) on the idea of seamless connectivity, which is made possible by cutting-edge communication technologies such as 5G and beyond. Because of their high speed and low latency, these networks make it possible for businesses and customers to interact in real time, regardless of the location or device (Sharma, M. et al., 2022a) of the customer. Whether they are using a mobile app to browse products, making purchases using a smart speaker, or receiving personalized recommendations while they are in-store, customers anticipate a seamless and consistent experience across all touchpoints. When it comes to businesses, seamless connectivity means having the ability to interact with customers in real time, optimize inventory and supply chain management, and react quickly to shifting market dynamics. By embracing seamless connectivity, businesses have the ability to maintain their agility, competitiveness, and responsiveness to the requirements of today's consumers who are empowered by digital technology.
3. *Integrated Ecosystems*: Commerce 5.0 facilitates the establishment of integrated ecosystems, wherein businesses, customers, suppliers, and partners engage in seamless collaboration. By utilizing interconnected platforms and APIs, businesses have the ability to exchange data, optimize (Pandey, D. et al., 2021b) operations, and generate services that provide additional value. The integration facilitates a comprehensive approach to commerce, wherein interactions among various stakeholders are seamless and devoid of obstacles. Integrated ecosystems improve efficiency, agility, and innovation throughout the entire value chain by enabling smooth payments, managing supply chain logistics, and facilitating cross-channel marketing campaigns.
4. *Augmented Reality (AR) and Virtual Reality (VR)*: Technologies play a crucial role in influencing the trajectory of commerce by providing consumers with immersive and interactive experiences. In the context of Commerce 5.0, enterprises utilize augmented reality (AR) and virtual reality (VR) technologies to establish virtual showrooms, interactive product demonstrations, and improved shopping experiences. Consumers have the ability to visually perceive products within authentic settings, engage in virtual clothing trials, or navigate virtual environments prior to finalizing their purchasing choices. These technologies have the dual effect of increasing user engagement and minimizing obstacles to online shopping through the provision of a more immersive and sensory-oriented experience. Businesses can distinguish themselves, enhance brand interaction, and generate impactful experiences that resonate with consumers by integrating augmented reality (AR) and virtual reality (VR) into their commerce strategies.
5. *Internet of Things (IoT) Integration*: Devices (Sharma, M. et al., 2022b) are essential components of Commerce 5.0 systems, facilitating instantaneous monitoring, anticipatory analysis, and tailored interactions. Internet of Things (IoT) devices, ranging from intelligent appliances and wearables to interconnected vehicles and industrial sensors (Du John, H. V. et al., 2022), produce substantial quantities of data that enterprises can utilize to optimize their operations and improve customer ex-

periences. IoT-enabled devices (Khan, B. et al., 2021) have the capability to offer valuable insights into patterns (Govindaraj, V. et al., 2023) of product usage, predict maintenance requirements, and initiate automated reordering procedures. By incorporating Internet of Things (IoT) (Pramanik, S. et al., 2023) data into their commercial strategies, enterprises have the potential to access novel sources of income, enhance operational effectiveness, and provide inventive offerings that cater to the changing demands of customers.

6. *Sustainability and Ethical Consumption*: Commerce 5.0 places a heightened focus on sustainability and ethical consumption practices, aligning with the increasing apprehensions of socially aware consumers. There is a growing trend among businesses to embrace environmentally conscious practices, procure sustainable materials, and establish transparent supply chains in order to satisfy consumer expectations for ethically manufactured products. Furthermore, technology assumes a pivotal role in facilitating transparency and accountability across the supply chain, thereby empowering consumers to make shopping decisions that are better informed. By adopting sustainable practices and engaging in ethical consumption, businesses have the opportunity to not only comply with regulatory standards but also cultivate trust, bolster brand reputation, and access an expanding consumer base of environmentally aware individuals.

Figure 1. Features of Commerce 5.0

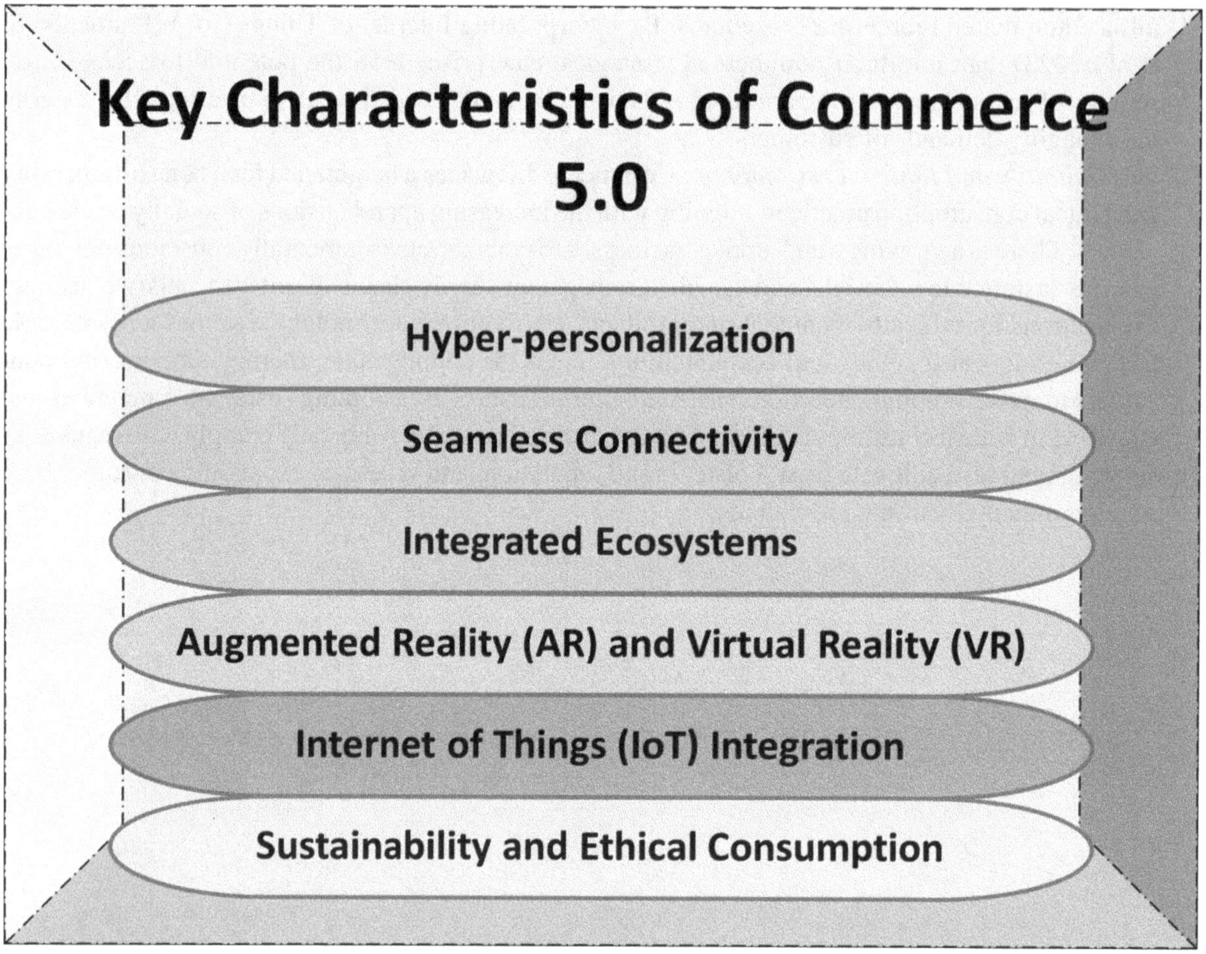

2.1 Tech's Role in Commerce 5.0

Technology is an essential component in the process of fostering innovation and transforming business models in order to conform to the constantly shifting landscape of commerce. Businesses are able to undergo digital transformation thanks in large part to the presence of technology. A transformation occurs in businesses when they adopt cutting-edge digital tools and platforms, which results in the automation of processes (Anand, R. et al., 2023) and the optimization of operations. Computing in the cloud, analytics on large amounts of data, and artificial intelligence (Pandey, D., & Pandey, B. K., 2022) all play an important part in that transformation. Using these technologies, businesses are able to access vast amounts of data, derive valuable insights from that data, and then use those insights to make educated decisions that improve performance and fuel expansion. Consider how this digital transformation can improve the efficiency of your operations, as well as maintain your company's agility and responsiveness to changes in the market. Technology also plays a significant part in the enhancement of customer experiences in the Commerce 5.0 environment. In order to acquire a comprehensive understanding of the preferences, behaviors, and purchasing patterns of their customers, businesses make use of technology. Through the utilization of customer relationship management (CRM) systems, data analytics, and marketing automation tools, businesses are able to customize their products, services, and marketing messages to cater to the specific requirements of each individual of their customers. By putting into action, a strategy that is centered on providing customers with individualized experiences, businesses have the ability to cultivate deeper connections with their customers, increase the level of involvement they have, and ultimately foster a sense of loyalty. In addition, technology gives businesses the ability to provide the customers with omni channel experiences that are seamless and integrated. This gives customers the opportunity to interact with brands through a variety of touch points and channels. It is of the utmost importance to ensure that customers have a consistent and seamless experience across all channels, whether they are accessing the product through the mobile app, browsing the website, or visiting the physical store. These expectations can be met by businesses through the use of technologies such as mobile commerce, social commerce, and voice commerce. This enhances customer satisfaction and fosters loyalty among customers. When it comes to the realm of business, technology is an essential component in the process of driving growth and change. In today's digital and interconnected landscape, it has the ability to empower businesses to adapt, evolve, and succeed.

III. EMERGENCE OF 6G SECURITY

3.1 6G Features and Risks

6G networks are expected to bring in a new era of connectivity with a plethora of cutting-edge features and functionalities are as shown in the figure 2. High-speed connectivity is the most important of these. With transmission rates (Devasenapathy, D. et al., 2024) predicted to exceed terabits per second (Tbps), 6G networks are expected to provide a major improvement in data transfer speeds compared to its predecessors. Due to the extremely fast and efficient connectivity, customers will be able to download huge files, stream video in high definition, and communicate in real time. Ultra-low latency is another essential component of 6G networks. 6G networks will make it possible to communicate and analyze data almost instantly, with reaction times as little as a few microseconds. For applications like remote surgery, driverless cars, and virtual reality gaming that demand real-time interactions, this extremely low latency is essential. 6G networks will open up new avenues for technical growth and innovation in a variety of industries by reducing data transmission delays (Webster, C., & Ivanov, S., 2020).

Figure 2. 6G features

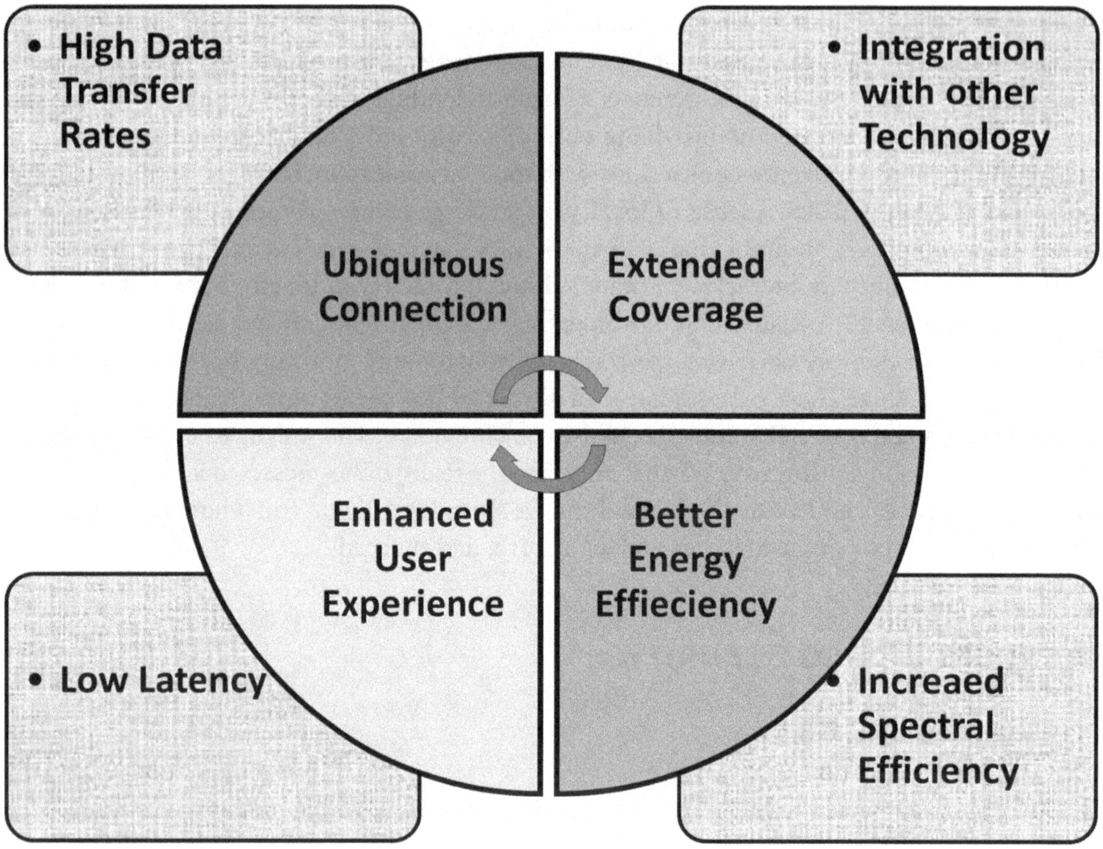

The Internet of Things (IoT) (Vinodhini, V. et al., 2022) ecosystem's expanding number of internet-connected devices and sensors will also be accommodated by 6G networks, which are anticipated to handle large device connectivity. Sixth-generation (6G) networks will offer the bandwidth and capacity required to enable smooth communication and data exchange across billions of devices, given the explosion of smart gadgets and sensors in homes, communities, and corporations. Due to the widespread device connectivity, smart cities, self-sufficient infrastructure, and interdependent ecosystems that improve productivity, sustainability, and quality of life will all be made possible. We expect 6G networks to provide increased resilience and durability together with ultra-low latency and ultra-high speed connectivity. In the event of network congestion or outages, 6G networks will be able to self-optimize and self-heal thanks to sophisticated network architecture and protocols. For mission-critical applications like telemedicine, industrial automation, and autonomous vehicles where delays or unavailability could have serious repercussions this enhanced reliability will be essential. Advanced security features are also anticipated to be included in 6G networks in order to safeguard data integrity and confidentiality and defend against cyberattacks. Businesses and network operators now place a high premium on security due to the increase in cyberattacks and the proliferation of linked devices. Network infrastructure security and dependability will be reinforced by 6G networks, which will use authentication, encryption (Pandey, D. et al., 2021c), and other security methods to protect data and stop illegal access. Environmental sustainability is a significant component of 6G networks. Energy-efficient and environmentally friendly technology development is becoming more and more important as worries about climate change and energy use grow. By optimizing network architecture, using renewable energy sources, and reducing environmental impact, 6G networks will place a high priority on energy efficiency and sustainability (Attaran, M., 2017). The implementation of 6G networks is expected to mitigate climate change and foster a more sustainable future by decreasing energy consumption and carbon emissions on a worldwide scale. Virtual reality (VR) and augmented reality (AR) technologies are also anticipated to enable immersive and interactive experiences via 6G networks. Users will be able to engage in real-time interactions with virtual objects, engage in remote gaming and collaboration, and experience immersive virtual reality environments thanks to ultra-low latency and ultra-high speed connectivity. Immersion experiences bring new opportunities for creativity, learning, and social interaction that will transform entertainment, education, training, and other fields (Rutter, P., & Keirstead, J., 2012).

3.2 Security Challenges

With the emergence of 6G networks, there are both notable security challenges and exciting opportunities that arise as the technology landscape continues to evolve. Having a clear understanding of these issues is essential to guarantee the security and reliability of data transmission and communication. Here are some important security considerations and potential advantages related to 6G networks:

1. *Dynamic Threat Landscape*: The ever-evolving nature of the threat landscape poses a substantial obstacle in ensuring the security of 6G networks. Cyber enemies are constantly adapting their strategies, methods, and protocols to take advantage of weaknesses and carry out advanced assaults. The advent of 6G networks brings forth novel technologies and functionalities, like edge computing and AI-driven services. This also gives rise to fresh avenues for cyber attacks, as they present new attack surfaces and potential entry points. In order to tackle this challenge, it is imperative for enterprises to embrace a proactive and adaptable strategy towards cybersecurity. This entails utilizing threat intelligence, machine learning, and automation to promptly identify and counter emerging threats.
2. *Complexity of Network Architecture*: Security practitioners have issues due to the intricate nature of 6G network architecture, which involves a wide range of networked devices, applications, and services. 6G networks exhibit distinct features like as distributed computing, edge computing, and software-defined networking (Kirubasri, G. et al., 2022), which give rise to novel security problems and difficulties, in contrast to conventional centralized designs. To ensure the security of this intricate system, it is necessary to adopt a comprehensive strategy that incorporates security measures throughout the whole process of designing, developing, and operating 6G networks. This includes implementing network segmentation, access controls, and encryption to safeguard data and reduce potential threats (Pandey, B. K. et al., 2023a).
3. *Privacy and Data Protection*: The increasing prevalence of interconnected devices and sensors within 6G networks gives rise to apprehensions regarding the safeguarding of privacy and data. The accumulation and transmission of extensive quantities of sensitive data, encompassing personal information and behavioral data, by these devices pose a potential threat of unauthorized access, data breaches, and infringements upon privacy. Organizations must establish strong data governance frameworks, encryption systems (Pandey, B. K. et al., 2022), and user consent procedures to safeguard sensitive

information and adhere to legislative obligations like GDPR and CCPA in order to guarantee privacy and data protection.

4. *Supply Chain Risks*: The successful implementation of 6G networks is contingent upon a sophisticated supply chain network that encompasses a diverse range of hardware components, software applications, and service providers procured from several vendors and suppliers around the globe. This phenomenon presents potential supply chain vulnerabilities, such as the presence of counterfeit components, malicious software, and reliance on third-party entities, which have the potential to undermine the integrity and security of 6G networks. In order to address these potential risks, it is imperative for companies to adopt supply chain security practices. These practices encompass the evaluation of suppliers, the execution of risk assessments, and the implementation of supply chain resilience measures. These measures are crucial for safeguarding the reliability and integrity of the supply chain system.
5. *Opportunities for Innovation*: Although 6G networks pose security issues, they also provide prospects for innovation and progress in cybersecurity. Zero-trust security, quantum-resistant encryption, and decentralized identification are technologies that provide innovative methods to improve security and resilience in 6G networks. Organizations may enhance their security stance, safeguard against emerging risks, and establish confidence in the reliability and security of 6G networks by adopting these cutting-edge solutions.
6. *Collaborative Security Initiatives*: The resolution of security concerns pertaining to 6G networks necessitates the establishment of collaborative and cooperative efforts among many stakeholders, encompassing government agencies, industry representatives, academic institutions, and cybersecurity experts. Collaborative security initiatives, such as platforms for sharing information, exchanges of threat intelligence, and collaborations between public and commercial entities, facilitate effective collaboration, knowledge sharing, and coordinated responses to cyber threats among companies. Through collaboration, stakeholders may bolster the robustness and safeguarding of 6G networks, alleviate vulnerabilities, and defend against cyber hazards in an ever more interconnected and digitalized society.

IV. FUTURE-PROOFING STRATEGIES

4.1 Adapting to 6G

a) Speed and Connectivity

Businesses in a variety of industries stand to gain a great deal from utilizing the high-speed connectivity provided by 6G networks. The capacity to perform real-time data analytics is one important benefit. Organizations are able to instantly gather, process, and analyze enormous volumes of data thanks to ultra-high-speed networking. This capability is transforming industries including manufacturing, healthcare (Tareke, S. A. et al., 2022), and finance by enabling real-time insights and decision-making. Healthcare practitioners may remotely monitor patients' vital signs (Pandey, D. et al., 2023) and swiftly address emergencies, financial institutions can execute trades in milliseconds based on real-time market data, and manufacturers can optimize production processes in reaction to real-time swings in supply and demand. Improved communication and cooperation between people and organizations are made possible by high-speed connectivity. 6G networks enable low-latency remote collaboration, virtual meetings, and high-definition video conferencing. This promotes creativity, productivity, and efficiency by facilitating easy communication and cooperation amongst geographically separated teams. The adoption of immersive technologies like virtual reality (VR) and augmented reality (AR) is made possible by fast internet. With these technologies, users may engage in virtual meetings, training sessions, and interactive experiences that have never been more realistic and immersive. By facilitating smooth connectivity and data exchange across billions of linked devices and sensors, high-speed connectivity strengthens the Internet of Things (IoT) ecosystem. IoT devices (Menon, V. et al., 2022) may transport data at extremely fast speeds via 6G networks, enabling real-time automation, control, and monitoring across a range of applications and sectors (Ghobakhloo, M., & Fathi, M., 2021). Through linked infrastructure and Internet of Things-enabled sensors, smart cities can, for instance, use high-speed connectivity to optimize energy use, monitor traffic patterns, and improve public safety. Similarly, high-speed connectivity-enabled supply chain optimization, predictive maintenance, and real-time asset monitoring can be advantageous for the retail, logistics, and agricultural sectors (Malhotra, P. et al., 2021). The media and entertainment sector, high-speed connectivity creates new avenues for content supply and consumption. With 6G networks, users can enjoy immersive gaming experiences, watch high-definition videos, and take part in live events with the least amount of latency and buffering. This improves user experience and opens up new sources of income for distributors and content creators. Additionally, the adoption of cutting-edge technology like virtual reality entertainment, cloud gaming, and streaming-based gaming services is made possible by fast internet, completely changing how consumers engage with digital material and entertainment (Di Silvestre, M. L. et al., 2021).

b) Edge Computing and IoT

Utilizing edge computing and IoT capabilities, along with the fast connectivity provided by 6G networks, offers a significant chance for enterprises in several industries to undergo a profound transformation. Edge computing entails the processing of data in close proximity to its origin, as opposed to depending on centralized data centers. When edge computing is integrated with the low-latency and high-bandwidth capabilities of 6G networks, its capabilities are further enhanced. By strategically placing edge computing nodes at the periphery of a network, companies can effectively evaluate and respond to data in real-time, thereby facilitating expedited decision-making processes and diminishing dependence on centralized infrastructure. In the industrial industry, the integration of edge computing and 6G connection enables the ability to monitor equipment performance in real-time, perform predictive maintenance, and ensure quality control. This integration results in enhanced operational efficiency and decreased periods of inactivity. Interconnected Internet of Things (IoT) devices, possessing the ability to gather and transmit data, assume a pivotal function across diverse sectors including healthcare (Abdulkarim, Y. I. et al., 2024), agriculture, transportation (Sahani, K. et al., 2023), and smart cities. The introduction of 6G networks enables IoT devices to communicate with greater efficiency and reliability, owing to its advanced features such as ultra-low latency and extensive device connectivity capabilities. In the healthcare field (Pandey, B. K. et al., 2011), wearable Internet of Things (IoT) devices that are integrated with biosensors have the capability to consistently monitor the vital signs of patients and transmit data to healthcare providers in real-time. This allows for remote patient monitoring and the early identification of health problems. Similarly, in the field of agriculture, Internet of Things (IoT) sensors that are integrated into soil can offer immediate information on the levels of moisture, temperature, and nutrient content. This allows farmers to enhance crop yields by optimizing irrigation and fertilizer consumption. Organizations can leverage edge computing and IoT capabilities, along with the high-speed connectivity provided by 6G networks, to access new possibilities for innovation, efficiency, and cost reduction in several fields. The integration of various technologies, such as real-time monitoring and control of industrial processes, optimization of supply chain logistics, and enhancement of customer experiences through personalized services, has significant potential to facilitate digital transformation and generate value within the dynamic digital environment. As enterprises increasingly adopt the capabilities of 6G networks, the incorporation of edge computing and IoT will have a crucial impact on the future of business and society. This integration will facilitate new applications, enhance operational effectiveness, and stimulate economic expansion (Mourtzis, D., et al., 2021).

4.2 Enhancing Security

a) Advanced Encryption

Ensuring the security and privacy of data transmitted over 6G networks is of utmost importance, and implementing advanced encryption protocols plays a vital role in achieving this. These protocols are essential for maintaining secure communication (Pandey, B. K. et al., 2023b) and safeguarding sensitive information from unauthorized access, interception, and tampering. To successfully implement advanced encryption protocols in the context of 6G networks, organizations need to adopt a comprehensive approach that includes different encryption techniques and secure key management practices. End-to-end encryption is a crucial element in ensuring the security of data transmission over 6G networks. With the implementation of end-to-end encryption, data is safeguarded and kept private from start to finish. By encrypting data at its source and decrypting it only at its intended destination, the confidentiality and security of the data are maintained throughout its entire journey. Utilizing strong encryption algorithms like AES or RSA, along with implementing secure key management practices (Pandey, B. K. et al., 2021), is crucial for ensuring end-to-end encryption. By implementing these measures, organizations can enhance the protection of sensitive information, preventing eavesdropping and unauthorized access. This will strengthen data security and privacy. With the ever-changing threat landscape, organizations need to be mindful of the potential risks that come with emerging technologies, like quantum computing. With the rise of quantum computers, it is crucial to consider the potential vulnerabilities that traditional encryption algorithms may face. As a result, the adoption of quantum-resistant cryptography becomes imperative. These cryptographic techniques utilize mathematical principles that are thought to be resistant to quantum attacks, guaranteeing security in the long run as technology progresses. In addition, post-quantum encryption algorithms provide advanced security against both classical and quantum threats, ensuring organizations have strong protection for their sensitive data in the age of 6G networks. Homomorphic encryption offers a fresh perspective on safeguarding data processing within the realm of 6G networks. With the ability to perform computations on encrypted data without the need for decryption, homomorphic encryption ensures the utmost confidentiality and privacy of sensitive information. With this solution, data can be processed securely in environments that are not trusted, like cloud computing platforms or edge devices, all while ensuring data confidentiality and privacy. Just like a systems analyst, zero-knowledge proofs provide a cryptographic method to verify the integrity and authenticity of transactions or identities without disclosing the underlying data. This enhances privacy and trust in transactions and communications over 6G networks (Zhang, N., et al., 2021). Ensuring proper key management is essential for successfully implementing advanced encryption protocols. Organizations need to implement strong measures to generate, store, and distribute encryption keys in order to safeguard them from unauthorized access or compromise. Hardware security modules (HSMs), key derivation techniques, and secure key exchange protocols are essential for ensuring the protection of encryption keys at every stage of their lifespan. Through the implementation of robust key management practices, organizations can safeguard the integrity and confidentiality of encryption keys, thus enhancing the overall security of their 6G networks.

b) AI for Threats

Utilizing advanced technology for threat detection and response is crucial in strengthening cybersecurity measures within the framework of 6G networks. AI technologies, such as machine learning and cognitive computing, have the ability to analyze large datasets, identify patterns, and detect anomalies that may indicate cyber threats. Utilizing AI for threat detection requires the implementation of advanced algorithms (Bessant, Y. A. et al., 2023) that can carefully examine network traffic, system logs, and user behavior in order to identify any deviations from typical patterns. Through the analysis of past data and continuous monitoring of network activity, these AI algorithms are able to detect and alert on any suspicious activities, including unauthorized access attempts, unusual data transfers, or the presence of malware. By taking a proactive approach, organizations can quickly detect potential threats and take immediate action to minimize risks before they become more serious. AI enables the automation of threat detection and response processes, enabling organizations to optimize their cybersecurity operations and effectively address threats. Through the automation of routine tasks like data analysis, incident triage, and response orchestration, AI-powered security systems (Deepa, R. et al., 2022) enable human resources to dedicate their efforts to more strategic initiatives and high-priority tasks. In addition, security solutions powered by AI have the capability to adapt and grow over time. They can learn from previous incidents and constantly enhance their ability to identify and address new threats. With its adaptive capability, this technology boosts the effectiveness of cybersecurity defenses, allowing organizations to proactively combat ever-changing cyber threats in the fast-paced world of 6G networks. With the help of advanced AI-powered threat intelligence platforms, organizations can acquire valuable insights into the strategies and methods used by cyber adversaries. This empowers them to proactively anticipate and protect against potential attacks. In addition, AI (Revathi, T. K. et al., 2022) can help facilitate the sharing of threat intelligence among organizations and security communities, encouraging collaborative efforts to collectively combat cyber threats. By adopting a collaborative approach, organizations can strengthen their cyber resilience and improve their ability to detect, respond to, and mitigate cyber threats in the interconnected ecosystem of 6G networks (Karnouskos, S., & De Holanda, T. N. et al., 2009).

4.3 Supply Chain Resilience

a) Diversification and Flexibility

Diversification and adaptability are critical factors for organizations attempting to navigate the intricate dynamics of the continuously developing 6G network environment. Adopting diversification involves distributing risks across a range of technologies, markets, and revenue sources in order to mitigate reliance on any one factor. This can be accomplished by integrating a variety of technologies, including wireless, fiber optic, and satellite technologies, into an organization's infrastructure, thereby assuring robust and dependable connectivity. In addition, the act of venturing into untapped markets and customer segments offers a safeguard against regulatory modifications and market volatility, thereby cultivating adaptability in the midst of competitive forces or economic uncertainties. Implementing a diversification strategy enables organizations to uphold stability and foster expansion through the utilization of a wide range of revenue streams and clientele, thereby protecting against unanticipated disruptions and obstacles. Flexibility serves as a valuable complement to diversification as it empowers organizations to promptly adjust to changing technological advancements, market conditions, and consumer preferences. It is imperative for organizations to foster agility within their operational processes and adopt iterative methodologies when it comes to de new business models. Agile methodologies and digital technologies enable organizations to rapidly test and evaluate new products, services, and distribution channels. This empowers them to maintain a competitive edge and exploit emergent opportunities within the ever-changing domain of 6G networks. In addition, business models that are adaptable permit organizations to swiftly change course in reaction to shifting market conditions, capitalizing on fresh sources of income and optimizing the distribution of resources to enhance productivity and financial gains. Organizations to efficiently implement and oversee network infrastructure, introduce ground breaking services, and deliver timely customer assistance, operational agility is of the utmost importance. Businesses have the potential to optimize processes, increase output, and elevate client contentment through the implementation of digital transformation initiatives and lean principles. Agile operations empower organizations to promptly address supply chain disruptions, customer demands, and competitive pressures, thereby guaranteeing adaptability and resilience within the rapidly evolving landscape of 6G networks. Operational flexibility enables organizations to adjust their operational scale in response to demand fluctuations, thereby optimizing resource allocation and ensuring sustained profitability and competitiveness.

CONCLUSION

The revolutionary effects of Commerce 5.0 in the developing context of 6G networks. We have outlined the salient features of Commerce 5.0, highlighting its dependence on digital innovation, high-speed connection, and technical convergence, via the prism of historical evolution. Simultaneously, our analysis of the 6G security environment has shed light on the intricacies and difficulties presented by new dangers and possibilities. Practical methods for companies to future-proof their operations in this changing environment by combining these ideas. Developing robust supply chains, embracing edge computing and IoT technologies, boosting security protocols, and utilizing high-speed internet are all essential tactics for innovation and adaptation. Furthermore, our analysis emphasizes how important it is to strategically invest in cybersecurity and technology in order to be proactive in navigating the complexity of Commerce 5.0 in the context of 6G networks. Practical advice and insights to help them deal with the challenges posed by Commerce 5.0 and take advantage of the ever-changing environment surrounding 6G networks. Businesses can position themselves for success and resilience in the future digital economy by adopting these tactics and utilizing emerging technology.

REFERENCES

Abdulkarim, Y. I., Awl, H. N., Muhammadsharif, F. F., Saeed, S. R., Sidiq, K. R., Khasraw, S. S., Dong, J., Pandey, B. K., & Pandey, D. (2024). Metamaterial-based sensors loaded corona-shaped resonator for COVID-19 detection by using microwave techniques. *Plasmonics*, 19(2), 595–610. 10.1007/s11468-023-02007-4

Anand, R., Khan, B., Nassa, V. K., Pandey, D., Dhabliya, D., Pandey, B. K., & Dadheech, P. (2023). Hybrid convolutional neural network (CNN) for kennedy space center hyperspectral image. *Aerospace Systems*, 6(1), 71–78. 10.1007/s42401-022-00168-4

Anand, R., Lakshmi, S. V., Pandey, D., & Pandey, B. K. (2024). An enhanced ResNet-50 deep learning model for arrhythmia detection using electrocardiogram biomedical indicators. *Evolving Systems*, 15(1), 83–97. 10.1007/s12530-023-09559-0

Attaran, M. (2017). The internet of things: Limitless opportunities for business and society. *Journal of Strategic Innovation and Sustainability*, 12(1), 11.

Bessant, Y. A., Jency, J. G., Sagayam, K. M., Jone, A. A. A., Pandey, D., & Pandey, B. K. (2023). Improved parallel matrix multiplication using Strassen and Urdhvatiryagbhyam method. *CCF Transactions on High Performance Computing*, 5(2), 102–115. 10.1007/s42514-023-00149-9

David, S., Duraipandian, K., Chandrasekaran, D., Pandey, D., Sindhwani, N., & Pandey, B. K. (2023). Impact of blockchain in healthcare system. In *Unleashing the Potentials of blockchain technology for healthcare industries* (pp. 37–57). Academic Press. 10.1016/B978-0-323-99481-1.00004-3

Deepa, R., Anand, R., Pandey, D., Pandey, B. K., & Karki, B. (2022). Comprehensive performance analysis of classifiers in diagnosis of epilepsy. *Mathematical Problems in Engineering*, 2022, 2022. 10.1155/2022/1559312

Devasenapathy, D., Madhumathy, P., Umamaheshwari, R., Pandey, B. K., & Pandey, D. (2024). Transmission-efficient grid-based synchronized model for routing in wireless sensor networks using Bayesian compressive sensing. *SN Computer Science*, 5(1), 1–11.

Di Silvestre, M. L., Favuzza, S., Sanseverino, E. R., & Zizzo, G. (2018). How Decarbonization, Digitalization and Decentralization are changing key power infrastructures. *Renewable & Sustainable Energy Reviews*, 93, 483–498. 10.1016/j.rser.2018.05.068

Du John, H. V., Jose, T., Jone, A. A. A., Sagayam, K. M., Pandey, B. K., & Pandey, D. (2022). Polarization insensitive circular ring resonator based perfect metamaterial absorber design and simulation on a silicon substrate. *Silicon*, 14(14), 9009–9020. 10.1007/s12633-021-01645-9

Ghobakhloo, M., & Fathi, M. (2021). Industry 4.0 and opportunities for energy sustainability. *Journal of Cleaner Production*, 295, 126427. 10.1016/j.jclepro.2021.126427

Govindaraj, V., Dhanasekar, S., Martinsagayam, K., Pandey, D., Pandey, B. K., & Nassa, V. K. (2023). Low-power test pattern generator using modified LFSR. *Aerospace Systems*, 1-8.

Iyyanar, P., Anand, R., Shanthi, T., Nassa, V. K., Pandey, B. K., George, A. S., & Pandey, D. (2023). A real-time smart sewage cleaning UAV assistance system using IoT. In *Handbook of Research on Data-Driven Mathematical Modeling in Smart Cities* (pp. 24–39). IGI Global.

Karnouskos, S., & De Holanda, T. N. (2009, November). Simulation of a smart grid city with software agents. In *2009 Third UKSim European Symposium on Computer Modeling and Simulation* (pp. 424-429). IEEE. 10.1109/EMS.2009.53

Khan, B., Hasan, A., Pandey, D., Ventayen, R. J. M., Pandey, B. K., & Gowwrii, G. (2021). Fusion of datamining and artificial intelligence in prediction of hazardous road accidents. In *Machine learning and iot for intelligent systems and smart applications* (pp. 201–223). CRC Press. 10.1201/9781003194415-12

Kirubasri, G., Sankar, S., Pandey, D., Pandey, B. K., Nassa, V. K., & Dadheech, P. (2022). Software-defined networking-based Ad hoc networks routing protocols. In *Software defined networking for Ad Hoc networks* (pp. 95–123). Springer International Publishing. 10.1007/978-3-030-91149-2_5

Kirubasri, G., Sankar, S., Pandey, D., Pandey, B. K., Singh, H., & Anand, R. (2021, September). A recent survey on 6G vehicular technology, applications and challenges. In *2021 9th International Conference on Reliability, Infocom Technologies and Optimization (Trends and Future Directions)(ICRITO)* (pp. 1-5). IEEE.

Kumar Pandey, B., Pandey, D., Nassa, V. K., Ahmad, T., Singh, C., George, A. S., & Wakchaure, M. A. (2021). Encryption and steganography-based text extraction in IoT using the EWCTS optimizer. *Imaging Science Journal*, 69(1-4), 38–56. 10.1080/13682199.2022.2146885

Kychkin, A., Deryabin, A., Neganova, E., & Markvirer, V. (2019, July). IoT-based energy management assistant architecture design. In *2019 IEEE 21st Conference on Business Informatics (CBI)* (Vol. 1, pp. 522-530). IEEE. 10.1109/CBI.2019.00067

Malhotra, P., Pandey, D., Pandey, B. K., & Patra, P. M. (2021). Managing agricultural supply chains in COVID-19 lockdown. *International Journal of Quality and Innovation*, 5(2), 109–118. 10.1504/IJQI.2021.117181

Menon, V., Pandey, D., Khosla, D., Kaur, M., Vashishtha, H. K., George, A. S., & Pandey, B. K. (2022). A Study on COVID–19, Its Origin, Phenomenon, Variants, and IoT-Based Framework to Detect the Presence of Coronavirus. In *IoT Based Smart Applications* (pp. 1–13). Springer International Publishing.

Mourtzis, D., Angelopoulos, J., & Panopoulos, N. (2021). A collaborative approach on energy-based offered services: Energy 4.0 ecosystems. *Procedia CIRP*, 104, 1638–1643. 10.1016/j.procir.2021.11.276

Pandey, B. K., Mane, D., Nassa, V. K. K., Pandey, D., Dutta, S., Ventayen, R. J. M., & Rastogi, R. (2021). Secure text extraction from complex degraded images by applying steganography and deep learning. In *Multidisciplinary approach to modern digital steganography* (pp. 146–163). IGI Global. 10.4018/978-1-7998-7160-6.ch007

Pandey, B. K., & Pandey, D. (2023). Parametric optimization and prediction of enhanced thermoelectric performance in co-doped CaMnO3 using response surface methodology and neural network. *Journal of Materials Science Materials in Electronics*, 34(21), 1589. 10.1007/s10854-023-10954-1

Pandey, B. K., Pandey, D., & Agarwal, A. (2022). Encrypted information transmission by enhanced steganography and image transformation. *International Journal of Distributed Artificial Intelligence*, 14(1), 1–14. 10.4018/IJDAI.297110

Pandey, B. K., Pandey, D., Alkhafaji, M. A., Güneşer, M. T., & Şeker, C. (2023a). A reliable transmission and extraction of textual information using keyless encryption, steganography, and deep algorithm with cuckoo optimization. In *Micro-Electronics and Telecommunication Engineering: Proceedings of 6th ICMETE 2022* (pp. 629–636). Springer Nature Singapore. 10.1007/978-981-19-9512-5_57

Pandey, B. K., Pandey, D., Gupta, A., Nassa, V. K., Dadheech, P., & George, A. S. (2023b). Secret data transmission using advanced morphological component analysis and steganography. In *Role of data-intensive distributed computing systems in designing data solutions* (pp. 21–44). Springer International Publishing. 10.1007/978-3-031-15542-0_2

Pandey, B. K., Pandey, S. K., & Pandey, D. (2011). A survey of bioinformatics applications on parallel architectures. *International Journal of Computer Applications*, 23(4), 21–25. 10.5120/2877-3744

Pandey, D., Hasan, A., Pandey, B. K., Lelisho, M. E., George, A. H., & Shahul, A. (2023). COVID-19 epidemic anxiety, mental stress, and sleep disorders in developing country university students. *CSI Transactions on ICT*, 11(2), 119–127. 10.1007/s40012-023-00383-0

Pandey, D., Nassa, V. K., Jhamb, A., Mahto, D., Pandey, B. K., George, A. H., & Bandyopadhyay, S. K. (2021a). An integration of keyless encryption, steganography, and artificial intelligence for the secure transmission of stego images. In *Multidisciplinary approach to modern digital steganography* (pp. 211–234). IGI Global. 10.4018/978-1-7998-7160-6.ch010

Pandey, D., Ogunmola, G. A., Enbeyle, W., Abdullahi, M., Pandey, B. K., & Pramanik, S. (2021b). COVID-19: A framework for effective delivering of online classes during lockdown. *Human Arenas*, 1-15.

Pandey, D., & Pandey, B. K. (2022). An efficient deep neural network with adaptive galactic swarm optimization for complex image text extraction. In *Process mining techniques for pattern recognition* (pp. 121–137). CRC Press. 10.1201/9781003169550-10

Pandey, D., Pandey, B. K., & Wairya, S. (2021c). Hybrid deep neural network with adaptive galactic swarm optimization for text extraction from scene images. *Soft Computing*, 25(2), 1563–1580. 10.1007/s00500-020-05245-4

Pandey, J. K., Jain, R., Dilip, R., Kumbhkar, M., Jaiswal, S., Pandey, B. K., & Pandey, D. (2022). Investigating role of iot in the development of smart application for security enhancement. In *IoT Based Smart Applications* (pp. 219–243). Springer International Publishing.

Pramanik, S., Pandey, D., Joardar, S., Niranjanamurthy, M., Pandey, B. K., & Kaur, J. (2023, October). An overview of IoT privacy and security in smart cities. In *AIP Conference Proceedings* (Vol. 2495, No. 1). AIP Publishing 10.1063/5.0123511

Revathi, T. K., Sathiyabhama, B., Sankar, S., Pandey, D., Pandey, B. K., & Dadeech, P. (2022). An intelligent model for coronary heart disease diagnosis. In *Networking Technologies in Smart Healthcare* (pp. 309–327). CRC Press. 10.1201/9781003239888-15

Rutter, P., & Keirstead, J. (2012). A brief history and the possible future of urban energy systems. *Energy Policy*, 50, 72–80. 10.1016/j.enpol.2012.03.072

Sahani, K., Khadka, S. S., Sahani, S. K., Pandey, B. K., & Pandey, D. (2023). A possible underground roadway for transportation facilities in Kathmandu Valley: A racking deformation of underground rectangular struct es. *Engineering Reports*, 12821. 10.1002/eng2.12821

Saxena, A., Agarwal, A., Pandey, B. K., & Pandey, D. (2024). Examination of the Criticality of Customer Segmentation Using Unsupervised Learning Methods. *Circular Economy and Sustainability*, 1–14. 10.1007/s43615-023-00336-4

Saxena, A., Sharma, N. K., Pandey, D., & Pandey, B. K. (2021). Influence of tourists satisfaction on future behavioral intentions with special reference to desert triangle of Rajasthan. *Augmented Human Research*, 6(1), 13. 10.1007/s41133-021-00052-4

Shah, K., Chadotra, S., Tanwar, S., Gupta, R., & Kumar, N. (2022). Blockchain for IoV in 6G environment: Review solutions and challenges. *Cluster Computing*, 25(3), 1927–1955. 10.1007/s10586-021-03492-0

Sharma, M., Pandey, D., Khosla, D., Goyal, S., Pandey, B. K., & Gupta, A. K. (2022a). Design of a GaN-based Flip Chip Light Emitting Diode (FC-LED) with au Bumps & Thermal Analysis with different sizes and adhesive materials for performance considerations. *Silicon*, 14(12), 7109–7120. 10.1007/s12633-021-01457-x

Sharma, M., Pandey, D., Palta, P., & Pandey, B. K. (2022b). Design and power dissipation consideration of PFAL CMOS V/S conventional CMOS based 2: 1 multiplexer and full adder. *Silicon*, 14(8), 4401–4410. 10.1007/s12633-021-01221-1

Sharma, S., Pandey, B. K., Pandey, D., Anand, R., Sharma, A., & Saini, S. (2023, March). Character Recognition Technique Implementation for Complicated Deteriorated Scene. In *2023 6th International Conference on Information Systems and Computer Networks (ISCON)* (pp. 1-4). IEEE. 10.1109/ISCON57294.2023.10112185

Tareke, S. A., Lelisho, M. E., Hassen, S. S., Seid, A. A., Jemal, S. S., Teshale, B. M., & Pandey, B. K. (2022). The prevalence and predictors of depressive, anxiety, and stress symptoms among Tepi town residents during the COVID-19 pandemic lockdown in Ethiopia. *Journal of Racial and Ethnic Health Disparities*, 1–13.35028903

Tripathi, R. P., Sharma, M., Gupta, A. K., Pandey, D., Pandey, B. K., Shahul, A., & George, A. H. (2023). Timely prediction of diabetes by means of machine learning practices. *Augmented Human Research*, 8(1), 1. 10.1007/s41133-023-00062-4

Vinodhini, V., Kumar, M. S., Sankar, S., Pandey, D., Pandey, B. K., & Nassa, V. K. (2022). IoT-based early forest fire detection using MLP and AROC method. *International Journal of Global Warming*, 27(1), 55–70. 10.1504/IJGW.2022.122794

Webster, C., & Ivanov, S. (2020). *Robotics, artificial intelligence, and the evolving nature of work.* Springer International Publishing. 10.1007/978-3-030-08277-2_8

Zhang, N., Sun, Q., Yang, L., & Li, Y. (2021). Event-triggered distributed hybrid control scheme for the integrated energy system. *IEEE Transactions on Industrial Informatics*, 18(2), 835–846. 10.1109/TII.2021.3075718

Chapter 9
E-Commerce Resilience Strategies for Mitigating 6G Security Threats

S. Sureshkumar
P.A. College of Engineering and Technology, India

R. Thamilselvan
Department of Management Studies, Sathyabama Institute of Science and Technology, Chennai, India

K. Usha Rani
Department of English, Koneru Lakshmiah Education Foundation, Vaddeswaram, India

Vellayan Srinivasan
Department of Master of Business Administration, S.A. Engineering College, Chennai, India

A. N. Arularasan
Department of Artificial Intelligence and Data Science, Panimalar Engineering College, Chennai, India

B. Yuvasri
R.M.K. College of Engineering and Technology, Puduvoyal, India

Pankaj Dadheech Dadheech
https://orcid.org/0000-0001-5783-1989
Swami Keshvanand Institute of Technology, Management, and Gramothan, India

ABSTRACT

With e-commerce constantly changing, the introduction of 6G technology presents both possibilities and difficulties. This chapter examines how e-commerce and 6G intersect, emphasizing how important it is to have strong security measures in place to counter new threats. The chapter starts with a summary of the 6G era's e-commerce environment and looks at the security issues that come with it before going into detail about the particular risks that 6G technology poses to e-commerce platforms. After that, the chapter turns its attention to methods for making e-commerce platforms more resilient to these attacks. It looks at how important it is to strengthen access controls and authentication, encrypt data for better security, and create effective disaster recovery plans.

DOI: 10.4018/979-8-3693-7421-4.ch009

I. INTRODUCTION

As we enter the 6G era, e-commerce is a key component of the digital economy (Swapna, H. R. et al., 2023), transforming how customers engage with companies and changing the face of international trade. The advent of 6G networks, which are distinguished by incredibly high speeds, minimal latency, and widespread connectivity, presents an opportunity for e-commerce to achieve unprecedented levels of innovation and productivity. The buying and selling of goods and services through the internet is referred to as electronic commerce, or e-commerce. Ever since its inception, e-commerce has grown at an exponential rate thanks to technological advancements, shifting consumer preferences, and the growing digitization of daily life. These days, e-commerce includes a broad variety of transactions, such as digital downloads, subscription services, and online retail purchases (George, W. K. et al., 2023). With 6G networks coming online, many of the drawbacks of earlier wireless technology (Devasenapathy, D. et al., 2024) generations will be removed, which should hasten the expansion and development of e-commerce. 6G (Kirubasri, G. et al., 2021) networks are expected to have speeds that are orders of magnitude faster than those of 5G (Sengupta, R. et al., 2021) networks. This means that real-time interactions, immersive experiences, and seamless connectivity will be possible everywhere in the world (Gupta, A. K. et al., 2023). This unparalleled degree of connectedness will open up new avenues for e-commerce companies, enabling them to provide customized, superior services to customers worldwide (Saxena, A. et al., 2024). E-commerce platforms will use cutting-edge technologies like augmented reality (AR), virtual reality (VR), and artificial intelligence (AI) (Anand, R. et al., 2023) in the 6G era to improve customer experiences and increase revenue. Before making a purchase, customers will be able to see products in real-world settings, try on virtual clothes, and test out furniture in their homes thanks to AR and VR technologies. Artificial intelligence (AI) (Anand, R. et al., 2024) driven chatbots and virtual assistants will make tailored recommendations, respond to consumer inquiries, and expedite the checkout process, resulting in a more seamless and enjoyable shopping experience. 6G networks will encourage the growth of Internet of Things (IoT) (Pramanik, S. et al., 2023) devices, allowing linked smart devices (Abdulkarim, Y. I. et al., 2023) to interact and communicate instantly. This networked ecosystem of machines, sensors (Du John, H. V. et al., 2023), and devices will open up new ways for e-commerce companies to collect data (JayaLakshmi, G. et al., 2024), streamline processes, and provide cutting-edge goods and services. For instance, wearable fitness trackers could suggest customized diet plans and supplements based on real-time health data (Singh, S. et al., 2023), and smart home appliances could automatically reorder necessities when supplies run low. The promise of e-commerce enabled by 6G brings with it new considerations and challenges for both consumers and businesses. As e-commerce transactions depend more and more on fast, low-latency networks, protecting sensitive data's security and privacy (Pandey, B. K. et al., 2023a) will become critical. Strong security measures and protocols are necessary because cybersecurity threats like data breaches (Sharma, S. et al., 2023), identity theft, and fraudulent transactions put e-commerce platforms and their users at serious risk. It will be crucial to guarantee inclusivity and accessibility for all customers as e-commerce develops internationally. To guarantee that everyone has an equal chance to engage in the digital economy, it will be imperative to close the digital divide and address inequalities in internet access and digital literacy (Meneghello, F. et al., 2019).

1.1 E-Commerce Evolution in 6G Era

E-commerce has been a major player in international trade long before the development of contemporary web browsers. It has grown along with the internet and become a part of our digital world (George, W. K. et al., 2024). Since its modest beginnings, e-commerce has grown rapidly, changing consumer behavior and conventional brick-and-mortar retail. Giants like Amazon now control a large share of global online retail sales, dominating the e-commerce scene. Indeed, in 2015 by itself, Amazon was responsible for more than half of the growth in e-commerce, demonstrating its unrivaled power in the sector. China is becoming a major force in e-commerce, with Alibaba emerging as a titan that eclipses even Amazon in the space. Due to its swift economic expansion and the technological advancements of its businesses, China is now regarded as a major force behind innovation and trial in the e-commerce industry. All one has to do to see into the future of e-commerce is follow the developments in China, where innovative technologies are changing the face of retail. Technological advancements in e-commerce are opening up digital retail platforms to a wider audience, enabling small businesses to take advantage of the infrastructure and technology provided by large e-commerce players. Mom-and-pop shops can now compete in the digital marketplace by providing them with strong retail logistics solutions through subscription-based models, which level the playing field. Lightning-fast delivery times have become the standard as a result of China's e-commerce ecosystem pushing the envelope in terms of efficiency and convenience (Matthess, M., & Kunkel, S., 2020). Thanks to sophisticated infrastructure and logistics networks, some areas boast grocery and other essentials delivered in less than thirty minutes. Global e-commerce ecosystems could soon be shaped by the innovative solutions being led by Chinese tech giants. In the context of e-commerce, sustainability becomes a critical issue in addition to speed and convenience. Even though customers are gravitating more and more toward businesses that practice ethics, supply chains still contribute significantly to waste and greenhouse gas emissions. Nevertheless, by streamlining their supply chains and implementing lean methodologies, e-commerce enterprises can be the agents of positive transformation. Cutting-edge technologies, like supply chain optimization tools and data analytics (Pandey, B. K. et al., 2023b), can help e-commerce businesses reduce waste and streamline operations, which has positive effects on the environment and the economy. Online retailers can improve customer satisfaction, cut costs, and promote sustainability all at the same time by managing their supply chains well. With the advent of 6G networks, transaction integrity becomes critical as connectivity and speed reach previously unheard-of heights. In the 6G ecosystem, consensus algorithms are essential to maintaining the security and integrity of transactions. These algorithms (Sahani, S. K. et al., 2024) create consensus among network users, which promotes trust and transparency and makes digital transactions safe and easy. Consensus algorithms play a more and more important role as e-commerce keeps changing and 6G networks usher in a new era of connectivity. E-commerce businesses can confidently (Pandey, D. et al., 2021) traverse the intricacies of the digital landscape by adopting these technologies and promoting innovation in transactional integrity, guaranteeing a smooth and secure experience for customers all over the world (Pouri, M. J., & Hilty, L. M., 2021).

1.2 Challenges of 6G Security

1. *Advanced Online Threats*: Cyber threats are evolving in the 6G era to more skillfully take advantage of e-commerce platform vulnerabilities. Attackers use cutting-edge strategies to target e-commerce companies, including supply chain compromises, ransomware, and AI-driven attacks. The confi-

dentiality, availability, and integrity of sensitive data (Tripathi, R. P. et al., 2023), such as financial transactions and customer information, are seriously jeopardized by these threats. To effectively reduce these risks, e-commerce platforms need to invest in strong cybersecurity measures like endpoint security solutions, intrusion detection systems, and frequent security audits. Proactive security measures are also required because the Internet of Things (IoT) (Pandey, B. K. et al., 2024) is growing, increasing the attack surface for cyber threats. To protect themselves from ever-changing cyber threats, e-commerce companies need to be alert and proactive in responding to cybercriminals' evolving tactics. To keep ahead of sophisticated cyber threats, you need to collaborate with cybersecurity experts, share threat intelligence, and engage in continuous monitoring. E-commerce companies can successfully reduce the risks presented by sophisticated cyber threats in the 6G era by putting in place a thorough cybersecurity strategy that incorporates technical controls, employee training, and incident response procedures.

2. *Payment Security Risks*: E-commerce platforms confront previously unheard-of difficulties in the 6G era with regard to data privacy and legal compliance. Data privacy and protection are becoming more and more important issues due to the volume and complexity of data that e-commerce platforms are collecting. Strict guidelines on the collection, storage, and processing of customer data are enforced by regulations like the GDPR, CCPA, and PCI DSS on e-commerce enterprises. E-commerce platforms must put strong data protection measures in place to comply with these regulations, including encryption, access controls, and data anonymization methods. E-commerce platforms also need to set up explicit data governance policies and processes in order to guarantee legal compliance and handle privacy issues. There are serious repercussions for breaking data privacy laws, such as fines, legal ramifications, and reputational harm. Data privacy and compliance must thus be given top priority by e-commerce companies and be integral parts of their operational and strategic plans. A proactive approach to data privacy and compliance can help e-commerce platforms reduce the risk of regulatory penalties, improve brand reputation, and foster customer trust (Schieferdecker, I., & Mattauch, W., 2018). E-commerce companies should also fund employee awareness and training initiatives to make sure staff members are aware of their responsibilities when it comes to protecting customer information.
3. *Identity Theft and Fraud Prevention*: Cybercriminals take advantage of holes in authentication systems to steal financial and personal data from unwary users. To effectively prevent fraudulent transactions and unauthorized access, e-commerce businesses need to implement fraud detection algorithms, biometric authentication, and multi-factor authentication. Ongoing observation of user accounts and transactional activity can aid in the identification and mitigation of possible security breaches. To lower the danger of fraud and identity theft, users must be informed about common phishing scams, security best practices, and the significance of password hygiene. To find and apprehend cybercriminals, e-commerce platforms should also work with financial institutions, law enforcement, and cybersecurity specialists. E-commerce platforms can safeguard their users' sensitive information and uphold confidence in the online marketplace by taking a proactive stance against identity theft and fraud prevention.
4. *Payment Security Risks*: Although secure payment processing is essential for online purchases, there are security risks associated with it. Cybercriminals looking to carry out fraudulent transactions frequently target payment data, including credit card numbers and banking details. Safeguard sensitive financial information and ensure the security of payment transactions, e-commerce platforms need to incorporate industry (Sharma, M. et al., 2024) standard encryption protocols like Transport

Layer Security (TLS). Tokenization and point-to-point encryption (P2PE) can also be used to further improve payment security by lowering the possibility of data theft and interception while in transit. Vulnerabilities in payment processing systems can be found and fixed with the aid of routine penetration tests and security assessments. To the requirements of the Payment Card Industry Data Security Standard (PCI DSS) is necessary to guarantee the safe processing and preservation of credit card information. E-commerce platforms can reduce the risk of payment fraud and safeguard their customers' financial interests by emphasizing payment security and implementing best practices in encryption (Kumar Pandey, B. et al., 2021), authentication, and compliance.

5. *Providence Chain Deficiencies*: Cybercriminals can take advantage of the vulnerabilities introduced by the global nature of e-commerce supply chains. Every stage of the supply chain, from production and warehousing to shipping and delivery, offers potential points of compromise for cybercriminals looking to undermine e-commerce operations. Supply chain risks must be evaluated and reduced by e-commerce companies through the use of best practices for supply chain security, frequent security audits, and supplier and vendor vetting. Within the supply chain ecosystem, unauthorized access and data breaches can be avoided with the help of access controls and the establishment of secure communication channels (Raja, D. et al., 2024). By producing an unchangeable record of transactions and interactions, supply chain management using blockchain technology (David, S. et al.,2023) can also improve security, traceability, and transparency. E-commerce platforms can secure their operations and maintain the integrity of their supply chains by proactively addressing supply chain vulnerabilities and putting strong security measures in place.
6. *Emerging Technologies and Security*: IoT, blockchain, and artificial intelligence (AI) (Pandey, B. K., & Pandey, D., 2023) are examples of emerging technologies that present new security risks in addition to providing creative e-commerce solutions. Though they can improve customer satisfaction, chatbots and virtual assistants driven by AI may also be open to abuse by unscrupulous parties. The Internet of Things (IoT) produces new avenues for cyberattacks and data breaches, thanks to wearable technology and smart home assistants. In order to maintain current with the constantly changing landscape of e-commerce security, this entails carrying out comprehensive security assessments, putting encryption and access controls in place, and keeping up with new threats and weaknesses. Systems should also give priority to patching, updating, and managing vulnerabilities in order to secure emerging technologies. E-commerce companies can take advantage of the advantages of emerging technology while successfully reducing the risks that go along with it by taking a proactive approach to cybersecurity and keeping up with the most recent advancements.

II. 6G SECURITY THREATS

2.1 Emerging Threat Vectors

To maintain cybersecurity, businesses must understand and address emerging threat vectors in the figure 1, which is ever-changing digital landscape. New cyber attack vectors emerge as technology advances, posing unique challenges for organizations across sectors. The proliferation of IoT devices is a major threat vector. Cybercriminals can exploit new vulnerabilities as IoT devices become more integrated into daily life and consumer lifestyles. Poor default settings, firmware updates, and authentication often cause these vulnerabilities. IoT devices are targeted by cybercriminals to gain network access, launch DDoS attacks, or steal sensitive data. Ransomware attacks, which have become more sophisticated and widespread, are another threat vector. Malicious actors encrypt sensitive data or lock users out of their systems and demand ransom for decryption keys or access restoration. These attacks can cripple operations, disrupt critical services, and cost companies a lot of money. Ransomware-as-a-service (RaaS) models allow even novice attackers to launch sophisticated ransomware campaigns. A powerful threat vector, supply chain attacks target organizations through their interconnected networks of suppliers, vendors, and service providers (Gensch, C. O. et al., 2017). Attackers can steal sensitive data, exploit system vulnerabilities, or spread malware across multiple organizations by infiltrating a trusted partner's network or compromising the software supply chain. Supply chain attacks can harm many stakeholders and undermine ecosystem trust. Insider threats also threaten organizations because malicious actors use their privileged access to internal systems and data to attack or steal sensitive data. Insider threats can come from disgruntled employees seeking revenge, negligent insiders compromising security, or malicious insiders working with external threat actors. Strong monitoring, access controls, and employee awareness training can identify suspicious insider behavior and prevent data breaches.

Figure 1. Emerging threat vectors

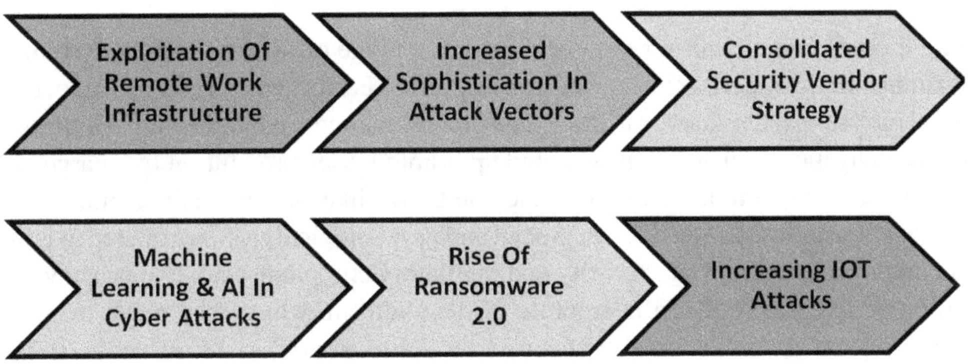

Cybercriminals also have new attack surfaces due to digital ecosystem interconnectivity and cloud computing adoption. Cloud services and infrastructure are scalable, flexible, and cost-effective. They also pose data privacy, identity management, and compliance security risks. Data breaches, unauthorized access, and regulatory violations can result from misconfigured cloud environments, weak authentication, and inadequate data encryption. Ransomware, phishing scams, zero-day exploits, fileless malware, and Denial-of-Service (DoS) attacks are increasing endpoint attack surfaces, making cybersecurity a major concern. These attacks exploit vulnerabilities in privileged computers, smartphones, and IoT devices, putting organizations and individuals at risk. Ransomware continues to threaten critical infrastructure and major companies worldwide. Recent attacks have targeted San Francisco's Bay Area Rapid Transit, Reddit, Dole Food Company, the US Marshals Service, Oregon, and Enzo Biochem. These incidents demonstrate how modern ransomware attacks use technical exploits and sophisticated social engineering to maximize impact and extortion. In a notable supply chain attack, North Korean threat actors compromised 3CX PABX. They used stealthy steganography to encode a payload in an image file and insert malicious code into 3CX endpoint clients as updates. This advanced attack shows how threat actors exploit network access and distribute malware, showing how cyber threats evolve. Digital identities have increased identity-based attacks on user identities, credentials, and authentication processes. These attacks use phishing, credential stuffing, identity theft, and SSO/MFA attacks to gain unauthorized access to sensitive data and systems. Espionage-motivated actors like STORM-0558 have mint session tokens for affected organizations' Microsoft services using Microsoft permissions. This attack shows how difficult it is to target digital trust and authentication mechanisms, emphasizing the need for strong security measures. Cyberattackers use weak access controls to break into cloud repositories and steal sensitive data. Data theft from vulnerable or misconfigured cloud services by financially motivated tools has increased, disrupting operations and compromising organizational integrity. Prompt injection techniques allow attackers to manipulate LLMs to bypass built-in safeguards and deceive models into producing malicious exploit codes. This emphasizes the need for increased security and monitoring to identify and mitigate new threats. IoT security protocols are expected to become more important, with strong authentication, advanced encryption, strict access controls, and regular software updates and patch management (von Kutzschenbach, M., & Daub, C. H., 2020). Industry collaboration will create standardized security frameworks for diverse IoT applications, making interconnected devices more resilient and secure and protecting transmitted data.

2.2 Risks to E-Commerce Platforms

Evaluating e-commerce platform risks encompasses a range of factors, such as system, psychological, social, financial, time, performance, and privacy risks. Performance risks are associated with the platform's capacity to manage user traffic in an efficient manner, guaranteeing seamless transaction processing and navigation. Financial risks include possible losses brought on by chargebacks, market swings, or fraudulent transactions. Time risks include things like website maintenance or order fulfillment delays that affect customer satisfaction. Social and psychological risks are related to how customers view a brand and its reputation. Data security and regulatory compliance are two privacy risks. System risks pertain to weaknesses in the infrastructure of the platform, which may result in cyberattacks or unavailability. To protect e-commerce platforms from these various risks, effective risk assessment and mitigation techniques are crucial. In the ever-changing digital landscape, e-commerce platforms are exposed to a wide range of risks, including those related to cybersecurity, supply chain disruptions, data privacy, fraud, customer service, and technological difficulties. The integrity, effectiveness, and reputation of e-commerce operations are seriously threatened by these risks, which calls for a thorough approach to risk management. One of the biggest risks facing e-commerce platforms is cybersecurity, which includes ransomware attacks, phishing scams, DDoS attacks, and data breaches. These nefarious actions have the potential to jeopardize confidential client information, interfere with company operations, and erode users' faith in the platform's security protocols. Due to the prevalence of fraudulent schemes like chargeback fraud, identity theft, and credit card fraud in online transactions, payment fraud poses a serious risk to e-commerce platforms. Due to the widespread use of digital payment methods, fraudsters are now more interested in targeting e-commerce platforms in an attempt to take advantage of weaknesses in payment processing systems. Disruptions to the supply chain, such as delays in shipping, stock shortages, or supplier bankruptcies, can affect customer satisfaction and loyalty in addition to impeding product availability and order fulfillment. E-commerce platforms are susceptible to supply chain disruptions because they depend on complex supply chains to source products and deliver goods to customers. E-commerce platforms constantly struggle with data privacy and compliance, especially in light of strict laws like the CCPA and GDPR. Robust data protection measures, open data handling procedures, and prompt notification of data breaches to relevant authorities and impacted parties are necessary for compliance with these regulations. The prevalence of dishonest vendors and fake goods needs to be addressed by e-commerce platforms since they damage customer confidence and brand integrity. Unauthorized sellers run the risk of breaking the law and upsetting customers by listing illegal or counterfeit goods on the platform. Reputation management and efficient customer service are crucial for preserving customer loyalty and trust. Negative customer feedback, fewer sales, and reputational harm can arise from poorly handled customer service, which includes mishandled returns, shipping mistakes, and insufficient handling of customer complaints. E-commerce platforms also have to deal with technical hazards like website crashes, server outages, or software bugs, which can cause disruptions in business and annoy customers. Rapid shifts in consumer preferences, industry trends, and competitive environments make it difficult for e-commerce platforms to effectively adapt and innovate. A comprehensive risk management strategy is needed to address these risks, one that includes strong cybersecurity defenses, compliance initiatives, resilient supply chains, efficient customer support procedures, and proactive market dynamics monitoring. E-commerce platforms can improve their resilience and guarantee the security, dependability, and prosperity of their operations in the face of constantly changing threats and challenges by giving priority to risk identification, assessment, and mitigation (Kirilenko, A. A., & Lo, A. W., 2013). Risks in E-commerce are as shown in the figure 2.

Figure 2. Risks in e-commerce

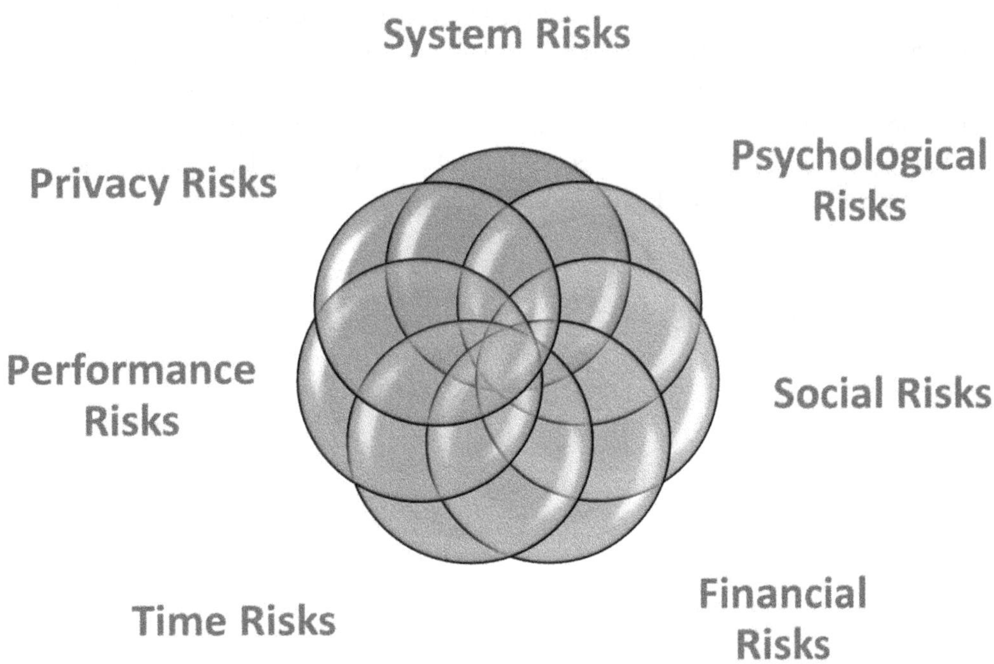

III. STRATEGIES FOR RESILIENT E-COMMERCE

3.1 Access Security Measures

In today's digital landscape, protecting organizational assets and data integrity requires strengthening authentication and access controls. Effective access control strategies are built around Access Control Policies (ACPs), which provide guidelines for allowing or prohibiting access to particular resources based on user identities and roles. A crucial component of access control is user identification, which guarantees that users are appropriately identified within the system. To confirm user identities, organizations can use a variety of identification techniques, such as advanced biometric authentication, employee IDs, and usernames. By adding an additional layer of validation to user identities, authentication mechanisms guarantee that only people with permission can access organizational resources. The authentication process is made more secure by using multi-factor authentication (MFA), which combines security tokens, passwords, or biometric verification. Users are given access based on authorization policies specified in the ACP after they have successfully authenticated. Authorization decisions are guided by the principle of least privilege, which makes sure that users only have access to the resources they need to carry out their duties. By controlling user access rights and permissions, access control techniques like Mandatory Access Control (MAC), Role-Based Access Control (RBAC), and Discretionary Access Control (DAC) uphold authorization policies. To identify and reduce possible security risks, access control measures must be routinely audited and monitored. Reviewing privileges and access logs on a regular basis will help organizations find vulnerabilities and fix them quickly (Rogers, D. L., 2016). Organizations can use cutting-edge technologies like artificial intelligence (AI) and machine learning (ML) (Muniandi, B. et al., 2024) in addition to conventional access control measures to improve authentication procedures and identify unusual user behavior. Organizations can strengthen their cybersecurity defenses, reduce the risk of unauthorized access and data breaches, and guarantee the integrity and confidentiality of their priceless assets by putting comprehensive access control policies into place and utilizing cutting-edge technologies. Figure 3 shows the key factors in access control.

Figure 3. Key factors in access control

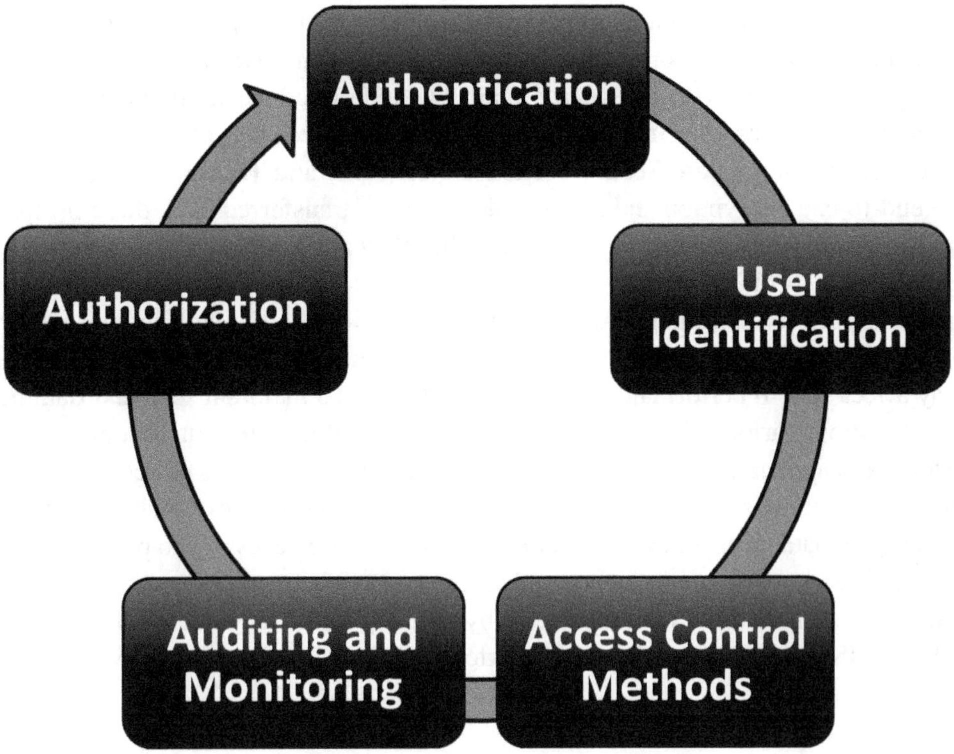

3.2 Encrypting Data for Enhanced Protection

Data encryption is an essential component of cybersecurity that protects private information from illegal access and guarantees the confidentiality and integrity of data. Encryption is a vital defense mechanism against potential vulnerabilities and exploits in the digital age, where data breaches and cyber threats are common. The significance of data encryption for improved security is discussed in this article, along with the different facets of data encryption in both stationary and mobile environments. Information that is stored on storage devices like hard drives, databases, or cloud servers is referred to as information at rest, and data encryption is essential to protecting this information. Encrypting data while it is at rest serves as a primary means of preventing unwanted access to the data in the event of a security breech (Pandey, B. K. et al., 2021a) or physical theft of the storage medium. The efficiency and simplicity of symmetric encryption make it a popular choice for encrypting data that is at rest. Symmetric encryption uses the same key for both encryption and decryption. With this encryption technique, you can be sure that even if someone else gains access to the storage device, they won't be able to decrypt the data without the encryption key. For data that is at rest, different levels of data encryption, such as full disk encryption, directory-level encryption, and file-level encryption, can be applied. By encrypting individual files or folders, file-level encryption offers fine-grained control over who can access which data sets. By extending this method to entire directories, directory-level encryption guarantees complete protection for several files kept inside a directory. Conversely, full-disk encryption encrypts every piece of data on the disk as well as the operating system, protecting the entire storage device. This guarantees that the data won't be accessible without the encryption key, even in the event that the storage device is lost, stolen, or compromised. Data encryption is crucial for protecting information while it is being transferred over networks or other communication channels, in addition to encryption while the data is at rest. Encrypting data while it's in transit guards against unauthorized parties intercepting or listening in on confidential information as it's being transmitted. Commonly used encryption protocols for protecting data in transit over the internet are Secure Sockets Layer (SSL) and Transport Layer Security (TLS). To guarantee end-to-end encryption and the confidentiality of transferred data, these protocols encrypt data packets prior to transmission and decrypt them after they are received. Data encryption adds complexity and concerns, especially with regard to performance, compatibility, and key management, even though it improves security and safeguards sensitive information. Particularly in high-volume settings, computational (Bessant, Y. A. et al., 2023) overhead and latency caused by encryption algorithms and protocols may affect system performance and response times. To maintain seamless data transmission and accessibility across various platforms and devices, compatibility and interoperability between encryption systems and applications are crucial. Data encryption also requires effective key management, which includes the creation, sharing, storing, and rotating of encryption keys. As the primary method of decrypting encrypted data, proper key management procedures are necessary to protect encryption keys from unauthorized access or compromise. Organizations can safely manage encryption keys and impose access controls to prevent unauthorized key access by utilizing key management solutions like hardware security modules (HSMs) and key management platforms (Esses, D., Csete, M. S., & Németh, B., 2021).

3.3 Disaster Recovery Planning

Organizations create disaster recovery plans (DRPs) as a documented strategy to help with the recovery of vital business IT infrastructure and operations in the case of an emergency. Disasters can wreak havoc on businesses, resulting in data loss, system outages, and monetary losses, whether they are caused by natural disasters or man-made events like cyberattacks or equipment failures. A well-thought-out DRP seeks to reduce these risks by offering a methodical framework for preventative measures, quick response strategies, and recovery operations after a disaster. The principal aim of a disaster recovery plan is to guarantee uninterrupted business operations by mitigating the effects of disruptions and expediting the reinstatement of crucial IT systems and services. Organizations can minimize downtime, speed up the recovery process, and streamline response efforts by establishing predefined protocols and guidelines. A thorough DRP covers many facets of disaster preparedness, such as resource allocation, communication tactics, and risk assessment, in order to handle a range of scenarios and emergencies. Business impact analysis (BIA) is an essential part of a disaster recovery plan that identifies the most important recovery priorities and evaluates the possible effects of disruptions on business operations. Recovery time objectives (RTOs) and recovery point objectives (RPOs), which specify the acceptable downtime and data loss thresholds for various systems and processes, can be established by organizations using business impact analysis (BIA). The foundation for creating customized recovery plans and allocating resources according to how important business operations are is this data. To create a strong disaster recovery plan, IT and business stakeholders must work together. When it comes to evaluating technology dependencies, spotting security holes, and putting in place technical protections like data backups, redundancy controls, and failover procedures, IT specialists are indispensable. However, business executives guarantee that IT recovery goals are in line with overarching business objectives by offering insights into crucial business processes, dependencies, and operational requirements. Several essential elements, each with a distinct function in the recovery process, are usually included in the structure of a disaster recovery plan. In order to guarantee data integrity and expedite recovery operations, comprehensive backup procedures are necessary. These procedures should include the frequency (Bruntha, P. M. et al., 2023), location, and techniques of backups. To effectively direct response efforts in the event of a cyberattack, a natural disaster, or an equipment malfunction, specific protocols and workflows for handling various disaster scenarios should be clearly documented. Determining backup locations, like hot or cold sites, where vital data and systems can be restored in case of an emergency, reduces downtime and guarantees business continuity. A disaster recovery plan should be regularly tested, trained, and updated in addition to these elements in order to stay current and efficient in handling new threats and technological developments. Organizations can improve their ability to withstand unanticipated disruptions, minimize downtime, and safeguard their valuable assets and reputation by allocating resources towards comprehensive disaster recovery planning (Imran, M. et al., 2022).

IV. IMPLEMENTATION AND BEST PRACTICES

4.1 Regular Security Assessments

Figure 4. Conducting regular security audits and assessments

Maintaining strong cybersecurity measures within organizations is largely dependent on conducting regular security audits and assessments (Pandey, B. K. et al., 2021b). Organizations can identify and address potential vulnerabilities that could endanger their systems and data by regularly conducting these evaluations. For efficient security audits and assessments, keep in mind the following important guidelines and best practices are shown in the figure 4.

- *Regular Audits*: Security audits should be carried out on a regular basis, preferably yearly, though more frequently if the organization handles sensitive data or operates in a high-risk environment (Iyyanar, P. et al., 2023). These audits assist in locating security holes that could be used by cybercriminals, such as out-of-date software, weak passwords, and incorrectly configured network devices.
- *Utilize Automated Tools*: Making use of automated tools can improve the thoroughness and efficiency of the security assessment procedure. These tools can notify organizations about the most recent cybersecurity trends and threats and can also identify vulnerabilities like unpatched software and improperly configured firewalls.
- *Planning for Incident Response*: To handle security breaches in an efficient manner, an incident response plan that is clearly defined is necessary. The actions to be taken in the case of a breach, such as notification protocols, system isolation, and the return of regular operations, should be outlined in this plan. The efficacy and preparedness of the incident response plan are guaranteed by routine testing.
- *Training of Employees*: Since employees are frequently the weakest link in cybersecurity, it is essential to regularly train them in best practices. Topics like password security, spotting phishing attempts, and abstaining from risky online conduct should all be included in training. For the purpose of effectively responding to security incidents, employees should also be conversant with the incident response plan.
- *Third-Party Auditors*: Hiring outside auditors can provide an unbiased evaluation of a company's security posture. These auditors provide recommendations for improvement based on industry best practices, bringing knowledge and insights that internal teams might miss.

Organizations can improve their cybersecurity defenses, lower the chance of security breaches, and protect sensitive data and systems from cyber threats by implementing these practices into their security protocols. In the end, regular security audits and assessments strengthen the organization's overall resilience against potential security incidents by ensuring that security measures remain effective and adaptable to changing cybersecurity landscapes. An organization's disaster recovery plan (DRP) and overall cybersecurity posture are greatly strengthened by conducting regular security audits and assessments. Organisations can systematically evaluate the efficacy of their security measures and detect any potential vulnerabilities or weaknesses within their IT infrastructure by regularly carrying out these assessments. Organizations can take proactive steps to address these risks and threats before they can be exploited by malicious actors by using these assessments to help identify potential risks and threats, which can range from insider threats and outdated software to misconfigured systems and compliance gaps (ElMassah, S., & Mohieldin, M., 2020). Regular security audits and assessments are also necessary to guarantee industry standards are met and regulations are followed. In order to protect sensitive data and maintain the integrity of their IT systems, many regulatory frameworks and standards mandate that organizations perform regular security audits and assessments. Organizations may show their dedication to security, reduce risk to the law and finances, and uphold the confidence of stakeholders, partners, and customers by following these guidelines and carrying out comprehensive assessments.

CONCLUSION

A major turning point in the development of e-commerce has been reached with the introduction of 6G technology, which brings with it complex security issues as well as new opportunities. This abstract explains why e-commerce in the 6G era requires proactive approaches like encrypting data for added security, strengthening authentication and access controls, and creating strong disaster recovery plans. Furthermore, it is crucial to stay ahead of evolving threats, as evidenced by the requirement for regular security audits and assessments. E-commerce platforms can strengthen their resilience and preparedness against changing 6G security environments by implementing these solutions and following best practices. As technology advances, it is more important than ever to proactively implement comprehensive security protocols to protect the accessibility, integrity, and confidentiality of e-commerce systems. Thus, enterprises can confidently traverse the constantly changing e-commerce landscape and ensure sustainability and longevity in the digital sphere by giving security top priority within the 6G paradigm.

REFERENCES

Abdulkarim, Y. I., Awl, H. N., Muhammadsharif, F. F., Saeed, S. R., Sidiq, K. R., Khasraw, S. S., & Pandey, D. (2023). Metamaterial-based sensors loaded corona-shaped resonator for COVID-19 detection by using microwave techniques. *Plasmonics*, 1–16.

Anand, R., Khan, B., Nassa, V. K., Pandey, D., Dhabliya, D., Pandey, B. K., & Dadheech, P. (2023). Hybrid convolutional neural network (CNN) for kennedy space center hyperspectral image. *Aerospace Systems*, 6(1), 71–78. 10.1007/s42401-022-00168-4

Anand, R., Lakshmi, S. V., Pandey, D., & Pandey, B. K. (2024). An enhanced ResNet-50 deep learning model for arrhythmia detection using electrocardiogram biomedical indicators. *Evolving Systems*, 15(1), 83–97. 10.1007/s12530-023-09559-0

Bessant, Y. A., Jency, J. G., Sagayam, K. M., Jone, A. A. A., Pandey, D., & Pandey, B. K. (2023). Improved parallel matrix multiplication using Strassen and Urdhvatiryagbhyam method. *CCF Transactions on High Performance Computing*, 5(2), 102–115. 10.1007/s42514-023-00149-9

. Bruntha, P. M., Dhanasekar, S., Hepsiba, D., Sagayam, K. M., Neebha, T. M., Pandey, D., & Pandey, B. K. (2023). Application of switching median filter with L 2 norm-based auto-tuning function for removing random valued impulse noise. *Aerospace Systems, 6*(1), 53-59.

David, S., Duraipandian, K., Chandrasekaran, D., Pandey, D., Sindhwani, N., & Pandey, B. K. (2023). Impact of blockchain in healthcare system. In *Unleashing the Potentials of blockchain technology for healthcare industries* (pp. 37–57). Academic Press. 10.1016/B978-0-323-99481-1.00004-3

Devasenapathy, D., Madhumathy, P., Umamaheshwari, R., Pandey, B. K., & Pandey, D. (2024). Transmission-efficient grid-based synchronized model for routing in wireless sensor networks using Bayesian compressive sensing. *SN Computer Science*, 5(1), 1–11.

Du John, H. V., Ajay, T., Reddy, G. M. K., Ganesh, M. N. S., Hembram, A., Pandey, B. K., & Pandey, D. (2023). Design and simulation of SRR-based tungsten metamaterial absorber for biomedical sensing applications. *Plasmonics*, 18(5), 1903–1912. 10.1007/s11468-023-01910-0

ElMassah, S., & Mohieldin, M. (2020). Digital transformation and localizing the sustainable development goals (SDGs). *Ecological Economics*, 169, 106490. 10.1016/j.ecolecon.2019.106490

Esses, D., Csete, M. S., & Németh, B. (2021). Sustainability and digital transformation in the visegrad group of central European countries. *Sustainability (Basel)*, 13(11), 5833. 10.3390/su13115833

Gensch, C. O., Prakash, S., & Hilbert, I. (2017). Is digitalisation a driver for sustainability? *Sustainability in a Digital World: New Opportunities Through New Technologies*, 117-129.

George, W. K., Ekong, M. O., Pandey, D., & Pandey, B. K. (2023). Pedagogy for Implementation of TVET Curriculum for the Digital World. In *Applications of Neuromarketing in the Metaverse* (pp. 117-136). IGI Global. 10.4018/978-1-6684-8150-9.ch009

George, W. K., Silas, E. I., Pandey, D., & Pandey, B. K. (2024). Utilization of Industry 4.0 Technologies in Nigerian Technical and Vocational Education: A Conundrum for Educators. In *Examining the Rapid Advance of Digital Technology in Africa* (pp. 270–293). IGI Global. 10.4018/978-1-6684-9962-7.ch014

Gupta, A. K., Sharma, R., Pandey, D., Nassa, V. K., Pandey, B. K., George, A. S., & Dadheech, P. (2023). Performance analysis of eight-channel WDM optical network with different optical amplifiers for industry 4.0. In *Innovation and Competitiveness in Industry 4.0 Based on Intelligent Systems* (pp. 197–212). Springer International Publishing. 10.1007/978-3-031-29775-5_9

Imran, M., Liu, X., Wang, R., Saud, S., Zhao, Y., & Khan, M. J. (2022). The influence of digital economy and society index on sustainable development indicators: The case of European union. *Sustainability (Basel)*, 14(18), 11130. 10.3390/su141811130

Iyyanar, P., Anand, R., Shanthi, T., Nassa, V. K., Pandey, B. K., George, A. S., & Pandey, D. (2023). A real-time smart sewage cleaning UAV assistance system using IoT. In *Handbook of Research on Data-Driven Mathematical Modeling in Smart Cities* (pp. 24–39). IGI Global.

JayaLakshmi, G., Pandey, D., Pandey, B. K., Kaur, P., Mahajan, D. A., & Dari, S. S. (2024). Smart Big Data Collection for Intelligent Supply Chain Improvement. In *AI and Machine Learning Impacts in Intelligent Supply Chain* (pp. 180-195). IGI Global.

Kirilenko, A. A., & Lo, A. W. (2013). Moore's law versus murphy's law: Algorithmic trading and its discontents. *The Journal of Economic Perspectives*, 27(2), 51–72. 10.1257/jep.27.2.51

Kirubasri, G., Sankar, S., Pandey, D., Pandey, B. K., Singh, H., & Anand, R. (2021, September). A recent survey on 6G vehicular technology, applications and challenges. In *2021 9th International Conference on Reliability, Infocom Technologies and Optimization (Trends and Future Directions)(ICRITO)* (pp. 1-5). IEEE.

Kumar Pandey, B., Pandey, D., Nassa, V. K., Ahmad, T., Singh, C., George, A. S., & Wakchaure, M. A. (2021). Encryption and steganography-based text extraction in IoT using the EWCTS optimizer. *Imaging Science Journal*, 69(1-4), 38–56. 10.1080/13682199.2022.2146885

Matthess, M., & Kunkel, S. (2020). Structural change and digitalization in developing countries: Conceptually linking the two transformations. *Technology in Society*, 63, 101428. 10.1016/j.techsoc.2020.101428

Meneghello, F., Calore, M., Zucchetto, D., Polese, M., & Zanella, A. (2019). IoT: Internet of threats? A survey of practical security vulnerabilities in real IoT devices. *IEEE Internet of Things Journal*, 6(5), 8182–8201. 10.1109/JIOT.2019.2935189

Muniandi, B., Nassa, V. K., Pandey, D., Pandey, B. K., Dadheech, P., & George, A. S. (2024). Pattern Analysis for Feature Extraction in Complex Images. In *Using Machine Learning to Detect Emotions and Predict Human Psychology* (pp. 145-167). IGI Global. 10.4018/979-8-3693-1910-9.ch007

Pandey, B. K., & Pandey, D. (2023). Parametric optimization and prediction of enhanced thermoelectric performance in co-doped CaMnO3 using response surface methodology and neural network. *Journal of Materials Science Materials in Electronics*, 34(21), 1589. 10.1007/s10854-023-10954-1

Pandey, B. K., Pandey, D., Alkhafaji, M. A., Güneşer, M. T., & Şeker, C. (2023a). A reliable transmission and extraction of textual information using keyless encryption, steganography, and deep algorithm with cuckoo optimization. In *Micro-Electronics and Telecommunication Engineering: Proceedings of 6th ICMETE 2022* (pp. 629–636). Springer Nature Singapore. 10.1007/978-981-19-9512-5_57

Pandey, B. K., Pandey, D., Dadheech, P., Mahajan, D. A., George, A. S., & Hameed, A. S. (2023b). Review on Smart Sewage Cleaning UAV Assistance for Sustainable Development. In *Handbook of Research on Safe Disposal Methods of Municipal Solid Wastes for a Sustainable Environment* (pp. 69–79). IGI Global. 10.4018/978-1-6684-8117-2.ch005

Pandey, B. K., Pandey, D., & Sahani, S. K. (2024). Autopilot control unmanned aerial vehicle system for sewage defect detection using deep learning. *Engineering Reports*, 12852. 10.1002/eng2.12852

Pandey, B. K., Pandey, D., Wairya, S., & Agarwal, G. (2021a). An advanced morphological component analysis, steganography, and deep learning-based system to transmit secure textual data. *International Journal of Distributed Artificial Intelligence*, 13(2), 40–62. 10.4018/IJDAI.2021070104

Pandey, B. K., Pandey, D., Wariya, S., & Agarwal, G. (2021b). A deep neural network-based approach for extracting textual images from deteriorate images. *EAI Endorsed Transactions on Industrial Networks and Intelligent Systems*, 8(28), e3–e3. 10.4108/eai.17-9-2021.170961

Pandey, D., Pandey, B. K., & Wairya, S. (2021). Hybrid deep neural network with adaptive galactic swarm optimization for text extraction from scene images. *Soft Computing*, 25(2), 1563–1580. 10.1007/s00500-020-05245-4

Pouri, M. J., & Hilty, L. M. (2021). The digital sharing economy: A confluence of technical and social sharing. *Environmental Innovation and Societal Transitions*, 38, 127–139. 10.1016/j.eist.2020.12.003

Pramanik, S., Pandey, D., Joardar, S., Niranjanamurthy, M., Pandey, B. K., & Kaur, J. (2023, October). An overview of IoT privacy and security in smart cities. In *AIP Conference Proceedings* (Vol. 2495, No. 1). AIP Publishing. 10.1063/5.0123511

Raja, D., Kumar, D. R., Santhiyakumari, N., Kumarganesh, S., Sagayam, K. M., Thiyaneswaran, B., Pandey, B. K., & Pandey, D. (2024). A compact dual-feed wide-band slotted antenna for future wireless applications. *Analog Integrated Circuits and Signal Processing*, 1–15. 10.1007/s10470-023-02233-0

Rogers, D. L. (2016). *The digital transformation playbook: Rethink your business for the digital age*. Columbia University Press. 10.7312/roge17544

Sahani, S. K., Pandey, B. K., & Pandey, D. (2024). *Single-valued Signals, Multi-valued Signals and Fixed-Point of Contractive Signals*. Mathematics Open. 10.1142/S2811007224500020

Saxena, A., Agarwal, A., Pandey, B. K., & Pandey, D. (2024). Examination of the Criticality of Customer Segmentation Using Unsupervised Learning Methods. *Circular Economy and Sustainability*, 1–14. 10.1007/s43615-023-00336-4

Schieferdecker, I., & Mattauch, W. (2018). ICT for smart cities: Innovative solutions in the public space. In *Computation for Humanity* (pp. 150–179). CRC Press.

Sengupta, R., Sengupta, D., Pandey, D., Pandey, B. K., Nassa, V. K., & Dadeech, P. (2021). A Systematic review of 5G opportunities, architecture and challenges. *Future Trends in 5G and 6G*, 247-269.

Sharma, M., Talwar, R., Pandey, D., Nassa, V. K., Pandey, B. K., & Dadheech, P. (2024). A Review of Dielectric Resonator Antennas (DRA)-Based RFID Technology for Industry 4.0. *Robotics and Automation in Industry*, 4(0), 303–324.

Sharma, S., Pandey, B. K., Pandey, D., Anand, R., Sharma, A., & Saini, S. (2023, March). Character Recognition Technique Implementation for Complicated Deteriorated Scene. In *2023 6th International Conference on Information Systems and Computer Networks (ISCON)* (pp. 1-4). IEEE. 10.1109/ISCON57294.2023.10112185

Singh, S., Madaan, G., Kaur, J., Swapna, H. R., Pandey, D., Singh, A., & Pandey, B. K. (2023). *Bibliometric Review on Healthcare Sustainability. Handbook of Research on Safe Disposal Methods of Municipal Solid Wastes for a Sustainable Environment*, 142-161. 10.4018/978-1-6684-8117-2.ch011

Swapna, H. R., Bigirimana, E., Madaan, G., Hasan, A., Pandey, B. K., & Pandey, D. (2023). Impact of neuromarketing on consumer psychology in digitally connected networks. In *Applications of Neuromarketing in the Metaverse* (pp. 193–205). IGI Global. 10.4018/978-1-6684-8150-9.ch015

Tripathi, R. P., Sharma, M., Gupta, A. K., Pandey, D., Pandey, B. K., Shahul, A., & George, A. H. (2023). Timely prediction of diabetes by means of machine learning practices. *Augmented Human Research*, 8(1), 1. 10.1007/s41133-023-00062-4

von Kutzschenbach, M., & Daub, C. H. (2020). Digital transformation for sustainability: A necessary technical and mental revolution. In *New Trends in Business Information Systems and Technology: Digital Innovation and Digital Business Transformation* (pp. 179–192). Springer International Publishing.

Chapter 10
Blockchain Commerce: Safeguarding Transactions in the Age of 6G

Shiv Kant Tiwari
Institute of Business Management, GLA University, India

S. Manjula
Department of Commerce, PSG College of Arts and Science, Coimbatore, India

Sibghatullah Nasir
Department of Commerce, B.S. Abdur Rahman Crescent Institute of Science and Technology, Chennai, India

K. Chokkanathan
Department of Artificial Intelligence, Madanapalle Institute of Technology and Science, India

S. Meenakshi
https://orcid.org/0000-0001-5075-6808
Department of Science and Humanities, R.M.K. Engineering College, Kavarapettai, India

Gourav Kalra
Maharishi Markandeshwar University (Deemed), India

Chetan M. Thakar
Savitribai Phule Pune University, India

ABSTRACT

Blockchain commerce and the start of 6G networks together mark the start of a new era of technological progress and safe online transactions. This chapter looks at the world of safe transactions by first looking at the basics of blockchain commerce and how important decentralization and cryptographic integrity are. Real-life examples show how useful and flexible blockchain technology is in today's business world. Moving on to the start of 6G networks, this chapter looks at the promise and potential of 6G beyond just connectivity, focusing on how it will change digital transactions. Sixth-generation networks change the way transactions work and create new ways to make digital transactions safe.

DOI: 10.4018/979-8-3693-7421-4.ch010

I. INTRODUCTION

In the era of 6G (Kirubasri, G. et al., 2021) networks, blockchain technology has proven to be an innovative tool for transaction security. Blockchain technology guarantees the safe and transparent storage and transfer of digital information (Swapna, H. R. et al., 2023) by functioning in a decentralized and distributed manner. With the help of this technology, transactions are verified and added to a blockchain a type of digital ledger using a consensus mechanism. An immutable record of transactions is formed by the cryptographic hash of each block in the chain. Because blockchain technology is decentralized, there is no longer a need for a central authority, ensuring transaction security and transparency. Blockchain technology, which offers trust, security (Pandey, B. K. et al., 2023a), and accountability, has found extensive application across multiple industries beyond its initial use in cryptocurrencies. Blockchain has promise, but before it is widely used, a number of issues need to be resolved. These difficulties include restrictions on scalability (Pandey, D. et al., 2021), worries about energy usage, intricate regulatory frameworks, problems with interoperability, and security threats. As transaction volumes rise, blockchain technology's scalability continues to be a major challenge. Blockchain networks' efficiency is hampered by congestion and slower processing times that arise from scalability constraints. Additionally, considering the substantial energy consumption linked to mining and transaction processing, guaranteeing energy efficiency is essential to the sustainability of blockchain networks. Adoption of blockchain is further complicated by regulatory compliance, which calls for a careful balancing act between innovation and respect to established legal frameworks when navigating regulations in various jurisdictions. The seamless exchange of assets and data (JayaLakshmi, G. et al., 2024) is impeded by gaps in interoperability across different blockchain platforms, which restricts the scalability and interoperability of blockchain networks. Constant threats to blockchain ecosystems are security flaws like smart contract bugs and hacking attempts. To effectively address these vulnerabilities and protect transactions, strong security practices and ongoing research are necessary. To tackle these obstacles, cooperative investigations and ongoing enhancements in protocols, infrastructure, and ecosystem are necessary. As blockchain technology develops, new approaches and best practices will emerge to realize its full potential in protecting transactions in the era of 6G networks. Blockchain technology has the potential to strengthen transaction security and integrity as 6G networks develop. Blockchain technology can be integrated with decentralized ledgers and cryptographic techniques to improve security in 6G networks. Blockchain technology's smart contracts allow for trustless transactions by automating contract execution under specified conditions. In 6G environments, the application of smart contracts can expedite transactions and guarantee accountability and transparency. Consensus algorithms reduce the possibility of fraud and manipulation by creating agreement among network users regarding the legitimacy of transactions (Wang, C. X. et al., 2023). Overcoming current obstacles and advancing R&D activities are necessary to fully realize blockchain's potential in the era of 6G. In blockchain networks, scalability techniques like sharding and layer 2 solutions can reduce congestion and boost transaction throughput.

1.1 Technological Convergence

Recent IoT (Pramanik, S. et al., 2023) systems integrate multiple heterogeneous sensors and objects in our smart living era to facilitate information exchange among all nodes. Traditional IoT systems failed to meet advanced efficacy, interoperability, network management, privacy, and security vulnerabilities, especially in complex data handling (Anand, R. et al., 2023), as network coverage expanded and smart devices evolved (Du John, H. V. et al., 2024). Centralized IoT architecture (Iyyanar, P. et al., 2023) is expensive to maintain, vulnerable to attacks, and unable to scale. To overcome these challenges, trusted users can participate independently in an autonomous distributed system Decentralised IoT reduces storage and computational complexity while participants copy blockchain leader to synchronize system. Smart contracts (when the contract clauses are met) in BC allowed IoT devices to cooperate without a middleman. Internet of Things (IoT) systems have revolutionized smart living by integrating heterogeneous sensors and objects and enabling information exchange among all nodes. As network coverage grows and smart devices become smarter, traditional IoT systems struggle to meet efficacy, interoperability, network management, privacy (Pandey, B. K. et al., 2021a), and security standards. Centralized IoT architectures are expensive, vulnerable to attacks, and limited in scalability. For these issues, an autonomous distributed system that lets trusted users participate independently is a better option. Distributing responsibilities among participants reduces storage load, computational complexity, and single point failures in this decentralized approach. Even with a node failure, multi-participant collaboration ensures system consistency. Blockchain offers a promising framework for decentralized IoT schemes. Blockchain's immutability, transparency, and decentralization allow IoT devices to interact autonomously without intermediaries. Smart contracts enable automatic execution of predefined actions when contract clauses are met, facilitating device cooperation. In the 6G era, blockchain and IoT enable secure (Kumar Pandey, B. et al., 2021) and efficient commerce. With their speed, low latency, and massive connectivity, 6G networks will boost blockchain-enabled IoT systems. Faster, safer, and more reliable transactions in this ecosystem enable innovative applications across industries. Data integrity (Sharma, S. et al., 2023) and authenticity are key benefits of blockchain and IoT. Blockchain records IoT ecosystem interactions transparently and immutably on a tamper-resistant distributed ledger. This encourages participant trust and streamlines auditing and compliance verification. By eliminating intermediaries and streamlining transactions, blockchain-enabled smart contracts reduce costs and increase efficiency. The convergence of blockchain and IoT could unlock new business models and revenue streams while improving security and efficiency. Supply chain management, logistics, healthcare (Tripathi, R. P. et al., 2023), and energy management can be transformed by blockchain-enabled IoT solutions' real-time data visibility, traceability, and automation (Treiblmaier & Sillaber, 2021).

1.2. Digital Age Essentials

Secure transactions are essential in today's fast-changing digital world. The need for strong security has never been greater as technology advances and digital interactions increase. Every aspect of modern life relies on secure and trustworthy transactions, from online purchases and financial transactions to data sharing and communication. At the heart of this landscape is the challenge of protecting sensitive data and transaction integrity amid evolving cybersecurity threats. With the rise of digital platforms and device interconnectivity, malicious actors' attack surface has grown exponentially. Businesses, governments, and individuals are constantly threatened by cyberattacks, fraud, and data breaches. These challenges have led to the development of digital transaction security technologies and protocols. Blockchain is a major player in this space. Blockchain, originally developed for cryptocurrencies like Bitcoin, now secures a wide range of digital transactions. Blockchain is a decentralized, distributed ledger that secures and verifies transactions. Blockchain uses cryptography and consensus mechanisms to make transactions transparent, immutable, and tamper-resistant. This makes it ideal for digital transaction security, where trust and transparency are crucial. Blockchain and other technologies like encryption, multi-factor authentication, machine learning (Pandey, B. K. et al., 2024) and biometrics secure digital transaction. For instance, encryption protects sensitive data during transmission, preventing unauthorized access. Multi-factor authentication requires multiple forms of identification before accessing accounts, adding security. Biometrics verifies a user's identity using unique physical traits like fingerprints or facial features, increasing security. Advanced cybersecurity solutions that detect and respond to cyber threats in real time have been developed using artificial intelligence (Anand, R. et al., 2024) and machine learning (Pandey, B. K., & Pandey, D., 2023). These technologies analyze massive amounts of data to identify patterns (Muniandi, B. et al., 2024) and anomalies that may indicate security breaches, allowing organizations to protect their systems and data (Ismanto, L. et al., 2019).

II. BLOCKCHAIN COMMERCE

2.1 Decentralization: Digital Security

An essential component of any effort to guarantee a genuinely open, equitable, and free internet is decentralization. Concerns about monopolistic practices, data privacy breaches, and content manipulation are becoming more prevalent in the current environment (Pandey, B. K. et al., 2023b), where a small number of people control a disproportionate amount of online space. On the other hand, decentralization presents a viable remedy, opening the door to true internet liberty and safety. The risks associated with centralized control are naturally reduced by a distributed, decentralized network. Malicious actors find it much more difficult to attack or manipulate the network when authority and control are distributed among numerous nodes. If a component fails or there is an attack, the system can still function normally because other nodes can take over and keep things running. This resilience is best demonstrated by Bitcoin, whose decentralized design makes it immune to hacking; in order to compromise the integrity of the network, an attacker would need to seize control of more than 51% of the network. It also encourages community members to take an active role and take ownership of their community. Decentralization fosters accountability and dedication by allowing people to participate in decision-making processes, which motivates group action toward common objectives. This spirit is best embodied by Decentralized Autonomous Organizations (DAOs), which give members direct control over initiatives, protocols, and projects. Blockchain networks prevent fraud and corruption by recording transactions on a public, distributed ledger that is open to all users. Centralized entities can improve transparency and accountability by guaranteeing equal access to the system for all participants by ceding control over participation. By empowering local communities, decentralized systems promote development and creativity. Organizations can leverage region-specific insights and needs by assigning authority to local teams and communities, allowing them to customize their growth strategies accordingly. With the help of this decentralized strategy, organizations can promote inclusivity and diversity while growing their presence in a variety of settings. It promotes diversity and creativity in solutions. Decentralized systems promote a wider range of ideas and results by enabling various entities within the network to test and apply novel approaches. This diversity of viewpoints stimulates original problem-solving and ongoing innovation throughout the ecosystem.

2.2 Cryptography: Trust Assurance

Protecting private data and guaranteeing the accuracy of digital transactions are critical in today's world that is becoming more and more digital. The foundation of online security is provided by cryptography and digital signatures, which maintain authenticity and secrecy in the digital domain. Let's examine the vital role that digital signatures and cryptography play in safeguarding our digital lives as we explore their complex realms. The art of information security, or cryptography, uses mathematical algorithms (Sahani, S. K. et al., 2024) to encrypt data so that only those who are meant to can access and decipher it. Cryptography is essentially a code that cannot be broken, protecting data and messages from prying eyes. When it comes to protecting sensitive information and ensuring secure communication (Pandey, B. K. et al., 2021b) across a variety of digital platforms, cryptography carries a significant amount of weight in today's world. Cryptography is a method of encrypting data by utilizing sophisticated mathematical algorithms (Bessant, Y. A. et al., 2023), which renders the data incomprehensible to outside parties. Protecting personal privacy, ensuring the safety of financial transactions, and protecting critical infrastructure from cyberattacks are all extremely important functions that can be provided by this technology. From a fundamental standpoint, cryptography is an indispensable tool for ensuring the confidentiality and integrity of data in the contemporary digital environment. Digital communication can be made private and secure by using cryptographic techniques, which encourages confidence and trust in online interactions. Digital signatures, which are an essential part of cryptographic integrity, offer a way to confirm the legitimacy and consistency of digital transactions and documents. Digital signatures guarantee the integrity of the document's contents during transmission and serve as a unique means of identifying the sender, much like handwritten signatures do. Utilizing cryptographic techniques, digital signatures produce a distinct "hash" or fingerprint of the document, which is subsequently encrypted with the sender's private key. The document has this encrypted hash appended to it so that recipients can check its authenticity and identify any changes. White-labeling and customization are the best ways to increase confidence in requests for digital signatures. Customization options also allow businesses to reinforce their commitment to professionalism and security while aligning the user experience with their brand identity. One example of how white labeling and customization can improve recognition and trustworthiness is SIGNiX's response to requests for digital signatures. By adding branding components and messaging that appeal to their target market, businesses can add a personal touch to the signing process. Electronic signatures are becoming more widely accepted and successful across a range of industries and contexts because signers are more likely to trust and interact with requests for digital signatures that are well-known and professionally branded. With its ability to protect sensitive data, guarantee privacy, and uphold data integrity, cryptography is essential to modern security. It shields data from unwanted access and thwarts cyberattacks with encryption techniques. Through the use of cryptographic protocols, businesses can send and store data in a secure manner, strengthening their defenses against constantly changing online threats. Because it ensures the confidentiality and integrity of digital transactions and communications, cryptography is a fundamental component of cybersecurity strategies for both individuals and businesses. Essential for Modern Security are as shown in the figure 1.

Figure 1. Essential for modern security

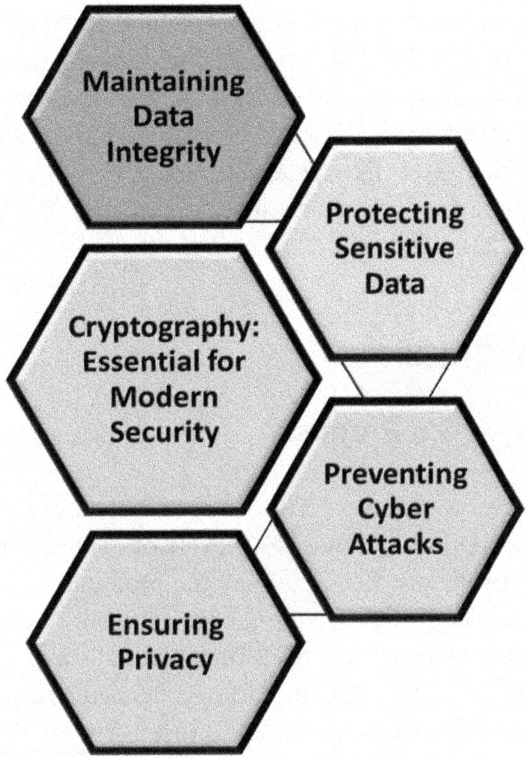

2.3 Real-World Blockchain Use

Once only associated with cryptocurrencies, blockchain technology has developed into a flexible instrument with a wide range of practical uses in numerous industries. Blockchain's distinctive qualities decentralization, transparency, and immutability offer revolutionary answers to persistent problems in the field of contemporary commerce. Supply chain management is one of the most well-known uses of blockchain technology in business. Utilizing the transparent and unchangeable ledger of blockchain technology, businesses can track product movement from manufacturer to final customer (Saxena, A. et al., 2024) with previously unheard-of efficiency and transparency. The blockchain records every ownership transfer and transaction, creating a comprehensive and verifiable audit trail. By enabling stakeholders to track the provenance of goods, confirm their legitimacy, and guarantee regulatory compliance, this eventually promotes trust and accountability along the supply chain. This is just another interesting way that blockchain technology is being used in business (Badotra, S., & Sundas, A., 2021). Conventional identity verification techniques frequently rely on centralized databases that are susceptible to identity theft and security lapses. By letting users keep control over their digital identities, blockchain provides a more secure and decentralized solution. Users can safely store and share personal information with trusted parties, lowering the risk of fraud and unauthorized access, with blockchain-based identity solutions. Blockchain technology has the potential to completely transform remittances and cross-border payments. Conventional international money transfers are frequently costly, time-consuming, and error-prone.

Blockchain-based payment solutions allow peer-to-peer transactions and do away with middlemen, making them a quicker and more affordable option. Cross-border payments using cryptocurrencies like Bitcoin and stablecoins are becoming more common, giving people and companies a safe and effective way to send money across borders. Tokenization of digital assets: In contemporary commerce, tokenization the act of representing physical assets as digital tokens on a blockchain is becoming more and more popular. Blockchain allows for increased accessibility to investment opportunities, increased liquidity, and fractional ownership by tokenizing assets like real estate, art, or commodities. By democratizing access to historically illiquid assets, tokenization enables investors to take part in new markets and diversify their holdings (Rahman, M., 2023).

III. UNVEILING 6G NETWORKS

3.1 Beyond Connectivity: 6G's Promise

Excitement is in the air as everyone looks forward to the arrival of 6G networks. While the switch from 4G to 5G brought with it previously unheard-of levels of connectivity and speed, the promise of 6G goes far beyond these improvements. Let's examine the profound possibilities of 6G networks and the various ways they could completely alter the digital environment. With its lightning-fast speeds, extremely low latency, and extensive connectivity, 6G is fundamentally a quantum leap forward in wireless communication (Devasenapathy, D. et al., 2024) technology. 6G networks are expected to transform how we interact with the digital world by reducing latency to just a few microseconds and reaching speeds of up to terabits per second. The possibilities are truly endless, ranging from realistic augmented reality applications and seamless virtual reality experiences to real-time remote surgeries and self-driving cars. 6G holds great potential for enabling ubiquitous connectivity, closing the digital divide and providing high-speed internet access to even the most remote areas of the world. 6G networks will offer high-speed internet access to all people and communities, giving them unprecedented opportunities for economic growth, healthcare, and education (Singh, S. et al., 2023). These networks will do this by utilizing cutting-edge technologies like satellite communication, high-altitude platforms, and sophisticated beamforming techniques (Raja, D. et al., 2024). 6G networks will function as the foundation for the developing Internet of Everything (IoE), seamlessly tying together machines, objects, people, and even ecosystems. Smart cities, autonomous infrastructure, personalized healthcare, and predictive maintenance are just a few of the cutting-edge uses made possible by this networked network of intelligent devices and systems (Anakath, A. S. et al., 2019). 6G networks will not only improve connectivity but also reshape communication by introducing novel concepts like ultra-reliable, low-latency communication (URLLC) and holographic telepresence. These developments are going to revolutionize a variety of industries, from gaming and entertainment to education and business, by enabling immersive, real-time collaboration experiences. By accelerating the growth of distributed intelligence and edge computing, 6G networks will bring processing power closer to the data generation point. 6G networks will make real-time decision-making, personalized services, and improved privacy and security possible by utilizing distributed computing resources and the combined intelligence of edge devices (Osita, G. C. et al., 2022).

3.2 Transaction Dynamics: 6G's Impact

We are about to witness a significant shift in digital transactions as we wait for the deployment of 6G networks. In addition to improving connectivity, 6G promises to completely alter the dynamics of how we conduct business online. 6G's Impact on Digital Transactions are shown in the figure 2.

- *Instantaneous Transactions*: 6G networks promise to transfer data at previously unheard-of speeds, surpassing terabits per second. Transactions will happen instantly with a microsecond latency, doing away with waiting times and other delays. The speed and efficiency of digital transactions will be redefined by this rapid data exchange, making them nearly instantaneous. The extremely quick speeds and low latency of 6G will be very advantageous to sectors like finance and healthcare (Sasidevi S et al., 2024) that depend on timely transactions. To improving user experience, instantaneous transactions will make it possible for cutting-edge applications that need instantaneous data transfer, like real-time gaming and remote surgery.
- *Expansion of Connectivity*: 6G networks will allow for the connection of a vast range of interconnected objects and systems, going beyond the boundaries of traditional devices. The emergence of the Internet of Everything (IoE) will link machines, sensors, infrastructure, and people in addition to devices and people. Machine-to-machine transactions will be made easier by this hyperconnected ecosystem, which will allow for smooth coordination and communication between different entities. Smart grids and driverless cars are two examples of automated processes that will need 6G connectivity to function effectively and safely. High-speed internet connectivity will be made available to rural and isolated areas, empowering locals and closing the digital divide.
- *Low-Latency, Ultra-Reliable Communication* (URLLC): High reliability and extremely low latency in communication, which are necessary for mission-critical transactions, will be ensured by URLLC in 6G networks. Applications that need to react quickly, like emergency response systems and financial trading, will profit from URLLC's dependability and speed. Even in difficult environments, critical transactions will be carried out promptly and without interruption thanks to 6G's URLLC capabilities. Digital transactions will become more trustworthy and dependable as a result of URLLC's dependability. Industries like manufacturing and healthcare, which require instantaneous communication for industrial automation and remote surgeries, will benefit from 6G's URLLC for increased productivity and security.
- *Customized Network Slicing*: With 6G, virtualized network instances that are suited to particular transaction needs can be created through network slicing. A dedicated network slice that is optimized for dependability, security, and performance can be assigned to each sort of transaction. Dynamic resource management and allocation will guarantee effective network resource use based on transaction demands. Businesses will be able to optimize user experience and performance by allocating network resources based on the priority of critical transactions. Without sacrificing speed or security, network slicing will support a wide range of transaction kinds and applications, from quick financial transactions to bandwidth-intensive multimedia streaming.
- *Integration of Distributed Ledger Technology* (DLT) and Blockchain: Digital transactions will be made more transparent and secure thanks to 6G's integration with blockchain and DLT. Transactions will be securely recorded and verified thanks to blockchain's decentralized and immutable ledger, which lowers the possibility of fraud and tampering. Smart contracts, made possible by blockchain technology, will further streamline procedures and eliminate the need for

middlemen by automating transaction execution based on predetermined conditions. Blockchain's traceability and transparency will improve digital transactions' dependability and trustworthiness, resulting in a more safe and effective transaction ecosystem. The combination of 6G and blockchain technology will be advantageous for sectors like supply chain management, where accountability and transparency are essential.

- *Autonomous Transactions*: As 6G rolls out, machine-to-machine transactions will grow more frequent. Transactions will be carried out automatically by smart devices and systems in accordance with pre-established protocols and conditions, removing the need for human intervention. Since repetitive jobs can be automated in sectors like logistics, this automation will optimize workflows and boost productivity. 6G's integration with blockchain will enable smart contracts, which will allow autonomous transactions by guaranteeing adherence to predetermined guidelines. Numerous economic sectors will experience increased scalability, reduced costs, and increased efficiency as autonomous transactions proliferate.
- *Enhanced Security and Transparency*: The security and transparency of digital transactions will be improved by the integration of DLT and blockchain with 6G. The integrity of transaction data will be ensured by safeguarding transactions recorded on a decentralized ledger against tampering or unauthorized access. The transparency of blockchain technology will allow participants to track and verify transactions in real-time, thereby augmenting trust and accountability. Blockchain technology will lower transaction costs and processing times by doing away with the need for middlemen, improving the efficiency and accessibility of digital transactions. Blockchain's security features coupled with 6G's connectivity will open the door to a new era of safe, open, and effective digital transactions.

Figure 2. Transaction dynamics

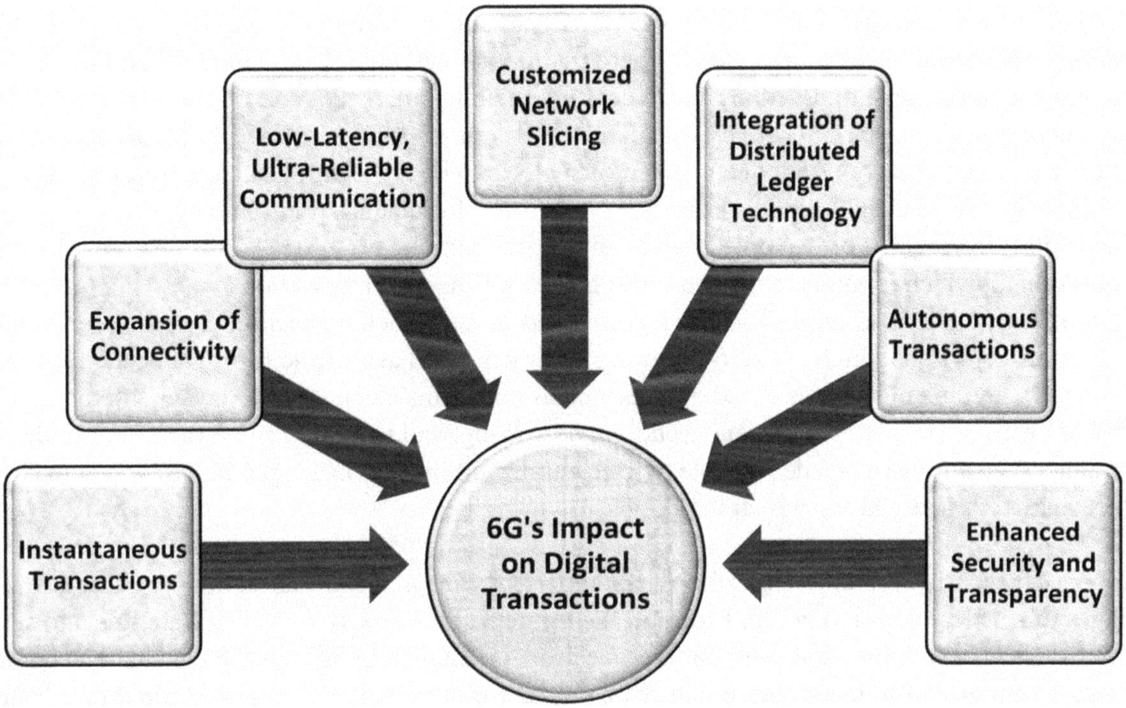

IV. FUSION OF BLOCKCHAIN AND 6G

4.1 Trustless Transactions: Smart Contracts

The use of smart contracts and blockchain technology to provide increased security, privacy, and efficiency in financial transactions is known as trustless transactions, which mark a paradigm shift in the industry (Saxena, A. et al., 2024).

1. *Enhanced Security and Privacy*: Cryptographic algorithms and decentralized networks are used in trustless transactions to protect user data. Cryptocurrencies such as Bitcoin use public-private key pairs to encrypt and authenticate transactions, thereby virtually preventing unauthorized access. A person's confidence in financial transactions made through trustless systems is increased by the increased security and privacy, which guard against fraud and identity theft.
2. *Elimination of Intermediaries*: Reduced expenses and delays result from the lack of intermediaries such as banks or payment processors in trustless transactions. Traditional financial systems have higher fees and longer settlement times because they depend on intermediaries to manage ledgers and facilitate transactions. Trustless transactions allow users to conduct business directly with one another, avoiding the possibility of manipulation or censorship and leading to quicker and more affordable exchanges.

3. *Global Accessibility*: Trustless transactions allow anyone to participate in the global economy, regardless of where they live or their financial situation. With only an internet connection and a digital wallet, people in underserved or unbanked areas can conduct economic activity. This accessibility enables people in developing nations, where traditional banking services may be hard to come by, to engage in financial transactions and access international markets.
4. *Immutable and Transparent Ledger:* To guarantee the immutability and traceability of every transaction, trustless transactions are documented on a blockchain, a decentralized and transparent ledger. Users can independently verify transactions thanks to blockchain's transparency, which lowers the possibility of fraud. For example, users can see the complete transaction history on Ethereum's blockchain, which promotes trust and transparency in financial transactions.
5. *Smart Contract Capabilities*: The utilisation of trustless transactions facilitates the implementation of smart contracts, which are self-executing contracts that have explicit terms encoded into their code. By automating actions based on preset conditions, smart contracts do away with the need for middlemen or outside enforcement. Lending, borrowing, and trading without the use of traditional financial institutions is made possible by Decentralized Finance (DeFi) platforms, which make use of smart contracts and trustless transactions.

Increased security, privacy, accessibility, and efficiency in financial transactions are just a few advantages of trustless transactions are shown in the figure 3. Trustless systems facilitate safe and secure transactions between individuals without the need for middlemen by utilizing blockchain technology and smart contracts. The increasing ubiquity of trustless transactions holds the potential to transform numerous sectors and create avenues for a more equitable and effective global economy.

Figure 3. Benefits of trustless transactions

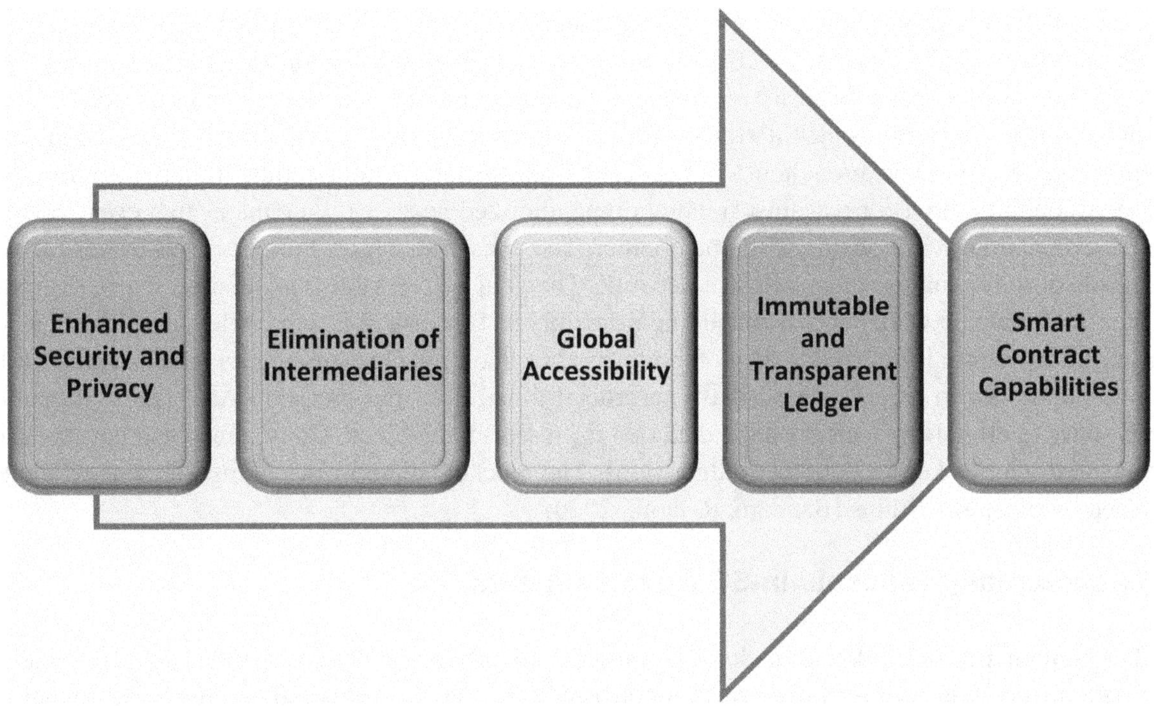

4.2 Integrity Assurance: Consensus Algorithms

Blockchain technology is a cornerstone of security and transparency in the digital sphere because of its well-known decentralized and immutable characteristics. Consensus algorithms, which are the foundation of this technology, are essential to preserving the integrity of transactions within blockchain networks. Recognizing the importance of consensus algorithms is critical to maintaining transaction security and dependability as we move toward the era of 6G networks. The foundation of blockchain security is consensus algorithms, which make sure that every member of the network comes to an understanding about the ledger's current state. By encouraging unity and cohesion, these algorithms help participants and peers from different backgrounds develop trust and dependability. Basis of Blockchain Security: Consensus algorithms serve as the cornerstone of blockchain security by guaranteeing that all network participants are in agreement regarding the ledger's current state. Blockchain networks reduce the possibility of fraud and manipulation by establishing trust and dependability among participants through consensus (Sarda, S. et al., 2022). Ensuring Common Agreement Consensus algorithms make it easier for peers in a network to come to a consensus. In order to verify and authenticate transactions and make sure that only legitimate transactions are added to the blockchain, participants work together through consensus. Critical Elements of Consensus Algorithms necessitate that all nodes in the network reach a consensus, putting aside individual interests for the good of the group. The goal of these algorithms is to reach the maximum degree of consensus within the network, encouraging dependability and confidence among users. The participants cooperate with one another in an egalitarian manner, giving each vote the same weight. Encouraging Cohesion and Reliability encourage cohesion among users by guaranteeing that each new block added to the blockchain is acknowledged as the authentic version by all. Consensus algorithms emphasize a win-win scenario for all parties involved rather than putting individual interests first, which promotes unity and cooperation within the blockchain network. Participation in Blockchain Security are essential for improving the consistency and security of blockchain data. These algorithms identify the nodes in charge of keeping track of transactions, guaranteeing integrity and consistency throughout the network. The integrity of transactions by encouraging trust and dependability, protecting against fraud and unauthorized access. It guarantees that every node in the Blockchain network concurs with one another. The consensus algorithm prioritizes cohesion over the needs of individual partners within a network. The goal is to establish a situation where everyone on the Blockchain network benefits, including its members. Because of its great relevance, Blockchain's consensus algorithm is referred to as its fundamental technology. Determining which particular nodes have the authority to record transactions is a crucial function of the protocol. As a result, it enables these nodes to effectively concur on the data that is present in the block. Consistency and data security are ensured via blockchain consensus algorithms. The blockchain network's computational efficiency is raised by these algorithms (Bandara, R. et al., 2020).

4.3 Accelerating Blockchain-6G Advancements

The combination of blockchain technology and 6G networks is a game-changer that could completely alter a number of industries in the quickly changing field of technology. This combination has the potential to unleash previously unheard-of levels of productivity, security, and creativity, propelling advancement in the digital age. Collaboration and strategic alliances are crucial for advancing developments at the nexus of blockchain and 6G. Blockchain developers, telecom providers, and other interested parties can form alliances to pool resources and expertise to investigate how blockchain technology can be integrated with 6G networks for increased security and efficiency. Initiatives for joint research and development have the potential to lead to ground-breaking discoveries that combine the strengths of both technologies. Research and development spending is essential to maximizing the benefits of blockchain-6G convergence. Important discoveries can result from providing funds and resources for studies that explore this synergy. Innovation must be pushed forward by funding universities, research facilities, and startups that are devoted to developing technologies that take advantage of the combination of blockchain (David, S. et al., 2023) and 6G. Key elements in guaranteeing the smooth integration of blockchain networks with 6G infrastructure are standardization and interoperability. By establishing industry standards and protocols (George, W. K. et al., 2024), effective data exchange across decentralized networks is made possible through interoperability. To fully realize the potential of blockchain-6G convergence, consensus mechanisms and communication protocols that are optimized for this integration must be developed. The establishment of regulatory frameworks and policy support is imperative in fostering an environment that is conducive to blockchain-6G innovation. It is crucial to work with legislators and regulatory agencies to create frameworks that support adoption and experimentation while addressing privacy, security, and data governance issues. Promoting laws that uphold the rights of stakeholders and encourage innovation is essential to advancing this field. Use case presentations and pilot projects are powerful tools for showcasing the advantages and real-world uses of blockchain-6G integration. Through the implementation of practical projects in domains like supply chain management, healthcare, finance, and smart cities, the game-changing influence of this convergence can be demonstrated. These projects show the real benefits of blockchain-6G solutions, which encourages adoption and yields insightful information. Initiatives to raise awareness and increase understanding of blockchain and 6G technologies are crucial. By funding educational initiatives and providing training opportunities, companies can equip professionals and developers with the know-how required to efficiently utilize blockchain and 6G advancements. Raising awareness among interested parties' industry (Sharma, M. et al., 2024), government, and the broader public creates an environment that is conducive to innovation. Grants, subsidies, and rewards systems are examples of incentive mechanisms that can promote innovation and adoption of blockchain-6G solutions. It is possible to accelerate the development and deployment of revolutionary applications at the nexus of blockchain and 6G by offering incentives to early adopters and innovators. These rewards promote experimentation and advancement in this quickly developing field. Global blockchain-6G convergence advancements must be accelerated through international cooperation and knowledge exchange. Stakeholders can address issues and advance innovation by leveraging global expertise and insights through forums, conferences, and cooperative projects that promote collaboration. The global development and adoption of blockchain-6G solutions is facilitated and accelerated by the sharing of best practices and lessons learned. We can fully realize the promise of blockchain-6G convergence by working together to catalyze action in these important areas and to create a more innovative, safe, and connected digital future Taherdoost, H., & Madanchian, M., 2023).

4.4 Promise Embrace: Secure Digital Future

The promise of safe transactions serves as a beacon in the rapidly changing technological landscape, pointing the way towards the digital economy of the future. Blockchain technology and 6G networks have made it possible for transactions to be more efficient and safer than before. This convergence offers never-before-seen levels of security, transparency, and trust in digital transactions, marking a revolutionary change. With its reputation for being decentralized and unchangeable, blockchain technology is at the core of this revolution. Blockchain functions as a distributed ledger, securely and transparently capturing transactions. Blockchain ensures the security and integrity of transactions by using consensus methods and cryptographic algorithms. This removes the need for middlemen and promotes participant trust. Blockchain technology's ability to work with 6G networks increases the possibility of safe transactions and opens the door to efficient and private real-time transactions. Transactions can happen instantly thanks to 6G's incredibly fast speeds and minimal latency, which decreases wait times and improves user experience. Furthermore, the enhanced connectivity of 6G guarantees worldwide accessibility, enabling people in various regions to engage in the digital economy.

Eliminating intermediaries, like banks or payment processors, which frequently cause delays and extra costs, is one of the main advantages of this convergence. Direct transactions between parties are possible with blockchain and 6G, making exchanges quicker and more affordable. This improves accessibility to financial services and streamlines procedures, especially in underserved or unbanked areas. The traceability and transparency that come with blockchain technology improve accountability and trust in online transactions. All participants can view every transaction that is recorded on the blockchain, which lowers the possibility of fraud and guarantees legal compliance. In industries such as supply chain management, where integrity and sustainability depend on the traceability of goods, this transparency is especially beneficial (Hongmei, Z., 2021). The addition of smart contracts improves the capabilities of blockchain-6G transactions in addition to security and transparency. Self-executing contracts with predetermined terms encoded into the blockchain are known as smart contracts. By automating transaction processes, these contracts ensure compliance and lessen the need for human intervention. Transactions can then be carried out more smoothly, accurately, and efficiently. Cooperation is necessary if secure transactions in the future digital economy (George, W. K. et al., 2023) are to live up to their full potential. It is imperative that stakeholders from various industries collaborate to propel innovation, establish guidelines, and tackle regulatory obstacles. To fully explore the potential of blockchain-6G convergence and its impact on various sectors, investments in R&D, education, and pilot projects are required.

CONCLUSION

A world full of opportunities for safe online transactions is revealed by investigating the technological convergence of blockchain technology and 6G networks. Through our analysis, we have clarified the fundamental ideas behind blockchain commerce, highlighting the significance of applications in the real world, decentralization, and cryptographic integrity. We have also explored the revolutionary potential of 6G networks, emphasizing how they can change the nature of transactions and open up new avenues for safe exchanges. Our analysis of the combination of blockchain technology and 6G has highlighted how crucial consensus algorithms are to maintaining the integrity of transactions in this ecosystem. We can improve security protocols and set the stage for a time when digital transactions will be primarily based on trust and dependability by incorporating blockchain technology into 6G networks. For blockchain-6G integration to progress more quickly, action must be catalyzed. Progress in this field is primarily driven by regulatory support, standardization initiatives, research investments, and strategic alliances. We can encourage cooperation and innovation and eventually create a more open, effective, and inclusive financial ecosystem by welcoming the promise of safe transactions in the digital economy of the future.

REFERENCES

Anakath, A. S., Rajakumar, S., & Ambika, S. (2019). Privacy preserving multi factor authentication using trust management. *Cluster Computing*, 22(S5, Suppl 5), 10817–10823. 10.1007/s10586-017-1181-0

Anand, R., Khan, B., Nassa, V. K., Pandey, D., Dhabliya, D., Pandey, B. K., & Dadheech, P. (2023). Hybrid convolutional neural network (CNN) for kennedy space center hyperspectral image. *Aerospace Systems*, 6(1), 71–78. 10.1007/s42401-022-00168-4

Anand, R., Lakshmi, S. V., Pandey, D., & Pandey, B. K. (2024). An enhanced ResNet-50 deep learning model for arrhythmia detection using electrocardiogram biomedical indicators. *Evolving Systems*, 15(1), 83–97. 10.1007/s12530-023-09559-0

Badotra, S., & Sundas, A. (2021). A systematic review on security of E-commerce systems. *International Journal of Applied Science and Engineering*, 18(2), 1–19.

Bandara, R., Fernando, M., & Akter, S. (2020). Privacy concerns in E-commerce: A taxonomy and a future research agenda. *Electronic Markets*, 30(3), 629–647. 10.1007/s12525-019-00375-6

Bessant, Y. A., Jency, J. G., Sagayam, K. M., Jone, A. A. A., Pandey, D., & Pandey, B. K. (2023). Improved parallel matrix multiplication using Strassen and Urdhvatiryagbhyam method. *CCF Transactions on High Performance Computing*, 5(2), 102–115. 10.1007/s42514-023-00149-9

David, S., Duraipandian, K., Chandrasekaran, D., Pandey, D., Sindhwani, N., & Pandey, B. K. (2023). Impact of blockchain in healthcare system. In *Unleashing the Potentials of blockchain technology for healthcare industries* (pp. 37–57). Academic Press. 10.1016/B978-0-323-99481-1.00004-3

Devasenapathy, D., Madhumathy, P., Umamaheshwari, R., Pandey, B. K., & Pandey, D. (2024). Transmission-efficient grid-based synchronized model for routing in wireless sensor networks using Bayesian compressive sensing. *SN Computer Science*, 5(1), 1–11.

Du John, H. V., Jose, T., Sagayam, K. M., Pandey, B. K., & Pandey, D. (2024). Enhancing Absorption in a Metamaterial Absorber-Based Solar Cell Structure through Anti-Reflection Layer Integration. *Silicon*, 1-11.

George, W. K., Ekong, M. O., Pandey, D., & Pandey, B. K. (2023). Pedagogy for Implementation of TVET Curriculum for the Digital World. In *Applications of Neuromarketing in the Metaverse* (pp. 117-136). IGI Global. 10.4018/978-1-6684-8150-9.ch009

George, W. K., Silas, E. I., Pandey, D., & Pandey, B. K. (2024). Utilization of Industry 4.0 Technologies in Nigerian Technical and Vocational Education: A Conundrum for Educators. In *Examining the Rapid Advance of Digital Technology in Africa* (pp. 270–293). IGI Global. 10.4018/978-1-6684-9962-7.ch014

Govindaraj, V., Dhanasekar, S., Martinsagayam, K., Pandey, D., Pandey, B. K., & Nassa, V. K. (2023). Low-power test pattern generator using modified LFSR. *Aerospace Systems*, 1-8.

Gupta, A. K., Sharma, R., Pandey, D., Nassa, V. K., Pandey, B. K., George, A. S., & Dadheech, P. (2023). Performance analysis of eight-channel WDM optical network with different optical amplifiers for industry 4.0. In *Innovation and Competitiveness in Industry 4.0 Based on Intelligent Systems* (pp. 197–212). Springer International Publishing. 10.1007/978-3-031-29775-5_9

Hongmei, Z. (2021). A cross-border e-commerce approach based on blockchain technology. *Mobile Information Systems*, 2021, 1–10. 10.1155/2021/2006082

Ismanto, L., Ar, H. S., Fajar, A. N., & Bachtiar, S. (2019, July). Blockchain as E-commerce platform in Indonesia. *Journal of Physics: Conference Series*, 1179(1), 012114. 10.1088/1742-6596/1179/1/012114

Iyyanar, P., Anand, R., Shanthi, T., Nassa, V. K., Pandey, B. K., George, A. S., & Pandey, D. (2023). A real-time smart sewage cleaning UAV assistance system using IoT. In *Handbook of Research on Data-Driven Mathematical Modeling in Smart Cities* (pp. 24–39). IGI Global.

JayaLakshmi, G., Pandey, D., Pandey, B. K., Kaur, P., Mahajan, D. A., & Dari, S. S. (2024). Smart Big Data Collection for Intelligent Supply Chain Improvement. In *AI and Machine Learning Impacts in Intelligent Supply Chain* (pp. 180-195). IGI Global.

Kirubasri, G., Sankar, S., Pandey, D., Pandey, B. K., Singh, H., & Anand, R. (2021, September). A recent survey on 6G vehicular technology, applications and challenges. In *2021 9th International Conference on Reliability, Infocom Technologies and Optimization (Trends and Future Directions)(ICRITO)* (pp. 1-5). IEEE.

Kumar Pandey, B., Pandey, D., Nassa, V. K., Ahmad, T., Singh, C., George, A. S., & Wakchaure, M. A. (2021). Encryption and steganography-based text extraction in IoT using the EWCTS optimizer. *Imaging Science Journal*, 69(1-4), 38–56. 10.1080/13682199.2022.2146885

Muniandi, B., Nassa, V. K., Pandey, D., Pandey, B. K., Dadheech, P., & George, A. S. (2024). Pattern Analysis for Feature Extraction in Complex Images. In *Using Machine Learning to Detect Emotions and Predict Human Psychology* (pp. 145-167). IGI Global. 10.4018/979-8-3693-1910-9.ch007

Osita, G. C., Chisom, C. D., Okoronkwo, M. C., Esther, U. N., & Vanessa, N. C. (2022). Application of Emerging Technologies in Mitigation of e-Commerce Security Challenges. *CCU J. Sci*, 2, 2734–3766.

Pandey, B. K., & Pandey, D. (2023). Parametric optimization and prediction of enhanced thermoelectric performance in co-doped CaMnO3 using response surface methodology and neural network. *Journal of Materials Science Materials in Electronics*, 34(21), 1589. 10.1007/s10854-023-10954-1

Pandey, B. K., Pandey, D., Alkhafaji, M. A., Güneşer, M. T., & Şeker, C. (2023a). A reliable transmission and extraction of textual information using keyless encryption, steganography, and deep algorithm with cuckoo optimization. In *Micro-Electronics and Telecommunication Engineering: Proceedings of 6th ICMETE 2022* (pp. 629–636). Springer Nature Singapore. 10.1007/978-981-19-9512-5_57

Pandey, B. K., Pandey, D., Dadheech, P., Mahajan, D. A., George, A. S., & Hameed, A. S. (2023b). Review on Smart Sewage Cleaning UAV Assistance for Sustainable Development. In *Handbook of Research on Safe Disposal Methods of Municipal Solid Wastes for a Sustainable Environment* (pp. 69–79). IGI Global. 10.4018/978-1-6684-8117-2.ch005

Pandey, B. K., Pandey, D., & Sahani, S. K. (2024). Autopilot control unmanned aerial vehicle system for sewage defect detection using deep learning. *Engineering Reports*, 12852. 10.1002/eng2.12852

Pandey, B. K., Pandey, D., Wairya, S., & Agarwal, G. (2021a). An advanced morphological component analysis, steganography, and deep learning-based system to transmit secure textual data. *International Journal of Distributed Artificial Intelligence*, 13(2), 40–62. 10.4018/IJDAI.2021070104

Pandey, B. K., Pandey, D., Wariya, S., & Agarwal, G. (2021b). A deep neural network-based approach for extracting textual images from deteriorate images. *EAI Endorsed Transactions on Industrial Networks and Intelligent Systems*, 8(28), e3–e3. 10.4108/eai.17-9-2021.170961

Pandey, D., Pandey, B. K., & Wairya, S. (2021). Hybrid deep neural network with adaptive galactic swarm optimization for text extraction from scene images. *Soft Computing*, 25(2), 1563–1580. 10.1007/s00500-020-05245-4

Pramanik, S., Pandey, D., Joardar, S., Niranjanamurthy, M., Pandey, B. K., & Kaur, J. (2023, October). An overview of IoT privacy and security in smart cities. In *AIP Conference Proceedings* (Vol. 2495, No. 1). AIP Publishing. 10.1063/5.0123511

Rahman, M. (2023). Prevention of E-Commerce Fraud in Bangladesh: A Critical Study on Legal and Institutional Framework. Available at *SSRN* 4477507. 10.2139/ssrn.4477507

Raja, D., Kumar, D. R., Santhiyakumari, N., Kumarganesh, S., Sagayam, K. M., Thiyaneswaran, B., Pandey, B. K., & Pandey, D. (2024). A compact dual-feed wide-band slotted antenna for future wireless applications. *Analog Integrated Circuits and Signal Processing*, 1–15. 10.1007/s10470-023-02233-0

Sahani, S. K., Pandey, B. K., & Pandey, D. (2024). *Single-valued Signals, Multi-valued Signals and Fixed-Point of Contractive Signals*. Mathematics Open. 10.1142/S2811007224500020

Sarda, S., Sharma, S., & Pal, R. (2022). Consumer Protection Regulation in Light of E-Commerce and Product Liability. *Indian JL & Legal Rsch., 4*, 1.

Sasidevi, S., Kumarganesh, S., Saranya, S., Thiyaneswaran, B., Shree, K. V. M., & Martin Sagayam, K. (2024, May 15). Binay Kumar Pandey & Digvijay Pandey. (2024). Design of Surface Plasmon Resonance (SPR) Sensors for Highly Sensitive Biomolecular Detection in Cancer Diagnostics. *Plasmonics*. Advance online publication. 10.1007/s11468-024-02343-z

Saxena, A., Agarwal, A., Pandey, B. K., & Pandey, D. (2024). Examination of the Criticality of Customer Segmentation Using Unsupervised Learning Methods. *Circular Economy and Sustainability*, 1–14. 10.1007/s43615-023-00336-4

Sharma, M., Talwar, R., Pandey, D., Nassa, V. K., Pandey, B. K., & Dadheech, P. (2024). A Review of Dielectric Resonator Antennas (DRA)-Based RFID Technology for Industry 4.0. *Robotics and Automation in Industry*, 4(0), 303–324.

Sharma, S., Pandey, B. K., Pandey, D., Anand, R., Sharma, A., & Saini, S. (2023, March). Character Recognition Technique Implementation for Complicated Deteriorated Scene. In *2023 6th International Conference on Information Systems and Computer Networks (ISCON)* (pp. 1-4). IEEE. 10.1109/ISCON57294.2023.10112185

Singh, S., Madaan, G., Kaur, J., Swapna, H. R., Pandey, D., Singh, A., & Pandey, B. K. (2023). *Bibliometric Review on Healthcare Sustainability. Handbook of Research on Safe Disposal Methods of Municipal Solid Wastes for a Sustainable Environment*, 142-161. 10.4018/978-1-6684-8117-2.ch011

Swapna, H. R., Bigirimana, E., Madaan, G., Hasan, A., Pandey, B. K., & Pandey, D. (2023). Impact of neuromarketing on consumer psychology in digitally connected networks. In *Applications of Neuromarketing in the Metaverse* (pp. 193–205). IGI Global. 10.4018/978-1-6684-8150-9.ch015

Taherdoost, H., & Madanchian, M. (2023). Blockchain-based e-commerce: A review on applications and challenges. *Electronics (Basel)*, 12(8), 1889. 10.3390/electronics12081889

Tripathi, R. P., Sharma, M., Gupta, A. K., Pandey, D., Pandey, B. K., Shahul, A., & George, A. H. (2023). Timely prediction of diabetes by means of machine learning practices. *Augmented Human Research*, 8(1), 1. 10.1007/s41133-023-00062-4

Wang, C. X., You, X., Gao, X., Zhu, X., Li, Z., Zhang, C., ... Hanzo, L. (2023). On the road to 6G: Visions, requirements, key technologies and testbeds. *IEEE Communications Surveys & Tutorials*.

Chapter 11
Supply Chain Security in 6G Networks:
Commerce's Critical Challenge

A. Shameem
AMET Business School, AMET University, India

Alok Jain
Lovely Professional University, India

C. Visvesvaran
Sri Krishna College of Engineering and Technology, Coimbatore, India

Ritesh Kumar Singhal
https://orcid.org/0000-0002-3690-0401
Ajay Kumar Garg Institute of Management, Ghaziabad, India

V. Revathi
https://orcid.org/0000-0002-8583-1916
Department of Applied Sciences, New Horizon College of Engineering, Bangalore, India

Joshuva Arockia Dhanraj
https://orcid.org/0000-0001-5048-7775
Dayananda Sagar University, India

ABSTRACT

A significant advancement in the field of wireless telecommunications is marked by the move towards 6G networks. Inheriting an unprecedented level of connectivity and technological advancement, 6G networks are the logical progression of 5G. The need for fast data transmission is growing, and new technologies are popping up all over the place, and these technologies require strong and dependable communication networks. Moving to 6G networks basically means creating and implementing state-of-the-art wireless infrastructure that can adapt to the changing demands of contemporary society.

I. INTRODUCTION

A significant advancement in the field of wireless telecommunications (Gupta, A. K. et al., 2023) is marked by the move towards 6G networks. Inheriting an unprecedented level of connectivity and technological advancement, 6G networks are the logical progression of 5G (Sengupta, R. et al., 2021). The need for fast data transmission (Pandey, B. K. et al., 2023a) is growing, and new technologies are popping up all over the place, and these technologies require strong and dependable communication networks. Moving to 6G networks basically means creating and implementing state-of-the-art wireless infrastructure (Devasenapathy, D. et al., 2024) that can adapt to the changing demands of contemporary

DOI: 10.4018/979-8-3693-7421-4.ch011

society. With data transmission speeds far faster than ever before imagined, 6G networks aim to go beyond current technological limitations, unlike their predecessors. Sixth generation (6G) networks are expected to reach terabit speeds, which could completely change the connectivity landscape and make a wide range of cutting-edge applications previously thought to be impossible possible. 6G networks are attractive because they are expected to have extremely low latency, which indicates that data will be exchanged quickly between devices (Sharma, M. et al., 2022) that are connected. 6G networks lay the foundation for a multitude of transformative applications by reducing latency to microseconds, allowing for instantaneous communication and responsiveness. The possibilities made possible by ultra-low latency are both revolutionary and vast, ranging from real-time remote surgery to immersive VR experiences. The security of the supply chain is very important for 6G networks because it protects the integrity, dependability, and resilience of the network infrastructure. The complicated and linked nature of 6G supply chains, which include many different parts, technologies, and people involved, makes it even more important to have strong security measures in place to reduce risks and holes. Because 6G networks depend on a wide range of vendors, manufacturers, and suppliers, any problem in the supply chain can have widespread effects. Any break or compromise in the supply chain can make the network infrastructure more vulnerable, which could mean that data integrity, privacy (Sharma, S. et al., 2023), and availability are at risk (Khan, B. et al., 2021). This can make users less likely to trust the site, hurt its reputation, and cost both businesses (Saxena, A. et al., 2021) and customers money. Supply chain security is very important to lower the chance that fake or tampered parts will get into the 6G network ecosystem. Because there are so many fake goods on the market and bad people trying to take advantage of weak spots in the global supply chain, the integrity of 6G network parts needs to be checked and confirmed very carefully. Not finding and getting rid of fake parts can hurt the performance and dependability of 6G networks. It can also lead to big security problems, like spying, data breaches, and breaks in the netwok (Hassija, V. et al., 2020). Malware, ransomware, and supply chain attacks are just some of the cyber threats that 6G networks can face as they become more connected and reliant on software-defined technologies. Bad people could use weaknesses in the supply chain to get into network infrastructure, add harmful code, or take down important systems, which would put the privacy, integrity, and availability of 6G services at risk. Telecommunications providers and network operators must use strong supply chain security practices to reduce the risk of not complying with regulations and meet their legal obligations because governments and regulatory bodies are putting in place strict security and privacy rules. If you don't follow the rules, you could face harsh punishments, legal problems, and damage to your reputation. This shows how important supply chain security is for 6G networks.

1.2 Commerce's Critical Challenge

The problem statement in the realm of commerce's critical challenge centers on the intricate and interdependent supply chains within the telecommunications industry, specifically during the shift to 6G networks. Commerce must address the pressing issue of maintaining supply chain security in the face of ever-changing telecommunications technology and the growing threat from malicious actors. Central to this challenge is the susceptibility of supply chains to a range of risks and threats, such as counterfeit components, cyberattacks, and dependencies within the supply chain. Understanding the complex network of suppliers, manufacturers, and vendors involved in the production and distribution of 6G network components is crucial in order to identify potential vulnerabilities that could be targeted by adversaries aiming to compromise network security. The increasing interconnectedness of supply chains poses a greater challenge in maintaining supply chain security. This is because telecommunications companies often depend on a wide range of suppliers and vendors spread across different parts of the world. Managing and mitigating supply chain risks has become increasingly challenging due to complexities related to regulatory compliance, cultural differences, and geopolitical tensions. The shift to 6G networks brings about more challenges and uncertainties, as the need for fast and reliable connectivity leads to the implementation of novel technologies and inventive approaches. The fast rate of innovation can sometimes surpass security measures, leaving supply chains exposed to new threats and vulnerabilities that may not have been properly addressed. Ensuring the security of supply chains is a crucial task for commerce. It is essential to implement strong practices that can effectively address risks, protect against cyber threats, and maintain the integrity and reliability of 6G networks. This necessitates cooperation among industry stakeholders, government agencies, and regulatory bodies to create and execute all-encompassing strategies for managing supply chain risks, sharing threat intelligence, and ensuring regulatory compliance. Not addressing the crucial issue of supply chain security during the transition to 6G networks can result in serious consequences for commerce. These consequences may include financial losses, damage to reputation (Mohamed-Iliasse, M. et al., 2020), and disruptions to critical services and infrastructure. Ensuring supply chain security is crucial for businesses to maintain resilience and continuity in the digital age (George, W. K. et al., 2023).

II. SUPPLY CHAIN VULNERABILITIES

2.1 Telecom Supply Chain

At a time when the landscape of telecommunications is undergoing rapid change and connectivity is the driving force behind modern commerce, supply chain security has emerged as a significant challenge for the industry (Ekong, M. O. et al., 2023). As a result of its multifaceted network of suppliers, which includes infrastructure providers, service operators, and equipment vendors, the telecommunications industry is able to successfully navigate the intricate web of dependencies that underpin its operations. A challenge that has taken on a greater significance as a result of the transition to 6G networks is the fundamental imperative to ensure the integrity, reliability, and security of the supply chain. This fundamental imperative is at the core of this intricate network. The ecosystem that makes up the supply chain of the telecommunications industry is comprised of a wide variety of stakeholders, each of whom plays an important part in the delivery of telecommunication services. On the other hand, infrastructure providers are responsible for the deployment and management of the physical infrastructure that is required for the transmission and delivery of telecommunication services. Equipment vendors are responsible for the manufacturing of the hardware and software components that are essential for network infrastructure. The provision of telecommunication services to businesses and households is overseen by service operators, who rely on a combination of owned and leased transmission networks and infrastructure (Hong, T. et al., 2021). Service operators are responsible for overseeing the availability of these services. The primary source of revenue for the telecommunications industry is the provision of telecommunication services to businesses and households. These services are also the foundation upon which modern communication and connectivity are built. Telecommunication services are the backbone of commerce, enabling seamless communication, collaboration, and commerce on a global scale. These services range from voice calls and messaging services to high-speed internet access and high-definition streaming of multimedia content. A significant portion of the revenue generated by the industry comes from the sale of products, equipment, and infrastructure services, in addition to the provision of services. This helps to fuel innovation and technological advancement in the field of telecommunications. In the midst of the ever-expanding scope and complexity of telecommunication services, supply chain security has emerged as a primary concern for commercial activity within the sector. When a supply chain relies on a diverse group of suppliers and vendors, it opens itself up to vulnerabilities and risks that have the potential to compromise its integrity and security. Counterfeit components, cyberattacks, and supply chain dependencies are all significant threats to the reliability and resilience of telecommunication networks. These threats undermine trust and confidence in the industry as a whole.

2.2 Identifying Vulnerabilities

In order to reduce risks and protect the integrity and security of the telecommunications infrastructure, it is imperative to identify potential vulnerabilities in 6G network supply chains. There are a number of supply chain vulnerabilities that should be carefully examined as the telecom sector moves to 6G networks. 6G network supply chains are seriously threatened by counterfeit components. The dependability and efficiency of network infrastructure can be jeopardized by counterfeit hardware and software, such as integrated circuits, routers, and antennas. Strong authentication procedures and supply chain tracking systems are necessary for the detection (KVM, S. et al., 2024) and mitigation of counterfeit components. Supply Chain Dependencies are another source of vulnerability. Dependencies are introduced into 6G network supply chains by the reliance on a wide range of vendors and suppliers. Network deployment delays and service outages can result from supply chain disruptions including natural disasters, geopolitical unrest, or manufacturing hold-ups that impede the flow of essential components and services. Supply chain dependencies can be lessened by diversifying suppliers and creating backup plans. Supply chains for 6G networks are also highly vulnerable to cybersecurity threat (Guo, F. et al., 2019). Threat actors may leverage weaknesses in supply chain procedures, like unsecured manufacturing facilities, hacked software packages, or unsafe firmware upgrades, to breach network security and jeopardize the confidentiality and integrity of data. To mitigate cyber threats within the supply chain, strong cybersecurity measures must be implemented. These measures include encryption (Pandey, D. et al., 2021a), access controls, and intrusion detection systems. Risks related to regulatory compliance are another difficulty. 6G network supply chains may face legal ramifications and reputational harm if they fail to adhere to industry standards and regulatory requirements. Numerous laws covering consumer protection, network security, and data privacy must be followed by telecommunications companies. There can be severe fines and penalties for breaking regulations, such as the Federal Communications Commission (FCC) rules or the General Data Protection Regulation (GDPR). A serious risk to the supply chains of 6G networks is intellectual property theft. Trade secrets, confidential data (Pandey, B. K. et al., 2023b), or proprietary technology pertaining to 6G network designs, algorithms (Bessant, Y. A. et al., 2023), or protocols may be targeted by rivals or malevolent parties. Strong intellectual property protection strategies, like trademarks, patents, and non-disclosure agreements, can be put into place to lessen the possibility of intellectual property theft in the supply chain (Ahmed, M. et al., 2021).

2.3 Examples of Past Supply Chain Security Breaches

Global supply chains are vulnerable, as shown by several security breaches. Breach-related industries include technology, retail, and healthcare (Deepa, R. et al., 2022). Some notable examples:

1. *2020 SolarWinds Cyberattack*: Hackers breached SolarWinds' software build and distribution system, one of the largest supply chain security breaches in recent years. The attackers inserted malicious code into SolarWinds' Orion software updates, which were distributed to thousands of customers, including government agencies and Fortune 500 companies. This breach allowed unauthorized access to sensitive data and possible espionage, showing the reach of supply chain attacks.
2. *2017 NotPetya Ransomware Attack*: NotPetya, a destructive ransomware attack, quickly spread through multinational corporations' supply chains, targeting software updates and distribution channels. A compromised update of a popular accounting software used by companies worldwide caused the attack. NotPetya disrupted operations, caused financial losses, and destroyed data, highlighting the vulnerability of interconnected supply chains to cyberattacks.
3. *Target Data Breach (2013)*: Cybercriminals breached Target's network using a third-party vendor's credentials in one of the largest retail data breaches. The attackers stole over 70 million customers' credit card and personal data from Target's payment system. This breach highlighted the risks of third-party vendor relationships and the need for strong retail supply chain security.
4. *Stuxnet Worm (2010)*: Iran's nuclear facilities' SCADA systems were targeted by Stuxnet, a sophisticated computer worm. The worm exploited industrial control system vulnerabilities and spread via infected USB drives, damaging uranium enrichment centrifuges. Stuxnet may have entered Iran's nuclear program through compromised supply chain components, showing how supply chain attacks can disrupt critical infrastructure.
5. *2019 Medtronic MyCareLink Patient Monitor Vulnerability*: Healthcare providers (Tareke, S. A. et al., 2022) remotely monitor cardiac patients with the Medtronic MyCareLink patient monitoring system, which researchers found vulnerabilities in. Attackers could intercept and modify patient data or disrupt critical medical services due to system vulnerabilities caused by a third-party component. This incident showed the importance of healthcare technology (Pandey, D. et al., 2023) supply chain security and third-party component vulnerabilities.

These examples demonstrate the variety of supply chain security breaches and the need to protect them from new threats. Implementing strong security measures, conducting thorough risk assessments, and collaborating with trusted partners can reduce supply chain vulnerabilities and improve operations resilience.

III. IMPLICATIONS OF INSECURITY

3.1 Economic and Industry Impact

The supply chain in the telecommunications sector is made up of a complicated web of organizations that are engaged in the manufacture, sale, and provision of telecom goods and services. Retail establishments, logistics and transportation companies, equipment and component makers, and telecom service providers are all included in this. In order to guarantee the smooth transfer of telecom goods and services from suppliers to end users, the supply chain is essential. It includes procedures like ordering, keeping track of goods, shipping, and customer support. It is crucial to comprehend the dynamics and elements of the telecom supply chain in order to maximize productivity, cut expenses, and provide clients with high-quality goods and service. Through GDP contribution, infrastructure investment, and job creation, the telecommunications sector has a major economic impact are as shown in the figure 1. It promotes innovation in a number of industries, trade, and communication. Modifications in the telecommunications sector may have a significant impact on international trade, the uptake of new technologies, and economic growth.

- *Financial Losses*: Supply chain security breaches often cause immediate and long-term financial losses for affected companies. Companies incur significant incident response, remediation, and recovery costs after a breach. These costs may include forensic investigations to determine the breach's scope and cause, cybersecurity experts to contain and mitigate it, and security upgrades to prevent future breaches. Notifying affected customers, providing credit monitoring, and meeting legal and regulatory compliance requirements may also cost companies. A supply chain security breach can quickly increase costs, affecting profitability and liquidity. Supply chain security breaches can also have long-term economic effects on affected companies. Reduced customer confidence, customer defection, or business disruptions can cost companies revenue. A breach can damage the company's brand and reputation, lowering its market value and shareholder confidence. The costs of implementing and maintaining strong supply chain security measures to prevent future breaches can also strain finances and lower profitability. Therefore, in today's interconnected business environment, supply chain security vulnerabilities must be addressed to mitigate financial risks and protect companies' economic viability.
- *Operational disruption*: Supply chain security breaches can cause downtime, production delays, and productivity loss. As they contain the incident, assess the impact, and implement remediation, companies may struggle to maintain operations after a breach. Companies may have to shut down if a cyberattack disrupts critical infrastructure or the flow of goods and services, resulting in financial losses and missed deadlines. Supply chain disruptions can delay production, affecting suppliers, distributors, and customers. Supply chain security breaches can also worsen operational disruptions by causing customer distrust, negative publicity, and stakeholder scrutiny. Customers may avoid companies with security breaches, lowering sales and revenue. Business partners and suppliers may reconsider their relationships with affected companies, complicating recovery. Supply chain security breaches have far-reaching operational effects, emphasizing the need for proactive measures to strengthen supply chain resilience and minimize disruptions in today's fast-paced and interconnected business landscape.
- *Reputation Damage*: Supply chain security breaches can harm a company's reputation, causing distrust among customers, investors, and partners. A breach can damage a company's brand, affecting customer loyalty and market perception. Customers may lose trust and avoid future business if they view the company as unreliable or insecure (Pramanik, S. et al., 2023). The company may also lose favor with investors and shareholders, lowering stock prices and market value. Rebuilding trust and reputation takes time and requires transparency, accountability, and proactive security and customer protection efforts. Supply chain security breaches can damage a company's reputation for years, affecting its ability to attract and retain customers, talent, and investment.

With promises of improved security and reliability, competitors may use the breach to steal customers from the affected company. The company's suppliers and partners may also reconsider their relationships, which could cost them opportunities and strain relations. The reputational damage caused by supply chain security breaches can be severe, emphasizing the need for proactive measures to protect the company's brand.

- *Market share loss*: As customers, suppliers, and partners seek safer and more reliable providers, supply chain security breaches can cost market share. A breach may cause customers to lose trust in a company's data security, resulting in customer defection and lower sales. Rivals may use the breach's vulnerabilities to lure customers with promises of better security and service. The company may lose market share and revenue, threatening its long-term viability and competitiveness. Market share loss from supply chain security breaches can also hurt the company's growth and industry position. This may cause suppliers and business partners to reconsider working with the affected company, worsening its market share decline and making it harder to secure new partnerships. The breach's reputational damage may deter customers and investors, limiting the company's growth. In today's dynamic and interconnected business environment, mitigating supply chain security breaches is crucial for market share and competitive advantage.
- *Costs of regulatory compliance*: Supply chain security breaches often lead to regulatory investigations and compliance costs for affected companies. Companies that violate data protection or cybersecurity regulations may face fines, penalties, and remediation. These costs can be high and include regulatory fines, litigation fees, and compliance remediation costs. Companies may also pay for audits, assessments, and monitoring to ensure regulatory compliance. Supply chain security and proactive compliance are crucial because regulatory noncompliance can lead to reputational damage, legal liabilities, and financial penalties.
- *Loss of Intellectual Property*: Affected companies face significant economic risks if supply chain security breaches steal or compromise sensitive intellectual property, trade secrets, and proprietary information. Intellectual property theft can cost companies revenue, market share, and competitive advantage as competitors gain access to valuable technology, research, and development. Companies may also face intellectual property infringement claims and litigation, compounding the financial impact of the breach. Loss of intellectual property can also hinder the company's ability to innovate and differentiate, affecting its long-term growth and sustainability. Encryption (Kumar Pandey, B. et al., 2021), access controls, and employee training are essential for reducing supply chain security risks and protecting the company's valuable intellectual property.

Figure 1. Economic and industry impact

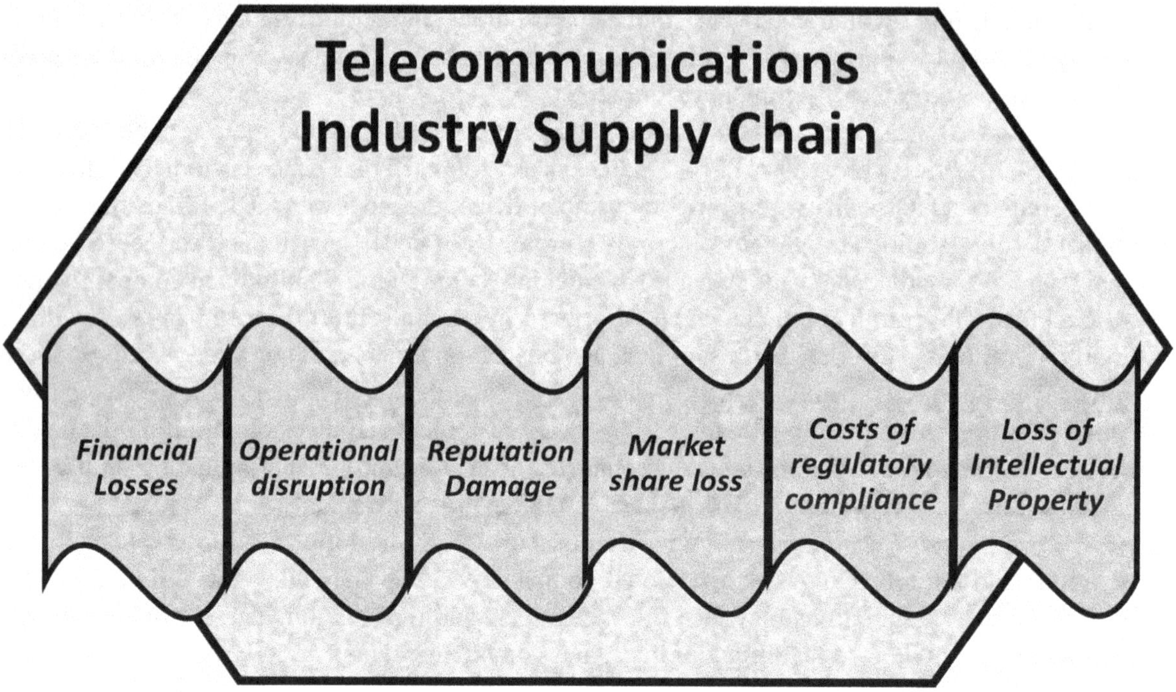

3.2 National Security Risks

The increasing frequency of cybersecurity attacks targeting vital national infrastructure has become a significant worry, since it has the potential to cause severe consequences for key sectors such as financial services, utilities, and transportation systems. Governments and affiliated organizations are acknowledging the pressing need to address these dangers by pursuing enhanced approaches to assess, oversee, and examine cybersecurity vulnerabilities that nation states and their critical infrastructure corporations are exposed to. Critical National Infrastructure have introduced subscription-based security ratings, which enable comprehensive analysis of crucial security performance indicators. These technological tools provide national security organizations and computer emergency response teams with enhanced capabilities to evaluate national security in a more efficient manner. By utilizing Bitsight, these groups are able to obtain essential information required for comprehending the risks associated with cybersecurity in vital infrastructure and assessing the security readiness of their nation. The number and severity of cyberattacks have been significantly increased due to the increasing interconnection resulting from digital transformation (Swapna, H. R. et al., 2023), rendering them as highly important risks to national security. Adversaries specifically focus on government networks and its reliable third-party vendors with the purpose of initiating catastrophic assaults on vital infrastructure, including energy systems (Du John, H. V. et al., 2024), water systems, aviation systems, and food and agriculture systems. Sophisticated cyberattacks have the potential to facilitate espionage activities, capture valuable intellectual property, and compromise networks for subsequent exploitation. In order to effectively address these cybersecurity risks, it is imperative for nations and government agencies to strengthen their capacities to assess, analyze, and understand the characteristics of these threats, as well as assess the effectiveness of their security programs and controls. The collection and analysis of cyber threat intelligence and the surveillance of security measures have been carried out manually, resulting in a limited understanding of cybersecurity in critical infrastructure. The continuous evolution of threats necessitates the development of more efficient methodologies for generating intelligence (Revathi, T. K. et al., 2022) that can effectively inform security strategy and policy. Cybersecurity for critical infrastructure refers to the comprehensive set of policies, protocols, and technologies designed to protect the vital infrastructure of nation states. Cybercriminals often focus their efforts on critical infrastructure sectors, including utilities, transportation systems (Sahani, K. et al., 2023), banking sectors, energy firms, and other entities that offer essential services to governments and individuals. Enhancing cybersecurity protections for critical infrastructure is of utmost significance, as the robustness of these systems is crucial for safeguarding national security, economic stability, and societal well-being.

3.3 Trust and Reputation Loss

The potential consequences of cybersecurity assaults on vital national infrastructure, such as the erosion of confidence and reputational harm, can have significant ramifications for various stakeholders, encompassing governments, enterprises, and citizens. When critical infrastructure systems experience a breach, stakeholders may see the entities involved as lacking reliability, security, and the ability to effectively meet their commitments. The erosion of trust can diminish confidence in the impacted organizations and weaken their credibility, resulting in complex reputational harm that may be difficult to rectify. The potential ramifications of governments experiencing a decline in trust and repute might be extensive, affecting their capacity to effectively carry out their fundamental responsibility of safeguarding the well-being and protection of their populace. When the integrity of critical infrastructure systems is compromised, it can lead to a decline in public trust regarding the government's capacity to safeguard vital services and successfully address emergency situations. The erosion of trust has the potential to compromise popular backing for governmental endeavors and strategies, so eroding the government's credibility and power. Enterprises engaged in the operation of vital infrastructure systems may experience detrimental effects on their reputation following instances of cybersecurity breaches. The affected businesses may face scrutiny from customers and stakeholders over their reliability and security, resulting in a decline in confidence in their products and services. The erosion of trust can lead to a decline in revenue, marginalization of market share, and detrimental effects on enduring relationships with customers and partners. Enterprises may encounter legal and regulatory consequences, so exacerbating their reputation and affecting their financial performance. The potential consequences of cybersecurity assaults on key infrastructure, such as the erosion of trust and reputational harm, can have profound ramifications for the safety, security, and overall welfare of individuals within a society. The disruption of vital services such as power, water, and transportation can lead to several negative consequences for individuals, including inconvenience, financial losses, and heightened susceptibility to other hazards. The erosion of trust in suppliers of key infrastructure has the potential to erode the faith of individuals in the capabilities of their communities to withstand and rebound from unforeseen events.

IV. ENHANCING SUPPLY CHAIN SECURITY

4.1 Stakeholder Collaboration

Working together, government agencies and sector players can effectively combat cybersecurity threats to vital national infrastructure. By working together, it is possible to combine knowledge, assets, and power to improve the security and resilience of crucial systems. Information sharing, which involves government agencies and industry stakeholders exchanging threat intelligence, cybersecurity best practices, and situational awareness, is a critical component of this partnership. This kind of sharing guarantees that pertinent stakeholders receive actionable information in a timely manner and helps with the fast discovery and reaction to cyber problems. Public-private partnerships and information sharing and analysis centers (ISACs) are examples of information sharing methods that facilitate this kind of interchange and promote coordinated incident response operations. Another important area where industry stakeholders and government organizations must work together is policy formulation. Governmental organizations can better understand the special needs and difficulties faced by vital infrastructure sectors by interacting with business. In turn, industry participants offer insightful commentary on new risks and technology advancements. Collaboration can be used to create laws and policies that balance innovation, security, and compliance while fostering a regulatory atmosphere that supports resilience. Building capacity is also essential, and government organizations should support programs that improve industry stakeholders' knowledge and provide them with training and online education (Pandey, D. e al., 2021b) in the field. Government organizations support the development of cybersecurity capabilities and resilience within critical infrastructure sectors by offering resources, money, and technical assistance. Industry stakeholders are empowered to acquire the skills and information required to effectively detect, respond to, and recover from cyber incidents through training programs, exercises, and seminars. Skills are further enhanced by cooperative research and development activities. Governmental organizations and industry participants collaborate on research projects and partnerships to propel innovation in tools, technology, and solutions. In order to meet new concerns, this cooperative strategy expedites the development of cutting-edge technology and encourages the useful use of research discoveries. Coordination of incident response is crucial during cyber disasters, and business stakeholders and government agencies must work together effectively to minimize damage and speed up recovery operations. Governmental organizations can provide technological know-how, threat intelligence, and regulatory advice to industry parties that are impacted. These organizations can lessen operational disruption, stop the spread of cyberattacks, and restore vital services by coordinating their response activities.

4.2 Risk Management Practices

SCRM is a strategic framework that proactively identifies, assesses, and mitigates supply chain risks that affect integrity, efficiency, and resilience. Its goal is to protect the supply chain and boost efficiency. Supplies are plagued by operational risks like equipment failures, labor disputes, and process inefficiencies. These tiny errors can cause major interruptions, lowering productivity and increasing operational costs. Currency fluctuations, loan availability, and interest rate volatility are financial risks. These financial undercurrents can quickly deplete liquidity, raise costs, and confuse planning. Strategic risks originate from firms aggressive market expansion, merger, or acquisition strategies. These enterprises promise new possibilities but may cause supply chain misalignments, resource allocation issues, and strategic vulnerabilities. Planning & Control Risk indicates a fault in demand forecasts and warehouse inventory management. Chaos reigns over stockouts, excess inventory, and production timelines. Quality risks threaten firms' main promise excellence. Failure to achieve quality standards can cause product recalls, brand damage, and customer distrust. Cultural Risk emphasises organisational and external harmony. Corporate cultural misalignments hinder communication, collaboration, and effectiveness. Cultural awareness training, inclusive settings, and effective change management are needed to bridge these gaps. SCRM involves prevention, preparedness, response, and recovery. Preventing dangers requires safety standards and frequent maintenance. Preparing for risk occurrences requires detailed planning and procedures, such as personnel training and company continuity plans. Crisis management teams and stakeholder coordination react quickly to risk situations during the Response phase. The Recovery phase restores activities and employs damage assessment and plan reviews to improve resilience (Siano, P. et al., 2019).

4.3 Emerging Tech Integration

Artificial Intelligence (AI) (Pandey, B. K., & Pandey, D., 2023) and Blockchain are two revolutionary technologies that have had a profound impact on various industries and how people interact with each other. Nevertheless, the convergence of these fields holds the potential to revolutionize numerous domains. This convergence has the potential to revolutionize industries such as supply chain logistics, healthcare (Pandey, B. K. et al., 2011), cybersecurity, and others, indicating a significant change in technological advancement. The convergence of AI (Saxena, A. et al., 2024) and Blockchain is rooted in their complementary nature. AI enables machines to make independent decisions and enhance human abilities, while Blockchain (David, S. et al., 2023) ensures a secure and transparent distributed ledger. Working in harmony, they create a powerful partnership that enhances their unique abilities, driving them towards uncharted territories of creativity and transformation. Integrating AI (Tripathi, R. P. et al., 2023) into Blockchain brings a heightened level of intelligence to data management and problem-solving. Utilizing hashing algorithms for data mining is a common practice in Blockchain (Troncia, M. et al., 2019). However, AI (Pandey, B. K. et al., 2024) simplifies and enhances this process by optimizing operations and reducing complexity. This optimization (Pandey, D., & Pandey, B. K., 2022) improves energy consumption efficiency within the Blockchain ecosystem and enhances scalability and transaction efficiency. This optimization helps improve energy efficiency, supporting sustainability and environmental responsibility in the ecosystem. AI brings in cutting-edge decentralized learning systems (Anand, R. et al., 2024) and innovative data-sharing techniques to tackle the scalability issue of Blockchain. This boosts efficiency and opens up new possibilities for startups and enterprises in the Blockchain ecosystem to effectively expand their operations. Blockchain is well-known for its strong security features. However, the incorporation of AI enhances security even further by utilizing natural language processing, image recognition, and real-time data transformation capabilities. This combination enhances the peer-to-peer linking of Blockchain, resulting in the creation of micro-economic environments that efficiently optimize data transactions with the adaptability offered by AI intelligence. With the rise of cutting-edge technologies like blockchain and artificial intelligence (AI), there is a world of possibilities for bolstering supply chain security and resilience. As this convergence continues to evolve, its impact on society and the economy are shown in the figure 2 which will be profound, reshaping the way we live, work, and interact with technology.

Figure 2. Impact of AI on blockchain

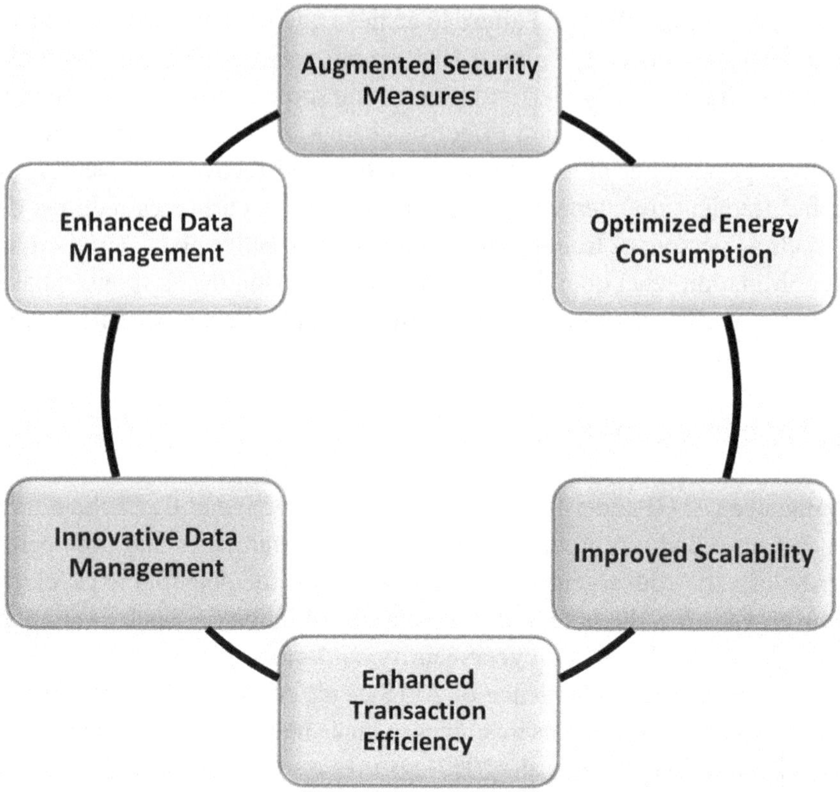

These cutting-edge technologies provide fresh solutions to tackle enduring issues in supply chain management, such as traceability, transparency, and risk mitigation. Blockchain technology is well-known for its decentralized and immutable ledger system, which offers a transparent and tamper-proof record of transactions throughout the supply chain. With the use of blockchain technology, organizations can achieve complete visibility and traceability of goods as they progress through different stages of production, transportation, and delivery. Every transaction or event is securely linked and time-stamped, ensuring a reliable audit trail that minimizes the chances of fraud, counterfeiting, and unauthorized alterations. In addition, blockchain technology allows for the secure sharing and collaboration of data among supply chain participants, all while ensuring the privacy and integrity of the information. With an improved level of transparency and trust, the ability to identify and address security threats is enhanced, resulting in a stronger supply chain security. With the help of cutting-edge artificial intelligence and machine learning technologies (Vinodhini, V. et al., 2022), businesses can now harness the power of advanced analytics to analyze large volumes of supply chain data in real-time. With the utilization of AI algorithms, organizations have the ability to identify patterns (Govindaraj, V. et al., 2023), anomalies, and potential security threats that might otherwise be overlooked by conventional approaches. Utilizing advanced predictive analytics, potential risks such as supplier disruptions, demand fluctuations, or cyber-security breaches can be anticipated and addressed proactively. AI-powered systems have the potential to streamline decision-making processes, optimize resource allocation, and automate repetitive tasks, resulting in increased operational efficiency and flexibility throughout the supply chain. The integration of blockchain and AI technologies can bring about significant advantages for enhancing supply chain security. As an expert in network architecture, one can utilize AI algorithms to analyze data stored on blockchain platforms and detect any suspicious patterns or anomalies that may indicate security breaches or fraudulent activities. Similarly, blockchain technology can improve the credibility and dependability of AI-generated insights by offering an unchangeable record of data origin and verifiability. With the integration, a robust ecosystem is formed, bringing together secure data sharing, predictive analytics, and automated decision-making to enhance supply chain security and resilience.

V. REGULATORY FRAMEWORKS AND POLICY

5.1 Navigating Supply Chain Security Regulations

Supply chain security regulations and standards encompass a wide range of legal frameworks, industry standards, and best practices, all designed to strengthen supply chains against various threats and vulnerabilities. The regulatory measures are carefully designed to ensure the stability, flexibility, and reliability of supply chains in response to changing security challenges. The Customs-Trade Partnership against Terrorism (C-TPAT) is a significant voluntary initiative led by the U.S. Customs and Border Protection (CBP). This program focuses on enhancing the security of international supply chains through collaborative partnerships with businesses. Authorized Economic Operator (AEO) programs are widely adopted by customs authorities worldwide to certify businesses as reliable and safe trading partners. These programs aim to improve supply chain security by providing benefits such as faster customs clearance and fewer inspections to businesses that consistently meet specific security criteria and compliance standards. The International Organization for Standardization (ISO) has played a crucial role in developing various standards related to supply chain security. These standards include ISO 28000 (Security Management Systems for the Supply Chain) and ISO 27001 (Information Security Management Systems). These standards provide detailed guidelines and requirements for implementing security management systems and effectively managing security risks in supply chains. The Transported Asset Protection Association (TAPA) is instrumental in developing industry-specific security standards and certification programs designed for the transportation and logistics sector (Fayyad, U. et al., 1996). The standards are carefully crafted to prevent cargo theft, tampering, and other security breaches by outlining the minimum security requirements for facilities, transport vehicles, and different supply chain processes. In the European Union (EU), various regulations and initiatives have been implemented to enhance supply chain security, such as the EU Customs Risk Management Framework and the EU Customs Security Program. The regulations aim to strengthen risk assessment and management practices, promote collaboration between customs authorities and businesses, and enhance supply chain security throughout the EU. The Safe Frameworks developed by the World Customs Organization (WCO) act as valuable resources, offering a collection of best practices and guidelines to strengthen the global supply chain against various security risks, including terrorism, smuggling, and illicit trade. These frameworks promote the importance of working together with customs administrations and other stakeholders to enhance supply chain security and streamline legitimate trade and travel. Various industries have developed their own regulations and guidelines to address specific supply chain security concerns. As an example, the pharmaceutical industry follows Good Distribution Practice (GDP) guidelines to guarantee the reliability and safety of pharmaceutical products during the supply chain. Just like a quantitative analyst, the food industry follows regulations like the Food Safety Modernization Act (FSMA) to prevent food contamination and adulteration.

5.2 Proposal for New Regulations

Supply chain security is crucial for the reliability and authenticity of 6G networks, which the entire world is waiting for with bated breath. 6G networks are a giant leap ahead in wireless communication (Raja, D. et al., 2024), and they have the ability to completely change industries and unleash new technologies. On the other hand, these networks' foundational supply chains pose a number of security risks because to their complexity and interconnection. This proposal therefore calls for new rules to be put in place to strengthen 6G ecosystem supply chain security. These rules are put in place to make sure that 6G supply chains are strong and reliable by reducing risks, making things more transparent, and encouraging stakeholders to work together. An essential part of the proposed rules is to create a consistent method for evaluating 6G network-related risks to the supply chain. There will be a focus on supplier dependencies, component vulnerabilities, and geopolitical issues within this framework. Organizations in the 6G supply chain can enhance their ability to detect and respond to risks by following these tips for performing thorough risk assessments. The supply chain of 6G networks relies on vendors and suppliers, and the new laws will impose strict due diligence obligations on them to guarantee their reliability and trustworthiness. Comprehensive security audits, compliance certifications, and background checks are all part of this process. Organizations can reduce the likelihood of fraudulent individuals penetrating the supply chain by thoroughly screening vendors and suppliers. The end-to-end supply chain of 6G networks must be made more transparent and traceable. Consequently, materials and components can be tracked in real-time throughout the supply chain thanks to the standards that will be put in place by the proposed laws. Utilizing technologies like blockchain, we will generate permanent records of transactions, guaranteeing openness and responsibility throughout the whole supply chain. Strong cybersecurity and data protection measures are crucial for 6G supply chain protection in light of the growing danger of cyber assaults and data breaches. The proposed rules aim to safeguard sensitive data from cybercriminals by mandating encryption technologies (Pandey, B. K. et al., 2022), access limitations, and frequent security assessments (Abdulkader, O. et al., 2019). Stakeholders in the 6G supply chain ecosystem must work together and share information if security issues are to be properly addressed. To promote the sharing of security insights, threat intelligence, and best practices, the new laws will set up industry forums, partnerships, and platforms for information sharing. Companies may better protect themselves from security threats and make 6G supply chains more resilient if they encourage a culture of teamwork.

5.3 International Cooperation

International cooperation and standards harmonization play a crucial role in ensuring the effectiveness and efficiency of regulations and policies related to supply chain security, particularly in the ever-changing realm of emerging technologies such as 6G networks. Collaborative efforts among countries and regions are crucial in addressing the common challenges and vulnerabilities posed by the interconnected nature of global supply chains. Through international cooperation, stakeholders can work together to utilize their collective expertise and resources in order to develop comprehensive strategies that effectively address risks and strengthen the resilience of supply chains. One of the main advantages of international cooperation is the encouragement of uniformity and harmony in regulations and standards across various jurisdictions. Ensuring standards are harmonized helps businesses in global supply chains avoid the hassle of conflicting or duplicative requirements. Instead, standardized processes promote interoperability between systems and technologies, enabling seamless integration and communication across supply chain networks. This harmonization helps to lower compliance costs and administrative burdens, creating a favorable environment for international trade and investment. International cooperation enhances the robustness of supply chains by promoting mutual aid and support in times of crisis or disruption. Through the exchange of valuable insights, experiences, and valuable tools, nations can collaboratively strengthen their ability to address crises and minimize the consequences of unforeseen events. This collaborative approach ensures that disruptions have minimal impact, allowing critical supply chain operations to continue smoothly and safeguarding economic stability and security. In the world of emerging technologies such as 6G networks, it is essential to have international cooperation to effectively tackle new security challenges that go beyond national borders. These technologies bring about intricate risks that necessitate synchronized action and expertise from stakeholders across the globe. Through the exchange of threat intelligence, collaborative research and development, and effective coordination of cybersecurity initiatives, nations can proactively address emerging threats and safeguard the security and durability of cutting-edge technologies. Standardized regulations and standards promote trade and encourage innovation by ensuring fair competition for businesses in international markets. Following internationally recognized standards allows companies to showcase their adherence to regulatory requirements and facilitates market access. This supports fair competition, promotes investment in research and development, and fosters innovation in supply chain security technologies and practices.

5.4 Supply Chain Security Evolution

Given the emergence of 6G networks, the realm of supply chain security is on the brink of experiencing substantial transformation. Anticipated is the integration of advanced technologies to enhance security measures. Cutting-edge technologies such as blockchain, artificial intelligence (AI) (Anand, R. et al., 2023), and Internet of Things (IoT) devices (Pandey, J. K. et al., 2022) will be seamlessly incorporated into supply chains to improve transparency, traceability, and proactive threat detection (Iyyanar, P. et al., 2023). For example, blockchain technology will allow for the creation of unchangeable records of transactions, guaranteeing the integrity of supply chain data. Additionally, artificial intelligence algorithms will analyze large sets of data to quickly detect anomalies and potential security risks. End-to-end visibility across supply chains (Malhotra, P. et al., 2021) is a significant trend that has gained prominence. 6G networks enable enhanced visibility and transparency, enabling organizations to monitor the movement of goods and information in real-time. This increased visibility will enable stakeholders to quickly identify possible security vulnerabilities and proactively implement risk mitigation measures. With the utilization of 6G networks, organizations can enhance the robustness of their supply chains to better withstand disruptions and threats. It is anticipated that supply chains operating in 6G networks will increasingly embrace the implementation of a zero trust security model. In a highly cautious environment, trust is never taken for granted, and stringent access controls are implemented. Organizations will adopt multi-factor authentication, encryption protocols, and micro segmentation strategies to safeguard critical resources and data, allowing only authorized users and devices (Du John, H. V. et al., 2022) to access them. This approach will help reduce the risk of insider threats and unauthorized access, strengthening the overall security of supply chains. Collaborative efforts in the field of cybersecurity are set to have a significant impact on bolstering supply chain security in the context of 6G networks. Various organizations from different sectors will work together to exchange information on potential threats, establish effective strategies, and carry out collaborative exercises to strengthen our overall defense against cyber threats. Through promoting collaboration and sharing of information, stakeholders can enhance the resilience of supply chains and facilitate swift responses to emerging security challenges. The evolution of supply chain security in 6G networks will be influenced by regulatory frameworks and compliance standards. Governments and regulatory bodies are set to implement mandatory security requirements, data protection regulations, and accountability measures for organizations operating within the supply chain. Organizations will be required to comply with these standards through regular audits, certifications, and penalties for non-compliance. This will encourage them to prioritize security and follow best practices. There will be an increased emphasis on incorporating resilience into supply chains operating within 6G networks. Organizations prioritize investing in redundant systems, diversifying sourcing strategies, and implementing contingency plans to effectively manage and minimize the impact of disruptions, including natural disasters, geopolitical tensions, and cyber attacks. By taking a proactive approach to resilience, supply chains can quickly adapt and recover from unexpected events, guaranteeing uninterrupted business operations and customer satisfaction.

CONCLUSION

6G networks are a revolutionary step forward for the telecoms industry, providing unmatched speed, connectedness, and innovative possibilities. But supply networks now face more sophisticated security issues as a result of this advancement. Supply chain security is a major concern for both national security and business, as we have emphasized throughout this abstract. It is especially important in the context of 6G networks. 6G networks' salient characteristics and prospective advantages is crucial to realizing their full potential and reducing related dangers, as becomes clear as we delve deeper into their nuances. A proactive approach to supply chain security is required due to the rising complexity of 6G networks, which presents new risks and vulnerabilities. Supply chain security can only be improved by stakeholders working together and putting strong plans into place. Developing legal frameworks specifically suited to the special features of 6G networks, this also entails embracing cutting-edge technology like blockchain and AI. Assuring uniformity and interoperability throughout supply chains globally depends on promoting international collaboration and standardization of standards. We can traverse the move to 6G networks with confidence, protecting vital infrastructure, financial stability, and stakeholder trust, by emphasizing supply chain security and adopting creative solutions. As we set out on this road, let's not lose sight of our goals and be flexible and attentive to creating robust supply chains that can resist the demands of the digital landscape of future.

REFERENCES

Abdulkader, O., Bamhdi, A. M., Thayananthan, V., & Elbouraey, F. (2019, July). Ibmsdc: Intelligent blockchain based management system for protecting digital currencies transactions. In *2019 Third World Conference on Smart Trends in Systems Security and Sustainablity (WorldS4)* (pp. 363-367). IEEE.

Ahmed, M., Farooq, M. S., Ibrar-ul-Haque, M., Ahmed, M., Maqbool, H., & Yousaf, A. (2021, October). Application of blockchain in green energy for sustainable future. In *2021 International Conference on Engineering and Emerging Technologies (ICEET)* (pp. 1-6). IEEE. 10.1109/ICEET53442.2021.9659727

Anand, R., Khan, B., Nassa, V. K., Pandey, D., Dhabliya, D., Pandey, B. K., & Dadheech, P. (2023). Hybrid convolutional neural network (CNN) for kennedy space center hyperspectral image. *Aerospace Systems*, 6(1), 71–78. 10.1007/s42401-022-00168-4

Anand, R., Lakshmi, S. V., Pandey, D., & Pandey, B. K. (2024). An enhanced ResNet-50 deep learning model for arrhythmia detection using electrocardiogram biomedical indicators. *Evolving Systems*, 15(1), 83–97. 10.1007/s12530-023-09559-0

Bessant, Y. A., Jency, J. G., Sagayam, K. M., Jone, A. A. A., Pandey, D., & Pandey, B. K. (2023). Improved parallel matrix multiplication using Strassen and Urdhvatiryagbhyam method. *CCF Transactions on High Performance Computing*, 5(2), 102–115. 10.1007/s42514-023-00149-9

David, S., Duraipandian, K., Chandrasekaran, D., Pandey, D., Sindhwani, N., & Pandey, B. K. (2023). Impact of blockchain in healthcare system. In *Unleashing the Potentials of blockchain technology for healthcare industries* (pp. 37–57). Academic Press. 10.1016/B978-0-323-99481-1.00004-3

Deepa, R., Anand, R., Pandey, D., Pandey, B. K., & Karki, B. (2022). Comprehensive performance analysis of classifiers in diagnosis of epilepsy. *Mathematical Problems in Engineering*, 2022, 2022. 10.1155/2022/1559312

Devasenapathy, D., Madhumathy, P., Umamaheshwari, R., Pandey, B. K., & Pandey, D. (2024). Transmission-efficient grid-based synchronized model for routing in wireless sensor networks using Bayesian compressive sensing. *SN Computer Science*, 5(1), 1–11.

Du John, H. V., Jose, T., Jone, A. A. A., Sagayam, K. M., Pandey, B. K., & Pandey, D. (2022). Polarization insensitive circular ring resonator based perfect metamaterial absorber design and simulation on a silicon substrate. *Silicon*, 14(14), 9009–9020. 10.1007/s12633-021-01645-9

Du John, H. V., Jose, T., Sagayam, K. M., Pandey, B. K., & Pandey, D. (2024). Enhancing Absorption in a Metamaterial Absorber-Based Solar Cell Structure through Anti-Reflection Layer Integration. *Silicon*, 1-11.

Ekong, M. O., George, W. K., Pandey, B. K., & Pandey, D. (2023). Enhancing the Fundamentals of Industrial Safety Management in TVET for Metaverse Realities. In *Applications of Neuromarketing in the Metaverse* (pp. 19-41). IGI Global. 10.4018/978-1-6684-8150-9.ch002

Fayyad, U., Piatetsky-Shapiro, G., & Smyth, P. (1996). The KDD process for extracting useful knowledge from volumes of data. *Communications of the ACM*, 39(11), 27–34. 10.1145/240455.240464

George, W. K., Ekong, M. O., Pandey, D., & Pandey, B. K. (2023). Pedagogy for Implementation of TVET Curriculum for the Digital World. In *Applications of Neuromarketing in the Metaverse* (pp. 117-136). IGI Global. 10.4018/978-1-6684-8150-9.ch009

. Govindaraj, V., Dhanasekar, S., Martinsagayam, K., Pandey, D., Pandey, B. K., & Nassa, V. K. (2023). Low-power test pattern generator using modified LFSR. *Aerospace Systems*, 1-8.

Guo, F., Yu, F. R., Zhang, H., Ji, H., Liu, M., & Leung, V. C. (2019). Adaptive resource allocation in future wireless networks with blockchain and mobile edge computing. *IEEE Transactions on Wireless Communications*, 19(3), 1689–1703. 10.1109/TWC.2019.2956519

Gupta, A. K., Sharma, R., Pandey, D., Nassa, V. K., Pandey, B. K., George, A. S., & Dadheech, P. (2023). Performance analysis of eight-channel WDM optical network with different optical amplifiers for industry 4.0. In *Innovation and Competitiveness in Industry 4.0 Based on Intelligent Systems* (pp. 197–212). Springer International Publishing. 10.1007/978-3-031-29775-5_9

Hassija, V., Chamola, V., Gupta, V., Jain, S., & Guizani, N. (2020). A survey on supply chain security: Application areas, security threats, and solution architectures. *IEEE Internet of Things Journal*, 8(8), 6222–6246. 10.1109/JIOT.2020.3025775

Hong, T., Lv, M., Zheng, S., & Hong, H. (2021). Key technologies in 6G SAGS IoT: Shape-adaptive antenna and radar-communication integration. *IEEE Network*, 35(5), 150–157. 10.1109/MNET.001.2100148

Iyyanar, P., Anand, R., Shanthi, T., Nassa, V. K., Pandey, B. K., George, A. S., & Pandey, D. (2023). A real-time smart sewage cleaning UAV assistance system using IoT. In *Handbook of Research on Data-Driven Mathematical Modeling in Smart Cities* (pp. 24–39). IGI Global.

Khan, B., Hasan, A., Pandey, D., Ventayen, R. J. M., Pandey, B. K., & Gowwrii, G. (2021). Fusion of datamining and artificial intelligence in prediction of hazardous road accidents. In *Machine learning and iot for intelligent systems and smart applications* (pp. 201–223). CRC Press. 10.1201/9781003194415-12

Kumar Pandey, B., Pandey, D., Nassa, V. K., Ahmad, T., Singh, C., George, A. S., & Wakchaure, M. A. (2021). Encryption and steganography-based text extraction in IoT using the EWCTS optimizer. *Imaging Science Journal*, 69(1-4), 38–56. 10.1080/13682199.2022.2146885

KVM, S., Pandey, B. K., & Pandey, D. (2024). Design of Surface Plasmon Resonance (SPR) Sensors for Highly Sensitive Biomolecular Detection in Cancer Diagnostics. *Plasmonics*, 1–13.

Malhotra, P., Pandey, D., Pandey, B. K., & Patra, P. M. (2021). Managing agricultural supply chains in COVID-19 lockdown. *International Journal of Quality and Innovation*, 5(2), 109–118. 10.1504/IJQI.2021.117181

Mohamed-Iliasse, M., Loubna, B., & Abdelaziz, B. (2020, October). Is machine learning revolutionizing supply chain? In *2020 5th International Conference on Logistics Operations Management (GOL)* (pp. 1-10). IEEE.

Pandey, B. K., & Pandey, D. (2023). Parametric optimization and prediction of enhanced thermoelectric performance in co-doped CaMnO3 using response surface methodology and neural network. *Journal of Materials Science Materials in Electronics*, 34(21), 1589. 10.1007/s10854-023-10954-1

Pandey, B. K., Pandey, D., & Agarwal, A. (2022). Encrypted information transmission by enhanced steganography and image transformation. *International Journal of Distributed Artificial Intelligence*, 14(1), 1–14. 10.4018/IJDAI.297110

Pandey, B. K., Pandey, D., Alkhafaji, M. A., Güneşer, M. T., & Şeker, C. (2023a). A reliable transmission and extraction of textual information using keyless encryption, steganography, and deep algorithm with cuckoo optimization. In *Micro-Electronics and Telecommunication Engineering: Proceedings of 6th ICMETE 2022* (pp. 629–636). Springer Nature Singapore. 10.1007/978-981-19-9512-5_57

Pandey, B. K., Pandey, D., Gupta, A., Nassa, V. K., Dadheech, P., & George, A. S. (2023b). Secret data transmission using advanced morphological component analysis and steganography. In *Role of data-intensive distributed computing systems in designing data solutions* (pp. 21–44). Springer International Publishing. 10.1007/978-3-031-15542-0_2

Pandey, B. K., Pandey, D., & Sahani, S. K. (2024). Autopilot control unmanned aerial vehicle system for sewage defect detection using deep learning. *Engineering Reports*, 12852. 10.1002/eng2.12852

Pandey, B. K., Pandey, S. K., & Pandey, D. (2011). A survey of bioinformatics applications on parallel architectures. *International Journal of Computer Applications*, 23(4), 21–25. 10.5120/2877-3744

Pandey, D., Hasan, A., Pandey, B. K., Lelisho, M. E., George, A. H., & Shahul, A. (2023). COVID-19 epidemic anxiety, mental stress, and sleep disorders in developing country university students. *CSI Transactions on ICT*, 11(2), 119–127. 10.1007/s40012-023-00383-0

Pandey, D., Nassa, V. K., Jhamb, A., Mahto, D., Pandey, B. K., George, A. H., & Bandyopadhyay, S. K. (2021a). An integration of keyless encryption, steganography, and artificial intelligence for the secure transmission of stego images. In *Multidisciplinary approach to modern digital steganography* (pp. 211–234). IGI Global. 10.4018/978-1-7998-7160-6.ch010

Pandey, D., Ogunmola, G. A., Enbeyle, W., Abdullahi, M., Pandey, B. K., & Pramanik, S. (2021b). COVID-19: A framework for effective delivering of online classes during lockdown. *Human Arenas*, 1-15.

Pandey, D., & Pandey, B. K. (2022). An efficient deep neural network with adaptive galactic swarm optimization for complex image text extraction. In *Process mining techniques for pattern recognition* (pp. 121–137). CRC Press. 10.1201/9781003169550-10

Pandey, J. K., Jain, R., Dilip, R., Kumbhkar, M., Jaiswal, S., Pandey, B. K., & Pandey, D. (2022). Investigating role of iot in the development of smart application for security enhancement. In *IoT Based Smart Applications* (pp. 219–243). Springer International Publishing.

Pramanik, S., Pandey, D., Joardar, S., Niranjanamurthy, M., Pandey, B. K., & Kaur, J. (2023, October). An overview of IoT privacy and security in smart cities. In *AIP Conference Proceedings* (Vol. 2495, No. 1). AIP Publishing 10.1063/5.0123511

Raja, D., Kumar, D. R., Santhiyakumari, N., Kumarganesh, S., Sagayam, K. M., Thiyaneswaran, B., Pandey, B. K., & Pandey, D. (2024). A compact dual-feed wide-band slotted antenna for future wireless applications. *Analog Integrated Circuits and Signal Processing*, 118(2), 1–15. 10.1007/s10470-023-02233-0

Revathi, T. K., Sathiyabhama, B., Sankar, S., Pandey, D., Pandey, B. K., & Dadeech, P. (2022). An intelligent model for coronary heart disease diagnosis. In *Networking Technologies in Smart Healthcare* (pp. 309–327). CRC Press. 10.1201/9781003239888-15

Sahani, K., Khadka, S. S., Sahani, S. K., Pandey, B. K., & Pandey, D. (2023). A possible underground roadway for transportation facilities in Kathmandu Valley: A racking deformation of underground rectangular struct es. *Engineering Reports*, 12821. 10.1002/eng2.12821

Saxena, A., Agarwal, A., Pandey, B. K., & Pandey, D. (2024). Examination of the Criticality of Customer Segmentation Using Unsupervised Learning Methods. *Circular Economy and Sustainability*, 1–14. 10.1007/s43615-023-00336-4

Saxena, A., Sharma, N. K., Pandey, D., & Pandey, B. K. (2021). Influence of tourists satisfaction on future behavioral intentions with special reference to desert triangle of Rajasthan. *Augmented Human Research*, 6(1), 13. 10.1007/s41133-021-00052-4

Sengupta, R., Sengupta, D., Pandey, D., Pandey, B. K., Nassa, V. K., & Dadeech, P. (2021). A Systematic review of 5G opportunities, architecture and challenges. *Future Trends in 5G and 6G*, 247-269.

Sharma, M., Pandey, D., Khosla, D., Goyal, S., Pandey, B. K., & Gupta, A. K. (2022). Design of a GaN-based Flip Chip Light Emitting Diode (FC-LED) with au Bumps & Thermal Analysis with different sizes and adhesive materials for performance considerations. *Silicon*, 14(12), 7109–7120. 10.1007/s12633-021-01457-x

Sharma, S., Pandey, B. K., Pandey, D., Anand, R., Sharma, A., & Saini, S. (2023, March). Character Recognition Technique Implementation for Complicated Deteriorated Scene. In *2023 6th International Conference on Information Systems and Computer Networks (ISCON)* (pp. 1-4). IEEE. 10.1109/ISCON57294.2023.10112185

Siano, P., De Marco, G., Rolán, A., & Loia, V. (2019). A survey and evaluation of the potentials of distributed ledger technology for peer-to-peer transactive energy exchanges in local energy markets. *IEEE Systems Journal*, 13(3), 3454–3466. 10.1109/JSYST.2019.2903172

Swapna, H. R., Bigirimana, E., Madaan, G., Hasan, A., Pandey, B. K., & Pandey, D. (2023). Impact of neuromarketing on consumer psychology in digitally connected networks. In *Applications of Neuromarketing in the Metaverse* (pp. 193–205). IGI Global. 10.4018/978-1-6684-8150-9.ch015

Tareke, S. A., Lelisho, M. E., Hassen, S. S., Seid, A. A., Jemal, S. S., Teshale, B. M., & Pandey, B. K. (2022). The prevalence and predictors of depressive, anxiety, and stress symptoms among Tepi town residents during the COVID-19 pandemic lockdown in Ethiopia. *Journal of Racial and Ethnic Health Disparities*, 1–13.35028903

Tripathi, R. P., Sharma, M., Gupta, A. K., Pandey, D., Pandey, B. K., Shahul, A., & George, A. H. (2023). Timely prediction of diabetes by means of machine learning practices. *Augmented Human Research*, 8(1), 1. 10.1007/s41133-023-00062-4

Troncia, M., Galici, M., Mureddu, M., Ghiani, E., & Pilo, F. (2019). Distributed ledger technologies for peer-to-peer local markets in distribution networks. *Energies*, 12(17), 3249. 10.3390/en12173249

Vinodhini, V., Kumar, M. S., Sankar, S., Pandey, D., Pandey, B. K., & Nassa, V. K. (2022). IoT-based early forest fire detection using MLP and AROC method. *International Journal of Global Warming*, 27(1), 55–70. 10.1504/IJGW.2022.122794

Chapter 12
Security Roadmap for Industry 5.0:
Managing Risks in the 6G Landscape

Ila Dixit
Department of Management, Maharaja Agrasen International College, Raipur, India

M. S. Kishan Varma
Department of Management Studies, VFSTR University (Deemed), India

Ashutosh Singh
Institute of Business Management, GLA University, India

B. Charith
AMET Business School, AMET University, India

Mallikarjun
Department of Management, Maharaja Agrasen International College, Raipur, India

H. Mickle Aancy
Department of Master of Business Administration, Panimalar Engineering College, Chennai, India

Chetan M. Thakar
Savitribai Phule Pune University, India

ABSTRACT

The coming together of Industry 5.0 and 6G technology represents a paradigm shift that has the potential to bring about unprecedented levels of connectivity, efficiency, and innovation. On the other hand, these advancements bring with them significant challenges in terms of ensuring the security and resilience of digital infrastructure. The purpose of this chapter is to investigate the intersection of Industry 5.0 and 6G technology, with a particular focus on the critical importance of security regarding the changing landscape. The chapter sheds light on the intricate dynamics that are influencing the digital future by conducting an analysis of the essential components of 6G technology, the evolution from Industry 4.0, and the key features of Industry 5.0. In addition to this, it presents an analysis of the threat landscape in the era of 6G, which includes cyber threats, system vulnerabilities, and the influence of hyper-connectivity.

DOI: 10.4018/979-8-3693-7421-4.ch012

I. INTRODUCTION

The most recent stage in the development of industrial processes (Saxena, A. et al., 2021), known as "industry 5.0," is distinguished from its predecessors by emphasizing human-centered innovation and the harmonious integration of cutting-edge technologies. Industry 5.0 (Ekong, M. O. et al., 2023) aims to balance human and machine capabilities, encouraging teamwork and collaboration on the factory floor, in contrast to previous stages that prioritized efficiency and automation (Tripathi, R. P. et al., 2023). The advent of 6G (Kirubasri, G. et al., 2021) technology, which promises previously unheard-of levels of connectedness, speed, and innovation, is set to completely transform the global telecom scene. Research endeavors to shape the future of 6G in accordance with national needs and aspirations are actively being undertaken by countries and consortiums worldwide due to its potential impact on lives, livelihoods, and productivity, among other aspects of society. Next G Alliance is leading a significant initiative in North America that includes a wide range of stakeholders, including universities, startups, and vendors and service providers. With the help of this cooperative effort, 6G technology research and development will be accelerated, paving the way for regional adoption and deployment. North America aims to lead the 6G revolution by promoting collaboration amongst a wide range of stakeholders. By doing so, it hopes to use its resources and experience to open up new avenues for technological advancement and economic expansion. Aiming for global leadership in the field, South Korea has unveiled a comprehensive plan for 6G research and development. The strategy, which is in place until 2025, places a strong emphasis on the creation of innovative technologies, active involvement in global standards-setting processes, and the construction of a strong foundation for 6G industry and research. By the end of the decade, South Korea intends to launch 14 Low Earth Orbit (LEO) satellites as part of its strategy, improving connectivity and opening the door for cutting-edge 6G services and applications. Europe is putting itself in a leadership position for the 6G era thanks to its long history of telecom research and innovation. The continent's dedication to attaining independence, sovereignty, and dependability in 6G network solutions and services is emphasized by the European 6G Vision. Europe wants to ensure its competitiveness in the global telecommunications (Bruntha, P. M. et al., 2023) market by establishing safe and reliable access to essential technologies through the identification of

The Vision 2030 white chapter, which outlines the Integrated Optical and Wireless Network (IOWN) Forum's vision for the future of telecommunications in Japan, was published. Japan aims to spearhead innovation in 6G and beyond, catering to the increasing need for fast, low-latency connectivity and opening up fresh avenues for digital transformation (Swapna, H. R. et al., 2023). It does this by leveraging its proficiency in optical and wireless networking technologies (Khan, R. et al., 2019). China, a dominant force in the world of telecommunications, is also developing 6G technology at a rapid pace. Important advancements in 6G technology have been identified, and initiatives are in place to promote innovation and research in this quickly developing field. China is positioned to be a key player in defining the direction of 6G and propelling its widespread adoption due to its sizable market and advanced technological capabilities.

1.1 Security in the 6G Landscape

In today's changing business environment, security (Pandey, J. K. et al., 2022) is essential to guaranteeing the availability, confidentiality, and integrity of data and systems (Sharma, S. et al., 2023) . Strong security measures are becoming more and more important as technologies develop and become more interconnected (Pandey, B. K. et al., 2023a). Security becomes even more crucial in the context of Industry5.0, when human-machine collaboration (Pandey, D. et al., 2022) is crucial to protecting sensitive data from potential threats. The mitigation of cyber threats is a primary reason why security is so important in today's world. The Internet of Things (IoT) (Iyyanar, P. et al., 2023) and the proliferation of linked devices increase the attack surface for possible cyberattacks. Vulnerabilities in networked systems (Devasenapathy, D. et al., 2024) may be used by malicious actors to obtain unauthorized access, steal confidential information, or interfere with operations. Strong security measures that are put in place aid in thwarting these threats and guaranteeing the ongoing operations. The digital ecosystem's (George, W. K. et al., 2023) ability to retain confidence and trust depends on security. Businesses mainly depend on data in Industry 5.0, where customized products and personalized manufacturing are essential, to comprehend consumer preferences and adjust product offerings. On the other hand, trust may be undermined and brand reputation may suffer if this data is compromised as a result of a security breach. Organizations can show their dedication to safeguarding customer (Saxena, A. et al., 2024) privacy and upholding data integrity by placing a high priority on security. Security is also essential for risk management and regulatory compliance. Strict security standards and guidelines are necessary for industries operating in highly regulated sectors, like healthcare (Singh, S. et al., 2023) and finance, to guarantee compliance with industry regulations and safeguard confidential data. There may be severe financial penalties and reputational harm if these requirements are not met. By putting strong security measures in place, organizations can reduce regulatory risks and prove that they are in compliance with all relevant laws and regulations. Breakdowns in vital systems can have far-reaching effects on business operations, public safety, and well-being in Industry 5.0, where automation and digitization are ubiquitous. Organizations can reduce their exposure to cyberattack risks and lessen the possible impact of disruptions by making investments in security infrastructure and putting proactive monitoring and response mechanisms in place.

II. INDUSTRY 5.0 AND 6G TECHNOLOGY

2.1 Industry 5.0

The most recent iteration of industrialization, known as "industry 5.0," signifies a dramatic change in the way manufacturing and production are done. Industry 5.0 stresses the integration of human-centered approaches alongside cutting-edge technologies, building upon the developments of Industry 4.0, which brought automation and data exchange in manufacturing technologies. Industry 5.0 emphasizes human-machine collaboration more than its predecessor, which concentrated mainly on automation and machine-to-machine communication (Anand, R. et al., 2023). The goal is to use the complementary abilities of both to boost productivity and innovation. The idea of human-machine collaboration, in which people and machines cooperate to accomplish shared objectives, is at the core of Industry 5.0. This collaborative approach acknowledges the unique strengths of machines and humans: machines provide precision, efficiency, and scalability, while humans contribute creativity, intuition, and adaptability. Industry 5.0 aims to unleash new levels of productivity, agility, and competitiveness in manufacturing and beyond by fusing human ingenuity with the capabilities of cutting-edge technologies like artificial intelligence (Pandey, B. K. et al., 2021), robotics, and the Internet of Things (IoT) (Pramanik, S. et al., 2023). Industry 5.0's salient characteristics encompass the amalgamation of cutting-edge technologies and human-centric design principles, prioritizing personalized and customized manufacturing processes, and embracing adaptable and nimble production systems (De Alwis, C. et al., 2021). Industry 5.0 welcomes flexibility and customization in contrast to traditional manufacturing models (Revathi, T. K. et al., 2022), which place a premium on mass production and standardization. This enables the development of customized goods and services that are suited to the particular requirements and tastes of each client. A strong emphasis on environmental responsibility and sustainability, with a particular emphasis on waste reduction, resource optimization, and environmental impact minimization. Industry 5.0 uses cutting-edge technologies like smart resource management systems, renewable energy sources, and green manufacturing techniques to develop more environmentally friendly and sustainable production processes that promote long-term environmental stewardship. The need for production systems that are both adaptable and agile, so that they can effectively respond to shifting market dynamics and unexpected disruptions. Resilience is another essential aspect of Industry 5.0. Industry 5.0 enables manufacturers to quickly adapt to shifting consumer preferences, disruptions in supply chain, and other challenges. This ensures the resilience and viability of their operations in a world that is becoming increasingly volatile and uncertain. Industry 5.0 is characterized by its embrace of flexibility and customization are as shown in the Figure 1.

Figure 1. 5.0 HCRS framework

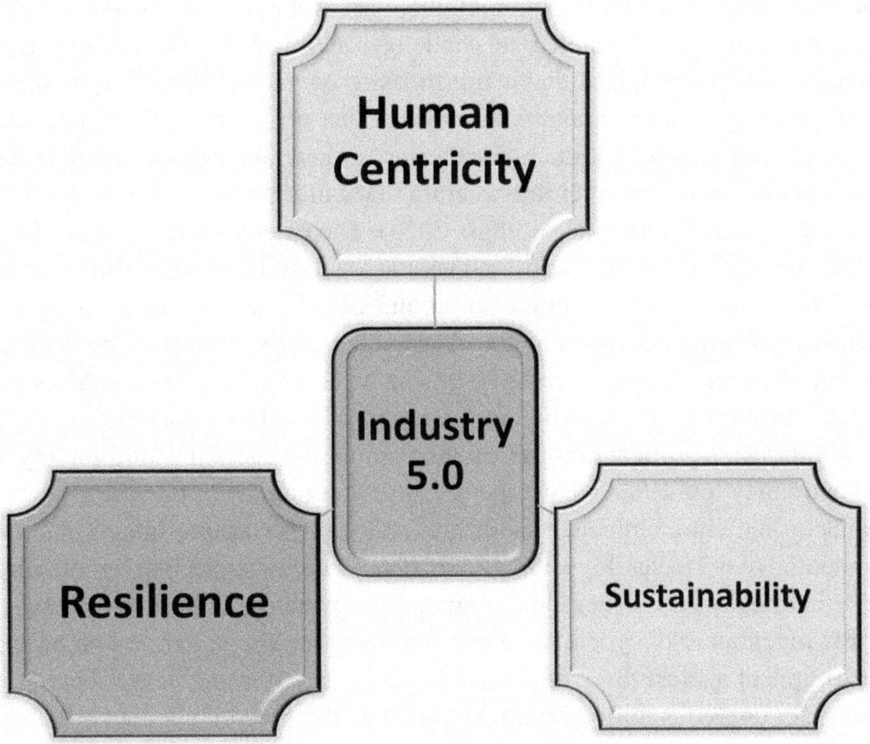

2.3 6G Technology

Experts are praising 6G technology as the next big thing in telecom innovation, and there is a tangible sense of excitement surrounding it. 6G, the cellular technology that replaces 5G (Sengupta, R. et al., 2021), is expected to bring in a new era of connectivity with speeds that are 50 times faster than 5G. The commercial launch of 6G is anticipated to occur between 2028 and 2030, signaling a fundamental change in the wireless communication landscape (Gupta, A. K. et al., 2023). 6G's ability to operate at higher frequencies than 5G networks, which allows it to deliver noticeably higher capacity and noticeably lower latency, is central to its allure. In contrast to its forerunners, 6G promises to enable communication with a latency of only one microsecond, signifying a significant advancement in terms of responsiveness and real-time engagement (Govindaraj, V. et al., 2023). With a latency 1,000 times faster than a millisecond throughput, this audacious goal highlights the revolutionary potential of 6G technology. Utilizing the terahertz band of frequency, a comparatively unexplored resource in the electromagnetic spectrum, is the foundation of 6G's capabilities. Terahertz waves are in the middle of the infrared and microwave spectrums, providing a plethora of options for extremely quick data transfer. Although terahertz waves are small and sensitive by nature, there is a lot of available spectrums in this frequency range, which could lead to amazing data rates and further advance 6G's effectiveness and performance (Deepa, R. et al., 2022). Even though 6G technology has a lot of potential, there are still a number of obstacles in the way of its implementation. Overcoming the technological challenges involved in using terahertz waves for wireless communication is one major obstacle. Reliable transmission over long distances is hampered by terahertz signals' high susceptibility to attenuation, which means that obstacles in their path can easily absorb (Du John, H. V. et al., 2022) or scatter them. Furthermore, there are significant engineering challenges in developing compatible hardware and infrastructure that can support terahertz-based communication, which need to be addressed (Du John, H. V. et al., 2024). The extensive integration of 6G technology is contingent upon the creation of worldwide guidelines and legal structures that oversee its implementation and functioning. Interoperability, spectrum allocation, and international regulatory compliance will require concerted efforts from industry players, regulatory agencies, and legislators. The smooth integration of 6G into the current telecommunications ecosystems can be facilitated by stakeholders working together to promote global cooperation and coordination. Beyond its technical capabilities, the introduction of 6G technology will have a significant impact on innovation, the economy, and society. 6G's extremely fast speeds and extremely low latency have the potential to completely transform a variety of sectors, including manufacturing, entertainment, healthcare, and transportation (Sahani, K. et al., 2023). The revolutionary potential of 6G technology will greatly benefit applications like remote surgery, driverless cars, and rich virtual reality experiences, opening up new avenues for human endeavor and economic expansion. A growing number of cyberattacks are concentrating their attention on networks of varying kinds. In order to protect against these attacks, it is necessary to implement robust security solutions because of their sheer unpredictability. Jamming is one of the potential dangers that will be protected against by 6G networks. When developing new mixed-reality environments that incorporate digital representations of both real and virtual objects, it is necessary to take into consideration concerns regarding privacy (Ray, P. P. et al., 2021). The next generation of wireless communication, or 6G technology, is primarily concerned with achieving ultra-high frequency data transmission (Pandey, B. K. et al., 2023b). Researchers working on 6G are investigating the use of waves in the terahertz (THz) or hundreds of GHz range, in contrast to 5G, which operates within the frequency range up to about 100GHz. The enormous amount of available spectrum in the upper atmosphere presents the possibility of extremely fast data rates, even with the difficulties presented by the fragile nature of these waves. In order to implement 6G technology, one of the main obstacles is the creation of semiconductor materials with multiple THz operating frequencies. In addition, large arrays of tiny aerial (Pandey, B. K. et al., 2024) antennas might need to be deployed by researchers in order to transmit data at these frequencies (Raja, D. et al., 2024). To overcome impediments like ambient water vapor, which reflects and scatters THz signals, complex models must be developed in order to facilitate data transmission via winding routes. 6G technology seeks to enable simultaneous transmission and reception in the same frequency as existing wireless systems, which can only allow for one of two things to happen at once: transmission or reception on any given frequency. This might greatly improve spectrum efficiency, but it might cause problems for networks that are already in place. Moreover, 6G might enable mesh networking, which would let gadgets help each other out by boosting each other's data, improving coverage and connectivity (Gui, G. et al., 2020). With the aim of obtaining latency below 1 ms, latency reduction is another area of advancement in 6G technology. Split computing, in which part of the data is processed locally on semiconductor devices (Dhanasekar, S. et al., 2023) and the remainder is processed and transmitted elsewhere, is made more efficient by lower latency. This is especially important for applications like augmented reality that need to process data in real time. Augmented reality glasses could send and receive data in real time with ease using 6G, improving user experiences and opening up new possibilities for split computing applications.

2.4 Intersection of Industry 5.0 and 6G

The coming together of Industry 5.0 and 6G technology is a meeting of two paradigm-shifting ideas that are each about to change their own fields. Industry 5.0 focuses on personalized manufacturing and collaboration between humans and machines. It aims to use new technologies to make production processes faster, more adaptable, and more efficient. On the other hand, 6G technology promises to bring about a new era of wireless communication with speeds, capacities, and connections that have never been seen before. When Industry 5.0 and 6G come together, they could spur innovation in many fields, from healthcare and manufacturing to transportation and entertainment. Industry 5.0 apps can be more responsive and efficient by using the very fast speeds and very low latency of 6G networks. This lets people in industrial settings communicate and make decisions in real time. For instance, in smart manufacturing settings, 6G-enabled sensors (Abdulkarim, Y. I. et al., 2023) and devices can send huge amounts of data in real time. This lets for planned maintenance, better production schedules, and easy communication between humans and machines. Industry 5.0's vision of people and machines working together seamlessly to reach common goals can't come true without this level of connectivity and responsiveness. Adding 6G technology to Industry 5.0 ecosystems also makes it possible for personalized and on-demand manufacturing to happen in new ways. With communication latency as low as one microsecond, 6G networks make it easy to quickly change and customize production processes to meet changing customer needs or market conditions. This speed and adaptability are very important to Industry 5.0, where mass customization and personalized products are very important for making money. Another thing that Industry 5.0 and 6G technology can do together is change the way supply chains and logistics work. Companies can improve the efficiency of their supply chains by using real-time data and analytics from 6G-enabled semiconductor (Du John, H. V. et al., 2023) devices to better manage their inventory, make transportation routes more efficient, and manage their deliveries more effectively. Better visibility and control make it easier to deal with problems quickly and make the system more resilient when problems come up out of the blue. When Industry 5.0 and 6G technology come together, they have huge effects on the future of healthcare delivery. 6G networks make it possible for ultra-low latency communication, which makes it easier to monitor patients from afar, have telemedicine consultations, and have immersive virtual reality experiences. With these features, healthcare providers can give patients high-quality care from anywhere, which cuts down on the need for in-person visits and makes medical services easier to get (Letaief, K. B. et al., 2019).

III. THREAT LANDSCAPE IN THE 6G ERA

3.1 Cyber Threats

In the digital age, cyber threats are increasingly dangerous to individuals, organizations, and societies. Cybercriminals use a variety of malicious methods to compromise systems, steal data, disrupt operations, or cause harm. From data breaches and ransomware attacks to phishing scams and malware infections, cyber threats can cause significant financial, reputational, and social harm. Malware, which infects computers, networks, and devices, is a major cyber threat. Viral, worm, Trojan, and ransomware are spread via email attachments, malicious websites, or infected files. Malware can steal data, encrypt files, and hijack computing (Bessant, Y. A. et al., 2023) resources once installed. Another common cyber threat is phishing, which uses deceptive emails, messages, or websites to steal login credentials or financial information. Phishing attacks are hard to detect and resist because they look like legitimate emails from trusted sources. Cybercriminals use psychology and social engineering to trick unsuspecting users into sharing sensitive information or clicking on malicious links. In recent years, ransomware attacks have devastated individuals, businesses, and critical infrastructure. Ransomware attacks encrypt files and systems and demand a ransom to decrypt them. These attacks can cripple operations, disrupt essential services, and cause significant financial and reputational damage. DDoS attacks flood a target system or network with traffic, making it inaccessible to legitimate users. Organizations can lose money and time due to DDoS attacks on websites, services, and communication channels. Cybercriminals may launch DDoS attacks for extortion, revenge, or ideology. Insider threats—malicious or accidental actions by employees, contractors, or trusted individuals with access to sensitive systems and information—also pose a cybersecurity risk to organizations. Insider threats can involve unauthorized access, data theft, or system and network sabotage due to negligence, disgruntlement, or malicious intent. Technical controls, employee training, and monitoring are needed to detect and mitigate insider threats. Cybersecurity must be multilayered to combat growing threats. Firewalls, antivirus software, encryption, and intrusion detection systems are used to protect against external threats and vulnerabilities. Organizations must also invest in employee training and awareness programs to teach users cybersecurity best practices and help them identify and respond to threats. To effectively combat cyber threats, government agencies, law enforcement, industry partners, and cybersecurity organizations must collaborate and share information. Shared threat intelligence, best practices, and resources can help stakeholders detect, prevent, and respond to cyber attacks faster. To respond quickly and effectively to cyber incidents, organizations must create and update incident response plans. These plans should outline roles and responsibilities, communication protocols, and remediation procedures to reduce cyber attack damage and aid recovery. Organizations can identify incident response gaps and improve their processes through regular testing and drills.

3.2 System Vulnerabilities

System vulnerabilities threaten data and system integrity, confidentiality, and availability, making cybersecurity a major issue. Software (Kirubasri, G. et al., 2022) bugs, misconfigurations, and design flaws allow cyber attackers to exploit and compromise systems. Cybercriminals use software vulnerabilities, misconfigured settings, insecure protocols, and outdated systems to gain unauthorized access to sensitive data or disrupt operations. Software vulnerabilities, caused by code or application flaws, are common system vulnerabilities. Attackers can use buffer overflows, injection attacks, insecure deserialization, and other coding errors to execute arbitrary code, escalate privileges, or gain unauthorized access to systems. Software vulnerabilities can be introduced during development, deployment, or maintenance of operating systems, web applications, third-party libraries, or firmware. Another common system vulnerability is misconfigured settings and insecure configurations, often caused by human error or oversight during deployment or maintenance. Poor passwords, open ports, unnecessary services, and lack of security controls can expose systems to unauthorized access, exploitation, and compromise. Insecure configurations in network devices, cloud services, or IoT devices (Vinodhini, V. et al., 2022) allow cyberattackers to infiltrate networks, steal data, or attack other systems. Systemic vulnerabilities caused by system and application design and architectural flaws are hard to detect and mitigate. Poor design, threat modeling, or security controls can lead to systemic vulnerabilities that cyber attackers can exploit. Lack of input validation, insecure authentication, or insufficient access controls can allow attackers to easily compromise systems. Outdated systems and unpatched software may contain known vulnerabilities that have not been patched, making them cybersecurity risks (Yang, H. et al., 2020). Cybercriminals exploit outdated systems and software with known vulnerabilities to gain unauthorized access, steal data, or attack other systems. Proactive vulnerability management and patch management are crucial because failing to apply security patches and updates leaves systems vulnerable to exploitation and compromise. To combat system vulnerabilities, organizations must take a proactive, multi-layered cybersecurity approach. Firewalls, intrusion detection systems, and endpoint protection solutions are used to protect against known vulnerabilities and emerging threats. Organizations should also perform regular vulnerability assessments, penetration testing, and security audits to prioritize vulnerability remediation. These programs should include vulnerability scanning, risk assessment, patch management, remediation, and vulnerability exposure tracking. A proactive and systematic vulnerability management strategy can reduce cyber threats and strengthen systems and infrastructure against exploitation and compromise.

3.3 Hyper-Connectivity Impact

Technology and the proliferation of interconnected devices and systems have created hyper-connectivity, which has a major impact on society, the economy, and daily life. Being constantly connected to networks and devices allows instant communication, information sharing, and access to digital services anytime, anywhere. Hyper-connectivity offers unprecedented opportunities for innovation, collaboration, and efficiency, but it also poses significant challenges and risks that must be addressed to realize its full potential. Hyper-connectivity revolutionizes communication and collaboration, enabling real-time interaction across borders. Technology like social media, messaging apps, and video conferencing allows people and organizations to communicate instantly, fostering global collaboration, knowledge sharing, and cultural exchange. Hyper-connectivity has transformed communication, collaboration, and work, removed barriers and enabling unprecedented collaboration. Hyper-connectivity has modernized commerce and business models, boosting e-commerce, digital marketplaces, and online payment systems. Hyper-connected ecosystems allow businesses to reach customers worldwide, personalize their offerings, and provide seamless digital experiences across channels and devices. Businesses can now make agile, data-driven decisions and better adapt to changing market dynamics and customer preferences thanks to hyper-connectivity. Hyper-connected platforms and streaming services provide on-demand access to music, videos, news, and educational resources, keeping people informed, entertained, and connected. Hyper-connectivity has also enabled smart cities, connected vehicles, and intelligent transportation systems. Cities can optimize traffic flow, public transportation, and urban mobility for residents and commuters with IoT sensors (Du John, H. V. et al., 2021), GPS technology, and real-time data analytics. Hyper-connected transportation systems reduce urban congestion, emissions, and travel times with real-time monitoring, predictive maintenance, and dynamic routing. Hyper-connectivity has many benefits, but it also poses significant challenges and risks that must be addressed to ensure its sustainability and resilience. Hyper-connected ecosystems are vulnerable to data breaches, ransomware attacks, and IoT (Menon, V. et al., 2022) botnets, making cybersecurity a major issue. Encryption, authentication, and intrusion detection systems are needed to secure sensitive data, connected devices, and critical infrastructure from cyberattacks. Hyper-connectivity raises concerns about data privacy, surveillance, and digital rights as companies and governments collect, analyze, and monetize personal data. Privacy and security in hyper-connected environments require strong data protection laws, transparent data practices, and user consent mechanisms to empower individuals to control their personal data and digital identities. Hyper-connectivity also worsens digital inequality and access disparities because not everyone has high-speed internet, digital semiconductor devices (Du John, H. V. et al., 2023), and online services. An inclusive and equitable digital society requires bridging the digital divide and providing universal access to digital resources and opportunities.

IV. SECURITY ROADMAP COMPONENTS

4.1 Secure Design for 6G-Enabled Systems

To make systems safe for the era of 6G, you need a proactive, multi-layered approach to cybersecurity that includes strong security measures, threat modeling, and safe design principles. As the next generation of cell phones after 5G, 6G systems need to be built with security in mind from the start to effectively protect against new threats and holes. By using secure design practices, businesses can make 6G systems more reliable and protect themselves from cyberattacks and security holes. Defense-in-depth is one of the most important principles of secure design for 6G-enabled systems. This means putting in place multiple layers of security controls to protect against a wide range of threats and attack vectors. Strong encryption, authentication, and access controls are all part of this approach to keep data safe while it's being sent and while it's being stored. In addition, businesses should set up intrusion detection and prevention systems, network segmentation, and secure configurations to lessen the effects of security incidents and stop possible breaches. Also, designing secure systems that can connect to 6G networks requires a deep knowledge of the threats and possible attack scenarios. Organizations should do full threat modeling exercises to find and rank possible threats and holes in their systems throughout their entire lifecycle. Organizations can make 6G systems safer and more resilient by looking at possible attack vectors, threat actors, and security holes and then creating strong security controls and countermeasures. To find and fix security flaws early in the development process, organizations should follow secure coding standards, review their code regularly, and do both static and dynamic code analysis. Also, businesses should use secure software development lifecycle (SDLC) practices like threat modeling, secure coding training, and secure deployment procedures to make sure that security is part of the whole development process. Strong identity and access management (IAM) controls are also needed for secure design of 6G-enabled systems to safely authenticate and authorize users, devices, and applications. To keep people from getting to sensitive data and resources, businesses should use least privilege, multi-factor authentication, and role-based access controls. Companies should also use strong encryption and digital signatures to keep data safe and make sure that users and systems can talk to each other safely. To safely monitor and manage network traffic, businesses should set up firewalls, intrusion detection systems, and virtual private networks (VPNs). Also, businesses should use safe protocols like Transport Layer Security (TLS) and Internet Protocol Security (IPsec) to encrypt data while it's being sent and keep others from listening in or messing with it. To make sure that security controls and countermeasures work, secure design for 6G-enabled systems needs to be constantly tested, monitored, and confirmed. Regular security assessments, penetration tests, and vulnerability scans should be done by organizations to find and fix any security holes or weak spots in their systems. Additionally, businesses should create incident response plans and procedures to effectively find, deal with, and recover from security incidents.

4.2 Communication Protocols

In the digital age, communication protocols are essential for enabling data and information exchange between devices, systems, and networks. In order to provide interoperability, dependability, and security in contemporary computing environments, these protocols specify the guidelines and norms controlling how data is transferred, formatted, and understood across communication channels. The seamless connectivity and operation of digital systems and services are supported by communication protocols, which are used in wired and wireless networks, cloud computing, and the Internet of Things (IoT). The Transmission Control Protocol/Internet Protocol (TCP/IP), which forms the basis of the Internet and contemporary networking, is one of the most extensively used communication protocols. Using IP addresses and port numbers, TCP/IP offers a standardized framework for packet-switched communication, allowing devices to send data across networks that are connected. Protocols like File Transfer Protocol (FTP) for file transfers, Simple Mail Transfer Protocol (SMTP) for email correspondence, and Hypertext Transfer Protocol (HTTP) for web browsing are all part of TCP/IP. The Hypertext Transfer Protocol Secure (HTTPS) protocol adds encryption and authentication mechanisms to the functionality of HTTP. Secure Sockets Layer (SSL) or Transport Layer Security (TLS) protocols are used by HTTPS to encrypt data, guaranteeing the integrity and confidentiality of data transferred between web servers and clients. Because it protects against tampering and eavesdropping, HTTPS is widely used for sensitive data transmission, e-commerce websites, and secure online transactions. These protocols, which are each suited to particular use cases and requirements of Internet of Things applications, include Bluetooth Low Energy (BLE), Zigbee, Z-Wave, and LoRaWAN. For instance, LoRaWAN is perfect for long-range, low-power communication in smart city and industrial IoT deployments, while BLE is frequently used for short-range wireless communication between smartphones and wearable devices. The foundation of both wired and wireless networking is communication protocols like Ethernet (IEEE 802.3) and Wi-Fi (IEEE 802.11), which allow devices to connect to local area networks (LANs) and the Internet. While Ethernet protocols enable wired communication over physical cables like fiber optic or twisted pair, Wi-Fi protocols support wireless communication between devices within a constrained range. For a variety of devices and applications, these protocols provide high-speed data transmission, network connectivity, and Internet access.

4.3 Incident Response for 6G Environments

In the future's hyperconnected landscape, incident response in 6G environments entails a proactive and all-encompassing approach to identifying, containing, and mitigating security incidents and breaches. 6G cellular technology, which replaces 5G, brings with it new risks and challenges. As a result, enterprises must modify their incident response plans to properly handle new threats. In order to reduce risks and safeguard vital assets and infrastructure, incident response in 6G environments needs to be flexible, resilient, and adaptive. This includes being able to handle sophisticated cyberattacks, supply chain vulnerabilities, quantum computing, and AI-driven threats. Proactive threat detection and monitoring, which uses machine learning (ML) (Pandey, B. K., & Pandey, D., 2023), artificial intelligence (AI) (Anand, R. et al., 2024), and advanced security analytics to instantly detect unusual activity and possible security incidents, is one of the most important components of incident response in 6G environments. Organizations can minimize the impact of security incidents and prevent potential breaches by effectively detecting and responding to security threats through continuous monitoring of system logs, network traffic, and user activity.

In order to respond to security incidents, organizations should set up incident response plans and procedures that specify roles and responsibilities, communication guidelines, and escalation procedures. Organizations can reduce operational disruption and expedite incident response efforts by instituting clear channels of communication and coordination. Incident response in 6G environments involves gathering evidence, fixing vulnerabilities, and conducting forensics and investigations to determine the underlying cause of security incidents and stop them from happening again. In order to effectively analyze compromised systems, find indicators of compromise (IOCs), and attribute attacks to threat actors, organizations should make use of digital forensics tools and techniques. Organizations should also hold lessons learned sessions and post-incident reviews to pinpoint areas that need work and gradually improve their incident response capabilities. Stakeholders can improve their combined capacity to quickly and effectively detect, stop, and respond to cyberattacks by exchanging threat intelligence, best practices, and resources. Organizations should also take part in tabletop, cyber, and simulation exercises to test incident response plans and strengthen their resistance to new threats (Goyal, J., 2020).

V. IMPLEMENTATION STRATEGIES

5.1 Collaborative Approaches

Bringing together stakeholders from different organizations, sectors, and regions to jointly address shared cybersecurity challenges, share threat intelligence, and develop best practices and standards to improve overall security posture are examples of collaborative approaches for industry-wide security initiatives. These cooperative initiatives seek to promote knowledge exchange, group defense, and group resilience against cyberthreats that could impact several enterprises in a given sector or industry. There are a number of cooperative strategies and programs in place to support industry-wide security initiatives are as shown in the Figure 2.

Figure 2. Collaborative approaches

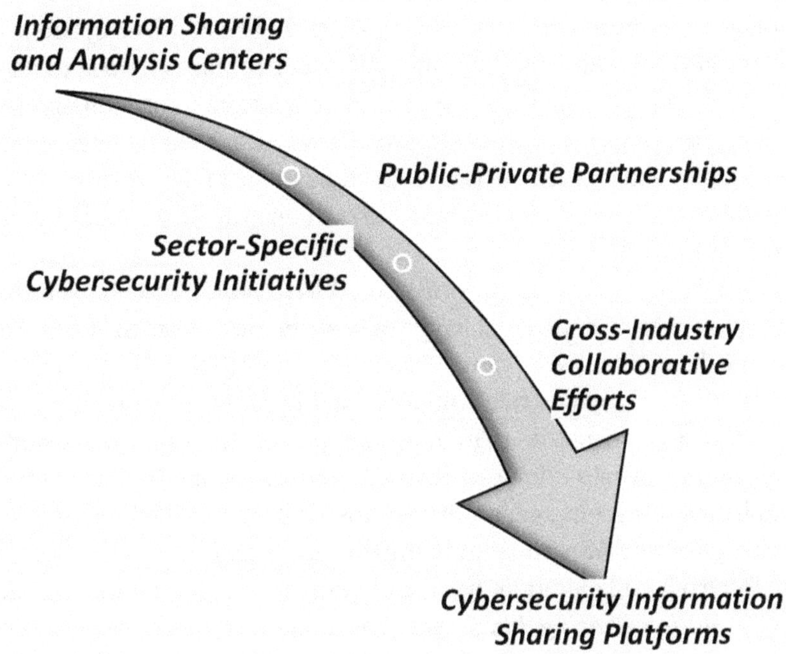

1. *Information Sharing and Analysis Centers (ISACs)*: These centers provide a forum for businesses to share threat intelligence, insights, and best practices. They are essential hubs for industry-specific cybersecurity (Pandey, B. K. et al., 2022) collaboration. By facilitating real-time information sharing on new vulnerabilities, cyberthreats, and attack trends, these centers help members improve their situational awareness and response skills. Organizations can proactively defend against cyber threats and mitigate risks by using ISACs to access timely alerts, advisories, and actionable intelligence. ISACs frequently coordinate cooperative efforts, like cooperative exercises, workshops, and working groups, to tackle shared issues and create cybersecurity solutions tailored to particular industries. The industry's overall security posture is strengthened by members working together on incident response strategies, exchanging lessons learned, and taking advantage of peer-to-peer networking opportunities.
2. *Public-Private Partnerships*: In order to jointly address cybersecurity challenges, public-private partnerships facilitate cooperation between government agencies, industry associations, and private sector organizations. Through these collaborations, cybersecurity resilience is improved across important industries and critical infrastructure sectors by utilizing the complementary strengths and resources of public and private entities. Public-private partnerships facilitate information sharing and collaboration on risk management and cybersecurity strategy development by exchanging threat

intelligence, organizing incident response activities, and holding joint exercises. Public-private partnerships increase awareness, develop cybersecurity expertise, and fortify the industry's overall security posture through cooperative projects like training programs, cybersecurity awareness campaigns, and capacity-building exercises.

3. *Sector-Specific Cybersecurity Initiatives*: These efforts aim to work together on cybersecurity strategy development, risk management, and incident response planning by bringing together relevant industry stakeholders. These projects concentrate on creating customized cybersecurity frameworks, guidelines, and standards as well as addressing cybersecurity issues unique to particular industries. Participants in sector-specific initiatives improve their knowledge of industry-specific threats and vulnerabilities by exchanging best practices, lessons learned, and threat intelligence. This facilitates proactive risk mitigation and incident response. Organizations in the sector cooperate on cybersecurity initiatives to improve their security posture and resilience against cyber threats through working groups, task forces, and workshops.
4. *Cross-Industry Collaborative Efforts*: In order to address common cybersecurity challenges and encourage information sharing and the exchange of best practices, organizations from various sectors collaborate. Through these initiatives, diverse stakeholders pool their collective expertise and resources to identify new threats, develop creative solutions, and improve cyber resilience across industries. Organizations from various industries gain important perspectives on cybersecurity challenges and solutions by exchanging insights, lessons learned, and threat intelligence. This strengthens risk management and incident response capabilities. Cross-industry collaborative efforts strengthen the overall cybersecurity posture of participating organizations and improve collective defense against cyber threats by fostering collaboration, trust, and information sharing among stakeholders.
5. *Cybersecurity Information Sharing Platforms*: These platforms give businesses access to online discussion boards, portals, and other resources so they can exchange best practices and resources, work together on incident response, and share threat intelligence. Members can collaborate and communicate in real time on these platforms, which speeds up the process of responding to cyberthreats and vulnerabilities. Cybersecurity information sharing platforms help organizations better detect and address new threats by utilizing automation and advanced analytics. Organizations improve their collective defense capabilities and situational awareness through cooperative efforts like sharing threat intelligence, coordinating incident response, and launching community-driven projects, which fortify overall cybersecurity resilience.

5.2 Training Programs for Industry 5.0 Workforce

Security awareness training and education are essential for Industry 5.0 workers to understand and mitigate cybersecurity risks. Industrial 5.0's rapid integration of advanced technologies and hyperconnectivity requires organizations to prioritize cybersecurity awareness and education to equip employees with cyber-defense skills. These programs educate employees about cybersecurity best practices, foster a security culture, and equip them to identify and respond to security threats. Interactive training modules are essential for engaging employees with real-world scenarios, case studies, and simulations of cybersecurity threats and attacks (Zhang, S. et al., 2019). Phishing awareness, password hygiene, social engineering, and safe browsing are covered in these modules to help employees identify and address security threats. Role-based training programs also customize security awareness modules to each employee's job function and address specific cybersecurity risks and challenges. Employees need regular cybersecurity training refreshers to stay current on threats and best practices. Quarterly or bi-annual training sessions reinforce key concepts, introduce new security measures, and address emerging threats, keeping employees aware of security. Phishing simulations also test employees' susceptibility to phishing attacks and emphasize the need for vigilance and skepticism when dealing with emails, links, and attachments. These simulations identify areas for improvement and offer targeted training to improve employees' phishing detection and reporting. Gamification and rewards can boost employee engagement in security awareness training. Leaderboards, badges, and rewards for completing training modules or reporting security incidents encourage personnel to participate in cybersecurity initiatives and practice good security. Mobile-friendly training platforms let employees access security awareness training content on their smartphones and tablets anytime, anywhere. To reduce legal and regulatory risks, employees must understand their roles in protecting sensitive data, complying with data protection laws, and following security protocols. Continuous feedback and evaluation mechanisms gather employee feedback on security awareness training programs and use it to improve them. Training content and delivery are optimized by regularly assessing employee awareness, behavior change, and incident response readiness. Comprehensive security awareness training and education programs help Industry 5.0 workers identify and mitigate cybersecurity risks, promoting security and resilience across the organization (Li, Y. et al., 2021).

5.3 Leveraging Blockchain Technology

Blockchain (David, S. et al., 2023) technology can improve data integrity and trust across many industries and applications. Blockchain, a decentralized and distributed ledger technology, records transactions securely and immutably on a network of computers. Its cryptographic principles and consensus mechanisms keep ledger data tamper-proof, transparent, and verifiable, boosting digital transaction trust. Blockchain immutability is a major advantage. Without network consensus, blockchain data is nearly impossible to change or delete. This inherent immutability ensures data integrity over time, providing a reliable audit trail of transactions and preventing unauthorized changes. Blockchain's decentralized network architecture eliminates the need for intermediaries or central authorities to validate transactions. Decentralization reduces single points of failure and increases stakeholder transparency and accountability. Independent verification of data authenticity and accuracy builds trust when all participants have access to a shared ledger of transactions. Another key feature of blockchain is security. Blockchain cryptography secures data and transactions from tampering and fraud (Kato, N. et al., 2020). Blockchain blocks are cryptographically linked, forming an immutable chain that protects data. Blockchain consensus mechanisms like PoW and PoS are crucial to transaction validation and confirmation. These mechanisms securely and transparently verify and add transactions to the blockchain, boosting data integrity trust. Blockchain technology has created smart contracts, self-executing contracts with predefined rules and conditions. When predefined conditions are met, these programmable contracts automatically execute and enforce the agreement, eliminating intermediaries and increasing trust in contractual agreements. Blockchain technology can improve data integrity and trust in supply chain management, financial transactions, identity verification, and healthcare records. Blockchain-based systems foster trust, transparency, and accountability in the digital age, enabling transformative innovation and collaboration across industries.

CONCLUSION

Industry 5.0 and 6G technology usher in a new era of innovation, connectivity, and productivity. Despite advancement promises, digital infrastructure security and resilience are difficult. The transition from Industry 4.0 to Industry 5.0 emphasizes human-machine collaboration and hyper-connectivity, while 6G technology promises unprecedented speed and capabilities, requiring strong security. The 6G threat landscape must include cyber threats, system vulnerabilities, and hyper-connectivity's transformative impact. Organisations must address these issues to protect their digital assets and infrastructure. Secure system design, resilient communication protocols, and effective incident response mechanisms are essential to a 6G security roadmap. Prioritizing these components reduces risks and strengthens cyber resilience. Collaborative approaches, Industry 5.0 workforce training, and blockchain technology can improve 6G security. Building a secure and resilient future requires stakeholder collaboration, employee security awareness training, and blockchain for data integrity and trust.

REFERENCES

Abdulkarim, Y. I., & Awl, H. N., Muhammad Sharif, F. F., Saeed, S. R., Sidiq, K. R., Khasraw, S. S., ... Pandey, D. (2023). Metamaterial-based sensors loaded corona-shaped resonator for COVID-19 detection by using microwave techniques. *Plasmonics*, 1–16.

Anand, R., Khan, B., Nassa, V. K., Pandey, D., Dhabliya, D., Pandey, B. K., & Dadheech, P. (2023). Hybrid convolutional neural network (CNN) for kennedy space center hyperspectral image. *Aerospace Systems*, 6(1), 71–78. 10.1007/s42401-022-00168-4

Anand, R., Lakshmi, S. V., Pandey, D., & Pandey, B. K. (2024). An enhanced ResNet-50 deep learning model for arrhythmia detection using electrocardiogram biomedical indicators. *Evolving Systems*, 15(1), 83–97. 10.1007/s12530-023-09559-0

Bessant, Y. A., Jency, J. G., Sagayam, K. M., Jone, A. A. A., Pandey, D., & Pandey, B. K. (2023). Improved parallel matrix multiplication using Strassen and Urdhvatiryagbhyam method. *CCF Transactions on High Performance Computing*, 5(2), 102–115. 10.1007/s42514-023-00149-9

Bruntha, P. M., Dhanasekar, S., Hepsiba, D., Sagayam, K. M., Neebha, T. M., Pandey, D., & Pandey, B. K. (2023). Application of switching median filter with L 2 norm-based auto-tuning function for removing random valued impulse noise. *Aerospace Systems, 6*(1), 53-59.

David, S., Duraipandian, K., Chandrasekaran, D., Pandey, D., Sindhwani, N., & Pandey, B. K. (2023). Impact of blockchain in healthcare system. In *Unleashing the Potentials of blockchain technology for healthcare industries* (pp. 37–57). Academic Press. 10.1016/B978-0-323-99481-1.00004-3

De Alwis, C., Kalla, A., Pham, Q. V., Kumar, P., Dev, K., Hwang, W. J., & Liyanage, M. (2021). Survey on 6G frontiers: Trends, applications, requirements, technologies and future research. *IEEE Open Journal of the Communications Society*, 2, 836–886. 10.1109/OJCOMS.2021.3071496

Deepa, R., Anand, R., Pandey, D., Pandey, B. K., & Karki, B. (2022). Comprehensive performance analysis of classifiers in diagnosis of epilepsy. *Mathematical Problems in Engineering*, 2022, 2022. 10.1155/2022/1559312

Devasenapathy, D., Madhumathy, P., Umamaheshwari, R., Pandey, B. K., & Pandey, D. (2024). Transmission-efficient grid-based synchronized model for routing in wireless sensor networks using Bayesian compressive sensing. *SN Computer Science*, 5(1), 1–11.

Dhanasekar, S., Martin Sagayam, K., Pandey, B. K., & Pandey, D. (2023). Refractive Index Sensing Using Metamaterial Absorbing Augmentation in Elliptical Graphene Arrays. *Plasmonics*, 1–11. 10.1007/s11468-023-02152-w

Du John, H. V., Ajay, T., Reddy, G. M. K., Ganesh, M. N. S., Hembram, A., Pandey, B. K., & Pandey, D. (2023). Design and simulation of SRR-based tungsten metamaterial absorber for biomedical sensing applications. *Plasmonics*, 18(5), 1903–1912. 10.1007/s11468-023-01910-0

Du John, H. V., Jose, T., Jone, A. A. A., Sagayam, K. M., Pandey, B. K., & Pandey, D. (2022). Polarization insensitive circular ring resonator based perfect metamaterial absorber design and simulation on a silicon substrate. *Silicon*, 14(14), 9009–9020. 10.1007/s12633-021-01645-9

Du John, H. V., Jose, T., Sagayam, K. M., Pandey, B. K., & Pandey, D. (2024). Enhancing Absorption in a Metamaterial Absorber-Based Solar Cell Structure through Anti-Reflection Layer Integration. *Silicon*, 1-11.

Du John, H. V., Moni, D. J., Ponraj, D. N., Sagayam, K. M., Pandey, D., & Pandey, B. K. (2021). Design of Si based nano strip resonator with polarization-insensitive metamaterial (MTM) absorber on a glass substrate. *Silicon*, 1-10.

Du John, H. V., Sagayam, K. M., Jose, T., Pandey, D., Pandey, B. K., Kotti, J., & Kaur, P. (2023). Design simulation and parametric investigation of a metamaterial light absorber with tungsten resonator for solar cell applications using silicon as dielectric layer. *Silicon*, 15(9), 4065–4079. 10.1007/s12633-023-02321-w

Ekong, M. O., George, W. K., Pandey, B. K., & Pandey, D. (2023). Enhancing the Fundamentals of Industrial Safety Management in TVET for Metaverse Realities. In *Applications of Neuromarketing in the Metaverse* (pp. 19-41). IGI Global. 10.4018/978-1-6684-8150-9.ch002

George, W. K., Ekong, M. O., Pandey, D., & Pandey, B. K. (2023). Pedagogy for Implementation of TVET Curriculum for the Digital World. In *Applications of Neuromarketing in the Metaverse* (pp. 117-136). IGI Global. 10.4018/978-1-6684-8150-9.ch009

Govindaraj, V., Dhanasekar, S., Martinsagayam, K., Pandey, D., Pandey, B. K., & Nassa, V. K. (2023). Low-power test pattern generator using modified LFSR. *Aerospace Systems*, 1-8.

Goyal, J., Singla, K., Akashdeep, & Singh, S. (2020). A survey of wireless communication technologies from 1G to 5G. In *Second International Conference on Computer Networks and Communication Technologies: ICCNCT 2019* (pp. 613-624). Springer International Publishing. 10.1007/978-3-030-37051-0_69

Gui, G., Liu, M., Tang, F., Kato, N., & Adachi, F. (2020). 6G: Opening new horizons for integration of comfort, security, and intelligence. *IEEE Wireless Communications*, 27(5), 126–132. 10.1109/MWC.001.1900516

Gupta, A. K., Sharma, R., Pandey, D., Nassa, V. K., Pandey, B. K., George, A. S., & Dadheech, P. (2023). Performance analysis of eight-channel WDM optical network with different optical amplifiers for industry 4.0. In *Innovation and Competitiveness in Industry 4.0 Based on Intelligent Systems* (pp. 197–212). Springer International Publishing. 10.1007/978-3-031-29775-5_9

Iyyanar, P., Anand, R., Shanthi, T., Nassa, V. K., Pandey, B. K., George, A. S., & Pandey, D. (2023). A real-time smart sewage cleaning UAV assistance system using IoT. In *Handbook of Research on Data-Driven Mathematical Modeling in Smart Cities* (pp. 24–39). IGI Global.

Kato, N., Mao, B., Tang, F., Kawamoto, Y., & Liu, J. (2020). Ten challenges in advancing machine learning technologies toward 6G. *IEEE Wireless Communications*, 27(3), 96–103. 10.1109/MWC.001.1900476

Khan, R., Kumar, P., Jayakody, D. N. K., & Liyanage, M. (2019). A survey on security and privacy of 5G technologies: Potential solutions, recent advancements, and future directions. *IEEE Communications Surveys and Tutorials*, 22(1), 196–248. 10.1109/COMST.2019.2933899

Kirubasri, G., Sankar, S., Pandey, D., Pandey, B. K., Nassa, V. K., & Dadheech, P. (2022). Software-defined networking-based Ad hoc networks routing protocols. In *Software defined networking for Ad Hoc networks* (pp. 95–123). Springer International Publishing. 10.1007/978-3-030-91149-2_5

Kirubasri, G., Sankar, S., Pandey, D., Pandey, B. K., Singh, H., & Anand, R. (2021, September). A recent survey on 6G vehicular technology, applications and challenges. In *2021 9th International Conference on Reliability, Infocom Technologies and Optimization (Trends and Future Directions)(ICRITO)* (pp. 1-5). IEEE.

Letaief, K. B., Chen, W., Shi, Y., Zhang, J., & Zhang, Y. J. A. (2019). The roadmap to 6G: AI empowered wireless networks. *IEEE Communications Magazine*, 57(8), 84–90. 10.1109/MCOM.2019.1900271

Li, Y., Yu, Y., Susilo, W., Hong, Z., & Guizani, M. (2021). Security and privacy for edge intelligence in 5G and beyond networks: Challenges and solutions. *IEEE Wireless Communications*, 28(2), 63–69. 10.1109/MWC.001.2000318

Menon, V., Pandey, D., Khosla, D., Kaur, M., Vashishtha, H. K., George, A. S., & Pandey, B. K. (2022). A Study on COVID–19, Its Origin, Phenomenon, Variants, and IoT-Based Framework to Detect the Presence of Coronavirus. In *IoT Based Smart Applications* (pp. 1–13). Springer International Publishing.

Pandey, B. K., & Pandey, D. (2023). Parametric optimization and prediction of enhanced thermoelectric performance in co-doped CaMnO3 using response surface methodology and neural network. *Journal of Materials Science Materials in Electronics*, 34(21), 1589. 10.1007/s10854-023-10954-1

Pandey, B. K., Pandey, D., & Agarwal, A. (2022). Encrypted information transmission by enhanced steganography and image transformation. *International Journal of Distributed Artificial Intelligence*, 14(1), 1–14. 10.4018/IJDAI.297110

Pandey, B. K., Pandey, D., Alkhafaji, M. A., Güneşer, M. T., & Şeker, C. (2023a). A reliable transmission and extraction of textual information using keyless encryption, steganography, and deep algorithm with cuckoo optimization. In *Micro-Electronics and Telecommunication Engineering: Proceedings of 6th ICMETE 2022* (pp. 629–636). Springer Nature Singapore. 10.1007/978-981-19-9512-5_57

Pandey, B. K., Pandey, D., Gupta, A., Nassa, V. K., Dadheech, P., & George, A. S. (2023b). Secret data transmission using advanced morphological component analysis and steganography. In *Role of data-intensive distributed computing systems in designing data solutions* (pp. 21–44). Springer International Publishing. 10.1007/978-3-031-15542-0_2

Pandey, B. K., Pandey, D., & Sahani, S. K. (2024). Autopilot control unmanned aerial vehicle system for sewage defect detection using deep learning. *Engineering Reports*, 12852. 10.1002/eng2.12852

Pandey, B. K., Pandey, D., Wairya, S., & Agarwal, G. (2021). An advanced morphological component analysis, steganography, and deep learning-based system to transmit secure textual data. *International Journal of Distributed Artificial Intelligence*, 13(2), 40–62. 10.4018/IJDAI.2021070104

Pandey, D., Wairya, S., Sharma, M., Gupta, A. K., Kakkar, R., & Pandey, B. K. (2022). An approach for object tracking, categorization, and autopilot guidance for passive homing missiles. *Aerospace Systems*, 5(4), 553–566. 10.1007/s42401-022-00150-0

Pandey, J. K., Jain, R., Dilip, R., Kumbhkar, M., Jaiswal, S., Pandey, B. K., & Pandey, D. (2022). Investigating role of iot in the development of smart application for security enhancement. In *IoT Based Smart Applications* (pp. 219–243). Springer International Publishing.

Pramanik, S., Pandey, D., Joardar, S., Niranjanamurthy, M., Pandey, B. K., & Kaur, J. (2023, October). An overview of IoT privacy and security in smart cities. In *AIP Conference Proceedings* (Vol. 2495, No. 1). AIP Publishing. 10.1063/5.0123511

Raja, D., Kumar, D. R., Santhiyakumari, N., Kumarganesh, S., Sagayam, K. M., Thiyaneswaran, B., Pandey, B. K., & Pandey, D. (2024). A compact dual-feed wide-band slotted antenna for future wireless applications. *Analog Integrated Circuits and Signal Processing*, 1–15. 10.1007/s10470-023-02233-0

Ray, P. P., Kumar, N., & Guizani, M. (2021). A vision on 6G-enabled NIB: Requirements, technologies, deployments, and prospects. *IEEE Wireless Communications*, 28(4), 120–127. 10.1109/MWC.001.2000384

Revathi, T. K., Sathiyabhama, B., Sankar, S., Pandey, D., Pandey, B. K., & Dadeech, P. (2022). An intelligent model for coronary heart disease diagnosis. In *Networking Technologies in Smart Healthcare* (pp. 309–327). CRC Press. 10.1201/9781003239888-15

Sahani, K., Khadka, S. S., Sahani, S. K., Pandey, B. K., & Pandey, D. (2023). A possible underground roadway for transportation facilities in Kathmandu Valley: A racking deformation of underground rectangular structures. *Engineering Reports*, 12821. 10.1002/eng2.12821

Saxena, A., Agarwal, A., Pandey, B. K., & Pandey, D. (2024). Examination of the Criticality of Customer Segmentation Using Unsupervised Learning Methods. *Circular Economy and Sustainability*, 1–14. 10.1007/s43615-023-00336-4

Saxena, A., Sharma, N. K., Pandey, D., & Pandey, B. K. (2021). Influence of tourists satisfaction on future behavioral intentions with special reference to desert triangle of Rajasthan. *Augmented Human Research*, 6(1), 13. 10.1007/s41133-021-00052-4

Sengupta, R., Sengupta, D., Pandey, D., Pandey, B. K., Nassa, V. K., & Dadeech, P. (2021). A Systematic review of 5G opportunities, architecture and challenges. *Future Trends in 5G and 6G*, 247-269.

Sharma, S., Pandey, B. K., Pandey, D., Anand, R., Sharma, A., & Saini, S. (2023, March). Character Recognition Technique Implementation for Complicated Deteriorated Scene. In *2023 6th International Conference on Information Systems and Computer Networks (ISCON)* (pp. 1-4). IEEE. 10.1109/ISCON57294.2023.10112185

Singh, S., Madaan, G., Kaur, J., Swapna, H. R., Pandey, D., Singh, A., & Pandey, B. K. (2023). *Bibliometric Review on Healthcare Sustainability. Handbook of Research on Safe Disposal Methods of Municipal Solid Wastes for a Sustainable Environment*, 142-161. 10.4018/978-1-6684-8117-2.ch011

Swapna, H. R., Bigirimana, E., Madaan, G., Hasan, A., Pandey, B. K., & Pandey, D. (2023). Impact of neuromarketing on consumer psychology in digitally connected networks. In *Applications of Neuromarketing in the Metaverse* (pp. 193–205). IGI Global. 10.4018/978-1-6684-8150-9.ch015

Tripathi, R. P., Sharma, M., Gupta, A. K., Pandey, D., Pandey, B. K., Shahul, A., & George, A. H. (2023). Timely prediction of diabetes by means of machine learning practices. *Augmented Human Research*, 8(1), 1. 10.1007/s41133-023-00062-4

Vinodhini, V., Kumar, M. S., Sankar, S., Pandey, D., Pandey, B. K., & Nassa, V. K. (2022). IoT-based early forest fire detection using MLP and AROC method. *International Journal of Global Warming*, 27(1), 55–70. 10.1504/IJGW.2022.122794

Yang, H., Alphones, A., Xiong, Z., Niyato, D., Zhao, J., & Wu, K. (2020). Artificial-intelligence-enabled intelligent 6G networks. *IEEE Network*, 34(6), 272–280. 10.1109/MNET.011.2000195

Zhang, S., Wang, Y., & Zhou, W. (2019). Towards secure 5G networks: A Survey. *Computer Networks*, 162, 106871. 10.1016/j.comnet.2019.106871

Chapter 13
Smart Farming in 6G Navigating Security Challenges for Agricultural Innovations

Satyanarayana Tirlangi
Visakha Institute of Engineering and Technology, India

Bachina Harish Babu
VNR Vignana Jyothi Institute of Engineering and Technology, India

S. Meenakshi
https://orcid.org/0000-0001-5075-6808
Department Science and Humanities, R.M.K. Engineering College, India

D. Sugumar
https://orcid.org/0000-0001-9652-2062
Karunya Institute of Technology and Sciences (Deemed), India

R. Manikandan
https://orcid.org/0000-0002-2055-6634
Department Electronics and Communication Engineering, Panimalar Engineering College, Chennai, India

Joshuva Arockia Dhanraj
https://orcid.org/0000-0001-5048-7775
Chandigarh University, India

ABSTRACT

The coming together of smart farming and 6G technology is a big change in the way agriculture is innovated. It opens new ways to improve productivity, sustainability, and resilience that have never been seen before. This chapter looks into the complex connection between smart farming methods and the rise of 6G technology, stressing how important security is for improving farming technologies. The introduction gives a full picture of smart farming and how important it is for solving modern farming problems.

I. INTRODUCTION

As the world's population has grown, agriculture, the backbone of human civilization, has had to adapt continuously. The sector has experienced tremendous changes from subsistence farming to contemporary agribusiness, mostly due to changes in environmental conditions (Pandey, B. K. et al., 2023a) and technology breakthroughs. Farmers face a multitude of challenges in the modern agricultural landscape, from the effects of climate change to the complexities of the supply chain. But in the middle of all of

DOI: 10.4018/979-8-3693-7421-4.ch013

these difficulties is innovation, which offers hope. This talk examines the security risks that agricultural innovations face as well as the proactive steps that farmers have taken to overcome these obstacles. Adaptive measures are also required to maintain agricultural productivity in the face of environmental volatility due to changing temperature regimes and precipitation patterns (Govindaraj, V. et al., 2023). In this situation, adopting cutting-edge tools and techniques to reduce the risks associated with climate change allows farmers to innovate as a primary means of fostering resilience. The innovative method of precision agriculture is being adopted by progressive farmers as a means of increasing productivity and maximizing resource use. Precision agriculture is made possible by the utilization of sensor (Du John, H. V. et al., 2023) technologies and data analytics to monitor crop health parameters in real-time. This allows for the precise application of fertilizer and irrigation to meet the individual needs of each crop. Thus, this precision-based strategy supports prudent water management, which is important given the depletion of water supplies, while also increasing yields. Drones and other aerial technologies have become essential monitoring and management tools for crops. Drones with multispectral imaging capabilities and high-resolution cameras give farmers an aerial perspective of their fields, facilitating the early identification of anomalies such as nutrient deficiencies and pest infestations. Farmers can address agronomic problems proactively, preventing possible yield losses and optimizing resource allocation, by quickly identifying areas that need attention. Farm management procedures are streamlined, operational resilience is strengthened, and farmers are encouraged to adopt these cutting-edge technologies thanks in large part to Bivatec Ltd. There is a risk to farmers' livelihoods and food security when there are disruptions anywhere in the supply chain. So, in an effort to improve supply chain transparency and traceability, farmers are increasingly relying on technology-enabled solutions like blockchain (David, S. et al., 2023). The agricultural value chain can benefit from a strong framework for transparent and secure transaction records established by blockchain technology, which is recognized for its decentralized architecture and unchangeable ledger system. Through the creation of a tamper-proof digital ledger that documents every transaction, from the purchase of seeds to the distribution of finished goods, blockchain fosters trust and accountability and empowers farmers to track the progress of their products and spot possible problems with quality. With soil degradation posing a serious threat to long-term agricultural productivity, soil health (Singh, S. et al., 2023) emerges as a critical concern in sustainable agriculture. The fertility and resilience of soil are compromised by conventional farming practices, which are typified by heavy tillage and chemical inputs. They also frequently worsen soil erosion and nutrient draining. Regenerative farming methods, which put soil health restoration and biodiversity conservation first, are becoming more and more popular among farmers in response (Monteiro, A. et al., 2021). A range of agroecological techniques known as "regenerative farming" are used to grow crops and soil microorganisms in a symbiotic relationship, increase soil organic matter, and improve water retention. Regenerative farming practices, which include crop rotation and cover crops, help reduce soil degradation and encourage carbon sequestration, which aids in the fight against climate change.

1.1 6G in Agriculture

The progress in telecommunications technology has brought us into a time of digital (George, W. K. et al., 2023) transformation and connectivity that has never been seen before. The world has seen amazing progress in communication networks (Devasenapathy, D. et al., 2024) since 5G infrastructure, the fifth generation of mobile technology, was widely put in place. Even though 5G technology has a lot of great features, it also has some problems. Because of the high cost of infrastructure and worries about security, scientists and engineers are looking into what 6G (Kirubasri, G. et al., 2021) technology can do. As millions of 5G base stations appear around the world, the technology's inherent flaws have become clear. One important limitation is the large amount of infrastructure needed for full coverage. 5G base stations have a much smaller coverage area than their predecessors. This means that more of them are needed to fully cover the network. Additionally, security holes, especially in new technologies like software-defined networks (SDNs), make 5G networks very problematic for their reliability. Because of these problems, countries like China, the EU, and others have started to set the stage for the creation of 6G technology. People see 6G technology as the start of a new era of connectivity, intelligence, and sensing. It promises to go beyond the limits of its predecessors and bring about a complete digital transformation in every part of society. As a result of this change, the agricultural industry is in a prime position to use 6G technology to completely change the way farms work and make them more productive. The meeting of 6G technology and farming holds a lot of promise, giving us chances to solve some of the most important problems facing the world's food system that have never been seen before. A big part of this digital revolution (Swapna, H. R. et al., 2023) in agriculture is smart farming, which is a mix of information and data management technologies (JayaLakshmi, G. et al., 2024). The goal of smart farming is to improve farming systems by using software, sensors, and robotics to make them more productive and lower the risks of natural disasters and financial losses. As one of the most important industries in the world, agriculture feeds and supports people all over the world. Still, climate change, a lack of resources, and changing consumer tastes can all be problems for the industry (George, W. K. et al., 2024). This is why smart farming solutions, 5G networks, the Internet of Things (IoT) (Iyyanar, P. et al., 2023), and precision farming have come together to form Agriculture 4.0, also known as digital agriculture. Agriculture 4.0 is a big change in the way farming is done, and it's made possible by the seamless integration of new technologies. The main ideas behind this digital revolution are automation, operational optimization (Pandey, B. K. et al., 2023b), and making decisions based on data (Sharma, S. et al., 2023). These ideas help farmers handle the complicated world of modern agriculture more quickly and accurately. By bringing together new technologies, Agriculture 4.0 creates unmatched chances for long-term food production and environmental protection (Bhat, S. A., & Huang, N. F., 2021).

1.2 Advancing Agricultural Technologies

Technological developments are a major factor in modern agriculture's dynamic landscape, as they stimulate creativity, efficiency, and sustainability. The combination of cutting-edge technologies, such as machine learning and artificial intelligence (Anand, R. et al., 2023), has the potential to revolutionize farming methods and bring in a new era of resilience and productivity. Though there is much excitement about the potential of technology in agriculture, it is important to remember that security is a crucial component of agricultural technology advancement. Technological advancements have the potential to completely transform the agricultural industry and present farmers with never-before-seen possibilities for productivity and operational optimization (Pandey, D. et al., 2021). The extensive use of contemporary technology in agriculture makes it easier to obtain up-to-date farm data, giving farmers insightful knowledge about crop health, weather patterns, and soil conditions. Farmers are better equipped to adjust to changing market conditions and dynamic environmental conditions when they have immediate access to critical data that helps them make informed decisions about crop management, resource allocation, and risk mitigation. The prospect of higher productivity and efficiency is one of the main forces behind the adoption of new technologies in agriculture. Farmers can automate repetitive tasks, optimize resource utilization, and streamline labor-intensive tasks by utilizing advanced technologies like machine vision and artificial intelligence (Pandey, B. K., & Pandey, D., 2023). The integration of modern technology holds immense potential for changing agricultural practices and increasing yields, from autonomous farming equipment that improves operational efficiency to precision agriculture techniques that enable targeted irrigation and fertilization (Yazdinejad, A. et al., 2021). Farmers can stay connected and informed in real-time thanks to the ease with which modern agriculture technology facilitates connectivity and communication (Gupta, A. K. et al., 2023). Farmers can proactively manage risks and make timely decisions to protect their crops and livelihoods by having access to weather forecasts, disaster warnings, and market trends. Farmers are empowered to recognize patterns (Muniandi, B. et al., 2024), trends, and inefficiencies thanks to the availability of farm data and analytics tools, which promotes innovation and ongoing agricultural practice improvement. Notwithstanding the many advantages of technology in agriculture, it is critical to identify and handle the security risks these developments present. Agricultural systems are more susceptible to malicious attacks, data breaches, and cybersecurity threats as they become more digitalized and networked. To preserve farmers' livelihoods and guarantee the resilience of agricultural systems, the integrity and confidentiality of farm data, including sensitive information like crop yields, financial records, and market strategies, must be protected. The dependence on networked technologies presents possible weak points and points of failure that might interfere with agricultural activities and jeopardize food security. Every element of the agricultural technology ecosystem, from cloud-based data storage and analytics platforms to IoT (Pramanik, S. et al., 2023) sensors and autonomous machinery, needs to be protected against cyber threats and vulnerabilities. Furthermore, as the agricultural industry (Sharma, M. et al., 2024) grows more dependent on digital technologies, it is critical to close the digital gap and guarantee that all farmers, regardless of size or location, have equitable access to technology and cybersecurity resources.

II. SMART FARMING AND 6G

2.1 Components and Functions

Utilizing contemporary Information and Communication Technologies (ICT) (Raja, D. et al., 2024) to maximize resource input reduction and maximize productivity and efficiency, smart farming is a revolutionary approach to agricultural management. Modern farming is fueled by a multitude of innovative technologies that enable farmers to maximize their operations in the modern era. These technologies cover a wide range of instruments, including sensors that track important variables like temperature, humidity, light intensity (Du John, H. V. et al., 2023), soil moisture content, and water quality. Furthermore, farmers can benefit from priceless insights and decision-making support from customized software solutions designed for particular farm types or applications. Smooth data transfer and communication between farm devices (Abdulkarim, Y. I. et al., 2023) and central management systems are made possible by connectivity options ranging from cellular networks to LoRa. In addition, the accuracy of farming operations is improved by location-based technologies like GPS and satellite imagery, which allow for precise positioning and mapping. Further improving operational efficiency is the integration of robotics, which includes autonomous tractors and processing facilities, which streamline labour-intensive tasks. Data analytics tools are being used to supplement these technological advancements, allowing farmers to extract insights from large datasets for informed decision-making and ongoing farming practice improvement. All of these technologies work together to form the basis of smart farming, giving farmers the ability to maximize yields, improve production processes, and maintain the sustainability of agricultural operations. To maximize farming operations and boost productivity while reducing resource inputs, smart farming systems combine cutting-edge technologies with conventional agricultural methods (Cravero, A., & Sepúlveda, S., 2021). A wide range of elements and operations, each essential to revolutionizing agricultural management, are at the core of smart farming. The main elements and capabilities of smart farming systems are as shown in the figure 1.

Figure 1. Components of smart farming

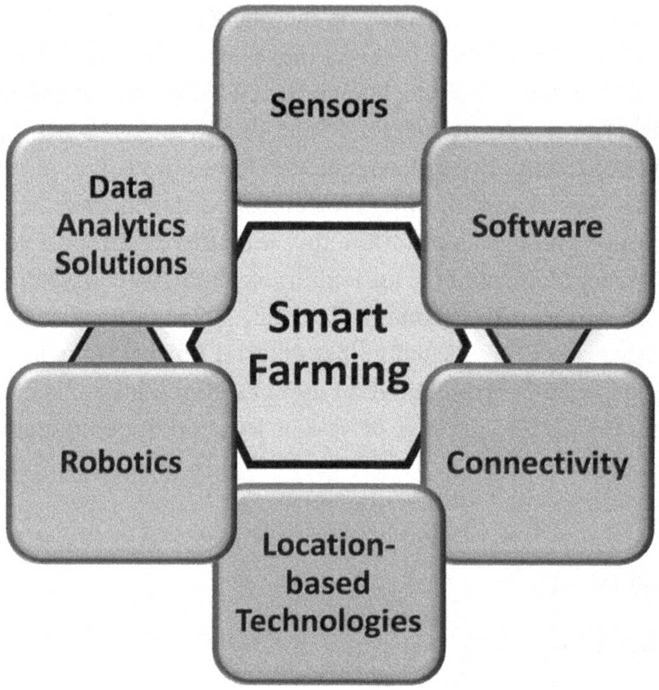

1. *Sensors*: The cornerstone of smart farming systems, sensors (Du John, H. V. et al., 2024) offer real-time data on a range of environmental parameters essential to crop productivity and health. With the use of soil sensors, one can precisely control irrigation and fertilization by monitoring soil temperature, moisture content, and nutrient levels. Water sensors enable effective management of water resources by keeping an eye on water quality and consumption. Light sensors also monitor light intensity, which aids in maximizing crop growth and photosynthesis. Temperature and humidity sensors help manage pests and diseases by providing information about microclimatic conditions.
2. *Software*: Advanced analytics, decision support, and remote monitoring features are provided by specialized software solutions, which are essential to smart farming systems. With the use of farm management software, farmers can plan their work, keep track of their inventory, and keep an eye on the health of their crops all from a single interface. By analyzing past data, predictive analytics

software forecasts crop yields, optimizes planting schedules, and reduces risks related to weather variations and market dynamics.

3. *Connectivity*: Interaction between farm equipment, sensors, and central management systems is made possible by connectivity, which is essential to smart farming systems. Even in remote or rural areas, cellular networks, satellite communication, and low-power wide-area networks (LPWANs) like LoRa enable dependable and ubiquitous connectivity across agricultural landscapes. With real-time data transmission and remote monitoring made possible by high-speed internet connectivity, farmers are better equipped to make decisions and act quickly in the event of changing circumstances.
4. *Location-based Technologies*: Accurate positioning and mapping capabilities are crucial for precision agriculture applications, and location-based technologies, such as satellite imagery and the GPS (Global Positioning System), give farmers this ability. Tractors and other equipment guided by GPS reduces overlap and maximizes inputs during field operations and navigation. With the help of satellite imagery, farmers can monitor crop growth and pinpoint problem areas by learning more about vegetation indices, soil variability, and crop health.
5. *Robotics*: By automating labor-intensive tasks and enhancing operational efficiency, robotics is becoming an increasingly important component of smart farming systems. Precise planting, seeding, and tillage are made possible by autonomous tractors fitted with GPS and sensor technologies, which lowers labor costs and fuel consumption. Drones and robotic arms improve precision and reduce environmental impact by making agricultural spraying, pest detection, and crop monitoring easier. Robotic harvesting systems also reduce post-harvest losses and improve yield consistency by streamlining harvesting operations.
6. *Data Analytics Solutions*: A key element of smart farming systems, data analytics solutions allow farmers to extract meaningful insights from massive datasets. These solutions evaluate historical and current data using sophisticated algorithms and machine learning techniques (Tripathi, R. P. et al., 2023) to find trends, patterns, and correlations that help with decision-making. Farmers can enhance resource allocation, minimize risks, and optimize crop management techniques by incorporating data analytics into smart farming systems. Moreover, farmers are better equipped to make educated decisions and adjust to changing agricultural environments with increased accuracy and efficiency thanks to predictive analytics tools, which forecast crop yields, market trends, and weather.

2.2 6G's Agricultural Impact

Communication technologies are evolving quickly as the world enters the digital era, drastically changing a number of industries, including agriculture. Although 5G technology has established a strong basis for enhanced connectivity and data transfer, the advent of 6G technology has the potential to transform agricultural innovation to previously unheard-of proportions. 6G technology is set to transform connectivity by outperforming its predecessors in terms of ultra-high-speed data transmission. 6G networks will enable instantaneous communication and data exchange between agricultural devices, sensors (Bruntha, P. M. et al., 2023), and central management systems at speeds predicted to reach terabits per second. Real-time monitoring, analysis, and decision-making will be possible thanks to this unheard-of speed and bandwidth, enabling farmers to optimize farm operations with unmatched accuracy and efficiency. 6G technology promises ultra-low latency, which lowers the time between data transmission and reception, in addition to high-speed connectivity. Applications needing real-time control and feedback, like robotic systems and autonomous farming equipment, depend on this almost instantaneous response time. 6G networks will make it possible to seamlessly integrate robotics, artificial intelligence (Anand, R. et al., 2024), and Internet of Things devices, cutting latency to microseconds or even nanoseconds. This will improve the agility and responsiveness of agricultural operations. It is anticipated that 6G technology will enable massive connectivity, allowing billions of devices (Jayapoorani, S. et al., 2023) and sensors to be connected at once. Precision agriculture applications benefit greatly from this scalability because a large network of sensors is used to monitor crop health, environmental conditions, and equipment status over large areas of farmland. Farmers can use a wide range of networked devices (KVM, S., 2024) with 6G networks, which allows for unprecedented coverage and granularity in the monitoring and management of agricultural assets. The incorporation of sensing and intelligence capabilities into 6G technology is one of its most exciting features. In order to gather, process, and analyze data at the network edge, 6G networks will make use of cutting-edge sensor technologies, such as edge computing (Bessant, Y. A. et al., 2023) devices and sensors driven by artificial intelligence (Pandey, B. K. et al., 2024). Because of the autonomous decision-making and adaptive control made possible by distributed intelligence, agricultural systems are able to adapt quickly to changing circumstances and allocate resources as efficiently as possible. 6G technology blurs the distinction between digital and physical environments by bringing immersive extended reality (XR) experiences. XR technologies, like virtual reality (VR) and augmented reality (AR), open up new training, simulation, and visualization opportunities in agriculture. AR overlays can be used by farmers to simulate equipment operations in a virtual environment, visualize crop growth patterns, and pinpoint areas of nutrient deficiency. With virtual reality (VR) simulations, farmers can experiment with novel farming techniques and investigate various farming scenarios without taking on real-world risks or costs.

III. SECURITY CHALLENGES IN AGRICULTURAL INNOVATIONS

3.1 Data Privacy Concerns in Smart Farming

By utilizing cutting-edge technologies like sensors, data analytics, and connectivity solutions, smart farming has a great deal of promise to improve productivity and optimize agricultural operations. Notwithstanding the enthusiasm surrounding the implementation of these technologies, it is crucial to recognize and tackle the data privacy issues that are intrinsic to smart farming systems. Data ownership and control is one of the main issues. The ownership and usage rights of the massive amounts of data that farmers generate and collect about crop yields, soil health, and farm operations are a source of concern. There's a chance that information gathered by smart farming systems will be used for profit without the farmers' permission. Therefore, it is essential to protect farmers' privacy and guarantee just compensation for the use of their data by making sure they maintain ownership and control over it. Not to mention the possibility of data breaches, data security presents major challenges for smart farming. Vulnerabilities arise when sensitive agricultural data is transmitted via networks and interconnected devices, which could be used by hostile actors to obtain unauthorized access. Data breaches in smart farming systems could have serious repercussions, including jeopardizing food security, compromising farmers' privacy, and disrupting farm operations. Thus, it is crucial to put strong security measures in place, such as encryption and access controls, to safeguard agricultural data and stop illegal access. It becomes clear that consent and transparency are important factors to take into account. In order for farmers to make decisions regarding the gathering, utilizing, and sharing of their data within smart farming systems, they need to be sufficiently informed and empowered. There is a chance, though, that farmers won't fully understand the consequences of data collection and will unintentionally agree to the sharing of their information with outside parties (Liu, Y. et al., 2021). Obtaining informed consent from farmers requires ensuring transparency and giving clear information about data collection practices and purposes. In smart farming, data aggregation and profiling raise additional privacy issues. Although combined data can provide insightful information for improving farming methods, there's a chance it could be misused to compile in-depth descriptions of specific farmers and their businesses. Concerns about privacy are raised by this kind of data profiling, which could result in discrimination against farmers or targeted marketing. Proper data anonymization and aggregation techniques are essential to protecting farmers' privacy and obtaining insightful information that can be used to make decisions. Regulatory compliance plays a critical role in resolving privacy issues with data in smart farming. The swift advancement of smart farming technologies may surpass the capabilities of current data protection regulations. Thus, safeguarding farmers' rights to privacy requires adherence to legal frameworks like the CCPA in the US and the GDPR in Europe. In the digital age, policymakers must also proactively address new privacy issues and create suitable regulatory frameworks to protect farmers' privacy (Trivelli, L. et al., 2019).

3.2 Cybersecurity Risks

The incorporation of digital technologies into agricultural practices has resulted in notable progress in terms of efficiency, productivity, and sustainability in recent times. But this digital revolution also means that agricultural infrastructure is more susceptible to cybersecurity threats and dangers. It is crucial to comprehend and evaluate these risks in order to protect farming operations and guarantee the robustness of the food supply chain. Cyberattacks that target networks and connected devices are one of the main cybersecurity threats to agricultural infrastructure. Cybercriminals now have a much larger attack surface thanks to the widespread use of Internet of Things (IoT) devices in agriculture, including sensors, drones, and autonomous machinery (Pandey, B. K. et al., 2021a). These devices have vulnerabilities that could be used to compromise sensitive data, interfere with operations, or allow unauthorized access to agricultural systems. Agricultural infrastructure is also vulnerable to network-based threats like Man-in-the-Middle (MitM) and Distributed Denial of Service (DDoS) attacks due to its dependence on digital communication networks. These attacks have the ability to obstruct data transmission, interfere with communication channels, or intercept private information being transferred between systems and devices. The reliance of agricultural operations on remote monitoring and real-time data exchange has made network-based attacks particularly dangerous. Data breaches and identity theft pose a further cybersecurity risk (Pandey, B. K. et al., 2021b) to agricultural infrastructure. The value of agricultural data extends beyond farmers to competitors, researchers, and other stakeholders. Examples of this include crop yields, assessments of the quality of the soil, and farm management practices. Unauthorized access to this information may result in theft of intellectual property, manipulation of the market, or harm to the reputation of farmers and agricultural organizations. New cybersecurity issues are brought about by the expanding use of cloud computing and data analytics platforms in agriculture (Sahani, S. K. et al., 2024). These technologies have the potential to be vulnerable to cybercriminals, even though they also provide scalability, flexibility, and advanced analytics capabilities. Weak authentication procedures, improperly configured systems, or insufficient security measures could allow unauthorized access or manipulation of private agricultural data kept in the cloud. Agricultural infrastructure cybersecurity risks and threats necessitate a multifaceted strategy that includes organizational and technical controls. By putting strong cybersecurity measures in place, such as intrusion detection systems, firewalls, and encryption (Kumar Pandey, B. et al., 2021), the risk of cyberattacks and illegal access can be reduced. To find and fix possible vulnerabilities in agricultural networks and systems, regular security audits and vulnerability assessments are crucial. Promoting a culture of cybersecurity awareness and resilience also requires educating farmers, agricultural employees, and industry stakeholders about cybersecurity best practices and offering them training in them. Agricultural organizations can enable their workforce to identify and effectively handle cybersecurity incidents by providing education on common cyber threats, phishing scams, and security hygiene practices. To combat cyber threats to agricultural infrastructure, cooperation and information sharing among government agencies, industry (Saxena, A. et al., 2024) associations, and cybersecurity specialists are also crucial. Proactive threat detection and response can be facilitated by forming public-private partnerships and exchanging threat intelligence, allowing the agriculture sector to remain ahead of evolving cyber threats and safeguard vital infrastructure (Shin, J. et al., 2022).

IV. STRATEGIES FOR NAVIGATING SECURITY CHALLENGES

4.1 Strong Encryption

Protecting private information and conversations from illegal access or interception requires robust encryption. Information is encoded using sophisticated algorithms so that anyone lacking the necessary decryption keys cannot understand it. This technology is necessary to guarantee the confidentiality of personal and business information, secure online transactions, and protect privacy. Data leaks and cyberattacks would put people, companies, and even national security at serious risk if there was weak encryption. The Role of Encryption and Protective Measures are as shown in the Figure 2.

Figure 2. Encryption and data protection measures

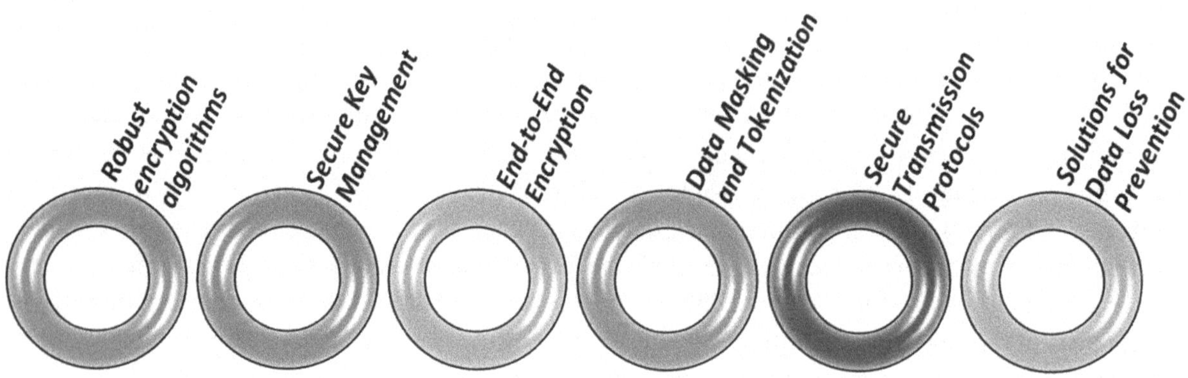

- *Robust encryption algorithms*: By transforming sensitive data into unintelligible ciphertext, encryption algorithms such as RSA (Rivest–Shamir–Adleman) and AES (Advanced Encryption Standard) are essential to the security of sensitive data. Particularly AES is well known for its reliability and effectiveness in encrypting data, making it very difficult for unauthorized parties to decode without the necessary decryption key. To guarantee that these algorithms are effective against different types of cyber threats, such as cryptographic vulnerabilities and brute force attacks, they go through a rigorous testing and analysis process. Continuous developments in encryption technology result in the creation of ever-stronger algorithms that can withstand new security threats as they arise, giving enterprises better protection for their data assets.
- *Secure Key Management*: To guarantee the security of encrypted data, efficient key management is necessary. Encryption keys are generated, stored, and distributed using secure key management techniques to reduce the possibility of unauthorized access or compromise. Key rotation is a widely used technique wherein encryption keys are substituted on a regular basis to lessen the effects of key exposure. Furthermore, to prevent theft or tampering, hardware security modules (HSMs) offer a safe environment for managing and storing encryption keys. Organizations can improve the overall security posture of their encryption systems and shield confidential data from illegal access or decryption by putting secure key management procedures into place.
- *End-to-End Encryption*: E2EE prevents data from being decrypted at any stage of the process and guarantees that it stays encrypted from the sender to the recipient. This indicates that the decryption key needed to unlock and access the encrypted data is unique to the intended recipient. E2EE stops intermediaries from accessing or intercepting private data sent between users, such as cloud or internet service providers. E2EE is used by well-known messaging apps like Signal and WhatsApp to secure user communications, protecting confidentiality and privacy from monitoring or eavesdropping.
- *Data Masking and Tokenization*: These methods safeguard private information while maintaining its applicability for authorized uses. Data masking is the process of substituting fake or obscure values for sensitive data, such as financial or personally identifiable information (PII). Because of this, companies can exchange data for analytics, testing, and development without disclosing private information. Tokenization, on the other hand, effectively anonymizes the original data while maintaining its referential integrity by replacing sensitive data with distinct tokens or identifiers. These techniques are frequently used in settings where it's necessary to share data with outside parties or have it processed by external systems while still protecting privacy rights and maintaining confidentiality.
- *Secure Transmission Protocols*: Data protection during network transit is greatly aided by secure transmission protocols like VPNs (Virtual Private Networks) and HTTPS (Hypertext Transfer Protocol Secure). By encrypting data exchanged between web browsers and servers, HTTPS protects sensitive data being transmitted over the internet and guarantees its integrity and confidentiality. By establishing encrypted tunnels, virtual private networks (VPNs) allow users to securely communicate with corporate networks and each other over public networks. Email, messaging, file transfers, and other internet-based applications can all benefit from secure communication channels provided by Transport Layer Security (TLS) protocols, which protect data from being intercepted or altered by unauthorized parties (Haneklaus, S. et al., 2016).
- *Solutions for Data Loss Prevention* (DLP): Data loss prevention (DLP) solutions use proactive monitoring, detection, and enforcement mechanisms to stop sensitive data from being shared or

leaked without authorization. By identifying and categorizing sensitive data in accordance with pre-established policies, content-aware DLP solutions stop confidential information from being shared or made public without authorization. Endpoint DLP solutions guard against data breaches brought on by compromised endpoints or insider threats by monitoring and managing data access on a per-device basis. By implementing DLP solutions, businesses can reduce the chance of data loss and continue to comply with data privacy laws, protecting their priceless information assets from misuse or illegal access.

4.2 Secure Communication

Communication protocols are the backbone of interconnected networks in the ever-expanding landscape of the Internet of Things (IoT). They make it possible for devices, sensors, and centralized systems to automatically exchange data with one another. Choosing the most appropriate communication protocol for Internet of Things deployments is of the utmost importance, given the abundance of protocols that are currently available. This is because the protocol has a direct influence on a variety of factors, including application range, power consumption, information bandwidth, latency, and quality of service, all while maintaining stringent security measures. Being able to comprehend the intricacies of these protocols is essential for ensuring that Internet of Things implementations are both efficient and secure. This is because Internet of Things devices utilize network standards and protocols to enable communication across cloud-connected physical objects. For the purpose of proactively identifying and mitigating potential security risks, the deployment of secure communication protocols necessitates continuous monitoring and vigilant threat detection. The use of sophisticated security information and event management (SIEM) solutions, in conjunction with anomaly detection algorithms and behavior analytics, makes it possible to monitor network traffic, suspicious activities, and potential security breaches within real time. Agricular organizations have the ability to improve their cyber resilience and remain one step ahead of evolving cybersecurity threats if they make use of threat intelligence platforms that are driven by artificial intelligence. Internet of Things devices primarily make use of network protocols and standards in order to establish communication pathways. These protocols and standards define the language that various network devices use to communicate with one another. Alternate connectivity options, such as Bluetooth, NFC (Near-Field Communication), and others, offer localized connections with varying characteristics. While the Internet Protocol (IP) is the most common method by which devices connect to the internet, other options include Bluetooth and NFC. In order to determine whether or not a particular protocol is suitable for a particular Internet of Things application, these distinctions, which include power consumption, range, and CPU usage, play a significant role. Although IP connections are difficult to use and require a lot of resources, they provide an unlimited range, which makes them an excellent choice for widespread deployments (Hedley, 2015). When it comes to situations where power efficiency and localized communication are of the utmost importance, protocols such as Bluetooth, which are characterized by their simplicity and lower resource requirements, perform exceptionally well. An approach that incorporates multiple layers of defense is required in order to successfully implement secure communication protocols. The incorporation of blockchain technology is becoming increasingly important in agricultural supply chains, in addition to the use of strong encryption methods such as AES and RSA. This is being done in order to improve the immutability and integrity of data. Farmers are able to authenticate the origin of agricultural products, establish the provenance of those products, and guarantee transparency throughout the production process by utilizing communication protocols that are based on blockchain technology. The Internet of Things (IoT) applications require specialized protocols that are tailored to meet unique requirements such as bandwidth, latency, and coverage distance. Traditional network protocols are sufficient for communication using conventional devices such as smartphones and personal computers. Despite the ease with which Internet of Things devices can be deployed, the communication protocols that sit beneath them need to be able to effectively bridge the gap between the inherent limitations in processing power, range, and reliability that are present in the internet infrastructure that is currently accessible. Because of this, choosing the appropriate communication protocol becomes a strategic decision that requires striking a balance between the technical considerations and the particular requirements of Internet of Things deployments (Hundal, G. S. et al., 2023).

4.3 Collaborative Solutions

A key part of improving cybersecurity in the agricultural sector is getting technology companies and government agencies to work together. Both sides' knowledge, resources, and skills are combined in this alliance so that comprehensive plans can be made to strengthen digital infrastructure and keep sensitive agricultural data safe. Stakeholders can combine their knowledge to make new cybersecurity solutions that meet the needs of the agricultural industry through joint research and development projects. Working together speeds up the creation of cutting-edge technologies like secure communication protocols, intrusion detection systems, and threat intelligence platforms, which are very important for protecting against new cyber threats. Setting up ways for people to share information and talk about threats is also very important for improving situational awareness and finding potential risks before they happen. Technology companies, government agencies, and people involved in agriculture can share real-time threat intelligence, signs of compromise, and best practices by setting up collaborative platforms and networks. This proactive approach helps everyone find and deal with cyber threats better, which lowers the damage from any attacks or breaches that might happen. The policies and rules that govern cybersecurity in the agricultural sector are largely made by government agencies. These government agencies can make rules that encourage best practices in cybersecurity, following standards, and protecting data by working together with tech companies and other important people in the industry. Stakeholders make sure that cybersecurity stays a priority and an important part of agricultural operations by making sure that regulatory requirements are in line with new technologies. Building people's skills and knowledge is important for making agricultural professionals more aware of and good at cybersecurity. Stakeholders can teach farmers, agribusinesses, and agricultural extension agents about best practices for cybersecurity, risk management, and how to handle an incident by holding workshops, seminars, and training sessions (Ma, M. et al., 2021). Giving people in agriculture the knowledge and skills they need to deal with cybersecurity issues in a good way encourages a culture of security awareness and resilience in the industry. Working together also makes it easier to do cybersecurity checks and risk management activities that are specific to the needs of the agricultural sector. Stakeholders can find weak spots, evaluate possible threats, and come up with ways to protect important assets and infrastructure by doing thorough risk assessments. To make sure that digital ecosystems are strong, the government gives advice and resources to help people involved in agriculture use best practices for cybersecurity and risk management frameworks. For incident response and cyber crisis management to work well in the event of a cyber incident or security breach, technology providers, government agencies, and agricultural stakeholders must work together. Stakeholders can lessen the effects of cyber threats, get operations back up and running, and stop more damage to agricultural systems and networks by working together, sharing information, and getting resources ready. This way of working together makes the sector safer and more resilient when it comes to cybersecurity. This encourages innovation, growth, and sustainability in agriculture (Sendros et al., 2022).

CONCLUSION

The convergence of smart farming and 6G technology represents a critical turning point in agricultural innovation, with the potential to bring about revolutionary improvements in resilience, sustainability, and productivity. But with increased technological convergence also comes a host of security issues that need to be properly resolved in order to protect data integrity, operational continuity, and agricultural infrastructure. Stakeholders can establish secure communication protocols, enact strong encryption and data protection measures, and form cooperative partnerships by realizing how crucial security is to advancing agricultural advancements. A thorough security plan for agricultural innovations must address data privacy issues, evaluate cybersecurity threats, and handle complex regulatory issues. Enabling the agricultural sector to fully realize the potential of 6G technology and smart farming requires putting security first as it navigates the challenges of digital transformation. Stakeholders can leverage these innovations to improve decision-making abilities, maximize resource utilization, and guarantee the sustainability of agricultural systems in the face of changing threats and challenges by combining forces and making calculated investments.

REFERENCES

Abdulkarim, Y. I., Awl, H. N., Muhammadsharif, F. F., Saeed, S. R., Sidiq, K. R., Khasraw, S. S., & Pandey, D. (2023). Metamaterial-based sensors loaded corona-shaped resonator for COVID-19 detection by using microwave techniques. *Plasmonics*, 1–16.

Anand, R., Khan, B., Nassa, V. K., Pandey, D., Dhabliya, D., Pandey, B. K., & Dadheech, P. (2023). Hybrid convolutional neural network (CNN) for kennedy space center hyperspectral image. *Aerospace Systems*, 6(1), 71–78. 10.1007/s42401-022-00168-4

Anand, R., Lakshmi, S. V., Pandey, D., & Pandey, B. K. (2024). An enhanced ResNet-50 deep learning model for arrhythmia detection using electrocardiogram biomedical indicators. *Evolving Systems*, 15(1), 83–97. 10.1007/s12530-023-09559-0

Bessant, Y. A., Jency, J. G., Sagayam, K. M., Jone, A. A. A., Pandey, D., & Pandey, B. K. (2023). Improved parallel matrix multiplication using Strassen and Urdhvatiryagbhyam method. *CCF Transactions on High Performance Computing*, 5(2), 102–115. 10.1007/s42514-023-00149-9

Bhat, S. A., & Huang, N. F. (2021). Big data and ai revolution in precision agriculture: Survey and challenges. *IEEE Access : Practical Innovations, Open Solutions*, 9, 110209–110222. 10.1109/ACCESS.2021.3102227

Bruntha, P. M., Dhanasekar, S., Hepsiba, D., Sagayam, K. M., Neebha, T. M., Pandey, D., & Pandey, B. K. (2023). Application of switching median filter with L 2 norm-based auto-tuning function for removing random valued impulse noise. *Aerospace Systems, 6*(1), 53-59.

Cravero, A., & Sepúlveda, S. (2021). Use and adaptations of machine learning in big data—Applications in real cases in agriculture. *Electronics (Basel)*, 10(5), 552. 10.3390/electronics10050552

David, S., Duraipandian, K., Chandrasekaran, D., Pandey, D., Sindhwani, N., & Pandey, B. K. (2023). Impact of blockchain in healthcare system. In *Unleashing the Potentials of blockchain technology for healthcare industries* (pp. 37–57). Academic Press. 10.1016/B978-0-323-99481-1.00004-3

Devasenapathy, D., Madhumathy, P., Umamaheshwari, R., Pandey, B. K., & Pandey, D. (2024). Transmission-efficient grid-based synchronized model for routing in wireless sensor networks using Bayesian compressive sensing. *SN Computer Science*, 5(1), 1–11.

Du John, H. V., Ajay, T., Reddy, G. M. K., Ganesh, M. N. S., Hembram, A., Pandey, B. K., & Pandey, D. (2023). Design and simulation of SRR-based tungsten metamaterial absorber for biomedical sensing applications. *Plasmonics*, 18(5), 1903–1912. 10.1007/s11468-023-01910-0

Du John, H. V., Jose, T., Sagayam, K. M., Pandey, B. K., & Pandey, D. (2024). Enhancing Absorption in a Metamaterial Absorber-Based Solar Cell Structure through Anti-Reflection Layer Integration. *Silicon*, 1-11.

Du John, H. V., Sagayam, K. M., Jose, T., Pandey, D., Pandey, B. K., Kotti, J., & Kaur, P. (2023). Design simulation and parametric investigation of a metamaterial light absorber with tungsten resonator for solar cell applications using silicon as dielectric layer. *Silicon*, 15(9), 4065–4079. 10.1007/s12633-023-02321-w

George, W. K., Ekong, M. O., Pandey, D., & Pandey, B. K. (2023). Pedagogy for Implementation of TVET Curriculum for the Digital World. In *Applications of Neuromarketing in the Metaverse* (pp. 117-136). IGI Global. 10.4018/978-1-6684-8150-9.ch009

George, W. K., Silas, E. I., Pandey, D., & Pandey, B. K. (2024). Utilization of Industry 4.0 Technologies in Nigerian Technical and Vocational Education: A Conundrum for Educators. In *Examining the Rapid Advance of Digital Technology in Africa* (pp. 270–293). IGI Global. 10.4018/978-1-6684-9962-7.ch014

Govindaraj, V., Dhanasekar, S., Martinsagayam, K., Pandey, D., Pandey, B. K., & Nassa, V. K. (2023). Low-power test pattern generator using modified LFSR. *Aerospace Systems*, 1-8.

Gupta, A. K., Sharma, R., Pandey, D., Nassa, V. K., Pandey, B. K., George, A. S., & Dadheech, P. (2023). Performance analysis of eight-channel WDM optical network with different optical amplifiers for industry 4.0. In *Innovation and Competitiveness in Industry 4.0 Based on Intelligent Systems* (pp. 197–212). Springer International Publishing. 10.1007/978-3-031-29775-5_9

Haneklaus, S., Lilienthal, H., & Schnug, E. (2016, July). 25 years Precision Agriculture in Germany–a retrospective. In *13th International Conference on Precision Agriculture*, St. Louis, MO.

Hundal, G. S., Laux, C. M., Buckmaster, D., Sutton, M. J., & Langemeier, M. (2023). Exploring barriers to the adoption of internet of things-based precision agriculture practices. *Agriculture*, 13(1), 163. 10.3390/agriculture13010163

Iyyanar, P., Anand, R., Shanthi, T., Nassa, V. K., Pandey, B. K., George, A. S., & Pandey, D. (2023). A real-time smart sewage cleaning UAV assistance system using IoT. In *Handbook of Research on Data-Driven Mathematical Modeling in Smart Cities* (pp. 24–39). IGI Global.

JayaLakshmi, G., Pandey, D., Pandey, B. K., Kaur, P., Mahajan, D. A., & Dari, S. S. (2024). Smart Big Data Collection for Intelligent Supply Chain Improvement. In *AI and Machine Learning Impacts in Intelligent Supply Chain* (pp. 180-195). IGI Global.

Jayapoorani, S., Pandey, D., Sasirekha, N. S., Anand, R., & Pandey, B. K. (2023). Systolic optimized adaptive filter architecture designs for ECG noise cancellation by Vertex-5. *Aerospace Systems*, 6(1), 163–173. 10.1007/s42401-022-00177-3

Kirubasri, G., Sankar, S., Pandey, D., Pandey, B. K., Singh, H., & Anand, R. (2021, September). A recent survey on 6G vehicular technology, applications and challenges. In *2021 9th International Conference on Reliability, Infocom Technologies and Optimization (Trends and Future Directions)(ICRITO)* (pp. 1-5). IEEE.

Kumar Pandey, B., Pandey, D., Nassa, V. K., Ahmad, T., Singh, C., George, A. S., & Wakchaure, M. A. (2021). Encryption and steganography-based text extraction in IoT using the EWCTS optimizer. *Imaging Science Journal*, 69(1-4), 38–56. 10.1080/13682199.2022.2146885

KVM, S., Pandey, B. K., & Pandey, D. (2024). Design of Surface Plasmon Resonance (SPR) Sensors for Highly Sensitive Biomolecular Detection in Cancer Diagnostics. *Plasmonics*, 1–13.

Liu, Y., Ma, X., Shu, L., Hancke, G. P., & Abu-Mahfouz, A. M. (2020). From industry 4.0 to agriculture 4.0: Current status, enabling technologies, and research challenges. *IEEE Transactions on Industrial Informatics*, 17(6), 4322–4334. 10.1109/TII.2020.3003910

Ma, M., Liu, J., Liu, M., Zeng, J., & Li, Y. (2021). Tree species classification based on sentinel-2 imagery and random forest classifier in the eastern regions of the Qilian mountains. *Forests*, 12(12), 1736. 10.3390/f12121736

Monteiro, A., Santos, S., & Gonçalves, P. (2021). Precision agriculture for crop and livestock farming—Brief review. *Animals (Basel)*, 11(8), 2345. 10.3390/ani1108234534438802

Muniandi, B., Nassa, V. K., Pandey, D., Pandey, B. K., Dadheech, P., & George, A. S. (2024). Pattern Analysis for Feature Extraction in Complex Images. In *Using Machine Learning to Detect Emotions and Predict Human Psychology* (pp. 145-167). IGI Global. 10.4018/979-8-3693-1910-9.ch007

Pandey, B. K., & Pandey, D. (2023). Parametric optimization and prediction of enhanced thermoelectric performance in co-doped CaMnO3 using response surface methodology and neural network. *Journal of Materials Science Materials in Electronics*, 34(21), 1589. 10.1007/s10854-023-10954-1

Pandey, B. K., Pandey, D., Alkhafaji, M. A., Güneşer, M. T., & Şeker, C. (2023a). A reliable transmission and extraction of textual information using keyless encryption, steganography, and deep algorithm with cuckoo optimization. In *Micro-Electronics and Telecommunication Engineering: Proceedings of 6th ICMETE 2022* (pp. 629–636). Springer Nature Singapore. 10.1007/978-981-19-9512-5_57

Pandey, B. K., Pandey, D., Dadheech, P., Mahajan, D. A., George, A. S., & Hameed, A. S. (2023b). Review on Smart Sewage Cleaning UAV Assistance for Sustainable Development. In *Handbook of Research on Safe Disposal Methods of Municipal Solid Wastes for a Sustainable Environment* (pp. 69–79). IGI Global. 10.4018/978-1-6684-8117-2.ch005

Pandey, B. K., Pandey, D., & Sahani, S. K. (2024). Autopilot control unmanned aerial vehicle system for sewage defect detection using deep learning. *Engineering Reports*, 12852. 10.1002/eng2.12852

Pandey, B. K., Pandey, D., Wairya, S., & Agarwal, G. (2021a). An advanced morphological component analysis, steganography, and deep learning-based system to transmit secure textual data. *International Journal of Distributed Artificial Intelligence*, 13(2), 40–62. 10.4018/IJDAI.2021070104

Pandey, B. K., Pandey, D., Wariya, S., & Agarwal, G. (2021b). A deep neural network-based approach for extracting textual images from deteriorate images. *EAI Endorsed Transactions on Industrial Networks and Intelligent Systems*, 8(28), e3–e3. 10.4108/eai.17-9-2021.170961

Pandey, D., Pandey, B. K., & Wairya, S. (2021). Hybrid deep neural network with adaptive galactic swarm optimization for text extraction from scene images. *Soft Computing*, 25(2), 1563–1580. 10.1007/s00500-020-05245-4

Pramanik, S., Pandey, D., Joardar, S., Niranjanamurthy, M., Pandey, B. K., & Kaur, J. (2023, October). An overview of IoT privacy and security in smart cities. In *AIP Conference Proceedings* (Vol. 2495, No. 1). AIP Publishing. 10.1063/5.0123511

Raja, D., Kumar, D. R., Santhiyakumari, N., Kumarganesh, S., Sagayam, K. M., Thiyaneswaran, B., Pandey, B. K., & Pandey, D. (2024). A compact dual-feed wide-band slotted antenna for future wireless applications. *Analog Integrated Circuits and Signal Processing*, 118(2), 1–15. 10.1007/s10470-023-02233-0

Sahani, S. K., Pandey, B. K., & Pandey, D. (2024). *Single-valued Signals, Multi-valued Signals and Fixed-Point of Contractive Signals*. Mathematics Open. 10.1142/S2811007224500020

Saxena, A., Agarwal, A., Pandey, B. K., & Pandey, D. (2024). Examination of the Criticality of Customer Segmentation Using Unsupervised Learning Methods. *Circular Economy and Sustainability*, 1–14. 10.1007/s43615-023-00336-4

Sharma, M., Talwar, R., Pandey, D., Nassa, V. K., Pandey, B. K., & Dadheech, P. (2024). A Review of Dielectric Resonator Antennas (DRA)-Based RFID Technology for Industry 4.0. *Robotics and Automation in Industry*, 4(0), 303–324.

Sharma, S., Pandey, B. K., Pandey, D., Anand, R., Sharma, A., & Saini, S. (2023, March). Character Recognition Technique Implementation for Complicated Deteriorated Scene. In *2023 6th International Conference on Information Systems and Computer Networks (ISCON)* (pp. 1-4). IEEE. 10.1109/ISCON57294.2023.10112185

Shin, J., Mahmud, M. S., Rehman, T. U., Ravichandran, P., Heung, B., & Chang, Y. K. (2022). Trends and prospect of machine vision technology for stresses and diseases detection in precision agriculture. *AgriEngineering*, 5(1), 20–39. 10.3390/agriengineering5010003

Singh, S., Madaan, G., Kaur, J., Swapna, H. R., Pandey, D., Singh, A., & Pandey, B. K. (2023). *Bibliometric Review on Healthcare Sustainability. Handbook of Research on Safe Disposal Methods of Municipal Solid Wastes for a Sustainable Environment*, 142-161. 10.4018/978-1-6684-8117-2.ch011

Swapna, H. R., Bigirimana, E., Madaan, G., Hasan, A., Pandey, B. K., & Pandey, D. (2023). Impact of neuromarketing on consumer psychology in digitally connected networks. In *Applications of Neuromarketing in the Metaverse* (pp. 193–205). IGI Global. 10.4018/978-1-6684-8150-9.ch015

Tripathi, R. P., Sharma, M., Gupta, A. K., Pandey, D., Pandey, B. K., Shahul, A., & George, A. H. (2023). Timely prediction of diabetes by means of machine learning practices. *Augmented Human Research*, 8(1), 1. 10.1007/s41133-023-00062-4

Trivelli, L., Apicella, A., Chiarello, F., Rana, R., Fantoni, G., & Tarabella, A. (2019). From precision agriculture to Industry 4.0: Unveiling technological connections in the agrifood sector. *British Food Journal*, 121(8), 1730–1743. 10.1108/BFJ-11-2018-0747

Yazdinejad, A., Zolfaghari, B., Azmoodeh, A., Dehghantanha, A., Karimipour, H., Fraser, E., Green, A. G., Russell, C., & Duncan, E. (2021). A review on security of smart farming and precision agriculture: Security aspects, attacks, threats and countermeasures. *Applied Sciences (Basel, Switzerland)*, 11(16), 7518. 10.3390/app11167518

Chapter 14
Digital Fields:
Securing Agriculture 5.0 in the 6G Landscape

Ashok Kumar Koshariya
College of Agriculture and Research Station, Indira Gandhi Krishi Vishwavidyalaya, Fingeshwar, India

S. Meenakshi
https://orcid.org/0000-0001-5075-6808
Department of Science and Humanities, R.M.K. Engineering College, Kavarapettai, India

R. Rajesh
School of Computer Science and Engineering, Vellore Institute of Technology, Chennai, India

M. Sakthivel
Department of ECE, Velammal College of Engineering and Technology, Madurai, India

Arjoo Pandey
Department of Computer Science and Engineering, Government Engineering College, Raipur, India

R. Manikandan
https://orcid.org/0000-0002-2055-6634
Department of ECE, Panimalar Engineering College, India

Chetan M. Thakar
Savitribai Phule Pune University, India

ABSTRACT

The incorporation of cutting-edge technology like 5G and 6G into the ever-changing digital world will have far-reaching consequences for the farming industry. This chapter delves into the importance of safeguarding Agriculture 5.0 in the 6G landscape, taking into account the development of agricultural technology, the difficulties in guaranteeing cybersecurity, and the tactics to utilize new technologies for better protection. From its inception to the present age of digitalization, the chapter explores the evolution of agricultural technology. It begins with an overview of Agriculture 5G and the 6G landscape.

I. INTRODUCTION

The agricultural industry is undergoing a radical transition towards Agriculture 5.0 in the fast-paced digital age, utilizing cutting-edge technologies to improve efficiency, sustainability, and productivity. To protect agricultural operations and data (Pandey, B. K. et al., 2024), however, strong cybersecurity

DOI: 10.4018/979-8-3693-7421-4.ch014

measures are imperative in light of this digital evolution. In order to ensure the security of agricultural systems, the integration of Agriculture 5.0 within the developing 6G landscape offers both enormous opportunities and challenges.

The most recent stage of farming evolution, known as "agriculture 5.0," is defined by a heavy reliance on automation, robotics, data analytics, and the Internet of Things (IoT) (Pramanik, S. et al., 2023). Precision agriculture is made possible by this paradigm shift, allowing farmers to maximize yields while minimizing their impact on the environment. Farmers can monitor crop health in real-time (KVM, S. et al., 2024), optimize resource management, and make data-driven decisions. However, agricultural systems are also vulnerable to a wide range of cybersecurity threats due to their growing connectedness and reliance on digital technologies. The upcoming 6G network infrastructure is expected to transform communication and connectivity in a number of industries, including agriculture, by offering previously unheard-of speed, capacity, and low latency. Sixth generation (6G) networks are predicted to have data transmission speeds of up to terabits per second, which will enable the real-time sharing and easy integration of enormous volumes of agricultural data. Despite these developments, 6G-enabled agricultural ecosystems' interconnectedness creates new opportunities for cyberattacks, calling for creative security solutions. Preserving sensitive agricultural data from theft, tampering, or unauthorized access is one of the main obstacles to securing Agriculture 5.0 in the context of 6G. Maintaining data availability, confidentiality, and integrity is crucial as agricultural operations become more digitally integrated. Cutting-edge encryption (Pandey, B. K. et al., 2023a) methods like quantum-resistant cryptography and homomorphic encryption will be essential for protecting data privacy and reducing the likelihood of cyberattacks. The widespread use of IoT devices and sensors (Abdulkarim, Y. I. et al., 2023) in smart farming creates security holes that malevolent actors may take advantage (Iyyanar, P. et al., 2023). These networked devices, which range from autonomous tractors and irrigation systems to unmanned aerial vehicles (UAVs) for crop monitoring, are the foundation of Agriculture 5.0, but they also pose a risk for cyberattacks. Robust authentication protocols, access controls, and intrusion detection systems must be put in place in order to guard against unwanted access and guarantee the security of agricultural infrastructure enabled by the Internet of Things. Agriculture 5.0's implementation of machine learning (ML) (Anand, R. et al., 2024) and artificial intelligence (AI) algorithms creates new security risks pertaining to data poisoning, adversarial attacks, and algorithmic bias. AI model (Devasenapathy, D. et al., 2024) flaws could be used by adversaries to influence judgment calls or interfere with vital agricultural operations. Consequently, combining cybersecurity and AI-driven anomaly detection can strengthen agricultural systems' resistance to new online threats. Edge computing appears as a key technology in the 6G landscape to improve the security and robustness of Agriculture 5.0. Edge computing (Bessant, Y. A. et al., 2023) minimizes latency, lessens dependency on centralized data centers, and lessens the effects of network outages or cyberattacks by processing and analyzing data closer to its source. Agricultural stakeholders can use edge computing capabilities (Sahani, S. K. et al., 2024) to detect and mitigate cyber threats in real-time by implementing localized security measures like anomaly detection, threat intelligence, and intrusion detection.

1.1 6G Landscape

Agriculture of the 5th Generation (5G) represents a significant shift in farming practices, as it makes use of advanced digital technologies (Swapna, H. R. et al., 2023) to revolutionize the methods that have been used traditionally. Precision agriculture is made possible by the integration of data analytics, automation, robotics, and the internet of things (IoT) in agriculture 5G (Sengupta, R. et al., 2021). This allows farmers to monitor and manage their operations with an unprecedented level of accuracy and efficiency. Farmers are able to collect, analyze, and interpret vast amounts of data related to the health of the soil, weather patterns (Govindaraj, V. et al., 2023), crop growth, and market trends thanks to the application of data analytics (Sharma, S. et al., 2023), which plays an essential role in Agriculture 5G. This method, which is driven by data, gives farmers the ability to make educated decisions about planting schedules, irrigation levels, fertilization, and pest control. As a result, they are able to maximize crop yields while simultaneously minimizing costs and the impact on the environment (Sahani, K. et al., 2023). The implementation of automation and robotics technologies is an essential part of Agriculture 5G, which aims to streamline labor-intensive tasks and improve operational efficiency. These technologies, which include autonomous tractors and robotic harvesters, as well as drones and intelligent (JayaLakshmi, G. et al., 2024) irrigation systems, automate tasks that are repetitive in nature, reduce the need for manual labor, and increase overall productivity. It is possible for farmers to achieve higher levels of precision, consistency, and scalability in their operations through the utilization of automation and robotics, which ultimately results in increased yields and profitability. The Internet of Things is an essential component of Agriculture 5G, as it enables devices, sensors, and agricultural machinery to connect with one another in a seamless manner. Sensors (Du John, H. V. et al., 2024) that are enabled by the Internet of Things and are spread out across agricultural fields monitor a variety of parameters in real time, including soil moisture, temperature, humidity, and crop health. Because of this continuous monitoring, farmers are able to detect anomalies, recognize potential problems, and promptly take corrective actions. Irrigation systems that are controlled by Internet of Things sensors are able to optimize water usage, thereby reducing waste and conserving valuable resources (Zhang, L. et al., 2019). Internet of Things-connected drones offer aerial imagery and crop surveillance, which enables farmers to identify areas of concern and implement targeted interventions. In terms of connectivity, the 6th Generation (6G) of wireless communication (Raja, D. et al., 2024) technology represents a paradigm shift that surpasses the capabilities of the 5G networks that are currently in use. With data transmission rates reaching terabit-per-second levels and ultra-low latency, 6G (Kirubasri, G. et al., 2021) networks make it possible to communicate in real time and exchange data on a scale that has never been seen before. One of the defining characteristics of the 6G landscape is hyper-connectivity, which makes it possible to establish seamless connectivity between billions of devices, sensors (Du John, H. V. et al., 2023), and autonomous systems. The proliferation of Internet of Things applications, smart cities, and intelligent infrastructure is made easier by this ecosystem's interconnectedness. Intelligent networking capabilities, which are powered by artificial intelligence (Pandey, B. K., & Pandey, D., 2023) and machine learning algorithms (Saxena, A. et al., 2024), allow for the autonomous optimization (Pandey, D. et al., 2021) of network resources, the routing of traffic, and the mitigation of network congestion. Self-organizing networks are able to dynamically adapt to changing conditions, which ensures that communication is both efficient and reliable across a wide range of environments (Pandey, B. K. et al., 2023b). The boundaries between the digital and physical worlds are blurred by pervasive computing, which is made possible by 6G networks. This results in computing experiences that are both immersive and ubiquitous. In the field of agriculture, 6G networks make it possible to perform autonomous operation of agricultural machinery, real-time monitoring of crop health, and predictive analytics for weather patterns (Rahman, I. et al., 2021).

1.2 Securing Agriculture in the Digital Era

The implementation of digital technologies is ushering in a new era of innovation and efficiency in the ever-changing landscape of agriculture. This is analogous to the transformative impact that steam power had during the industrial revolution. Farming practices are being reshaped from the ground up as a result of the convergence of technologies such as the Internet of Things (IoT), artificial intelligence (AI) (Saxena, A. et al., 2024), cloud data storage, and advancements in satellite and weather technology. This is resulting in the optimization of food production and distribution processes. Due to the rapid adoption of digital technology in agriculture, it is more important than ever to ensure that agricultural systems are protected in this digital era. One of the most important aspects of the paradigm shift toward digital agriculture is the proliferation of data and Internet of Things devices, which make it possible to collect enormous amounts of information on a scale that has never been seen before. The foundation of a digital framework that provides insights into sustainability, crop management, and field testing is comprised of these data points. This framework opens up new opportunities for agricultural research and innovation. Cloud storage and artificial intelligence (Anand, R. et al., 2023) are breaking down data silos and democratizing access to valuable agricultural insights. The applications of digital agriculture span across a wide range of farm sizes, from smallholder farms to broad-acre operations. Not only in response to technological advancements, but also in response to public pressure and regulatory demands for environmentally sustainable practices, digital agriculture is becoming increasingly popular. An increasing number of consumers are looking for food products that are of higher quality, sourced in a sustainable manner, and have a higher nutritional value. This has resulted in an increased emphasis on the necessity of sustainable agricultural practices. In this context, digital agriculture provides a multitude of innovations that enable farmers to optimize irrigation, fertilizer applications, equipment automation, and robotic processes. As a result, farmers are able to reduce costs and their impact on the environment while simultaneously increasing their productivity and profitability. As a result of the crucial part that food security plays in ensuring the sustainability of the global community, it is absolutely necessary to ensure the safety of agriculture in the digital age. With an estimated 800 million people lacking basic food security, the digitalization of agriculture has the potential to address this pressing challenge by increasing efficiency, optimizing resource allocation, and enhancing agricultural productivity (Ji, B. et al., 2021). Digitalization of agriculture has the potential to address this pressing challenge. Given that it is anticipated that the demand for food on a global scale will double by the year 2050, it is absolutely necessary for digital innovations in agriculture to keep pace with the growing demand in order to guarantee food security for everyone. It is important to note that the problem of climate change is intricately connected to the intersection of digital agriculture and issues of sustainability. There is no denying the fact that there is a need for improved monitoring and adaptation to climate variability, despite the fact that opinions may differ regarding the causes of climate change. Farmers are able to more effectively monitor climate and weather patterns (Muniandi, B. et al., 2024), which in turn enables them to adapt to challenges such as temperature fluctuations, droughts, and flooding. This, in turn, improves food security and resilience in the face of risks related to climate change.

II. AGRICULTURE IN THE 5G

2.1 Evolution of Agriculture (1.0 to 5.0)

Figure 1. Advancements in agriculture: From 1.0 to 5.0

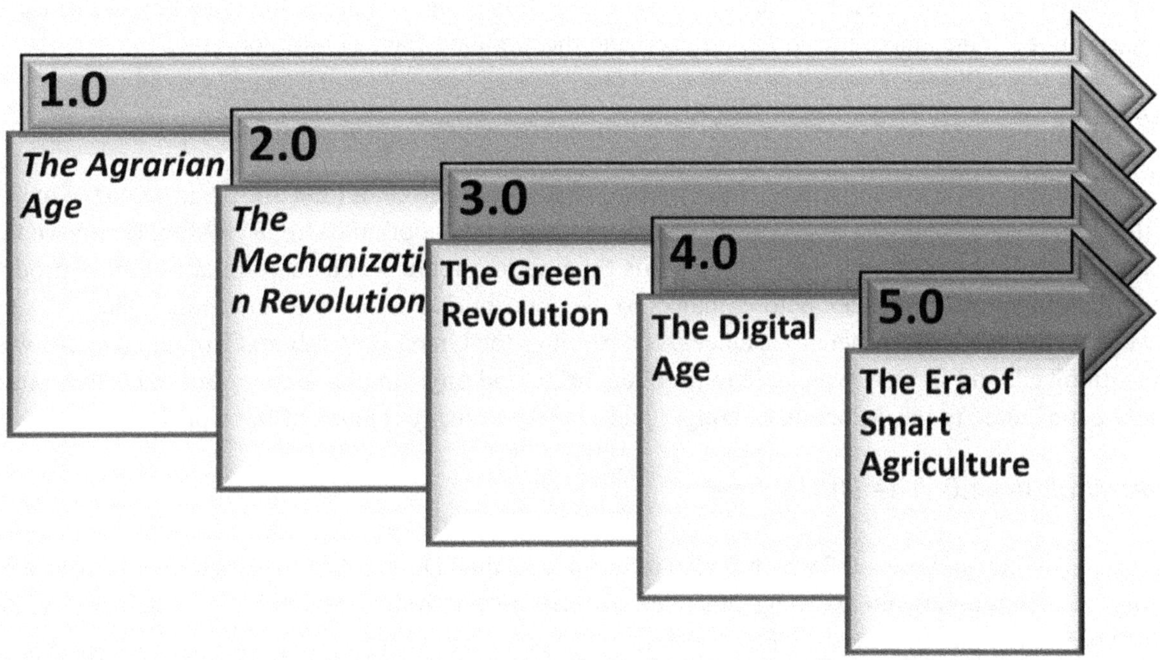

Agriculture can be broken down into several distinct phases, each of which is characterized by significant technological advancements and changes in farming practices. These phases can be traced back to early times. Throughout its history, agriculture has been characterized by a process of adaptation and innovation, beginning with the early days of subsistence farming and continuing into the modern era of precision agriculture. This is a summary of the progression of agriculture from Agriculture 1.0 to Agriculture 5.0, are as shown in the figure 1.

1. Agriculture 1.0: The Agrarian Age

Agriculture 1.0, also known as the Agrarian Age, is the period that marks the beginning of organized agriculture and the transition from a society of hunter-gatherers to communities of settled farmers from the beginning of the agricultural revolution. Domestication of plants and animals, cultivation of crops, and the establishment of permanent settlements all began during this time period from the human perspective. Early farmers were able to till the soil, plant seeds, and harvest crops thanks to the invention of fundamental tools such as stone axes and hoes. This laid the groundwork for agricultural practices that would continue to be used for millennia.

2. Agriculture 2.0: The Mechanization Revolution

The introduction of mechanized farming equipment that was powered by steam engines and, later, internal combustion engines led to the emergence of Agriculture 2.0, which is also referred to as the Mechanization Revolution. This revolution occurred during the 18th and 19th centuries. Plows, seed drills, reapers, and threshers were some of the agricultural implements that brought about a revolution in farming practices, leading to increased efficiency, productivity, and scale. It was possible for farmers to cultivate larger areas of land thanks to the mechanization of agriculture, which resulted in significant increases in both the amount of food produced and the amount of agricultural output.

3. Agriculture 3.0: The Green Revolution

Agriculture 3.0, also known as the Green Revolution, was a period of time that occurred in the middle of the 20th century and was distinguished by the widespread adoption of high-yielding crop varieties, synthetic fertilizers, and pesticides. During this time period, there was a surge in agricultural productivity that had never been seen before, thanks to the contributions of scientific research, technological advancements, and government assistance. As a result of the Green Revolution, farming practices were revolutionized, and farmers were able to produce more food on a smaller amount of land. This significantly contributed to the reduction of hunger and poverty in many regions of the world.

4. Agriculture 4.0: The Digital Age

The term "Agriculture 4.0," which is also referred to as the "Digital Age," refers to the incorporation of digital technologies into farming practices in order to maximize productivity, sustainability, and profitability. Technology such as GPS-guided tractors, precision farming equipment, and remote sensing technologies began to emerge in the latter half of the 20th century, which coincided with the beginning of the fourth industrial revolution in agriculture. These technological advancements made it possible for farmers to collect and analyze data on the conditions of the soil, weather patterns, and the health of their crops, which resulted in more precise management of resources and inputs among farmers. The foundation for the subsequent stage of agricultural evolution, which is referred to as Agriculture 5.0, was laid by Agriculture 4.0.

5. Agriculture 5.0: The Era of Smart Agriculture

The most recent phase in the evolution of agriculture is known as Agriculture 5.0. This phase represents the convergence of digital technologies such as the Internet of Things (IoT), artificial intelligence (AI), robotics, and automation in order to revolutionize farming practices. During the implementation of Agriculture 5.0, farmers are provided with access to a vast amount of data and insights, which enables them to make decisions that are informed and timely. On the other hand, drones and satellite imagery provide aerial views of fields and crops, while sensors (Du John, H. V. et al., 2023) connected to the internet of things monitor soil moisture, temperature, and nutrient levels. These data are analyzed by AI algorithms, which then optimize planting schedules, irrigation, and pest control, which ultimately results in increased yields, decreased costs, and significantly improved sustainability. A shift toward farming practices that are more efficient, resilient, and environmentally friendly is what is meant by the term "agriculture 5.0." This shift will ensure that future generations will have access to food and will be able to sustain themselves.

The progression of agriculture from Agriculture 1.0 to Agriculture 5.0 is a reflection of humanity's ongoing quest to feed a growing population while simultaneously adapting to changing environmental and technological landscapes. The relentless pursuit of progress, along with inventiveness and innovation, has been a defining characteristic of each phase. Agriculture 5.0 holds the promise of a more sustainable, efficient, and resilient agricultural system that is capable of meeting the challenges of the 21st century and beyond. This is something that we can look forward to as we look towards the future.

2.1 Characteristics of Agriculture 5G

The introduction of 5G technology holds the potential to usher in a new era of innovation and efficiency in the field of agriculture, which is at the heart of matters pertaining to the sustenance of humanity. It is remarkable that even in the 21st century, agriculture continues to rely heavily on manual labor. This is contrary to the fact that farming plays a crucial role in the survival of humans. On the other hand, the introduction of 5G in the agricultural sector represents a paradigm shift because it makes it possible to automate labor-intensive and repetitive tasks. This could potentially usher in a new era of farming practices that are revolutionary. As a result of the need for more intelligent farming practices to address the challenges of resource scarcity and production demands, sustainability has emerged as a prominent issue that has become increasingly urgent in recent times. A promising solution to improve food crop production while ensuring environmental stewardship is emerging in the form of smart farming, which makes use of the power of 5G, edge computing, and artificial intelligence (AI). The integration of these technologies makes it possible to achieve connectivity at higher speeds and with lower latency, thereby paving the way for decisions in agriculture that are driven by data in real time. When compared to its predecessor, 4G technology, the 5G technology represents a significant leap forward in terms of the speed and capacity of the network. 5G promises to provide lag-free data connectivity and enables seamless data sharing across billions of connected devices. Its network speed is approximately twenty times faster than that of 4G, and it offers download and upload speeds of up to ten gigabits per second and one gigabit per second, respectively. This ground-breaking capability has the potential to revolutionize the agricultural sector in a variety of ways, which would be to the advantage of consumers, farmers, agribusiness companies, and other stakeholders alike. Precision agriculture is one of the most promising applications of 5G in agriculture. This type of agriculture seeks to maximize agricultural productivity while simultaneously optimizing resource utilization and minimizing environmental impact (Naqvi, S. M. Z. A et al., 2022). The importance of utilizing 5G technology to address a variety of challenges pertaining to soil health, crop management, post-harvesting management, and livestock monitoring is highlighted by initiatives such as the network program on precision agriculture that is being implemented by the Indian Council of Agriculture Research (ICAR). Variable Rate Technologies (VRTs), which are made possible by 5G, give farmers the ability to make optimal use of resources such as fertilizers, pesticides, water, and other resources across a variety of soil types. This allows them to improve agricultural production while simultaneously preserving the environment and lowering costs. In the context of real-time monitoring of crop and soil characteristics, sensors powered by 5G play a pivotal role. These sensors provide farmers with valuable insights that enable them to make informed decisions. The use of modular Internet of Things gateways that are powered by 5G enables comprehensive monitoring of livestock, climate conditions, pest control, crop health, soil moisture, and other aspects of agriculture. The data that is gathered from these sources is then transmitted in real time and seamlessly to the cloud. Once there, it is analyzed by artificial intelligence and machine learning (Pandey, B. K. et al., 2024) algorithms in order to provide farmers and other stakeholders in the agribusiness with insights that can be put into action. When it comes to precision agriculture, 5G technology makes it easier to deploy drones that are fitted with sophisticated sensors. These drones can perform tasks such as digital soil mapping, pest detection, disease surveillance, and crop monitoring. The high bandwidth of 5G services ensures the transmission of high-quality visual data, which enables drones to identify anomalies and implement targeted interventions based on real-time data. In addition to increasing agricultural productivity, this also helps to promote sustainability by lowering the amount of reliance on chemical inputs and maintaining the quality of the crops. Weather stations that are powered by 5G make it possible for farmers to monitor weather updates in real time, which enables them to take preventative measures to reduce risks related to the weather and improve agricultural operations. Similarly, the implementation of 5G technology makes it possible to monitor water quality parameters in aquaculture ponds, such as pH levels, dissolved oxygen levels, and temperature. This not only improves yield but also fosters a healthy (Singh, S. et al., 2023) environment for aquatic life (Balaji, G. N. et al., 2018).

2.2 Key Technologies Driving Agriculture 5G

The agricultural sector is at a crossroads as the world enters the third decade of the 21st century. It is poised for a transformative leap forward that will be fueled by the convergence of digital technologies. The emergence of Agriculture 5G represents a watershed moment in the history of modern farming. This is because as concerns about sustainability, resource scarcity, and the need to feed a growing global population continue to grow, the need to feed these populations is becoming more pressing. This revolution is being driven by a constellation of key technologies that are driving the adoption and integration of 5G in agriculture. These technologies provide the foundation for this revolution. These technologies, which include edge computing and artificial intelligence (AI) as well as sensors and drones connected to the Internet of Things (IoT), are reshaping farming practices, optimizing resource management, and revolutionizing crop production and management (Mohapatra, D., & Subudhi, B., 2022).

- *5G Connectivity*: It should come as no surprise that the revolutionary connectivity that 5G networks offer is at the heart of the agriculture 5G initiative. 5G enables seamless data transmission and real-time communication across vast agricultural landscapes. Its speeds are up to 20 times faster than those of 4G, and it has a significantly lower latency. The backbone of digital agriculture is comprised of this high-speed, low-latency connectivity, which makes it possible for sensors, devices, machinery, and cloud-based platforms to share data with one another. Precision agriculture, livestock management, and supply chain logistics are just some of the areas that stand to benefit from the implementation of 5G connectivity in agriculture, which has the potential to revolutionize many farming practices. When it comes to monitoring soil moisture levels, temperature fluctuations, and crop health in real time, for instance, farmers can deploy Internet of Things sensors throughout their fields at any given time. This data is instantly transmitted through 5G networks to centralized platforms, where it is analyzed by artificial intelligence algorithms in order to provide farmers with insights and recommendations that they can put into action. In addition, drones that are equipped with wireless technology (Gupta, A. K. et al., 2023) can be used for aerial surveillance, which gives farmers the ability to detect crop diseases, pest infestations, and other irregularities with an accuracy that is unmatched.

- *Edge Computing*: Alongside the introduction of 5G connectivity comes the development of edge computing, which brings computing power closer to the source of the data. This brings about a reduction in latency and makes it possible to process agricultural data in real time. The deployment of edge computing devices, such as Internet of Things gateways and edge servers, directly on the farm enables farmers to perform data analysis on a local level, which in turn enables them to make decisions more quickly and operate agricultural machinery independently. Additionally, edge computing improves data privacy and security by reducing the amount of sensitive information that must be transmitted to centralized cloud servers. The use of edge computing has the potential to significantly improve the scalability, efficiency, and dependability of agricultural 5G systems. Edge computing reduces the reliance on centralized cloud infrastructure by processing data closer to its source. This results in a reduction in latency and an improvement in response times. This is especially important in time-sensitive applications such as precision agriculture, where making decisions in a timely manner is of the utmost importance in order to maximize crop yields and minimize resource waste. Additionally, edge computing makes it possible for agricultural systems to operate offline, which ensures that they continue to function normally even in regions with limited or intermittent connectivity. This resilience is essential for maintaining productivity and mitigating risks in agricultural settings that are located in remote or rural areas.
- *Artificial Intelligence (AI) and Machine Learning (ML)*: Unlocking actionable insights from the flood of agricultural data generated by sensors, drones, and other Internet of Thing's devices is one of the most important roles that artificial intelligence and machine learning (Tripathi, R. P. et al., 2023) technologies play in Agriculture 5G. For the purpose of providing farmers with personalized recommendations and management strategies that are optimized, AI-powered systems are able to analyze soil health, crop conditions, weather patterns, and pest infestations. This is accomplished through the utilization of advanced algorithms and predictive analytics. Additionally, AI-driven solutions make it possible for agricultural machinery to operate on its own, for fertilizers and pesticides to be sprayed with pinpoint accuracy, and for crop diseases to be identified at an earlier stage. Farmers are provided with the ability to make decisions based on data through the incorporation of artificial intelligence and machine learning into agriculture 5G systems. This gives them the ability to maximize crop yields, optimize resource allocation, and reduce input costs. Artificial intelligence algorithms, for instance, are able to examine historical weather data and crop performance metrics in order to forecast the best times to plant crops and the types of crops that should be grown in particular countries. In the same vein, machine learning models have the ability to identify patterns in soil moisture levels and nutrient concentrations, which allows them to recommend precise irrigation and fertilization schedules. This helps to reduce the amount of water used and the impact on the environment. Drones that are powered by artificial intelligence are also capable of autonomously patrolling agricultural fields. This allows for the early detection of crop diseases and pest infestations, which in turn enables targeted interventions to reduce yield losses (Saravanan, K., & Saraniya, S, 2017).
- *Internet of Things (IoT) Sensors*: Sensors connected to the internet of things are the driving force behind precision agriculture. These sensors enable real-time monitoring and measurement of a wide range of environmental parameters, including soil moisture, temperature, humidity, and nutrient levels. The dissemination of these sensors across agricultural fields and livestock farms

allows for the collection of data at granular levels, which in turn enables farmers to optimize their practices regarding irrigation, fertilization, and livestock management. It is now possible for Internet of Things sensors to transmit data at higher speeds and with lower latency thanks to the introduction of Agriculture 5G. This will improve the scalability and efficiency of precision agriculture systems. These sensors provide farmers with actionable insights into the health of the soil, the conditions of the crop, and environmental factors. Using soil moisture sensors, for instance, it is possible to monitor the amount of water present in the soil and activate automated irrigation systems when the water level falls below the optimal thresholds. Similarly, temperature and humidity sensors are able to detect microclimatic variations within fields, which enables farmers to adjust planting schedules and crop management practices in accordance with the findings. Farmers can maximize crop yields, optimize resource utilization, and minimize input costs by utilizing real-time data from Internet of Things sensors. This allows them to maintain environmental sustainability while also optimizing resource utilization.

- *Drones and Unmanned Aerial Vehicles (UAVs)*: As a result of providing farmers with a bird's-eye view of their fields and crops, drones have distinguished themselves as indispensable tools in the field of agriculture 5G. Drones, which are equipped with high-resolution cameras, multispectral sensors, and thermal imaging technology, are able to capture detailed aerial imagery, detect crop stress, identify pest infestations, and evaluate plant health with an accuracy that is unmatched by other methods. Drones are able to transmit real-time data to farmers and agricultural experts by utilizing 5G connectivity. This enables timely decision-making and targeted interventions, which in turn optimizes crop yields and minimizes the impact on the environment. The incorporation of drones into agriculture 5G systems gives farmers the ability to monitor the health of their crops and identify potential problems at a scale and level of granularity that has never been seen before. For instance, multispectral sensors that are mounted on drones have the ability to detect almost imperceptible shifts in the reflectance spectrum of crops, which can indicate nutrient deficiencies, pest infestations, or water stress. Through the use of thermal imaging cameras, farmers are able to identify areas that are experiencing heat stress or disease outbreaks, which enables them to take prompt corrective actions. Furthermore, drones that are fitted with LiDAR sensors are able to generate high-resolution three-dimensional maps of agricultural fields. This offers the opportunity for precise topographical analysis as well as soil mapping. By harnessing the power of drones and 5G connectivity, farmers are able to maximize yields, minimize crop losses, and optimize (Jayapoorani, S., 2023) resource allocation in a manner that is both environmentally sustainable and efficient (Zhang, S. et al., 2020).

III. CHALLENGES IN SECURING AGRICULTURE 5G

There are a number of issues with 5G agriculture security that must be resolved in order to guarantee the availability, confidentiality, and integrity of agricultural systems and data. These difficulties are caused by the ever-changing threat landscape, the intricate agricultural ecosystem, and the interconnectedness of smart farming technologies. It is imperative to comprehend and address these issues in order to preserve agriculture's future and guarantee food security for the world's expanding population. Navigating security challenges in implementing 5G in agriculture are shown in the figure 2.

1. *Diverse ecosystem*: An agricultural ecosystem is made up of many different types of people and groups, including farmers, agronomists, suppliers, vendors, and government agencies. No two people or groups in the agricultural supply chain are exactly the same. They all help make, distribute, and manage agricultural resources. But this variety also makes it hard to make sure that all parts of the ecosystem are protected in the same way. It can be hard to agree on security policies and procedures because different stakeholders may have different priorities, resources, and levels of technical knowledge. Also, the fact that the agricultural industry is so fragmented can make it harder for people to work together and coordinate their efforts, which makes it even harder to deal with cybersecurity problems effectively. To get around these problems, everyone involved needs to work together to make plans and guidelines for putting security measures into agriculture. When farmers, suppliers, government agencies, and industry (George, W. K. et al., 2024) groups work together, they can find common security risks and come up with standard ways to deal with them. Giving stakeholders resources and training can also help them learn more about cybersecurity risks and best practices, which gives them the power to protect their operations on their own. By encouraging people to work together and share their knowledge, stakeholders can make the agricultural ecosystem more resilient and lessen the damage that cyber threats do to food production and distribution.
2. *Interconnected Technologies*: Smart farming technologies have led to a lot of devices, sensors, and systems in agriculture that are all connected to each other. IoT sensors gather information about the health of crops, the weather, and the state of the soil. This information is then processed and used by cloud-based platforms and edge computing devices. Unfortunately, these technologies make it easier for bad people to do bad things, even though they make things more efficient and productive. Because agricultural systems are linked to each other, they can be attacked by cyber threats like data breaches, malware infections, and supply chain compromises. To deal with these problems, operators of Agriculture 5G networks need to put in place strong security measures that cover the whole network infrastructure. Software must be updated and patched on a regular basis to address known vulnerabilities, data must be encrypted while in transit and at rest, and intrusion detection and prevention systems must be deployed. Using network segmentation can also help separate important agricultural systems from less secure parts, making them less vulnerable to cyberattacks.
3. *Privacy and compliance with data*: Concerns about data privacy and following data protection rules are raised by the collection and processing of agricultural data. Agriculture: 5G creates a lot of private data about crop yields, soil conditions, and operational metrics. This data needs to be handled and stored safely to keep privacy and confidentiality safe. On the other hand, smart farming's dispersed data storage and processing, along with the necessity to share data with various stakeholders while still meeting privacy regulations, can make data privacy assurance a real challenge. In order to overcome these obstacles, 5G operators in the agriculture sector must establish stringent data encryption (Kumar Pandey, B. et al., 2021) and access control protocols to guarantee that no one other than authorized personnel can access or alter agricultural data. Also, in order to be in line with data protection rules, you need to have open data handling practices and give people power over their data. This means they can ask to see, edit, or erase their data if they want to. Agriculture 5G operators can build trust with customers and stakeholders while lowering their risk of fines and penalties from regulators by putting data privacy and compliance first.
4. *Attacks and threats on the internet*: There are many cyber threats and attacks that can happen to agriculture 5G systems because they use connected technologies and create a lot of sensitive data. Bad people could use weaknesses in agricultural systems to stop work, steal private information,

or damage important infrastructure. There are many threats that Agriculture 5G operators might have to deal with, such as data breaches, malware infections, ransomware attacks, and supply chain compromises. Agriculture 5G operators need to take action to lower these risks by using a proactive cybersecurity plan that includes ongoing monitoring, threat intelligence, and the ability to respond to incidents. It is important to use security tools and technologies that can find and stop cyber threats in real time. It is also important to make incident response plans to stop and lessen the effects of any possible breaches or attacks. Getting stakeholders to work together and share information can also help find new threats and weak spots, which lets you take proactive steps to protect yourself from cyber threats.

5. *Limitations on resources*: A lot of farmers and agricultural groups are on tight budgets and might not have the tools, knowledge, or knowledge of what to do to set up strong cybersecurity measures. To keep agriculture 5G safe, money needs to be spent on cybersecurity training, programs to raise awareness, and technical solutions that are specifically made for the agricultural sector's needs and skills. It is very important to give farmers access to low-cost cybersecurity tools and services and to teach them about cybersecurity risks and best practices through training programs. Public-private partnerships can also help fill in gaps in resources by funding and supporting cybersecurity efforts in agriculture. This way, farmers can be sure they have the tools they need to keep their operations and data safe. Stakeholders can help farmers and agricultural organizations become more resistant to cyber threats and protect the future of agriculture by addressing resource limitations and promoting cybersecurity education and awareness (Coffin, A. et al., 2021).
6. *New Technologies and Their Dangers*: Because technology is changing so quickly in agriculture, 5G brings about new security risks and problems that need to be dealt with ahead of time. New technologies, like self-driving drones, blockchain (David, S. et al., 2023), and analytics powered by AI, can make farming more efficient, productive, and environmentally friendly. But these technologies also bring about new ways to attack, holes in security, and risks that need to be carefully managed. In order to deal with this problem, Agriculture 5G operators need to keep up with new technology-related threats and weaknesses. It is very important to put money into research and development to come up with new cybersecurity solutions that are specifically designed for Agriculture 5G. Working together with partners in the industry (Sharma, M. et al., 2024) and cybersecurity experts can also help find and reduce the risks that come with new technologies. This will help make sure that Agriculture 5G stays safe and strong as cyber threats change. By being open to new ideas and putting security first, everyone involved can use the full power of new technologies to promote long-term growth and innovation in agriculture (Akitsu, T. et al., 2017).

Figure 2. Navigating security challenges in implementing 5G in agriculture

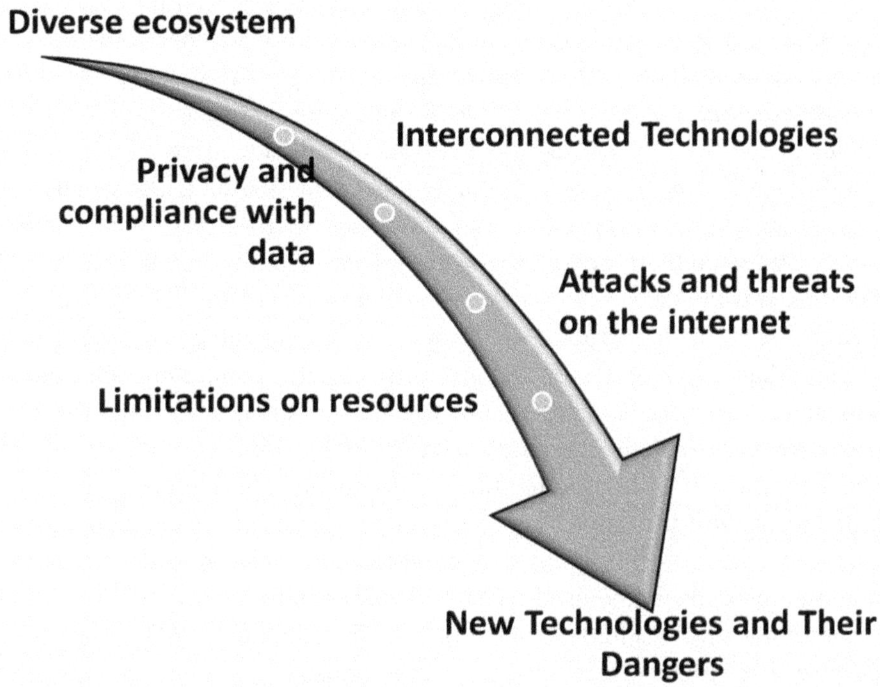

IV. STRATEGIES FOR SECURING AGRICULTURE 5G IN THE 6G LANDSCAPE

Comprehensive strategy that addresses the unique challenges and opportunities presented by advanced networking technologies is required to secure Agriculture 5G in the 6G landscape. Stakeholders can improve the sustainability, resilience, and security of agricultural systems in the 6G era by coordinating collaborative efforts, establishing policy frameworks, and implementing technical solutions. For the 6G era of agriculture, here are a few ways to secure 5G. 5G operators in agriculture need to put multi-layered security measures in place to protect against a wide range of cyberthreats that are common in the digital world. To strengthen data transmission and storage systems, this calls for the implementation of a variety of strong authentication methods, encryption techniques (Pandey, B. K. et al., 2021a), and access controls. Furthermore, network segmentation is essential for separating vital agricultural systems from less secure components, and the implementation of intrusion detection and prevention systems (IDPS) is crucial for promptly identifying and addressing possible security breaches. Agriculture 5G operators can ensure the integrity and resilience of agricultural operations in the 6G landscape and considerably strengthen their defenses against evolving cyber threats by implementing a multi-layered security approach (Lacerda, L. N. et al., 2022). Agribusiness 5G operators need to put policies in place to guarantee compliance with these standards in order to address the growing concerns about data privacy and compliance with strict regulations like GDPR and CCPA. This entails putting in place open and honest data handling procedures, giving people detailed control over their data, and carrying out frequent audits to ensure compliance. Furthermore, the implementation of encryption technologies and anonymization strategies protects private and confidential information related to agriculture by preventing unauthorized access and disclosure. This benefits farmers and other stakeholders. Agriculture 5G operators can build trust among stakeholders and reduce the risk of fines or reputational harm by putting data privacy and compliance first. In order to strengthen access controls and thwart unauthorized access attempts, 5G operators in the agriculture industry are increasingly relying on advanced authentication mechanisms like biometric authentication, multi-factor authentication (MFA), and certificate-based authentication (Pandey, B. K. et al., 2021b). Agricultural 5G operators can improve the security posture of their operations by reducing the likelihood of credential theft, unauthorized access, and identity-based attacks by putting strong authentication mechanisms in place. Agriculture 5G operators can effectively protect vital agricultural systems and data assets from malicious actors in the 6G landscape by integrating these advanced authentication measures into their security framework. Adoption of edge computing solutions is essential for Agriculture 5G to enable real-time data processing and analysis close to the data source. However, 5G operators in agriculture must implement secure edge computing solutions with strong security features in order to guarantee the security of edge computing environments. This includes putting access controls, data encryption, and secure boot procedures in place on edge computing devices to prevent tampering and unwanted access. Furthermore, by encrypting data transferred between edge devices and central servers, the use of secure communication protocols like TLS/SSL strengthens security measures and increases the resilience of agricultural operations in the context of 6G. The adoption of 6G networks offers a chance to greatly improve security protocols as the agriculture industry continues to embrace technological innovations. By providing faster and more dependable connectivity, sophisticated encryption protocols, and cutting-edge security features catered to the particular requirements of the sector, 6G technology has the potential to completely transform agricultural security. Unprecedented speed and bandwidth are promised by 6G networks, allowing for massive real-time data processing and transmission. In agriculture, where timely access to data can significantly impact crop management, resource allocation, and decision-making, this increased connectivity is especially advantageous. Farmers can easily incorporate drones, IoT sensors, and other smart devices into their operations with 6G, enabling ongoing agricultural data monitoring and analysis. By enabling proactive risk management and response, this real-time visibility helps to minimize the impact of potential security threats. Novel security features tailored to the agriculture industry will soon be available on 6G networks. To improve transparency and traceability across the agricultural ecosystem, distributed ledger technology (DLT) and blockchain-based solutions, for instance, can offer unchangeable records of supply chain operations, data exchanges, and agricultural transactions. Through the utilization of blockchain technology, stakeholders can authenticate and ensure the integrity of agricultural data, thereby mitigating the likelihood of fraudulent activities, fake goods, and manipulation of data. Advanced cybersecurity analytics and threat detection capabilities can be more easily implemented with the help of 6G networks. Agricultural stakeholders can identify potential security threats, anomalies, and patterns suggestive of malicious activity by analyzing large amounts of data in real-time using artificial intelligence (AI) and machine learning algorithms (Crawford, S. E. et al., 2021). By taking a proactive approach to cybersecurity, the risk of security lapses and data breaches is reduced and new threats can be quickly identified and countered. The use of 6G technology presents new possibilities for improving agricultural security, to conclude. 6G networks can assist those involved in agriculture in safeguarding sensitive data, reducing security risks, and ensuring the robustness and integrity of agricultural operations through improved connectivity, faster speeds, and new security features. To secure food security for an expanding global population and preserve the future of agriculture, the move to 6G networks is vital, especially as the agricultural sector embraces digital transformation (George, W. K. et al., 2023).

CONCLUSION

The security of Agriculture 5.0 is a critical priority in the digital landscape of the 6G era. This is because it is necessary to guarantee the availability, integrity, and confidentiality of agricultural systems and data through the implementation of Agriculture 5.0. It is becoming increasingly difficult to secure agriculture as technology continues to advance, but it is absolutely necessary to do so in order to maintain global food production and guarantee food security for a population that is growing. As a result of the evolution from Agriculture 1.0 to Agriculture 5.0, which was driven by innovations such as the Internet of Things (IoT), artificial intelligence (AI), and cloud computing, the agricultural sector has experienced a transformation that has never been seen before, paving the way for increased efficiency, productivity, and sustainability. There are, however, inherent cybersecurity risks and challenges that come along with these advancements. These risks and challenges range from vulnerabilities in Internet of Things devices to threats from malicious actors. In the process of transitioning into the realm of 6G technology, there is a tremendous potential to leverage advanced security features and capabilities in order to strengthen Agriculture 5.0 against new cyber threats. Enhanced connectivity, real-time data processing, and innovative security solutions that are tailored to the specific requirements of the agricultural industry are all possibilities that become available as a result of the integration of 6G networks with agricultural systems. By harnessing the power of end-to-end encryption, blockchain technology, continuous monitoring, and collaboration with cybersecurity experts and agencies, stakeholders can mitigate risks, detect threats, and safeguard agricultural operations in the digital era.

REFERENCES

Abdulkarim, Y. I., Awl, H. N., Muhammadsharif, F. F., Saeed, S. R., Sidiq, K. R., Khasraw, S. S., & Pandey, D. (2023). Metamaterial-based sensors loaded corona-shaped resonator for COVID-19 detection by using microwave techniques. *Plasmonics*, 1–16.

Akitsu, T., Nasahara, K. N., Hirose, Y., Ijima, O., & Kume, A. (2017). Quantum sensors for accurate and stable long-term photosynthetically active radiation observations. *Agricultural and Forest Meteorology*, 237, 171–183. 10.1016/j.agrformet.2017.01.011

Anand, R., Khan, B., Nassa, V. K., Pandey, D., Dhabliya, D., Pandey, B. K., & Dadheech, P. (2023). Hybrid convolutional neural network (CNN) for kennedy space center hyperspectral image. *Aerospace Systems*, 6(1), 71–78. 10.1007/s42401-022-00168-4

Anand, R., Lakshmi, S. V., Pandey, D., & Pandey, B. K. (2024). An enhanced ResNet-50 deep learning model for arrhythmia detection using electrocardiogram biomedical indicators. *Evolving Systems*, 15(1), 83–97. 10.1007/s12530-023-09559-0

Balaji, G. N., Nandhini, V., Mithra, S., Priya, N., & Naveena, R. (2018). IoT based smart crop monitoring in farm land. *Imperial Journal of Interdisciplinary Research*, 4(1), 88–92.

Bessant, Y. A., Jency, J. G., Sagayam, K. M., Jone, A. A. A., Pandey, D., & Pandey, B. K. (2023). Improved parallel matrix multiplication using Strassen and Urdhvatiryagbhyam method. *CCF Transactions on High Performance Computing*, 5(2), 102–115. 10.1007/s42514-023-00149-9

Coffin, A., Bonnefoy-Claudet, C., Chassaigne, M., Jansen, A., & Gée, C. (2021). PARADe: A low-cost open-source device for photosynthetically active radiation (PAR) measurements. *Smart Agricultural Technology*, 1, 100018. 10.1016/j.atech.2021.100018

Crawford, S. E., Shugayev, R. A., Paudel, H. P., Lu, P., Syamlal, M., Ohodnicki, P. R., Chorpening, B., Gentry, R., & Duan, Y. (2021). Quantum sensing for energy applications: Review and perspective. *Advanced Quantum Technologies*, 4(8), 2100049. 10.1002/qute.202100049

David, S., Duraipandian, K., Chandrasekaran, D., Pandey, D., Sindhwani, N., & Pandey, B. K. (2023). Impact of blockchain in healthcare system. In *Unleashing the Potentials of blockchain technology for healthcare industries* (pp. 37–57). Academic Press. 10.1016/B978-0-323-99481-1.00004-3

Devasenapathy, D., Madhumathy, P., Umamaheshwari, R., Pandey, B. K., & Pandey, D. (2024). Transmission-efficient grid-based synchronized model for routing in wireless sensor networks using Bayesian compressive sensing. *SN Computer Science*, 5(1), 1–11.

Du John, H. V., Ajay, T., Reddy, G. M. K., Ganesh, M. N. S., Hembram, A., Pandey, B. K., & Pandey, D. (2023). Design and simulation of SRR-based tungsten metamaterial absorber for biomedical sensing applications. *Plasmonics*, 18(5), 1903–1912. 10.1007/s11468-023-01910-0

Du John, H. V., Jose, T., Sagayam, K. M., Pandey, B. K., & Pandey, D. (2024). Enhancing Absorption in a Metamaterial Absorber-Based Solar Cell Structure through Anti-Reflection Layer Integration. *Silicon*, 1-11.

Du John, H. V., Sagayam, K. M., Jose, T., Pandey, D., Pandey, B. K., Kotti, J., & Kaur, P. (2023). Design simulation and parametric investigation of a metamaterial light absorber with tungsten resonator for solar cell applications using silicon as dielectric layer. *Silicon*, 15(9), 4065–4079. 10.1007/s12633-023-02321-w

George, W. K., Ekong, M. O., Pandey, D., & Pandey, B. K. (2023). Pedagogy for Implementation of TVET Curriculum for the Digital World. In *Applications of Neuromarketing in the Metaverse* (pp. 117-136). IGI Global. 10.4018/978-1-6684-8150-9.ch009

George, W. K., Silas, E. I., Pandey, D., & Pandey, B. K. (2024). Utilization of Industry 4.0 Technologies in Nigerian Technical and Vocational Education: A Conundrum for Educators. In *Examining the Rapid Advance of Digital Technology in Africa* (pp. 270–293). IGI Global. 10.4018/978-1-6684-9962-7.ch014

Govindaraj, V., Dhanasekar, S., Martinsagayam, K., Pandey, D., Pandey, B. K., & Nassa, V. K. (2023). Low-power test pattern generator using modified LFSR. *Aerospace Systems*, 1-8.

Gupta, A. K., Sharma, R., Pandey, D., Nassa, V. K., Pandey, B. K., George, A. S., & Dadheech, P. (2023). Performance analysis of eight-channel WDM optical network with different optical amplifiers for industry 4.0. In *Innovation and Competitiveness in Industry 4.0 Based on Intelligent Systems* (pp. 197–212). Springer International Publishing. 10.1007/978-3-031-29775-5_9

Iyyanar, P., Anand, R., Shanthi, T., Nassa, V. K., Pandey, B. K., George, A. S., & Pandey, D. (2023). A real-time smart sewage cleaning UAV assistance system using IoT. In *Handbook of Research on Data-Driven Mathematical Modeling in Smart Cities* (pp. 24–39). IGI Global.

JayaLakshmi, G., Pandey, D., Pandey, B. K., Kaur, P., Mahajan, D. A., & Dari, S. S. (2024). Smart Big Data Collection for Intelligent Supply Chain Improvement. In *AI and Machine Learning Impacts in Intelligent Supply Chain* (pp. 180-195). IGI Global.

Jayapoorani, S., Pandey, D., Sasirekha, N. S., Anand, R., & Pandey, B. K. (2023). Systolic optimized adaptive filter architecture designs for ECG noise cancellation by Vertex-5. *Aerospace Systems*, 6(1), 163–173. 10.1007/s42401-022-00177-3

Ji, B., Han, Y., Liu, S., Tao, F., Zhang, G., Fu, Z., & Li, C. (2021). Several key technologies for 6G: Challenges and opportunities. *IEEE Communications Standards Magazine*, 5(2), 44–51. 10.1109/MCOMSTD.001.2000038

Kirubasri, G., Sankar, S., Pandey, D., Pandey, B. K., Singh, H., & Anand, R. (2021, September). A recent survey on 6G vehicular technology, applications and challenges. In *2021 9th International Conference on Reliability, Infocom Technologies and Optimization (Trends and Future Directions)(ICRITO)* (pp. 1-5). IEEE.

Kumar Pandey, B., Pandey, D., Nassa, V. K., Ahmad, T., Singh, C., George, A. S., & Wakchaure, M. A. (2021). Encryption and steganography-based text extraction in IoT using the EWCTS optimizer. *Imaging Science Journal*, 69(1-4), 38–56. 10.1080/13682199.2022.2146885

KVM, S., Pandey, B. K., & Pandey, D. (2024). Design of Surface Plasmon Resonance (SPR) Sensors for Highly Sensitive Biomolecular Detection in Cancer Diagnostics. *Plasmonics*, 1–13.

Lacerda, L. N., Snider, J. L., Cohen, Y., Liakos, V., Gobbo, S., & Vellidis, G. (2022). Using UAV-based thermal imagery to detect crop water status variability in cotton. *Smart Agricultural Technology*, 2, 100029. 10.1016/j.atech.2021.100029

Mohapatra, D., & Subudhi, B. (2022). Development of a cost-effective IoT-based weather monitoring system. *IEEE Consumer Electronics Magazine*, 11(5), 81–86. 10.1109/MCE.2021.3136833

Muniandi, B., Nassa, V. K., Pandey, D., Pandey, B. K., Dadheech, P., & George, A. S. (2024). Pattern Analysis for Feature Extraction in Complex Images. In *Using Machine Learning to Detect Emotions and Predict Human Psychology* (pp. 145-167). IGI Global. 10.4018/979-8-3693-1910-9.ch007

Naqvi, S. M. Z. A., Saleem, S. R., Tahir, M. N., Li, S., Hussain, S., Ul Haq, S. I., & Awais, M. (2022). Role of 5G and 6G Technology in Precision Agriculture. *Environmental Sciences Proceedings*, 23(1), 3.

Pandey, B. K., & Pandey, D. (2023). Parametric optimization and prediction of enhanced thermoelectric performance in co-doped CaMnO3 using response surface methodology and neural network. *Journal of Materials Science Materials in Electronics*, 34(21), 1589. 10.1007/s10854-023-10954-1

Pandey, B. K., Pandey, D., Alkhafaji, M. A., Güneşer, M. T., & Şeker, C. (2023a). A reliable transmission and extraction of textual information using keyless encryption, steganography, and deep algorithm with cuckoo optimization. In *Micro-Electronics and Telecommunication Engineering: Proceedings of 6th ICMETE 2022* (pp. 629–636). Springer Nature Singapore. 10.1007/978-981-19-9512-5_57

Pandey, B. K., Pandey, D., Dadheech, P., Mahajan, D. A., George, A. S., & Hameed, A. S. (2023b). Review on Smart Sewage Cleaning UAV Assistance for Sustainable Development. In *Handbook of Research on Safe Disposal Methods of Municipal Solid Wastes for a Sustainable Environment* (pp. 69–79). IGI Global. 10.4018/978-1-6684-8117-2.ch005

Pandey, B. K., Pandey, D., & Sahani, S. K. (2024). Autopilot control unmanned aerial vehicle system for sewage defect detection using deep learning. *Engineering Reports*, 12852. 10.1002/eng2.12852

Pandey, B. K., Pandey, D., Wairya, S., & Agarwal, G. (2021a). An advanced morphological component analysis, steganography, and deep learning-based system to transmit secure textual data. *International Journal of Distributed Artificial Intelligence*, 13(2), 40–62. 10.4018/IJDAI.2021070104

Pandey, B. K., Pandey, D., Wariya, S., & Agarwal, G. (2021b). A deep neural network-based approach for extracting textual images from deteriorate images. *EAI Endorsed Transactions on Industrial Networks and Intelligent Systems*, 8(28), e3–e3. 10.4108/eai.17-9-2021.170961

Pandey, D., Pandey, B. K., & Wairya, S. (2021). Hybrid deep neural network with adaptive galactic swarm optimization for text extraction from scene images. *Soft Computing*, 25(2), 1563–1580. 10.1007/s00500-020-05245-4

Pramanik, S., Pandey, D., Joardar, S., Niranjanamurthy, M., Pandey, B. K., & Kaur, J. (2023, October). An overview of IoT privacy and security in smart cities. In *AIP Conference Proceedings* (Vol. 2495, No. 1). AIP Publishing. 10.1063/5.0123511

Rahman, I., Razavi, S. M., Liberg, O., Hoymann, C., Wiemann, H., Tidestav, C., Schliwa-Bertling, P., Persson, P., & Gerstenberger, D. (2021). 5G evolution toward 5G advanced: An overview of 3GPP releases 17 and 18. *Ericsson Technology Review*, 2021(14), 2–12. 10.23919/ETR.2021.9904665

Raja, D., Kumar, D. R., Santhiyakumari, N., Kumarganesh, S., Sagayam, K. M., Thiyaneswaran, B., Pandey, B. K., & Pandey, D. (2024). A compact dual-feed wide-band slotted antenna for future wireless applications. *Analog Integrated Circuits and Signal Processing*, 118(2), 1–15. 10.1007/s10470-023-02233-0

Sahani, K., Khadka, S., Sahani, S. K., Pandey, B. K., & Pandey, D. (2023). *A Possible Underground Roadway for Transportation Facilities in Kathmandu Valley Ring Road: A Racking Deformation of Underground Rectangular Structures*. Academic Press.

Sahani, S. K., Pandey, B. K., & Pandey, D. (2024). *Single-valued Signals, Multi-valued Signals and Fixed-Point of Contractive Signals*. Mathematics Open. 10.1142/S2811007224500020

Saravanan, K., & Saraniya, S. (2017). Cloud IOT based novel livestock monitoring and identification system using UID. *Sensor Review*, 38(1), 21–33.

Saxena, A., Agarwal, A., Pandey, B. K., & Pandey, D. (2024). Examination of the Criticality of Customer Segmentation Using Unsupervised Learning Methods. *Circular Economy and Sustainability*, 1–14. 10.1007/s43615-023-00336-4

. Sengupta, R., Sengupta, D., Pandey, D., Pandey, B. K., Nassa, V. K., & Dadeech, P. (2021). A Systematic review of 5G opportunities, architecture and challenges. *Future Trends in 5G and 6G*, 247-269.

Sharma, M., Talwar, R., Pandey, D., Nassa, V. K., Pandey, B. K., & Dadheech, P. (2024). A Review of Dielectric Resonator Antennas (DRA)-Based RFID Technology for Industry 4.0. *Robotics and Automation in Industry*, 4(0), 303–324.

Sharma, S., Pandey, B. K., Pandey, D., Anand, R., Sharma, A., & Saini, S. (2023, March). Character Recognition Technique Implementation for Complicated Deteriorated Scene. In *2023 6th International Conference on Information Systems and Computer Networks (ISCON)* (pp. 1-4). IEEE. 10.1109/ISCON57294.2023.10112185

Singh, S., Madaan, G., Kaur, J., Swapna, H. R., Pandey, D., Singh, A., & Pandey, B. K. (2023). *Bibliometric Review on Healthcare Sustainability. Handbook of Research on Safe Disposal Methods of Municipal Solid Wastes for a Sustainable Environment*, 142-161. 10.4018/978-1-6684-8117-2.ch011

Swapna, H. R., Bigirimana, E., Madaan, G., Hasan, A., Pandey, B. K., & Pandey, D. (2023). Impact of neuromarketing on consumer psychology in digitally connected networks. In *Applications of Neuromarketing in the Metaverse* (pp. 193–205). IGI Global. 10.4018/978-1-6684-8150-9.ch015

Tripathi, R. P., Sharma, M., Gupta, A. K., Pandey, D., Pandey, B. K., Shahul, A., & George, A. H. (2023). Timely prediction of diabetes by means of machine learning practices. *Augmented Human Research*, 8(1), 1. 10.1007/s41133-023-00062-4

Zhang, L., Liang, Y. C., & Niyato, D. (2019). 6G Visions: Mobile ultra-broadband, super internet-of-things, and artificial intelligence. *China Communications*, 16(8), 1–14. 10.23919/JCC.2019.08.001

Zhang, S., Liu, J., Guo, H., Qi, M., & Kato, N. (2020). Envisioning device-to-device communications in 6G. *IEEE Network*, 34(3), 86–91. 10.1109/MNET.001.1900652

Chapter 15
IoT Solutions for Crop Protection:
Safeguarding Agricultural 6G Networks

Chetan Shelke
Alliance College of Engineering and Design, Alliance University, Bangalore, India

C. Rakesh
Department of Mechanical Engineering, New Horizon College of Engineering, Bangalore, India

I. E. S. Naidu
https://orcid.org/0000-0001-7950-6386
GITAM University (Deemed), India

Alok Jain
Lovely Professional University, India

Modi Himabindu
Institute of Aeronautical Engineering, Dundigal, India

Joshuva Arockia Dhanraj
https://orcid.org/0000-0001-5048-7775
Chandigarh University, India

ABSTRACT

The convergence of internet of things (IoT) solutions and agricultural practices has resulted in revolutionary alterations in crop management and protection. With the emergence of sophisticated connectivity technologies such as 6G networks, the capacity to protect agricultural assets and improve crop protection has reached unparalleled levels. The current period of swift technological progress presents an opportunity for the incorporation of internet of things (IoT) solutions into the upcoming 6G networks. This integration has the potential to significantly transform crop protection techniques, guarantee food security, and optimize agricultural productivity.

I. INTRODUCTION

The convergence of Internet of Things (IoT) (Pandey, J. K. et al., 2022) solutions and agricultural practices has resulted in revolutionary alterations in crop management and protection. With the emergence of sophisticated connectivity technologies such as 6G (Kirubasri, G. et al., 2021) networks, the capacity to protect agricultural assets and improve crop protection has reached unparalleled levels. The current period of swift technological progress presents an opportunity for the incorporation of Internet of Things (IoT) solutions (Vinodhini, V. et al., 2022) into the upcoming 6G networks. This integration

DOI: 10.4018/979-8-3693-7421-4.ch015

has the potential to significantly transform crop protection techniques, guarantee food security, and optimize agricultural productivity. Traditional agricultural practices frequently encounter various obstacles, including pest infestations, diseases, and unfavorable environmental conditions, all of which can have a substantial influence on both the quantity and quality of crops. Nevertheless, IoT solutions (Iyyanar, P. et al., 2023) have arisen as a promising solution for tackling these challenges by facilitating instantaneous monitoring, data-informed (Khan, B. et al., 2021) decision-making, and accurate interventions (Pandey, B. K. et al., 2023a). Farmers can acquire significant knowledge regarding crop health, soil conditions, and weather patterns (Govindaraj, V. et al., 2023) by utilizing sensors, drones, and other Internet of Things (IoT) devices (Pramanik, S. et al.,2023). This enables them to effectively implement specific strategies for crop protection and management. With the ongoing increase in global population, the agricultural sector is facing unprecedented pressure to achieve sustainable food production. The aforementioned requires the implementation of novel technologies that can enhance the efficient use of resources, mitigate adverse environmental effects, and guarantee the robustness of agricultural systems. The potential of 6G networks, the upcoming generation of wireless communication technology (Devasenapathy, D. et al., 2024), lies in their ability to provide extremely fast connectivity, minimal delay, and extensive device (Sharma, M. et al., 2022) connectivity. Through leveraging the capabilities of 6G networks, the effectiveness and efficiency of IoT solutions for crop protection can be significantly enhanced. By utilizing faster data transmission and response times, along with improved network reliability and coverage, IoT devices (Sharma, M. et al., 2022) enabled by 6G technology can provide immediate insights and facilitate prompt action to address crop threats (Patle, K. S. et al., 2021). The scalability of 6G networks guarantees uninterrupted connectivity, even in geographically isolated agricultural regions, thereby addressing the digital divide and promoting equal access to cutting-edge agricultural technologies. The integration of IoT solutions for crop protection with the protection of agricultural 6G networks signifies a fundamental change in agricultural practices. The convergence of various factors not only presents the potential to improve crop yields and profitability for farmers, but also plays a significant role in advancing global food security and sustainability objectives. As we commence this endeavor to harness the complete capabilities of the Internet of Things (IoT) and 6G technology in the agricultural sector, it is crucial to confront a range of obstacles, such as security, privacy (David, S. et al., 2023), and regulatory factors, in order to guarantee the smooth and conscientious implementation of these technologies (Tzounis, A. et al., 2017).

1.1 IoT in Agriculture

Agriculture is not an exception to the rule that the Internet of Things (IoT) has already revolutionized a variety of industries. The Internet of Things (IoT) has led to the development of smart agriculture products in recent years, which provide farmers with innovative solutions to monitor crop fields and automate irrigation systems. Agricultural practices can be made more efficient and productive through the use of this technology, which enables farmers and associated brands to remotely monitor the conditions of the field. Throughout the centuries, ever since the beginning of the industrial revolution in the 1800s, automation has undergone continuous development in order to manage complex tasks and boost production. The agricultural sector, on the other hand, has been confronted with difficulties such as a lack of available labor, particularly in regions such as the United States of America, where crop production has been significantly decreased. A decrease in crop production that is estimated to be worth approximately $3.1 billion annually is a direct result of labor shortages, according to estimates. Agricultural robots, also known as agrobots, have recently gained popularity among farmers as a potential solution to the challenges that they face. With the advancements that have been made in artificial intelligence (AI) (Pandey, B. K., & Pandey, D., 2023) technology and sensor technology, agrobots are a promising solution. The reliance on manual labor in agricultural fields is reduced thanks to the capabilities of these robots, which can navigate and carry out tasks. There is a tremendous amount of potential for the Internet of Things in agriculture, despite the fact that we are still in the beginning stages of the ag-robotics revolution. There are a lot of Internet of Things products that are currently going through experiments and research and development phases, which indicates that this technology has a bright future in the agricultural sector. The ability to access and control these devices (Du John, H. V. et al., 2022) remotely is made possible by this connectivity, which in turn improves automation and efficiency. As a means of providing comprehensive solutions for crop and soil monitoring, Internet of Things (IoT) systems in agriculture make use of a variety of technologies, including artificial intelligence (Anand, R. et al., 2023), sensors, networking, and cloud messaging. It is anticipated that the demand for food production will significantly increase since it is anticipated that the global population will reach approximately 10 billion by the year 2050. Technology must be embraced by agriculture in order to maximize productivity and reduce waste in order to satisfy this expectation. In order to accomplish these objectives and make smart farming practices possible, Internet of Things (IoT) systems play a significant role (Tzounis et al., 2017). The Internet of Things enables farmers to monitor their fields in real time by utilizing sensors (Dhanasekar, S. et al., 2023) that provide information on a variety of parameters, including the temperature, the moisture content of the soil, and the overall health of the crop. The availability of this information enables farmers to make informed decisions, which in turn allows them to maximize yields and optimize (Pandey, D. et al., 2021a) resource allocation. In addition, the Internet of Things makes it possible to conduct predictive analytics (Tripathi, R. P. et al., 2023), which enables proactive intervention and the identification of potential problems before they become more severe.

1.2 Crop Protection Importance

Protection of crops from pests, diseases, weeds, and other harmful organisms is an important part of farming. There are many different methods and strategies used to protect crops from these problems. You can't say enough good things about crop protection because it has a direct effect on the long-term viability, profitability, and food security of farming systems around the world. There are many things that can hurt agricultural fields, from weeds and small animals to pests, diseases, and pathogens. If these things aren't stopped, they can do a lot of damage to crops, which can lower yields, cost money, and even cause food crises. So, effective crop protection measures must be used throughout the whole farming process, from getting ready for planting to storing crops after harvest. Throughout the history of farming, there are many examples of crops that were destroyed by pests and diseases. In the 1840s, the famous Irish Potato Famine happened because of the spread of Late blight, which killed many people and caused a lot of people to go hungry. Also, after World War I, Late blight and insect infestations caused a huge failure of crops in Germany, which caused a lot of suffering and made things hard for the economy. Since the beginning of farming, farmers have had to fight off pests, diseases, and weeds all the time. The fight has become more intense since the development of modern farming methods, since more intensive farming methods often make crops more vulnerable to damage. Because of this, farmers have always been looking for proactive ways to protect their crops so that they don't lose as much and grow better. Pathogens, pests, and weeds are always a danger to crops' health and yield. Without good crop protection, diseases, pest insects, and weeds can destroy huge amounts of crops. Studies show that if farming methods don't change, diseases could destroy up to 16.7% of wheat crops around the world, insect pests could destroy 11.3%, and weeds would destroy 23.9%. In Southern Africa, too, about 15% of crop losses are thought to be caused by diseases, 30% by insects, and 20% by weeds. Crop protection products are very important for reducing these losses and making sure that crop yields are reliable and high-quality. Aggressive pesticides, herbicides, fungicides, and other crop protection agents help farmers control pests and diseases while reducing the competition from weeds. These products give farmers useful tools to keep crops healthy, get the most out of their crops, and meet the needs of a growing world population in a way that doesn't harm the environment. Progress in agricultural science and technology has led to the creation of new ways to protect crops (Figueiredo e Silva, P. et al., 2018). Integrated pest management (IPM) methods, for instance, stress the use of several methods, such as biological control, cultural practices, and chemical treatments, to reduce the number of pests while causing the least amount of damage to the environment. Biotechnological tools, like genetically modified crops that are naturally resistant to pests and diseases, are also promising ways to make crops safer and more resilient.

1.3 6G Networks in Agriculture

The emergence of 6G networks is poised to revolutionize a variety of industries, including agriculture, as a result of the ongoing development of communication technologies. In terms of speed, reliability, and connectivity, 6G networks are the next generation of wireless communication technology. They offer services that have never been seen before. The potential impact of 6G networks on Internet of Things (IoT) solutions is particularly significant in the field of agriculture. These networks possess the potential to improve efficiency, productivity, and sustainability in the agricultural sector. When it comes to the agricultural industry, where real-time data collection, analysis, and decision-making are of the utmost importance, this game-changing technology shows promise for mitigating the specific challenges that are faced by the sector. 6G networks have the potential to revolutionize crop management, monitoring, and protection applications within the context of agricultural Internet of Things solutions. The deployment of advanced sensors, drones, and other Internet of Thing's devices across agricultural landscapes can be made easier by 6G networks, which enable seamless connectivity and data transmission (Pandey, B. K. et al., 2023b). This provides farmers with insights into crop health, soil conditions, and environmental parameters that have never been offered before. As an additional benefit, the ultra-low latency of 6G networks guarantees nearly instantaneous data processing (Deepa, R. et al., 2022) and response times, which enables timely interventions and maximizes the utilization of available resources. In the field of crop protection, where prompt action is required to mitigate the impact of pests, diseases, and adverse weather events on crop yields, this capability makes a particularly important contribution (Zhang, Z. et al., 2019). Even in remote rural areas, where traditional connectivity solutions may be limited, the scalability of 6G networks ensures that an all-encompassing coverage is present. To bridge the digital divide and promote inclusivity in agriculture, this democratization of connectivity provides farmers with access to advanced agricultural technologies, regardless of their geographic location. This empowers farmers to make use of these technologies.

II. CHALLENGES IN CROP PROTECTION

2.1 Pests and Diseases

Agricultural productivity and global food security are seriously threatened by pests and diseases, which pose formidable obstacles to crop protection. To minimize crop losses and uphold sustainable agricultural practices, managing these challenges effectively necessitates the implementation of attentive monitoring, preventative measures, and prompt interventions. Out of all the challenges that crop protection poses, pest and disease problems are among the most important. Primary obstacles in the field of crop protection are identification and monitoring. For management plans to be successful, it is essential to accurately identify and track disease and pest populations. Identifying particular threats to crops can be difficult, though, because pests and diseases have a wide range of characteristics and staged life cycles. Monitoring these populations over large agricultural landscapes also necessitates the application (Pandey, B. K. et al., 2011) of effective and economical techniques to identify outbreaks early and stop their spread. Protecting crops is made more difficult by the rapid spread of diseases and pests. Invasive pests and diseases spread quickly due to a number of factors, including globalization, trade between countries, and climate change. The swift expansion of the disease makes it more challenging to contain and regulate, so preventive actions are needed to stop its spread and lessen the harm it causes to agricultural productivity. Another big obstacle to crop protection is resistance development. Chemical pesticides and other control methods have not been able to stop pests and diseases from evolving remarkable resistance over time (Palattella, M. R. et al., 2016). The emergence of resistance is accelerated when control measures are based exclusively on a single mode of action or chemical class. For crop protection measures to remain effective and prevent resistance development, it is imperative to apply integrated pest management (IPM) strategies that integrate various techniques such as chemical interventions, biological control, and cultural practices. Concerns over how crop protection methods affect the environment are becoming more widespread. Utilizing synthetic control techniques and chemical pesticides can have negative consequences on the ecosystem, such as contaminating water sources, harming non-target organisms, and deteriorating soil health. In addition to endangering human health, persistent pesticide residues can have long-term ecological effects. Sustainable crop protection methods like biological control, precision agriculture, and organic farming are being used more often to manage pests and diseases and reduce environmental impact in response to these environmental concerns. For crop protection stakeholders, regulatory compliance poses still another difficulty. The safety, effectiveness, and environmental sustainability of crop protection products are ensured by strict regulatory requirements. Following strict procedures and guidelines during the production, distribution, and application of crop protection products is necessary to comply with regulatory standards, which can be difficult and complex to follow. Ensuring regulatory compliance in crop protection requires striking a balance between the need for efficient pest and disease control (Imoize, A. L. et al., 2021) and the protection of the environment and human health (Tareke, S. A. et al., 2022).

2.2 Environmental Factors

Environmental factors, which include a wide range of variables including weather patterns and soil conditions, present significant challenges in the context of crop protection. Agricultural productivity and food security are both impacted as a result of these factors because they have a significant impact on the growth, development, and susceptibility of crops to diseases and pests. Variations in the weather, such as temperature extremes, levels of precipitation, and humidity, can create conditions that are conducive to the spread of diseases and pests, which can result in significant losses to crops. In contrast, drought, flooding, and other extreme weather events can cause stress to crops, which in turn weakens their defenses against diseases and pests and makes them more susceptible to damage. Crop health and resilience are also significantly influenced by the conditions of the soil, which include the availability of nutrients, the pH levels, and the moisture content of the soil. It is possible for crops to be more susceptible to diseases and decreased in their ability to withstand the pressure of pests if the soil fertility is not balanced, soilborne pathogens are present, and conditions are waterlogged. In order to effectively manage environmental factors, a comprehensive approach is required. This approach should incorporate agronomic practices, climate-smart technologies, and resilient crop varieties that are adapted to the specific conditions of the area. Farmers have the ability to improve crop protection and facilitate the development of resilient agricultural systems by addressing environmental challenges through the implementation of sustainable soil management practices, irrigation methods, and weather forecasting tools. Furthermore, the advancement of research and innovation in climate-resilient agriculture and precision farming technologies can provide farmers with the ability to adapt to shifting environmental conditions and reduce the impact of environmental factors on crop health and productivity. The implementation of regulatory frameworks and policies that encourage sustainable land use practices, conservation agriculture, and ecosystem-based approaches is also essential for the purpose of protecting the environment and improving crop protection in the face of environmental challenges. In conclusion, environmental factors present significant challenges in crop protection, which calls for proactive measures and innovative solutions to mitigate the impact that these factors have on agricultural productivity and food security. It is possible for farmers to effectively manage environmental risks and promote resilient agricultural systems that are capable of maintaining crop production over the long term if they adopt sustainable practices, leverage technology, and foster collaboration among stakeholders (Huang, K. et al., 2020).

2.3 Resource Management

Weather conditions and soil health are significant environmental factors that have a profound impact on crop protection strategies. These factors present both challenges and opportunities for achieving agricultural sustainability. The complex relationship between environmental factors and crop health is characterized by the profound influence of weather patterns and soil conditions on the susceptibility of crops to pests and diseases. The presence of weather fluctuations, such as extreme temperatures, droughts, floods, and storms, presents significant obstacles in the field of crop protection. These weather phenomena can disturb the physiological processes of plants, compromise their natural defenses, and create advantageous circumstances for the occurrence of pest infestations and disease outbreaks. One example of the impact of prolonged periods of high humidity is the promotion of fungal diseases, whereas drought stress increases the vulnerability of crops to insect attacks. The challenges are further intensified by the unpredictable weather patterns linked to climate change, which require the implementation of adaptive strategies to reduce risks and improve resilience in agricultural systems. Soil health is a crucial factor that significantly impacts crop protection outcomes, as it greatly affects plant strength, resistance to diseases, and vulnerability to pests. Soil characteristics, including pH levels, nutrient availability, and organic matter content, are crucial factors that significantly influence plant growth and resilience. The compromised health of crops can result from imbalanced soil fertility, nutrient deficiencies, and the presence of soilborne pathogens, ultimately leading to decreased yields and heightened pest pressures. Consequently, the implementation of soil management techniques such as crop rotation, cover cropping, and organic amendments is imperative in order to maximize soil health, bolster plant resilience, and mitigate the potential hazards posed by pests and diseases. Resource management, specifically the management of water and fertilizers, plays a crucial role in ensuring efficient crop protection and promoting sustainable agriculture. The challenges associated with water scarcity and inefficient irrigation practices have significant implications for maintaining optimal soil moisture levels, which in turn have a direct impact on plant health and susceptibility to pests. The excessive application of fertilizers can result in imbalances in nutrient levels, degradation of soil quality, and heightened occurrences of pest infestations, thereby requiring the implementation of prudent strategies for nutrient management. The utilization of precision irrigation techniques, soil moisture sensors, and nutrient management plans allows farmers to effectively allocate resources, practice water conservation, and reduce environmental consequences, all while improving crop protection outcomes.

Technological progress, including remote sensing, satellite imaging, and weather forecasting, provides valuable instruments for monitoring environmental conditions and predicting pest and disease outbreaks. Integrative pest management (IPM) strategies, which encompass the integration of biological, cultural, and chemical control techniques, empower farmers to effectively address pest pressures while simultaneously mitigating potential environmental hazards. The adoption of sustainable agricultural methods, including agroecology, organic farming, and conservation agriculture, has been shown to have positive effects on the overall well-being of the environment, the proliferation of biodiversity, and the development of resilience within agricultural systems (Ragazou, K. et al., 2022).

2.4 IoT Limitations

A number of obstacles prevent current IoT solutions in agriculture from fully tackling the complex issues raised by crop protection, resource management, and environmental factors. Technological limitations, infrastructure impediments, and socio-economic factors are some of the causes of these limitations.

- *Complexity of Data Integration and Analysis*: Large volumes of heterogeneous data are produced by IoT solutions from a variety of sources, such as sensors, drones, and satellite imagery. However, it can be difficult and resource-intensive to integrate and analyze this data in a way that makes sense and can be put to use. The capacity to obtain significant insights and forecast models for well-informed decision-making in crop protection and resource management is hampered by inadequate data integration capabilities and analytical tools.
- *Power Supply and Energy Efficiency*: Numerous Internet of Things (IoT) devices in the agricultural sector are dependent on solar or battery-powered systems, which may have limited dependability and energy efficiency, especially in isolated or off-grid areas. The continuity and efficacy of Internet of Things (IoT)-based monitoring and control systems can be jeopardized by inadequate power supply and battery life, which can lead to downtime and data loss.
- *Scalability and Localized Solutions*: Certain Internet of Things solutions are tailored to particular crops, areas, or farming methods, which restricts their scalability and application in a variety of agricultural contexts. The lack of standardization and interoperability in customized IoT solutions may prevent their wider adoption and integration into current agricultural supply chains and workflows.

- *Policy and Regulatory Frameworks*: Cross-border data exchange and collaboration are complicated by the disparate legal frameworks and policies that regulate data privacy, ownership, and sharing in the agricultural industry across different jurisdictions. Investment and innovation in IoT solutions may be discouraged by a lack of clarity and harmonization in regulatory requirements, especially in areas with strict data protection laws.
- *Digital Divide and Accessibility*: Differences in technology access, infrastructure, and digital literacy make it harder for some people to adopt and profit from IoT solutions in agriculture. It is possible that farmers in underserved or remote areas lack the knowledge, resources, and connectivity needed to implement and use IoT technologies efficiently, which would increase the digital divide and exacerbate socioeconomic differences in agricultural resilience and productivity.
- *Ethical and Environmental Sustainability Considerations*: IoT solutions' environmental impact, which includes carbon emissions, energy use, and electronic waste, raises questions about their long-term viability and moral implications. It takes comprehensive analyses and mitigation techniques to reduce negative externalities in order to strike a balance between the potential advantages of IoT technologies in improving resource management and crop protection and their environmental effects.
- *Multidisciplinary Cooperation and Involvement of Stakeholders*: Interdisciplinary cooperation and stakeholder engagement throughout the agricultural value chain including farmers, researchers, legislators, and technology providers are necessary for the effective deployment and adoption of IoT solutions in agriculture. Maximizing the effectiveness and sustainability of IoT interventions in crop protection and sustainable agriculture requires developing partnerships, establishing trust, and working together to co-create solutions that address end users' needs and priorities.

Governments, academia (Pandey, D. et al., 2021b), business, and civil society must work together to invest in R&D, encourage entrepreneurship and innovation, and create supportive environments for the responsible use and deployment of IoT solutions in agriculture in order to address these constraints. IoT technologies have the potential to improve crop resilience, optimize (Pandey, D., & Pandey, B. K., 2022) resource use, and advance sustainable agricultural practices for the benefit of current and future generations by overcoming these obstacles.

III. LEVERAGING IOT FOR CROP PROTECTION

3.1 Sensor Integration

Modern farmers use sensors for real-time monitoring to understand environmental conditions, crop health, and pest dynamics. Farmers can use IoT technologies to establish a network of sensors across their fields to collect real-time data on numerous aspects for informed decision-making and proactive management. Integrating sensors for real-time monitoring in agriculture is difficult, but addressing these problems is necessary to maximize IoT solutions in crop protection and resource management. Data accuracy and dependability are major problems when integrating sensors for real-time farm monitoring. Temperature, humidity, and soil variability affect sensor performance in tough agricultural situations. Calibration drift, signal interference, and environmental noise (Bruntha, P. M. et al., 2023) can skew data, affecting monitoring system reliability. Farmers must buy high-quality sensors, calibrate and maintain their equipment, and use redundancy (Jayapoorani, S. et al., 2023) to assure data integrity and accuracy. Another barrier in integrating sensors for real-time agriculture monitoring is connectivity, especially in isolated or rural locations with insufficient network infrastructure. Transmission of sensor data to centralized platforms requires reliable and fast connectivity for rapid decision-making and action. Poor network coverage, signal degradation, and bandwidth limits might delay or disrupt monitoring systems. Farmers may use satellite or LoRaWAN networks and modify infrastructure to improve network reliability and coverage to solve connectivity issues. Scalability and affordability are crucial when establishing sensor networks for real-time monitoring of huge agricultural fields. Small-scale farmers and those on a budget may find sensors, data management systems, and connectivity infrastructure too expensive. IoT implementations across large agricultural areas require careful planning and investment in infrastructure, logistics, and staff training. Farmers may phase in IoT adoption, prioritize high-value crops or sensor deployment regions, and use cost-sharing mechanisms or government incentives to reduce early investment costs to meet scalability and affordability issues. Compatibility and interoperability difficulties can also limit agriculture sensor integration for real-time monitoring, especially with different sensor kinds, connection protocols, and data formats (Zhai, Z. et al., 2020). Integrating and analyzing data from many sources may be difficult due to incompatible hardware and software (Kirubasri, G. et al., 2022). Standardisation, open-source platforms, and APIs can let sensor systems communicate, allowing farmers to monitor and analyse data from disparate sources. Given the sensitive nature of agricultural data acquired by IoT devices (Sasidevi S et al., 2024), data privacy and security are important in real-time agriculture monitoring sensor integration. Farmers must secure sensor networks with data encryption (Kumar Pandey, B. et al., 2021), access controls, and cybersecurity to prevent unwanted access, data breaches, and malicious attacks. For farmer privacy, IP, and business competitiveness, data protection standards and best practices must be followed.

3.2 Data Analytics and Predictive Modelling

Data analytics and predictive modelling in agriculture transform early detection (Abdulkarim, Y. I. et al., 2024) and decision-making, helping farmers anticipate and manage hazards. Farmers can proactively manage crop protection and resource allocation using sensor readings, satellite photography, and historical trends. The successful deployment of these technologies requires overcoming hurdles and adopting new methods. Agricultural data quality and reliability are major challenges. Sensor errors, environmental variability, and data gathering methods make agricultural datasets complex and inconsistent. These difficulties demand strong quality control, data validation, and ongoing monitoring to assure data veracity and integrity. Farmers may improve data analytics and decision-making by investing in data quality assurance. Data source integration and interoperability are also important. Sensors, machines, weather stations, and farm management software generate agricultural data in different formats and protocols. Interoperable data platforms, defined data schemas, and smooth data exchange protocols are needed to integrate heterogeneous data. Interoperability, open-source frameworks, and data sharing agreements can help farmers maximize their data assets. Extracting insights from agricultural data and constructing predictive models requires advanced analytical and computational tools. Machine learning algorithms (Anand, R. et al., 2024), statistical models, and geospatial analysis help farmers spot data patterns, trends, and anomalies, identifying dangers and possibilities early. These methods involve computational resources, data science and analytics skills, and competence. Capacity building, research partnerships, and technology adoption can help farmers use sophisticated analytics and make better decisions. To protect agricultural data from unauthorised access, breaches, and misuse, data privacy and security must be prioritized. Cyberattackers target agricultural data because it contains sensitive information about crop yields, land use, and farm activities. For data confidentiality, integrity, and availability, farmers must use strong data encryption (Pandey, D. et al., 2021c) access restrictions, and cybersecurity. To build trust in data-driven decision-making, data protection standards and best practices must be followed (Abbasi, R. et al., 2022).

3.3 Automation and Smart Interventions

Agricultural practices are being reshaped by automation and intelligent interventions (Revathi, T. K. et al., 2022), which provide crop protection and resource management with precise and focused treatment administration. The way farmers manage their crops is about to change dramatically thanks to these cutting-edge technologies that take advantage of advances in robotics, artificial intelligence (AI), and the Internet of Things (IoT). Farmers may increase productivity, cut down on wasted inputs, and improve the efficacy of crop protection tactics by automating processes and implementing clever interventions. The capacity of automation to enable accurate application of treatments, such as pesticides, fertilizers, and water, is one of the main advantages for agriculture. Sensitive, actuating, GPS-enabled automated equipment may target specific field segments with accuracy, supplying inputs at the right volumes and positions. This focused strategy maximizes treatment effectiveness while lowering environmental impact by minimizing input overlap, cutting waste, and guaranteeing that treatments are applied only where necessary. Automation also enables real-time monitoring and decision-making, giving farmers the ability to react quickly to pest pressures and changing environmental circumstances. Drones, satellite imaging, and sensor networks give farmers practical information on pest populations, soil moisture content, and crop health. Farmers may optimize crop protection tactics for optimum performance by making educated decisions regarding treatment timing, dose, and application techniques by combining these data sources with AI-driven analytics and predictive modeling. Cost, complexity, and compatibility issues, however, make automation and intelligent interventions in agriculture difficult to implement. Infrastructure and equipment investments must be made up front before automation technologies like robotic systems and driverless cars can be put into use. It could also take technical assistance and specialized knowledge to integrate automation technologies with current farm operations and workflows. Data interchange and seamless integration also depend on the compatibility and interoperability of various automation systems and equipment. In order for farmers to fully utilize automation for precision agriculture, standardization initiatives, open protocols, and interoperability frameworks can help to promote communication and cooperation amongst various automation technologies.

IV. THE EMERGENCE OF 6G NETWORKS

4.1 Potential Agricultural Applications

Real-time monitoring of crop health and environmental conditions, as well as precision agriculture techniques for precise treatment application that are shown in the figure 1, autonomous machinery and drones for farm operations, data-driven decision-making using artificial intelligence analytics, and enhanced connectivity for remote farming areas are some of the potential applications of sixth-generation wireless technology in agriculture and crop protection.

Figure 1. Potential agricultural applications

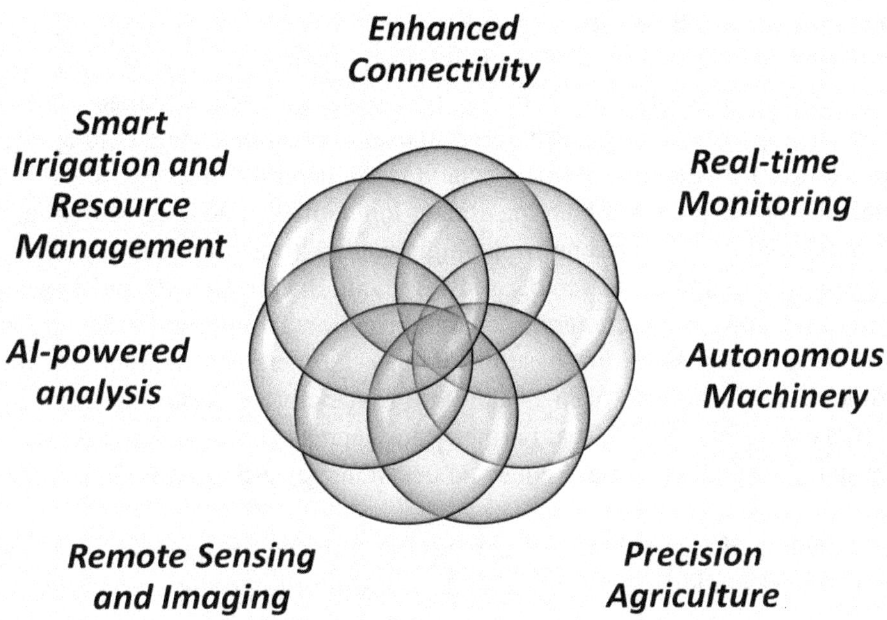

- *Enhanced Connectivity*: In comparison to earlier generations, 6G networks offer unmatched speed, dependability, and coverage, marking a substantial progress in connectivity. Farmers are able to remotely monitor and operate agricultural operations from any location thanks to these networks' flawless connectivity and data sharing capabilities. Farmers may depend on 6G networks to provide constant communication between their agricultural gadgets, sensors, and machinery whether they are located in far-off rural locations or across vast agricultural landscapes. Because of the increased connectivity, farmers are better able to make decisions quickly in response to changing conditions and optimize their farming methods for increased efficiency and productivity.
- *Real-time Monitoring*: Farmers can now keep an eye on important agricultural factors including crop health, soil moisture levels, and environmental variables in real time thanks to 6G networks' high-speed data transfer capabilities. Farmers may get real-time information about the condition of their crops and soil thanks to the continuous data collection of advanced sensors and Internet of Things devices in the field. Farmers are able to take prompt remedial action to safeguard their crops and maximize yields by utilizing this real-time monitoring capabilities to identify problems such as pest infestations, nutritional deficits, or water stress early on.
- *Autonomous Machinery*: The use of drones and other autonomous technology in agriculture is becoming more dependable and efficient with the help of 6G networks. With the use of sophisti-

cated sensors, cameras, and AI algorithms, these machines can function independently and carry out efficient and accurate operations like planting, spraying, and harvesting. Farmers can remotely monitor and manage these self-sufficient equipment using 6G connectivity, guaranteeing their safe and efficient operation in the field. Farmers benefit from greater production and profitability as a result of the automation of agricultural chores, which also lowers labor expenses and human error.

- *Precision Agriculture*: Precision agriculture methods can now be maximized for effectiveness thanks to 6G networks. These networks enable farmers to accurately apply treatments like pesticides and fertilizers, reducing waste and environmental effect, by offering exact geolocation and positioning services. To customize their treatment plans for particular fields, farmers can gather information on crop growth, pest infestations, and soil conditions using cutting-edge sensors and Internet of Things (IoT) devices. Farmers benefit from increased crop yields and profitability as a result of this focused approach, which maximizes input effectiveness while minimizing expenses.
- *Remote Sensing and Imaging*: 6G networks high bandwidth and low latency make it possible to use high-resolution imaging and remote sensing methods like LiDAR and hyperspectral imaging. Farmers may now obtain comprehensive information about crop health, growth trends, and environmental variables thanks to these technology. Farmers can monitor soil moisture levels, identify illnesses, and evaluate plant health with remarkable precision by evaluating data from remote sensors and imaging devices. Farmers may increase crop health and yield by using this comprehensive information to make educated decisions regarding pest control, fertilization, and irrigation.
- *AI-powered analysis*: Large volumes of agricultural data can be processed and analyzed in real-time by 6G networks, allowing cutting-edge AI algorithms to produce predictive models and actionable insights. Farmers may forecast yield results, optimize crop management procedures, and reduce risks more successfully by utilizing machine learning and data analytics tools (Saxena, A. etal., 2024). Farmers can now make data-driven decisions that optimize output, reduce input costs, and guarantee environmental sustainability thanks to these AI-driven insights. Farmers can seize new chances for innovation and expansion in agriculture by utilizing AI-driven data.
- *Smart Irrigation and Resource Management*: The development of intelligent irrigation systems that dynamically modify water usage based on current environmental circumstances is made possible by 6G connectivity. These systems optimize the distribution of water to crops by using data from sensors, weather forecasts, and soil moisture sensors to make sure the proper amount of water is applied at the right time. Smart irrigation systems assist farmers preserve water resources and limit their impact on the environment while preserving crop yields by decreasing water waste and increasing water efficiency. This strategic approach to resource management ensures the long-term profitability of farming operations by fostering resilience and sustainability in the agricultural sector.

4.2 limitations of IoT Solutions

6G networks can improve connectivity, speed, reliability, capacity, and energy efficiency for agricultural IoT olutions. Agriculture IoT solutions have connectivity concerns, especially in isolated or rural areas with low network coverage. SixG networks provide better coverage and reliability, allowing agricultural

IoT equipment to communicate and share data regardless of location. This improved connectivity lets farmers monitor and control farm operations in real time, improving agricultural resource management.

6G networks speed up data transfer, lowering latency and enabling real-time data processing and analysis. Current IoT solutions may not have fast enough data transmission speeds for rapid decision-making. 6G allows agricultural IoT devices to transfer enormous amounts of data rapidly and efficiently, allowing farmers to monitor crop status, environmental parameters, and machinery performance in real time. Farmers can make informed decisions quickly and optimize crop management and yields with real-time monitoring and analysis. Advanced beam forming, network slicing, and massive MIMO improve 6G network resilience. These systems shield agricultural IoT devices against signal interference, network congestion, and data loss. So, farmers may use 6G networks for continual connectivity and data exchange, improving their agricultural IoT solutions. Current IoT networks struggle to scale, but 6G networks can accommodate more devices and data-intensive applications. Agriculture IoT systems can handle more sensors, drones, and autonomous machinery with 6G's increased capacity without sacrificing performance or economy. Scalability allows farmers to use additional IoT sensors and apps to monitor and control their agricultural operations, improving productivity and sustainability (Zambon, I. et al., 2019).

V. SAFEGUARDING AGRICULTURAL 6G NETWORKS

Maintaining the dependability, security, and resilience of digital infrastructure in the farming industry depends critically on the protection of agricultural 6G networks. The agricultural sector is becoming more and more dependent on 6G networks for connectivity and modern technology. Therefore, safeguarding these networks from potential threats and vulnerabilities is crucial to preserving farming practices sustainability, productivity, and efficiency. Making sure strong cybersecurity measures are in place to guard against cyber threats and attacks is one of the main factors in protecting agricultural 6G networks. As agricultural data sharing and connected device proliferation increase, 6G networks become more attractive to malevolent actors who aim to breach system integrity, steal confidential data, or interfere with operations. Strong cybersecurity measures, like intrusion detection systems, authentication (Pandey, B. K. et al., 2022), and encryption, can be put in place to assist reduce these risks and protect agricultural 6G networks from cyberattacks. Resolving physical security issues is necessary to protect agricultural 6G networks from unwanted access, manipulation, or infrastructure damage. Protecting vital infrastructure elements from physical assaults and guaranteeing the continuous functioning of 6G networks in agricultural environments are achieved by securing base stations, antennas, and network equipment. Agricultural 6G networks physical security posture is improved by deploying security measures including perimeter fencing, access controls, and surveillance cameras, which lowers the possibility of disruption or sabotage. Resilience and redundancy solutions are needed to protect agricultural 6G networks from potential disturbances such natural catastrophes, equipment malfunctions, or network outages. The implementation of redundant network paths, failover methods, and backup systems guarantees uninterrupted operations and reduces downtime in the event of unanticipated catastrophes. By regularly testing, maintaining, and monitoring network infrastructure, vulnerabilities can be found early on and fixed, strengthening the resilience of agricultural 6G networks against outages. Making sure industry standards and legal criteria for network security and data privacy are followed is another way to protect agricultural 6G networks. Sensitive data is protected and legal and regulatory requirements are met when established rules and best practices such as the General Data Protection Regulation (GDPR) and industry-specific security frameworks are followed. Raising awareness and promoting a security-conscious culture in the agriculture industry can be achieved through teaching farmers and network operators about cybersecurity threats and best practices.

CONCLUSION

The incorporation of Internet of Things (IoT) solutions in agriculture has transformed crop security methods through supplying real-time monitoring, data analytics, and automated procedures to address a variety of challenges. The scalability, connection, and dependability of current IoT solutions are restricted, which limits their potential to effectively handle intricate agricultural problems. With the introduction of ultra-high-speed, low-latency connection that can support sophisticated IoT applications in agriculture, 6G networks offer an exciting chance to get past these constraints. Farmers are better able to secure their crops through automation, data analytics, and real-time monitoring when they take advantage of 6G network capabilities. More productivity and sustainable agricultural methods are made possible by 6G networks, which also allow for early disease and pest detection, targeted treatment application, and improved resource management. The safety and integrity of agricultural IoT systems can also be guaranteed by 6G networks, which have the ability to handle privacy problems, security challenges, and legal requirements. To ensure the dependability, security, and robustness of digital infrastructure in the farming industry, agricultural 6G networks must be safeguarded. Agricultural 6G networks can be safeguarded against a range of risks and vulnerabilities by stakeholders through the implementation of strong cybersecurity measures, improved physical security, network resilience, and adherence to regulatory requirements. In the end, the coming together of IoT and 6G technology promises to advance innovation, revolutionize agriculture, and tackle issues related to global food security.

REFERENCES

Abbasi, R., Martinez, P., & Ahmad, R. (2022). The digitization of agricultural industry–a systematic literature review on agriculture 4.0. *Smart Agricultural Technology*, 2, 100042. 10.1016/j.atech.2022.100042

Abdulkarim, Y. I., Awl, H. N., Muhammadsharif, F. F., Saeed, S. R., Sidiq, K. R., Khasraw, S. S., Dong, J., Pandey, B. K., & Pandey, D. (2024). Metamaterial-based sensors loaded corona-shaped resonator for COVID-19 detection by using microwave techniques. *Plasmonics*, 19(2), 595–610. 10.1007/s11468-023-02007-4

Anand, R., Khan, B., Nassa, V. K., Pandey, D., Dhabliya, D., Pandey, B. K., & Dadheech, P. (2023). Hybrid convolutional neural network (CNN) for kennedy space center hyperspectral image. *Aerospace Systems*, 6(1), 71–78. 10.1007/s42401-022-00168-4

Anand, R., Lakshmi, S. V., Pandey, D., & Pandey, B. K. (2024). An enhanced ResNet-50 deep learning model for arrhythmia detection using electrocardiogram biomedical indicators. *Evolving Systems*, 15(1), 83–97. 10.1007/s12530-023-09559-0

Bruntha, P. M., Dhanasekar, S., Hepsiba, D., Sagayam, K. M., Neebha, T. M., Pandey, D., & Pandey, B. K. (2023). Application of switching median filter with L 2 norm-based auto-tuning function for removing random valued impulse noise. *Aerospace Systems, 6*(1), 53-59.

David, S., Duraipandian, K., Chandrasekaran, D., Pandey, D., Sindhwani, N., & Pandey, B. K. (2023). Impact of blockchain in healthcare system. In *Unleashing the Potentials of blockchain technology for healthcare industries* (pp. 37–57). Academic Press. 10.1016/B978-0-323-99481-1.00004-3

Deepa, R., Anand, R., Pandey, D., Pandey, B. K., & Karki, B. (2022). Comprehensive performance analysis of classifiers in diagnosis of epilepsy. *Mathematical Problems in Engineering*, 2022, 2022. 10.1155/2022/1559312

Devasenapathy, D., Madhumathy, P., Umamaheshwari, R., Pandey, B. K., & Pandey, D. (2024). Transmission-efficient grid-based synchronized model for routing in wireless sensor networks using Bayesian compressive sensing. *SN Computer Science*, 5(1), 1–11.

Dhanasekar, S., Martin Sagayam, K., Pandey, B. K., & Pandey, D. (2023). Refractive Index Sensing Using Metamaterial Absorbing Augmentation in Elliptical Graphene Arrays. *Plasmonics*, 1–11. 10.1007/s11468-023-02152-w

Du John, H. V., Jose, T., Jone, A. A. A., Sagayam, K. M., Pandey, B. K., & Pandey, D. (2022). Polarization insensitive circular ring resonator based perfect metamaterial absorber design and simulation on a silicon substrate. *Silicon*, 14(14), 9009–9020. 10.1007/s12633-021-01645-9

Figueiredo e Silva, P., Kaseva, V., & Lohan, E. S. (2018). Wireless positioning in IoT: A look at current and future trends. *Sensors (Basel)*, 18(8), 2470. 10.3390/s1808247030061535

Govindaraj, V., Dhanasekar, S., Martinsagayam, K., Pandey, D., Pandey, B. K., & Nassa, V. K. (2023). Low-power test pattern generator using modified LFSR. *Aerospace Systems*, 1-8.

Huang, K., Shu, L., Li, K., Yang, F., Han, G., Wang, X., & Pearson, S. (2020). Photovoltaic agricultural internet of things towards realizing the next generation of smart farming. *IEEE Access : Practical Innovations, Open Solutions*, 8, 76300–76312. 10.1109/ACCESS.2020.2988663

Imoize, A. L., Adedeji, O., Tandiya, N., & Shetty, S. (2021). 6G enabled smart infrastructure for sustainable society: Opportunities, challenges, and research roadmap. *Sensors (Basel)*, 21(5), 1709. 10.3390/s2105170933801302

Iyyanar, P., Anand, R., Shanthi, T., Nassa, V. K., Pandey, B. K., George, A. S., & Pandey, D. (2023). A real-time smart sewage cleaning UAV assistance system using IoT. In *Handbook of Research on Data-Driven Mathematical Modeling in Smart Cities* (pp. 24–39). IGI Global.

Jayapoorani, S., Pandey, D., Sasirekha, N. S., Anand, R., & Pandey, B. K. (2023). Systolic optimized adaptive filter architecture designs for ECG noise cancellation by Vertex-5. *Aerospace Systems*, 6(1), 163–173. 10.1007/s42401-022-00177-3

Khan, B., Hasan, A., Pandey, D., Ventayen, R. J. M., Pandey, B. K., & Gowwrii, G. (2021). Fusion of datamining and artificial intelligence in prediction of hazardous road accidents. In *Machine learning and iot for intelligent systems and smart applications* (pp. 201–223). CRC Press. 10.1201/9781003194415-12

Kirubasri, G., Sankar, S., Pandey, D., Pandey, B. K., Nassa, V. K., & Dadheech, P. (2022). Software-defined networking-based Ad hoc networks routing protocols. In *Software defined networking for Ad Hoc networks* (pp. 95–123). Springer International Publishing. 10.1007/978-3-030-91149-2_5

Kirubasri, G., Sankar, S., Pandey, D., Pandey, B. K., Singh, H., & Anand, R. (2021, September). A recent survey on 6G vehicular technology, applications and challenges. In *2021 9th International Conference on Reliability, Infocom Technologies and Optimization (Trends and Future Directions)(ICRITO)* (pp. 1-5). IEEE.

Kumar Pandey, B., Pandey, D., Nassa, V. K., Ahmad, T., Singh, C., George, A. S., & Wakchaure, M. A. (2021). Encryption and steganography-based text extraction in IoT using the EWCTS optimizer. *Imaging Science Journal*, 69(1-4), 38–56. 10.1080/13682199.2022.2146885

Palattella, M. R., Dohler, M., Grieco, A., Rizzo, G., Torsner, J., Engel, T., & Ladid, L. (2016). Internet of things in the 5G era: Enablers, architecture, and business models. *IEEE Journal on Selected Areas in Communications*, 34(3), 510–527. 10.1109/JSAC.2016.2525418

Pandey, B. K., & Pandey, D. (2023). Parametric optimization and prediction of enhanced thermoelectric performance in co-doped CaMnO3 using response surface methodology and neural network. *Journal of Materials Science Materials in Electronics*, 34(21), 1589. 10.1007/s10854-023-10954-1

Pandey, B. K., Pandey, D., & Agarwal, A. (2022). Encrypted information transmission by enhanced steganography and image transformation. *International Journal of Distributed Artificial Intelligence*, 14(1), 1–14. 10.4018/IJDAI.297110

Pandey, B. K., Pandey, D., Alkhafaji, M. A., Güneşer, M. T., & Şeker, C. (2023a). A reliable transmission and extraction of textual information using keyless encryption, steganography, and deep algorithm with cuckoo optimization. In *Micro-Electronics and Telecommunication Engineering: Proceedings of 6th ICMETE 2022* (pp. 629–636). Springer Nature Singapore. 10.1007/978-981-19-9512-5_57

Pandey, B. K., Pandey, D., Gupta, A., Nassa, V. K., Dadheech, P., & George, A. S. (2023b). Secret data transmission using advanced morphological component analysis and steganography. In *Role of data-intensive distributed computing systems in designing data solutions* (pp. 21–44). Springer International Publishing. 10.1007/978-3-031-15542-0_2

Pandey, B. K., Pandey, S. K., & Pandey, D. (2011). A survey of bioinformatics applications on parallel architectures. *International Journal of Computer Applications*, 23(4), 21–25. 10.5120/2877-3744

Pandey, D., Nassa, V. K., Jhamb, A., Mahto, D., Pandey, B. K., George, A. H., & Bandyopadhyay, S. K. (2021a). An integration of keyless encryption, steganography, and artificial intelligence for the secure transmission of stego images. In *Multidisciplinary approach to modern digital steganography* (pp. 211–234). IGI Global. 10.4018/978-1-7998-7160-6.ch010

Pandey, D., Ogunmola, G. A., Enbeyle, W., Abdullahi, M., Pandey, B. K., & Pramanik, S. (2021b). COVID-19: A framework for effective delivering of online classes during lockdown. *Human Arenas*, 1-15.

Pandey, D., & Pandey, B. K. (2022). An efficient deep neural network with adaptive galactic swarm optimization for complex image text extraction. In *Process mining techniques for pattern recognition* (pp. 121–137). CRC Press. 10.1201/9781003169550-10

Pandey, D., Pandey, B. K., & Wairya, S. (2021c). Hybrid deep neural network with adaptive galactic swarm optimization for text extraction from scene images. *Soft Computing*, 25(2), 1563–1580. 10.1007/s00500-020-05245-4

Pandey, J. K., Jain, R., Dilip, R., Kumbhkar, M., Jaiswal, S., Pandey, B. K., & Pandey, D. (2022). Investigating role of iot in the development of smart application for security enhancement. In *IoT Based Smart Applications* (pp. 219–243). Springer International Publishing.

Patle, K. S., Saini, R., Kumar, A., & Palaparthy, V. S. (2021). Field evaluation of smart sensor system for plant disease prediction using LSTM network. *IEEE Sensors Journal*, 22(4), 3715–3725. 10.1109/JSEN.2021.3139988

Pramanik, S., Pandey, D., Joardar, S., Niranjanamurthy, M., Pandey, B. K., & Kaur, J. (2023, October). An overview of IoT privacy and security in smart cities. In *AIP Conference Proceedings* (Vol. 2495, No. 1). AIP Publishing 10.1063/5.0123511

Ragazou, K., Garefalakis, A., Zafeiriou, E., & Passas, I. (2022). Agriculture 5.0: A new strategic management mode for a cut cost and an energy efficient agriculture sector. *Energies*, 15(9), 3113. 10.3390/en15093113

Revathi, T. K., Sathiyabhama, B., Sankar, S., Pandey, D., Pandey, B. K., & Dadeech, P. (2022). An intelligent model for coronary heart disease diagnosis. In *Networking Technologies in Smart Healthcare* (pp. 309–327). CRC Press. 10.1201/9781003239888-15

Sasidevi, S., Kumarganesh, S., Saranya, S., Thiyaneswaran, B., Shree, K. V. M., & Martin Sagayam, K. (2024, May 15). Design of Surface Plasmon Resonance (SPR) Sensors for Highly Sensitive Biomolecular Detection in Cancer Diagnostics. *Plasmonics*. Advance online publication. 10.1007/s11468-024-02343-z

Saxena, A., Agarwal, A., Pandey, B. K., & Pandey, D. (2024). Examination of the Criticality of Customer Segmentation Using Unsupervised Learning Methods. *Circular Economy and Sustainability*, 1–14. 10.1007/s43615-023-00336-4

Sharma, M., Pandey, D., Khosla, D., Goyal, S., Pandey, B. K., & Gupta, A. K. (2022). Design of a GaN-based Flip Chip Light Emitting Diode (FC-LED) with au Bumps & Thermal Analysis with different sizes and adhesive materials for performance considerations. *Silicon*, 14(12), 7109–7120. 10.1007/s12633-021-01457-x

Sharma, M., Pandey, D., Palta, P., & Pandey, B. K. (2022). Design and power dissipation consideration of PFAL CMOS V/S conventional CMOS based 2: 1 multiplexer and full adder. *Silicon*, 14(8), 4401–4410. 10.1007/s12633-021-01221-1

Tareke, S. A., Lelisho, M. E., Hassen, S. S., Seid, A. A., Jemal, S. S., Teshale, B. M., & Pandey, B. K. (2022). The prevalence and predictors of depressive, anxiety, and stress symptoms among Tepi town residents during the COVID-19 pandemic lockdown in Ethiopia. *Journal of Racial and Ethnic Health Disparities*, 1–13.35028903

Tripathi, R. P., Sharma, M., Gupta, A. K., Pandey, D., Pandey, B. K., Shahul, A., & George, A. H. (2023). Timely prediction of diabetes by means of machine learning practices. *Augmented Human Research*, 8(1), 1. 10.1007/s41133-023-00062-4

Tzounis, A., Katsoulas, N., Bartzanas, T., & Kittas, C. (2017). Internet of Things in agriculture, recent advances and future challenges. *Biosystems Engineering*, 164, 31–48. 10.1016/j.biosystemseng.2017.09.007

Vinodhini, V., Kumar, M. S., Sankar, S., Pandey, D., Pandey, B. K., & Nassa, V. K. (2022). IoT-based early forest fire detection using MLP and AROC method. *International Journal of Global Warming*, 27(1), 55–70. 10.1504/IJGW.2022.122794

Zambon, I., Cecchini, M., Egidi, G., Saporito, M. G., & Colantoni, A. (2019). Revolution 4.0: Industry vs. agriculture in a future development for SMEs. *Processes (Basel, Switzerland)*, 7(1), 36. 10.3390/pr7010036

Zhai, Z., Martínez, J. F., Beltran, V., & Martínez, N. L. (2020). Decision support systems for agriculture 4.0: Survey and challenges. *Computers and Electronics in Agriculture*, 170, 105256. 10.1016/j.compag.2020.105256

Zhang, Z., Xiao, Y., Ma, Z., Xiao, M., Ding, Z., Lei, X., Karagiannidis, G. K., & Fan, P. (2019). 6G wireless networks: Vision, requirements, architecture, and key technologies. *IEEE Vehicular Technology Magazine*, 14(3), 28–41. 10.1109/MVT.2019.2921208

Chapter 16
Securing Future Harvests:
A Comprehensive Review of IoT Solutions for Crop Protection in Agricultural 6G Networks

Isha Chopra
Department of CSE, Maharishi Markandeshwar (Deemed), India

Amit Kumar Bindal
https://orcid.org/0000-0002-2624-8077
Department of CSE, Maharishi Markandeshwar (Deemed), India

Zatin Gupta
Galgotias University, India

ABSTRACT

Crop protection is essential to agricultural sustainability because it keeps farming systems resilient and productive all over the world. Nevertheless, conventional techniques frequently prove inadequate in tackling the diverse obstacles presented by pests, illnesses, and environmental conditions. Advances in technology like the internet of things (IoT) and the upcoming 6G networks have brought new opportunities for agricultural innovation in recent years. This thorough analysis aims to investigate the revolutionary possibilities of IoT solutions in the context of agricultural 6G networks, emphasizing the improvement of crop protection techniques.

I. INTRODUCTION

Crop protection is essential to agricultural sustainability because it keeps farming systems resilient and productive all over the world. Nevertheless, conventional techniques frequently prove inadequate in tackling the diverse obstacles presented by pests, illnesses, and environmental conditions. Advances in technology like the Internet of Things (IoT) and the upcoming 6G (Kirubasri, G. et al., 2021) networks have brought new opportunities for agricultural innovation in recent years. This thorough analysis aims to investigate the revolutionary possibilities of IoT (Iyyanar, P. et al., 2023) solutions in the context of

DOI: 10.4018/979-8-3693-7421-4.ch016

agricultural 6G networks, emphasizing the improvement of crop protection techniques. The agricultural industry has long struggled with the challenges of protecting crops from various threats, such as invasive pests, deadly diseases, and erratic weather patterns. Conventional methods of crop protection, which depend on manual observation and reactive measures, frequently fall short in offering prompt and focused solutions to new problems. With the ability to provide real-time monitoring, data-driven (Khan, B. et al., 2021) insights, and precision interventions to support crop resilience and yield, the emergence of IoT technologies in this context represents a paradigm shift.

IoT solutions cover a wide range of instruments and methods, from data analytics platforms and automated control systems to sensor (Abdulkarim, Y. I. et al., 2023) networks and drones. With the use of these technologies, farmers can keep an eye on the health of their crops from a distance, spot disease outbreaks or pest infestations early on, and take preventative measures to manage their crops. Farmers can promote sustainable and environmentally friendly farming practices by optimizing resource utilization, minimizing chemical inputs, and mitigating the environmental impact of agricultural practices by leveraging the power of the Internet of Things. The forthcoming deployment of 6G networks presents significant opportunities for agricultural data exchange and connectivity. IoT devices (Dhanasekar, S. et al., 2023) deployed in agricultural settings have the potential to revolutionize communication and collaboration through the use of 6G networks, which offer ultra-fast speeds, low latency, and high capacity. The efficient and effective implementation of crop protection measures is made possible by the seamless data transmission (Pandey, B. K. et al., 2023a), automated control systems (Pandey, B. K. et al., 2024), and real-time decision-making made possible by the integration of IoT with 6G networks. The revolutionary potential of IoT solutions in protecting crop health and guaranteeing food security by thoroughly analyzing them in the context of agricultural 6G networks. Farmers can adopt sustainable farming practices that are resistant to changing environmental challenges, embrace data-driven approaches, and optimize resource allocation by utilizing the capabilities of IoT and 6G networks. Ultimately, a new era of crop protection innovation and resilience is heralded by the integration of IoT (Pandey, J. K. et al., 2022) solutions within agricultural 6G networks, opening the door to a more productive and sustainable agricultural future (Nguyen, D. C. et al., 2021).

1.1 Relevance of Crop Protection

Protecting crops from pests, diseases, and weeds is essential to agriculture. These risks must be mitigated and plant growth and yield optimized (Jayapoorani, S. et al., 2023) by timely preventive measures. Agriculture's crop protection goes beyond protection to conserve biodiversity, optimize resource use, and improve food security. Crop protection focuses on maintain agricultural productivity. Farmers face challenges from pests, diseases, and weeds that reduce crop yields. Farmers can minimize crop losses and optimize production on smaller land areas by taking timely preventive measures like IPM. This boosts agricultural profits and helps meet global food demand. Crop protection can also preserve biodiversity and soil health in agricultural ecosystems. Pest and disease control help maintain ecosystem balance and minimize disruptions to native flora and fauna. Organic farming and biological control agents build soil fertility and microbial diversity for long-term soil health and productivity. Agriculture resource optimization depends on crop protection. By reducing pest and disease losses, farmers can increase yields with fewer inputs, reducing their environmental impact. Integrating biological control with pesticide use reduces resource waste and maximizes water, land, and labor use. Food quality and safety depend on crop protection, which maintains productivity and biodiversity. Controlling pests and diseases reduces crop contaminants and toxins, improving food safety and consumer health (Pandey, B. K. et al., 2011). Food quality and marketability are maintained by effective crop protection measures that preserve nutritional value and taste. The role that crop protection plays in preserving the environment and promoting ecological sustainability is a significant fact that highlights the significance of crop protection in the agricultural sector. Through the implementation of sustainable crop protection practices, such as organic farming techniques and the utilization of pesticides that are friendly to the environment, the negative impact that agricultural activities have on the ecosystems that are in the surrounding area is reduced. Farmers are able to reduce pollution, protect natural habitats, and promote the conservation of biodiversity if they adopt practices that are based on nature and reduce their use of synthetic chemicals. Protecting crops helps agricultural systems become more resilient and adaptable in the face of shifting environmental conditions and new dangers. This is because crop protection ensures that crops are protected from harm. The incidence of pest infestations, disease outbreaks, and the introduction of invasive species is anticipated to increase as a result of the rise in climate change and globalization. Farmers have the ability to anticipate and respond to these challenges, which ensures the long-term viability and sustainability of agricultural production. Effective crop protection strategies, which are informed by scientific research and technological innovation, enable farmers at this level (Cirillo, F. et al., 2020).

1.2 IoT in Agriculture

Technological progress has brought about a new era of innovation, revolutionizing multiple industries, including agriculture. The agricultural industry has experienced a significant transformation towards enhanced productivity, sustainability, and efficiency due to the advent of the Internet of Things (IoT), which refers to a network of interconnected devices and sensors (Du John, H. V. et al., 2022). This essay examines the impact of IoT solutions on crop protection, the utilization of data-driven methods to optimize agricultural practices and enhance overall efficiency. Smart agriculture, alternatively referred to as precision agriculture or agro technology, utilizes sophisticated technologies and data-centric methodologies to optimize agricultural methodologies and augment operational effectiveness. At the core of intelligent (Revathi, T. K. et al., 2022) agriculture resides the incorporation of Internet of Things (IoT) solutions, which facilitate the continuous monitoring, collection, and analysis of data in real-time, thereby facilitating well-informed decision-making procedures. Through the implementation of a network of interconnected devices and sensors (Sharma, M. et al., 2022), farmers and agribusinesses can acquire valuable knowledge regarding soil conditions, crop health, and environmental factors. This, in turn, contributes to the improvement of crop protection measures. The acquisition and dissemination of data from diverse sources, such as soil, crops, machinery, and livestock, constitute a fundamental element of Internet of Things (IoT) solutions (Vinodhini, V. et al., 2022) within the agricultural sector. These Internet of Things (IoT) devices, equipped with sensors, continuously monitor essential parameters such as temperature, humidity, soil moisture, nutrient levels, and animal behavior in real-time. By collecting this data, farmers can acquire a more profound comprehension of their agricultural operations and make well-informed decisions regarding irrigation, fertilization, disease prevention, and overall farm management. Farmers have the ability to remotely monitor their fields and promptly respond to any necessary actions by accessing real-time data on soil conditions and crop health through their smartphones or tablets. By achieving a high degree of precision and control, farmers are able to enhance resource utilization, optimize fertilizer efficiency, and enhance crop yields, all while mitigating environmental consequences. The global Internet of Things (IoT) and agriculture market is currently undergoing significant expansion due to several factors. These factors include the rising need for agricultural products, advancements in IoT and artificial intelligence (AI) technology (Anand, R. et al., 2023), and an increasing emphasis on livestock monitoring and disease detection (Tzounis, A. et al., 2017). According to market projections, it is anticipated that the valuation of the agriculture industry will reach USD 26.93 Billion by the year 2027. This highlights the considerable importance of IoT solutions in driving its transformation. The incorporation of Industrial Internet of Things (IIoT) has had a substantial impact on the transformation of conventional farming methods, facilitating the advent of intelligent agricultural practices. The utilization of remote monitoring techniques enables farmers to optimize efficiency and productivity by monitoring soil conditions, weather patterns, crop health, and equipment performance. Smart irrigation systems utilize real-time data to optimize watering schedules, thereby optimizing the timing and quantity of water provided to crops. This approach effectively conserves water resources and reduces wastage. Internet of Things (IoT) solutions facilitate improved surveillance of crops and identification of diseases, thereby empowering farmers to promptly detect initial indications of illness, nutrient insufficiencies, or pest infestations. Real-time monitoring and management systems for livestock are designed to track various parameters, including body temperature, heart rate, feeding patterns, and location. These systems facilitate proactive interventions aimed at ensuring the health and well-being of livestock. The utilization of IoT solutions in agriculture offers a significant advantage in the form of data-driven decision-making. Through the utilization of insights obtained from data generated by the Internet of Things (IoT), farmers have the ability to enhance production processes, efficiently allocate resources, and effectively manage risks. In addition, supply chain optimization (Malhotra, P. et al., 2021) is achieved by ensuring visibility and traceability from start to finish, which guarantees transparency, quality control, and food safety across the entire agricultural supply chain (Polymeni, S. et al., 2022).

1.3 Potential of 6G Networks

Many regions of the world are still implementing 5G networks, scientists and engineers are already planning for the creation of 6G networks, which are expected to completely transform a number of industries, including agriculture. Regarding the agricultural Internet of Things (IoT), 6G networks are extremely promising in terms of revolutionizing farm operations, improving productivity, and opening up new applications. The potential effects of 6G networks on the Internet of Things in agriculture are shown in the figure 1, which can be examined in a number of important domains.

Figure 1. 6G-enabled agricultural advancements

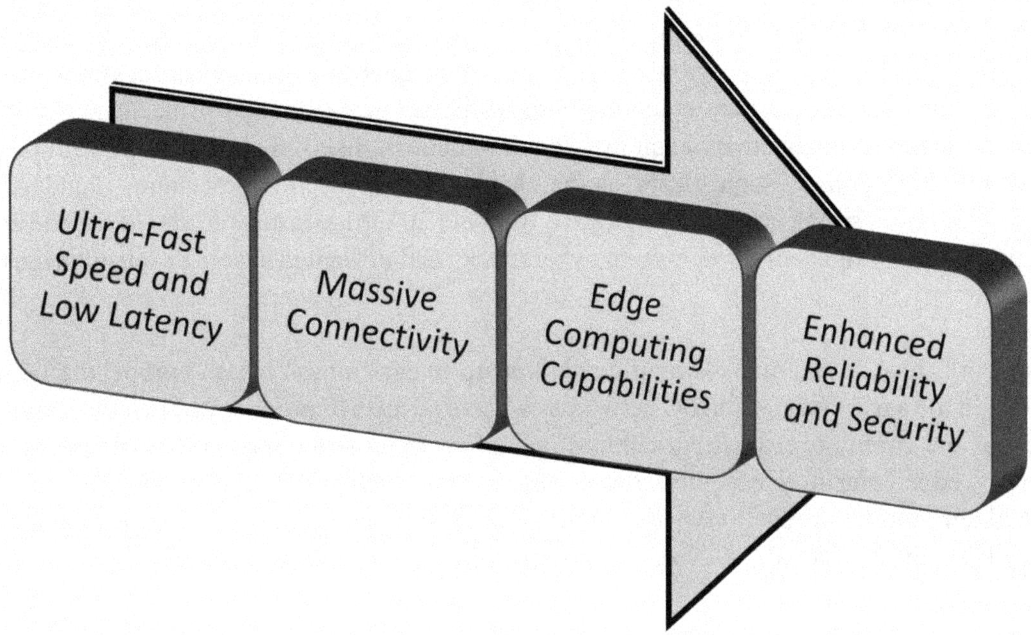

- *Ultra-Fast Speed and Low Latency*: In comparison to existing wireless technologies (Devasenapathy, D. et al., 2024), 6G networks are anticipated to offer ultra-fast speeds and much reduced latency. This implies that real-time monitoring and control of agricultural processes will be possible due to nearly instantaneous data transmission between IoT devices and the cloud. For instance, sensors placed in fields can gather information on crop health, soil moisture, and meteorological conditions; these data can then be instantly transmitted to farmers or self-sufficient agricultural equipment. This real-time data sharing enables timely interventions to maximize crop protection measures and supports quick decision-making.
- *Massive Connectivity*: The proliferation of IoT devices in agriculture is made possible by 6G networks, which are built to support a massive number of connected devices per square kilometer. Large-scale monitoring and management of agricultural operations are made possible by 6G networks, which can support a dense network of sensors, actuators, drones, and other IoT devices. With this degree of connectivity, IoT solutions can be easily integrated into the current farm infrastructure, improving precision farming techniques and facilitating data-driven decision-making throughout the whole agricultural value chain.
- *Edge Computing Capabilities*: It is anticipated that 6G networks will make use of edge computing capabilities, which will enable data processing and analysis to be carried out closer to the location where the data is generated. This decentralized computing method is perfect for time-sensitive agricultural applications because it lowers latency and bandwidth requirements. Edge computing, for instance, can enable IoT sensors placed in remote field locations to perform data analytics

on-device, doing away with the need to send raw data to centralized servers for processing. This lowers the cost of data transmission while improving data security (David, S. et al., 2023) and privacy (Pandey, B. K. et al., 2021), two important factors in agricultural IoT deployments.

- *Enhanced Reliability and Security*: 6G networks are better suited for mission-critical applications in agriculture because they are built to provide better reliability and security features than earlier generations. 6G networks are equipped with resilience and redundancy mechanisms that allow them to maintain connectivity even in difficult situations, like remote locations with poor infrastructure. Furthermore, sophisticated authentication and encryption procedures (Pandey, B. K. et al., 2022a) offer strong security (Pandey, B. K. et al., 2023b) measures to shield private and intellectual property rights of farmers from cyberattacks and unwanted access to sensitive agricultural data.

6G networks has the potential to significantly transform agricultural IoT and propel digital transformation within the agriculture sector. 6G networks can give farmers unprecedented levels of connectivity, intelligence, and control over their agricultural operations by utilizing their ultra-fast speeds, massive connectivity, edge computing capabilities, and improved reliability and security features. In crop protection and agricultural production, 6G technology is set to open up new possibilities for innovation, efficiency (Pandey, B. K. et al., 2022b), and sustainability as it develops further.

II. CROP RISKS

2.1 Pest and Disease Management

The management of pests and diseases is an essential component of agriculture. This is due to the fact that weeds, agricultural pests, and plant diseases all pose significant risks to the health and productivity of crops. Despite the fact that some people have traditionally supported the use of chemical solutions, there has been a shift toward more sustainable farming practices as a result of concerns regarding the long-term effects that these solutions have on human health (Tareke, S. A. et al., 2022) and the environment. The practice of natural pest management, which is also referred to as integrated pest management (IPM), is a holistic approach to the control of pests and diseases. It involves working in harmony with nature to maintain a balance between crops, pests, beneficial organisms, and the health of the soil. The primary objective of natural pest management strategies is to reduce the use of harmful chemicals while simultaneously preventing the occurrence of pest and disease problems. By fostering the development of wholesome ecosystems and decreasing reliance on chemical substances, these practices contribute to the preservation of the environment and the viability of agriculture over the long term. In this article, we will discuss the fundamentals and practices of natural pest management, as well as the role that these can play in improving crop protection. There is a strong emphasis placed on maintaining the health of plants, which is one of the fundamental principles of natural pest management. The foundation of plant health is healthy soil, which supplies the plant with essential nutrients and creates an environment that is conducive to the growth of beneficial soil organisms. In order to improve soil structure, fertility, and microbial diversity, farmers can improve soil health by adopting practices such as composting, crop rotation, and cover cropping. These practices are important for promoting soil health. Plants that are in good health are more resistant to damage from diseases and pests, which makes them less likely to be affected by infestations and outbreaks. Another important strategy in natural pest management is the selection of crop varieties that are resistant to the pest. Farmers can reduce the need for chemical interventions and promote crop resilience by selecting seeds that are naturally resistant to common pests and diseases. This reduces the amount of chemical intervention that is required. The selection of resistant varieties that are well-suited to the growing conditions of the local area can be facilitated by extension agents and seed suppliers, who can provide valuable guidance. When it comes to natural pest management, the timing and spacing of plants are two of the most important considerations. By restricting the flow of air and the amount of sunlight (Du John, H. V. et al., 2021) that can reach the plants, planting crops too closely together can create conditions that are conducive to the development of pests and diseases. On the other hand, if crops are spaced with an excessive amount of distance between them, gaps may be left that allow weeds to flourish and compete for resources. Farmers are required to strike a balance by experimenting with various spacing configurations and planting schedules in order to maximize the nutritional value and yield of their crops. Not only does natural pest management involve the utilization of cultural practices, but it also includes the utilization of biological control methods in order to manage pest populations. Beneficial insects, such as ladybugs, lacewings, and parasitic wasps, play an important part in the management of pest populations by either feeding on pests or parasitizing them. The presence of these beneficial insects can be encouraged by farmers through the conservation of natural habitats and the reduction of pesticide use, which in turn strengthens the effectiveness of these insects in controlling pests. Monitoring crops on a regular basis is necessary in order to detect outbreaks of diseases and pests at an earlier stage. It is important for farmers to conduct routine inspections of their crops to look for signs of damage caused by pests, such as chewed leaves, wilting, or discoloration. Farmers are able to implement timely interventions, such as the release of beneficial insects or the application of natural pesticides, to implement in order to prevent further damage and protect crop yields. This is accomplished by monitoring pest populations and understanding the life cycles of the pests. Pesticides that are natural, meaning they are derived from plant extracts or microbial agents, provide an efficient alternative to synthetic chemicals that are used for pest control. These naturally occurring compounds are less harmful to the environment and to organisms that are beneficial to the environment, which makes them ideal for use in farming systems that are organic and sustainable. It is essential to use natural pesticides in a prudent manner and to adhere to the application guidelines that are recommended in order to minimize the risks to human health and to organisms that are not the intended targets (Qadir, Z. et al., 2022).

2.2 Environmental Influences

Numerous environmental factors have a significant impact on the nutritional status of crops as well as their productivity. There is a wide range of natural elements that are included in these factors, such as climate, soil quality, water availability, and topography. There are human-induced factors that are included, such as pollution and land management practices. When it comes to optimizing crop health, resilience, and yield, having a solid understanding of the interplay between these environmental factors is absolutely necessary. Crop health and productivity are both significantly influenced by climate in a significant way. The growth and development of crops are all affected by a variety of factors, including temperature, patterns (Govindaraj, V. et al., 2023) of rainfall, levels of humidity, and exposure to sunlight. Variations from optimal conditions can result in stress, decreased yields, and increased susceptibility to pests and diseases. The temperature and moisture requirements of various crops are different, and these variations can have a significant impact on the agricultural industry. In the event that they are not adequately managed, extreme weather events such as droughts, floods, and heatwaves present significant challenges to the health of crops and have the potential to result in crop failures. The impact of climate variability on crop production can be mitigated through the implementation of adaptation strategies. These strategies include the selection of climate-resilient crop varieties, as well as the implementation of irrigation and water management systems. The quality of the soil is an important environmental factor that has a direct impact on the health and productivity of your crops. The fact that soil supplies plants with required nutrients, water, and support for their growth, the composition and structure of soil are critical factors in determining the performance of crops. A number of factors, including soil pH, organic matter content, nutrient levels, and soil texture, have an impact on the availability of nutrients, the development of roots, and the activity of soil microbes, all of which are essential for the optimal health of crops. The growth and yield of crops can be negatively impacted by degraded soils, which are characterized by phenomena such as erosion, compaction, salinity, or nutrient depletion. Therefore, the resilience of crops to environmental stressors can be improved through the implementation of soil conservation practices such as conservation tillage, cover cropping, and organic amendments. These practices help improve the health and fertility of the soil. It is absolutely necessary to have access to sufficient water in order to maintain the growth and development of crops. Crops can experience water stress as a result of insufficient water supply, which can be caused by drought or inefficient irrigation practices. This stress can lead to stunted growth, decreased yields, and increased susceptibility to diseases and pests. On the other hand, having an excessive amount of water, such as when there is flooding or waterlogging, can suffocate plant roots and encourage the growth of pathogens, which can result in damage and loss of crops. Strategies for water management, such as drip irrigation, mulching, and rainwater harvesting, help maximize the efficiency with which water is used and reduce the amount of stress that crops experience as a result of water-related issues (Palattella, M. R. et al., 2016). The selection of crop varieties that are able to withstand drought and the implementation of technologies that save water are both factors that contribute to the sustainable management of water in agriculture. The health of crops and their productivity are also impacted by topography, which includes elements such as elevation, slope, and aspect characteristics. The slope of the land can have an effect on the rate of water drainage and erosion, while elevation and aspect can have an effect on the temperature and the amount of sunlight encountered. Farmers are able to implement appropriate land management practices, such as contour farming, terracing, and agroforestry, when they have a thorough understanding of the topographical characteristics of a region. These practices help farmers reduce the risk of soil erosion, conserve soil moisture, and maximize the amount of sunlight that crops receive. It is possible for farmers to maximize crop production while simultaneously minimizing the amount of environmental degradation they cause by utilizing the natural features of the landscape.

III. IOT TECHNOLOGIES IN AGRICULTURE

3.1 IoT Fundamentals in Agriculture

The Internet of Things serves as a facilitator for smart agriculture, which includes a variety of applications and sensors that are specifically designed to improve agricultural processes. The following are the most important fundamentals are shown in the Figure 2.

1. *Weather Monitoring*: Internet of Things weather sensors not only collect environmental data such as temperature, humidity, and precipitation, but they also monitor wind speed, solar radiation, and air pressure. Utilizing this extensive data, farmers are able to evaluate weather trends, forecast the occurrence of extreme weather events, and adjust irrigation schedules and crop protection measures in accordance with these findings.
2. *Automation of greenhouses*: Monitoring external conditions, Internet of Things sensors installed in greenhouses are able to monitor both the levels of carbon dioxide and the concentrations of nutrients in hydroponic systems, as well as the rates at which plants are growing. Automated systems have the ability to alter the intensity and duration of lighting, control irrigation and fertilization, and regulate ventilation in order to generate optimal growing conditions for a variety of crops throughout their growth cycle.
3. *Crop Management*: Internet of Things sensors installed in fields give constant monitoring of soil moisture levels, nutrient content, and pH levels. This enables farmers to accurately regulate irrigation and fertilization. Advanced sensors are also able to identify early indicators of pest infestations or nutrient deficits, which can then prompt timely interventions such as the application of targeted pesticides or the supplementing of nutrients in order to avoid crop damage and maximize output.
4. *Monitoring cattle*: Internet of Things sensors that are linked to cattle not only monitor vital signals like heart rate, body temperature, and activity levels, but they also track feeding behavior and rumination patterns. With the help of this information, farmers are able to identify early warning indications of illness or discomfort, provide prompt veterinary care, and adjust feeding techniques in order to increase animal health and productivity.
5. *Agricultural Drones*: The use of agricultural drones that are equipped with multispectral cameras allows for the collection of data on crop health indicators such as chlorophyll levels, leaf area index, and crop biomass. This goes beyond the capabilities of aerial imaging. With the help of this precise imaging, farmers are able to detect regions of their fields that are experiencing stress or illness, evaluate the uniformity of their crops, and optimize the application of irrigation and fertilizer through targeted interventions.
6. *Predictive Analytics*: Algorithms (Bessant, Y. A. et al., 2023) that use predictive analytics are able to identify future trends and dangers in agricultural output by examining past data on weather patterns, soil health, crop performance, and the incidence of pests. With the help of these projections, farmers are able to make proactive decisions regarding planting schedules, techniques for pest management, and post-harvest handling in order to maximize yields and reduce losses.
7. *End-to-end farm management systems*: It is possible to obtain full insights into farm operations by utilizing integrated farm management solutions, which combine data from a variety of Internet of Things devices and sensors with powerful analytics tools. The use of these platforms, which provide capabilities such as crop planning and rotation suggestions, inventory management, supply chain optimization, and financial analysis, enables farmers to make decisions based on data in order to maximize profitability and sustainability across their whole business.

Figure 2. IoT essentials for agricultural applications

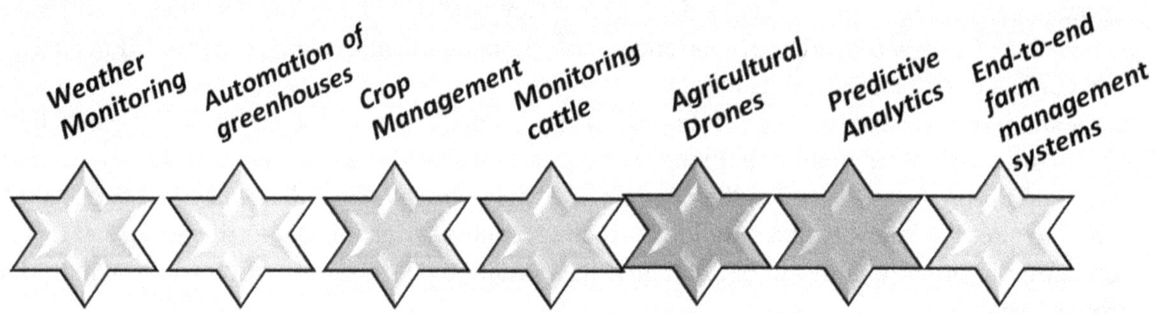

3.2 Current Adoption Status

The current state of crop protection IoT adoption shows a revolutionary movement toward using cutting-edge technologies to maximize agricultural practices. An important development in farmlands is the growing use of Internet of Things (IoT) sensors, which allow for real-time monitoring of crop status, soil health, and environmental variables. With the ability to gather vital information on temperature, humidity, soil moisture, and insect activity, these sensors are great instruments that provide farmers with useful information to improve crop protection tactics. The adoption of IoT technologies is driving the growth of precision agriculture techniques. Farmers can use targeted interventions like variable-rate fertilization and precision irrigation to minimize input usage and maximize crop health and output by utilizing data from IoT devices. Sustainable agricultural practices are supported by this method's ability to allocate resources more effectively and control pest pressures better. Integrated pest management (IPM) approaches are becoming more widely used, which is in keeping with the ideals of sustainable agriculture and is made possible by IoT technologies. These methods place a focus on controlling pests with a variety of techniques while lowering the need for chemical pesticides. IoT sensors make it possible to identify pest infestations early on, giving farmers the ability to implement targeted interventions like pheromone traps and biocontrol agents, reducing their negative effects on the environment and fostering ecosystem balance. Crop security tactics are being transformed by IoT-driven, data-driven decision-making. Farmers may evaluate risks, identify patterns, and improve pest management tactics in real time by utilizing extensive datasets and analytics tools. The efficiency and efficacy of crop protection initiatives are increased by this data-driven strategy, which eventually raises agricultural productivity and health in general. One important advancement in IoT-enabled crop protection is the rise of smart pest monitoring systems. Utilizing Internet of Things sensors, AI, and machine learning algorithms (Saxena, A. et al., 2024), these systems track pest populations over time, forecast outbreaks, and advise farmers on when to take action. Intelligent pest monitoring systems maximize resource efficiency and reduce crop loss by offering proactive pest control solutions. Continued improvements in IoT technology, along with a rise in stakeholder collaboration and knowledge exchange, present encouraging chances to get past these obstacles and hasten the use of IoT in crop protection. IoT solutions are positioned to be crucial in determining the direction of crop protection and sustainable agriculture as the agriculture sector continues to embrace digitization (Huang, K. et al., 2020).

IV. 6G NETWORKS IN AGRICULTURE

4.1 Capabilities of 6G

Rapid advancements in telecommunications network (Kirubasri, G. et al., 2022) evolution are driven by the growing global dependence on connectivity. The next generation of wireless communication technology, or 6G networks, has the potential to completely change how we engage with digital services and gadgets. 6G networks, which build on the groundwork set by earlier generations, promise hitherto unseen capabilities that will spur innovation across a range of industries and facilitate game-changing applications. 6G denotes the generation of wireless communication technologies that comes after 5G networks, or the sixth generation. Researchers and industry stakeholders are already establishing the foundation for 6G, imagining a future where connectivity is faster, more dependable, and more widespread than ever before, while 5G networks are still being deployed globally. It is anticipated that 6G networks would be tens of times more capable than their predecessors. 6G promises to deliver ultra-high-speed, low-latency connectivity that will support a wide range of emerging technologies, from artificial intelligence (AI) (Deepa, R. et al., 2022) and the Internet of Things (IoT) to augmented reality (AR) and virtual reality (VR), with projected data transfer speeds reaching terabits per second. The capacity of 6G networks to utilize a wide variety of frequency bands, including terahertz (THz) frequencies, is one of its distinguishing characteristics (Ragazou, K. et al., 2022). In contrast to earlier generations, which mostly used the millimeter-wave and sub-6 GHz bands, 6G networks are anticipated to make use of the extensive spectrum found in the THz range, providing previously unheard-of speeds and bandwidth. 6G networks are intended to provide extremely low latency, with reaction times measured in microseconds or even nanoseconds, in addition to lightning-fast speeds. Applications requiring real-time engagement, including remote surgery, immersive gaming, and autonomous vehicles, will depend heavily on this near-instantaneous communication delay.

4.2 Integration With IoT Solutions

The convergence of 6G networks and the Internet of Things (IoT) has the potential to greatly transform crop protection methods in agriculture. Through the utilization of the advanced functionalities of 6G networks and the connectivity facilitated by IoT devices (Tripathi, R. P. et al., 2023), farmers may implement cutting-edge solutions to efficiently monitor, control, and safeguard their crops with unprecedented effectiveness. An important benefit of combining 6G with IoT for crop protection is the exceptional speed and bandwidth provided by 6G networks. 6G networks, with their terabit-per-second data transfer speeds and minimal latency, facilitate immediate communication and data processing (Singh, H. et al., 2022). This enables farmers to promptly get information on crop conditions and fast respond to emerging risks. Internet of Things (IoT) devices integrated into fields have the capability to gather extensive data on environmental conditions, soil moisture levels, pest activity, and crop health. These devices encompass a range of technologies such as sensors, drones, and automated monitoring systems, all of which are interconnected through the 6G network. Through the continual monitoring of these characteristics and the real-time transmission of data over 6G networks, farmers acquire vital insights into the condition of their crops and can detect possible problems before they worsen. The exceptional dependability and little delay of 6G networks enable the deployment of self-governing or partially self-governing crop protection systems. Autonomous drones, connected with IoT sensors, may monitor fields, identify indications of pest infestation or disease, and promptly respond by performing targeted spraying or releasing beneficial insects, all without the need for human participation. 6G's seamless connectivity guarantees efficient operation and speedy response to changing conditions for these technologies. Integrating 6G with IoT for crop security has the advantage of utilizing new technologies like artificial intelligence (AI) (Pandey, B. K., & Pandey, D., 2023) and machine learning (Zhai, Z. et al., 2020). Through the analysis of extensive data gathered from Internet of Things (IoT) devices, artificial intelligence (AI) algorithms have the capability to detect patterns, forecast future risks, and suggest enhanced methods for safeguarding crops. AI-powered systems can utilize drone imagery analysis to identify initial indications of agricultural stress or pest damage, allowing for proactive interventions to reduce risks and minimize output losses. 6G networks facilitate the incorporation of various Internet of Things (IoT) devices and sensors into comprehensive platforms for managing farms. These platforms offer farmers the ability to centrally regulate and monitor several aspects of crop protection, including irrigation, fertilization, pest control, and disease management, all from one interface. Through the optimization of agricultural operations and decision-making processes, these integrated solutions improve overall efficiency and productivity.

V. IMPLEMENTING IOT FOR CROP PROTECTION

The early detection of agricultural stress, pest infestations, and illnesses is made possible by the integration of remote sensing technologies with Internet of Things devices. Farmers are able to discern small changes in crop health and vegetation patterns by using drones that are equipped with multispectral sensors. These drones are able to gather high-resolution imagery for use in agricultural fields. The Internet of Things (IoT) sensors (Pramanik, S. et al., 2023) that are spread out across the field collect data on environmental conditions, soil moisture levels, and pest activity. This data provides useful insights that have the potential to aid in early detection. In order to minimize crop damage and maximize production potential, farmers can take preventative measures to address emergent concerns by assessing this data in real time. These interventions may include the use of targeted pesticides or adjustments to irrigation systems. To improve crop protection, strategies for precision agriculture that are enabled by the Internet of Things optimize resource use and crop management behaviors. In order to apply accurate irrigation schedules, variable-rate fertilization schemes, and localized pest management interventions, farmers can leverage the data that is collected via Internet of Things sensors (Nehrey et al., 2023). Farmers are able to modify irrigation to correctly meet the water requirements of their crops because to the real-time feedback that soil moisture sensors provide on the levels of soil moisture. At the same time, Internet of Things-enabled technology, such as smart sprayers, may distribute pesticides or fertilizers precisely where they are required, so minimizing waste and the impact on the environment while simultaneously increasing efficiency. Through the examination of both historical data and data collected by sensors in real time, machine learning models are able to recognize patterns, forecast the occurrence of pest outbreaks, and suggest crop protection techniques that were optimized. In the case of pest movement patterns, for instance, predictive models (Anand, R. et al., 2024) can estimate these patterns based on environmental variables. This provides farmers with the ability to implement preventative actions in order to reduce the risks. In addition, data analytics platforms offer farmers ideas and insights that can be put into action, which enables them to make well-informed decisions that will effectively preserve their farming products. Innovative solutions for crop protection activities are offered by automation and robotics technologies, which are driven by the Internet of Things (IoT). These technologies reduce the need for manual labor and increase levels of efficiency. The ability to patrol fields and detect weeds or pests with a high degree of precision is made possible by automated devices such as robotic weeders or autonomous drones. By providing real-time feedback on crop conditions, the Internet of Things sensors that are integrated into these devices make it possible to implement tailored interventions. For example, robotic weeders that are integrated with artificial intelligence algorithms (Pandey, D., & Pandey, B. K., 2022) are able to discern between crops and weeds, allowing them to target weeds with pinpoint accuracy while reducing the amount of harm they cause to crops (Tang, Y. et al., 2021). Also, autonomous drones can quickly survey huge areas of farmland, allowing for the identification of pest hotspots and the application of pesticides in a tailored manner, hence minimizing the need for broad-spectrum chemical treatments.

CONCLUSION

IoT solutions and 6G networks can transform crop protection in agriculture. IoT technology help farmers combat pests, illnesses, and environmental conditions better than ever. Farmers can protect their crops by using remote sensing to spot dangers early. Precision agriculture, enabled by IoT technology, optimizes resource use and targets interventions to maximize crop health and output while minimizing input waste. Data analytics and machine learning algorithms enable farmers to forecast and minimize hazards before they worsen. IoT device integration and real-time communication are made possible by 6G networks unprecedented connectivity and bandwidth. This convergence between 6G and IoT could revolutionize crop management and protection. Technology and a better understanding of agricultural ecosystems will accelerate the adoption of IoT solutions for crop protection in the future. Farmers may improve production, sustainability, and resilience to changing environmental and economic problems by adopting these advances, assuring food security for future generations.

REFERENCES

Abdulkarim, Y. I., Awl, H. N., Muhammadsharif, F. F., Saeed, S. R., Sidiq, K. R., Khasraw, S. S., & Pandey, D. (2023). Metamaterial-based sensors loaded corona-shaped resonator for COVID-19 detection by using microwave techniques. *Plasmonics*, 1–16.

Anand, R., Khan, B., Nassa, V. K., Pandey, D., Dhabliya, D., Pandey, B. K., & Dadheech, P. (2023). Hybrid convolutional neural network (CNN) for kennedy space center hyperspectral image. *Aerospace Systems*, 6(1), 71–78. 10.1007/s42401-022-00168-4

Anand, R., Lakshmi, S. V., Pandey, D., & Pandey, B. K. (2024). An enhanced ResNet-50 deep learning model for arrhythmia detection using electrocardiogram biomedical indicators. *Evolving Systems*, 15(1), 83–97. 10.1007/s12530-023-09559-0

Bessant, Y. A., Jency, J. G., Sagayam, K. M., Jone, A. A. A., Pandey, D., & Pandey, B. K. (2023). Improved parallel matrix multiplication using Strassen and Urdhvatiryagbhyam method. *CCF Transactions on High Performance Computing*, 5(2), 102–115. 10.1007/s42514-023-00149-9

Cirillo, F., Gómez, D., Diez, L., Maestro, I. E., Gilbert, T. B. J., & Akhavan, R. (2020). Smart city IoT services creation through large-scale collaboration. *IEEE Internet of Things Journal*, 7(6), 5267–5275. 10.1109/JIOT.2020.2978770

David, S., Duraipandian, K., Chandrasekaran, D., Pandey, D., Sindhwani, N., & Pandey, B. K. (2023). Impact of blockchain in healthcare system. In *Unleashing the Potentials of blockchain technology for healthcare industries* (pp. 37–57). Academic Press. 10.1016/B978-0-323-99481-1.00004-3

Deepa, R., Anand, R., Pandey, D., Pandey, B. K., & Karki, B. (2022). Comprehensive performance analysis of classifiers in diagnosis of epilepsy. *Mathematical Problems in Engineering*, 2022, 2022. 10.1155/2022/1559312

Devasenapathy, D., Madhumathy, P., Umamaheshwari, R., Pandey, B. K., & Pandey, D. (2024). Transmission-efficient grid-based synchronized model for routing in wireless sensor networks using Bayesian compressive sensing. *SN Computer Science*, 5(1), 1–11.

Dhanasekar, S., Martin Sagayam, K., Pandey, B. K., & Pandey, D. (2023). Refractive Index Sensing Using Metamaterial Absorbing Augmentation in Elliptical Graphene Arrays. *Plasmonics*, •••, 1–11. 10.1007/s11468-023-02152-w

Du John, H. V., Jose, T., Jone, A. A. A., Sagayam, K. M., Pandey, B. K., & Pandey, D. (2022). Polarization insensitive circular ring resonator based perfect metamaterial absorber design and simulation on a silicon substrate. *Silicon*, 14(14), 9009–9020. 10.1007/s12633-021-01645-9

Du John, H. V., Moni, D. J., Ponraj, D. N., Sagayam, K. M., Pandey, D., & Pandey, B. K. (2021). Design of Si based nano strip resonator with polarization-insensitive metamaterial (MTM) absorber on a glass substrate. *Silicon*, 1-10.

Govindaraj, V., Dhanasekar, S., Martinsagayam, K., Pandey, D., Pandey, B. K., & Nassa, V. K. (2023). Low-power test pattern generator using modified LFSR. *Aerospace Systems*, 1-8.

Huang, K., Shu, L., Li, K., Yang, F., Han, G., Wang, X., & Pearson, S. (2020). Photovoltaic agricultural internet of things towards realizing the next generation of smart farming. *IEEE Access : Practical Innovations, Open Solutions*, 8, 76300–76312. 10.1109/ACCESS.2020.2988663

Iyyanar, P., Anand, R., Shanthi, T., Nassa, V. K., Pandey, B. K., George, A. S., & Pandey, D. (2023). A real-time smart sewage cleaning UAV assistance system using IoT. In *Handbook of Research on Data-Driven Mathematical Modeling in Smart Cities* (pp. 24–39). IGI Global.

Jayapoorani, S., Pandey, D., Sasirekha, N. S., Anand, R., & Pandey, B. K. (2023). Systolic optimized adaptive filter architecture designs for ECG noise cancellation by Vertex-5. *Aerospace Systems*, 6(1), 163–173. 10.1007/s42401-022-00177-3

Khan, B., Hasan, A., Pandey, D., Ventayen, R. J. M., Pandey, B. K., & Gowwrii, G. (2021). Fusion of datamining and artificial intelligence in prediction of hazardous road accidents. In *Machine learning and iot for intelligent systems and smart applications* (pp. 201–223). CRC Press. 10.1201/9781003194415-12

Kirubasri, G., Sankar, S., Pandey, D., Pandey, B. K., Nassa, V. K., & Dadheech, P. (2022). Software-defined networking-based Ad hoc networks routing protocols. In *Software defined networking for Ad Hoc networks* (pp. 95–123). Springer International Publishing. 10.1007/978-3-030-91149-2_5

Kirubasri, G., Sankar, S., Pandey, D., Pandey, B. K., Singh, H., & Anand, R. (2021, September). A recent survey on 6G vehicular technology, applications and challenges. In *2021 9th International Conference on Reliability, Infocom Technologies and Optimization (Trends and Future Directions)(ICRITO)* (pp. 1-5). IEEE.

Malhotra, P., Pandey, D., Pandey, B. K., & Patra, P. M. (2021). Managing agricultural supply chains in COVID-19 lockdown. *International Journal of Quality and Innovation*, 5(2), 109–118. 10.1504/IJQI.2021.117181

Nguyen, D. C., Ding, M., Pathirana, P. N., Seneviratne, A., Li, J., Niyato, D., Dobre, O., & Poor, H. V. (2021). 6G internet of things: A comprehensive survey. *IEEE Internet of Things Journal*, 9(1), 359–383. 10.1109/JIOT.2021.3103320

Palattella, M. R., Dohler, M., Grieco, A., Rizzo, G., Torsner, J., Engel, T., & Ladid, L. (2016). Internet of things in the 5G era: Enablers, architecture, and business models. *IEEE Journal on Selected Areas in Communications*, 34(3), 510–527. 10.1109/JSAC.2016.2525418

Pandey, B. K., & Pandey, D. (2023). Parametric optimization and prediction of enhanced thermoelectric performance in co-doped CaMnO3 using response surface methodology and neural network. *Journal of Materials Science Materials in Electronics*, 34(21), 1589. 10.1007/s10854-023-10954-1

Pandey, B. K., Pandey, D., & Agarwal, A. (2022). Encrypted information transmission by enhanced steganography and image transformation. *International Journal of Distributed Artificial Intelligence*, 14(1), 1–14. 10.4018/IJDAI.297110

Pandey, B. K., Pandey, D., Alkhafaji, M. A., Güneşer, M. T., & Şeker, C. (2023a). A reliable transmission and extraction of textual information using keyless encryption, steganography, and deep algorithm with cuckoo optimization. In *Micro-Electronics and Telecommunication Engineering: Proceedings of 6th ICMETE 2022* (pp. 629–636). Springer Nature Singapore. 10.1007/978-981-19-9512-5_57

Pandey, B. K., Pandey, D., Gupta, A., Nassa, V. K., Dadheech, P., & George, A. S. (2023b). Secret data transmission using advanced morphological component analysis and steganography. In *Role of data-intensive distributed computing systems in designing data solutions* (pp. 21–44). Springer International Publishing. 10.1007/978-3-031-15542-0_2

Pandey, B. K., Pandey, D., & Sahani, S. K. (2024). Autopilot control unmanned aerial vehicle system for sewage defect detection using deep learning. *Engineering Reports*, 12852. 10.1002/eng2.12852

Pandey, B. K., Pandey, D., Wairya, S., & Agarwal, G. (2021a). An advanced morphological component analysis, steganography, and deep learning-based system to transmit secure textual data. [*International Journal of Distributed Artificial Intelligence*, 13(2), 40–62. 10.4018/IJDAI.2021070104

Pandey, B. K., Pandey, D., Wairya, S., Agarwal, G., Dadeech, P., Dogiwal, S. R., & Pramanik, S. (2022b). Application of integrated steganography and image compressing techniques for confidential information transmission. *Cyber Security and Network Security*, 169-191.

Pandey, B. K., Pandey, S. K., & Pandey, D. (2011). A survey of bioinformatics applications on parallel architectures. *International Journal of Computer Applications*, 23(4), 21–25. 10.5120/2877-3744

Pandey, D., & Pandey, B. K. (2022). An efficient deep neural network with adaptive galactic swarm optimization for complex image text extraction. In *Process mining techniques for pattern recognition* (pp. 121–137). CRC Press. 10.1201/9781003169550-10

Pandey, J. K., Jain, R., Dilip, R., Kumbhkar, M., Jaiswal, S., Pandey, B. K., & Pandey, D. (2022). Investigating role of iot in the development of smart application for security enhancement. In *IoT Based Smart Applications* (pp. 219–243). Springer International Publishing.

Polymeni, S., Skoutas, D. N., Kormentzas, G., & Skianis, C. (2022). Findeas: A fintech-based approach on designing and assessing iot systems. *IEEE Internet of Things Journal*, 9(24), 25196–25206. 10.1109/JIOT.2022.3195770

Pramanik, S., Pandey, D., Joardar, S., Niranjanamurthy, M., Pandey, B. K., & Kaur, J. (2023, October). An overview of IoT privacy and security in smart cities. In *AIP Conference Proceedings* (Vol. 2495, No. 1). AIP Publishing. 10.1063/5.0123511

Qadir, Z., Le, K. N., Saeed, N., & Munawar, H. S. (2023). Towards 6G Internet of Things: Recent advances, use cases, and open challenges. *ICT Express, 9*(3), 296-312.

Ragazou, K., Garefalakis, A., Zafeiriou, E., & Passas, I. (2022). Agriculture 5.0: A new strategic management mode for a cut cost and an energy efficient agriculture sector. *Energies*, 15(9), 3113. 10.3390/en15093113

Revathi, T. K., Sathiyabhama, B., Sankar, S., Pandey, D., Pandey, B. K., & Dadeech, P. (2022). An intelligent model for coronary heart disease diagnosis. In *Networking Technologies in Smart Healthcare* (pp. 309–327). CRC Press. 10.1201/9781003239888-15

Saxena, A., Agarwal, A., Pandey, B. K., & Pandey, D. (2024). Examination of the Criticality of Customer Segmentation Using Unsupervised Learning Methods. *Circular Economy and Sustainability*, 1–14. 10.1007/s43615-023-00336-4

Sharma, M., Pandey, D., Khosla, D., Goyal, S., Pandey, B. K., & Gupta, A. K. (2022). Design of a GaN-based Flip Chip Light Emitting Diode (FC-LED) with au Bumps & Thermal Analysis with different sizes and adhesive materials for performance considerations. *Silicon*, 14(12), 7109–7120. 10.1007/s12633-021-01457-x

Singh, H., Pandey, B. K., George, S., Pandey, D., Anand, R., Sindhwani, N., & Dadheech, P. (2022, July). Effective overview of different ML models used for prediction of COVID-19 patients. In *Artificial Intelligence on Medical Data: Proceedings of International Symposium, ISCMM 2021* (pp. 185-192). Singapore: Springer Nature Singapore.

Tang, Y., Dananjayan, S., Hou, C., Guo, Q., Luo, S., & He, Y. (2021). A survey on the 5G network and its impact on agriculture: Challenges and opportunities. *Computers and Electronics in Agriculture*, 180, 105895. 10.1016/j.compag.2020.105895

Tareke, S. A., Lelisho, M. E., Hassen, S. S., Seid, A. A., Jemal, S. S., Teshale, B. M., & Pandey, B. K. (2022). The prevalence and predictors of depressive, anxiety, and stress symptoms among Tepi town residents during the COVID-19 pandemic lockdown in Ethiopia. *Journal of Racial and Ethnic Health Disparities*, 1–13.35028903

Tripathi, R. P., Sharma, M., Gupta, A. K., Pandey, D., Pandey, B. K., Shahul, A., & George, A. H. (2023). Timely prediction of diabetes by means of machine learning practices. *Augmented Human Research*, 8(1), 1. 10.1007/s41133-023-00062-4

Tzounis, A., Katsoulas, N., Bartzanas, T., & Kittas, C. (2017). Internet of Things in agriculture, recent advances and future challenges. *Biosystems Engineering*, 164, 31–48. 10.1016/j.biosystemseng.2017.09.007

Vinodhini, V., Kumar, M. S., Sankar, S., Pandey, D., Pandey, B. K., & Nassa, V. K. (2022). IoT-based early forest fire detection using MLP and AROC method. *International Journal of Global Warming*, 27(1), 55–70. 10.1504/IJGW.2022.122794

Zhai, Z., Martínez, J. F., Beltran, V., & Martínez, N. L. (2020). Decision support systems for agriculture 4.0: Survey and challenges. *Computers and Electronics in Agriculture*, 170, 105256. 10.1016/j.compag.2020.105256

Chapter 17
Intelligent Healthcare in 6G:
Addressing Security and Privacy Concerns

Syed Jahangir Badashah
Sreenidhi Institute of Science and Technology, Hyderabad, India

S. Asokkumar
Department of Management Studies, Mahendra Engineering College, Namakkal, India

D. Balasubramaniam
Vel Tech Rangarajan Dr. Sagunthala R&D Institute of Science and Technology, Chennai, India

R. Saravanakumar
Saveetha Institute of Medical and Technical Sciences, Saveetha University, Chennai, India

K. Karthik
Velammal College of Engineering and Technology, Madurai, India

R. Manikandan
https://orcid.org/0000-0002-2055-6634
Department Electronics and Communication Engineering, Panimalar Engineering College, India

S. B. G. Tilak Babu
Department of ECE, Aditya Engineering College, Surampalem, India

ABSTRACT

In the era of 6G technology, intelligent healthcare represents a paradigm shift in the delivery of healthcare. It is distinguished by unprecedented connectivity, data accessibility, and technological advancements throughout the industry. Through the use of real-time data exchange, advanced analytics, and remote monitoring, this chapter examines the definition of intelligent healthcare in 6G as well as its scope. The chapter also highlights the potential of this technology to revolutionize patient care. This chapter, however, delves into the critical importance of addressing security and privacy concerns that are inherent in this evolving landscape, alongside the promises that it makes.

I. INTRODUCTION

The integration of cutting-edge technologies, like 6G (Kirubasri, G. et al., 2021, September) networks, promises a paradigm shift towards more effective and efficient healthcare delivery in the quickly changing healthcare landscape. The emergence of 6G, which offers extremely high data rates, extremely low

DOI: 10.4018/979-8-3693-7421-4.ch017

latency, and extensive connectivity, raises the possibility of intelligent healthcare solutions. To maintain the integrity and confidence of healthcare systems, it is crucial to address security and privacy (Pandey, D. et al., 2021) issues as they become more interconnected and dependent on data-driven technologies. The inherent security flaws in greater connectivity and data sharing that come with 6G are one of the main obstacles to using it for intelligent healthcare. Healthcare networks and devices that are interconnected offer a greater surface area for cyberattacks, increasing the risk of ransomware, malware, and unwanted access. Furthermore, hackers find healthcare data which includes patient medical records and personal information—to be a lucrative target due to its sensitive nature. In a 6G-enabled healthcare system, a single security breach could have disastrous effects, jeopardizing patient privacy, causing delays in medical services, and even posing a threat to life.

Concerns about privacy are also very real in the age of healthcare enabled by 6G. These systems generate and exchange enormous amounts of personal health data, which presents serious ethical and legal issues. Patients want the highest level of care and secrecy when handling their medical information, but the interconnectedness of 6G networks makes data privacy (Sharma, S. et al., 2023) more difficult to maintain. Furthermore, privacy risks are exacerbated by the spread of data-driven healthcare technologies like wearables and remote monitoring systems, which further obfuscate the distinction between personal and medical data. A diversified strategy is needed to address these security and privacy issues. First and foremost, the whole healthcare ecosystem needs to be outfitted with strong security measures. This entails implementing intrusion detection and prevention systems to instantly identify and neutralize possible cyberthreats, as well as the deployment of encryption (Pandey, B. K. et al., 2023) and authentication protocols to secure data transmission (Pandey, B. K. et al., 2021a). Moreover, security-by-design guidelines ought to be incorporated throughout the healthcare technology development process to guarantee that security concerns are given top priority right away. Privacy-enhancing technologies and practices must be implemented in 6G healthcare systems to protect patient privacy. Sensitive medical data can be anonymized with the use of techniques like differential privacy, which adds noise (Bruntha, P. M. et al., 2023) to data to protect privacy while allowing for meaningful analysis. Furthermore, establishing thorough frameworks for data governance that place a high priority on patient consent, accountability, and transparency is essential for fostering a culture of trust and guaranteeing adherence to privacy laws.

1.1 Intelligent Healthcare in 6G

When discussing 6G networks, the term "intelligent healthcare" refers to the application of emerging technologies and methods that are driven by data in order to improve the quality of healthcare services, as well as their accessibility and efficiency. A healthcare system that is enabled with 6G technology allows for the transmission and analysis of data in real time by interconnecting various components, such as medical devices, sensors (Abdulkarim, Y. I. et al., 2023), and patient records, through networks that are extremely fast and have a low latency. The implementation of intelligent healthcare solutions that are powered by artificial intelligence (AI) (Anand, R. et al., 2023), machine learning (ML), and the Internet of Things (IoT) (Pramanik, S. et al.,) is made possible by this interconnectedness. These solutions have the ability to automate processes, personalize treatments, and improve patient outcomes. With the implementation of 6G technology in the healthcare industry (George, W. K. et al., 2024), there is a significant possibility that the delivery of medical services will undergo a revolutionary change. Sixth-generation wireless networks (Devasenapathy, D. et al., 2024), which feature extremely high data transfer rates and low latency, make it possible for healthcare providers to communicate (Raja, D. et al.,

2024) and collaborate without interruption, regardless of where they are physically located. Patients are able to receive timely care and consultations without having to leave the comfort of their own homes thanks to the facilitation of telemedicine and remote monitoring applications. In addition, the massive connectivity of 6G networks makes it possible for the proliferation of wearable devices and medical sensors (Du John, H. V. et al., 2023). These devices are able to continuously monitor the vital signs and health metrics of patients, which provides valuable insights for the early detection and prevention of diseases from occurring. It is essential to address security and privacy concerns in order to ensure the trust, integrity, and adoption of these systems in order to take advantage of the transformative potential of intelligent healthcare and 6G. A variety of security risks, such as cyberattacks, data breaches, and unauthorized access, are made possible by the interconnected nature of healthcare networks that are enabled with 6G technology. The compromise of sensitive patient data, disruption of medical services, and even potential threat to patient safety could all be the result of a single security breach in a healthcare system. As a result, the implementation of highly effective security measures, such as encryption (Kumar Pandey, B. et al., 2021), authentication, and intrusion detection systems, is absolutely necessary in order to protect the confidentiality, integrity, and availability of healthcare data. Several significant privacy concerns are raised as a result of the enormous amount of personal health data that is generated and shared within 6G healthcare systems. However, the interconnectedness and data-driven nature of 6G networks introduce complications in the process of ensuring data privacy. Patients have the expectation that their medical information will be handled with the utmost care and confidentiality. This could result in violations of patient privacy, identity theft, and discrimination if unauthorized individuals gain access to sensitive healthcare information. Protecting the privacy rights of patients and adhering to regulatory requirements necessitates the implementation of technologies and practices that enhance privacy, such as the anonymization of data, the management of consent, and transparency.

II. INTELLIGENT HEALTHCARE IN 6G

2.1 Potential Benefits of 6G in Healthcare

An important development in telecommunications technology (Gupta, A. K. et al., 2023), the rollout of 6G networks holds the potential to completely transform a number of sectors, including healthcare. 6G has the potential to completely change the way healthcare services are provided and accessed because of its extremely high data transmission speeds, extremely low latency, and extensive connectivity capabilities. Innovative healthcare solutions that can improve patient care, streamline clinical workflows, and spur medical advancements are made possible by this next-generation network technology. Healthcare providers, especially those in underserved and remote areas, can overcome long-standing obstacles to care delivery and access by utilizing the capabilities of 6G networks. This will also create opportunities for the development of new healthcare technologies and applications are shown in the Figure 1.

Figure 1. Advantages of 6G technology in the healthcare sector

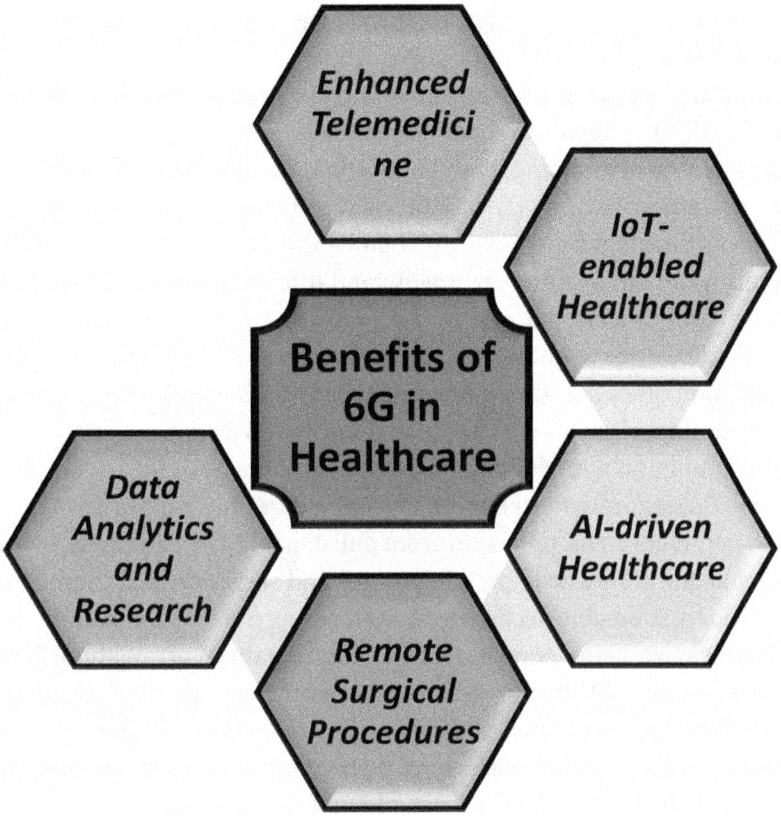

- *Enhanced Telemedicine*: 6G networks are driving the advancement of telemedicine, which promises to completely transform the way healthcare is delivered by providing previously unheard-of capabilities for remote monitoring, diagnostics, and consultations. Patients and healthcare professionals can have real-time, high-definition video consultations thanks to 6G's ultra-high speed and low latency connectivity, which creates a virtual healthcare environment that mimics in-person interactions. 6G makes it easier to conduct remote interventions and surgeries, giving surgeons the ability to precisely and accurately carry out difficult operations from a distance. By enabling prompt interventions and treatments, this improved telemedicine capability not only improves patient outcomes by improving access to healthcare services for people living in remote or rural areas.
- *IoT-enabled Healthcare*: The Internet of Things (IoT) (Iyyanar, P. et al., 2023), which enables a vast ecosystem of interconnected medical devices, sensors (Du John, H. V. et al., 2024), and systems, becomes a cornerstone of healthcare innovation in the era of 6G networks. The deployment of IoT-enabled devices by healthcare providers for remote patient monitoring, disease management, and preventive care is made possible by 6G's massive machine-type communication capabilities. Personalized healthcare interventions and early health issue detection are made possible by these devices, which continuously gather and transmit patient health data in real-time.

Furthermore, real-time insights and decision-making based on IoT-generated data are made possible by 6G networks' support for advanced data analytics at the edge. Through the use of IoT in healthcare, providers can provide more proactive, effective, and patient-centered care, which will ultimately improve health outcomes and lower costs.

- *AI-driven Healthcare*: 6G networks are enabling the integration of artificial intelligence (AI) (Anand, R. et al., 2024) in healthcare, which offers revolutionary potential in the areas of personalized medicine, treatment planning, and diagnostics. Healthcare providers can use AI algorithms to analyze massive amounts of medical data, such as patient records, imaging scans, and genetic information, in real-time thanks to 6G's high bandwidth and low latency. This makes it possible to diagnose patients more quickly and accurately and to create treatment regimens that are specific to each patient's requirements. In addition, AI-powered predictive analytics can identify populations at risk, predict disease outbreaks, and allocate resources optimally, all of which improve population health outcomes and streamline healthcare delivery. Healthcare organizations can gain new insights, streamline clinical workflows, and ultimately enhance patient care and outcomes by utilizing AI in conjunction with 6G networks.
- *Remote Surgical Procedures*: 6G networks make it possible for surgeons to perform complex operations with confidence and precision from a distance. 6G's extremely low latency guarantees real-time communication between operating rooms and surgeons, and augmented reality (AR) and high-definition video streaming technologies offer improved visualization and guidance during procedures. This feature helps patients receive high-quality care without having to relocate or travel, which is especially helpful in situations where access to specialized surgical expertise is limited. Furthermore, 6G networks' ability to support remote surgery creates new avenues for healthcare professionals to collaborate across geographic borders, facilitating the exchange of knowledge and skills that will enhance surgical outcomes and patient care everywhere.
- *Data Analytics and Research*: By enabling healthcare organizations and researchers to fully utilize big data analytics, 6G networks will accelerate the advancement of medical research and innovation. 6G's high data throughput makes it possible to analyze big healthcare datasets in real time, such as genomic data, patient records, and clinical trials. This analysis produces new insights that improve disease prevention, diagnosis, and treatment. Researchers can find previously undiscovered patterns (Govindaraj, V. et al., 2023), trends, and correlations in healthcare data by utilizing sophisticated analytics tools like machine learning (Pandey, B. K. et al., 2024) and predictive modelling (Muniandi, B. et al., 2024). This makes it possible to create targeted interventions, precision medicine strategies, and personalized therapies that enhance patient outcomes and quality of life. 6G-enabled data analytics also make it easier for academics and organizations to collaborate, which promotes innovation and discovery in the healthcare sector.

III. SECURITY CONCERNS IN INTELLIGENT HEALTHCARE

3.1 Data Breach and Cyberattack Risks

Organizations in a variety of sectors, including the healthcare industry, are at serious risk from data breaches and cyberattacks. These risks carry serious repercussions that can include trust erosion, compromised sensitive information, financial losses, and reputational harm. Data breaches and cyberattacks can have especially serious repercussions in the healthcare industry, where patient data protection is of utmost importance. In order to mitigate potential threats and implement effective cybersecurity measures, healthcare organizations must have a thorough understanding of these risks. Unauthorized access to private information, including financial information, personal identifiers, and medical records, is known as a data breach (Bessant, Y. A. et al., 2023). Numerous techniques, such as hacking, phishing, malware infections, and insider threats, can result in these breaches. The compromised data may be used for fraud, identity theft, or other nefarious purposes after a breach happens. Data breaches in the healthcare industry can have serious repercussions, including jeopardizing patient privacy and exposing organizations to fines and legal obligations. Conversely, intentional attempts to interfere with or compromise computer networks, systems, or data are known as cyberattacks. Malware infections, ransomware, and denial-of-service (DoS) attacks are just a few of the many possible forms that these attacks can take (Habibzadeh, H. et al., 2019). Cybercriminals may target healthcare institutions in an effort to extort ransom payments, disrupt medical services, or steal confidential patient data. Cyberattacks in the healthcare industry can have far-reaching effects on hospital operations, patient care delivery, and the confidentiality and integrity of medical records. The compromise of patient privacy is one of the main risks connected to data breaches and cyberattacks in the healthcare industry. Sensitive information found in medical records, such as diagnoses, treatment histories, and personal identifiers, needs to be safeguarded in order to abide by privacy laws like the Health Insurance Portability and Accountability Act (HIPAA). A breach of patient privacy can harm healthcare organizations' reputations by undermining patients' faith in the confidentiality of their medical records. Furthermore, if patients' private medical information is mishandled or leaked, they could experience financial loss or psychological distress. Potential financial losses and legal repercussions are another risk associated with data breaches and cyberattacks in the healthcare industry. When a data breach occurs, healthcare organizations may have to pay a large amount of money to investigate and fix the breach, notify the individuals who were impacted, and put cybersecurity safeguards in place to stop similar incidents in the future. Financial losses may also be exacerbated by fines and penalties that regulatory bodies like the Office for Civil Rights (OCR) may levy for HIPAA violations. The resources of healthcare organizations may be strained, which may affect their capacity to provide high-quality patient care. Cyberattacks and data breaches can interfere with medical services and jeopardize patient security. Disruptions to computer systems or networks can have major repercussions in healthcare settings, where prompt access to vital information and medical records is necessary for delivering high-quality care. Delays in the delivery of medication, treatment, or test results could have a negative impact on the patient. Cyberattacks like ransomware can also encrypt vital data, including medical records, making them unusable until a ransom is paid. This increases disruptions and jeopardizes the quality of patient care (Alshehri, F., & Muhammad, G., 2020).

3.2 Healthcare Security Incidents

Cybercriminals have been going after healthcare organizations more and more in recent years. This has led to a lot of security problems that have put patient data at risk and slowed down medical services. These events show that healthcare systems are open to cyber threats and stress how important strong cybersecurity measures are for keeping private data and patient privacy safe.

As an example of a major security incident in healthcare, the WannaCry ransomware attack in 2017 infected thousands of computers around the world, some of which belonged to healthcare organizations. The ransomware took advantage of flaws in the Microsoft Windows operating system to encrypt files and demand money in exchange for keys that could unlock them. The attack happened at a number of hospitals and other healthcare facilities, which caused problems with patient care and the temporary closure of some medical services. WannaCry showed how vulnerable healthcare systems are to ransomware attacks and how important it is to take proactive cybersecurity steps to stop and lessen these kinds of problems (Dian, F. J. et al., 2020).

The data breach at Anthem Inc., one of the biggest health insurance companies in the US, was another major security event. In 2015, hackers got into Anthem's computer systems without permission and stole personal information about almost 80 million people. This included names, addresses, Social Security numbers, and medical ID numbers. The breach, which was one of the biggest in the history of healthcare, made private patient information public and caused people to worry about the safety of electronic health records (EHRs) and protected health information (PHI). The Anthem breach made it clear how important strong data protection measures and following the rules are for protecting patient privacy and stopping people from getting to private healthcare information without permission.

The rise of insider threats has made things very hard for healthcare organizations, since workers who have access to private information can compromise security on purpose or by accident. In 2018, a former worker at a Florida healthcare system was charged with illegally accessing patient records, which let thousands of people's personal and medical information get out. Negligence, bad intentions, or not enough security training can all lead to insider threats. This shows how important it is to use access controls, monitoring systems, and employee education programs to lower the risk of insider breaches (Qadri, Y. A. et al., 2020).

More and more medical IoT devices are being used, which has made cybersecurity harder for healthcare organizations because hackers may be able to take advantage of these devices. Hackers have been going after medical devices like insulin pumps and pacemakers in recent years, which has made people worry about patient safety and the reliability of medical devices. Healthcare organizations need to protect IoT devices with strong security measures, like encryption, authentication, and intrusion detection systems, to keep patients safe and stop cyber threats.

IV. PRIVACY CONCERNS IN INTELLIGENT HEALTHCARE

4.1 Protecting Patient Data Privacy

The digitization of medical records and the widespread use of digital healthcare technologies have made privacy issues in the industry (Sharma, M. et al., 2024) more complicated and difficult to manage. A vast amount of patient data, including medical histories, test results, treatment plans, and personal identifiers, has been accumulated as a result of the switch from paper-based to electronic health records (EHRs). While there are many advantages to digital records (George, W. K. et al., 2023), including increased efficiency, accessibility, and interoperability, there are also new privacy risks. Unauthorized access to patient information is a major privacy concern in the healthcare industry. Sensitive medical information may become public knowledge through healthcare data breaches brought on by insider threats, cyberattacks, or human error. In addition to jeopardizing patient privacy, these breaches also raise questions about financial fraud, identity theft, and harm to healthcare organizations' reputations. Additionally, as digital (Swapna, H. R. et al., 2023) healthcare technologies proliferate and include wearables, mobile health apps, and telemedicine platforms, the attack surface for cybercriminals has grown, raising the risk of privacy violations and data breaches. Sharing patient data between healthcare providers, insurers, and outside vendors is another privacy concern in the healthcare industry. While sharing patient data can help with treatment planning, expedite administrative procedures, and enhance care coordination, it also brings up moral and legal issues with consent and data privacy. There could be possible breaches of confidentiality and trust if patients are not fully informed about how their information is shared or used. Furthermore, the inability of healthcare IT systems to be standardized and interoperable can make data sharing even more difficult and prevent the safe transfer of patient information between various healthcare organizations. Data processing, algorithmic bias, and predictive modeling privacy issues are brought about by the use of artificial intelligence (AI) (Pandey, B. K., & Pandey, D., 2023) and data analytics in the healthcare industry. In order to evaluate massive datasets, spot trends, and forecast patient outcomes, healthcare companies are depending more and more on AI algorithms. Disparities in healthcare outcomes and delivery could result from these algorithms unintentionally maintaining prejudices or discrimination. Concerns regarding individual privacy and consent are also raised by the gathering and analysis of patient data for research or public health objectives, since patients might not have control over how their data is used for unrelated purposes. Ensuring the confidentiality, integrity, and trustworthiness of the healthcare system depends critically on protecting patient data privacy. Patients put their most private information in the hands of healthcare providers, believing that the information will be protected from unwanted access or disclosure and that their privacy will be upheld. Healthcare organizations and patients alike may suffer grave repercussions if patient data privacy is not protected. Legally and administratively, healthcare organizations must abide by strict privacy laws, such as the General Data Protection Regulation (GDPR) in the European Union and the Health Insurance Portability and Accountability Act (HIPAA) in the United States. These laws establish stringent fines, sanctions, and legal ramifications for breaking the requirements governing the protection of patient health information. Healthcare organizations have an ethical duty to protect patient rights and dignity in addition to being required by law to comply with privacy regulations. Healthcare organizations may face severe financial consequences from breaches of patient data privacy. These costs may include those associated with looking into and resolving security incidents, informing those who were impacted, and putting preventative measures in place to avoid similar incidents in the future. Beyond the financial and legal ramifications, patient data privacy violations can have a significant emotional and psychological impact on those who are impacted. When privacy is violated, patients may feel vulnerable, violated, and betrayed. This can cause mistrust and make them reluctant to seek medical attention. Furthermore, since marginalized populations may be disproportionately affected by discrimination and confidentiality breaches, privacy violations can worsen already-existing disparities in healthcare outcomes and access.

4.2 Regulatory Frameworks and Compliance Requirements

Data privacy and security in the healthcare industry are shaped in large part by regulatory frameworks and compliance requirements, which play an important role in the process. The Health Insurance Portability and Accountability Act (HIPAA) contains comprehensive regulations that are designed to protect protected health information (PHI) and guarantee its availability, integrity, and confidentiality. These regulations are enacted in the United States. HIPAA's Privacy Rule is responsible for establishing guidelines for the use and disclosure of protected health information (PHI) by covered entities. These entities include healthcare providers, health plans, and healthcare clearinghouses. Individuals are also granted certain rights, such as the right to access their medical records and the right to request amendments to make corrections to inaccurate information. Further, the HIPAA Security Rule requires the implementation of administrative, physical, and technical safeguards to protect electronic protected health information (ePHI) from being accessed, altered, or destroyed by unauthorized parties. In order to ensure that they are in compliance with these requirements, healthcare organizations that are subject to HIPAA are required to undergo periodic audits (Ullah, A. et al., 2021). An analogous regulation, known as the General Data Protection Regulation (GDPR), governs the processing and protection of personal data in the European Union (EU), which includes data pertaining to healthcare. The General Data Protection Regulation (GDPR) applies to any and all organizations anywhere in the world that process the personal data of EU residents. The General Data Protection Regulation (GDPR) mandates that healthcare organizations must obtain individuals' express consent before processing their personal data, which may include information related to their health. In addition to this, they are required to develop and implement suitable organizational and technical safeguards in order to guarantee the safety and privacy of personal information. Fines of up to 4% of a company's global annual revenue or €20 million, whichever is higher, may be imposed on businesses that fail to comply with the General Data Protection Regulation (GDPR). A Data Protection Officer (DPO) may be appointed, data protection impact assessments (DPIAs) may be carried out, and data breach notification procedures may be established in order for healthcare organizations to be in compliance with the General Data Protection Regulation (GDPR) (Malamas, V. et al., 2021).

Additional regulatory frameworks and standards, such as the Health Information Technology for Economic and Clinical Health (HITECH) Act in the United States and the ISO/IEC 27001 standard for information security management systems (ISMS), offer additional guidance and requirements for the purpose of ensuring the privacy and security of data in the healthcare industry. The HITECH Act seeks to expand upon the provisions of the Health Insurance Portability and Accountability Act of 1996 (HIPAA) by bolstering enforcement mechanisms and encouraging the adoption of electronic health records (EHRs) and health information exchange (HIE) technologies. As an additional requirement, it mandates breach notification requirements, which stipulate that covered entities are obligated to notify affected individuals as well as the Department of Health and Human Services (HHS) in the event of a data breach. A similar framework is provided by the ISO/IEC 27001 standard, which enables an information security management system (ISMS) to be established, implemented, maintained, and continuously improved in order to effectively manage information security risks. In order to demonstrate their dedication to safeguarding patient information and adhering to regulatory requirements, healthcare (Singh, S. et al., 2023) organizations may choose to obtain certification under the ISO/IEC 27001 standard (Bhatia, H., 2020).

V. SECURITY CONCERNS IN 6G HEALTHCARE

The development and application of cutting-edge healthcare technologies must take privacy concerns into account in 6G healthcare. Massive connectivity, low latency, and ultra-fast data speeds are what 6G networks promise, and they make it easier to exchange and analyze enormous volumes of private patient data. But more connectivity and data sharing (JayaLakshmi, G. et al., 2024) also means a higher chance of privacy violations and illegal access to private medical records. Ensuring the security and confidentiality of patient data is one of the main obstacles to resolving privacy concerns in 6G healthcare. Healthcare organizations need to protect patient privacy by implementing strong encryption, authentication, and access controls as they utilize 6G networks to deploy wearable sensors (Du John, H. V. et al., 2023),

IoT devices, and other connected healthcare technologies. Pseudonymization and data anonymization are two more techniques that can reduce the possibility of re-identification and illegal access to private medical records. There are privacy concerns arising from the interoperability of healthcare systems and the sharing of patient data among various stakeholders. To control the gathering, use, and sharing of patient data, healthcare institutions must set up explicit consent procedures and data governance frameworks. In order to ensure informed consent and respect patient autonomy, it is imperative that patients are communicated with transparently about the goals and implications of data sharing (Amin, S. U., & Hossain, M. S., 2020). The moral application of AI and machine learning algorithms (Tripathi, R. P. et al., 2023) is a further facet of privacy concerns in 6G healthcare. Concerns about algorithmic bias, fairness, and transparency must be addressed by healthcare organizations as they use AI-driven technologies to analyze patient data and assist in clinical decision-making. To prevent biases and disparities in healthcare delivery, healthcare providers must make sure AI algorithms are trained on representative and diverse datasets. Furthermore, to improve accountability and trust in the application of AI in healthcare, clear documentation of the decision-making processes of AI algorithms is required. The resolution of privacy issues in 6G healthcare depends critically on regulatory compliance. To protect patient privacy and stay out of trouble with the law, healthcare organizations must abide by privacy regulations like HIPAA, GDPR, and other local data protection laws. To guarantee patient data protection and adherence to privacy best practices, compliance with these regulations necessitates continual risk assessments, security audits, and employee training programs (Jolfaei, A. A. et al., 2021).

VI. ETHICAL CONSIDERATIONS IN INTELLIGENT HEALTHCARE

As intelligent healthcare technologies advance, ethical considerations become more important for responsible and equitable use. Prioritizing patient autonomy and informed consent in health data collection, use, and sharing is ethical. Healthcare providers must explain how their data will be used and shared and respect patients' right to control their health information. Bias and discrimination in AI-driven healthcare systems are another ethical issue. Machine learning algorithms may perpetuate biases in training data, resulting in healthcare disparities. Healthcare providers must carefully evaluate and mitigate AI algorithm biases to treat all patients equally, regardless of demographics. Intelligent healthcare systems raise ethical concerns about patient data privacy and security. Healthcare organizations must implement strong security measures to protect patient privacy and prevent unauthorized access to sensitive health information. Maintaining patient trust in healthcare systems requires transparency and accountability. Several new trends and technologies could improve intelligent healthcare system security (Taimoor, N., & Rehman, S., 2021). Blockchain technology is being used to securely and transparently record healthcare transactions and data exchanges. A decentralized, tamper-proof ledger like blockchain (David, S. et al., 2023) can prevent data tampering and unauthorized access. Federation learning, which allows healthcare institutions to train models without sharing data, is another emerging technology. Federated learning (Saxena, A. et al., 2024) lets healthcare providers share knowledge while protecting patient data. Healthcare systems that use homomorphic encryption can process and analyze encrypted data without decrypting it. Secure computation (Pandey, B. K. et al., 2021b). A deep neural network-based approach for extracting textual images from deteriorate images.) and data privacy make homomorphic encryption a good choice for health data protection. Smart healthcare system security and privacy policies are shaped by governments and regulators. Clear healthcare data protection and cybersecurity guidelines are one policy recommendation. To encourage healthcare organizations to prioritize security and privacy, governments should require compliance and penalize noncompliance. Healthcare regulators should also promote transparency and accountability in AI-driven technologies. To ensure fairness, accuracy, and ethical compliance, healthcare providers should disclose their algorithms and undergo regular audits. To advance cybersecurity technologies and encourage healthcare, technology, and policy experts to collaborate, governments should fund research and development. Governments can promote innovation and knowledge-sharing to create secure, privacy-preserving intelligent healthcare systems. Several research priorities can improve 6G healthcare security and privacy. To secure healthcare systems and patient data, authentication and access control must be improved. To improve security, explore biometric authentication, multi-factor authentication, and behavioral analytics (Barua, A. et al., 2022). Intelligent healthcare systems should also incorporate privacy-preserving technologies like differential privacy and secure multi-party computation. These technologies allow data analysis and sharing without compromising patient privacy. Research is needed to address the ethical implications of AI-driven healthcare technologies and develop frameworks for evaluating and mitigating AI algorithm biases. Interdisciplinary computer science, ethics, and healthcare research can identify ethical issues and develop responsible technology development and deployment strategies (Ali, M. et al., 2022).

CONCLUSION

The exploration of Intelligent Healthcare within the context of 6G technology highlights a paradigm shift in the delivery of healthcare, which is characterized by unprecedented connectivity, data accessibility, and technological innovation. We have, throughout the entirety of this chapter, outlined the complex landscape of security and privacy concerns that are inherent in this rapidly evolving domain. The definition of Intelligent Healthcare in 6G lays the groundwork for a dynamic ecosystem that will redefine the boundaries of healthcare delivery through the convergence of real-time data exchange, advanced analytics, and remote patient monitoring. On the other hand, in addition to its promises, there is a significant need to address concerns regarding privacy and security. Comprehensive security strategies that include encryption, authentication protocols, and intrusion detection mechanisms are required in order to address a wide range of security challenges, including data breaches and cyberattacks. Similarly, concerns regarding privacy highlight the significance of safeguarding patient information by adhering to stringent regulatory compliance, implementing transparent consent management practices, and incorporating technologies that protect privacy. For the purpose of guiding the ethical development and deployment of intelligent healthcare in 6G, ethical considerations serve as a cornerstone. In order to preserve trust and integrity within the healthcare ecosystem, it is essential to uphold the rights of patients to privacy, to guarantee that artificial intelligence algorithms are fair, and to encourage practices that are transparent and accountable.

REFERENCES

Abdulkarim, Y. I., Awl, H. N., Muhammadsharif, F. F., Saeed, S. R., Sidiq, K. R., Khasraw, S. S., & Pandey, D. (2023). Metamaterial-based sensors loaded corona-shaped resonator for COVID-19 detection by using microwave techniques. *Plasmonics*, 1–16.

Ali, M., Naeem, F., Tariq, M., & Kaddoum, G. (2022). Federated learning for privacy preservation in smart healthcare systems: A comprehensive survey. *IEEE Journal of Biomedical and Health Informatics*, 27(2), 778–789. 10.1109/JBHI.2022.318182335696470

Alshehri, F., & Muhammad, G. (2020). A comprehensive survey of the Internet of Things (IoT) and AI-based smart healthcare. *IEEE Access : Practical Innovations, Open Solutions*, 9, 3660–3678. 10.1109/ACCESS.2020.3047960

Amin, S. U., & Hossain, M. S. (2020). Edge intelligence and Internet of Things in healthcare: A survey. *IEEE Access : Practical Innovations, Open Solutions*, 9, 45–59. 10.1109/ACCESS.2020.3045115

Anand, R., Khan, B., Nassa, V. K., Pandey, D., Dhabliya, D., Pandey, B. K., & Dadheech, P. (2023). Hybrid convolutional neural network (CNN) for kennedy space center hyperspectral image. *Aerospace Systems*, 6(1), 71–78. 10.1007/s42401-022-00168-4

Anand, R., Lakshmi, S. V., Pandey, D., & Pandey, B. K. (2024). An enhanced ResNet-50 deep learning model for arrhythmia detection using electrocardiogram biomedical indicators. *Evolving Systems*, 15(1), 83–97. 10.1007/s12530-023-09559-0

Barua, A., Al Alamin, M. A., Hossain, M. S., & Hossain, E. (2022). Security and privacy threats for bluetooth low energy in iot and wearable devices: A comprehensive survey. *IEEE Open Journal of the Communications Society*, 3, 251–281. 10.1109/OJCOMS.2022.3149732

Bessant, Y. A., Jency, J. G., Sagayam, K. M., Jone, A. A. A., Pandey, D., & Pandey, B. K. (2023). Improved parallel matrix multiplication using Strassen and Urdhvatiryagbhyam method. *CCF Transactions on High Performance Computing*, 5(2), 102–115. 10.1007/s42514-023-00149-9

Bhatia, H., Panda, S. N., & Nagpal, D. (2020, June). Internet of things and its applications in healthcare-A survey. In *2020 8th International Conference on Reliability, Infocom Technologies and Optimization (Trends and Future Directions)(ICRITO)* (pp. 305-310). IEEE. 10.1109/ICRITO48877.2020.9197816

Bruntha, P. M., Dhanasekar, S., Hepsiba, D., Sagayam, K. M., Neebha, T. M., Pandey, D., & Pandey, B. K. (2023). Application of switching median filter with L 2 norm-based auto-tuning function for removing random valued impulse noise. *Aerospace Systems, 6*(1), 53-59.

David, S., Duraipandian, K., Chandrasekaran, D., Pandey, D., Sindhwani, N., & Pandey, B. K. (2023). Impact of blockchain in healthcare system. In *Unleashing the Potentials of blockchain technology for healthcare industries* (pp. 37–57). Academic Press. 10.1016/B978-0-323-99481-1.00004-3

Devasenapathy, D., Madhumathy, P., Umamaheshwari, R., Pandey, B. K., & Pandey, D. (2024). Transmission-efficient grid-based synchronized model for routing in wireless sensor networks using Bayesian compressive sensing. *SN Computer Science*, 5(1), 1–11.

Dian, F. J., Vahidnia, R., & Rahmati, A. (2020). Wearables and the Internet of Things (IoT), applications, opportunities, and challenges: A Survey. *IEEE Access : Practical Innovations, Open Solutions*, 8, 69200–69211. 10.1109/ACCESS.2020.2986329

Du John, H. V., Ajay, T., Reddy, G. M. K., Ganesh, M. N. S., Hembram, A., Pandey, B. K., & Pandey, D. (2023). Design and simulation of SRR-based tungsten metamaterial absorber for biomedical sensing applications. *Plasmonics*, 18(5), 1903–1912. 10.1007/s11468-023-01910-0

Du John, H. V., Jose, T., Sagayam, K. M., Pandey, B. K., & Pandey, D. (2024). Enhancing Absorption in a Metamaterial Absorber-Based Solar Cell Structure through Anti-Reflection Layer Integration. *Silicon*, 1-11.

Du John, H. V., Sagayam, K. M., Jose, T., Pandey, D., Pandey, B. K., Kotti, J., & Kaur, P. (2023). Design simulation and parametric investigation of a metamaterial light absorber with tungsten resonator for solar cell applications using silicon as dielectric layer. *Silicon*, 15(9), 4065–4079. 10.1007/s12633-023-02321-w

George, W. K., Ekong, M. O., Pandey, D., & Pandey, B. K. (2023). Pedagogy for Implementation of TVET Curriculum for the Digital World. In *Applications of Neuromarketing in the Metaverse* (pp. 117-136). IGI Global. 10.4018/978-1-6684-8150-9.ch009

George, W. K., Silas, E. I., Pandey, D., & Pandey, B. K. (2024). Utilization of Industry 4.0 Technologies in Nigerian Technical and Vocational Education: A Conundrum for Educators. In *Examining the Rapid Advance of Digital Technology in Africa* (pp. 270–293). IGI Global. 10.4018/978-1-6684-9962-7.ch014

Govindaraj, V., Dhanasekar, S., Martinsagayam, K., Pandey, D., Pandey, B. K., & Nassa, V. K. (2023). Low-power test pattern generator using modified LFSR. *Aerospace Systems*, 1-8.

Gupta, A. K., Sharma, R., Pandey, D., Nassa, V. K., Pandey, B. K., George, A. S., & Dadheech, P. (2023). Performance analysis of eight-channel WDM optical network with different optical amplifiers for industry 4.0. In *Innovation and Competitiveness in Industry 4.0 Based on Intelligent Systems* (pp. 197–212). Springer International Publishing. 10.1007/978-3-031-29775-5_9

Habibzadeh, H., Dinesh, K., Shishvan, O. R., Boggio-Dandry, A., Sharma, G., & Soyata, T. (2019). A survey of healthcare Internet of Things (HIoT): A clinical perspective. *IEEE Internet of Things Journal*, 7(1), 53–71. 10.1109/JIOT.2019.294635933748312

Iyyanar, P., Anand, R., Shanthi, T., Nassa, V. K., Pandey, B. K., George, A. S., & Pandey, D. (2023). A real-time smart sewage cleaning UAV assistance system using IoT. In *Handbook of Research on Data-Driven Mathematical Modeling in Smart Cities* (pp. 24–39). IGI Global.

JayaLakshmi, G., Pandey, D., Pandey, B. K., Kaur, P., Mahajan, D. A., & Dari, S. S. (2024). Smart Big Data Collection for Intelligent Supply Chain Improvement. In *AI and Machine Learning Impacts in Intelligent Supply Chain* (pp. 180-195). IGI Global.

Jolfaei, A. A., Aghili, S. F., & Singelee, D. (2021). A survey on blockchain-based IoMT systems: Towards scalability. *IEEE Access : Practical Innovations, Open Solutions*, 9, 148948–148975. 10.1109/ACCESS.2021.3117662

Kirubasri, G., Sankar, S., Pandey, D., Pandey, B. K., Singh, H., & Anand, R. (2021, September). A recent survey on 6G vehicular technology, applications and challenges. In *2021 9th International Conference on Reliability, Infocom Technologies and Optimization (Trends and Future Directions)(ICRITO)* (pp. 1-5). IEEE.

Kumar Pandey, B., Pandey, D., Nassa, V. K., Ahmad, T., Singh, C., George, A. S., & Wakchaure, M. A. (2021). Encryption and steganography-based text extraction in IoT using the EWCTS optimizer. *Imaging Science Journal*, 69(1-4), 38–56. 10.1080/13682199.2022.2146885

Malamas, V., Chantzis, F., Dasaklis, T. K., Stergiopoulos, G., Kotzanikolaou, P., & Douligeris, C. (2021). Risk assessment methodologies for the internet of medical things: A survey and comparative appraisal. *IEEE Access : Practical Innovations, Open Solutions*, 9, 40049–40075. 10.1109/ACCESS.2021.3064682

Muniandi, B., Nassa, V. K., Pandey, D., Pandey, B. K., Dadheech, P., & George, A. S. (2024). Pattern Analysis for Feature Extraction in Complex Images. In *Using Machine Learning to Detect Emotions and Predict Human Psychology* (pp. 145-167). IGI Global. 10.4018/979-8-3693-1910-9.ch007

Pandey, B. K., & Pandey, D. (2023). Parametric optimization and prediction of enhanced thermoelectric performance in co-doped CaMnO3 using response surface methodology and neural network. *Journal of Materials Science Materials in Electronics*, 34(21), 1589. 10.1007/s10854-023-10954-1

Pandey, B. K., Pandey, D., Alkhafaji, M. A., Güneşer, M. T., & Şeker, C. (2023). A reliable transmission and extraction of textual information using keyless encryption, steganography, and deep algorithm with cuckoo optimization. In *Micro-Electronics and Telecommunication Engineering: Proceedings of 6th ICMETE 2022* (pp. 629–636). Springer Nature Singapore. 10.1007/978-981-19-9512-5_57

Pandey, B. K., Pandey, D., & Sahani, S. K. (2024). Autopilot control unmanned aerial vehicle system for sewage defect detection using deep learning. *Engineering Reports*, 12852. 10.1002/eng2.12852

Pandey, B. K., Pandey, D., Wairya, S., & Agarwal, G. (2021a). An advanced morphological component analysis, steganography, and deep learning-based system to transmit secure textual data. *International Journal of Distributed Artificial Intelligence*, 13(2), 40–62. 10.4018/IJDAI.2021070104

Pandey, B. K., Pandey, D., Wariya, S., & Agarwal, G. (2021b). A deep neural network-based approach for extracting textual images from deteriorate images. *EAI Endorsed Transactions on Industrial Networks and Intelligent Systems*, 8(28), e3–e3. 10.4108/eai.17-9-2021.170961

Pandey, D., Pandey, B. K., & Wairya, S. (2021). Hybrid deep neural network with adaptive galactic swarm optimization for text extraction from scene images. *Soft Computing*, 25(2), 1563–1580. 10.1007/s00500-020-05245-4

Pramanik, S., Pandey, D., Joardar, S., Niranjanamurthy, M., Pandey, B. K., & Kaur, J. (2023, October). An overview of IoT privacy and security in smart cities. In *AIP Conference Proceedings* (Vol. 2495, No. 1). AIP Publishing. 10.1063/5.0123511

Qadri, Y. A., Nauman, A., Zikria, Y. B., Vasilakos, A. V., & Kim, S. W. (2020). The future of healthcare internet of things: A survey of emerging technologies. *IEEE Communications Surveys and Tutorials*, 22(2), 1121–1167. 10.1109/COMST.2020.2973314

Raja, D., Kumar, D. R., Santhiyakumari, N., Kumarganesh, S., Sagayam, K. M., Thiyaneswaran, B., Pandey, B. K., & Pandey, D. (2024). A compact dual-feed wide-band slotted antenna for future wireless applications. *Analog Integrated Circuits and Signal Processing*, 118(2), 1–15. 10.1007/s10470-023-02233-0

Saxena, A., Agarwal, A., Pandey, B. K., & Pandey, D. (2024). Examination of the Criticality of Customer Segmentation Using Unsupervised Learning Methods. *Circular Economy and Sustainability*, 1–14. 10.1007/s43615-023-00336-4

Sharma, M., Talwar, R., Pandey, D., Nassa, V. K., Pandey, B. K., & Dadheech, P. (2024). A Review of Dielectric Resonator Antennas (DRA)-Based RFID Technology for Industry 4.0. *Robotics and Automation in Industry*, 4(0), 303–324.

Sharma, S., Pandey, B. K., Pandey, D., Anand, R., Sharma, A., & Saini, S. (2023, March). Character Recognition Technique Implementation for Complicated Deteriorated Scene. In *2023 6th International Conference on Information Systems and Computer Networks (ISCON)* (pp. 1-4). IEEE. 10.1109/ISCON57294.2023.10112185

Singh, S., Madaan, G., Kaur, J., Swapna, H. R., Pandey, D., Singh, A., & Pandey, B. K. (2023). *Bibliometric Review on Healthcare Sustainability. Handbook of Research on Safe Disposal Methods of Municipal Solid Wastes for a Sustainable Environment*, 142-161. 10.4018/978-1-6684-8117-2.ch011

Swapna, H. R., Bigirimana, E., Madaan, G., Hasan, A., Pandey, B. K., & Pandey, D. (2023). Impact of neuromarketing on consumer psychology in digitally connected networks. In *Applications of Neuromarketing in the Metaverse* (pp. 193–205). IGI Global. 10.4018/978-1-6684-8150-9.ch015

Taimoor, N., & Rehman, S. (2021). Reliable and resilient AI and IoT-based personalised healthcare services: A survey. *IEEE Access : Practical Innovations, Open Solutions*, 10, 535–563. 10.1109/ACCESS.2021.3137364

Tripathi, R. P., Sharma, M., Gupta, A. K., Pandey, D., Pandey, B. K., Shahul, A., & George, A. H. (2023). Timely prediction of diabetes by means of machine learning practices. *Augmented Human Research*, 8(1), 1. 10.1007/s41133-023-00062-4

Ullah, A., Azeem, M., Ashraf, H., Alaboudi, A. A., Humayun, M., & Jhanjhi, N. Z. (2021). Secure healthcare data aggregation and transmission in IoT—A survey. *IEEE Access : Practical Innovations, Open Solutions*, 9, 16849–16865. 10.1109/ACCESS.2021.3052850

Chapter 18
Telemedicine in 6G:
A Secure Frontier for Healthcare Transformation

Shivkumar P. Mantri
Hitkarini Dental College and Hospital, Jabalpur, India

Maurya Manjunath
JSS Dental College and Hospital, JSS Academy of Higher Education and Research, Mysuru, India

S. Bathrinath
https://orcid.org/0000-0002-5502-6203
Kalasalingam Academy of Research and Education, Krishnankoil, India

N. Kavitha
Hindusthan College of Engineering and Technology, Coimbatore, India

M. Sakthivel
Velammal College of Engineering and Technology, Madurai, India

R. Manikandan
https://orcid.org/0000-0002-2055-6634
Panimalar Engineering College, Tamil Nadu, India

S. B. G. Tilak Babu
Aditya Engineering College, Surampalem, India

ABSTRACT

The development of 6G technology is driving telemedicine, which has the potential to completely transform the way that healthcare is delivered by facilitating remote consultations, diagnosis, and treatment. This study examines how telemedicine and 6G technology interact, with an emphasis on how these developments could change patient care, increase accessibility, and strengthen security. The authors begin by explaining what telemedicine is and giving a general review of 6G technology, emphasizing its extraordinarily dependable, latency-free communication capabilities. The thesis that telemedicine in 6G presents a secure frontier for transforming healthcare is emphasized, as is the significance of security in telemedicine.

DOI: 10.4018/979-8-3693-7421-4.ch018

I. INTRODUCTION

Telemedicine is the application of electronic information and communication technologies to provide medical care from a distance. It is the nexus of cutting-edge and mainstream technological developments. Telemedicine is a broad term for a variety of applications (Bruntha, P. M. et al., 2023) ranging from conventional telephone consultations to state-of-the-art telesurgery, all of which are intended to get around geographic barriers to healthcare delivery. Still, as telemedicine develops, it becomes more and more entwined with the quick development of communication technologies (Gupta, A. K. et al., 2023), especially with the introduction of 6G (Kirubasri, G. et al., 2021) systems. With its unprecedented speeds, ultra-reliable low latency, and massive connectivity, 6G technology is the next big thing in wireless communication (Devasenapathy, D. et al., 2024). 6G has the potential to significantly improve the capabilities and reach of telemedicine. It is positioned to revolutionize a number of industries, including healthcare. 6G has the potential to revolutionize the delivery of healthcare remotely by enabling real-time interactions, high-definition video streaming, and advanced data transmission (JayaLakshmi, G. et al., 2024). Ensuring patient data availability, confidentiality, and integrity is critical as telemedicine depends more and more on digital (George, W. K. et al., 2023) platforms and interconnected networks. Robust security measures are vital to protect patient privacy and trust, as evidenced by the convergence of sophisticated communication technologies and sensitive medical information. Beyond just safeguarding data, security in telemedicine is crucial because it affects the acceptability, usability, and standard of remote medical care. To fully participate in virtual consultations and remote monitoring, patients need to feel secure (Pandey, B. K. et al., 2021b) in the telemedicine platforms' security. Similarly, assurance that private patient data is protected during the telemedicine process is needed by healthcare providers. Without sufficient security measures, worries about data breaches and privacy (Pandey, B. K. et al., 2021a) violations may outweigh the potential advantages of telemedicine in terms of bettering healthcare outcomes and access. Given these factors, especially with regard to 6G technology, a thorough assessment framework is necessary to determine the efficacy and significance of telemedicine initiatives. Stakeholder satisfaction, cost-effectiveness, security, and clinical outcomes must all be taken into account in these assessments. These assessments are essential for decision-making regarding the adoption and use of telemedicine solutions by policymakers, physicians, patients, and healthcare administrators. The assessment framework needs to change to account for the various technological applications and settings as telemedicine develops and diversifies further. From telemedicine consultations to telesurgery and beyond, each modality offers different opportunities and challenges that call for specific security protocols and evaluation standards.

1.1 Security in Telemedicine

A crucial component of telemedicine security is ensuring compliance with applicable regulations. Healthcare organizations are required to comply with stringent regulations, such as the Health Insurance Portability and Accountability Act (HIPAA) in the United States, which mandate the protection of patient health information. It is possible to incur severe penalties and suffer damage to one's reputation if one does not comply with these specifications. Healthcare providers are able to ensure compliance with regulatory standards, protect patient data, and maintain the integrity of their organizations by implementing stringent security protocols. Assurance of confidentiality is of the utmost importance in telemedicine because of the sensitive nature of the information that is being transmitted online. If appropriate safety precautions are not taken, the transmission of personal health information through digital channels, which is a component of telemedicine, leaves the data vulnerable to unauthorized access (Sharma, S. et al., 2023). In addition to undermining the trust of patients, breaches in confidentiality introduce significant legal risks for those who provide medical care. The confidentiality of patients can be maintained and the integrity of healthcare services can be protected if healthcare organizations put in place stringent security protocols. When it comes to successful interactions in the healthcare industry, especially in telemedicine, trust building is absolutely necessary. Before participating in a remote consultation, patients need to have the assurance that their private medical information is protected and secure. Security breaches have the potential to undermine the trust of patients and discourage individuals from participating in telemedicine services. For the purpose of fostering trust and confidence in telemedicine platforms, healthcare providers can prioritize security measures. This will encourage greater patient participation and engagement in remote healthcare services. In order to protect telemedicine platforms from the ever-evolving cybersecurity risks, it is essential to put cyber threat prevention into action. It is possible for healthcare providers to experience significant disruptions and compromises in the security of patient data as a result of the proliferation of cyber threats such as ransomware attacks and data breaches. For the purpose of mitigating these risks and protecting telemedicine infrastructure from malicious actors, it is essential to make investments in cybersecurity measures such as encryption (Kumar Pandey, B. et al., 2021) and access controls. When it comes to telemedicine, maintaining data integrity is absolutely necessary in order to guarantee the precision and dependability of digital medical records. Changing or manipulating medical records without authorization can have severe repercussions for the health and well-being of patients as well as the results of their treatment. Keeping data integrity intact and preventing unauthorized access to sensitive information are two of the most important roles that security measures like encryption (Pandey, B. K. et al., 2023) and data validation play (Taleb, H. et al., 2021). Putting security at the forefront of telemedicine practices is emphasized by the concept of ethical responsibility. Healthcare providers have a moral and ethical obligation to put the patient's well-being and privacy at the forefront of their priority list. When healthcare organizations demonstrate a commitment to ethical conduct and responsible patient care by integrating robust security measures into telemedicine operations, they are able to uphold their reputation and promote patient well-being in the context of the technological landscape of healthcare.

II. EVOLUTION OF TELEMEDICINE

2.1 Historical Background

The use of radio to connect emergency medical personnel to medical facilities and the common practice of using the phone to facilitate patient-clinician consultations fall into the commonplace category. Telesurgery, which uses tactile and visual cues to guide robotic instruments to perform surgery at a remote location, is an example of an experimental advancement that falls on the opposite end of the telemedicine spectrum. Applications and technologies for data, audio, and video transmission can be found in the space between these two extremes. There are some that let doctors see, hear, examine, question, and counsel patients who are far away in "real-time" for diagnostic and therapeutic purposes. These include the somewhat pricey interactive video conferencing systems. Others relying on "store and forward" technologies allow digital (Swapna, H. R. et al., 2023) photos and other data to be saved and sent at a reasonable cost to consultants who can receive and analyze them at a convenient time, giving schedule flexibility to both parties. These diverse technologies can be used in a wide range of fields, including public health, professional education, research, and administration, aside from patient care. Expensive information and communications investments may be able to spread their costs more widely thanks to these numerous applications. The dearth of comprehensive analyses of telemedicine applications for patient care served as the impetus for this study. It argues for more methodical and thorough evaluations of the effects of telemedicine applications on health care quality, accessibility, costs, and acceptability in comparison to alternative services. It also provides a broad framework for assessing telemedicine's clinical applications. Such assessments are crucial for telemedicine, as they are for any other health technology or service, for a number of reasons. They are capable of Inform health plan managers about the viability, affordability, and patient and clinician acceptance of clinical telemedicine. Support policymakers debating whether to promote telemedicine by encouraging infrastructure development, funding specific telemedicine programs, or lowering policy barriers. Provide clinicians and patients with appropriate reassurance or caution about telemedicine applications. The evaluation framework proposed here will need to be modified to fit various applications and environments because telemedicine is actually a family of quite diverse technologies and applications, and because telemedicine uses and benefits may be interwoven with important educational, research, public health, and administrative uses (Smith-Bindman, R. et al., 2012). Incorporating links to other clinical and nonclinical programs that utilize some of the same technical and human resources may also require modifications. A set of guiding principles and techniques that serve as the cornerstone for both evaluation research in general and health services research in particular are incorporated into the evaluation framework, despite these modifications and changes. This study aims to connect those ideas and approaches to the unique difficulties and issues associated with telemedicine evaluation. It is intended mainly for managers, policymakers, physicians, and patients, but it should also give researchers and evaluators who are interested in evaluating information and telecommunications technologies some background and assistance.

2.2 Advancements in Telecommunication Technologies

The evolution of telemedicine has been significantly influenced by developments in telecommunication technologies, which have made it possible to provide healthcare services to patients located in remote locations with an unprecedented level of efficiency and competence. The capabilities of telemedicine have been expanded and improved over the years as a result of several significant technological advancements are shown in the figure 1.

1. *High-Speed Internet Connectivity*: By facilitating smooth communication between medical professionals and patients, the general availability of high-speed internet has revolutionized telemedicine. Healthcare practitioners can work remotely with colleagues, share medical records and images instantly, and conduct real-time video consultations thanks to broadband and fiber-optic networks. Fast connectivity guarantees seamless, responsive telemedicine interactions that support efficient diagnosis and treatment planning. High-speed internet connectivity also makes it possible to send massive amounts of medical data—like clear, high-definition pictures and videos—without any hiccups or delays, which improves the caliber and dependability of remote healthcare services.

2. *Mobile Technology*: Patients can now obtain healthcare services at any time and from any location thanks to the development of mobile devices like smartphones and tablets, which has completely changed the telemedicine landscape. Patients can use built-in sensors (Abdulkarim, Y. I. et al., 2023) in mobile health applications to track their health parameters, make appointment appointments, and text or video chat with healthcare providers. From the comfort of their homes, patients can conveniently track their treatment progress, get timely medical advice, and follow their medication regimens thanks to these mobile technologies. Furthermore, telemedicine overcomes geographical barriers to healthcare access by being more accessible to underserved populations and people living in remote or rural areas due to the portability and prevalence of mobile devices.
3. *Teleconferencing Platforms*: By giving medical professionals flexible tools for virtual consultations and remote collaboration, cutting-edge teleconferencing platforms and software applications have completely transformed the field of telemedicine. These platforms enable smooth communication and information exchange between healthcare providers and patients by providing features like interactive whiteboards, document sharing, and screen sharing. Additionally, teleconferencing platforms facilitate the coordination of patient care among various healthcare settings and specialties, as well as allow multidisciplinary care teams to work together on complex cases and share expertise. Telemedicine providers can offer patients comprehensive and integrated healthcare services, independent of their medical needs or location, by utilizing these collaborative tools.
4. *Remote Monitoring Devices*: Wearable sensors (Du John, H. V. et al., 2023), smartwatches, and home monitoring kits are examples of technological advancements in remote monitoring devices that have revolutionized telemedicine by enabling continuous monitoring of patients' health parameters outside of conventional clinical settings. Patients can monitor vital signs like blood pressure, heart rate, and blood glucose levels with these devices, and they can send real-time data for remote monitoring and analysis to healthcare providers. By enabling early diagnosis and prompt intervention, remote monitoring devices enable patients to actively manage their health and chronic conditions. Furthermore, by remotely monitoring patients' progress, modifying treatment plans as necessary, and acting quickly in an emergency, remote monitoring helps healthcare providers improve patient outcomes and lower readmission rates to hospitals (Stefanova-Pavlova, M. et al., 2017).
5. *Cloud Computing*: By offering scalable and secure storage options for medical data and applications, cloud computing technologies have completely transformed telemedicine. With the flexibility, scalability, and accessibility that cloud-based telemedicine platforms provide, healthcare providers can safely access patient records, diagnostic reports, and medical imaging from any internet-enabled device. Healthcare providers can collaborate and share information easily thanks to cloud computing, regardless of where they are located or what institution they work for. Additionally, cloud-based telemedicine platforms make data integration and interoperability easier, which helps healthcare organizations increase the effectiveness of healthcare delivery overall, optimize (Pandey, D. et al., 2021) administrative procedures, and improve care coordination.
6. *Artificial Intelligence (AI) and Machine Learning*: By automating processes, evaluating medical data, and offering clinical decision support, AI (Anand, R. et al., 2023) and machine learning algorithms have improved telemedicine capabilities. Thanks to these cutting-edge technologies, healthcare professionals can now use vast amounts of patient data—such as genetic, medical image, and electronic health record data—to gain insights and make informed decisions. AI (Pandey, B. K., & Pandey, D., 2023) powered telemedicine solutions can help medical professionals diagnose patients, forecast their prognoses, and customize treatment regimens according to the unique needs and preferences of

each patient. AI systems are also capable of analyzing medical images, including MRIs and X-rays, to find anomalies and help radiologists correctly interpret complex results. Telemedicine providers can increase the quality of patient care overall, optimize (Jayapoorani, S. et al., 2023) treatment outcomes, and improve diagnostic accuracy by utilizing AI and machine learning (Pandey, B. K. et al., 2024).

7. *Virtual Reality (VR) and Augmented Reality (AR):* By establishing dynamic and immersive virtual worlds for patient education, medical simulation, and training, VR and AR technologies have revolutionized telemedicine. Healthcare professionals can practice clinical skills in a safe and controlled environment, conduct virtual surgeries, and simulate medical procedures thanks to these technologies. Furthermore, patients can visualize their medical conditions, comprehend available treatments, and engage in collaborative decision-making with healthcare providers thanks to VR and AR applications. VR and AR technologies improve health literacy, foster better patient-provider communication, and increase patient engagement by submerging patients in lifelike virtual environments. VR and AR can also be used to improve procedural skills, simulate medical emergencies, and train healthcare professionals. This way, providers will be prepared to provide high-quality care in telemedicine settings.

Figure 1. Advances in telemedicine technology

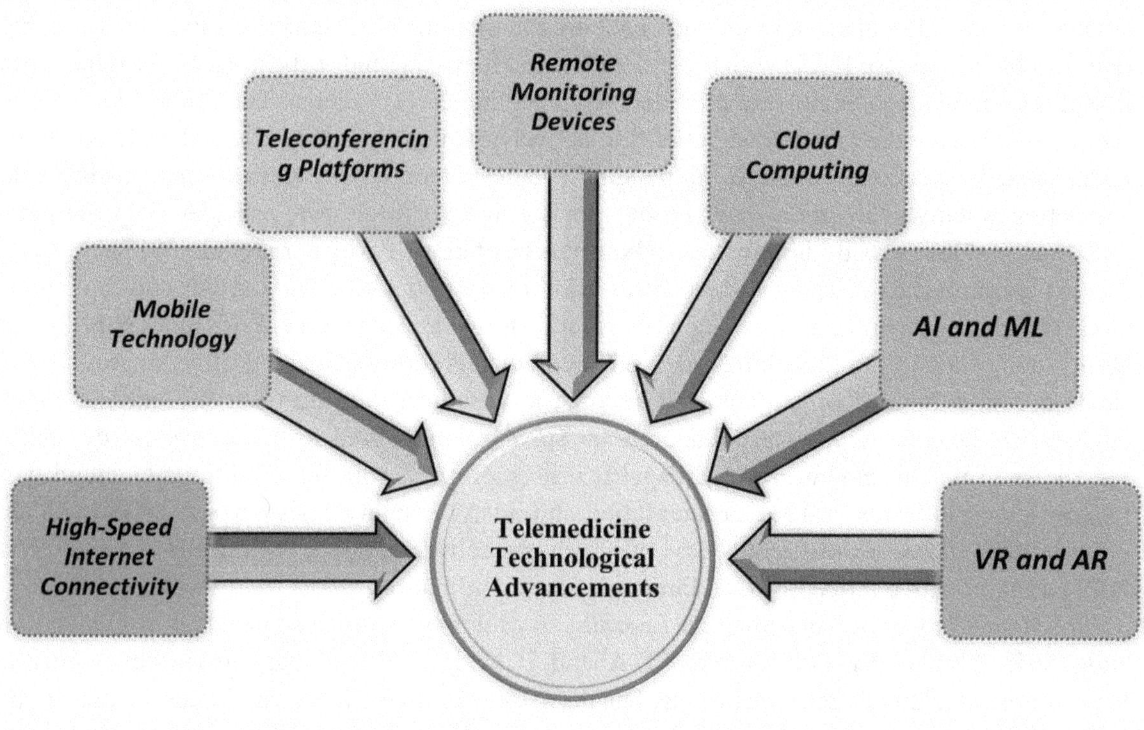

2.3 Potential of 6G in Enhancing Telemedicine

There is a tremendous possibility that 6G technology will revolutionize telemedicine. It will provide capabilities that have never been seen before, which could significantly improve the delivery of healthcare remotely in the in the future. How could 6G revolutionize the field of telemedicine? Ultra-reliable low latency communication (URLLC) is anticipated to be provided by 6G, which will make it possible to transmit medical data in real time with a minimal amount of delay. These applications of telemedicine, which require instant feedback, such as remote surgery and emergency consultations, are extremely dependent on this extremely low latency. With the advent of 6G, medical professionals will be able to carry out intricate medical procedures remotely with increased precision and responsiveness, thereby enhancing the outcomes for patients and increasing access to specialized care in areas that are yet to be adequately served. The 6G technology is designed to support massive machine type communications (mMTC), which enables seamless connectivity between a large number of devices and sensors (Du John, H. V. et al., 2024). These capabilities are in addition to the low latency that the technology offers. The capabilities of mMTC could make it easier to deploy a wide variety of remote monitoring devices and wearable sensors (Du John, H. V. et al., 2023) in the field of telemedicine. This would make it possible to continuously monitor the health parameters and vital signs of your patients. This real-time data collection and analysis makes it possible to detect health problems at an earlier stage, to take preventative measures, and to develop individualized treatment plans, which ultimately leads to better patient outcomes and lower overall prices for medical care (Kashani, M. H. et al., 2021). The technology known as network slicing, which enables the creation of virtualized network segments that are tailored to specific applications and user requirements, is anticipated to be supported by 6G networks. Through the use of network slicing, healthcare providers are able to prioritize critical healthcare traffic in telemedicine. This ensures that communication for remote consultations, medical imaging, and data transmission becomes dependable and secure. The quality of service for telemedicine applications can be optimized by 6G networks through the dynamic allocation of network resources based on healthcare priorities. This results in an overall improvement in the reliability and performance of remote healthcare delivery. The ability to perform data processing and analysis closer to the point of care is made possible by edge computing, which is another important feature of the 6G technology infrastructure. Remote diagnostics and patient monitoring are two examples of time-sensitive telemedicine applications that require real-time data processing. This distributed computing architecture reduces latency and bandwidth requirements, making it an ideal choice for these applications. A healthcare provider is able to analyze medical data locally, make clinical decisions in a timely manner, and respond promptly to patient needs when they harness the resources of edge computing. This is possible even in environments where resources are limited. It is anticipated that the deployment of 6G technology will allow for the direct incorporation of artificial intelligence (AI) (Anand, R. et al., 2024) and machine learning (ML) algorithms into telemedicine platforms, thereby enabling intelligent decision support and predictive analytics capabilities. Using artificial intelligence, telemedicine solutions are able to analyze vast amounts of patient data, such as medical records, diagnostic images, and genetic information, in order to provide assistance to medical professionals in the areas of diagnosis, treatment planning, and risk predictability (Bhuiyan, M. N. et al., 2021). The utilization of artificial intelligence and machine learning algorithms (Saxena, A. et al., 2024) enables 6G telemedicine platforms to improve clinical decision-making, optimize treatment outcomes, and enhance the quality and efficiency of patient care.

III. KEY COMPONENTS OF TELEMEDICINE IN 6G

3.1 Ultra-Reliable Low Latency Communication (URLLC)

A key element of the 5G network architecture is Ultra-Reliable Low Latency Communication (URLLC), which is intended to guarantee extremely effective scheduling of data transfers with the least amount of latency. In order to achieve extremely low latency, it works by streamlining transmission procedures, making use of bigger subcarriers, and even planning overlapping transmissions. For applications like remote surgery and driverless cars that need real-time data transfer, this 5G feature is especially crucial. URLLC coexists with two other important 5G service areas, Enhanced Mobile Broadband (eMBB) and Massive Machine-Type Communications (mMTC), within the larger framework. Although eMBB targets higher download speeds and better user experiences for high-bandwidth applications like streaming and augmented/virtual reality (AR/VR), mMTC concentrates on connecting a large number of devices to advance the Internet of Things (IoT) industry (George, W. K. et al., 2024). Conversely, mission-critical applications like autonomous driving and smart factories that require a guaranteed connection with low latency are the focus of URLLC. One of the main applications for URLLC is autonomous driving, where cars need incredibly dependable connections to exchange real-time information with roadside systems and other cars. This guarantees smooth coordination and improves safety by reducing the possibility of mishaps brought on by a breakdown in communication. Comparably, sectors such as smart manufacturing depend on low-latency systems to facilitate instantaneous communication between robotics and machinery, thereby enhancing overall efficiency and streamlining production procedures. Beyond the manufacturing and automotive industries, URLLC has enormous potential in fields like cloud-based gaming and entertainment, smart electricity distribution, and remote healthcare (Aghdam, Z. N. et al., 2021). For example, URLLC enables augmented reality applications and remote surgeries in the healthcare industry, allowing surgeons to operate precisely and accurately from a distance. In the meantime, URLLC facilitates smart grid technologies in the energy distribution sector, guaranteeing dependable and effective management of electrical networks. Network slicing, a technology that permits each service area to operate independently within the same physical network infrastructure, is how URLLC functions within the 5G ecosystem. With unique requirements for quality of service, security, and provisioning, each slice functions as a separate network, guaranteeing that mission-critical applications are given priority and access to resources. By dividing up the network's resources, URLLC use cases can communicate effectively and dependably, ensuring extremely low latency and high dependability for crucial applications (Da Fonseca, M. H. et al., 2021).

3.2 Massive Machine Type Communications (mMTC)

Massive Machine Type Communications (mMTC) is an important part of 5G technology, which was developed by the 3rd Generation Partnership Project (3GPP) to change the way we talk on the phone by making room for the growing Internet of Things (IoT) (Iyyanar, P. et al., 2023). This group of 5G technologies includes enhanced mobile broadband (eMBB), ultra-reliable low latency communication (uRLLC), and massive Internet of Things (mIoT) applications. It's designed to work in situations where a lot of devices need to be connected but data speeds are limited. Our main goal at mMTC is to build a strong wide area network that can connect a huge number of Internet of Things (IoT) (Pramanik, S. et al., 2023) devices and provide them with fast, low-latency, and low-cost communication services. mMTC's ability to improve network performance is one of its most important benefits. mMTC makes sure that a lot of devices have the best performance possible, even when the network is busy, by using software-defined networks and network slicing. This optimization leads to better performance for apps that use the 5G network, which results in a better experience for users. Additionally, mMTC tries to cut down on latency by a large amount. Using the latest developments in 5G technology and low-latency protocols, mMTC creates ultra-low latency connections between IoT devices. This lets applications respond faster and more reliably than ever before. mMTC also helps to lower the amount of energy that is used. By providing better connectivity, mMTC makes it easier for IoT devices to work efficiently, which lowers energy use and increases battery life. This makes IoT deployments more sustainable and long-lasting. The way mMTC works is controlled by a special network topology, which requires specialized base stations and more coverage across the network. In addition, a lot of low-bandwidth backhaul links are set up, and a lot of distributed access points, or "hubs," are put in place. These all work together to reduce message latency and increase network capacity. A key part of mMTC is that it uses new radio access technologies, like LTE-M or NB-IoT, that are designed to support large-scale wireless transmissions (Raja, D. et al., 2024) with low power. To cut down on the time and effort needed to send data, messages are compressed and broken up into packets. The LTE-M or NB-IoT infrastructure then routes these packets efficiently, making data transmission more efficient. It's important to note that mMTC is based on network protocols that were carefully created to support high throughput, low latency, and low power needs (Govindaraj, V. et al., 2023). These protocols are very important for making sure that data can be sent reliably to and from many devices, with the least amount of delay and the highest level of reliability. When it comes to mMTC, security is very important because it needs safe connections between IoT devices and the network infrastructure. To do this, mMTC networks use strong security authentication protocols to make sure that messages are sent over secure channels, which lowers the chances of them being tampered with or intercepted. The usefulness of mMTC is very large and varied, encompassing areas like smart energy grids, self-driving factories, and intelligent transportation systems (Sahani, K. et al., 2023). mMTC is great for supporting areas with lots of people and devices because it has low-latency connections and a lot of capacity. So, mMTC makes it easier to keep an eye on and control things related to public safety, the environment, and infrastructure, which helps make cities smarter and more efficient. It is expected that mMTC will have a huge effect on smart cities and the IoT ecosystem as it continues to grow and change (Taha, A. E. M., 2021). Using the revolutionary power of 5G technology, mMTC promises connections with very low latency, better network performance, and low energy use for a wide range of IoT uses. mMTC is already making progress in deploying in a number of regions. It is set to change the way IoT devices connect, ushering in a time of unmatched innovation and efficiency.

3.3 Edge Computing for Real-Time Processing

Edge Computing revolutionizes distributed computing by bringing computation (Bessant, Y. A. et al., 2023) and data storage closer to data generation. Edge Computing moves computation to the "edge" of the network, where data originates, instead of centralizing data processing in remote data centers. This architectural shift enables real-time processing and analysis, benefiting applications across industries. Several fundamental principles underpin Edge Computing's functionality and efficacy. The principle of proximity requires data processing to occur near its source, minimizing latency and eliminating the need for data to travel long distances to centralized data centers. Edge Computing improves workflow efficiency and response times by reducing the physical distance between data processing nodes and data sources. Edge Computing optimizes bandwidth by processing and filtering data at the edge to send only relevant data to the cloud or data center. Data transmission infrastructures scale better, bandwidth usage decreases, and network congestion decreases. Edge Computing emphasizes real-time responsiveness for instantaneous data processing and decision-making. Edge Computing supports real-time decision-making and low latency by processing data near its source. Edge Computing is especially important in smart transportation, industrial automation (Sharma, M. et al., 2024), and healthcare, where split-second decisions can affect safety, efficiency, and customer satisfaction. Edge Computing also supports offline operation, allowing edge devices to operate without a network. This resilience reduces network outage and latency risks in remote or disconnected environments. It has many benefits across many domains due to its core principles and architecture. It reduces the need to send massive amounts of raw data to cloud infrastructures, improving efficiency. By processing data at the edge and transmitting only actionable information, Edge Computing optimizes bandwidth, reduces network congestion, and improves operational efficiency. Real-time data processing and analysis for applications that require immediate responses. Edge Computing helps automotive, manufacturing, and healthcare companies make faster, safer, and more satisfying decisions. It keeps sensitive data close to its source and reduces data transmission over external networks, improving data privacy and security. Edge Computing reduces data breaches and unauthorized access by processing and analyzing data locally, boosting data privacy and compliance. Edge Computing also distributes computational resources across edge devices, making it scalable and cost-effective for growing data volumes and processing needs without straining cloud infrastructures. Edge Computing is a cost-effective solution for diverse applications because its decentralized data processing optimizes resource utilization and reduces data transfer costs. By processing data from edge sensors and devices, Edge Computing improves traffic flow, public safety, and real-time event response in smart cities. Automakers use Edge Computing for real-time vehicle decision-making to ensure safety and reliability in dynamic environments. Real-time personalization and targeted advertising based on customer behavior and preferences improve retail customer experience with Edge Computing. Healthcare uses Edge Computing for remote patient monitoring, real-time health data analysis, and faster diagnosis and intervention, improving patient outcomes and lowering costs (Khattak, S. B. A., 2022).

3.4 AI and Machine Learning Integration

Integration of AI and Machine Learning (ML) (Tripathi, R. P. et al., 2023) is a significant development in contemporary technology that ushers in a new era of intelligent systems and applications in a variety of fields. By enhancing the capabilities and functionalities of current systems, processes, and applications through the use of AI algorithms and ML models, this integration opens up a wide range of advantages and opportunities for both individuals and organizations. AI integration is the process of integrating AI capabilities into different technology domains, such as hardware systems and devices, software platforms, and applications. By allowing systems to behave in a "smart" way that is, to be able to see, think, learn, and act on their own this integration enhances human capabilities and optimizes workflows. This integration is made possible by machine learning, a branch of artificial intelligence that allows systems to learn from data, spot patterns (Muniandi, B. et al., 2024), and make judgment calls or predictions without the need for explicit programming. Numerous advantages are available to a wide range of sectors and industries when AI and machine learning are integrated. Increased efficiency and automation is one of the main benefits. Organizations can increase productivity and cut expenses by automating repetitive tasks, optimizing resource allocation, and streamlining workflows with the help of AI algorithms and ML models. AI-driven predictive maintenance systems, for instance, can evaluate sensor data from machinery to foresee probable malfunctions and proactively schedule maintenance, reducing downtime and optimizing operational effectiveness. Recommendations and tailored experiences across digital platforms (Swapna, H. R. et al., 2023) and services are made easier by AI integration. AI-powered recommendation systems can provide individualized content, product recommendations, and services based on user preferences and interests by examining user data and behavior patterns. This customized approach increases customer loyalty and retention while also improving user engagement and satisfaction. AI integration is used by social media, streaming, and e-commerce platforms to provide recommendations and personalized experiences that increase customer satisfaction and spur business expansion. AI integration encourages creativity and innovation by facilitating the creation of intelligent systems and applications with cutting-edge features and functionalities, in addition to automation, personalization, and analytics. AI-powered technologies are driving innovation and changing industries in a variety of fields, from medical diagnostics systems and driverless cars to smart home appliances and virtual assistants. Artificial intelligence (AI)-driven diagnostic systems, for instance, can evaluate medical imaging data to help physicians diagnose conditions and determine the best course of treatment, ultimately improving patient outcomes and cutting costs. But integrating AI is not without its difficulties and concerns, especially when it comes to security, privacy, and ethics. Concerns concerning algorithmic (Sahani, S. K. et al., 2024) bias, data privacy, and unforeseen consequences are brought up by the application of ML models and AI algorithms. As a result, businesses need to embrace moral AI concepts and procedures, guarantee accountability and transparency in AI systems, and give data security and privacy top priority (Istepanian, R. S., & Al-Anzi, T., 2018).

3.5 Enhanced Virtual Reality (VR) and Augmented Reality (AR) Capabilities

Immersive technology has advanced, changing how people interact with digital content and the real world. A wide range of technological innovations improve the realism, interactivity, and functionality of VR and AR experiences, opening up new possibilities across industries and applications. Improved VR and AR visual fidelity and realism are key. Hi-resolution screens, wide-field-of-view optics, and high refresh rates make virtual environments more realistic. These advances improve VR and AR clarity, depth, and detail, blurring the virtual and physical worlds. VR games feel more realistic and engaging with higher visual fidelity. To include motion sensing and spatial tracking innovations. These advances allow seamless interaction with virtual objects and environments by tracking user movements and interactions more precisely and responsively. Tracking hand gestures, body movements, and eye movements helps users manipulate virtual objects, navigate virtual spaces, and interact more precisely. Training simulations, architectural visualization, and virtual prototyping require realistic and intuitive virtual environment interaction, so this level of immersion and interactivity is beneficial. Audio technology advances like spatial audio and realistic sound rendering. These advances make VR and AR audio more immersive and realistic. Spatial audio simulates sound from different directions and distances, creating a more realistic audio environment. Spatial audio enhances VR immersion by matching auditory cues to visual stimuli. In VR training simulations, spatial audio can guide users' attention and improve situational awareness. It includes haptic feedback technologies that let users touch and interact with virtual objects and environments. Gloves, vests, and controllers simulate touch, texture, and force feedback. Users can interact with virtual objects more realistically and precisely with haptic feedback in VR and AR, increasing immersion and presence. In VR surgical simulations, haptic feedback devices let trainee surgeons feel tissue manipulation and instrument interaction. Advanced content creation tools and development platforms allow developers to create more engaging VR and AR experiences. These tools offer 3D modeling software, animation tools, and development frameworks to help developers create immersive and interactive content faster. Additionally, cloud-based rendering and streaming technologies enable the delivery of high-quality VR and AR content to smartphones, tablets, and VR headsets, improving accessibility and scalability.

IV. SECURITY MEASURES AND SOLUTIONS

Cyber threats threaten individuals, organizations, and governments in today's interconnected digital world, making security measures and solutions essential. Due to data breaches, ransomware attacks, and other cyber threats, strong security measures are needed to protect sensitive data, business continuity, and digital assets. Implementing strong authentication and access control is essential to security. To verify user identities and control access to sensitive systems and data, multi-factor authentication, biometric authentication, and cryptography are used. Using multiple forms of authentication reduces the risk of unauthorized access and credential-based attacks like phishing and password theft. Protection of data in transit and at rest depends on encryption. Cryptography technologies like SSL and TLS protect data from eavesdropping and interception over networks. Full-disk and file-level encryption protect data on devices and servers from unauthorized access even if the storage media is compromised. Malware, phishing, and DDoS attacks can be prevented by implementing strong network security solutions. Installing firewalls, IDPS, and antivirus software to monitor and filter network traffic, detect malicious activity, and block (David, S. et al., 2023) or mitigate threats in real time. In addition, network segmentation and least privilege access controls can reduce critical asset exposure and security breaches. To identify and fix infrastructure and application security vulnerabilities, organizations must prioritize security assessments and vulnerability management. Regular penetration testing, vulnerability scanning, and code reviews identify and fix security vulnerabilities before attackers can exploit them. Identifying and fixing security vulnerabilities can help organisations prevent data breaches and cyberattacks. Employee training and awareness programs and technical security measures. Employee education about cyber threats, security best practices, and data security can reduce human error and insider threats. Phishing simulations, incident response drills, and security awareness training can help employees recognize and respond to security threats. Proactive incident response and disaster recovery planning to address security incidents and data breaches. To minimise security incidents' impact on business operations and financial and reputational damage, incident response plans, communication protocols, and data backup and recovery procedures are needed (Istepanaian & Zhang, 2012).

V. BENEFITS OF SECURE TELEMEDICINE IN 6G

In 6G, secure telemedicine ensures the privacy, availability, and integrity of medical services in a digital setting, among many other advantages that go beyond the capabilities of earlier telecommunications technology generations. With its ultra-reliable, low-latency communication (URLLC) capabilities and cutting-edge security features, 6G, the next generation of wireless technology, promises to completely transform telemedicine. This will improve patient care, make healthcare more accessible, and protect patient privacy and confidentiality.

- *Improved Results and Patient Care*: 6G secure telemedicine uses cutting-edge technologies to transform patient care. Healthcare providers are able to perform real-time consultations, diagnostics, and treatments remotely with ultra-reliable, low-latency communication (URLLC). This allows for prompt interventions that have a substantial impact on patient outcomes. Large-scale patient data analysis is made possible by the combination of AI and ML algorithms, which enhances clinical decision-making and results in more individualized treatment regimens.
- *Enhanced Healthcare Accessibility*: 6G telemedicine not only provides excellent care but also greatly improves healthcare accessibility, especially in rural or underprivileged areas. Patients in remote or isolated areas can receive virtual consultations, remote monitoring, and specialized care without having to travel far thanks to high-speed, low-latency communication capabilities. Geographical barriers are lessened, and everyone, wherever they may be, is encouraged to have equitable access to healthcare services.
- *Privacy and security of data*: Security is still a primary concern in telemedicine, particularly with regard to patient confidentiality. For the purpose of protecting medical data both during transmission and storage, 6G networks use sophisticated encryption algorithms and safe authentication procedures. In addition, strong security protocols guarantee adherence to strict healthcare laws like HIPAA, safeguarding patient confidentiality and promoting confidence in telemedicine platforms.
- *Healthcare Innovation and Collaboration*: New technologies such as AI, ML, and AR are incorporated into healthcare delivery through the use of secure telemedicine in 6G, which stimulates innovation. In addition to enabling more precise diagnoses and prognoses, AI-powered diagnostic tools and predictive analytics enable remote surgical assistance and medical education. Collaborative platforms facilitate smooth collaboration among multidisciplinary teams, which in turn leads to better treatment outcomes and better patient care.
- *Healthcare Regulation Compliance*: To guarantee patient data security and privacy, 6G telemedicine platforms follow stringent regulatory requirements. These platforms preserve patient information and maintain regulatory compliance by putting strong security measures and compliance protocols in place to reduce the risk of data breaches and cyberattacks. In order to guarantee continued compliance with healthcare laws, continuous monitoring and auditing also assist in locating and addressing possible security vulnerabilities.
- *Robust Healthcare Infrastructure*: 6G networks' robustness guarantees telemedicine services remain accessible even in difficult situations or when there are network outages. As traditional infrastructure may be unreliable in remote or disaster-affected areas, resilience is essential for providing continuous healthcare (Singh, S. et al., 2023) services. 6G telemedicine platforms guarantee prompt medical care to patients in spite of outside circumstances by offering dependable connectivity (Kim et al., 2008).
- *Efficient Healthcare Delivery*: With 6G, secure telemedicine reduces the need for physical infrastructure and lowers patient travel expenses, providing efficient healthcare delivery options. Healthcare resource optimization, clinical workflow streamlining, and overall cost reduction are achieved through virtual consultations and remote monitoring services. Long-term patient out-

comes are improved and the strain on the healthcare system is lessened thanks to telemedicine's ability to provide early intervention and preventive care.

- *Healthcare Providers and Patients Empowerment*: By providing patients with more control over their healthcare experiences, 6G telemedicine empowers both healthcare providers and patients. Clinical outcomes can be enhanced by providers through the provision of individualized care, access to remote expertise, and improved collaboration with colleagues. Conversely, patients have the ability to actively manage their healthcare by getting timely medical advice, following up on their health remotely (Sasidevi, S. et al., 2024), and engaging in joint decision-making.
- *The scalability and adaptability*: 6G telemedicine platforms facilitate the easy integration of novel technologies and services in response to evolving healthcare requirements. Since telemedicine solutions are scalable, they can adapt to changing healthcare needs, expanding patient populations, and new technical developments. Telemedicine platforms can also accommodate a variety of use cases and applications, from remote consultations to real-time medical monitoring and diagnostics, thanks to the adaptability of 6G networks.
- *Impact and Reach Worldwide*: By addressing healthcare delivery disparities and advancing health equity globally, secure telemedicine in 6G has the potential to have a major impact on the world. 6G telemedicine has the potential to improve population health by decreasing healthcare disparities, improving health outcomes, and reaching underserved populations with healthcare services. In addition, 6G telemedicine advances global healthcare standards and practices, which eventually benefits people and communities everywhere by promoting cross-border collaboration and information exchange.

CONCLUSION

Telemedicine in 6G allows healthcare to be transformed using telecommunications and IT advances. Telemedicine, which uses remote healthcare delivery via electronic information and communications technologies, will revolutionize patient care by leveraging URLLC, mMTC, edge computing, AI, and AR/VR integration. The history and current technology of telemedicine have made 6G integration possible. The ultra-reliable, low-latency communication infrastructure of 6G allows real-time interactions between healthcare providers and patients, improving diagnosis, treatment, and monitoring. Telemedicine in 6G uses URLLC, mMTC, network slicing, and edge computing to process and analyze healthcare data in real time. Clinical decision-making is improved by AI and machine learning, and AR and VR provide immersive medical training and surgical assistance. 6G telemedicine's transformative potential, security is paramount. Protecting patient data requires data privacy, authentication, network security, and regulatory compliance. End-to-end encryption, blockchain technology, and biometric authentication are necessary to protect cybersecurity. Secure telemedicine in 6G can unlock many benefits for healthcare stakeholders. Patient outcomes, accessibility, cost-effectiveness, doctor-patient communication, and global scalability are benefits. Secure telemedicine transforms healthcare delivery and gives people access to high-quality care when and where they need it.

REFERENCES

Abdulkarim, Y. I., Awl, H. N., Muhammadsharif, F. F., Saeed, S. R., Sidiq, K. R., Khasraw, S. S., & Pandey, D. (2023). Metamaterial-based sensors loaded corona-shaped resonator for COVID-19 detection by using microwave techniques. *Plasmonics*, 1–16.

Aghdam, Z. N., Rahmani, A. M., & Hosseinzadeh, M. (2021). The role of the Internet of Things in healthcare: Future trends and challenges. *Computer Methods and Programs in Biomedicine*, 199, 105903. 10.1016/j.cmpb.2020.10590333348073

Anand, R., Khan, B., Nassa, V. K., Pandey, D., Dhabliya, D., Pandey, B. K., & Dadheech, P. (2023). Hybrid convolutional neural network (CNN) for kennedy space center hyperspectral image. *Aerospace Systems*, 6(1), 71–78. 10.1007/s42401-022-00168-4

Anand, R., Lakshmi, S. V., Pandey, D., & Pandey, B. K. (2024). An enhanced ResNet-50 deep learning model for arrhythmia detection using electrocardiogram biomedical indicators. *Evolving Systems*, 15(1), 83–97. 10.1007/s12530-023-09559-0

Bessant, Y. A., Jency, J. G., Sagayam, K. M., Jone, A. A. A., Pandey, D., & Pandey, B. K. (2023). Improved parallel matrix multiplication using Strassen and Urdhvatiryagbhyam method. *CCF Transactions on High Performance Computing*, 5(2), 102–115. 10.1007/s42514-023-00149-9

Bhuiyan, M. N., Rahman, M. M., Billah, M. M., & Saha, D. (2021). Internet of things (IoT): A review of its enabling technologies in healthcare applications, standards protocols, security, and market opportunities. *IEEE Internet of Things Journal*, 8(13), 10474–10498. 10.1109/JIOT.2021.3062630

Bruntha, P. M., Dhanasekar, S., Hepsiba, D., Sagayam, K. M., Neebha, T. M., Pandey, D., & Pandey, B. K. (2023). Application of switching median filter with L 2 norm-based auto-tuning function for removing random valued impulse noise. *Aerospace Systems, 6*(1), 53-59.

Da Fonseca, M. H., Kovaleski, F., Picinin, C. T., Pedroso, B., & Rubbo, P. (2021, September). E-health practices and technologies: a systematic review from 2014 to 2019. In *Healthcare* (Vol. 9, No. 9, p. 1192). MDPI.

David, S., Duraipandian, K., Chandrasekaran, D., Pandey, D., Sindhwani, N., & Pandey, B. K. (2023). Impact of blockchain in healthcare system. In *Unleashing the Potentials of blockchain technology for healthcare industries* (pp. 37–57). Academic Press. 10.1016/B978-0-323-99481-1.00004-3

Devasenapathy, D., Madhumathy, P., Umamaheshwari, R., Pandey, B. K., & Pandey, D. (2024). Transmission-efficient grid-based synchronized model for routing in wireless sensor networks using Bayesian compressive sensing. *SN Computer Science*, 5(1), 1–11.

Du John, H. V., Ajay, T., Reddy, G. M. K., Ganesh, M. N. S., Hembram, A., Pandey, B. K., & Pandey, D. (2023). Design and simulation of SRR-based tungsten metamaterial absorber for biomedical sensing applications. *Plasmonics*, 18(5), 1903–1912. 10.1007/s11468-023-01910-0

Du John, H. V., Jose, T., Sagayam, K. M., Pandey, B. K., & Pandey, D. (2024). Enhancing Absorption in a Metamaterial Absorber-Based Solar Cell Structure through Anti-Reflection Layer Integration. *Silicon*, 1-11.

Du John, H. V., Sagayam, K. M., Jose, T., Pandey, D., Pandey, B. K., Kotti, J., & Kaur, P. (2023). Design simulation and parametric investigation of a metamaterial light absorber with tungsten resonator for solar cell applications using silicon as dielectric layer. *Silicon*, 15(9), 4065–4079. 10.1007/s12633-023-02321-w

George, W. K., Ekong, M. O., Pandey, D., & Pandey, B. K. (2023). Pedagogy for Implementation of TVET Curriculum for the Digital World. In *Applications of Neuromarketing in the Metaverse* (pp. 117-136). IGI Global. 10.4018/978-1-6684-8150-9.ch009

George, W. K., Silas, E. I., Pandey, D., & Pandey, B. K. (2024). Utilization of Industry 4.0 Technologies in Nigerian Technical and Vocational Education: A Conundrum for Educators. In *Examining the Rapid Advance of Digital Technology in Africa* (pp. 270–293). IGI Global. 10.4018/978-1-6684-9962-7.ch014

. Govindaraj, V., Dhanasekar, S., Martinsagayam, K., Pandey, D., Pandey, B. K., & Nassa, V. K. (2023). Low-power test pattern generator using modified LFSR. *Aerospace Systems*, 1-8.

Gupta, A. K., Sharma, R., Pandey, D., Nassa, V. K., Pandey, B. K., George, A. S., & Dadheech, P. (2023). Performance analysis of eight-channel WDM optical network with different optical amplifiers for industry 4.0. In *Innovation and Competitiveness in Industry 4.0 Based on Intelligent Systems* (pp. 197–212). Springer International Publishing. 10.1007/978-3-031-29775-5_9

Istepanian, R. S., & Al-Anzi, T. (2018). m-Health 2.0: New perspectives on mobile health, machine learning and big data analytics. *Methods (San Diego, Calif.)*, 151, 34–40. 10.1016/j.ymeth.2018.05.01529890285

Iyyanar, P., Anand, R., Shanthi, T., Nassa, V. K., Pandey, B. K., George, A. S., & Pandey, D. (2023). A real-time smart sewage cleaning UAV assistance system using IoT. In *Handbook of Research on Data-Driven Mathematical Modeling in Smart Cities* (pp. 24–39). IGI Global.

JayaLakshmi, G., Pandey, D., Pandey, B. K., Kaur, P., Mahajan, D. A., & Dari, S. S. (2024). Smart Big Data Collection for Intelligent Supply Chain Improvement. In *AI and Machine Learning Impacts in Intelligent Supply Chain* (pp. 180-195). IGI Global.

Jayapoorani, S., Pandey, D., Sasirekha, N. S., Anand, R., & Pandey, B. K. (2023). Systolic optimized adaptive filter architecture designs for ECG noise cancellation by Vertex-5. *Aerospace Systems*, 6(1), 163–173. 10.1007/s42401-022-00177-3

Kashani, M. H., Madanipour, M., Nikravan, M., Asghari, P., & Mahdipour, E. (2021). A systematic review of IoT in healthcare: Applications, techniques, and trends. *Journal of Network and Computer Applications*, 192, 103164. 10.1016/j.jnca.2021.103164

Khattak, S. B. A., Nasralla, M. M., & Rehman, I. U. (2022, September). The role of 6g networks in enabling future smart health services and applications. In *2022 IEEE International Smart Cities Conference (ISC2)* (pp. 1-7). IEEE.

Kirubasri, G., Sankar, S., Pandey, D., Pandey, B. K., Singh, H., & Anand, R. (2021, September). A recent survey on 6G vehicular technology, applications and challenges. In *2021 9th International Conference on Reliability, Infocom Technologies and Optimization (Trends and Future Directions)(ICRITO)* (pp. 1-5). IEEE.

Kumar Pandey, B., Pandey, D., Nassa, V. K., Ahmad, T., Singh, C., George, A. S., & Wakchaure, M. A. (2021). Encryption and steganography-based text extraction in IoT using the EWCTS optimizer. *Imaging Science Journal*, 69(1-4), 38–56. 10.1080/13682199.2022.2146885

Muniandi, B., Nassa, V. K., Pandey, D., Pandey, B. K., Dadheech, P., & George, A. S. (2024). Pattern Analysis for Feature Extraction in Complex Images. In *Using Machine Learning to Detect Emotions and Predict Human Psychology* (pp. 145-167). IGI Global. 10.4018/979-8-3693-1910-9.ch007

Pandey, B. K., & Pandey, D. (2023). Parametric optimization and prediction of enhanced thermoelectric performance in co-doped CaMnO3 using response surface methodology and neural network. *Journal of Materials Science Materials in Electronics*, 34(21), 1589. 10.1007/s10854-023-10954-1

Pandey, B. K., Pandey, D., Alkhafaji, M. A., Güneşer, M. T., & Şeker, C. (2023). A reliable transmission and extraction of textual information using keyless encryption, steganography, and deep algorithm with cuckoo optimization. In *Micro-Electronics and Telecommunication Engineering: Proceedings of 6th ICMETE 2022* (pp. 629–636). Springer Nature Singapore. 10.1007/978-981-19-9512-5_57

Pandey, B. K., Pandey, D., & Sahani, S. K. (2024). Autopilot control unmanned aerial vehicle system for sewage defect detection using deep learning. *Engineering Reports*, 12852. 10.1002/eng2.12852

Pandey, B. K., Pandey, D., Wairya, S., & Agarwal, G. (2021a). An advanced morphological component analysis, steganography, and deep learning-based system to transmit secure textual data. *International Journal of Distributed Artificial Intelligence*, 13(2), 40–62. 10.4018/IJDAI.2021070104

Pandey, B. K., Pandey, D., Wariya, S., & Agarwal, G. (2021b). A deep neural network-based approach for extracting textual images from deteriorate images. *EAI Endorsed Transactions on Industrial Networks and Intelligent Systems*, 8(28), e3–e3. 10.4108/eai.17-9-2021.170961

Pandey, D., Pandey, B. K., & Wairya, S. (2021). Hybrid deep neural network with adaptive galactic swarm optimization for text extraction from scene images. *Soft Computing*, 25(2), 1563–1580. 10.1007/s00500-020-05245-4

Pramanik, S., Pandey, D., Joardar, S., Niranjanamurthy, M., Pandey, B. K., & Kaur, J. (2023, October). An overview of IoT privacy and security in smart cities. In *AIP Conference Proceedings* (Vol. 2495, No. 1). AIP Publishing. 10.1063/5.0123511

Raja, D., Kumar, D. R., Santhiyakumari, N., Kumarganesh, S., Sagayam, K. M., Thiyaneswaran, B., Pandey, B. K., & Pandey, D. (2024). A compact dual-feed wide-band slotted antenna for future wireless applications. *Analog Integrated Circuits and Signal Processing*, 1–15. 10.1007/s10470-023-02233-0

Sahani, K., Khadka, S. S., Sahani, S. K., Pandey, B. K., & Pandey, D. (2023). A possible underground roadway for transportation facilities in Kathmandu Valley: A racking deformation of underground rectangular structures. *Engineering Reports*, 12821. 10.1002/eng2.12821

Sahani, S. K., Pandey, B. K., & Pandey, D. (2024). *Single-valued Signals, Multi-valued Signals and Fixed-Point of Contractive Signals*. Mathematics Open. 10.1142/S2811007224500020

Sasidevi, S., Kumarganesh, S., Saranya, S., Thiyaneswaran, B., & Shree, K. V. M. (2024, May 15). Design of Surface Plasmon Resonance (SPR) Sensors for Highly Sensitive Biomolecular Detection in Cancer Diagnostics. *Plasmonics*. Advance online publication. 10.1007/s11468-024-02343-z

Saxena, A., Agarwal, A., Pandey, B. K., & Pandey, D. (2024). Examination of the Criticality of Customer Segmentation Using Unsupervised Learning Methods. *Circular Economy and Sustainability*, 1–14. 10.1007/s43615-023-00336-4

Sharma, M., Talwar, R., Pandey, D., Nassa, V. K., Pandey, B. K., & Dadheech, P. (2024). A Review of Dielectric Resonator Antennas (DRA)-Based RFID Technology for Industry 4.0. *Robotics and Automation in Industry*, 4(0), 303–324.

Sharma, S., Pandey, B. K., Pandey, D., Anand, R., Sharma, A., & Saini, S. (2023, March). Character Recognition Technique Implementation for Complicated Deteriorated Scene. In *2023 6th International Conference on Information Systems and Computer Networks (ISCON)* (pp. 1-4). IEEE. 10.1109/ISCON57294.2023.10112185

Singh, S., Madaan, G., Kaur, J., Swapna, H. R., Pandey, D., Singh, A., & Pandey, B. K. (2023). *Bibliometric Review on Healthcare Sustainability. Handbook of Research on Safe Disposal Methods of Municipal Solid Wastes for a Sustainable Environment*, 142-161. 10.4018/978-1-6684-8117-2.ch011

Smith-Bindman, R., Miglioretti, D. L., Johnson, E., Lee, C., Feigelson, H. S., Flynn, M., Greenlee, R. T., Kruger, R. L., Hornbrook, M. C., Roblin, D., Solberg, L. I., Vanneman, N., Weinmann, S., & Williams, A. E. (2012). Use of diagnostic imaging studies and associated radiation exposure for patients enrolled in large integrated health care systems, 1996-2010. *Journal of the American Medical Association*, 307(22), 2400–2409. 10.1001/jama.2012.596022692172

. Stefanova-Pavlova, M., Andonov, V., Stoyanov, T., Angelova, M., Cook, G., Klein, B., ... Stefanova, E. (2017). Modeling telehealth services with generalized nets. *Recent Contributions in Intelligent Systems*, 279-290.

Swapna, H. R., Bigirimana, E., Madaan, G., Hasan, A., Pandey, B. K., & Pandey, D. (2023). Impact of neuromarketing on consumer psychology in digitally connected networks. In *Applications of Neuromarketing in the Metaverse* (pp. 193–205). IGI Global. 10.4018/978-1-6684-8150-9.ch015

Taha, A. E. M. (2021). Quality of experience in 6G networks: Outlook and challenges. *Journal of Sensor and Actuator Networks*, 10(1), 11. 10.3390/jsan10010011

Taleb, H., Nasser, A., Andrieux, G., Charara, N., & Motta Cruz, E. (2021). Wireless technologies, medical applications and future challenges in WBAN: A survey. *Wireless Networks*, 27(8), 5271–5295. 10.1007/s11276-021-02780-2

Tripathi, R. P., Sharma, M., Gupta, A. K., Pandey, D., Pandey, B. K., Shahul, A., & George, A. H. (2023). Timely prediction of diabetes by means of machine learning practices. *Augmented Human Research*, 8(1), 1. 10.1007/s41133-023-00062-4

Chapter 19
A Recent Survey on 6G Vehicular Technology:
Applications and Challenges

Binay Kumar Pandey
https://orcid.org/0000-0002-4041-1213
Department of Information Technology, College of Technology, Govind Ballabh Pant University of Agriculture and Technology, India

Mukundan Appadurai Paramashivan
https://orcid.org/0009-0009-5608-4788
Aligarh Muslim University, India & Champions Group, India

Digvijay Pandey
https://orcid.org/0000-0003-0353-174X
Department of Technical Education, Government of Uttar Pradesh, India

A.Shaji George
https://orcid.org/0000-0002-8677-3682
Almarai Company, Riyadh, Saudi Arabia

Ashi Agarwal
Department of Computer Science, ABES Engineering College, Ghaziabad, India

Pankaj Dadheech
https://orcid.org/0000-0001-5783-1989
Swami Keshvanand Institute of Technology, Management, and Gramothan, India

Darshan A. Mahajan
https://orcid.org/0000-0002-1239-6343
NICMAR University, Pune, India

ABSTRACT

Most cars of the future might be intelligent and self-driving. 6G will be the main technology used in automobiles. An overview of 6G-enabling technologies is presented in this current study and their future application. The primary role that 6G will play in automotive technology is to accomplish this. Furthermore, a new technology called 6G wireless connection is on the rise and has the potential to completely transform automotive technology. It is anticipated that more items will be connected in the future via the new 6G technology. Therefore, it must outperform more contemporary, cutting-edge communication technologies like 5G in terms of performance. Heterogeneous object connectivity, ultra-low latency, high throughput, low power consumption, and high data reliability are the main characteristics of 6G technology. Additionally, it will use artificial intelligence to facilitate secure and intelligent communication.

DOI: 10.4018/979-8-3693-7421-4.ch019

1. INTRODUCTION

Over the years, advances in wireless communication technologies (Devasenapathy, D. et al., 2024) have been made. Fifth generation (5G) technology advances with the advent of digital technology (Swapna, H. R. et al., 2023) and requires future communication technology because it cannot meet all future requirements (Chettri, L., & Bera, R., 2019). Sixth generation (6G) (Kirubasri, G. et al., 2021) is a promising new mobile communication technology (Raja, D. et al., 2024) that could revolutionize the globe starting in 2030 and going forward. 5G has already been implemented in many nations and is causing significant economic growth (Chen, S. et al., 2020). At the moment, 6G wireless communication technology (Gupta, A. K. et al., 2023) is the focus of research. The 6G (David, K. et al., 2019) specifications are very different from the 5G ones. Therefore, 6G's features will enable a wealth of cutting-edge applications and knowledge (Khalaf, O. I., & Abdulsahib, G. M., 2021).

Specifically, 6G is a well-known innovator in the fields of commercial, healthcare, and automotive technologies. The research community, developers, and manufacturers were drawn to the emerging uses of 6G, which resulted in the publication of numerous research concepts in a variety of articles (Gui, G.et al., 2020). The main obstacles to integrating AI with 6G have been recognized, along with significant trends in 6G communications (David, K., & Berndt, H., 2018). A comprehensive overview of AI-assisted 6G communication is provided in (Raddo, T. R. et al., 2021). A number of barriers and difficulties must be overcome in order to achieve the expectations of 6G communication technology. Although the worldwide rollout of 6G is expected to occur in 2030, deploying the technology in rural and hazardous environments remains a significant problem (De Alwis, C. et al., 2021). As a result, the current 5G scenario on campus addresses the difficulties.

The Quality of Service (QoS) is currently limited by transmission technology requirements that include more than one Tbps data rate, minimum delay, and highly dependable operation. Numerous cutting-edge applications and a wide range of research topics might be imagined in response to the needs and potential of 6G communications. Thus, 6G will blossom into a global financial system, civilization, and way of life. A number of current technologies will be redefined and changed over the 6G communication era. Modernizing existing technology will bring about changes to industry, the environment, and human living. The Internet of Everything (IoE) will be the primary moniker for the internet of things (IoT) (Pandey, J. K. et al., 2022), which is now giving rise to many new technologies. The Internet of Everything (IoE) will play a major role in 6G communications, enabling wearable technology, smart cities, smart healthcare (Singh, S. et al., 2023).

6G's ultra-high density networks, compact cell networks (Bi, Q., 2019), low cost, increased spectrum efficiency, and the ability to shift heavy traffic indoors are its salient features. Low device cost, low deployment cost, high security (Pandey, B. K. et al., 2021), high privacy, high energy efficiency (Sennan, S. et al., 2021), etc. are some of its other crucial needs.

Since its inception in 1979, cellular communication has expanded globally along with advancements in communication technology. Since 1980, it has developed into a new generation of technology in each decade.

Voice calls predominate in first generation communication. During the second generation, voice calls and plain text mail applications are both feasible. Third-generation cellular communication allows for the sharing of multimedia data, including audio, images, music, and video, as well as I-mode data. Fourth-generation mobile communication is expanding thanks to sophisticated Long-Term Evolution (LTE), with a maximum transmission rate of 1 Gbps. The world is opened up by fifth generation technology, which also makes it possible for networked devices (Dhanasekar, S. et al., 2023) to communicate with one another. This generation has seen the emergence of the Internet of Things and Artificial Intelligence (Pandey, B. K., & Pandey, D., 2023), which connect devices quickly. With new technologies, multimedia communication services are launched and grow quickly. Users of 5G (Sengupta, R. et al., 2021) are benefiting greatly from mobile internet technology for a wide range of uses, such as online shopping, electronic payments, booking tickets, smart home and healthcare applications, entertainment, and multimedia applications. Following the 5G standardization process, the technology has begun to roll out globally, with the majority of 5G's city launches occurring in South Korea. The number of devices processing massive amounts of data (Deepa, R. et al., 2022) online is increasing, which raises the daily requirement for bandwidth. Applications can be served in the current decade with the available mm-wave spectrum, but in the future, it won't be enough. In order to increase spatial spectrum efficiency and provide additional frequency bands for foreseeable application requirements, the 6G concept was developed. The vision for 6G technology is shown in Figure 1.

The following are the paper's contributions:

- Important features and specifications of 6G technology;
- 6G communication supporting technologies.
- 6G vehicular technology applications;
- Research difficulties for the future and workable VT solutions.

Figure 1. 6G technology vision and requirements

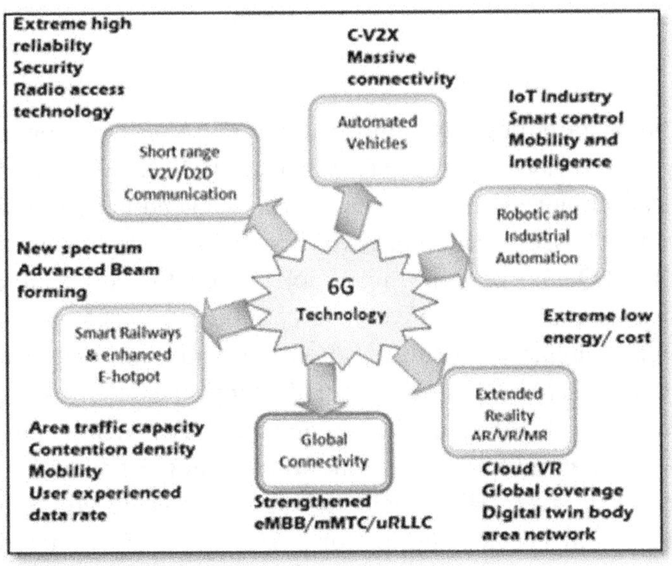

Synopsis of 6G

The objectives of intellect, economy, civilization, and industry can be changed by 6G communication technologies. 5G's primary objective is to enable high-reliability and significantly reduced latency communication. Furthermore, 6G offers services like navigation, automation, sensing, and visualization. The maintenance of self-supporting systems depends on these processes. Sixth sense communication is the core of 6G communication. Numerous nations have already begun their research initiatives, including the United States, Finland, Russia, China, and Japan. In particular, in order to achieve the data speeds that applications require, 6G will operate in Tera Hertz and at wavelength frequencies between 300μm and 100μm. The amount of study being done on potential spectrum sharing and redistribution is growing.

Paradigm Shift From Smart to Intelligent

There are currently a number of reuse strategies available, such as cognitive radio, which enables many wireless systems to share the same frequency. Temporary usage of unlicensed airwaves is possible in this spectrum sharing. The operations of 6G based wireless communication confront several obstacles, despite the introduction of a breakthrough method dubbed symbiotic radio with effective spectrum sharing for heterogeneous wireless networks and intelligent support systems (Revathi, T. K. et al., 2022). The goal of 6G is to offer true AI-driven communication technology. High levels of safety and anonymity are made possible by the 3D communication method known as time, space, and frequency. All of the smart devices utilized in VT are genuinely AI-controlled smart devices, as 6G involves the Internet of Everything. Devices using 6G applications can therefore operate intelligently through peer-to-peer communication, sensing, forecasting, and delaying.

QoS Anticipation

A minimum of 1 Tbps data throughput, ultra-massive machine-type communications, extremely dependable, low latency, long-distance, low-power (Govindaraj, V. et al., 2023), high-mobility communications, and communications are among the features that 6G technology promises to deliver in terms of QoS for 6G applications. Thus, 6G technology will be revolutionary in a number of areas. Excellent Quality of Service (QoS) and Quality of Everything (QoE) enable for user-centered communication and many online services, including telesurgery. Five sense communications, holographic communications, tactile Internet technologies, augmented reality, and virtual reality are integrated with 6G to produce promising aspects of current 6G applications. Along with many other changes, QoE will bring about the transition of smart devices, cars, drones, ambulances, and more. Excellent quality can only be achieved by utilizing 6G technology in all relevant areas. Likewise, Quality of Life (QoL) uses QoS and QoE to enhance health-conscious lifestyles. High quality of life can be achieved through mobile technology thanks to 6G technologies. Intelligent Hospital-to-Home (H2H) services, remote patient health monitors (including those for elderly patients), intelligent accident detection, and accurate medication are among the key components of QoL.

6G Enabling Technology

Internet of Everything (IoE)

The six characteristics that 6G technology aims to achieve are capture, caching, cognition, control, compute, and communication. Using digital input data (Ekong, M. O. et al., 2023), cognition aids in the formulation of useful conclusions. These are wise choices that streamline processing, and computed data is sent to intelligent devices so that device activity may be tracked (George, W. K. et al., 2023). IoE will employ the combined and enhanced eMBB and mMTC service when an alarm is triggered. In order to enable touch interactions, the 6G IoE needs include a significant capacity for connecting millions of intelligent devices at greater data speeds. The URLLC and mMTC core services have been combined and enhanced for use in Industrial IoT (IIoT) (Iyyanar, P. et al., 2023). The key issues include having excellent communication capabilities to connect sensors (Abdulkarim, Y. I. et al., 2023), actuators (Vinodhini, V. et al., 2022), and personnel, as well as low latency to enable smooth interaction between them. In order to calculate (Bessant, Y. A. et al., 2023) and analyze the data when 6G is commercially available, a supercomputer running Big Data 2.0 is required.

Table 1. 6G technology requirements

6G Key Performance Factors	Enabling Technology Requirement
Data Rate	1 Tbps
Reliability	10-9 packet error rate
Delay	0.1 ms
Traffic Capacity	1 to 10 Gbps/m2
Frequency Bands	Non-RF bands(VLC, Optical) MM-wave for mobile access Exploration of THz band
Localization Precision	1 cm on 3D
Energy Efficiency	1000 x in bps/Hz/m3
Mobility	1000 km/h
Jitter latency	10 ms
Max Channel BW	100 GHz
Connection Density	107 Devices/km
Peak Spectral Efficiency	60 b/s/ Hz

Edge Intelligence

In order to incorporate cloud functions into intelligent nodes, edge computing will be utilized in 6G. It offers sophisticated gadgets for constant, fast Internet access. Real-time data collection, computation, and analysis take place on Edge nodes. To further reduce transmission and processing costs, the edge node filters (Bruntha, P. M. et al., 2023) the data and only sends essential storage data to the cloud. Additional benefits include low latency, reliability, flexibility, scalability, and privacy (Pandey, B. K. et al., 2023). With all of these advantages, 6G is able to meet its high-quality standards. AI and Edge computers are combined into Edge Intelligence. Edge Analytics uses AI algorithms to analyze Edge devices. AI may be used by Edge devices to generate images, data, and movies. AI algorithm implementation necessitates a high processing power and limited energy consumption in the Edge Nodes. Edge intelligent devices—which compute and analyze real-time data (Jayapoorani, S. et al., 2023) will be reported by 6G. The different requirements of 6G enabling technologies are displayed in Table 1.

Artificial Intelligence

In fact, 6G is an AI network that enables the system to self-recognize, compute, and make decisions for itself in the context of AI-led communication systems. Global coverage is the primary objective of 6G, and this can be accomplished by combining AI and communication intelligence. AI helps with adaptive encryption and decoding, intelligent beam shaping, automated modulation and categorization, and channel state estimation and prediction on the physical layer of the network. In a similar vein, 6G communication technology's physical layer security (Pandey, B. K. et al., 2023) is essential.

Figure 2. Intelligent vehicular communication using 6G technology

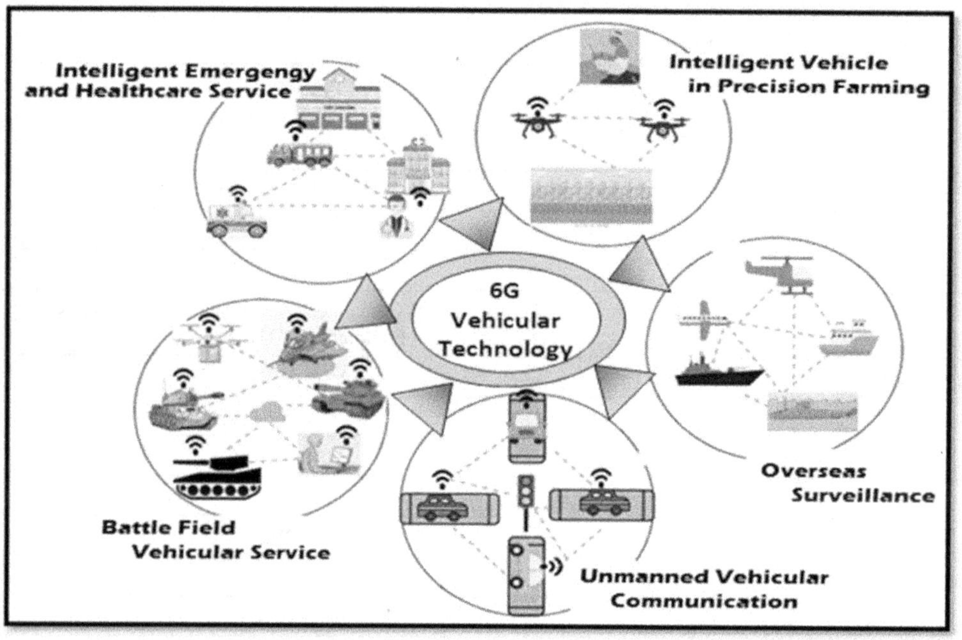

Deep reinforcement learning is improved by resource allocation at the data connection layer. At the transport level, intelligent vehicle forecast techniques and route computation are also used. 6G will explore dynamic access to spectrums and will use artificial intelligence (AI) to provide next-generation services with high computational demands.

6G on Vehicular Applications

Because of the effective real-time services offered by 6G, intelligent vehicles offer a comfortable travel from the source to the destination in terms of fuel consumption, route finding, and obstacle recognition. Artificial Intelligence (AI) (Anand, R. et al., 2024) with high-speed vehicular connectivity will be the foundation of the future car. The many application scenarios of 6G intelligent vehicular devices are shown in Figure 2.

Intelligent Transportation

The implementation of intelligent (Anand, R. et al., 2023) transportation is a difficult undertaking due of the multiple algorithms involved. Intelligent transportation activities include, but are not limited to, route planning, autonomous driving, vehicle tracking, and obstacle identification. Intelligent transportation (Saxena, A. et al., 2021) needs a high data transfer rate, dependable connectivity, and low latency to accomplish these duties. Therefore, 6G technology offers these features.

Domestic Intelligent Transportation

Throughout the journey, a sophisticated domestic transportation system (Sahani, K. et al., 2023) is linked to the 6G internet. High data transfer rates, extensive coverage, and little latency are all offered by 6G to ensure a trouble-free trip. In order to cut down on waiting time, it provides the passenger with trustworthy and up-to-date data. The motorist can benefit from this real-time information by being alert of oncoming traffic and obstructions (Sharma, S. et al., 2023). The driver can reroute the car to go to the location based on the real-time data. Security is another crucial factor. The police can utilize the camera in public transportation to identify the suspicious vehicle.

International Intelligent Transportation

The car that passes the adjacent country border can be tracked with the use of 6G. As a result, it will lower the nation's crime rate. Furthermore, the ship and aircraft are linked to the 6G-enabled Internet of Things (IoT) (Pramanik, S. et al., 2023). Real-time monitoring and prediction of natural disasters, including climate change, are made possible by IoT technology (Menon, V. et al., 2022) based on 6G. This fully automated intelligent transportation system. In the event of an emergency, the real-time monitoring will benefit the passengers by providing food, medical attention, and rescue assistance.

Table 2. 6G enabling technology communication challenges and possible solutions

6G Communication Challenges	Solutions
Superior Intelligence causes loss of privacy and Increased network complexity	• An agent is needed to function between AI algorithms and Private data.
	• Intelligent device structures are improved with advanced technology.
End-to-end security consumes bandwidth and More complex computations involved in security	• Standardizing encryption algorithms to meet out the advanced security need
	• Implement PHY security technology
	• AI algorithms should be designed with early warning security policy
Achieving Spectral Efficiency and Energy Efficiency	• Innovative route-breaking, energy-harvesting technology
	• Ubiquitous intelligent device technology
Higher Bandwidth requirement (THz)	• Innovative transceiver design with advanced features to handle transmission distance and limited power in 6G mobile environment
Optimization in protocol design for 6G 3D environment	• AI-driven protocols for signaling, scheduling, and coordination
	• Novel dynamic multiple access and handover protocols
	• Designing new authentication and identification protocols
Integration of multiple functions and Lack of prior models	• Design of 3CLS metrics and Joint 3CLS optimization
	• AI-enabled 3CL and Energy efficient 3CLS
Operating highly mobile systems and in Short range	• Effective mobility management for mmWave and THz systems
	• Coverage and range improvement

Intelligent Connected Cars

Its AI foundation allows it to drive without a steering wheel. In addition to acting as a smart ambulance to transport passengers to the closest hospital, the intelligent cars will keep an eye on their vital signs, such as blood pressure and temperature. 6G will accomplish everything. The batteries will be charged via wireless technology. Complete intelligent driving is a difficult challenge to accomplish since it combines several intricate algorithms. Numerous modules, including course planning, vehicle monitoring, automated driving, obstacle identification, etc., make up these intricate algorithms. But it requires low latency, steady connectivity, and quick data throughput.

Unmanned Aerial Vehicles

UAVs will be used in the developing areas for front- and back-haul operations. Drone to Drone (D2D) and Drone to Infrastructure (D2I) wireless connection can be established using drones. The done can be used for necessary operations in places that are inaccessible to humans in difficult circumstances. The drone can be used by the police to apprehend the thief. Furthermore, the surveillance drones are always keeping an eye on the areas where people live, spotting events like fires, accidents, etc. Drones can also be used to identify chemicals in agricultural applications.

6G Research Challenges on Vehicular Technology

Ultra-Low Latency

One of the main requirements for 6G technology in cars is this. One of the main requirements for developing the ultra-low latency support architecture is to maintain the reliability between the short latency and fast data transmission rate. In order to examine the effects of latency and reliability in 5G car networks, this paper suggested a reliability and latency join function. The Monte Carlo approach is used to derive the link between latency and reliability. The service and function slicing principles are used in this work to further improve latency and reliability. As a result, the vehicular communication's latency and dependability have improved. Table 2 outlined the 6G communication technology research difficulties and potential answers.

Ultra-low latency in vehicular communication based on reinforcement learning was proposed by (Yang, H. et al.,2019). In order to enhance learning (Saxena, A. et al., 2024) capacity and accomplish dependable and delay-aware vehicular communication in the Internet of vehicles, this work advocated the use of an Efficient Transfer Actor Critic (ETAC) learning model. When compared to previous methods, the convergence speed and stability of the vehicle network are thus improved. For 6G IoV (Zhou, F. et al., 2021). suggested DRL-based low-latency aware content delivery. This work built a Q-learning based deep reinforcement learning framework. As a result, the throughput is maximized and the vehicle latency is reduced.

Decentralization Networks

These days, decentralized networks rather than centralized ones underpin vehicular communication. Blockchain technology (David, S. et al., 2023) serves as the foundation for the decentralized network. This network, which is built on a blockchain, is still in its infancy. In order to overcome the shortcomings of the centralized network system, (Qiao, X. et al., 2020) presented an AI-driven decentralized network for vehicular communication. They also suggested a 6G-based decentralized network system for vehicular communication. A decentralized multi-agent reinforcement learning method was introduced by Pervez and Lin. To enhance vehicle performance, this work introduced the software-defined (Kirubasri, G. et al., 2022), energy-efficient vehicular edge network. The decentralized vehicle network is still being developed, though.

Trust, Privacy, and Security

Reliability, throughput, and latency were often the three key priorities of the cellular network. 5G networks use the public-key cryptography technique known as Rivest Shamir-Adleman (RSA) to maintain security. The RSA has been vulnerable in recent years as a result of the data's explosive proliferation across numerous applications. A decision-based tree-making system is developed in this study to classify the device into several groups. An extensive analysis of the application of several machine learning techniques to vehicular communication is presented in this work. AI data security based on blockchain was introduced by Li et al. Vehicle communication based on 6G. The 6G architecture was first introduced in this chapter. Afterwards, AI-enabled applications are covered, including indoor location and driverless vehicles in 6G vehicular communication. Therefore, security in the 6G-based vehicle network is still a challenge. Therefore, in order to short out the problem in the 6G based vehicular network, a novel security technique is needed.

CONCLUSION

The fundamentals of 6G wireless communication are covered first in this essay. Next, the effect of 6G communication on automotive technologies was discussed. The different enabling technologies for 6G technology are also covered. It focused mostly on the difficulties associated with integrating 6G technology into automotive applications. It is now official that 6G technology will revolutionize vehicle communication.

REFERENCES

Abdulkarim, Y. I., Awl, H. N., Muhammadsharif, F. F., Saeed, S. R., Sidiq, K. R., Khasraw, S. S., & Pandey, D. (2023). Metamaterial-based sensors loaded corona-shaped resonator for COVID-19 detection by using microwave techniques. *Plasmonics*, 1–16.

Anand, R., Khan, B., Nassa, V. K., Pandey, D., Dhabliya, D., Pandey, B. K., & Dadheech, P. (2023). Hybrid convolutional neural network (CNN) for kennedy space center hyperspectral image. *Aerospace Systems*, 6(1), 71–78. 10.1007/s42401-022-00168-4

Anand, R., Lakshmi, S. V., Pandey, D., & Pandey, B. K. (2024). An enhanced ResNet-50 deep learning model for arrhythmia detection using electrocardiogram biomedical indicators. *Evolving Systems*, 15(1), 83–97. 10.1007/s12530-023-09559-0

Bessant, Y. A., Jency, J. G., Sagayam, K. M., Jone, A. A. A., Pandey, D., & Pandey, B. K. (2023). Improved parallel matrix multiplication using Strassen and Urdhvatiryagbhyam method. *CCF Transactions on High Performance Computing*, 5(2), 102–115. 10.1007/s42514-023-00149-9

Bi, Q. (2019). Ten trends in the cellular industry and an outlook on 6G. *IEEE Communications Magazine*, 57(12), 31–36. 10.1109/MCOM.001.1900315

Bruntha, P. M., Dhanasekar, S., Hepsiba, D., Sagayam, K. M., Neebha, T. M., Pandey, D., & Pandey, B. K. (2023). Application of switching median filter with L 2 norm-based auto-tuning function for removing random valued impulse noise. *Aerospace Systems, 6*(1), 53-59.

Chen, S., Liang, Y. C., Sun, S., Kang, S., Cheng, W., & Peng, M. (2020). Vision, requirements, and technology trend of 6G: How to tackle the challenges of system coverage, capacity, user data-rate and movement speed. *IEEE Wireless Communications*, 27(2), 218–228. 10.1109/MWC.001.1900333

Chettri, L., & Bera, R. (2019). A comprehensive survey on Internet of Things (IoT) toward 5G wireless systems. *Science China. Information Sciences*, 64, 1–74.

David, K., & Berndt, H. (2018). 6G vision and requirements: Is there any need for beyond 5G? *IEEE Vehicular Technology Magazine*, 13(3), 72–80. 10.1109/MVT.2018.2848498

David, K., Elmirghani, J., Haas, H., & You, X. H. (2019). Defining 6G: Challenges and opportunities [from the guest editors]. *IEEE Vehicular Technology Magazine*, 14(3), 14–16. 10.1109/MVT.2019.2922512

David, S., Duraipandian, K., Chandrasekaran, D., Pandey, D., Sindhwani, N., & Pandey, B. K. (2023). Impact of blockchain in healthcare system. In *Unleashing the Potentials of blockchain technology for healthcare industries* (pp. 37–57). Academic Press. 10.1016/B978-0-323-99481-1.00004-3

De Alwis, C., Kalla, A., Pham, Q. V., Kumar, P., Dev, K., Hwang, W. J., & Liyanage, M. (2021). Survey on 6G frontiers: Trends, applications, requirements, technologies and future research. *IEEE Open Journal of the Communications Society*, 2, 836–886. 10.1109/OJCOMS.2021.3071496

Deepa, R., Anand, R., Pandey, D., Pandey, B. K., & Karki, B. (2022). Comprehensive performance analysis of classifiers in diagnosis of epilepsy. *Mathematical Problems in Engineering*, 2022, 2022. 10.1155/2022/1559312

Devasenapathy, D., Madhumathy, P., Umamaheshwari, R., Pandey, B. K., & Pandey, D. (2024). Transmission-efficient grid-based synchronized model for routing in wireless sensor networks using Bayesian compressive sensing. *SN Computer Science*, 5(1), 1–11.

Dhanasekar, S., Martin Sagayam, K., Pandey, B. K., & Pandey, D. (2023). Refractive Index Sensing Using Metamaterial Absorbing Augmentation in Elliptical Graphene Arrays. *Plasmonics*, 1–11. 10.1007/s11468-023-02152-w

Ekong, M. O., George, W. K., Pandey, B. K., & Pandey, D. (2023). Enhancing the Fundamentals of Industrial Safety Management in TVET for Metaverse Realities. In *Applications of Neuromarketing in the Metaverse* (pp. 19-41). IGI Global. 10.4018/978-1-6684-8150-9.ch002

George, W. K., Ekong, M. O., Pandey, D., & Pandey, B. K. (2023). Pedagogy for Implementation of TVET Curriculum for the Digital World. In *Applications of Neuromarketing in the Metaverse* (pp. 117-136). IGI Global. 10.4018/978-1-6684-8150-9.ch009

Govindaraj, V., Dhanasekar, S., Martinsagayam, K., Pandey, D., Pandey, B. K., & Nassa, V. K. (2023). Low-power test pattern generator using modified LFSR. *Aerospace Systems*, 1-8.

Gui, G., Liu, M., Tang, F., Kato, N., & Adachi, F. (2020). 6G: Opening new horizons for integration of comfort, security, and intelligence. *IEEE Wireless Communications*, 27(5), 126–132. 10.1109/MWC.001.1900516

Gupta, A. K., Sharma, R., Pandey, D., Nassa, V. K., Pandey, B. K., George, A. S., & Dadheech, P. (2023). Performance analysis of eight-channel WDM optical network with different optical amplifiers for industry 4.0. In *Innovation and Competitiveness in Industry 4.0 Based on Intelligent Systems* (pp. 197–212). Springer International Publishing. 10.1007/978-3-031-29775-5_9

Iyyanar, P., Anand, R., Shanthi, T., Nassa, V. K., Pandey, B. K., George, A. S., & Pandey, D. (2023). A real-time smart sewage cleaning UAV assistance system using IoT. In *Handbook of Research on Data-Driven Mathematical Modeling in Smart Cities* (pp. 24–39). IGI Global.

Jayapoorani, S., Pandey, D., Sasirekha, N. S., Anand, R., & Pandey, B. K. (2023). Systolic optimized adaptive filter architecture designs for ECG noise cancellation by Vertex-5. *Aerospace Systems*, 6(1), 163–173. 10.1007/s42401-022-00177-3

Khalaf, O. I., & Abdulsahib, G. M. (2021). Optimized dynamic storage of data (ODSD) in IoT based on blockchain for wireless sensor networks. *Peer-to-Peer Networking and Applications*, 14(5), 2858–2873. 10.1007/s12083-021-01115-4

Kirubasri, G., Sankar, S., Pandey, D., Pandey, B. K., Nassa, V. K., & Dadheech, P. (2022). Software-defined networking-based Ad hoc networks routing protocols. In *Software defined networking for Ad Hoc networks* (pp. 95–123). Springer International Publishing. 10.1007/978-3-030-91149-2_5

Kirubasri, G., Sankar, S., Pandey, D., Pandey, B. K., Singh, H., & Anand, R. (2021, September). A recent survey on 6G vehicular technology, applications and challenges. In *2021 9th International Conference on Reliability, Infocom Technologies and Optimization (Trends and Future Directions)(ICRITO)* (pp. 1-5). IEEE.

Menon, V., Pandey, D., Khosla, D., Kaur, M., Vashishtha, H. K., George, A. S., & Pandey, B. K. (2022). A Study on COVID–19, Its Origin, Phenomenon, Variants, and IoT-Based Framework to Detect the Presence of Coronavirus. In *IoT Based Smart Applications* (pp. 1–13). Springer International Publishing.

Pandey, B. K., & Pandey, D. (2023). Parametric optimization and prediction of enhanced thermoelectric performance in co-doped CaMnO3 using response surface methodology and neural network. *Journal of Materials Science Materials in Electronics*, 34(21), 1589. 10.1007/s10854-023-10954-1

Pandey, B. K., Pandey, D., Alkhafaji, M. A., Güneşer, M. T., & Şeker, C. (2023). A reliable transmission and extraction of textual information using keyless encryption, steganography, and deep algorithm with cuckoo optimization. In *Micro-Electronics and Telecommunication Engineering: Proceedings of 6th ICMETE 2022* (pp. 629–636). Springer Nature Singapore. 10.1007/978-981-19-9512-5_57

Pandey, B. K., Pandey, D., Gupta, A., Nassa, V. K., Dadheech, P., & George, A. S. (2023). Secret data transmission using advanced morphological component analysis and steganography. In *Role of data-intensive distributed computing systems in designing data solutions* (pp. 21–44). Springer International Publishing. 10.1007/978-3-031-15542-0_2

Pandey, B. K., Pandey, D., Wairya, S., & Agarwal, G. (2021). An advanced morphological component analysis, steganography, and deep learning-based system to transmit secure textual data. *International Journal of Distributed Artificial Intelligence*, 13(2), 40–62. 10.4018/IJDAI.2021070104

Pandey, J. K., Jain, R., Dilip, R., Kumbhkar, M., Jaiswal, S., Pandey, B. K., & Pandey, D. (2022). Investigating role of iot in the development of smart application for security enhancement. In *IoT Based Smart Applications* (pp. 219–243). Springer International Publishing.

Pramanik, S., Pandey, D., Joardar, S., Niranjanamurthy, M., Pandey, B. K., & Kaur, J. (2023, October). An overview of IoT privacy and security in smart cities. In *AIP Conference Proceedings* (Vol. 2495, No. 1). AIP Publishing. 10.1063/5.0123511

Qiao, X., Huang, Y., Dustdar, S., & Chen, J. (2020). 6G vision: An AI-driven decentralized network and service architecture. *IEEE Internet Computing*, 24(4), 33–40. 10.1109/MIC.2020.2987738

Raddo, T. R., Rommel, S., Cimoli, B., Vagionas, C., Perez-Galacho, D., Pikasis, E., Grivas, E., Ntontin, K., Katsikis, M., Kritharidis, D., Ruggeri, E., Spaleniak, I., Dubov, M., Klonidis, D., Kalfas, G., Sales, S., Pleros, N., & Tafur Monroy, I. (2021). Transition technologies towards 6G networks. *EURASIP Journal on Wireless Communications and Networking*, 2021(1), 100. 10.1186/s13638-021-01973-9

Raja, D., Kumar, D. R., Santhiyakumari, N., Kumarganesh, S., Sagayam, K. M., Thiyaneswaran, B., Pandey, B. K., & Pandey, D. (2024). A compact dual-feed wide-band slotted antenna for future wireless applications. *Analog Integrated Circuits and Signal Processing*, 118(2), 1–15. 10.1007/s10470-023-02233-0

Revathi, T. K., Sathiyabhama, B., Sankar, S., Pandey, D., Pandey, B. K., & Dadeech, P. (2022). An intelligent model for coronary heart disease diagnosis. In *Networking Technologies in Smart Healthcare* (pp. 309–327). CRC Press. 10.1201/9781003239888-15

Sahani, K., Khadka, S. S., Sahani, S. K., Pandey, B. K., & Pandey, D. (2023). A possible underground roadway for transportation facilities in Kathmandu Valley: A racking deformation of underground rectangular structures. *Engineering Reports*, 12821. 10.1002/eng2.12821

Saxena, A., Agarwal, A., Pandey, B. K., & Pandey, D. (2024). Examination of the Criticality of Customer Segmentation Using Unsupervised Learning Methods. *Circular Economy and Sustainability*, 1–14. 10.1007/s43615-023-00336-4

Saxena, A., Sharma, N. K., Pandey, D., & Pandey, B. K. (2021). Influence of tourists satisfaction on future behavioral intentions with special reference to desert triangle of Rajasthan. *Augmented Human Research*, 6(1), 13. 10.1007/s41133-021-00052-4

Sengupta, R., Sengupta, D., Pandey, D., Pandey, B. K., Nassa, V. K., & Dadeech, P. (2021). A Systematic review of 5G opportunities, architecture and challenges. *Future Trends in 5G and 6G*, 247-269.

Sennan, S., Somula, R., Luhach, A. K., Deverajan, G. G., Alnumay, W., Jhanjhi, N. Z., Ghosh, U., & Sharma, P. (2021). Energy efficient optimal parent selection based routing protocol for Internet of Things using firefly optimization algorithm. *Transactions on Emerging Telecommunications Technologies*, 32(8), e4171. 10.1002/ett.4171

Sharma, S., Pandey, B. K., Pandey, D., Anand, R., Sharma, A., & Saini, S. (2023, March). Character Recognition Technique Implementation for Complicated Deteriorated Scene. In *2023 6th International Conference on Information Systems and Computer Networks (ISCON)* (pp. 1-4). IEEE. 10.1109/ISCON57294.2023.10112185

Singh, S., Madaan, G., Kaur, J., Swapna, H. R., Pandey, D., Singh, A., & Pandey, B. K. (2023). *Bibliometric Review on Healthcare Sustainability. Handbook of Research on Safe Disposal Methods of Municipal Solid Wastes for a Sustainable Environment,* 142-161. 10.4018/978-1-6684-8117-2.ch011

Swapna, H. R., Bigirimana, E., Madaan, G., Hasan, A., Pandey, B. K., & Pandey, D. (2023). Impact of neuromarketing on consumer psychology in digitally connected networks. In *Applications of Neuromarketing in the Metaverse* (pp. 193–205). IGI Global. 10.4018/978-1-6684-8150-9.ch015

Tripathi, R. P., Sharma, M., Gupta, A. K., Pandey, D., Pandey, B. K., Shahul, A., & George, A. H. (2023). Timely prediction of diabetes by means of machine learning practices. *Augmented Human Research*, 8(1), 1. 10.1007/s41133-023-00062-4

Vinodhini, V., Kumar, M. S., Sankar, S., Pandey, D., Pandey, B. K., & Nassa, V. K. (2022). IoT-based early forest fire detection using MLP and AROC method. *International Journal of Global Warming*, 27(1), 55–70. 10.1504/IJGW.2022.122794

Yang, H., Xie, X., & Kadoch, M. (2019). Intelligent resource management based on reinforcement learning for ultra-reliable and low-latency IoV communication networks. *IEEE Transactions on Vehicular Technology*, 68(5), 4157–4169. 10.1109/TVT.2018.2890686

Zhou, F., Feng, L., Yu, P., Li, W., Que, X., & Meng, L. (2021). DRL-based low-latency content delivery for 6G massive vehicular IoT. *IEEE Internet of Things Journal*, 9(16), 14551–14562. 10.1109/JIOT.2021.3064874

Compilation of References

Abbasi, R., Martinez, P., & Ahmad, R. (2022). The digitization of agricultural industry–a systematic literature review on agriculture 4.0. *Smart Agricultural Technology*, 2, 100042. 10.1016/j.atech.2022.100042

Abdulkader, O., Bamhdi, A. M., Thayananthan, V., & Elbouraey, F. (2019, July). Ibmsdc: Intelligent blockchain based management system for protecting digital currencies transactions. In *2019 Third World Conference on Smart Trends in Systems Security and Sustainablity (WorldS4)* (pp. 363-367). IEEE.

Abdulkarim, Y. I., Awl, H. N., Muhammadsharif, F. F., Saeed, S. R., Sidiq, K. R., Khasraw, S. S., Dong, J., Pandey, B. K., & Pandey, D. (2024). Metamaterial-based sensors loaded corona-shaped resonator for COVID-19 detection by using microwave techniques. *Plasmonics*, 19(2), 595–610. 10.1007/s11468-023-02007-4

Adamopoulou, E., & Moussiades, L. (2020). Chatbots: History, technology, and applications. *Machine Learning with Applications*, 2, 100006. 10.1016/j.mlwa.2020.100006

Aghdam, Z. N., Rahmani, A. M., & Hosseinzadeh, M. (2021). The role of the Internet of Things in healthcare: Future trends and challenges. *Computer Methods and Programs in Biomedicine*, 199, 105903. 10.1016/j.cmpb.2020.10590333348073

Ahmed, M., Farooq, M. S., Ibrar-ul-Haque, M., Ahmed, M., Maqbool, H., & Yousaf, A. (2021, October). Application of blockchain in green energy for sustainable future. In *2021 International Conference on Engineering and Emerging Technologies (ICEET)* (pp. 1-6). IEEE. 10.1109/ICEET53442.2021.9659727

Akhtar, M. W., Hassan, S. A., Ghaffar, R., Jung, H., Garg, S., & Hossain, M. S. (2020). The shift to 6G communications: Vision and requirements. *Human-centric Computing and Information Sciences*, 10(1), 1–27. 10.1186/s13673-020-00258-2

Akitsu, T., Nasahara, K. N., Hirose, Y., Ijima, O., & Kume, A. (2017). Quantum sensors for accurate and stable long-term photosynthetically active radiation observations. *Agricultural and Forest Meteorology*, 237, 171–183. 10.1016/j.agrformet.2017.01.011

Ali, M., Naeem, F., Tariq, M., & Kaddoum, G. (2022). Federated learning for privacy preservation in smart healthcare systems: A comprehensive survey. *IEEE Journal of Biomedical and Health Informatics*, 27(2), 778–789. 10.1109/JBHI.2022.318182335696470

Alshammari, S. (2021). Determining the factors that affect the use of virtual classrooms: A modification of the UTAUT model. *Journal of Information Technology Education*, 20, 117–135. 10.28945/4709

Alshehri, F., & Muhammad, G. (2020). A comprehensive survey of the Internet of Things (IoT) and AI-based smart healthcare. *IEEE Access : Practical Innovations, Open Solutions*, 9, 3660–3678. 10.1109/ACCESS.2020.3047960

Amin, S. U., & Hossain, M. S. (2020). Edge intelligence and Internet of Things in healthcare: A survey. *IEEE Access : Practical Innovations, Open Solutions*, 9, 45–59. 10.1109/ACCESS.2020.3045115

Anakath, A. S., Rajakumar, S., & Ambika, S. (2019). Privacy preserving multi factor authentication using trust management. *Cluster Computing*, 22(S5, Suppl 5), 10817–10823. 10.1007/s10586-017-1181-0

Anand, R., Khan, B., Nassa, V. K., Pandey, D., Dhabliya, D., Pandey, B. K., & Dadheech, P. (2023). Hybrid convolutional neural network (CNN) for kennedy space center hyperspectral image. *Aerospace Systems*, 6(1), 71–78. 10.1007/s42401-022-00168-4

Anand, R., Lakshmi, S. V., Pandey, D., & Pandey, B. K. (2024). An enhanced ResNet-50 deep learning model for arrhythmia detection using electrocardiogram biomedical indicators. *Evolving Systems*, 15(1), 83–97. 10.1007/s12530-023-09559-0

Arksey, H., & O'malley, L. (2005). Scoping studies: Towards a methodological framework. *International Journal of Social Research Methodology*, 8(1), 19–32. 10.1080/1364557032000119616

Attaran, M. (2017). The internet of things: Limitless opportunities for business and society. *Journal of Strategic Innovation and Sustainability*, 12(1), 11.

Badotra, S., & Sundas, A. (2021). A systematic review on security of E-commerce systems. *International Journal of Applied Science and Engineering*, 18(2), 1–19.

Balaji, G. N., Nandhini, V., Mithra, S., Priya, N., & Naveena, R. (2018). IoT based smart crop monitoring in farm land. *Imperial Journal of Interdisciplinary Research*, 4(1), 88–92.

Bandara, R., Fernando, M., & Akter, S. (2020). Privacy concerns in E-commerce: A taxonomy and a future research agenda. *Electronic Markets*, 30(3), 629–647. 10.1007/s12525-019-00375-6

Baraković, S., & Skorin-Kapov, L. (2013). Survey and challenges of QoE management issues in wireless networks. *Journal of Computer Networks and Communications*, 2013, 165146. 10.1155/2013/165146

Barua, A., Al Alamin, M. A., Hossain, M. S., & Hossain, E. (2022). Security and privacy threats for bluetooth low energy in iot and wearable devices: A comprehensive survey. *IEEE Open Journal of the Communications Society*, 3, 251–281. 10.1109/OJCOMS.2022.3149732

Belkhir, L., & Elmeligi, A. (2018). Assessing ICT global emissions footprint: Trends to 2040 & recommendations. *Journal of Cleaner Production*, 177, 448–463. 10.1016/j.jclepro.2017.12.239

Bessant, Y. A., Jency, J. G., Sagayam, K. M., Jone, A. A. A., Pandey, D., & Pandey, B. K. (2023). Improved parallel matrix multiplication using Strassen and Urdhvatiryagbhyam method. *CCF Transactions on High Performance Computing*, 5(2), 102–115. 10.1007/s42514-023-00149-9

Bhatia, H., Panda, S. N., & Nagpal, D. (2020, June). Internet of things and its applications in healthcare-A survey. In *2020 8th International Conference on Reliability, Infocom Technologies and Optimization (Trends and Future Directions) (ICRITO)* (pp. 305-310). IEEE. 10.1109/ICRITO48877.2020.9197816

Bhat, S. A., & Huang, N. F. (2021). Big data and ai revolution in precision agriculture: Survey and challenges. *IEEE Access : Practical Innovations, Open Solutions*, 9, 110209–110222. 10.1109/ACCESS.2021.3102227

Bhuiyan, M. N., Rahman, M. M., Billah, M. M., & Saha, D. (2021). Internet of things (IoT): A review of its enabling technologies in healthcare applications, standards protocols, security, and market opportunities. *IEEE Internet of Things Journal*, 8(13), 10474–10498. 10.1109/JIOT.2021.3062630

Bi, Q. (2019). Ten trends in the cellular industry and an outlook on 6G. *IEEE Communications Magazine*, 57(12), 31–36. 10.1109/MCOM.001.1900315

Borenstein, J., & Howard, A. (2021). Emerging challenges in AI and the need for AI ethics education. *AI and Ethics*, 1(1), 61–65. 10.1007/s43681-020-00002-738624388

Brito, J. M. C., Mendes, L. L., & Gontijo, J. G. S. (2020, March). Brazil 6G project-an approach to build a national-wise framework for 6G networks. In *2020 2nd 6G Wireless Summit (6G SUMMIT)* (pp. 1-5). IEEE.

Bruntha, P. M., Dhanasekar, S., Hepsiba, D., Sagayam, K. M., Neebha, T. M., Pandey, D., & Pandey, B. K. (2023). Application of switching median filter with L 2 norm-based auto-tuning function for removing random valued impulse noise. *Aerospace Systems, 6*(1), 53-59.

Burns, R., Fast, V., Levenda, A., & Miller, B. (2021). Smart cities: Between worlding and provincialising. *Urban Studies (Edinburgh, Scotland)*, 58(3), 461–470. 10.1177/0042098020975982

Cao, K., Hu, S., Shi, Y., Colombo, A. W., Karnouskos, S., & Li, X. (2021). A survey on edge and edge-cloud computing assisted cyber-physical systems. *IEEE Transactions on Industrial Informatics*, 17(11), 7806–7819. 10.1109/TII.2021.3073066

Chard, R., Chard, K., Wolski, R., Madduri, R., Ng, B., Bubendorfer, K., & Foster, I. (2017). Cost-aware cloud profiling, prediction, and provisioning as a service. *IEEE Cloud Computing*, 4(4), 48–59. 10.1109/MCC.2017.3791025

Chaudhary, S., & Amphawan, A. (2014). The role and challenges of free-space optical systems. *Journal of Optical Communications*, 35(4), 327–334. 10.1515/joc-2014-0004

Chen, S., Liang, Y. C., Sun, S., Kang, S., Cheng, W., & Peng, M. (2020). Vision, requirements, and technology trend of 6G: How to tackle the challenges of system coverage, capacity, user data-rate and movement speed. *IEEE Wireless Communications*, 27(2), 218–228. 10.1109/MWC.001.1900333

Chen, Y., Wu, K., & Zhang, Q. (2014). From QoS to QoE: A tutorial on video quality assessment. *IEEE Communications Surveys and Tutorials*, 17(2), 1126–1165. 10.1109/COMST.2014.2363139

Chettri, L., & Bera, R. (2019). A comprehensive survey on Internet of Things (IoT) toward 5G wireless systems. *IEEE Internet of Things Journal*, 7(1), 16–32. 10.1109/JIOT.2019.2948888

Chettri, L., & Bera, R. (2019). A comprehensive survey on Internet of Things (IoT) toward 5G wireless systems. *Science China. Information Sciences*, 64, 1–74.

Chowdhury, M. Z., Shahjalal, M., Ahmed, S., & Jang, Y. M. (2020). 6G wireless communication systems: Applications, requirements, technologies, challenges, and research directions. *IEEE Open Journal of the Communications Society*, 1, 957–975. 10.1109/OJCOMS.2020.3010270

Cirillo, F., Gómez, D., Diez, L., Maestro, I. E., Gilbert, T. B. J., & Akhavan, R. (2020). Smart city IoT services creation through large-scale collaboration. *IEEE Internet of Things Journal*, 7(6), 5267–5275. 10.1109/JIOT.2020.2978770

Coffin, A., Bonnefoy-Claudet, C., Chassaigne, M., Jansen, A., & Gée, C. (2021). PARADe: A low-cost open-source device for photosynthetically active radiation (PAR) measurements. *Smart Agricultural Technology*, 1, 100018. 10.1016/j.atech.2021.100018

Cravero, A., & Sepúlveda, S. (2021). Use and adaptations of machine learning in big data—Applications in real cases in agriculture. *Electronics (Basel)*, 10(5), 552. 10.3390/electronics10050552

Crawford, S. E., Shugayev, R. A., Paudel, H. P., Lu, P., Syamlal, M., Ohodnicki, P. R., Chorpening, B., Gentry, R., & Duan, Y. (2021). Quantum sensing for energy applications: Review and perspective. *Advanced Quantum Technologies*, 4(8), 2100049. 10.1002/qute.202100049

Da Fonseca, M. H., Kovaleski, F., Picinin, C. T., Pedroso, B., & Rubbo, P. (2021, September). E-health practices and technologies: a systematic review from 2014 to 2019. In *Healthcare* (Vol. 9, No. 9, p. 1192). MDPI.

Dang, S., Amin, O., Shihada, B., & Alouini, M. S. (2020). What should 6G be? *Nature Electronics*, 3(1), 20–29. 10.1038/s41928-019-0355-6

Dao, N. N. (2023). Internet of wearable things: Advancements and benefits from 6G technologies. *Future Generation Computer Systems*, 138, 172–184. 10.1016/j.future.2022.07.006

David, K., & Berndt, H. (2018). 6G vision and requirements: Is there any need for beyond 5G? *IEEE Vehicular Technology Magazine*, 13(3), 72–80. 10.1109/MVT.2018.2848498

David, K., Elmirghani, J., Haas, H., & You, X. H. (2019). Defining 6G: Challenges and opportunities [from the guest editors]. *IEEE Vehicular Technology Magazine*, 14(3), 14–16. 10.1109/MVT.2019.2922512

David, S., Duraipandian, K., Chandrasekaran, D., Pandey, D., Sindhwani, N., & Pandey, B. K. (2023). Impact of blockchain in healthcare system. In *Unleashing the Potentials of blockchain technology for healthcare industries* (pp. 37–57). Academic Press. 10.1016/B978-0-323-99481-1.00004-3

De Alwis, C., Kalla, A., Pham, Q. V., Kumar, P., Dev, K., Hwang, W. J., & Liyanage, M. (2021). Survey on 6G frontiers: Trends, applications, requirements, technologies and future research. *IEEE Open Journal of the Communications Society*, 2, 836–886. 10.1109/OJCOMS.2021.3071496

De Mattos, W. D., & Gondim, P. R. (2016). m-health solutions using 5G networks and M2M communications. *IT Professional*, 18(3), 24–29. 10.1109/MITP.2016.52

Deepa, R., Anand, R., Pandey, D., Pandey, B. K., & Karki, B. (2022). Comprehensive performance analysis of classifiers in diagnosis of epilepsy. *Mathematical Problems in Engineering*, 2022, 2022. 10.1155/2022/1559312

Devasenapathy, D., Madhumathy, P., Umamaheshwari, R., Pandey, B. K., & Pandey, D. (2024). Transmission-efficient grid-based synchronized model for routing in wireless sensor networks using Bayesian compressive sensing. *SN Computer Science*, 5(1), 1–11.

Dhanasekar, S., Martin Sagayam, K., Pandey, B. K., & Pandey, D. (2023). Refractive Index Sensing Using Metamaterial Absorbing Augmentation in Elliptical Graphene Arrays. *Plasmonics*, 1–11. 10.1007/s11468-023-02152-w

Di Silvestre, M. L., Favuzza, S., Sanseverino, E. R., & Zizzo, G. (2018). How Decarbonization, Digitalization and Decentralization are changing key power infrastructures. *Renewable & Sustainable Energy Reviews*, 93, 483–498. 10.1016/j.rser.2018.05.068

Dian, F. J., Vahidnia, R., & Rahmati, A. (2020). Wearables and the Internet of Things (IoT), applications, opportunities, and challenges: A Survey. *IEEE Access : Practical Innovations, Open Solutions*, 8, 69200–69211. 10.1109/ACCESS.2020.2986329

Doughan, Z., Al Mubasher, H., El Bizri, M., & Haidar, A. (2022). The metaverse: A virtual world in the palm of your hand. *BAU Journal-Science and Technology*, 4(1), 10. 10.54729/KXRC1143

Du John, H. V., Jose, T., Sagayam, K. M., Pandey, B. K., & Pandey, D. (2024). Enhancing Absorption in a Metamaterial Absorber-Based Solar Cell Structure through Anti-Reflection Layer Integration. *Silicon*, 1-11.

Du John, H. V., Moni, D. J., Ponraj, D. N., Sagayam, K. M., Pandey, D., & Pandey, B. K. (2021). Design of Si based nano strip resonator with polarization-insensitive metamaterial (MTM) absorber on a glass substrate. *Silicon*, 1-10.

Du John, H. V., Ajay, T., Reddy, G. M. K., Ganesh, M. N. S., Hembram, A., Pandey, B. K., & Pandey, D. (2023). Design and simulation of SRR-based tungsten metamaterial absorber for biomedical sensing applications. *Plasmonics*, 18(5), 1903–1912. 10.1007/s11468-023-01910-0

Du John, H. V., Jose, T., Jone, A. A. A., Sagayam, K. M., Pandey, B. K., & Pandey, D. (2022). Polarization insensitive circular ring resonator based perfect metamaterial absorber design and simulation on a silicon substrate. *Silicon*, 14(14), 9009–9020. 10.1007/s12633-021-01645-9

Du John, H. V., Sagayam, K. M., Jose, T., Pandey, D., Pandey, B. K., Kotti, J., & Kaur, P. (2023). Design simulation and parametric investigation of a metamaterial light absorber with tungsten resonator for solar cell applications using silicon as dielectric layer. *Silicon*, 15(9), 4065–4079. 10.1007/s12633-023-02321-w

Ekong, M. O., George, W. K., Pandey, B. K., & Pandey, D. (2023). Enhancing the Fundamentals of Industrial Safety Management in TVET for Metaverse Realities. In *Applications of Neuromarketing in the Metaverse* (pp. 19-41). IGI Global. 10.4018/978-1-6684-8150-9.ch002

Elliott, D., Keen, W., & Miao, L. (2019). Recent advances in connected and automated vehicles. *Journal of Traffic and Transportation Engineering (English Edition), 6*(2), 109-131.

ElMassah, S., & Mohieldin, M. (2020). Digital transformation and localizing the sustainable development goals (SDGs). *Ecological Economics*, 169, 106490. 10.1016/j.ecolecon.2019.106490

Elmeadawy, S., & Shubair, R. M. (2019, November). 6G wireless communications: Future technologies and research challenges. In *2019 international conference on electrical and computing technologies and applications (ICECTA)* (pp. 1-5). IEEE.

Esses, D., Csete, M. S., & Németh, B. (2021). Sustainability and digital transformation in the visegrad group of central European countries. *Sustainability (Basel)*, 13(11), 5833. 10.3390/su13115833

Fayyad, U., Piatetsky-Shapiro, G., & Smyth, P. (1996). The KDD process for extracting useful knowledge from volumes of data. *Communications of the ACM*, 39(11), 27–34. 10.1145/240455.240464

Fiedler, M., Hossfeld, T., & Tran-Gia, P. (2010). A generic quantitative relationship between quality of experience and quality of service. *IEEE Network*, 24(2), 36–41. 10.1109/MNET.2010.5430142

Figueiredo e Silva, P., Kaseva, V., & Lohan, E. S. (2018). Wireless positioning in IoT: A look at current and future trends. *Sensors (Basel)*, 18(8), 2470. 10.3390/s1808247030061535

Gensch, C. O., Prakash, S., & Hilbert, I. (2017). Is digitalisation a driver for sustainability? *Sustainability in a Digital World: New Opportunities Through New Technologies*, 117-129.

George, W. K., Ekong, M. O., Pandey, D., & Pandey, B. K. (2023). Pedagogy for Implementation of TVET Curriculum for the Digital World. In *Applications of Neuromarketing in the Metaverse* (pp. 117-136). IGI Global. 10.4018/978-1-6684-8150-9.ch009

George, W. K., Silas, E. I., Pandey, D., & Pandey, B. K. (2024). Utilization of Industry 4.0 Technologies in Nigerian Technical and Vocational Education: A Conundrum for Educators. In *Examining the Rapid Advance of Digital Technology in Africa* (pp. 270–293). IGI Global. 10.4018/978-1-6684-9962-7.ch014

Ghobakhloo, M., & Fathi, M. (2021). Industry 4.0 and opportunities for energy sustainability. *Journal of Cleaner Production*, 295, 126427. 10.1016/j.jclepro.2021.126427

Giordani, M., Polese, M., Mezzavilla, M., Rangan, S., & Zorzi, M. (2020). Toward 6G networks: Use cases and technologies. *IEEE Communications Magazine*, 58(3), 55–61. 10.1109/MCOM.001.1900411

González-Calatayud, V., Prendes-Espinosa, P., & Roig-Vila, R. (2021). Artificial intelligence for student assessment: A systematic review. *Applied Sciences (Basel, Switzerland)*, 11(12), 5467. 10.3390/app11125467

Govindaraj, V., Dhanasekar, S., Martinsagayam, K., Pandey, D., Pandey, B. K., & Nassa, V. K. (2023). Low-power test pattern generator using modified LFSR. *Aerospace Systems*, 1-8.

Goyal, J., Singla, K., Akashdeep, & Singh, S. (2020). A survey of wireless communication technologies from 1G to 5G. In *Second International Conference on Computer Networks and Communication Technologies: ICCNCT 2019* (pp. 613-624). Springer International Publishing. 10.1007/978-3-030-37051-0_69

Gui, G., Liu, M., Tang, F., Kato, N., & Adachi, F. (2020). 6G: Opening new horizons for integration of comfort, security, and intelligence. *IEEE Wireless Communications*, 27(5), 126–132. 10.1109/MWC.001.1900516

Guo, F., Yu, F. R., Zhang, H., Ji, H., Liu, M., & Leung, V. C. (2019). Adaptive resource allocation in future wireless networks with blockchain and mobile edge computing. *IEEE Transactions on Wireless Communications*, 19(3), 1689–1703. 10.1109/TWC.2019.2956519

Gupta, A. K., Sharma, R., Pandey, D., Nassa, V. K., Pandey, B. K., George, A. S., & Dadheech, P. (2023). Performance analysis of eight-channel WDM optical network with different optical amplifiers for industry 4.0. In *Innovation and Competitiveness in Industry 4.0 Based on Intelligent Systems* (pp. 197–212). Springer International Publishing. 10.1007/978-3-031-29775-5_9

Habibzadeh, H., Dinesh, K., Shishvan, O. R., Boggio-Dandry, A., Sharma, G., & Soyata, T. (2019). A survey of healthcare Internet of Things (HIoT): A clinical perspective. *IEEE Internet of Things Journal*, 7(1), 53–71. 10.1109/JIOT.2019.294635933748312

Han, C., Wu, Y., Chen, Z., & Wang, X. (2019). Terahertz communications (TeraCom): Challenges and impact on 6G wireless systems. arXiv preprint arXiv:1912.06040.

Haneklaus, S., Lilienthal, H., & Schnug, E. (2016, July). 25 years Precision Agriculture in Germany–a retrospective. In *13th International Conference on Precision Agriculture*, St. Louis, MO.

Hassija, V., Chamola, V., Gupta, V., Jain, S., & Guizani, N. (2020). A survey on supply chain security: Application areas, security threats, and solution architectures. *IEEE Internet of Things Journal*, 8(8), 6222–6246. 10.1109/JIOT.2020.3025775

Henrique, P. S. R., & Prasad, R. (2020). The Road for 6G Multimedia Applications. *Proceedings of the 2020 23rd International Symposium on Wireless Personal Multimedia Communications (WPMC)*, 1–6.

Holland, J., Kingston, L., McCarthy, C., Armstrong, E., O'Dwyer, P., Merz, F., & McConnell, M. (2021). Service robots in the healthcare sector. *Robotics (Basel, Switzerland)*, 10(1), 47. 10.3390/robotics10010047

Hongmei, Z. (2021). A cross-border e-commerce approach based on blockchain technology. *Mobile Information Systems*, 2021, 1–10. 10.1155/2021/2006082

Hong, T., Lv, M., Zheng, S., & Hong, H. (2021). Key technologies in 6G SAGS IoT: Shape-adaptive antenna and radar-communication integration. *IEEE Network*, 35(5), 150–157. 10.1109/MNET.001.2100148

Hong, W., Jiang, Z. H., Yu, C., Hou, D., Wang, H., Guo, C., Hu, Y., Kuai, L., Yu, Y., Jiang, Z., Chen, Z., Chen, J., Yu, Z., Zhai, J., Zhang, N., Tian, L., Wu, F., Yang, G., Hao, Z.-C., & Zhou, J. Y. (2021). The role of millimeter-wave technologies in 5G/6G wireless communications. *IEEE Journal of Microwaves*, 1(1), 101–122. 10.1109/JMW.2020.3035541

Huang, K., Shu, L., Li, K., Yang, F., Han, G., Wang, X., & Pearson, S. (2020). Photovoltaic agricultural internet of things towards realizing the next generation of smart farming. *IEEE Access : Practical Innovations, Open Solutions*, 8, 76300–76312. 10.1109/ACCESS.2020.2988663

Hundal, G. S., Laux, C. M., Buckmaster, D., Sutton, M. J., & Langemeier, M. (2023). Exploring barriers to the adoption of internet of things-based precision agriculture practices. *Agriculture*, 13(1), 163. 10.3390/agriculture13010163

Hwang, G. J., & Chang, C. Y. (2023). A review of opportunities and challenges of chatbots in education. *Interactive Learning Environments*, 31(7), 4099–4112. 10.1080/10494820.2021.1952615

Imoize, A. L., Adedeji, O., Tandiya, N., & Shetty, S. (2021). 6G enabled smart infrastructure for sustainable society: Opportunities, challenges, and research roadmap. *Sensors (Basel)*, 21(5), 1709. 10.3390/s2105170933801302

Imran, M., Liu, X., Wang, R., Saud, S., Zhao, Y., & Khan, M. J. (2022). The influence of digital economy and society index on sustainable development indicators: The case of European union. *Sustainability (Basel)*, 14(18), 11130. 10.3390/su141811130

Ismail, L., & Materwala, H. (2021). IoT-edge-cloud computing framework for QoS-aware computation offloading in autonomous mobile agents: modeling and simulation. In *Mobile, Secure, and Programmable Networking: 6th International Conference, MSPN 2020, Paris, France, October 28–29, 2020, Revised Selected Papers 6* (pp. 161-176). Springer International Publishing. 10.1007/978-3-030-67550-9_11

Ismail, L., & Materwala, H. (2019). A review of blockchain architecture and consensus protocols: Use cases, challenges, and solutions. *Symmetry*, 11(10), 1198. 10.3390/sym11101198

Ismanto, L., Ar, H. S., Fajar, A. N., & Bachtiar, S. (2019, July). Blockchain as E-commerce platform in Indonesia. *Journal of Physics: Conference Series*, 1179(1), 012114. 10.1088/1742-6596/1179/1/012114

Istepanian, R. S., & Al-Anzi, T. (2018). m-Health 2.0: New perspectives on mobile health, machine learning and big data analytics. *Methods (San Diego, Calif.)*, 151, 34–40. 10.1016/j.ymeth.2018.05.01529890285

Iyyanar, P., Anand, R., Shanthi, T., Nassa, V. K., Pandey, B. K., George, A. S., & Pandey, D. (2023). A real-time smart sewage cleaning UAV assistance system using IoT. In *Handbook of Research on Data-Driven Mathematical Modeling in Smart Cities* (pp. 24–39). IGI Global.

JayaLakshmi, G., Pandey, D., Pandey, B. K., Kaur, P., Mahajan, D. A., & Dari, S. S. (2024). Smart Big Data Collection for Intelligent Supply Chain Improvement. In *AI and Machine Learning Impacts in Intelligent Supply Chain* (pp. 180-195). IGI Global.

Jayapoorani, S., Pandey, D., Sasirekha, N. S., Anand, R., & Pandey, B. K. (2023). Systolic optimized adaptive filter architecture designs for ECG noise cancellation by Vertex-5. *Aerospace Systems*, 6(1), 163–173. 10.1007/s42401-022-00177-3

Ji, B., Han, Y., Liu, S., Tao, F., Zhang, G., Fu, Z., & Li, C. (2021). Several key technologies for 6G: Challenges and opportunities. *IEEE Communications Standards Magazine*, 5(2), 44–51. 10.1109/MCOMSTD.001.2000038

Jolfaei, A. A., Aghili, S. F., & Singelee, D. (2021). A survey on blockchain-based IoMT systems: Towards scalability. *IEEE Access : Practical Innovations, Open Solutions*, 9, 148948–148975. 10.1109/ACCESS.2021.3117662

Karnouskos, S., & De Holanda, T. N. (2009, November). Simulation of a smart grid city with software agents. In *2009 Third UKSim European Symposium on Computer Modeling and Simulation* (pp. 424-429). IEEE. 10.1109/EMS.2009.53

Kashani, M. H., Madanipour, M., Nikravan, M., Asghari, P., & Mahdipour, E. (2021). A systematic review of IoT in healthcare: Applications, techniques, and trends. *Journal of Network and Computer Applications*, 192, 103164. 10.1016/j.jnca.2021.103164

Kato, N., Mao, B., Tang, F., Kawamoto, Y., & Liu, J. (2020). Ten challenges in advancing machine learning technologies toward 6G. *IEEE Wireless Communications*, 27(3), 96–103. 10.1109/MWC.001.1900476

Katz, M., Matinmikko-Blue, M., & Latva-Aho, M. (2018, November). 6Genesis flagship program: Building the bridges towards 6G-enabled wireless smart society and ecosystem. In *2018 IEEE 10th Latin-American Conference on Communications (LATINCOM)* (pp. 1-9). IEEE.

Khalaf, O. I., & Abdulsahib, G. M. (2021). Optimized dynamic storage of data (ODSD) in IoT based on blockchain for wireless sensor networks. *Peer-to-Peer Networking and Applications*, 14(5), 2858–2873. 10.1007/s12083-021-01115-4

Khan, B., Hasan, A., Pandey, D., Ventayen, R. J. M., Pandey, B. K., & Gowwrii, G. (2021). Fusion of datamining and artificial intelligence in prediction of hazardous road accidents. In *Machine learning and iot for intelligent systems and smart applications* (pp. 201–223). CRC Press. 10.1201/9781003194415-12

Khan, R., Kumar, P., Jayakody, D. N. K., & Liyanage, M. (2019). A survey on security and privacy of 5G technologies: Potential solutions, recent advancements, and future directions. *IEEE Communications Surveys and Tutorials*, 22(1), 196–248. 10.1109/COMST.2019.2933899

Khan, W. Z., Rehman, M. H., Zangoti, H. M., Afzal, M. K., Armi, N., & Salah, K. (2020). Industrial internet of things: Recent advances, enabling technologies and open challenges. *Computers & Electrical Engineering*, 81, 106522. 10.1016/j.compeleceng.2019.106522

Khattak, S. B. A., Nasralla, M. M., & Rehman, I. U. (2022, September). The role of 6g networks in enabling future smart health services and applications. In *2022 IEEE International Smart Cities Conference (ISC2)* (pp. 1-7). IEEE.

Kirilenko, A. A., & Lo, A. W. (2013). Moore's law versus murphy's law: Algorithmic trading and its discontents. *The Journal of Economic Perspectives*, 27(2), 51–72. 10.1257/jep.27.2.51

Kirubasri, G., Sankar, S., Pandey, D., Pandey, B. K., Singh, H., & Anand, R. (2021, September). A recent survey on 6G vehicular technology, applications and challenges. In *2021 9th International Conference on Reliability, Infocom Technologies and Optimization (Trends and Future Directions)(ICRITO)* (pp. 1-5). IEEE.

Kirubasri, G., Sankar, S., Pandey, D., Pandey, B. K., Nassa, V. K., & Dadheech, P. (2022). Software-defined networking-based Ad hoc networks routing protocols. In *Software defined networking for Ad Hoc networks* (pp. 95–123). Springer International Publishing. 10.1007/978-3-030-91149-2_5

Kumar Pandey, B., Pandey, D., Nassa, V. K., Ahmad, T., Singh, C., George, A. S., & Wakchaure, M. A. (2021). Encryption and steganography-based text extraction in IoT using the EWCTS optimizer. *Imaging Science Journal*, 69(1-4), 38–56. 10.1080/13682199.2022.2146885

KVM, S., Pandey, B. K., & Pandey, D. (2024). Design of Surface Plasmon Resonance (SPR) Sensors for Highly Sensitive Biomolecular Detection in Cancer Diagnostics. *Plasmonics*, 1-13.

Kychkin, A., Deryabin, A., Neganova, E., & Markvirer, V. (2019, July). IoT-based energy management assistant architecture design. In *2019 IEEE 21st Conference on Business Informatics (CBI)* (Vol. 1, pp. 522-530). IEEE. 10.1109/CBI.2019.00067

Lacerda, L. N., Snider, J. L., Cohen, Y., Liakos, V., Gobbo, S., & Vellidis, G. (2022). Using UAV-based thermal imagery to detect crop water status variability in cotton. *Smart Agricultural Technology*, 2, 100029. 10.1016/j.atech.2021.100029

Laubenbacher, R., Sluka, J. P., & Glazier, J. A. (2021). Using digital twins in viral infection. *Science*, 371(6534), 1105–1106. 10.1126/science.abf337033707255

Lee, B. H., & Park, S. H. (2021). *A study on the NCS based curriculum for educating Technical Director for VFX industry with Artificial Intelligence*. Cartoon and Animation Studies.

Letaief, K. B., Chen, W., Shi, Y., Zhang, J., & Zhang, Y. J. A. (2019). The roadmap to 6G: AI empowered wireless networks. *IEEE Communications Magazine*, 57(8), 84–90. 10.1109/MCOM.2019.1900271

Liu, H., Tai, Y., Lin, H., & Du, X. (2022, January). Analysis of technology hotspots in artificial intelligence field based on Patent Map. In *2022 International Seminar on Computer Science and Engineering Technology (SCSET)* (pp. 141-144). IEEE. 10.1109/SCSET55041.2022.00041

Liu, Y., Ma, X., Shu, L., Hancke, G. P., & Abu-Mahfouz, A. M. (2020). From industry 4.0 to agriculture 4.0: Current status, enabling technologies, and research challenges. *IEEE Transactions on Industrial Informatics*, 17(6), 4322–4334. 10.1109/TII.2020.3003910

Liu, Y., Wei, X., Xiao, J., Liu, Z., Xu, Y., & Tian, Y. (2020). Energy consumption and emission mitigation prediction based on data center traffic and PUE for global data centers. *Global Energy Interconnection*, 3(3), 272–282. 10.1016/j.gloei.2020.07.008

Li, Y., Yu, Y., Susilo, W., Hong, Z., & Guizani, M. (2021). Security and privacy for edge intelligence in 5G and beyond networks: Challenges and solutions. *IEEE Wireless Communications*, 28(2), 63–69. 10.1109/MWC.001.2000318

Lopes, D., Coelho, L., & Silva, M. F. (2023). Development of a collaborative robotic platform for autonomous auscultation. *Applied Sciences (Basel, Switzerland)*, 13(3), 1604. 10.3390/app13031604

Luo, X., & Xie, L. (2018, January). Research on artificial intelligence-based sharing education in the era of Internet+. In *2018 International conference on intelligent transportation, big data & smart city (ICITBS)* (pp. 335-338). IEEE.

Malamas, V., Chantzis, F., Dasaklis, T. K., Stergiopoulos, G., Kotzanikolaou, P., & Douligeris, C. (2021). Risk assessment methodologies for the internet of medical things: A survey and comparative appraisal. *IEEE Access : Practical Innovations, Open Solutions*, 9, 40049–40075. 10.1109/ACCESS.2021.3064682

Malhotra, P., Pandey, D., Pandey, B. K., & Patra, P. M. (2021). Managing agricultural supply chains in COVID-19 lockdown. *International Journal of Quality and Innovation*, 5(2), 109–118. 10.1504/IJQI.2021.117181

Ma, M., Liu, J., Liu, M., Zeng, J., & Li, Y. (2021). Tree species classification based on sentinel-2 imagery and random forest classifier in the eastern regions of the Qilian mountains. *Forests*, 12(12), 1736. 10.3390/f12121736

Materwala, H., Ismail, L., Shubair, R. M., & Buyya, R. (2022). Energy-SLA-aware genetic algorithm for edge–cloud integrated computation offloading in vehicular networks. *Future Generation Computer Systems*, 135, 205–222. 10.1016/j.future.2022.04.009

Matthess, M., & Kunkel, S. (2020). Structural change and digitalization in developing countries: Conceptually linking the two transformations. *Technology in Society*, 63, 101428. 10.1016/j.techsoc.2020.101428

Meneghello, F., Calore, M., Zucchetto, D., Polese, M., & Zanella, A. (2019). IoT: Internet of threats? A survey of practical security vulnerabilities in real IoT devices. *IEEE Internet of Things Journal*, 6(5), 8182–8201. 10.1109/JIOT.2019.2935189

Menon, V., Pandey, D., Khosla, D., Kaur, M., Vashishtha, H. K., George, A. S., & Pandey, B. K. (2022). A Study on COVID–19, Its Origin, Phenomenon, Variants, and IoT-Based Framework to Detect the Presence of Coronavirus. In *IoT Based Smart Applications* (pp. 1–13). Springer International Publishing.

Mohamed-Iliasse, M., Loubna, B., & Abdelaziz, B. (2020, October). Is machine learning revolutionizing supply chain? In *2020 5th International Conference on Logistics Operations Management (GOL)* (pp. 1-10). IEEE.

Mohapatra, D., & Subudhi, B. (2022). Development of a cost-effective IoT-based weather monitoring system. *IEEE Consumer Electronics Magazine*, 11(5), 81–86. 10.1109/MCE.2021.3136833

Monteiro, A., Santos, S., & Gonçalves, P. (2021). Precision agriculture for crop and livestock farming—Brief review. *Animals (Basel)*, 11(8), 2345. 10.3390/ani1108234534438802

Mourtzis, D., Angelopoulos, J., & Panopoulos, N. (2021). A collaborative approach on energy-based offered services: Energy 4.0 ecosystems. *Procedia CIRP*, 104, 1638–1643. 10.1016/j.procir.2021.11.276

Muniandi, B., Nassa, V. K., Pandey, D., Pandey, B. K., Dadheech, P., & George, A. S. (2024). Pattern Analysis for Feature Extraction in Complex Images. In *Using Machine Learning to Detect Emotions and Predict Human Psychology* (pp. 145-167). IGI Global. 10.4018/979-8-3693-1910-9.ch007

Munn, Z., Peters, M. D., Stern, C., Tufanaru, C., McArthur, A., & Aromataris, E. (2018). Systematic review or scoping review? Guidance for authors when choosing between a systematic or scoping review approach. *BMC Medical Research Methodology*, 18(1), 1–7. 10.1186/s12874-018-0611-x30453902

Muñoz-Saavedra, L., Miró-Amarante, L., & Domínguez-Morales, M. (2020). Augmented and virtual reality evolution and future tendency. *Applied Sciences (Basel, Switzerland)*, 10(1), 322. 10.3390/app10010322

Mutichiro, B., Tran, M. N., & Kim, Y. H. (2021). QoS-based service-time scheduling in the IoT-edge cloud. *Sensors (Basel)*, 21(17), 5797. 10.3390/s2117579734502688

Naqvi, S. M. Z. A., Saleem, S. R., Tahir, M. N., Li, S., Hussain, S., Ul Haq, S. I., & Awais, M. (2022). Role of 5G and 6G Technology in Precision Agriculture. *Environmental Sciences Proceedings*, 23(1), 3.

Nayak, S., & Patgiri, R. (2020). 6G communication: Envisioning the key issues and challenges. arXiv preprint arXiv:2004.04024.

Nguyen, D. C., Ding, M., Pathirana, P. N., Seneviratne, A., Li, J., Niyato, D., Dobre, O., & Poor, H. V. (2021). 6G internet of things: A comprehensive survey. *IEEE Internet of Things Journal*, 9(1), 359–383. 10.1109/JIOT.2021.3103320

Nicolescu, L., & Tudorache, M. T. (2022). Human-computer interaction in customer service: The experience with AI chatbots—a systematic literature review. *Electronics (Basel)*, 11(10), 1579. 10.3390/electronics11101579

Okonkwo, C. W., & Ade-Ibijola, A. (2021). Chatbots applications in education: A systematic review. *Computers and Education: Artificial Intelligence*, 2, 100033. 10.1016/j.caeai.2021.100033

Osita, G. C., Chisom, C. D., Okoronkwo, M. C., Esther, U. N., & Vanessa, N. C. (2022). Application of Emerging Technologies in Mitigation of e-Commerce Security Challenges. *CCU J. Sci*, 2, 2734–3766.

Palattella, M. R., Dohler, M., Grieco, A., Rizzo, G., Torsner, J., Engel, T., & Ladid, L. (2016). Internet of things in the 5G era: Enablers, architecture, and business models. *IEEE Journal on Selected Areas in Communications*, 34(3), 510–527. 10.1109/JSAC.2016.2525418

Pandey, B. K., Pandey, D., Wairya, S., Agarwal, G., Dadeech, P., Dogiwal, S. R., & Pramanik, S. (2022b). Application of integrated steganography and image compressing techniques for confidential information transmission. *Cyber Security and Network Security*, 169-191.

Pandey, D., Ogunmola, G. A., Enbeyle, W., Abdullahi, M., Pandey, B. K., & Pramanik, S. (2021b). COVID-19: A framework for effective delivering of online classes during lockdown. *Human Arenas*, 1-15.

Pandey, B. K., & Pandey, D. (2023). Parametric optimization and prediction of enhanced thermoelectric performance in co-doped CaMnO3 using response surface methodology and neural network. *Journal of Materials Science Materials in Electronics*, 34(21), 1589. 10.1007/s10854-023-10954-1

Pandey, B. K., Pandey, D., & Agarwal, A. (2022). Encrypted information transmission by enhanced steganography and image transformation. *International Journal of Distributed Artificial Intelligence*, 14(1), 1–14. 10.4018/IJDAI.297110

Pandey, B. K., Pandey, D., Alkhafaji, M. A., Güneşer, M. T., & Şeker, C. (2023a). A reliable transmission and extraction of textual information using keyless encryption, steganography, and deep algorithm with cuckoo optimization. In *Micro-Electronics and Telecommunication Engineering: Proceedings of 6th ICMETE 2022* (pp. 629–636). Springer Nature Singapore. 10.1007/978-981-19-9512-5_57

Pandey, B. K., Pandey, D., Dadheech, P., Mahajan, D. A., George, A. S., & Hameed, A. S. (2023b). Review on Smart Sewage Cleaning UAV Assistance for Sustainable Development. In *Handbook of Research on Safe Disposal Methods of Municipal Solid Wastes for a Sustainable Environment* (pp. 69–79). IGI Global. 10.4018/978-1-6684-8117-2.ch005

Pandey, B. K., Pandey, D., Gupta, A., Nassa, V. K., Dadheech, P., & George, A. S. (2023b). Secret data transmission using advanced morphological component analysis and steganography. In *Role of data-intensive distributed computing systems in designing data solutions* (pp. 21–44). Springer International Publishing. 10.1007/978-3-031-15542-0_2

Pandey, B. K., Pandey, D., & Sahani, S. K. (2024). Autopilot control unmanned aerial vehicle system for sewage defect detection using deep learning. *Engineering Reports*, 12852. 10.1002/eng2.12852

Pandey, B. K., Pandey, D., Wairya, S., & Agarwal, G. (2021a). An advanced morphological component analysis, steganography, and deep learning-based system to transmit secure textual data. *International Journal of Distributed Artificial Intelligence*, 13(2), 40–62. 10.4018/IJDAI.2021070104

Pandey, B. K., Pandey, D., Wariya, S., & Agarwal, G. (2021b). A deep neural network-based approach for extracting textual images from deteriorate images. *EAI Endorsed Transactions on Industrial Networks and Intelligent Systems*, 8(28), e3–e3. 10.4108/eai.17-9-2021.170961

Pandey, B. K., Pandey, S. K., & Pandey, D. (2011). A survey of bioinformatics applications on parallel architectures. *International Journal of Computer Applications*, 23(4), 21–25. 10.5120/2877-3744

Pandey, D., Hasan, A., Pandey, B. K., Lelisho, M. E., George, A. H., & Shahul, A. (2023). COVID-19 epidemic anxiety, mental stress, and sleep disorders in developing country university students. *CSI Transactions on ICT*, 11(2), 119–127. 10.1007/s40012-023-00383-0

Pandey, D., Nassa, V. K., Jhamb, A., Mahto, D., Pandey, B. K., George, A. H., & Bandyopadhyay, S. K. (2021a). An integration of keyless encryption, steganography, and artificial intelligence for the secure transmission of stego images. In *Multidisciplinary approach to modern digital steganography* (pp. 211–234). IGI Global. 10.4018/978-1-7998-7160-6.ch010

Pandey, D., & Pandey, B. K. (2022). An efficient deep neural network with adaptive galactic swarm optimization for complex image text extraction. In *Process mining techniques for pattern recognition* (pp. 121–137). CRC Press. 10.1201/9781003169550-10

Pandey, D., Pandey, B. K., & Wairya, S. (2021). Hybrid deep neural network with adaptive galactic swarm optimization for text extraction from scene images. *Soft Computing*, 25(2), 1563–1580. 10.1007/s00500-020-05245-4

Pandey, D., Wairya, S., Sharma, M., Gupta, A. K., Kakkar, R., & Pandey, B. K. (2022). An approach for object tracking, categorization, and autopilot guidance for passive homing missiles. *Aerospace Systems*, 5(4), 553–566. 10.1007/s42401-022-00150-0

Patle, K. S., Saini, R., Kumar, A., & Palaparthy, V. S. (2021). Field evaluation of smart sensor system for plant disease prediction using LSTM network. *IEEE Sensors Journal*, 22(4), 3715–3725. 10.1109/JSEN.2021.3139988

Pesek, I., Nosović, N., & Krašna, M. (2022, June). The Role of AI in the Education and for the Education. In *2022 11th Mediterranean Conference on Embedded Computing (MECO)* (pp. 1-4). IEEE. 10.1109/MECO55406.2022.9797189

Pollock, D., Tricco, A. C., Peters, M. D., Mclnerney, P. A., Khalil, H., Godfrey, C. M., Alexander, L. A., & Munn, Z. (2022). Methodological quality, guidance, and tools in scoping reviews: A scoping review protocol. *JBI Evidence Synthesis*, 20(4), 1098–1105. 10.11124/JBIES-20-0057034446668

Polymeni, S., Skoutas, D. N., Kormentzas, G., & Skianis, C. (2022). Findeas: A fintech-based approach on designing and assessing iot systems. *IEEE Internet of Things Journal*, 9(24), 25196–25206. 10.1109/JIOT.2022.3195770

Pouri, M. J., & Hilty, L. M. (2021). The digital sharing economy: A confluence of technical and social sharing. *Environmental Innovation and Societal Transitions*, 38, 127–139. 10.1016/j.eist.2020.12.003

Pramanik, S., Pandey, D., Joardar, S., Niranjanamurthy, M., Pandey, B. K., & Kaur, J. (2023, October). An overview of IoT privacy and security in smart cities. In *AIP Conference Proceedings* (Vol. 2495, No. 1). AIP Publishing 10.1063/5.0123511

Qadir, Z., Le, K. N., Saeed, N., & Munawar, H. S. (2023). Towards 6G Internet of Things: Recent advances, use cases, and open challenges. *ICT Express, 9*(3), 296-312.

Qadri, Y. A., Nauman, A., Zikria, Y. B., Vasilakos, A. V., & Kim, S. W. (2020). The future of healthcare internet of things: A survey of emerging technologies. *IEEE Communications Surveys and Tutorials*, 22(2), 1121–1167. 10.1109/COMST.2020.2973314

Qamar, F., Hindia, M. N., Abbas, T., Dimyati, K. B., & Amiri, I. S. (2019). Investigation of QoS performance evaluation over 5G network for indoor environment at millimeter wave bands. *International Journal of Electronics and Telecommunications*, 65(1), 95–101. 10.24425/ijet.2019.126288

Qiao, X., Huang, Y., Dustdar, S., & Chen, J. (2020). 6G vision: An AI-driven decentralized network and service architecture. *IEEE Internet Computing*, 24(4), 33–40. 10.1109/MIC.2020.2987738

Raddo, T. R., Rommel, S., Cimoli, B., Vagionas, C., Perez-Galacho, D., Pikasis, E., Grivas, E., Ntontin, K., Katsikis, M., Kritharidis, D., Ruggeri, E., Spaleniak, I., Dubov, M., Klonidis, D., Kalfas, G., Sales, S., Pleros, N., & Tafur Monroy, I. (2021). Transition technologies towards 6G networks. *EURASIP Journal on Wireless Communications and Networking*, 2021(1), 100. 10.1186/s13638-021-01973-9

Ragazou, K., Garefalakis, A., Zafeiriou, E., & Passas, I. (2022). Agriculture 5.0: A new strategic management mode for a cut cost and an energy efficient agriculture sector. *Energies*, 15(9), 3113. 10.3390/en15093113

Rahman, I., Razavi, S. M., Liberg, O., Hoymann, C., Wiemann, H., Tidestav, C., Schliwa-Bertling, P., Persson, P., & Gerstenberger, D. (2021). 5G evolution toward 5G advanced: An overview of 3GPP releases 17 and 18. *Ericsson Technology Review*, 2021(14), 2–12. 10.23919/ETR.2021.9904665

Rahman, M. (2023). Prevention of E-Commerce Fraud in Bangladesh: A Critical Study on Legal and Institutional Framework. Available at *SSRN* 4477507. 10.2139/ssrn.4477507

Raja, D., Kumar, D. R., Santhiyakumari, N., Kumarganesh, S., Sagayam, K. M., Thiyaneswaran, B., Pandey, B. K., & Pandey, D. (2024). A compact dual-feed wide-band slotted antenna for future wireless applications. *Analog Integrated Circuits and Signal Processing*, 1–15. 10.1007/s10470-023-02233-0

Rani, S., Bhambri, P., & Kataria, A. (2023). Integration of IoT, Big Data, and Cloud Computing Technologies: Trend of the Era. In *Big Data, Cloud Computing and IoT* (pp. 1-21). Chapman and Hall/CRC.

Rappaport, T. S., Xing, Y., Kanhere, O., Ju, S., Madanayake, A., Mandal, S., Alkhateeb, A., & Trichopoulos, G. C. (2019). Wireless communications and applications above 100 GHz: Opportunities and challenges for 6G and beyond. *IEEE Access : Practical Innovations, Open Solutions*, 7, 78729–78757. 10.1109/ACCESS.2019.2921522

Ray, P. P., Kumar, N., & Guizani, M. (2021). A vision on 6G-enabled NIB: Requirements, technologies, deployments, and prospects. *IEEE Wireless Communications*, 28(4), 120–127. 10.1109/MWC.001.2000384

Revathi, T. K., Sathiyabhama, B., Sankar, S., Pandey, D., Pandey, B. K., & Dadeech, P. (2022). An intelligent model for coronary heart disease diagnosis. In *Networking Technologies in Smart Healthcare* (pp. 309–327). CRC Press. 10.1201/9781003239888-15

Rogers, D. L. (2016). *The digital transformation playbook: Rethink your business for the digital age*. Columbia University Press. 10.7312/roge17544

Rudolph, J., Tan, S., & Tan, S. (2023). ChatGPT: Bullshit spewer or the end of traditional assessments in higher education? *Journal of Applied Learning and Teaching, 6*(1), 342-363.

Rutter, P., & Keirstead, J. (2012). A brief history and the possible future of urban energy systems. *Energy Policy*, 50, 72–80. 10.1016/j.enpol.2012.03.072

Saad, W., Bennis, M., & Chen, M. (2019). A vision of 6G wireless systems: Applications, trends, technologies, and open research problems. *IEEE Network*, 34(3), 134–142. 10.1109/MNET.001.1900287

Sahani, K., Khadka, S., Sahani, S. K., Pandey, B. K., & Pandey, D. (2023). *A Possible Underground Roadway for Transportation Facilities in Kathmandu Valley Ring Road: A Racking Deformation of Underground Rectangular Structures*. Academic Press.

Sahani, K., Khadka, S. S., Sahani, S. K., Pandey, B. K., & Pandey, D. (2023). A possible underground roadway for transportation facilities in Kathmandu Valley: A racking deformation of underground rectangular structures. *Engineering Reports*, 12821. 10.1002/eng2.12821

Sahani, S. K., Pandey, B. K., & Pandey, D. (2024). *Single-valued Signals, Multi-valued Signals and Fixed-Point of Contractive Signals*. Mathematics Open. 10.1142/S2811007224500020

Salameh, A. I., & El Tarhuni, M. (2022). From 5G to 6G—Challenges, technologies, and applications. *Future Internet*, 14(4), 117. 10.3390/fi14040117

Santos, J. A., Lopes, M. R., Viegas, J. L., Vieira, S. M., & Sousa, J. M. (2020). Internal supply chain digital twin of a pharmaceutical company. *IFAC-PapersOnLine*, 53(2), 10797–10802. 10.1016/j.ifacol.2020.12.2864

Saravanan, K., & Saraniya, S. (2017). Cloud IOT based novel livestock monitoring and identification system using UID. *Sensor Review*, 38(1), 21–33.

Sarda, S., Sharma, S., & Pal, R. (2022). Consumer Protection Regulation in Light of E-Commerce and Product Liability. *Indian JL & Legal Rsch., 4*, 1.

Sasidevi, S., Kumarganesh, S., Saranya, S., Thiyaneswaran, B., Shree, K. V. M., & Martin Sagayam, K. (2024, May 15). Design of Surface Plasmon Resonance (SPR) Sensors for Highly Sensitive Biomolecular Detection in Cancer Diagnostics. *Plasmonics*. Advance online publication. 10.1007/s11468-024-02343-z

Saxena, A., Agarwal, A., Pandey, B. K., & Pandey, D. (2024). Examination of the Criticality of Customer Segmentation Using Unsupervised Learning Methods. *Circular Economy and Sustainability*, 1–14. 10.1007/s43615-023-00336-4

Saxena, A., Sharma, N. K., Pandey, D., & Pandey, B. K. (2021). Influence of tourists satisfaction on future behavioral intentions with special reference to desert triangle of Rajasthan. *Augmented Human Research*, 6(1), 13. 10.1007/s41133-021-00052-4

Saxena, N., Rastogi, E., & Rastogi, A. (2021). *6G Use Cases, Requirements, and Metrics. In 6G Mobile Wireless Networks.* Springer.

Schieferdecker, I., & Mattauch, W. (2018). ICT for smart cities: Innovative solutions in the public space. In *Computation for Humanity* (pp. 150–179). CRC Press.

Schwendimann, R., Blatter, C., Dhaini, S., Simon, M., & Ausserhofer, D. (2018). The occurrence, types, consequences and preventability of in-hospital adverse events–a scoping review. *BMC Health Services Research*, 18(1), 1–13. 10.1186/s12913-018-3335-z29973258

Sengupta, R., Sengupta, D., Pandey, D., Pandey, B. K., Nassa, V. K., & Dadeech, P. (2021). A Systematic review of 5G opportunities, architecture and challenges. *Future Trends in 5G and 6G*, 247-269.

Sennan, S., Somula, R., Luhach, A. K., Deverajan, G. G., Alnumay, W., Jhanjhi, N. Z., Ghosh, U., & Sharma, P. (2021). Energy efficient optimal parent selection based routing protocol for Internet of Things using firefly optimization algorithm. *Transactions on Emerging Telecommunications Technologies*, 32(8), e4171. 10.1002/ett.4171

Shah, K., Chadotra, S., Tanwar, S., Gupta, R., & Kumar, N. (2022). Blockchain for IoV in 6G environment: Review solutions and challenges. *Cluster Computing*, 25(3), 1927–1955. 10.1007/s10586-021-03492-0

Sharma, S., Pandey, B. K., Pandey, D., Anand, R., Sharma, A., & Saini, S. (2023, March). Character Recognition Technique Implementation for Complicated Deteriorated Scene. In *2023 6th International Conference on Information Systems and Computer Networks (ISCON)* (pp. 1-4). IEEE. 10.1109/ISCON57294.2023.10112185

Sharma, M., Pandey, D., Khosla, D., Goyal, S., Pandey, B. K., & Gupta, A. K. (2022). Design of a GaN-based Flip Chip Light Emitting Diode (FC-LED) with au Bumps & Thermal Analysis with different sizes and adhesive materials for performance considerations. *Silicon*, 14(12), 7109–7120. 10.1007/s12633-021-01457-x

Sharma, M., Pandey, D., Palta, P., & Pandey, B. K. (2022b). Design and power dissipation consideration of PFAL CMOS V/S conventional CMOS based 2: 1 multiplexer and full adder. *Silicon*, 14(8), 4401–4410. 10.1007/s12633-021-01221-1

Sharma, M., Talwar, R., Pandey, D., Nassa, V. K., Pandey, B. K., & Dadheech, P. (2024). A Review of Dielectric Resonator Antennas (DRA)-Based RFID Technology for Industry 4.0. *Robotics and Automation in Industry*, 4(0), 303–324.

Shin, J., Mahmud, M. S., Rehman, T. U., Ravichandran, P., Heung, B., & Chang, Y. K. (2022). Trends and prospect of machine vision technology for stresses and diseases detection in precision agriculture. *AgriEngineering*, 5(1), 20–39. 10.3390/agriengineering5010003

Siano, P., De Marco, G., Rolán, A., & Loia, V. (2019). A survey and evaluation of the potentials of distributed ledger technology for peer-to-peer transactive energy exchanges in local energy markets. *IEEE Systems Journal*, 13(3), 3454–3466. 10.1109/JSYST.2019.2903172

Singh, H., Pandey, B. K., George, S., Pandey, D., Anand, R., Sindhwani, N., & Dadheech, P. (2022, July). Effective overview of different ML models used for prediction of COVID-19 patients. In *Artificial Intelligence on Medical Data: Proceedings of International Symposium, ISCMM 2021* (pp. 185-192). Singapore: Springer Nature Singapore.

Singh, S., Madaan, G., Kaur, J., Swapna, H. R., Pandey, D., Singh, A., & Pandey, B. K. (2023). *Bibliometric Review on Healthcare Sustainability. Handbook of Research on Safe Disposal Methods of Municipal Solid Wastes for a Sustainable Environment*, 142-161. 10.4018/978-1-6684-8117-2.ch011

Sithipolvanichgul, J., Chen, C., Land, J., & Ractham, P. (2021). Factors affecting cloud computing adoption and continuance intention of students in Thailand. *International Journal on Management of Innovation & Technology*, 18(07), 2150037. 10.1142/S0219877021500371

Smith-Bindman, R., Miglioretti, D. L., Johnson, E., Lee, C., Feigelson, H. S., Flynn, M., Greenlee, R. T., Kruger, R. L., Hornbrook, M. C., Roblin, D., Solberg, L. I., Vanneman, N., Weinmann, S., & Williams, A. E. (2012). Use of diagnostic imaging studies and associated radiation exposure for patients enrolled in large integrated health care systems, 1996-2010. *Journal of the American Medical Association*, 307(22), 2400–2409. 10.1001/jama.2012.596022692172

Snehi, J., Snehi, M., Prasad, D., Simaiya, S., Kansal, I., & Baggan, V. (2022). SDN-Based Cloud Combining Edge Computing for IoT Infrastructure. *Software Defined Networks: Architecture and Applications*, 497-540.

Sodhro, A. H., Zahid, N., Pirbhulal, S., Garcia, N. M., & Wang, L. (2020). Towards QoE Optimization in Medical Multimedia Services for Decentralized IoT-based Applications. *Proceedings of the 2020 IEEE 91st Vehicular Technology Conference (VTC2020-Spring),* 1–5. 10.1109/VTC2020-Spring48590.2020.9129227

Soodtoetong, N., & Rattanasiriwongwut, M. (2022). Educational Transformation with Virtual Classroom: Integrated between TTF and Social Motivation. *TEM Journal*, 11(1), 439–445. 10.18421/TEM111-56

Strinati, E. C., Barbarossa, S., Gonzalez-Jimenez, J. L., Ktenas, D., Cassiau, N., Maret, L., & Dehos, C. (2019). 6G: The next frontier: From holographic messaging to artificial intelligence using subterahertz and visible light communication. *IEEE Vehicular Technology Magazine*, 14(3), 42–50. 10.1109/MVT.2019.2921162

Swapna, H. R., Bigirimana, E., Madaan, G., Hasan, A., Pandey, B. K., & Pandey, D. (2023). Impact of neuromarketing on consumer psychology in digitally connected networks. In *Applications of Neuromarketing in the Metaverse* (pp. 193–205). IGI Global. 10.4018/978-1-6684-8150-9.ch015

Taha, A. E. M. (2021). Quality of experience in 6G networks: Outlook and challenges. *Journal of Sensor and Actuator Networks*, 10(1), 11. 10.3390/jsan10010011

Taherdoost, H., & Madanchian, M. (2023). Blockchain-based e-commerce: A review on applications and challenges. *Electronics (Basel)*, 12(8), 1889. 10.3390/electronics12081889

Taimoor, N., & Rehman, S. (2021). Reliable and resilient AI and IoT-based personalised healthcare services: A survey. *IEEE Access : Practical Innovations, Open Solutions*, 10, 535–563. 10.1109/ACCESS.2021.3137364

Taleb, H., Nasser, A., Andrieux, G., Charara, N., & Motta Cruz, E. (2021). Wireless technologies, medical applications and future challenges in WBAN: A survey. *Wireless Networks*, 27(8), 5271–5295. 10.1007/s11276-021-02780-2

Tang, Y., Dananjayan, S., Hou, C., Guo, Q., Luo, S., & He, Y. (2021). A survey on the 5G network and its impact on agriculture: Challenges and opportunities. *Computers and Electronics in Agriculture*, 180, 105895. 10.1016/j.compag.2020.105895

Tareke, S. A., Lelisho, M. E., Hassen, S. S., Seid, A. A., Jemal, S. S., Teshale, B. M., & Pandey, B. K. (2022). The prevalence and predictors of depressive, anxiety, and stress symptoms among Tepi town residents during the COVID-19 pandemic lockdown in Ethiopia. *Journal of Racial and Ethnic Health Disparities*, 1–13.35028903

Tataria, H., Shafi, M., Molisch, A. F., Dohler, M., Sjöland, H., & Tufvesson, F. (2021). 6G wireless systems: Vision, requirements, challenges, insights, and opportunities. *Proceedings of the IEEE*, 109(7), 1166–1199. 10.1109/JPROC.2021.3061701

Terzopoulos, G., & Satratzemi, M. (2019, September). Voice assistants and artificial intelligence in education. In *Proceedings of the 9th Balkan Conference on Informatics* (pp. 1-6). 10.1145/3351556.3351588

Tripathi, R. P., Sharma, M., Gupta, A. K., Pandey, D., Pandey, B. K., Shahul, A., & George, A. H. (2023). Timely prediction of diabetes by means of machine learning practices. *Augmented Human Research*, 8(1), 1. 10.1007/s41133-023-00062-4

Trivelli, L., Apicella, A., Chiarello, F., Rana, R., Fantoni, G., & Tarabella, A. (2019). From precision agriculture to Industry 4.0: Unveiling technological connections in the agrifood sector. *British Food Journal*, 121(8), 1730–1743. 10.1108/BFJ-11-2018-0747

Troncia, M., Galici, M., Mureddu, M., Ghiani, E., & Pilo, F. (2019). Distributed ledger technologies for peer-to-peer local markets in distribution networks. *Energies*, 12(17), 3249. 10.3390/en12173249

Tzounis, A., Katsoulas, N., Bartzanas, T., & Kittas, C. (2017). Internet of Things in agriculture, recent advances and future challenges. *Biosystems Engineering*, 164, 31–48. 10.1016/j.biosystemseng.2017.09.007

Ullah, A., Azeem, M., Ashraf, H., Alaboudi, A. A., Humayun, M., & Jhanjhi, N. Z. (2021). Secure healthcare data aggregation and transmission in IoT—A survey. *IEEE Access : Practical Innovations, Open Solutions*, 9, 16849–16865. 10.1109/ACCESS.2021.3052850

Vaswani, A., Shazeer, N., Parmar, N., Uszkoreit, J., Jones, L., & Gomez, A. N. (2017, December). Attention Is All You Need, Adv. Neural Inf. Process. Syst. In *Neural Inf. Process. Syst* (pp. 5999-6009). Academic Press.

Vinodhini, V., Kumar, M. S., Sankar, S., Pandey, D., Pandey, B. K., & Nassa, V. K. (2022). IoT-based early forest fire detection using MLP and AROC method. *International Journal of Global Warming*, 27(1), 55–70. 10.1504/IJGW.2022.122794

von Kutzschenbach, M., & Daub, C. H. (2020). Digital transformation for sustainability: A necessary technical and mental revolution. In *New Trends in Business Information Systems and Technology: Digital Innovation and Digital Business Transformation* (pp. 179–192). Springer International Publishing.

Wang, C. X., You, X., Gao, X., Zhu, X., Li, Z., Zhang, C., ... Hanzo, L. (2023). On the road to 6G: Visions, requirements, key technologies and testbeds. *IEEE Communications Surveys & Tutorials*.

Wang, J., Wang, C. X., Huang, J., & Chen, Y. (2022). 6G THz propagation channel characteristics and modeling: Recent developments and future challenges. *IEEE Communications Magazine*.

Wang, K. J., Lee, Y. H., & Angelica, S. (2021). Digital twin design for real-time monitoring–a case study of die cutting machine. *International Journal of Production Research*, 59(21), 6471–6485. 10.1080/00207543.2020.1817999

Webster, C., & Ivanov, S. (2020). *Robotics, artificial intelligence, and the evolving nature of work*. Springer International Publishing. 10.1007/978-3-030-08277-2_8

Yang, Y., & Yu, D. (2022, January). Research and Exploration on the Training of New Engineering Personnel from the Perspective of Artificial Intelligence. In *2022 2nd Asia Conference on Information Engineering (ACIE)* (pp. 102-106). IEEE 10.1109/ACIE55485.2022.00029

Yang, H., Alphones, A., Xiong, Z., Niyato, D., Zhao, J., & Wu, K. (2020). Artificial-intelligence-enabled intelligent 6G networks. *IEEE Network*, 34(6), 272–280. 10.1109/MNET.011.2000195

Yang, H., Xie, X., & Kadoch, M. (2019). Intelligent resource management based on reinforcement learning for ultra-reliable and low-latency IoV communication networks. *IEEE Transactions on Vehicular Technology*, 68(5), 4157–4169. 10.1109/TVT.2018.2890686

Yang, P., Xiao, Y., Xiao, M., & Li, S. (2019). 6G wireless communications: Vision and potential techniques. *IEEE Network*, 33(4), 70–75. 10.1109/MNET.2019.1800418

Yazdinejad, A., Zolfaghari, B., Azmoodeh, A., Dehghantanha, A., Karimipour, H., Fraser, E., Green, A. G., Russell, C., & Duncan, E. (2021). A review on security of smart farming and precision agriculture: Security aspects, attacks, threats and countermeasures. *Applied Sciences (Basel, Switzerland)*, 11(16), 7518. 10.3390/app11167518

You, X., Wang, C. X., Huang, J., Gao, X., Zhang, Z., Wang, M., Huang, Y., Zhang, C., Jiang, Y., Wang, J., Zhu, M., Sheng, B., Wang, D., Pan, Z., Zhu, P., Yang, Y., Liu, Z., Zhang, P., Tao, X., & Liang, Y.-C. (2021). Towards 6G wireless communication networks: Vision, enabling technologies, and new paradigm shifts. *Science China. Information Sciences*, 64(1), 1–74. 10.1007/s11432-020-2955-6

Zambon, I., Cecchini, M., Egidi, G., Saporito, M. G., & Colantoni, A. (2019). Revolution 4.0: Industry vs. agriculture in a future development for SMEs. *Processes (Basel, Switzerland)*, 7(1), 36. 10.3390/pr7010036

Zeng, X., Garg, S., Barika, M., Zomaya, A. Y., Wang, L., Villari, M., Chen, D., & Ranjan, R. (2020). SLA management for big data analytical applications in clouds: A taxonomy study. *ACM Computing Surveys*, 53(3), 1–40. 10.1145/3383464

Zhai, Z., Martínez, J. F., Beltran, V., & Martínez, N. L. (2020). Decision support systems for agriculture 4.0: Survey and challenges. *Computers and Electronics in Agriculture*, 170, 105256. 10.1016/j.compag.2020.105256

Zhang, L., Liang, Y. C., & Niyato, D. (2019). 6G Visions: Mobile ultra-broadband, super internet-of-things, and artificial intelligence. *China Communications*, 16(8), 1–14. 10.23919/JCC.2019.08.001

Zhang, N., Sun, Q., Yang, L., & Li, Y. (2021). Event-triggered distributed hybrid control scheme for the integrated energy system. *IEEE Transactions on Industrial Informatics*, 18(2), 835–846. 10.1109/TII.2021.3075718

Zhang, S., Liu, J., Guo, H., Qi, M., & Kato, N. (2020). Envisioning device-to-device communications in 6G. *IEEE Network*, 34(3), 86–91. 10.1109/MNET.001.1900652

Zhang, S., Wang, Y., & Zhou, W. (2019). Towards secure 5G networks: A Survey. *Computer Networks*, 162, 106871. 10.1016/j.comnet.2019.106871

Zhang, Z., Xiao, Y., Ma, Z., Xiao, M., Ding, Z., Lei, X., Karagiannidis, G. K., & Fan, P. (2019). 6G wireless networks: Vision, requirements, architecture, and key technologies. *IEEE Vehicular Technology Magazine*, 14(3), 28–41. 10.1109/MVT.2019.2921208

Zhao, J. (2019). A survey of intelligent reflecting surfaces (IRSs): Towards 6G wireless communication networks. arXiv preprint arXiv:1907.04789.

Zhao, Y., Zhao, J., Zhai, W., Sun, S., Niyato, D., & Lam, K. Y. (2021). A survey of 6G wireless communications: Emerging technologies. *Proceedings of the Future of Information and Communication Conference*, 150–170. 10.1007/978-3-030-73100-7_12

Zhou, F., Feng, L., Yu, P., Li, W., Que, X., & Meng, L. (2021). DRL-based low-latency content delivery for 6G massive vehicular IoT. *IEEE Internet of Things Journal*, 9(16), 14551–14562. 10.1109/JIOT.2021.3064874

Zou, J., & Chen, Y. (2022, December). Online Aesthetic Education Information Teaching System Based On Big Data Cloud Platform. In *2022 International Conference on Knowledge Engineering and Communication Systems (ICKES)* (pp. 1-6). IEEE. 10.1109/ICKECS56523.2022.10059986

About the Contributors

* * *

Joshuva Arockia Dhanraj is currently working as an Associate Professor in Computer Science Cluster (AI&ML), School of Engineering at Dayanada Sagar University. He is also associated as Adjunct Faculty in University Centre for Research & Development (UCRD), Chandigarh University, Mohali, Punjab, India. He has totally 5.5 years of teaching experience, 3 years of research experience and 1 year of post-doc experience. He has published 160+ papers in peer-reviewed/SCI/Scopus indexed international journals and he filed nearly 10 National and 5 International Patents. His research area is in the field of Machine Learning, Machine Fault Diagnosis and Prognosis, Structural Health and Condition Monitoring, Renewable Energy Applications towards SDG Development.

A. N. Arularasan is a faculty member in the Department of Artificial Intelligence and Data Science at Panimalar Engineering College, located in Chennai, India.

Amit Kumar Bindal is an Associate Professor in the Department of Computer Science & Engineering, M. M. Engineering College, M. M. (Deemed to be University) Mullana, Ambala, Haryana, India. Dr. Bindal received Ph.D. from Maharishi Markandeshwar University, M. Tech (Computer Engineering) from Kurukshetra University and B. Tech. in Computer Engineering .from Kurukshetra University Kurukshetra. Dr. Bindal is in teaching and Research & Development since 2005. He has published about 60 research papers in International, National Journals and Refereed International Conferences. His current research interests are in Wireless Sensor Networks, Underwater Wireless Sensor Networks, Sensors, and IoT, etc.

B. Charith holds a Doctorate in Management, Possess Good 18+ Years of total work experience and Specifically 9+ yrs in the Leadership Hiring with proven results and repeated success in multiple units and assignment handled, building good client relationship and value, driving vision and achieving critical strategic goals towards the Organization's growth. Valued contributor to key strategic improvements and highly successful new set ups. Personally hold a Track record in placing Leaders for leading Giants in India across functions like ITES operations, HR, Quality, Transition, Presales and Solution Design etc. Been instrumental in closing Niche mandates at Leadership band and successful on boarding of critical resources who are now in the Executive Band of Fortune 100 Companies. Apart from Heading Leadership hiring directly, personally being a part of the Golden Opportunities Management group, being instrumental in terms of important decision making, Process Improvement, MIS, Overall key account management and Global Revenue management as well.

Pankaj Dadheech is currently working as a Professor & Deputy Head in the Department of Computer Science & Engineering (NBA Accredited), Swami Keshvanand Institute of Technology, Management & Gramothan (SKIT), Jaipur, Rajasthan, India (Accredited by NAAC A++ Grade). He has more than 19 years of experience in teaching. He is currently working a Professor & Dy. HOD in the Department of Computer Science & Engineering (NBA Accredited), Swami Keshvanand Institute of Technology, Management & Gramothan (SKIT), Jaipur, Rajasthan, India. He has published 25 Patents at Intellectual Property India, Office of the Controller General of Patents, Design and Trade Marks, Department of Industrial Policy and Promotion, Ministry of Commerce and Industry, Government of India. He has published 8 International Patents (USA, South African, Australian, Germany) & 2 Copyrights. He has 80 publications in various International & National Journals, 63 papers in various National & International conferences. He has published 9 Books & 40 Book Chapters.

A. Shaji George is a highly respected and accomplished figure in the fields of education and the ICT industry. With over 30 years of experience in designing and deploying large-scale projects, Dr. George has made significant contributions to industry. He has a passion for working with clients to help them overcome complex business challenges, drive innovation, and deliver results. Dr. George is recognized as an expert in the field of ICT and has published over 250 research papers in national and international journals and conferences. He is also the author of 30 books that have been published by reputed international publishers. His extensive contributions to the field have earned him 20 awards, recognizing his outstanding achievements and contributions to the industry. Dr. George is the founder of PU Publications, PUIRJ, PUIIJ and PUIRP International Journal. He has a keen interest in wireless networking, cloud computing, big data analytics, the Internet of Things, and industrial automation systems. He works with clients from a wide range of industries to develop strategies and implement next-generation solutions that transform their businesses. Dr. George's wealth of knowledg3.

About the Contributors

Sandeep Gupta received his B.Tech. degree in Electrical and Electronics Engineering from UPTU Lucknow in the year 2006. He has completed his Ph.D. from NIT Allahabad in the area of control and power systems with AI techniques. He is presently working as an Associate Professor at Graphic Era (Deemed to be University), Dehradun (India). He has a total of 15 years of experience. His areas of interest in research are the application of artificial intelligence to power system control design, FACTS devices, renewable energy, power electronics, and stability of power systems with machine learning. He is a member of numerous professional organizations, including IE, IRED, IDES, IAENG, IAER, and the Society of Professional Engineers. He has been the author or co-author of 80 papers published in international journals and presented at different national and international conferences. He is currently guiding 4 research scholars under Machine Learning, Control & Power Systems, Wireless Technology, and Internet of Things.

R. Manikandan completed his undergraduate studies in Electronics and Instrumentation Engineering at Annamalai University, Chidambaram in 2002. In 2008, he earned his master's degree in Applied Electronics from Anna University, Chennai. Later, in 2014, he successfully obtained his Ph.D. in Image/Video Processing from the Department of Advanced Sports Training and Technology at Tamil Nadu Physical Education and Sports University, Chennai. He has more than 21 years of experience in teaching and is a life member of ISTE. His primary research interests encompass automation, computer vision, and image/video processing. Presently, he holds the position of a Professor in the Department of Electronics and Communication Engineering at Panimalar Engineering College, Chennai.

K. Sankara Moorthy is an AIMA Certified Management Teacher in Marketing Domain and SEBI Certified Research Analyst . He has Published around 15 research articles in scopus indexed and refereed journals. Added to the teaching assignments, he is also serving as a resident mentor at SRM Innovation Incubation and Entrepreneurship Centre(SIIEC) in motivating budding entrepreneurs. He had served as a core member in Alumni Activities, Research Coordination, Exam Coordination. He has completed various certifications in the Coursera, Udemy and NPTEL platforms in the areas of Consumer Behaviour, Social Media and Fintech.

|I. E. S. Naidu served as Assistant professor in EEE Department of ANITS, STIET and GITAM, working as Associate Professor from 2008 in GITAM, Visakhapatnam campus. Acquired a B.Tech Degree in EEE from JNTU Hyderabad, an M.Tech in Power Systems from JNTU Kakinada and a Ph.D. in Electrical Engineering from Andhra University. My areas of interest include power system stability, power system security, smart and microgrids.

Thamil Selvan R. is presently Associate Professor, Faculty of Business Administration Sathyabama University, Chennai, India. He has more than 23 years of experience in teaching Management Accounting, Financial Accounting, Corporate Accounting, Cost accounting, Financial Management and Security Analysis and Portfolio Management at undergraduate and post graduate level in Sathyabama University. He has attended and presented papers at national and international level conferences. He has published articles in national and international journals. He guided 4 Ph.D scholars, 20 M.Phil., Scholars and Supervising 3 PhD scholars. He is examiner in various universities/autonomous colleges and professional bodies.

Bathrinath Sankaranarayanan's areas of interests are Industrial Engineering, Production Scheduling and Optimization, Supply Chain Management, Industrial Safety. He obtained his Post Doctoral Fellowship in University of Southern Denmark. He has several publications in the area of Industrial Engineering.

D. Sugumar is an Associate Professor of Electronics and Communication Engineering Department, Karunya Institute of Technology and Sciences (Deemed University) with teaching experience of 20 years. He has received the B.E. degree in Electronics & Communication Engineering from Bharathiar University, M.E. degree in Communication Systems from Anna University, Chennai, Ph.D degree in Information and Communication Engineering, Anna University, PGP in AI and ML from The University of Texas at Austin and Master of Data Sciences from Deakin University, Australia. Research interest includes 1) Blind Source Separation, 2) AI-ML based Signal Processing and 5G communication and 3) Wearables, Flexible & Metamaterial based Antennas for RF/Wireless Communication and medical applications. He is a life member of AMIE, ISTE, IAENG, IACSIT and Senior member of IEEE (Signal Processing Society, Microwave Theory and Techniques Society, & Antenna & Propagation Society). He has published 49 national and international conferences papers and 38 journal articles. (Out of that 43- Scopus/WOS indexed articles). He also authored 3 books, 6 book chapters and filed 3 Patents. He has received the best teacher award in the year 2010, innovative professional award in the year 2016, Dedicated faculty international a6ward in the year 2017 and young achiever Award in the year 2019. He has contributed as a reviewer for the Interscience and Elsevier Journals. He has organized several workshops, trainings, guest lectures and seminars, also has contributed as a chair person and resource person in various international conferences, Workshops, Add on programs and seminars. Doing RF & Antenna Design Consultancy for the past 8 Years and generated fund 3.0 Lakhs. He was the PI and Co-PI for 7 different seed money projects funded by government and non-government agencies.

S. Thilaga is currently working as Assistant Professor at Coimbatore Institute of Technology, Coimbatore. She has more than 13+ years of experience in teaching and she has undertaken various training and consultancy projects for organisations. She has over 3 years of industrial experience in the field of Marketing. She completed her Doctoral degree in the field of Marketing. She is a topper in her MBA Program from GRD College of Arts and Science and a University Rank holder in her Under Graduation program. Her interests are in the area of Marketing, Finance, Logistics and Entrepreneurship. In addition, she has also published scholarly articles both in National and International Journals. She has been certified by the University of Virginia for the completion of their course on Marketing Analytics. She has completed TA 101 course conducted by International Transactional Analysis Association. Her teaching interests are in Marketing Management, Consumer Behaviour, Organisational Behaviour, Strategic Management, Business Research Methods and Data Analysis and Business Modelling. Her research interest is in the area of consumer behavior. She completed her Master's degree in Business Administration and Marketing Management, Post Graduate in International Business and has also qualified UGC -NET and SET.

Index

Symbols

A

B

C

D

E

H

I

L

M

P

S

T

U

V

www.ingramcontent.com/pod-product-compliance
Lightning Source LLC
LaVergne TN
LVHW062119300926
849161LV00010B/2497

* 9 7 9 8 3 6 9 3 7 4 2 1 4 *